A BOOK OF TRAVELLERS' TALES

A BOOK OF
TRAVELLERS'
TALES

assembled by
ERIC NEWBY

COLLINS
8 Grafton Street London w1
1985

William Collins Sons & Co. Ltd
London · Glasgow · Sydney · Auckland
Toronto · Johannesburg

BRITISH LIBRARY CATALOGUING IN PUBLICATION DATA
A book of travellers' tales.
1. Voyages and travels
I. Newby, Eric
910.4   G465

ISBN 0-00-217238-0

First published 1985
Introduction, arrangement and editorial material
copyright © 1985 by Eric Newby
For details of other copyright material reproduced
see *Sources and Acknowledgements*

Photoset in Linotron Sabon by
Rowland Phototypesetting Ltd
Bury St Edmunds, Suffolk
Made and printed in Great Britain by
William Collins Sons & Co. Ltd, Glasgow

To the travellers of the future

CONTENTS

CONTENTS

INTRODUCTION

As my principal intention in assembling this anthology has been to entertain rather than to instruct, there should be no need for a long introduction. Indeed, there is a duty to avoid one: it is too much like inviting guests to a feast and then asking them to read a preamble about how and why the dishes were prepared before allowing them to tuck in and find out for themselves.

Why then have an introduction at all? Anthologists are a particularly vulnerable breed. They can expect no mercy from the reading public or from reviewers. (I expect none when this anthology appears.) Yet there is a widespread delusion among them that with a few well-chosen words in an introduction they can deflect the fury of readers who have discovered that their favourite writers have been omitted in favour of what – to them – are utterly boring nonentities. To attempt to excuse oneself in this way is about as effective as taking refuge under a solitary tree during an electric storm in order to avoid being struck by lightning. Better and braver to follow the example of Jan Morris in her anthology on Oxford and quote Dr Jowett, Master of Balliol College: 'Never retreat. Never explain. Get it done and let them howl.'

That said, some explanation *is* necessary.

I have omitted from my anthology:

1. The majority of biblical travellers.

2. All sailors, or travellers by sea, out of sight of land. They need and deserve an anthology of their own.

3. Mountaineers, for the same reason.

4. Travellers whose narratives, although eminently worthy of inclusion, proved impossible to extract from because they would not reduce to a length which would enable them to be included even in a book of this size. An example taken at random is Gerald Brenan's account in *South from Granada* of transporting a reluctant Lytton Strachey by mule from Lanjarón to Yegen.

5. Travellers who, although illustrious, seemed either boring or condescending, a common nineteenth-century trait (goodbye Dickens in the United States).

The travellers that are included appear in chronological order by date of birth (where it is known). With the exception of the first chapter, which is devoted to advice to or from travellers, the material is arranged geographically. Mexico is included with South and Central America, and islands will be found with the nearest land mass. Asia provided such a wealth of traveller's accounts that I have divided it into three parts: Near, Middle and Far. Under my scheme, Middle Asia extends from longitude 62°E (the eastern borders of Iran) as far as the western borders of Burma (approximately 91°E), including Siberia eastwards from the Urals and as far north as the Arctic Circle and those parts of Asiatic Russia, Tibet, China and Mongolia included between these longitudes, as well as Afghanistan, Pakistan, India, Sri Lanka and the Himalayas.

The production of adequate maps for such a book as this is an insoluble problem. Those at the beginning of each section can show only a fraction of the places mentioned in the text, some of which are unidentifiable anyway. This will be another source of irritation (I once received an immensely long and abusive letter from a reader who complained that the map drawn for a book I had written about the Trans-Siberian Railway did not mark every station and halt on a line that is 5900 miles long and stretches over seven time zones). I can only refer readers to an atlas and wish them good luck.

Let me end by saying that in assembling this book my aim has been to produce a feast, even if it is a feast, like the Chinese variety, in which some offerings are more appetizing than others (remembering that not everything served up at a Chinese banquet is acceptable to squeamish foreign tastes). I shall be happy if, when putting the book down, readers feel that they have eaten their fill and that every course has provided at least one dish that surprised and pleased them. But perhaps, bearing in mind the obloquy that is inevitably heaped on the hapless anthologist, I should be satisfied if they do not feel tempted to echo the *cri de coeur* of Queen Victoria, benighted at an appalling inn at Dalwhinnie in the Scottish Highlands: 'No pudding, and no *fun*.'

ERIC NEWBY
April 1985

ACKNOWLEDGEMENTS

I would like to thank Wanda, my wife, for the great help she gave me with this book in its early, herculean scissors-and-paste stages; Joan Bailey of the London Library, now retired, who for more years than I can count has been of inestimable help to me; and Dan Franklin at Collins, who took over the editing and final shaping of the book after so many others had almost literally fallen by the wayside.

E.N.

ADVICE TO TRAVELLERS

SAMUEL JOHNSON
(1709–1784)

English scholar, critic and lexicographer.

Some rather conflicting observations on travel

All travel has its advantages. If the passenger visits better countries, he may learn to improve his own, and if fortune carries him to worse, he may learn to enjoy it.

You have often heard me complain of finding myself disappointed by books of travels; I am afraid travel itself will end likewise in disappointment. One town, one country, is very like another: civilized nations have the same customs, and barbarous nations have the same nature: there are indeed minute discriminations both of places and of manners, which perhaps are not unworthy of curiosity, but which a traveller seldom stays long enough to investigate and compare. The dull utterly neglect them, the acute see a little, and supply the rest with fancy and conjecture.

Books of travels will be good in proportion to what a man has previously in his mind; his knowing what to observe; his power of contrasting one mode of life with another. As the Spanish proverb says, 'He, who would bring home the wealth of the Indies, must carry the wealth of the Indies with him.'

PRINCE HERMANN PÜCKLER-MUSKAU
(1785–1871)

German prince. A great traveller, a gifted writer, a talented landscape gardener and a voracious lover.

Rules for the young traveller

Had I . . . to give a few universal rules to a young traveller, I should seriously counsel him thus: – In Naples, treat the people brutally; in Rome, be natural; in Austria, don't talk politics; in France, give yourself no airs; in Germany, a great many; and in England, don't spit.

SIR FRANCIS GALTON
(1822–1911)

English scientist. A man of extraordinary energy and breadth of interest. A cousin of Charles Darwin, he founded the science of eugenics, devised the correlation coefficient, originated the meteorological theory of the anticyclone, invented the system of fingerprinting now in universal use, made valuable contributions in the field of experimental psychology dealing with visual memory and visions, and produced a map showing the physical distribution of beauty in the British Isles. In 1850–1 he explored Damaraland, an almost completely unknown region of south-west Africa. His book *The Art of Travel*, which resulted from these journeys, is obligatory reading for any traveller (or non-traveller).

How to cope with snake bites

Tie a string tight above the part, suck the wound, and caustic it as soon as you can. Or, for want of caustic, explode gunpowder in the wound; or else do what Mr. Mansfield Parkyns well suggests, *i.e.*, cut away with a knife, and afterwards burn out with the end of your iron ramrod, heated as near a white heat as you can readily get it. The arteries lie deep, and as much flesh may, without much danger, be cut or burnt into, as the fingers can pinch up. The next step is to use the utmost energy, and even cruelty, to prevent the patient's giving way to that lethargy and drowsiness which is the usual effect of snake-poison, and too often ends in death.

Two methods of keeping warm on frosty nights

Mr. St. John tell us of an excellent way in which Highland poachers, when in a party, usually pass frosty nights on the moor-side. They cut quantities of heather, and strew part of it as a bed on the ground; then all the party lie down, side by side, excepting one man, whose place among the rest is kept vacant for him. His business is to spread plaids upon them as they lie, and to heap up the remainder of the heather upon the plaids. This being accomplished, the man wriggles and works himself into the gap that has been left for him in the midst of his comrades.

In Napoleon's retreat, after his campaign in Russia, many a soldier saved or prolonged his life by creeping within the warm and reeking carcase of a horse that had died by the way.

W. B. LORD
(*fl.* 1870s) and
THOMAS BAINES
(1822–1875)

English authors of *Shifts and Expedients of Camp Life, Travel and Exploration* (1876), an immense, unportable book illustrated with marvellously instructive drawings. Lord was an artillery officer, a veteran of the siege of Sebastapol. Baines was an artist and explorer who had been on expeditions in Australia and Africa.

When dying of thirst in the desert

In cases of extreme necessity, and when the preservation of human life depends on the obtainment of water, the supply to be found in the stomach of the camel should not be overlooked or forgotten.

During the Algerian campaign the French made some investigations in order to find out the quantity of water a dead camel's stomach would contain, and the result was that about 15 pints was the average arrived at. This water, although green and turbid, had no offensive smell. It is asserted by the Arabs that water of this character requires three days to clear itself. People, however, dying of thirst, are not very nice.

MURRAY'S HANDBOOK OF TRAVEL-TALK
(1874)

'Being a collection of questions, phrases, and vocabularies intended to serve as interpreter to English travellers abroad'.

On the road

Traveller – Postboy.	Reisender und Postillon.
T. Postilion, drive slowly.	Postillon (Schwager), fahren Sie langsam.
T. Take care you do not upset us.	Geben Sie Acht, dasz Sie uns nicht umwerfen.
T. Don't go to sleep, postilion.	Schlafen Sie nicht ein, Schwager.
T. Do not drive so near the river – (the precipice – the ditch.)	Fahren Sie doch nicht so nahe am Flusse – Abgrunde – Graben, hin.
T. The coachman (postilion) is drunk – impertinent – foolhardy.	Der Kutscher (Postillon) ist betrunken – impertinent – tollkühn.
T. The carriage is near the precipice.	Der Wagen ist ganz nah dem Abgrund.
T. One of the wheels is off.	Ein Rad ist losgegangen.
T. Oh, dear! The postilion has been thrown (off) down.	O weh! Der Postillon ist heruntergefallen.
T. I am afraid he has broken his leg – his arm.	Ich fürchte, er hat ein Bein – einen Arm gebrochen.
T. Ask for a surgeon.	Holen Sie einen Wundarzt.
T. It rains in torrents.	Es regnet in Strömen.
T. It lightens – it thunders.	Es blitzt – es donnert.

T. It is impossible to travel in such weather.	Man kann bei solchem Wetter nicht reisen.
T. The lightning has struck that tree.	Der Blitz hat in jenen Baum eingeschlagen.
T. This is quite a hurricane.	Das ist ja ein wahrer Orkan.
T. I am really much alarmed.	Ich bin in groszer Angst.

FRANK TATCHELL
(*fl.* 1920)

English clergyman. Vicar of Midhust, Sussex, in the 1920s, but if his charming book *The Happy Traveller: A Book for Poor Men* (1923) is anything to go by, he must have been a frequent absentee. One of the inspirations of my own childhood and youth, Tatchell must have lured countless Britons from their hearths in search of new horizons.

The real fun of travelling

The real fun of travelling can only be got by one who is content to go as a comparatively poor man. In fact, it is not money which travel demands so much as leisure, and anyone with a small, fixed income can travel all the time.

The beaten track is often the best track, but devote most of your time to the by-ways. In no other way can you so quickly reach the heart of a country. Yet, though I would have you do much of your journey by road, get a zest for travelling by railways. Just being in a train and rushing on to somewhere is extraordinarily nerve-soothing. Besides, a train goes through out-of-the-way places and enables you to surprise many intimate sights which you would miss from the highway. The track usually follows river valleys and a distraction can be found on a long journey in shooting the rapids in an imaginary canoe or in fishing likely pools. When there is no river, I take the hedges and ditches on a dream horse, or pretend that I am an airman and spot good landing places.

When I have to wait for a train, I amuse myself by scribbling down a list of the collective words in which our language is so rich, e.g., a *pack* of hounds, a *shoal* of fish, a *peal* of bells. There are about a hundred of them, but I can seldom think of more than fifty or sixty. Or I make out a list of what I consider to be really first-rate books of travel. How few there are! I begin with these:

> Kinglake's, 'Eöthen.'
> Borrow's, 'Bible in Spain.'
> Melville's, 'Moby Dick.'
> Butler's, 'Alps and Sanctuaries.'
> Doughty's, 'Arabia Deserta.'
> Anson's, 'Voyage Round the World.'
> Darwin's, 'Voyage of the "Beagle."'
> Bates's, 'Naturalist on the Amazons.'
> Wallace's, 'Malay Archipelago.'

Here I pause to weigh the claims of such books as 'Tom Cringle's Log,' the 'Cruise of the "Falcon,"' and 'Two Years before the Mast'; and, thinking the list is getting too nautical, I return ashore with Stevenson's 'Travels with a Donkey,' Curzon's 'Monasteries of the Levant,' and Ford's 'Gatherings from Spain.' Then the train comes in.

On various animals

An elephant . . . has a dislike to a white man approaching him from behind. Camels do not bite or kick (except when *must*), but they can give a violent sneeze of half-masticated cud, which is almost as bad. With them *oos, oos* means go on; *adda* turn; *ogf* stop; and *ch, ch, ch* lie down. They are the only animals in the world to move the legs of one side before the others move. A llama has but one method of attack or defence and that is to spit in your eye, and the ploughing buffaloes of Siam, though driven with ease by a tiny native child, resent the smell of a white man.

Playing the tramp

There are few beds more comfortable than a dry ditch in England in June.

The law is that you must not sleep within fifteen yards of the crown (or centre) of the road. To play the tramp in England have a blue handkerchief with white spots round your neck, wear a silver ring, and let your nails get dirty. Address an old man as 'old gentleman,' a woman as 'Missis,' and a quite ordinary man as 'Mister.' English tramps avoid blisters by putting fresh dock leaves in their socks every morning.

On being attacked

Should you be attacked by a mob in the East, hurt one of the crowd and hurt him quickly. The others will gather chattering round the injured man and you will be able to slip away. If attacked by one man, hold your umbrella round the top of the ribs and meet his charge with a thrust in the belly or throat. If you have a stick, hold it just below the handle and let him have it, *not* on the head, but on the collar-bone an inch or so away from the neck. Keep your hand low so as not to hit the pad of muscle behind the collar-bone, and stand as in fencing, with the right foot forward. Other vulnerable places are the outside of the forearm, the tip of the shoulder, and . . . the shins. When the man has a knife and you have time, get your coat off and wrap it round the left wrist as a pad, leaving part of it dangling. If you are camping when attacked, leap away from the fire into the dark and keep still. To catch the faintest sound, keep your mouth open, for our ear has an inward entrance as well as an outer, like the gill which gave it origin. If you have a companion and want to wake him without his speaking, press with your finger under his ear.

But I hope none of these alarming things will happen to you. You are much more likely to be attacked by a dog. The mongrel curs are a nuisance to the wayfarer in most foreign lands. It is useless to try and 'good dog' them. Instead, abuse them in the hoarsest voice at your command and with the worst language you can think of. They may slink off utterly ashamed of themselves, but, if one comes for you, try this method. Snatch off your hat and hold it out to him, when he will snap at it and seize it by the brim. Now the length of your hat and arm is exactly the length of your leg, and, if you kick out, he will get it just under the jaw, bite his tongue and go off howling. Approaching a dog sleeping in the road, I do so whistling. This wakes him up before I get close and helps to convince him that I am human, in spite of the bag on my shoulder and my outlandish smell.

MEMBERS OF THE ROYAL GEOGRAPHICAL SOCIETY

In 1854 the Royal Geographical Society published *Hints to Travellers*, another essential book for reading in the armchair or on the road. It has since expanded into two volumes and gone through at least eleven editions. Much of Volume II is made up of advice from members.

On giving and receiving presents

About twenty big savages stalked out and stared at me, so I shook hands with tremendous friendliness, and they just went on staring. Then I gave them all sticks of tobacco and they pretended I had not given them anything, which is the correct behaviour on receiving a present in Sara.

Mrs. Baker. New Hebrides.

On the usefulness of trick cycles in Haiti

I found here three bicycles left by a stranded Circus that went broke and was sold up. These belonged to a trick cycling act and only weighed 14 lb. apiece. They come completely to pieces almost at a touch by releasing two clips and pulling the tubular aluminium frame apart. They can be packed down into a small canvas bag 28 inches square and any depth according to the number of cycles one puts in one on top of another. The tyres are solid, but their cylindrical springs make even better riding than air-filled ones. There seems to be no limit to the load that can be put on these machines and although not highly geared they can be made to travel very fast over all kinds of country not too mountainous. These things save hours of walking when travelling or collecting. For surveying they could be put to all kinds of uses: small dynamos and things can be run off them; and if one wants to one can always carry them on one's back without any discomfort! Please put this in the *Hints*; I am sure many will bless you!

Letter from Ivan Sanderson from Haiti 2/8/37.

On reckoning distances in Equatoria

In Equatoria it is almost impossible to find out how far it is to anywhere. The answer is always in hours. But we learned great astuteness in turning hours into miles. The method is to have a look at your informant's legs: if they are long an hour means 4 miles; however short they are it is never less than two and a half. The sultan was a very big man, and he told us it was seven hours from his rest-house to the Shari ferry which would take us across to Fort Lamy. The distance by our speedometer worked out at 27 miles.

Tweedy. Central Africa.

HORACE KEPHART
(1862–1931)

American librarian and author of *Camping and Woodcraft* (1916), a compendium of useful information for every traveller.

Dog is No. 2

The Englishman Ruxton, who lived in the Far West in the time of Bridger and the Sublettes and Fitzpatrick, says: 'Throwing aside all the qualms and conscientious scruples of a fastidious stomach, it must be confessed that dog meat takes a high rank in the wonderful variety of cuisine afforded to the gourmand and the gourmet by the prolific mountains. Now, when the bill of fare offers such tempting viands as buffalo beef, venison, mountain mutton, turkey, grouse, wildfowl, hares, rabbits, beaver-tails, etc., etc., the station assigned to dog as No. 2 in the list can well be appreciated – No. 1, in delicacy of flavour, richness of meat, and other good qualities, being the flesh of panthers, which surpasses every other, and all put together.'

V. R. RAGAM
(fl. 1963)

Indian author of the *Pilgrim's Travel Guide* to North India and the Himalayas.

'A list of suggestive articles'

Religious

Japamala
Agarbattis
Camphor
Dhup Powder
Kumkuma
Sandalwood Powder

Wicks soaked in ghee and
    kundi
Sri Ramakoti Book
Asanam
Bhagavad Gita or any
    religious book for daily use.
    Bhajan Songs or Namavali

Eatables

Rice
Dhal
Dried Fruits, vegetables
Pickles, Chutneys
Tamarind
Sugar
Tea, Coffee
Ovaltine

Milk Powder
Sweets
Sugar–candy
Chilly Powders
Appadams
Odiyams
Ghee
Nut Powder

Utensils

Canvas Bucket
Cooker
Oven
One set of stainless
    steel-vessels
Ladle

Spoons–3
Fraid pan
Tiffin Carrier
Tumbler
Glass

Cloths

Rugs, Blanket
Muffler
Dhavali or Silk Dhoti
Dhoties 2
Shirts 4
Baniyans 2
Uppar Clothes 3
Towels 3

Waterproff cloth 2 yards.
Rotten cloth pieces 4
Coupeens 2
Cloth Bag for money to keep round the waist
Bedding
Mosquito Curtain

Medicines

Amrutanjan
Smelling salt
Vaseline bottle
J & J De Chane's Medical service set with its guide-book
Homeopathic Box and a guide booh
Diarrhoea pills
Dysentery pills

Indigestion pills
Malaria pills
Boric Powder
Cotton
Cloth (Plaster)
Bandage Cloth
Aspro Tablets
Purgative chacklets
Tooth powder or paste

Miscellaneous

Looking glass and comb
Soaps for bath and wash
Nails of all sizes
Locks 2
Cloth bags for food stuffs
Pen knife
Small gunny bag for coal
Wrist Watch
Umbrella
Hand stick
Visiting Cards
List of departed souls and their Gotras
Hand bags 2
Note book

Tongue Cleaner
Suit case or hand jip bag
Lock and chain
Pandari bag to carry things on shoulder
Safety pins
Change for Rs. 10–00
Setuvu from Rameswaram
Ganges from Allahabad, Haridwar or Gangottari.
Battery light with spare batteries
Thermos Flask
Hurricane Lamp
Match box

White Papers
Fountain pen and pencil
Candles
Needles and thread
Railway Guide
Pilgrim's Travel Guide
Rail and Road maps

Calender both Telugu and
  English
News Papers
Ink bottles
Postage stamps and cards
A small hand axe
Good Camera with flash
Movie (Cene) Camera

Cloths

Woolen Rugs 2 (can be had
  for hire at Takalkot)
Woolen shirt

Woolen dress for head, hands
  and legs.
Light water proof coat,
  Canvas Boots

Other things

Kerosine stove
Empty Tins with handles (for
  storing and heating water
  and also can be useful to
  carry things safely while on
  journey)
Iron pointed stick to walk on
  the slipping path or ice
A pair of goggles with side
  closers

Needles and thread balls to
  present them on the way to
  monks and hill tribes
Spring balance portable
A portable weighing machine
Some good corked bottles to
  fetch Holy water from
  Manas etc.

JOHN HATT
(1948–   )

English traveller and publisher. He has travelled to more
than fifty countries, reprinted some of the great travel
books (and done as much as anyone to inspire the current
revival of interest in travel writing) and written *The
Tropical Traveller* (1982), the modern equivalent of
Galton's *The Art of Travel*.

On farting

Farting anywhere in public is usually embarrassing for the perpetrator, but there are countries where it is treated as a disastrous breach of manners. There is a man in Lamu, Kenya, who is known as 'The man whose grandfather farted', and I have read of a traveller being forcibly ejected from a shop in Afghanistan on account of an involuntary fart. However, it hasn't always been a serious *faux pas* in every part of the world; I quote again from Mr Vaughan who recounts an episode at a Chinese dinner: 'The writer was astonished at the individual next to him indulging not only in loud sounds from his mouth but by explosions of a different nature. The writer looked at him with disgust – much to his amusement; and he excused himself by saying that unless guests showed their approval of the repast in this way, the host would fear that he hadn't given them a good dinner.'

Sound advice

So pack your bags and go on your travels before it is too late. There are still vast tracts of the world which beg to be visited; and travel will give you a wealth of experience and pleasure which can be drawn on for the rest of your life – a wealth, furthermore, which no government can ever take away. If the very worst happens and you are miserable on your travels (unlikely), at least you will have learnt to appreciate your own country. I have never regretted visiting a single country (though three days in Dubai were enough), and I have rarely met anyone who regretted going on their travels. Our greatest disappointments are nearly always for what we *haven't* done – not for what we *have* done. And don't let the feeble excuse of work keep you back; remember the Haitian proverb: If work is such a good thing, how come the rich haven't grabbed it all for themselves?

AFRICA

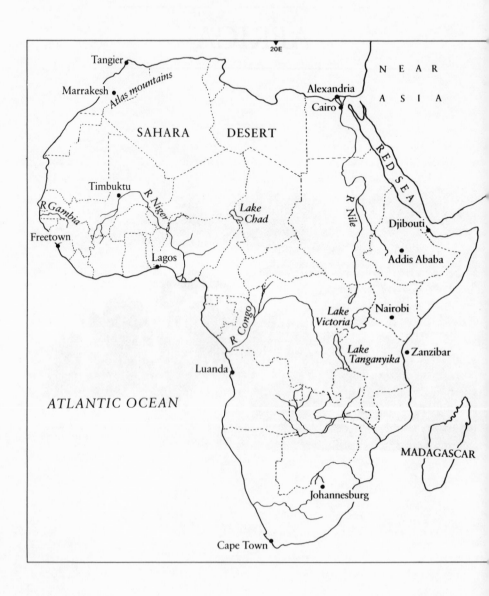

SUETONIUS PAULINUS
(d. after AD 69)

Roman general. In AD 61 he was the Roman commander in Britain and was responsible for suppressing Boadicea's revolt. Nineteen years earlier, when stationed in Mauretania under Claudius I, he became the first Roman to cross the Atlas Mountains (here described by Pliny the Elder).

The Atlas and beyond

Suetonius Paulinus, whom we have seen Consul in our own time, was the first Roman general who advanced a distance of some miles beyond Mount Atlas. . . . He informs us that the summit of this mountain is covered with snow even in summer, and says that having arrived there after a march of ten days, he proceeded some distance beyond it as far as a river which bears the name of Ger; the road being through deserts covered with a black sand, from which rocks that bore the appearance of having been exposed to the action of fire, projected every here and there; localities rendered quite uninhabitable by the intensity of the heat, as he himself experienced, although it was in the winter season that he visited them. We also learn from the same source that the people who inhabit the adjoining forests, which are full of all kinds of elephants, wild beasts, and serpents, have the name of Canarii; from the circumstance that they partake of their food in common with the canine race, and share with it the entrails of wild beasts.

FIDELIS
(*fl.* AD 762)

Irish monk. On his way to the Holy Land in *c.* AD 762 with a group of monks, he visited the Pyramids. Their journey was described by Dicuil, another Irish monk and the author of *De Mensura Orbis Terrae*, in the next century.

A visit to the Pyramids

... After a long voyage on the Nile they saw in the distance the Granaries made by Saint Joseph. There were seven of them, to match the number of years of plenty: they looked like mountains, four in one place and three in another. At this point, as they were going across to admire the three Granaries they found a dead lioness and, behind her, the dead bodies of eight men and women. The lioness had killed them by her strength and they had killed her with their spears and swords, for both the places in which the seven Granaries had been built were in the desert. Next [they] had a careful look at the three Granaries, and were once more amazed that from their foundation right up to their topmost point they were made entirely of stone. The lower part of them was rectangular, but the upper part was round, and the very top was as sharp as a needle.

This brother [Fidelis] we have mentioned measured one side of these Granaries, and it was four hundred paces from corner to corner.

IBN BATTUTA
(1304–1377)

A Berber born at Tangier, Ibn Battuta was the most indefatigable and indeed the greatest traveller in the history of the world – 'the traveller not of an age but of Islam'. It has been estimated that, at the very least, without taking detours into account, he travelled 75,000 miles. The first of his journeys began in 1325 and lasted twenty-four years. In the course of it he visited Egypt, the

Levant, Mecca (his original destination), Shiraz, Aden, East Africa, Caucasia, Siberia, Constantinople, the Hindu Kush, Delhi, Ceylon, Sumatra and China, seeing more of the known world than any man before him. On his return to Morocco in 1349, the Sultan provided him with a secretary to transcribe his account of his adventures. In 1352 he set out again, but this time his horizons were more limited: at the request of the Sultan, he went to visit Sulaiman, the Negro Muslim ruler of Melli (or Mali), whose kingdom extended from east of Timbuktu westwards to the Atlantic. His capital was at Niani, upstream from the present city of Bamako on the upper Niger.

Ibn Battuta's route took him over the Atlas Mountains to Sijilmasa, an important trading centre for gold and salt, and thence to Taghaza, twenty days' march to the south, where the salt mines were. At last he reached the Niger, which he believed to be the Nile.

An encounter with a crocodile

I saw a crocodile in this part of the Nile, close to the bank; it looked just like a small boat. One day I went down to the river to satisfy a need, and lo, one of the blacks came and stood between me and the river. I was amazed at such lack of manners and decency on his part and spoke of it to someone or other. He answered, 'His purpose in doing that was solely to protect you from the crocodile, by placing himself between you and it.'

At Niani, Ibn Battuta was granted an audience by the Negro Sultan. Also present were some cannibals from 'Wangara'.

A loathsome feast

The Sultan received them without honour and gave them as his hospitality gift a servant, a Negress. They killed and ate her, and having smeared their faces and hands with her blood, came to the Sultan to thank him.

From Niani he proceeded, along the caravan route to Egypt, to Takedda, where the 'women are the most perfect in beauty and the most shapely in figure of all women, of a pure white colour and very stout; nowhere in the world have I seen any who equal them in stoutness.' Ibn Battuta decided to buy one.

The difficulty of purchasing a female slave

When I arrived at Tagaddá I wished to buy an educated female slave, but could not find one. After a while the qádí sent me one who belonged to a friend of his, and I bought her for twenty-five *mithqáls*. Later on her master repented [of having sold her] and wished to have the sale rescinded, so I said to him, 'If you can show me where to find another, I shall cancel it for you.' He suggested a servant belonging to 'Alí Aghyúl, who was that very Maghrabin from Tádalá who had refused to carry any of my effects when my camel broke down, and to give my boy water when he was thirsty. So I bought her from him (she was better than the former one) and cancelled the sale with the first man. Afterwards this Maghrabin too repented of having sold the servant and wished to have the sale cancelled. He was very insistent about it but I refused, simply to pay him back for his vile conduct. He was like to go mad or die of grief, but afterwards I cancelled his bargain for him.

ALVISE DA CADAMOSTO
(1432?–1483)

Venetian navigator in the service of Prince Henry of Portugal, whose indefatigable endeavours in the field of exploration earned him the title The Navigator. In 1455 Cadamosto sailed to the Canary Islands and, with a Genoese, Antonio de Nola, went down the coast of Africa to the Gambia River. In Mauritania he met the Azanaghi (Azenegues/Tuaregs), who carried salt from the Moroccan border to Timbuktu and Mali, in Guinea, where it was exchanged for gold.

The silent trade in salt and gold

I enquired of them what the merchants of Melli did with this salt, and was told that a small quantity is consumed in their country. Since it is below the meridional and on the equinoctial, where the day is constantly about as long as the night, it is extremely hot at certain seasons of the year: this causes the blood of putrefy, so that were it not for this salt, they would die. The remedy they employ is as follows: they take a small piece of the salt, mix it in a jar with a little water, and drink it every day. . . . The remainder of this salt they carry away on a long journey in pieces as large as a man can, with a certain knack, bear on his head. . . . Those who carry it have two forked sticks, one in each hand: when they are tired, they plant them in the ground, and rest their load upon them. In this way they carry it until they reach certain waters: I could not learn from them whether it is fresh or sea water, so that I do not know if it is a river or the sea, though they consider it to be the sea. (I think however it must be a river, for were it the sea, in such a hot country there would be no lack of salt.) These Blacks are obliged to carry it in this way, because they have no camels or other beasts of burden, as these cannot live in the great heat. It may be imagined how many men are required to carry it on foot, and how many are those who consume it every year. Having reached these waters with the salt, they proceed in this fashion: all those who have the salt pile it in rows, each marking his own. Having made these piles, the whole caravan retires half a day's journey. Then there comes another race of blacks who do not wish to be seen or to speak. They arrive in large boats, from which it appears that they come from islands, and disembark. Seeing the salt, they place a large quantity of gold opposite each pile, and then turn back, leaving salt and gold. When they have gone, the Negroes who own the salt return: if they are satisfied with the quantity of gold, they leave the salt and retire with the gold. Then the blacks of the gold return, and remove those piles which are without gold. By the other piles of salt they place more gold, if it pleases them, or else they leave the salt. In this way, by long and ancient custom, they carry on their trade without seeing or speaking to each other.

VASCO DA GAMA
(1469?–1524)

Portuguese navigator. On a remarkable voyage, 1497–9,
he discovered the sea route from Portugal to India round
the Cape of Good Hope. A journal of the voyage, by an
unknown author, has survived.

Meeting a band of Hottentots at Mossel Bay near the Cape of Good Hope, December 1497

On Saturday about two hundred Negroes came, both young and
old. They brought with them about a dozen oxen and cows and four
or five sheep. As soon as we saw them we went ashore. They
forthwith began to play on four or five flutes, some producing high
notes and others low ones, thus making a pretty harmony for
Negroes who are not expected to be musicians; and they danced in
the style of Negroes. The captain-major then ordered the trumpets
to be sounded, and we, in the boats, danced, and the captain-major
did so likewise when he rejoined us. This festivity ended, we landed
where we had landed before, and bought a black ox for three
bracelets. This ox we dined off on Sunday. We found him very fat,
and his meat as toothsome as the beef of Portugal.

On Sunday many visitors came, and brought with them their
women and little boys, the women remaining on the top of a hill
near the sea. They had with them many oxen and cows. Having
collected in two spots on the beach, they played and danced as they
had done on Saturday. It is the custom of this people for the young
men to remain in the bush with their weapons. The [older] men
came to converse with us. They carried a short stick in the hand,
attached to which was a fox's tail, with which they fan the face.
Whilst conversing with them, by signs, we observed the young men
crouching in the bush, holding their weapons in their hands. The
captain-major then ordered Martin Affonso, who had formerly
been in Manicongo [Congo] to advance, and to buy an ox, for
which purpose he was supplied with bracelets. The natives, having
accepted the bracelets, took him by the hand, and, pointing to the
watering place, asked him why we took away their water, and
simultaneously drove their cattle into the bush. When the captain-

major observed this he ordered us to gather together, and called upon Martin Affonso to retreat, for he suspected some treachery. Having drawn together we proceeded [in our boats] to the place where we had been at first. The Negroes followed us. The captain-major then ordered us to land, armed with lances, assegais, and strung cross-bows, and wearing our breast-plates, for he wanted to show that we had the means of doing them an injury, although we had no desire to employ them. When they observed this they ran away.

LEO AFRICANUS
(1494?–1552)

Moorish traveller in Africa in the Middle East. His Arabic name was Al-Hassan Ibn Mohammed Al-Wezaz Al-Fasi. Captured by pirates, he was sent as a slave to Pope Leo X and was baptized as a Christian in Rome. There he wrote in Arabic *The History and Description of Africa and of the Notable Things Therein Contained*, which was published in Italian in 1550 and in English in 1600.

Wild life of the Congo

The Hippopotamus or water-horse is somewhat tawnie, of the colour of a lion; in the night he comes on lande to feed upon the grasse, and keepeth in the water all the day time. The Africans tame and manage some of these horses, and they prove exceeding swift; but a man must beware how he passe over deepe rivers with them, for they will sodainly dive under water. Also in these rivers of Ethiopia are bred a kinde of Oxen, which live every night upon the lande. Here likewise breedeth another strange creature, called in the Congonian language Ambize Angulo, that is to say, a hogge-fish, being so exceeding fatte, and of such greatnes, that some of them weie above five hundred pound. . . . Heere also, besides goates, sheepe, deere, Gugelle, conies, hares, civet-cats, and ostriches, are great swarmes of tigres, which are very hurtfull both to man and beast. The Zebra or Zabra of this countrey being about the bignes of a mule, is a beast of incomparable swiftnes, straked about the body, legges, eares, and other parts, with blacke, white and browne circles of three fingers broad; which do make a pleasant shew. Buffles, wilde asses, called by the Greekes Onagri, and Dantes (of whose hard skins they make all their targets) range in heards up and downe the woods. Also here are infinite store of elephants of such monstrous bignes, that by the report of sundrie credible persons, some of their teeth do weigh two hundred pounds, at sixteene ounces the pound: upon the plaines this beast is swifter than any horse, by reason of his long steps; onely he cannot turne with such celeritie. Trees he overturneth with the strength of his backe, or breaketh them between his teeth, or standeth upright upon his hinder feete, to browse upon the leaves and tender sprigs. The she elephants beare their brood in their wombes two yeeres before they bring foorth yoong ones: neither are they great with yoong, but onely from seven yeeres to seven yeeres. This creature is saide to live 150 yeeres; hee is of a gentle disposition; and relying upon his great strength, he hurteth none but such as do him iniurie; only he will in a sporting maner gently heave up with his snowte such persons as he meeteth.

ANONYMOUS ENGLISHMAN
(c. 1580)

Cairo and the Nile

The great pleasures of Cairo are in the moneth of August, when by meanes of the great raine in Ethiopia the river Nilus overfloweth and watereth all the countrey, and then they open the mouth of a great ditch, which extendeth into the river, and passeth through the midst of the citie, and entring there are innumerable barkes rowing to and fro laden with gallant girles and beautifull dames, which with singing, eating, drinking and feasting, take their solace. The women of this countrey are most beautifull, and goe in rich attire bedecked with gold, pretious stones, and jewels of great value, but chiefely perfumed with odours, and are very libidinous, and the men likewise, but foule and hard favoured.

Without the Citie, sixe miles higher into the land, are to be seene neere unto the river diverse Piramides, among which are three marvellous great, and very artificially wrought. Out of one of these are dayly digged the bodies of auncient men, not rotten but all whole, the cause whereof is the qualitie of the Egyptian soile, which will not consume the flesh of man, but rather dry and harden the same, and so alwayes conserveth it. And these dead bodies are the Mummie which the Phisitians and Apothecaries doe against our willes make us swallow.

ANDREW BATTEL
(*fl.* 1589–1614)

English adventurer. In 1589 Battel was captured by South American Indians who handed him over to the Portuguese. Eventually he was taken to Zaire on the Congo, where he was given a pinnace to collect ivory, wheat and palm-tree oil for his masters. After an unsuccessful escape attempt he was banished to the interior where he spent six years. After another attempt, equally unsuccessful, he was sent on an expedition against one of the local tribes, in the course of which he was badly injured in the leg. On another occasion he was left as a hostage with the Gagas, a cannibal tribe, equipped only with a musket. His marksmanship so impressed them, however, that they spared him. When he eventually escaped from the Portuguese he returned to England, after an absence of eighteen years, with many strange tales to tell.

Pongos and Engecos

The Woods are so covered with Baboones, Monkies, Apes, and Parrots, that it will feare any man to travaile in them alone. Here are also two kinds of Monsters, which are common in these Woods, and very dangerous.

The greatest of these two Monsters is called, *Pongo*, in their Language: and the lesser is called, *Engeco*. This *Pongo* is in all proportion like a man, but that he is more like a Giant in a stature, then a man: for he is very tall, a hath a mans face, hollow eyed, with long haire upon his browes. His face and eares are without haire, and his hands also. His bodie is full of haire, but not very thicke, and it is of a dunnish colour. He differeth not from a man, but in his legs, for they have no calfe. Hee goeth alwaies upon his legs, and carrieth his hands clasped on the nape of his necke, when he goeth upon the ground. . . . They goe many together, and kill many *Negroes* that travaile in the Woods. Many times they fall upon the Elephants, which come to feed where they be, and so beate them with their clubbed fists, and pieces of wood, that they will runne roaring away from them. Those *Pongoes* are never taken alive, because they are so strong, that ten men cannot hold one of them. . . .

JAMES BRUCE
(1730–1794)

Scottish explorer. An enormous, vain, red-headed Scot of great courage, James Bruce, the laird of Kinnaird, enjoyed travel for its own sake. In 1768 he set out to discover the source of the Nile. After many adventures, and having been provided with a troop of imperial horses by Ras Michael, the ruler of Abyssinia, he reached the Little Abbai, source of the Blue Nile. He believed it to be the main source of the Nile and, as such, thought that he was the first European to set eyes on it. (He was wrong: he had been preceded by two Jesuit priests – Father Pedro Paez in *c.* 1613, and Father Jeronimo Lobo, who lived in Abyssinia between 1624 and 1633. The latter described it as being 'two springs . . . each about five feet and a half deep, a stone's cast distant from one another'.)

A mere private Briton at the source of the Blue Nile

Half undressed as I was by the loss of my sash, and throwing my shoes off, I ran down the hill, towards the little island of green sods, which was about two hundred yards distant; the whole side of the hill was thick grown over with flowers, the large bulbous roots of which appearing above the surface of the ground, and their skins coming off on treading upon them, occasioned me two very severe falls before I reached the brink of the marsh; I after this came to the island of green turf, which was in the form of an altar, apparently the work of art, and I stood in rapture over the principal fountain which rises in the middle of it.

It is easier to guess than to describe the situation of my mind at that moment – standing in that spot which had baffled the genius, industry and inquiry of both ancients and moderns, for the course of near three thousand years. . . . Though a mere private Briton, I triumphed here, in my own mind, over kings and their armies; and every comparison was leading nearer and nearer to presumption, when the place itself where I stood, the object of my vain-glory, suggested what depressed my short-lived triumph. I was but a few minutes arrived at the sources of the Nile, through numberless dangers and sufferings, the least of which would have overwhelmed me, but for the continual goodness and protection of Providence; I was, however, but then half through my journey, and all those dangers which I had already passed, awaited me again on my return. I found a despondency gaining ground fast upon me, and blasting the crown of laurels I had too rashly woven for myself. I resolved, therefore, to divert, till I could, on more solid reflection, overcome its progress.

MUNGO PARK
(1771–1806)

Scottish explorer. Park went to Sumatra as a ship's surgeon for the East India Company after qualifying as a doctor at Edinburgh University. On his return, he was invited to undertake a journey in search of the source of the Niger. In July 1795 he arrived at Pisania, on the Gambia, and five months later set out for interior accompanied by a Negro servant named Johnson, a boy, two asses and one horse.

An encounter with some harpies between Buggil and Soobrudooka, 19 December 1795

We departed from Buggil, and travelled along a dry, stony height, covered with *mimosas*, till mid-day, when the land sloped towards the east, and we descended into a deep valley, in which I observed abundance of whin-stone and white quartz. Pursuing our course to the eastward, along this valley, in the bed of an exhausted river course, we came to a large village, where we intended to lodge. We found many of the natives dressed in a thin French gauze, which they called *byqui*; this being a light airy dress, and well calculated to display the shape of their persons, is much esteemed by the ladies. The manners of these females, however, did not correspond with their dress, for they were rude and troublesome in the highest degree; they surrounded me in numbers, begging for amber, beads, etc., and were so vehement in their solicitations, that I found it impossible to resist them. They tore my cloak, cut the buttons from my boy's clothes, and were proceeding to other outrages, when I mounted my horse and rode off, followed for half a mile by a body of these harpies.

First sight of the Niger at Segou, 21 July 1796

As we approached the town, I was fortunate enough to overtake the fugitive Kaartans, to whose kindness I had been so much indebted in my journey through Bambarra. They readily agreed to introduce me to the king; and we rode together through some marshy ground, where, as I was anxiously looking around for the river, one of them called out, geo affilli, (see the water); and looking forwards, I saw with infinite pleasure the great object of my mission; the long sought for, majestic Niger, glittering to the morning sun, as broad as the Thames at Westminster, and flowing slowly to the *eastward*. I hastened to the brink, and, having drank of the water, lifted up my fervent thanks in prayer, to the Great Ruler of all things, for having thus far crowned my endeavours with success.

The circumstance of the Niger's flowing towards the east, and its collateral points, did not, however, excite my surprise; for although I had left Europe in great hesitation on this subject, and rather believed that it ran in the contrary direction, I had made such frequent inquiries during my progress, concerning this river; and received from Negroes of different nations, such clear and decisive assurances that its general course was *towards the rising sun*, as scarce left any doubt on my mind.

Nine days later, 'worn down by sickness, exhausted with hunger and fatigue, half-naked, and without any article of value by which [he] might procure provisions, clothes, or lodging, [he] began to reflect seriously on [his] situation.' He turned for home, arriving back in Britain in 1797, where he worked as a country doctor in Scotland and published his Travels in the Interior Districts of Africa, *which became a best-seller.*

In 1805, accompanied by his brother-in-law and forty Europeans, thirty of whom were soldiers, Park embarked on a second expedition, to trace the Niger to its mouth. By the time the expedition reached the Niger only eleven Europeans were still alive. There was worse to come.

Mungo Park's last letter to his wife, from Sansanding on the Niger, 19 November 1805

It grieves me to the heart to write any thing that may give you uneasiness; but such is the will of him who *doeth all things well!* Your brother Alexander, my dear friend, is no more! He died of fever at Sansanding, on the morning of the 28th of October; for particulars I must refer you to your father.

I am afraid that, impressed with a woman's fears and the anxieties of a wife, you may be led to consider my situation as a great deal worse than it really is. It is true, my dear friends, Mr. Anderson and George Scott, have both bid adieu to the things of this world; and the greater part of the soldiers have died on the march during the rainy season; but you may believe me, I am in good health. The rains are completely over, and the healthy season has commenced, so that there is no danger of sickness: and I have still a sufficient force to protect me from any insult in sailing down the river, to the sea. . . .

I think it not unlikely but I shall be in England before you receive this. – You may be sure that I feel happy at turning my face towards home. We this morning have done with all intercourse with the natives; and the sails are now hoisting for our departure for the coast.

> *On the same day Park left Sansanding with the four surviving Europeans (one of them insane), three slaves and a guide. What happened next is known only from the testimony of the only survivor, one of the slaves. He reported that Park and the rest of the party had drowned in the Niger when their boat sank after an ambush.*

WILLIAM J. BURCHELL
(1782–1863)

English naturalist. A nurseryman's son, Burchell worked at Kew before being sent to St Helena as government botanist. He arranged for his fiancée to follow him, but on the voyage out she fell in love with the ship's captain and married him instead. Distraught, Burchell threw up his post and set off for South Africa, where in 1811–12 he undertook a remarkable journey into the interior. A meticulous naturalist, he collected over 63,000 objects of scientific interest, identified the white rhino and a new type of zebra that was duly named in his honour, and kept a meticulous log of his finds. He spent the rest of his life cataloguing and discussing his collections of animals and plants from Africa and South America – literally, for when, at the age of eighty-two, he completed the work, he committed suicide.

A bad night with a Boer meester, Graaffreynet, March 1812

This *meester*, as he was called, (that is; *schoolmeester*, or school-master) considered it part of his profession, like the meester at Pieter Jacobs's, to let every person know the extent of his acquirements. But this was done without any inordinate share of vanity; and, I confess, I was not sorry at his making this display; for, although there was nothing which any person but a Cape meester would boast of, it was an agreeable relief from the monotony of a conversation on agricultural subjects, the only topics which gener-ally are to be expected at such farm-houses. He exhibited some small drawings which, he told me, were done entirely with the juice of the petals of a species of *oxalis* producing a blue color, of the tint of indigo. He had very ingeniously made pencils from the hair of the springbuck; and as far as my present stock of drawing materials would permit, I was glad at being able to supply his wants, by furnishing him with a few camels-hair pencils and a piece of China-ink. With these he employed himself in the evening in making a copy of my drawing of the rhinoceros. His powers in penmanship were not despicable; and as a proof of steadiness of hand and of good sight, he gave me a piece of paper on which, by the naked eye, he had written the 'Lord's Prayer' twice in a circular space of less than seven tenths of an inch in diameter.

At night I sat down with the family to a hot supper of mutton; to which were added, a salad of cucumbers, and a large bowl of milk: this last being usually the concluding dish at a boor's supper.

. . . The rooms in the principal house being but three (that is, one in the middle in which the family sit and take their meals, and one bed-room at each end) a visitor could not be accommodated with a chamber to himself. A bed was therefore prepared for me, in the same apartment with the meester and his three scholars.

This tutor was in every respect, qualified for finishing their education, and for completing them for Dutch farmers; for a man who does not *smoke*, is a rare phenomenon in this colony, and is generally looked upon by the boors as an imperfect creature; a disadvantage which I myself laboured under, but which, for want of any natural talent for this accomplishment, I was never able to overcome. I might perhaps have partly retrieved my character in their estimation, could I even have shown them that I enjoyed it in taste; or even in smell, by exhibiting both nostrils blackened, and hermetically closed, with that elegant and fashionable dirt, called in England, *snuff*: but in both these arts, unfortunately, I was equally deficient.

This tutor, then, as soon as he was in bed, placed the candle by his side, as I at first thought and hoped, to extinguish it, that I might be left to close my eyes for that sleep which nature demanded after two days of fatigue with little intermediate rest. But finding that the light still remained, I turned my head towards it, and, to my double mortification, beheld the *meester* lying very quietly, with a short crooked German pipe hanging from one corner of his mouth, while from the other, arose clouds of smoke rapidly following each other, till the room was filled with the fume of tobacco, and myself almost suffocated.

At length when that pipe was finished, I had some little respite, but it was only while he was occupied in filling it again. In this interval, finding that I was not asleep, a circumstance not much to be wondered at, he began to relate to me some of his *adventures* in foreign parts; and these reminiscences afforded him so much satisfaction, that he allowed himself to talk and smoke in alternate fits, so that the second pipe, unfortunately, lasted twice as long as the first. But, as it would ill become a guest so hospitably received, to interrupt his entertainers' enjoyments, I endured it all with perfect patience till the last; though, at an hour when most mortals desire to be 'lulled into sweet oblivion,' his candle, his pipe, and his conversation, kept three of my senses in a state of continued irritation.

By degrees the smoking became fainter; the anecdotes of Malacca, Batavia, and Moccha, were at length all exhausted; he stretched forth his arm to put out the candle; and bade me *Goodnight*. But the long-wished-for hour of sleep was not yet come; and it now fell to his turn to be annoyed. Scarcely had we begun to doze, when repeated claps of the most violent thunder, roused us again; and flashes of lightning glaring through the window, gave us opportunities of beholding each other once more.

In a few minutes after this, the sound of the rain out of doors, pouring down in torrents, made me, notwithstanding the tobacco smoke, consider myself fortunate in being at such a time under the *shelter of a roof*. Presently, I heard the meester start up, and, with furious rattling, begin dragging his bed, with the frame which supported it, from one side of the room to the other. He cried out, in a mixed tone of lamentation and surprize, that the rain was running down upon him in a stream, from the *groot gat in het dak*; and truly enough; for on looking upwards, I saw, what I had not noticed before, a 'great hole in the roof,' just above the place whence he had so long been issuing his fumigations, and his anecdotes of Malacca, Batavia, and Moccha. When I saw this, I began to regret that the storm had not commenced an hour or two sooner.

JOHANN LUDWIG
BURCKHARDT
(1784–1817)

Swiss traveller. Discoverer of Petra and the great rock temple of Rameses II at Abu Simbel. In 1812 he set off, in disguise, on a camel journey which was to take him through the Nubian desert to the slave entrepôt of Shendi in the great bend of the Nile, then on to Suakin on the Red Sea and, ultimately, across the Red Sea to Jiddah and Mecca. All this was to provide himself with an alibi for a journey to the Niger from the Nile by way of Timbuktu, which he intended to make in the guise of a returning pilgrim. He died in 1817, in Cairo, before he could carry it out and was buried in the Muslim cemetery under the name he had used on the pilgrimage, Ibrahim ibn Abdallah.

A pilgrim's provisions

I appeared at Daraou in the garb of a poor trader, the only character in which I believe I could possibly have succeeded. It may not be superfluous that I should inform the reader in detail of the contents of my baggage, and of my provisions: at least it had always been, with me, a great desideratum in reading books of travels, to collect such information for my own use.

I was dressed in a brown loose woollen cloak, such as is worn by the peasants of Upper Egypt, called Thabout, with a coarse white linen shirt and trowsers, a Lebde, or white woollen cap, tied round with a common handkerchief, as a turban, and with sandals on my feet. I carried in the pocket of my Thabout, a small journal-book, a pencil, pocket-compass, pen-knife, tobacco-purse, and a steel for striking a light. The provisions I took with me were as follows: forty pounds of flour, twenty of biscuit, fifteen of dates, ten of lentils, six of butter, five of salt, three of rice, two of coffee beans, four of tobacco, one of pepper, some onions, and eighty pounds of Dhourra for my ass. Besides these I had a copper boiler, a copper plate, a coffee roaster, an earthen mortar to pound the coffee beans, two coffee cups, a knife and spoon, a wooden bowl for drinking and filling the water-skins, an axe, ten yards of rope, needles and thread, a large packing needle, one spare shirt, a comb, a coarse carpet, a woollen cloth (Heram) of Mogrebin manufactory for a night covering, a small parcel of medicines, and three spare water-skins.

I had also a small pocket Coran, bought at Damascus, which I lost afterwards on the day of the pilgrimage, 10th of November, 1814, among the crowds of Mount Arafat [at Mecca], – a spare journal-book and an inkstand, together with some loose sheets of paper, for writing amulets for the Negroes. My watch had been broken in Upper Egypt, where I had no means of getting another. The hours of march noted down in the journal are therefore merely by computation, and by observing the course of the sun.

The little merchandize I took with me consisted of twenty pounds of sugar, fifteen of soap, two of nutmegs, twelve razors, twelve steels, two red caps, and several dozen of wooden beads, which are an excellent substitute for coin in the southern countries. I had a gun, with three dozen of cartridges and some small shot, a pistol, and a large stick, called nabbout, strengthened with iron at either end, and serving either as a weapon, or to pound the coffee beans, and which, according to the custom of the country, was my constant companion. My purse, worn in a girdle under the Thabout, contained fifty Spanish dollars, including the twenty-five, the price of my camel, and I had besides sewed a couple of sequins in a small leathern amulet, tied round my elbow, thinking this to be the safest place for secreting them. . . . All my baggage and provisions were packed up in five leather bags or djerab, much in use among the slave-traders; those articles of which I stood in daily need, I put up in a small saddle-bag on my ass.

AUGUSTUS EARLE
(fl. 1815–1831)

English artist and traveller. After exploring the Mediterranean and North and South America between 1815 and 1824, Earle left Rio for the Cape of Good Hope, hoping to get a passage to India. Instead he found himself stranded on Tristan da Cunha, an island 1500 miles west of the Cape, then populated by seven men, two women and a few children. He later became the draughtsman on the *Beagle*, the ship on which Darwin was the naturalist.

Dismal thoughts in Tristan da Cunha

Our house is (and all are built nearly after the same model) a complete proof of the nationality of an Englishman, and his partiality for a comfortable fire-side. Though the latitude is temperate, each room is furnished with a noble fire-place; and in what we call 'The Government House,' we meet every night, and sit round a large and cheerful blaze, each telling his story, or adventures, or singing his song; and we manage to pass the time pleasantly enough.

Looking out from my abode, no spot in the world can be more desolate; particularly on a blowing night. The roar of the sea is almost deafening; and the wind rushing furiously down the perpendicular sides of the mountains, which are nearly nine hundred feet high, and are masses of craggy rocks, has the most extraordinary and almost supernatural effect. No sooner does night set in than the air is full of nocturnal birds, whose screams are particularly mournful; and then comes the painful reflection, that I am so many thousands of miles from every human haunt, and separated from all

48

my friends and family, who are in total ignorance of where I am, or what has become of me. But I force myself to struggle against dismal thoughts, unwilling that my comrades (who do every thing in their power to console me) should suspect how much I suffer. . . .

HUGH CLAPPERTON
(1788–1827)

British explorer, one of twenty-two children of a Scottish surgeon. In 1822, after service in the Royal Navy in East India and Canada (where he hunted with the Huron Indians and came close to marrying one of their princesses), Clapperton joined the Bornou Mission, an expedition setting off from Tripoli to the interior. His companions were Walter Oudney, a Scottish naval surgeon and botanist, and Major Dixon Denham, an unpleasant army officer who spent his time sending the British Consul at Tripoli scurrilous reports about Clapperton's alleged homosexual relations with his native servants. On 4 February 1823 they discovered Lake Chad; then the party split up, Clapperton and Oudney moving west towards Kano, Denham travelling south-east to reach the Chari River which feeds the lake. Oudney died *en route* and Clapperton reached Kano alone.

Clapperton enters Kano, 20 January 1824

At eleven o'clock we entered Kano, the great emporium of the kingdom of Haussa, but I had no sooner passed the gates than I felt grievously disappointed; for from the flourishing description of it given by the Arabs, I expected to see a city of surprising grandeur: I found, on the contrary, the houses nearly a quarter of a mile from the walls, and in many parts scattered into detached groups, between large stagnant pools of water. I might have spared all the pains I had taken with my toilet; for not an individual turned his head round to gaze at me, but all, intent on their own business, allowed me to pass by without notice or remark.

RÉNÉ CAILLIÉ
(1799–1838)

A penniless young Frenchman of humble parentage, Caillié, inspired to become an explorer after reading *Robinson Crusoe*, was obsessed with the idea of seeing Timbuktu. After eleven years' careful preparation, he set off in April 1827 from the Rio Nuñez, north of Sierra Leone. A year later, after a long and hazardous journey, he reached his goal and became the first European to reach the legendary city and return to tell the tale.

'An indescribable satisfaction' (and something of a disappointment)

. . . We arrived safely at Timbuctoo, just as the sun was touching the horizon. I now saw this capital of the Soudan, to reach which had so long been the object of my wishes. On entering this mysterious city, which is an object of curiosity and research to the civilised nations of Europe, I experienced an indescribable satisfaction. I never before felt a similar emotion and my transport was extreme. I was obliged, however to restrain my feelings, and to God alone did I confide my joy. With what gratitude did I return thanks to Heaven, for the happy result which attended my enterprise! How many grateful thanksgivings did I pour forth for the protection which God had vouchsafed to me, amidst obstacles and dangers which appeared insurmountable. This duty being ended, I looked around and found that the sight before me, did not answer my expectations. I had formed a totally different idea of the grandeur and wealth of Timbuctoo. The city presented, at first view, nothing but a mass of ill-looking houses, built of earth. Nothing was to be seen in all directions but immense plains of quicksand of a yellowish white colour. The sky was a pale red as far as the horizon: all nature wore a dreary aspect, and the most profound silence prevailed; not even the warbling of a bird was to be heard. Still, though I cannot account for the impression, there was something imposing in the aspect of a great city, raised in the midst of sands, and the difficulties surmounted by its founders cannot fail to excite admiration.

RICHARD LEMON LANDER
(1804–1834)

English explorer. A Cornishman, Lander accompanied Hugh Clapperton as his attendant on his second expedition into Africa. The party landed at Badagri in the Bight of Benin (near Lagos) in November 1825; their mission was to discover the mouth of the Niger. Of the five Englishman accompanying Clapperton, three died almost immediately and another left the expedition. Clapperton and Lander went on alone with some native servants.

The enormous widow Zuma

While we remained in the city of Wow Wow [Wawa, near the Niger], we were visited almost every day by a widow lady, of Arabic extraction, named *Zuma* (*Honey* in English), between thirty and forty years of age, who, if one might be allowed to judge from the remaining charms which were still visible in her countenance, had been really beautiful in her younger years. This individual was vastly rich, being the acknowledged mistress of a thousand slaves; and from her excessive plumpness, and extraordinary size was the exact counterpart of our bulky friend Ebo, the fat eunuch of Katunga. Zuma's affection for my master and myself was unbounded, and as it led to an adventure perhaps never equalled in novelty by any incident that has occurred to Europeans in the bosom of Africa, I hope I may be forgiven in attempting to trace its causes and effects, without which my narrative would be incomplete; for they are so intimately connected with each other, that it would be impossible to disunite them. . . .

It was the misfortune of the far-famed Zuma to fancy herself, for no reason in the world, to be extremely fair, and although she had certainly passed the 'Age of the Passions,' she took it into her head to fall desperately in love with me, whose complexion, she affirmed, rivalled her own in whiteness! The frequency of her visitations to our house nourished the tender feeling, which was encouraged by Captain Clapperton, who relished a joke with all his heart, and did his utmost to inflame the lady's passion, by passing a thousand unmeaning compliments on the regularity of my features, and the handsomeness of my person. 'See what beautiful eyes he has,' observed the Captain: 'if you were to search from Badagry to Wow Wow, you would not find such eyes.' . . .

For my own part I was but a novice in the art of courtship, and imagining it to be altogether in jest, took little pains to spoil the fun by shrinking from it. Besides, Zuma had behaved remarkably well to us in sending, repeatedly, presents of provisions, together with every luxury with which she was acquainted, and I was rather glad than otherwise to have her for our guest,

> ——'For the heart must
> Leap kindly back to kindness;'

and neither of us wished to offend a lady of her consequence by being morose and unsociable in manners, or by repelling her advances with ridicule and contempt.

For an hour together the widow would gaze intently on me, while the most amorous glances shot from her large, full, and certainly beautiful eyes, which confused and disconcerted me not a little, even though I was surrounded by strangers and in the heart of Africa; for I had been a wanderer from my childhood, and had had but few opportunities of mingling in the delightful company of the gentler sex in my own country, and consequently was excessively bashful on coming in contact with ladies, whether in the country of the Hottentots, or the birth-place of the widow Zuma.

As for my master, he was sensibly delighted with these interviews, and with his arms folded on his breast, while thick volumes of tobacco-smoke rolled from his pipe, he with the most impenetrable gravity enjoyed the scene, and looked as happy and as much at home as if he had been seated by his friends in his native Scotland. After the widow's departure, it was his usual custom, tapping me on the shoulder, to ask how I felt my heart, and observe what a boast I could make, on our return to England, of so magnificent a conquest.

All this I took in good part for some days; but things beginning, at length, to wear a more serious aspect than I had at first anticipated, I was resolved to bring this whimsical courtship to a conclusion as speedily as possible. I was the more inclined to do so, because I did not wish to wound the feelings of even a *black* lady (for black she most certainly was, although not quite so deep a sable as the aborigines), by trifling with them; nor did I forget the exclamation of the frog in the fable: – 'It may be sport to you, but it is death to us!'

Independently of the delicate state of my health, which incapacitated me from carrying on so curious an amour with the spirit and gallantry it required, I was positively afraid that, from the warmth and energy of Zuma's embraces, I should actually be pressed to death between her monstrous arms! I was but a youth, and my short residence in the country had certainly impaired a constitution originally robust and vigorous; by reason of which I was sadly apprehensive that one of her Brobdingnagian hugs would send me into the other world with very little ceremony. These reflexions I had seriously revolved in my mind; and on her next visit I candidly told the widow by signs, words, and gestures, that I could not love her; but she either did not or would not understand me. I remarked that I should never choose a *black* wife: she pointed to her face, and said she was a *white* woman. I then observed that it would be impossible for me to exist in her country, the heat being insupportable. Her reply was disinterested and tender: – 'Then I will quit it, and follow you to whichever part of the world you may be inclined to lead me to.' Thus beset on all sides, I hardly knew what to say next; but after a short pause, summing up all my resolution, I gave my greasy inamorata a flat refusal to see her again in the light of a lover, as it was out of her power to awaken in my breast a corresponding sensation to that which reigned in her own! and saying this I instantly left the apartment; whilst Zuma, poor lady,

> ——'Rais'd a sigh so piteous and profound,
> As it did seem to shatter all her bulk,
> And end her being!' . . .

Poor widow Zuma! I almost fancy I see her now, waddling into our house, a moving world of flesh, 'puffing and blowing like a blacksmith's bellows,' and the very pink and essence of African fashion. Her hair used to be carefully dyed with indigo, and of a rich and vivid blue; her feet and hands stained with hennah and an extract of the goora-nut, produced alternate streaks of red and yellow; and her teeth were also tinged with a delicate crimson stain. In the adornment of her person, likewise, the buxom widow evinced considerable taste. Her bared neck and bosom were ornamented with coral and gold beads, which, contrasted with the dingy colour of her skin, occasioned a truly captivating effect! while a dress of striped silk, hanging in graceful folds from the waist to the ancles, set off her *fairy form* to the best possible advantage! Thus beautified, the accomplished Zuma used to sit cross-legged on our mat, and chewing the goora-nut, or a little tobacco-snuff, she was without exception the most ravishing object that came across our path in all our wanderings!

> *On reaching Sokoto, Clapperton fell ill with fever. He died on 13 April 1827 and was buried by Lander on the outskirts of the town. 'Opening a prayer-book, amidst a shower of tears, I read the impressive funeral service of the Church of England over the remains of my valued master – the English flag waving slowly and mournfully over them at the same moment. Not a single soul listened to this peculiarly distressing ceremony; for the slaves were quarrelling with each other the whole of the time it lasted.' Lander returned to the coast, where he was subjected to a disagreeable experience by the local ruler.*

Ordeal by poison

The news of the white man's arrest, and approaching trial, spread like wild-fire through the town, and the inhabitants, assembling from all parts, armed with axes, spears, clubs, and bows and arrows, followed the procession to the dismal spot. On entering the hut, I beheld a number of priests and elders of the people, seated in a circle, who desired me to stand in the midst of them. When I had complied with their request, one of the priests arose, and presenting me with a bowl, containing about a quart of a clear liquid, scarcely distinguishable from water, cried out in a loud voice, and with much emphasis, 'You are accused, white man, of designs against our king and his government, and are therefore desired to drink the contents of this vessel, which, if the reports to your prejudice be true, will surely destroy you; whereas, if they be without foundation, you need not fear, Christian; the fetish will do you no injury, for our gods will do that which is right.'

I took the bowl in my trembling hand, and gazed for a moment on the sable countenances of my judges; but not a single look of compassion shone upon any of them; a dead silence prevailed in the gloomy sanctuary of skulls; every eye was intently fixed upon me; and seeing no possibility of escape, or of evading the piercing glance of the priests and elders, I offered up, internally, a short prayer to the Throne of Mercy, – to the God of Christians, – and hastily swallowed the fetish, dashing the poison-chalice to the ground. A low murmur ran through the assembly; they all thought I should instantly have expired, or at least have discovered symptoms of severe agony, but detecting no such tokens, they arose simultaneously, and made way for me to leave the hut. On getting into the open air, I found my poor slaves in tears; they had come, they said, to catch a last glimpse of their master; but when they saw me alive and at liberty, they leaped and danced for joy, and prepared a path for me through the dense mass of armed people. These set up an astounding shout at my unexpected appearance, and seemed greatly pleased, (if I might be allowed to judge;) that I had not fallen a victim to the influence of their fearful fetish. On arriving at my dwelling, I took instant and powerful means to eject the venomous potion from my stomach, and happily succeeded in the attempt.

I was told that the liquid I had swallowed was a decoction of the bark of a tree abounding in the neighbourhood, and that I was the only individual who, for a long season, had escaped its poisonous qualities. It had a disagreeably bitter taste, but I experienced no other ill effects from it than a slight dizziness, which wore off completely a few hours after the conclusion of the trial.

GÉRARD DE NERVAL
(1808–1855)

Pseudonym of Gérard Labrunie. French writer. In December 1842, shortly after the death of the great love of his life, Jenny Colon, Nerval left for the East. He visited Egypt, Lebanon, Greece and Turkey.

Buying a slave, Cairo, 1843

Early the following morning I set off with Abdullah to the slave bazaar at Souk-el-Ezzi. I had chosen a very handsome donkey, streaked like a zebra, for this occasion, and arranged my new costume with a measure of affectation. Buying women is no reason for frightening them, as I had learnt from the scornful laughter of the Negresses.

We arrived at a quite splendid house that must have once belonged to a kachef (bey's deputy) or a mameluke bey; the hall extended into a colonnaded gallery along one side of the courtyard, at the end of which was a wooden divan adorned with cushions.

Here a good-looking, elegantly dressed Muslim was holding court; nonchalantly he fingered his rosary of aloes, while a Negro boy rekindled his narghile for him; a Coptic scribe, seated at his feet, probably served him as a secretary.

'This,' Abdullah announced, 'is his honour Abd-el-Kerim, the most illustrious of slave-merchants. He can procure you the loveliest women, if he wants to . . . he's wealthy and he often keeps them for himself.' . . .

His features were refined and distinguished, his eyes penetrating, and his manners courteous; it was only natural that he should conduct me through his palace where he devoted himself, however, to a very dismal trade. He was an affable prince and at the same time a pitiless, resolute freebooter: a strange and fascinating mixture, indeed. He had to dominate the slaves with a fierce glance from his melancholy eyes, even make them suffer, and finally have them leave him full of regrets that he was no longer their master. Clearly enough, any woman sold to me by Abd-el-Kerim would leave him like a mistress forced to leave her lover, but this prospect didn't deter me, for I was already so struck myself by his character and expression that I was almost sure I would settle my business with him and no other. . . .

Abd-el-Kerim now invited me to enter the private section of his house, and Abdullah was discreet enough to remain behind at the foot of the staircase.

In a spacious room with a carved ceiling, which enriched a number of painted and gold arabesques, I saw lined up against the wall five quite beautiful women whose tints recalled the glowing bronze of Florence; their features were symmetrical, their noses straight, their mouths small; the perfect oval of their heads, the graceful lines of their necks and the serenity of their expression made them resemble those Italian paintings of the Madonna which time has faintly tarnished. They were Catholic Abyssinians, descendants, perhaps, of Father John or Queen Candicia.

To make a particular choice was by no means an easy matter, for they all looked alike, which is what generally occurs among these primitive races. Seeing me hesitate, Abd-el-Kerim thought they didn't attract me, so he had another one brought in; indolently, she walked towards the wall and then turned round to face us.

I was unable to suppress a cry of enthusiasm as I immediately recognized the almond-shaped eyes and the slanting eyelids of a Javanese, while her complexion confirmed that she belonged to the yellow race. Nor can I explain my sudden, overwhelming inclination for the strange and unexpected which quickly led me to decide in her favour. Moreover, she was extremely beautiful, and I didn't hesitate to admire her firm but supple body; the metallic glint of her eyes, the whiteness of her teeth, the elegance of her hands, and her dark mahogany-coloured hair, which she revealed when, obeying the merchant's orders, she insolently took off her tarboosh, far from offered me any cause to object to Abd-el-Kerim's eulogies:

'*Bono! Bono!*' he exclaimed.

We descended the staircase and discussed business, with Abdullah acting as interpreter. This woman had arrived the day before along with the caravan's retinue.

'But,' I said to Abdullah, 'if Abd-el-Kerim put her among his wives yesterday. . . .'

'But what? . . .' my dragoman insisted, looking at me with surprise.

I had evidently made a banal remark.

'Do you mean to say,' Abdullah exclaimed, finally understanding my line of thought, 'that his legitimate wives would allow him to flirt with another woman? . . . And then he's a merchant, just think for a moment! Why, if anything like that ever got known he'd lose all his clientele!'

That made sense enough, and Abdullah swore, moreover, that Abd-el-Kerim, as a good Muslim, must have spent the whole of the previous night praying at the mosque, to be ready for the solemn celebrations in honour of Mohammed.

One question remained, then: the price. Abd-el-Kerim asked for 625 francs; at first, I thought of offering only five hundred, but bargaining for a woman struck me as a rather squalid affair. And anyhow, Abdullah informed me, a Turkish merchant never has two prices.

I asked what her name was, for the price of her name would naturally be included in the net sum.

'Z't'n'b,' Abd-el-Kerim said.

'Z't'n'b,' Abdullah repeated with a tremendous nasal contraction.

I was unable to understand how the sneezing of four consonants represented a name; it took me some time to figure out that Z't'n'b could more reasonably be pronounced Zetnaybia.

FRANCIS OWEN
(fl. 1837)

English missionary. In 1836, while a curate in Yorkshire, he was inspired by a talk by Captain A. F. Gardiner about his missionary work among the Zulu. On Christmas Eve he sailed for Cape Town and by late summer he was installed, with his wife and sister, at the court of the great Zulu chieftain, Dingaan. Dingaan's territory in Natal was being encroached on by the Boers, led by Piet Retief, and he was anxious to obtain firearms to resist them. While Owen resisted his demands for a bullet-mould and did his best to preach the word of God, Dingaan prepared an elaborate trap for the Boers. The result was a terrible massacre of which Owen was an unwilling witness.

The seed falls on stony ground, Umgungundhlovu, Natal, November 1837

At length I told him [Dingaan] it was Sunday, whereupon he bid me to address his people and teach them the word of God. At the same time he sent Masipulu, his head servant to tell the Indoonas that they were all to be quiet and listen attentively to me. A dead pause immediately ensued. I went forward, feeling in my heart, that I was called to testify Christ publickly in this place for the last, and the only time!

Having advanced within a convenient distance from the men, the king sitting a good way behind, I commenced by telling them that they all knew that there was a great chief above the sky. Dingarn now sent a message to us to tell us to speak up, as we did at Nabamba. Raising our voices I proceeded to say that this king was greater than all kings, greater than my king, greater than their king: that they ought to fear their parents, they ought to fear their king, but much more ought they to fear the great God; they ought to do what their parents bid them, what their king bid them, and also what God bid them! We have none of us, however, done what God has told us to do. We are all sinners before him: He is displeased at us: each of us has a soul that must live for ever when the body is dead, but that our Souls, by reason of sin, are filthy and that they must be *washed*.

Until this moment the greatest stillness and attention prevailed, but now the contradiction began, and such a cavilling and stormy audience never did I before address. It is impossible to give an adequate idea of the dispute which lasted for nearly 2 hours; one cavil succeeded another or was repeated 10 times, whilst no reply was made to my answers. The indoonas and the king were the chief objectors, the latter sitting at some distance behind and speaking low, his servant Masipulu shouted out to my Interpreter all his remarks. First I had to turn to the Indoonas, then to the king as they successively opposed me. When I had begun to speak of the need of spiritual washing in order to introduce the Gospel the subject was treated with scorn. One asked if we were to be washed in the river. I said not with water, but with blood! Whose blood was the natural reply. The blood, I answered, of the Son of God, who was Jesus Christ. Where is he? they asked. In heaven, I said, but once he came down to earth, and . . . Whom did he leave behind to wash us. He washes us himself with his own blood. It is not our bodies that he washes, but our Souls. – He washes all who come to him by faith. Away, its all a lie. I persisted in crying that Jesus Christ shed his blood, and that if they believed in him, that he came down from heaven, that he died for them, their souls would be saved. They asked me how this person was killed and who killed him. I said, wicked men nailed him to a tree. Dingarn then asked if it was God that died. I said, the Son of God. Did not God die, he asked. I said God cannot die. If God does not die, he replied, why has he said that people must die? I told him it was because all people were sinners, and death was the punishment of sin, but he would raise us all again from the grave.

This gave rise to innumerable cavils. They wanted me to tell them the day and the hour when we should rise again, who would be witnesses of the resurrection, who would be alive at that day. They said if any generation had been seen to rise from their graves they would believe. I told them that Jesus Christ rose again the third day, and that he was seen by his 12 servants, and afterwards by 500 persons at once, and that his servants raised a great many other people. Dingarn asked me how many days Jesus Christ had been dead. If only 3 days (said he), it is very likely that he was not dead in reality but only *supposed* to be so! I said, that when he was on the tree a soldier pierced his side from which came forth blood, and that blood, I said, if believed in washes away sin.

After a great deal more combat they told me I need not speak anything more about the resurrection, for they would not believe it. They had no objection to God's word, but they did not believe in the resurrection. . . . This doctrine indeed now appeared to be 'foolishness' to them and as such utterly rejected: but I was encouraged to hope that the Spirit himself would hereafter unfold it to them, shewing them its true import and necessity. It might I hoped be a foundation on which to build at a future time, and doubtless they would remember more, than if my discourse had proceeded in a natural strain.

I many times broke away from their cavillings and exhorted them to believe instead of objecting. The king once asked if all men would go to heaven? I told them plainly, if you believe the words which I now speak you will go to heaven, but if you believe them not you will all go to hell. They wanted me to give a proof that Christ was now in heaven; as who had seen him there. What the persons who took him up into heaven said when they came back again. Umthela remarked that if he saw a bird fly ever so high in the air and he looked at it steadfastly it always came down again. I told them he went up by his own power, in the sight of his disciples and that he would surely come again, when every eye should see him.

ALEXANDER KINGLAKE
(1809–1891)

English historian and author of *Eothen*, a classic of travel-writing, which describes a journey to the Levant and the Near East in 1835. In 1854 Kinglake went to the Crimea with the British Expedition and fortuitously fell off his pony in front of Lord Raglan, who later commissioned him to write the history of the Crimean War. Kinglake did so – in great detail and at enormous length.

Cairo and the plague, 1835

Although the plague was now spreading quick and terrible havoc around him, I did not see very plainly any corresponding change in the looks of the streets until the seventh day after my arrival: I then first observed that the city was *silenced*. There were no outward signs of despair nor of violent terror, but many of the voices that had swelled the busy hum of men were already hushed in death, and the survivors, so used to scream and screech in their earnestness whenever they bought or sold, now showed an unwonted indifference about the affairs of this world: it was less worth while for men to haggle and haggle, and crack the sky with noisy bargains, when the Great Commander was there who could 'pay all their debts with the roll of his drum.'

At this time I was informed that of 25,000 people at Alexandria, 12,000 had died already; the Destroyer had come rather later to Cairo, but there was nothing of weariness in his strides. The deaths came faster than ever they befell in the plague of London: but the calmness of orientals under such visitations, and their habit of using biers for interment instead of burying coffins along with the bodies, rendered it practicable to dispose of the dead in the usual way, without shocking the people by any unaccustomed spectacle of horror. . . .

The funerals pouring through the streets were not the only public evidence of deaths. In Cairo this custom prevails: At the instant of a man's death (if his property is sufficient to justify the expense) professional howlers are employed. I believe that these persons are brought near to the dying man when his end appears to be approaching, and the moment that life is gone they lift up their voices and send forth a loud wail from the chamber of death. Thus I knew when my near neighbours died: sometimes the howls were near, sometimes more distant. Once I was awakened in the night by the wail of death in the next house, and another time by a like howl from the house opposite; and there were two or three minutes, I recollect, during which the howl seemed to be actually *running* along the street.

I happened to be rather teased at this time by a sore throat, and I thought it would be well to get it cured if I could before I again started on my travels. I therefore inquired for a Frank doctor, and was informed that the only one then at Cairo was a Bolognese refugee, a very young practitioner, and so poor that he had not been able to take flight as the other medical men had done. At such a time as this it was out of the question to *send* for a European physician; a person thus summoned would be sure to suppose that the patient was ill of the plague and would decline to come. I therefore rode to the young doctor's residence, ascended a flight or two of stairs, and knocked at his door. No one came immediately, but after some little delay the medico himself opened the door and admitted me. I of course made him understand that I had come to consult him, but before entering upon my throat grievance, I accepted a chair, and exchanged a sentence or two of commonplace conversation. Now the natural commonplace of the city at this season was of a gloomy sort – 'Come va la peste?' (how goes the plague?), and this was precisely the question I put. A deep sigh, and the words, 'Sette cento per giorno, signor' (seven hundred a day), pronounced in a tone of the deepest sadness and dejection, were the answer I received. The day was not oppressively hot, yet I saw that the doctor was transpiring profusely, and even the outside surface of the thick shawl dressing-gown in which he had wrapped himself appeared to be moist. He was a handsome, pleasant-looking young fellow, but the deep melancholy of his tone did not tempt me to prolong the conversation, and without further delay I requested that my throat might be looked at. The medico held my chin in the usual way, and examined my throat; he then wrote me a prescription, and almost immediately afterwards I bade him farewell, but as he conducted me towards the door, I observed an expression of strange and unhappy watchfulness in his rolling eyes. It was not the next day, but the next day but one, if I rightly remember, that I sent to request another interview with my doctor. In due time Dthemetri, my messenger, returned, looking sadly aghast. He had '*met* the medico,' for so he phrased it, 'coming out from his house – in a bier!'

JOHANN LUDWIG KRAPF
(1810–1881)

German Protestant missionary. After working for the Church Missionary Society in Ethiopia, he undertook the first serious modern attempt to introduce Christianity to East Africa. He worked there for eighteen years, and he and his colleague Johann Rebmann were the earliest explorers of the Kilimanjaro region and – in 1848 – the first to set eyes on East Africa's snow-covered peaks.

Dilbo, a slave, tells a missionary about the Pygmies

He told me that to the south of Kaffa and Susa there is a very sultry and humid country with many bamboo woods, inhabited by the race called Dokos, who are no bigger than boys of ten years old; that is, only four feet high. They have a dark, olive-coloured complexion, and live in a completely savage state, like the beasts; having neither houses, temples, nor holy trees, like the Gallas, yet possessing something like an idea of a higher being called Yer, to whom in moments of wretchedness and anxiety they pray – not in an erect posture, but reversed with the head on the ground, and the feet supported upright against a tree or stone. In prayer they say: 'Yer, if thou really dost exist, why dost thou allow us thus to be slain? We do not ask thee for food and clothing, for we live on serpents, ants, and mice. Thou hast made us, why dost thou permit us to be trodden underfoot?' The Dokos have no chief, no laws, no weapons; they do not hunt, nor till the ground, but live solely on fruits, roots, mice, serpents, ants, honey, and the like, climbing trees and gathering the fruits like monkeys, and both sexes go completely naked. They have thick, protruding lips, flat noses, and small eyes; the hair is not woolly, and is worn by the women over the shoulders. The nails on the hands and feet are allowed to grow like the talons of vultures, and are used in digging for ants, and in tearing to pieces the serpents which they devour raw, for they are unacquainted with fire. The spine of the snake is the only ornament worn round the neck, but they pierce the ears with a sharp-pointed piece of wood.

The Dokos multiply very rapidly, but have no regular marriages, the intercourse of the sexes leading to no settled home, each in perfect independence going whither fancy leads. The mother nurses her child only for a short time, accustoming it as soon as possible to the eating of ants and serpents; and as soon as the child can help itself, the mother lets it depart whither it pleases. Although these people live in thick woods, and conceal themselves amongst the trees, yet they become the prey of the slave-hunters of Susa, Kaffa, Dumbaro, and Kulla; for whole regions of their woods are encircled by the hunters, so that the Dokos cannot easily escape. When the slave-hunters come in sight of the poor creatures they hold up clothes of bright colours, singing and dancing, upon which the Dokos allow themselves to be captured, without resistance, knowing from experience that such resistance is fruitless and can lead only to their destruction. In this way thousands can be captured by a small band of hunters; and once captured they become quite docile. In slavery the Dokos retain their predilection for feeding on mice, serpents, and ants, although often on that account punished by their masters, who in other respects are attached to them, as they are docile and obedient, have few wants, and enjoy good health, for which reasons they are never sold as slaves beyond Enarea. As diseases are unknown among them, they die only of old age, or through the assaults of their enemies.

WILLIAM MAKEPEACE THACKERAY
(1811–1863)

English novelist. In the autumn of 1844 he sailed from Southampton on a P & O ship to visit Athens, Constantinople, Jerusalem and Cairo. Like many a penniless writer since, he managed to secure a free passage, and gratefully acknowledged the Peninsular and Oriental Company in his account of the journey. This transaction did not meet with universal approval, Carlyle comparing it to 'the practice of a blind fiddler going to and fro on a penny ferry-boat in Scotland, and playing tunes to the passengers for half-pence'.

From the top of a pyramid

It was nothing but joking and laughter, bullying of guides, shouting for interpreters, quarrelling about sixpences. We were acting a farce, with the Pyramids for the scene. There they rose up enormous under our eyes, and the most absurd, trivial things were going on under their shadow. The sublime had disappeared, vast as they were. Do you remember how Gulliver lost his awe of the tremendous Brobdingnag ladies? Every traveller must go through all sorts of chaffering, and bargaining, and paltry experiences, at this spot. You look up the tremendous steps, with a score of savage ruffians bellowing round you; you hear faint cheers and cries high up, and catch sight of little reptiles crawling upwards; or, having achieved the summit, they come hopping and bouncing down again from degree to degree, – the cheers and cries swell louder and more disagreeable; presently the little jumping thing, no bigger than an insect a moment ago, bounces down upon you expanded into a panting Major of Bengal cavalry. He drives off the Arabs with an oath, – wipes his red shining face with his yellow handkerchief , drops puffing on the sand in a shady corner, where cold fowl and hard eggs are awaiting him, and the next minute you see his nose plunged into a foaming beaker of brandy and soda-water. He can say now, and for ever, he has been up the Pyramid. There is nothing sublime in it. You cast your eye once more up that staggering perspective of a zigzag line, which ends at the summit, and wish you were up there – and down again. Forwards! – Up with you! It must be done. Six Arabs are behind you, who won't let you escape if you would.

The importunity of these ruffians is a ludicrous annoyance to which a traveller must submit. For two miles before you reach the Pyramids, they seize on you and never cease howling. Five or six of them pounce upon one victim, and never leave him until they have carried him up and down. Sometimes they conspire to run a man up the huge stair, and bring him, half-killed and fainting, to the top. Always a couple of brutes insist upon impelling you sternwards; from whom the only means to release yourself is to kick out vigorously and unmercifully, when the Arabs will possibly retreat. The ascent is not the least romantic, or difficult, or sublime: you walk up a great broken staircase, of which some of the steps are four feet high. It's not hard, only a little high. You see no better view from the top than you beheld from the bottom; only a little more river, and sand, and ricefield. You jump down the big steps at your leisure; but your meditations you must keep for after-times, – the cursed shrieking of the Arabs prevents all thought or leisure.

DAVID LIVINGSTONE
(1813–1873)

Scottish missionary and explorer. At the age of ten he started work in a cotton factory. Self-educated, he studied Greek and Divinity at Glasgow University before graduating in medicine from London University. He joined the London Missionary Society and was ordained in 1840. In May 1841 he landed in South Africa, beginning a career as a missionary that was to make him famous throughout the world.

Attacked by a lion

Starting, and looking half round, I saw the lion just in the act of springing upon me. I was upon a little height; he caught my shoulder as he sprang, and we both came to the ground below together. Growling horribly close to my ear, he shook me as a terrier dog does a rat. The shock produces a stupor similar to that which seems to be felt by a mouse after the first shake of the cat. It caused a sort of dreaminess, in which there was no sense of pain nor feeling of terror, though quite conscious of all that was happening. It was like what patients partially under the influence of chloroform describe, who see all the operation, but feel not the knife. This singular condition was not the result of any mental process. The shake annihilated fear, and allowed no sense of horror in looking round at the beast. This peculiar state is probably produced in all animals killed by the carnivora; and if so, is a merciful provision by our benevolent Creator for lessening the pain of death. Turning round to relieve myself of the weight, as he had one paw on the back of my head, I saw his eyes directed to Mebalwe, who was trying to shoot him at a distance of ten or fifteen yards. His gun, a flint one, missed fire in both barrels; the lion immediately left me, and, attacking Mebalwe, bit his thigh. Another man, whose life I had saved before, after he had been tossed by a buffalo, attempted to spear the lion while he was biting Mebalwe. He left Mebalwe and caught this man by the shoulder, but at that moment the bullets he had received took effect, and he fell down dead.

In November 1853 Livingstone set off from Linyanti, near the Chobe River, to cross the continent to the Atlantic. With him he had 27 porters and a number of canoes lent to him by Sekeletu, son of Sebituane, chief of the Makololo. He also carried a tent, five guns, scientific instruments and some ivory tusks for barter. They followed the Upper Zambesi, at first through lush country, then into the rain forest where they were permanently wet through and suffered from fever and dysentery. After traversing a terrible swampy plain, in February 1854 Livingstone crossed the watershed and descended into the Congo Basin. Having survived every imaginable privation and the attentions of savage tribes, he and his party finally reached the coast at Luanda, in Portuguese territory, on 31 May 1854.

The end of the world

As we were now drawing near to the sea, my companions were looking at everything in a serious light. One of them asked me if we should all have an opportunity of watching each other at Loanda. 'Suppose one went for water, would the others see if he were kidnapped?' I replied, 'I see what you are driving at; and if you suspect me, you may return, for I am as ignorant of Loanda as you are: but nothing will happen to you but what happens to myself. We have stood by each other hitherto, and will do so to the last.' The plains adjacent to Loanda are somewhat elevated and comparatively sterile. On coming across these we first beheld the sea: my companions looked upon the boundless ocean with awe. On describing their feelings afterwards, they remarked that 'we marched along with our father, believing that what the ancients had always told us was true, that the world has no end; but all at once the world said to us, "I am finished; there is no more of me!"' They had always imagined that the world was one extended plain without limit.

ROUALEYN GORDON CUMMING
(1820–1866)

Scottish big-game hunter. The second son of a Scottish aristocrat, Cumming first served in the Madras Cavalry, then joined the Royal Veteran Newfoundland Companies but found the life too tame; in 1843 he transferred to the Cape Mounted Rifles, but was similarly disappointed. Resigning his commission in 1844, he set off with his two cavalry chargers as hunting horses, and a Cockney ex-cab-driver for a servant, to shoot big game. Livingstone, whose missionary station he visited several times, called him 'a mad sort of Scotchman'. This was an understatement: Cumming's enthusiasm for the hunt bordered on the lunatic; he tore around South Africa, dressed in a kilt, shooting everything that moved. When he returned home in 1848 he brought thirty tons of souvenirs, many of which were displayed at the Great Exhibition of 1851. He died of drink in 1866.

The disadvantages of hunting quaggas by night

Night was now fast setting in, so we descended, and made for home; cantering along, we observed what we took to be a herd of quaggas and a bull wildebeest standing in front of us, upon which we jumped off our horses, and, bending our bodies, approached them to fire.

It being now quite dark, it was hard to tell what sort of game we were going to fire at; Strydom, however, whispered to me they were quaggas, and they certainly appeared to be such. His gun snapped three times at the wildebeest, upon which they all set off at a gallop; he was riding my stallion, and let go his bridle when he ran in to fire, taking advantage of which the horse set off after them. I then mounted 'The Cow,' and after riding hard for about a mile came up to them. They were now standing still, and the stallion in the middle of them. I made him out by his saddle, and, jumping off my horse in a state of intense excitement, ran forward, fired both barrels of my two-grooved rifle into the quaggas, and heard the bullets tell loudly. They then started off, but the stallion was soon once more fighting in the middle of them; I was astonished and delighted to remark how my horse was able to take up their attention, so that they appeared heedless of the reports of my rifle.

In haste I commenced loading, but to my dismay found that I had left my loading-rod with Hendrick. Mounting 'The Cow,' I rode nearer to the quaggas, and was delighted to find that they allowed my horse to come within easy shot. It was now very dark, but I set off in the hope to fall in with Hendrick on the wide plain, and galloped along shouting with all my might, but in vain. I then rode across the plain for the hill, to try to find some bush large enough to make a ramrod; in this, by the greatest chance, I succeeded, and, being provided with a knife, I cut a good ramrod, loaded my rifle, and rode off to seek the quaggas once more. I soon fell in with them, and, coming within shot, fired at them right and left, and heard both bullets tell, upon which they galloped across the plain with the stallion still after them. One of them, however, was very hard hit, and soon dropped astern – the stallion remained to keep him company.

About this time the moon shone forth faintly. I galloped on after the troop, and, soon coming up with them, rode on one side, when, dismounting and dropping on my knee, I sent a bullet through the shoulder of the last quagga; he staggered forward, fell to the ground with a heavy crash, and expired. The rest of the troop charged wildly around him, snorting and prancing like the wild horses in *Mazeppa*, and then set off at full speed across the plain; I did not wait to bleed the quagga, but, mounting my horse, galloped on after the troop, nevertheless I could not overtake them. Returning, I endeavoured to find the quagga that I had last shot, but owing to the darkness, and my having no mark to guide me on the plain, I failed to find him. I then set off to try for the quagga which had dropped astern with the stallion; having searched some time in vain, I dismounted, and, laying my head on the ground, made out two dark objects which turned out to be what I sought. On my approaching, the quagga tried to make off, when I sent a ball through his shoulder, which laid him low. Going up to him in the full expectation of inspecting for the first time one of these animals, what was my disappointment and vexation to find a fine brown gelding, with two white stars on his forehead! The truth now flashed upon me; Strydom and I had both been mistaken; instead of quaggas, the wagon-team of a neighbouring Dutchman had afforded me my evening's shooting!

An appalling storm

On the forenoon of the 19th we were visited by a most appalling thunder-storm; it burst close over my head with a report so sudden and tremendous, that I involuntarily trembled, and the sweat ran down my brow. The lightning fairly pained my eyes, and seemed so near, that I fancied every moment it must strike the waggons, which would certainly have proved extremely inconvenient, as 300 pounds of gunpowder were stowed in one of them beneath my bed. The storm passed away at sundown, having exquisitely purified the atmosphere, while the grateful earth and fragrant forest emitted a perfume of overpowering sweetness. Sauntering out with my rifle I shot a couple of shaggy old brindled gnoos, firing right and left. The storm set in again about ten P.M. with thunder and lightning, which continued throughout the greater part of the night.

LUCIE DUFF GORDON
(1821–1869)

English traveller. Born Lucie Austin, she was a friend of Dickens and Tennyson and famous for her wit, beauty and independence. During the 1850s she began to show symptoms of TB; she took up cigar-smoking and then, on doctor's advice, travel. She went first to South Africa, and then in 1862 to Egypt. She spent the next seven years there, chiefly in Luxor, the longest period any European had ever spent in Upper Egypt. Her regular letters to her family and husband were later published, enjoyed great success and created a fashion for wintering in Egypt.

An English hareem

I heard Seleem Effendi and Omar discussing English ladies one day lately while I was inside the curtain with Seleem's slave girl, and they did not know I heard them. Omar described Janet, and was of the opinion that a man who was married to her could want nothing more. 'By my soul, she rides like a Bedawee, she shoots with the gun and pistol, and rows the boat; she speaks many languages, works with the needle like an Efreet, and to see her hands run over the teeth of the music-box (keys of piano) amazes the mind, while her singing gladdens the soul. How then should her husband ever desire the coffee-shop? *Wallahy!* she can always amuse him at home. And as to my lady, the thing is not that she does not know. When I feel my stomach tightened, I go to the divan and say to her, 'Do you want anything, a pipe, or sherbet, or so and so?' and I talk till she lays down her book and talks to me, and I question her and amuse my mind, and, by God! if I were a rich man and could marry one English Hareem like that I would stand before her and serve her like her memlook. You see I am only this lady's servant, and I have not once sat in the coffee-shop because of the sweetness of her tongue. Is it not therefore true that the man who can marry such Hareem is rich more than with money?' Seleem seemed disposed to think a little more of looks, though he quite agreed with all Omar's enthusiasm, and asked if Janet were beautiful. Omar answered with decorous vagueness that she was a 'moon,' but declined mentioning her hair, eyes, etc. (it is a liberty to describe a woman minutely). I nearly laughed out at hearing Omar relate his manœuvres to make me 'amuse his mind'; it seems I am in no danger of being discharged for being dull.

HEINRICH BARTH
(1821–1865)

A German, the greatest and most scientifically minded of all the explorers beyond the Sahara in the 1850s, Barth was an Arabic-speaking archaeologist, historian, geographer and student of law. At the age of twenty-eight he set off on an expedition sponsored by the British Government to explore the regions around Lake Chad and westward to the Niger, before crossing the continent to Zanzibar. With two European companions, Barth left Tripoli in April 1850; by September 1853 when, after a series of extraordinary journeys and adventures, he reached Timbuktu, he was on his own.

Dr Barth suffers the extortions of his host in Timbuktu, the Sheik El Bakáy

On the morning of the 8th of September, the first news I heard was that Hammádi, the rival and enemy of El Bakáy, had informed the Fúlbe or Fullán that a Christian had entered the town, and that, in consequence, they had come to the determination of killing him. However, these rumours did not cause me any great alarm, as I entertained the false hope that I might rely on the person who, for the time, had undertaken to protect me; but my feeling of security was soon destroyed, this very man turning out my greatest tormentor. I had destined for him a very handsome gift, consisting of a fine cloth bernús, a cloth kaftán, and two tobes, one of silk and the other of indigo-dyed cotton, besides some smaller articles; but he was by no means satisfied with these, and peremptorily raised the present to the following formidable proportions:

	Shells.
Two blue bernúses of the best quality, worth	100,000
One kaftán	40,000
Two waistcoats; one red and one blue	15,000

Two silk tobes 35,000
Two Núpe tobes 30,000
A pair of small pistols, with 7 pounds of fine powder
Ten Spanish dollars . . . .
Two English razors, and many other articles . . . . . .

While levying this heavy contribution upon me, in order to take from the affair its vexatious character, my host stated that as their house and their whole establishment were at my disposal, so my property ought to be at theirs. But even this amount of property did not satisfy him, nor were his pretensions limited to this; for the following day he exacted an almost equal amount of considerable presents from me, such as two cloth kaftáns, two silk hamáil or sword belts, three other silk tobes, one of the species called jellábi, one of that called harír, and the third of the kind called filfil, one Núpe tobe, three túrkedís, a small six-barreled pistol, and many other things. . . .

Thus my first day in Timbúktu passed away, preparing me for a great deal of trouble and anxiety which I should have to go through; even those who professed to be my friends treating me with so little consideration.

SIR SAMUEL WHITE BAKER
(1821–1893)

British explorer. In 1862 he set out on an expedition of discovery in Central Africa, where he hoped he might encounter Speke and Grant, who were travelling north-wards from Lake Victoria (see p. 77). Together with his Hungarian mistress, the beautiful Florence von Sass (whom he had bought at a slave auction in Bulgaria), he set out from Khartoum at the end of that year, having already spent fourteen months exploring the Abyssinian tributaries of the Nile. In February 1863 the Bakers reached Gondoroko.

Hurrah for Old England!

My men rushed madly to my boat, with the report that two white men were with them who had come from the *sea*! Could they be Speke and Grant? Off I ran, and soon met them in reality. Hurrah for Old England! . . . All my men were perfectly mad with excitement. Firing salutes, as usual with ball-cartridges, they shot one of my donkeys – a melancholy sacrifice as an offering at the completion of this geographical discovery.

Speke appeared the more worn of the two: he was excessively lean, but in reality was in tough condition; he had walked the whole way from Zanzibar, never having once ridden during that wearying march. Grant was in honourable rags, his bare knees projecting through the remnants of trousers that were an exhibition of rough industry in tailor's work. He was looking tired and feverish, but both men had a fire in their eye, that showed the spirit that had led them through.

A disagreeable encounter with King Kamrasi of Unyoro on the way to Lake Albert, February 1864

I now requested Kamrasi to allow us to take leave, as we had not an hour to lose. In the coolest manner he replied, 'I will send you to the lake and to Shooa, as I have promised; but, *you must leave your wife with me!*'

At that moment we were surrounded by a great number of natives, and my suspicions of treachery at having been led across the Kafoor river appeared confirmed by this insolent demand. If this were to be the end of the expedition I resolved that it should also be the end of Kamrasi, and, drawing my revolver quietly, I held it within two feet of his chest, and looking at him with undisguised contempt, I told him that if I touched the trigger, not all his men could save him: and that if he dared to repeat the insult I would shoot him on the spot. At the same time I explained to him that in my country such insolence would entail bloodshed, and that I looked upon him as an ignorant ox who knew no better, and that this excuse alone could save him. My wife, naturally indignant, had risen from her seat, and, maddened with the excitement of the moment, she made him a little speech in Arabic (not a word of which he understood) with a countenance almost as amiable as the head of Medusa.

Altogether the *mise en scène* utterly astonished him; the woman Bacheeta, although savage, had appropriated the insult to her mistress, and she also fearlessly let fly at Kamrasi, translating as nearly as she could the complimentary address that 'Medusa' had just delivered.

Whether this little *coup de théâtre* had so impressed Kamrasi with British female independence that he wished to be let off his bargain, I cannot say, but with an air of complete astonishment, he said, 'Don't be angry! I had no intention of offending you by asking for your wife; I will give you a wife, if you want one, and I thought you might have no objection to give me yours; it is my custom to give visitors pretty wives, and I thought you might exchange. Don't make a fuss about it; if you don't like it, there's an end of it; I will never mention it again.' This very practical apology I received very sternly, and merely insisted upon starting. He seemed rather confused at having committed himself, and to make amends he called his people and ordered them to carry our loads. His men ordered a number of women, who had assembled out of curiosity, to shoulder the luggage and carry it to the next village, where they would be relieved. I assisted my wife upon her ox, and with a very cold adieu to Kamrasi, I turned my back most gladly on M'rooli.

GUSTAVE FLAUBERT
(1821–1880)

French novelist. In 1849 he left his home at Croisset for a tour of the 'Orient'. With his friend Maxime du Camp (whose own diaries of the expedition are worth looking into), Flaubert sampled as many of the sexual delights that came his way, leaving marvellous and sometimes hair-raising accounts of his adventures.

Kuchuk dances the Bee, Esna, Egypt, March 1850

... Kuchuk Hanem is a tall, splendid creature, lighter in colouring than an Arab; she comes from Damascus; her skin, particularly on her body, is slightly coffee-coloured. When she bends, her flesh ripples into bronze ridges. Her eyes are dark and enormous, her eyebrows black, her nostrils open and wide; heavy shoulders, full, apple-shaped breasts. She wore a large tarboosh, ornamented on the top with a convex gold disk, in the middle of which was a small green stone imitating emerald; the blue tassel of her tarboosh was spread out fanwise and fell down over her shoulders; just in front of the lower edge of the tarboosh, fastened to her hair and going from one ear to the other, she had a small spray of white artificial flowers.

Her black hair, wavy, unruly, pulled straight back on each side from a centre parting beginning at the forehead; small braids joined together at the nape of her neck. She has one upper incisor, right, which is beginning to go bad. For a bracelet she has two bands of gold, twisted together and interlaced, around one wrist. Triple necklace of large hollow gold beads. Earrings: gold disks, slightly convex, circumference decorated with gold granules. On her right arm is tattooed a line of blue writing.

She asks us if we would like a little entertainment, but Max says that first he would like to entertain himself alone with her, and they go downstairs. After he finishes, I go down and follow his example. Groundfloor room, with a divan and a *cafas* [an upturned palm-fibre basket] with a mattress.

Dance. The musicians arrive: a child and an old man, whose left eye is covered with a rag; they both scrape on the *rebabah*, a kind of small round violin with a metal leg that rests on the ground and two horse-hair strings. The neck of the instrument is very long in proportion to the rest. Nothing could be more discordant or disagreeable. The musicians never stop playing for an instant unless you shout at them to do so.

Kuchuk dances the Bee. First, so that the door can be closed, the women send away Farghali and another sailor, who up to now have been watching the dances and who, in the background, constituted the grotesque element of the scene. A black veil is tied around the eyes of the child, and a fold of his blue turban is lowered over those of the old man. Kuchuk shed her clothing as she danced. Finally she was naked except for a *fichu* which she held in her hands and behind which she pretended to hide, and at the end she threw down the *fichu*. That was the Bee. She danced it very briefly and said she does not like to dance that dance. Joseph, very excited, kept clapping his hands: '*La, eu, nia, oh! eu, nia, oh!*' Finally, after repeating for us the wonderful step she had danced in the afternoon, she sank down breathless on her divan, her body continuing to move slightly in rhythm. One of the women threw her her enormous white trousers striped with pink, and she pulled them on up to her neck. The two musicians were unblindfolded.

SIR RICHARD FRANCIS
BURTON
(1821–1890)

English explorer. After service with the East India Company and a famous journey, in various disguises, to
Mecca and Medina, in August 1857 Burton set off from
Bagamoyo on the east coast with John Hanning Speke, a
fellow officer of the Indian Army but of very different
temperament. The object of the expedition, according to
its sponsors the Royal Geographical Society, was 'to
make the best of your way to the reputed Lake Nyanza.
Having obtained all the information you require in this
quarter you are to proceed northwards towards the range
of mountains marked on our maps, as containing the
probable source of the Nile, which it will be your next
great object to discover.' On 13 February 1858, having
travelled 900 miles and suffered appalling hardships,
they looked out over the blue waters of Lake Tanganyika
in the Great Rift Valley, the second largest lake in Africa
and, after Lake Baikal, the deepest lake in the world. By
this time Burton was partly paralysed and suffering from
an abscess of the jaw, while Speke was partly blind. On
the return journey Speke, who had temporarily separated
from Burton (with whom he was already on bad terms),
discovered the lake which he named Victoria Nyanza.
Gazing out across it he was convinced (rightly) that he
had found the source of the Nile, but when he confided
this belief to Burton when he rejoined him six weeks later,
the latter was more than displeased and their estrange-
ment became even more bitter.

A serious difference of opinion in the heart of Africa

At length my companion had been successful, his 'flying trip' had
led him to the northern water, and he had found its dimensions
surpassing our most sanguine expectations. We had scarcely,
however, breakfasted, before he announced to me the startling fact
that he had discovered the sources of the White Nile. It was an
inspiration perhaps: the moment he sighted the Nyanza, he felt at
once no doubt but that the 'Lake at his feet gave birth to the

interesting river which had been the subject of so much speculation, and the object of so many explorers.' The fortunate discoverer's conviction was strong, his reasons were weak – were of the category alluded to by the damsel Luceter, when justifying her penchant in favour of 'the lovely gentleman' Sir Proteus:–

> 'I have no other but a woman's reason,
> I think him so because I think him so';

and probably his sources of the Nile grew in his mind as his Mountains of the Moon had grown under his hand. . . .

But difference of opinion was allowed to alter companionship. After a few days it became evident to me that not a word could be uttered upon the subject of the Lake, the Nile, and his *trouvaille* generally without offence. By a tacit agreement it was, therefore, avoided, and I should never have resumed it had my companion not stultified the results of the expedition by putting forth a claim which no geographer can admit and which is at the same time so weak and flimsy that no geographer has yet taken the trouble to contradict it.

JOHN HANNING SPEKE
(1827–1864)

English explorer. Speke reached England ahead of Burton, whom he left to wind up the affairs of the expedition at Aden. With almost indecent haste, and without waiting for Burton, he reported to the President of the Royal Geographical Society, addressed the members of the Society, obtained a grant of £2,500 for another expedition, and chose as his companion James Grant, a sportsman, zoologist, botanist and painter in watercolours. When Burton eventually arrived in London, his feelings can be imagined. Speke and Grant left Zanzibar for the interior in October 1860, and in November 1861, after great privations, reached Karagwe, west of Lake Victoria. There they were offered hospitality by Rumanika, chief of the Galla people.

A wonder of obesity

After a long and amusing conversation with Rŭmanika in the morning, I called on one of his sisters-in-law, married to an elder brother who was born before Dagara ascended the throne. She was another of those wonders of obesity, unable to stand excepting on all fours. I was desirous to obtain a good view of her, and actually to measure her, and induced her to give me facilities for doing so, by offering in return to show her a bit of my naked legs and arms. The bait took as I wished it, and after getting her to sidle and wriggle into the middle of the hut, I did as I promised, and then took her dimensions as noted below.[1] All of these are exact except the height, and I believe I could have obtained this more accurately if I could have her laid on the floor. Not knowing what difficulties I should have to contend with in such a piece of engineering, I tried to get her height by raising her up. This, after infinite exertions on the part of us both, was accomplished, when she sank down again, fainting, for her blood had rushed into her head. Meanwhile, the daughter, a lass of sixteen, sat stark-naked before us, sucking at a milk-pot, on which the father kept her at work by holding a rod in his hand, for as fattening is the first duty of fashionable female life, it must be duly enforced by the rod if necessary. I got up a bit of flirtation with missy, and induced her to rise and shake hands with me. Her features were lovely, but her body was as round as a ball.

[1] Round arm, 1 ft. 11 in.; chest, 4 ft. 4 in.; thigh, 2 ft. 7 in.; calf, 1 ft. 8 in.; height, 5 ft. 8 in.

In January 1862 Speke and Grant became the first Euro-peans to enter Uganda, where they stayed at the court of the young King Mtésa of Buganda, who extinguished human life with the indifference that another might display in swatting a fly.

At the palace of mad King Mtésa

At noon Mtésa sent his pages to invite me to his palace. I went, with my guard of honour and my stool, but found I had to sit waiting in an ante-hut three hours with his commander-in-chief and other high officers before he was ready to see me. . . . But, as rain fell, the court broke up, and I had nothing for it but to walk about under my umbrella, indulging in angry reflections against the haughty king for not letting me into his hut.

When the rain had ceased, and we were again called in, he was found sitting in state as before, but this time with the head of a black bull placed before him, one horn of which, knocked off, was placed alongside, whilst four living cows walked about the court.

I was now requested to shoot the four cows as quickly as possible; but having no bullets for my gun, I borrowed the revolving pistol I had given him, and shot all four in a second of time; but as the last one, only wounded, turned sharply upon me, I gave him the fifth and settled him. Great applause followed this *wonderful* feat, and the cows were given to my men. The king now loaded one of the carbines I had given him with his own hands, and giving it full-cock to a page, told him to go out and shoot a man in the outer court; which was no sooner accomplished than the little urchin returned to announce his success, with a look of glee such as one would see in the face of a boy who had robbed a bird's nest, caught a trout, or done any other boyish trick. The king said to him, 'And did you do it well?' 'Oh, yes, capitally.' He spoke the truth, no doubt, for he dared not have trifled with the king; but the affair created hardly any interest. I never heard, and there appeared no curiosity to know, what individual human being the urchin had deprived of life.

GEORG AUGUST SCHWEINFURTH
(1836–1925)

German botanist, ethnographer and zoologist. One of the outstanding African travellers of the age, he also had a great talent for drawing and his depictions of his finds are as accurate as photographs. In the course of his travels in Central Africa he discovered and described many strange tribes, and was the first man to confirm the existence of the Central African pygmies (he bought one, in exchange for a dog, but he died on the return journey).

The Shillooks of the Upper Nile, c.1868

Soon after the arrival of the boat, a great crowd of naked Shillooks, prompted by curiosity, assembled on the shore, my dog still being the chief attraction. The first sight of a throng of savages, suddenly presenting themselves in their native nudity, is one from which no amount of familiarity can remove the strange impression; it takes abiding hold upon the memory, and makes the traveller recall anew the civilisation he has left behind.

One of the Khartoom men disturbed my pensive contemplations

by pointing to the Shillooks, and making a remark that they looked like Christians. I punished him with the scornful reply to the effect that of whatever faith the savages were, I could answer for it that they had the good luck to be neither Jews nor Mohammedans.

A large *sombrero* of Mexican cut which protected my head from the rays of the sun, excited the curiosity of the Shillooks. On their own heads they wore a similar covering, except that theirs was made from their own hair. I called their attention to the great likeness between black men and white men, but very great was their astonishment when they saw that my hair could be taken off and put on again, which would be to them very incredible. It might almost be said that they are hardly born without their crests, which sometimes resemble the comb of a guinea-fowl, and at other times seem to be borrowed and designed from the aureoles which we admire in Greek sacred pictures. Even while they are infants at the breast, the hair is begun to be fastened into shape with gum-arabic and ashes, and in course of time is permanently brought into whatever form they please.

HENRY MORTON STANLEY
(1841–1904)

Anglo-American explorer and journalist. Originally named John Rowlands, he was born in Denbigh, Wales, and took the name of his adoptive father in New Orleans, where he went in 1857. After fighting on both sides of the American Civil War, he became a journalist. In 1871 the *New York Herald* commissioned him to lead an expedition in search of Livingstone, who, exploring the watersheds of the Nile, the Congo and the Zambesi, was rumoured to have died. Stanley undertook three subsequent expeditions to Africa, on one of which he followed the Congo River from its source to the Atlantic, reaching it 999 days after setting out from Zanzibar.

Meeting Dr Livingstone at Ujiji, near Lake Tanganyika,
10 November 1871

... I did that which I thought was most dignified. I pushed back the crowds, and, passing from the rear, walked down a living avenue of people, until I came in front of the semicircle of Arabs, in the front of which stood the white man with the grey beard. As I advanced slowly towards him I noticed he was pale, looked wearied, had a grey beard, wore a bluish cap with a faded gold band round it, had on a red-sleeved waistcoat, and a pair of grey tweed trousers. I would have run to him, only I was a coward in the presence of such a mob – would have embraced him, only, he being an Englishman, I did not know how he would receive me; so I did what cowardice and false pride suggested was the best thing – walked deliberately to him, took off my hat, and said:

'Dr Livingstone, I presume?'

'YES,' said he, with a kind smile, lifting his cap slightly.

I replace my hat on my head, and he puts on his cap, and we both grasp hands, and I then say aloud:

'I thank God, Doctor, I have been permitted to see you.'

He answered, 'I feel thankful that I am here to welcome you.'

JOSEPH THOMSON
(1858–1895)

Scottish geologist and explorer. In 1883, having already led one East African expedition, Thomas was commissioned by the Royal Geographical Society 'to ascertain if a practical direct route for European travellers exists through the Masai country from any one of the East African ports to Lake Victoria Nyanza'. He set off in March, from the coast opposite Zanzibar, with a Maltese sailor named James Martin, 130 porters and a few donkeys. The Masai gave Thomson a hard time; in addition to threatening him with worse treatment they made him take his boots off and wiggle his toes, pinched him and tried to take down his trousers. His only defence was the performance of a bit of Western magic – adding Enos fruit salts to a glass of water – which gave him some temporary reputation among these fearsome warriors.

Thomson's expedition reached the Great Rift Valley in July, survived a bad scare at Naivasha, where they were surrounded by bellicose Masai tribesmen, crossed the 13,000-foot Aberdare Range, saw Mount Kenya and finally reached Lake Victoria in December. The return journey was equally eventful, Thomson being badly gored by a buffalo which left him semi-conscious for six weeks. He finally reached Rabai, inland from Mombasa, on 24 May 1884, having travelled 3000 miles.

How not to shoot a buffalo

At last we were rewarded by the sight of couple of buffaloes feeding some distance ahead. Gliding up warily till I got within fifty yards, I gave one of them a bullet close to the region of the heart. This was not sufficient to bring the animal down, and off it lumbered. Following it up, we were soon once more at close quarters, with the result that a bullet from my Express passed through its shoulder. With the obstinacy and tenacity of life characteristic of its kind, however, it did not quietly succumb. I next tried it with a fair header. This obviously took effect, for after it had struggled forward some distance it lay down, clearly, as I thought, to die. My belief was quite correct, only I should not have disturbed its last moments. Concluding, very foolishly, that the buffalo was completely *hors de combat*, and that the game was mine, I, with the jaunty air of a conqueror, tucked my rifle under my arm, and proceeded to secure my prize. Brahim, with more sense, warned me that it was not finished yet; and indeed, if I had not been a fool – which the most sensible people will be sometimes – I might have concluded that with so much of the evil one in its nature the brute had still sufficient life to play me a mischief, for it still held its head erect and defiant, though we were unseen. Heedless of Brahim's admonition, I obstinately went forward, intending to give it its *quietus* at close quarters. I had got within six yards, and yet I remained unnoticed, the head of the buffalo being turned slightly from me, and I not making much noise. I was not destined to go much further. A step or two more and there was a rustling among some dead leaves. Simultaneously the buffalo's head turned in my direction. A ferocious, blood-curdling grunt instantly apprised me of the brute's resolution to be revenged. The next moment it was on its feet. Unprepared to fire, and completely taken by surprise, I had no time for thought. Instinctively I turned my back upon my infuriated enemy. As far as my recollections serve me, I had no feeling of fear while I was running away. I am almost confident that I was not putting my best foot foremost, and that I felt as if the whole affair was rather a well-played game. It was a game, however, that did not last long. I was aware of Brahim tearing away in front of me. There was a loud crashing behind me. Then something touched me on the thigh, and I was promptly propelled skyward.

My next recollection was finding myself lying dazed and bruised, with some hazy notion that I had better take care! With this indefinite sense of something unusual I slowly and painfully raised my head, and lo! there was the brutal avenger standing three yards off, watching his victim, but apparently disdaining to hoist an inert foe. I found I was lying with my head towards the buffalo. Strangely enough even then, though I was in what may be called the jaws of death, I had not the slightest sensation of dread; only the electric thought flashed through my brain, 'If he comes for me again I am a dead man.' It almost seemed to me as if my thought roused the buffalo to action. Seeing signs of life in my hitherto inanimate body, he blew a terrible blast through his nostrils, and prepared to finish me off. Stunned and bruised as I was, I could make no fight for life. I simply dropped my head down among the grass in the vague hope that it might escape being pounded into jelly. Just at that moment a rifle-shot rang through the forest, which caused me to raise my head once more. With glad surprise I found the buffalo's tail presented to my delighted contemplation. Instinctively seizing the unexpected moment of grace, I with a terrible effort pulled myself together and staggered away a few steps. As I did so, I happened to put my hand down to my thigh, and there I felt something warm and wet; exploring further, my fingers found their way into a big hole in my thigh. As I made this discovery there was quite a volley, and I saw my adversary drop dead. . . .

MARY KINGSLEY
(1862–1900)

English author and intrepid traveller. She received no formal education, but taught herself at home in Highgate and Bexley, Kent, experimenting in mechanics and studying chemistry, electricity, ethnography and anthropology. In 1893, filled with enthusiasm for foreign travel, she decided to visit West Africa, where she collected beetles and freshwater fishes, travelling through appalling swamps in their pursuit. She also explored a hitherto unknown part of the Congo, negotiating the deadly rapids of the Ogowé River in a canoe, and climbed the Great Cameroon, the highest mountain in West Africa.

She died at Simonstown, South Africa, while nursing Boer prisoners of war. Of her Rudyard Kipling said: 'Being human, she must have been afraid of something, but one never found out what it was.'

The blessings of a good thick skirt

About five o'clock I was off ahead and noticed a path which I had been told I should meet with, and when met with, I must follow. The path was slightly indistinct, but by keeping my eye on it I could see it. Presently I came to a place where it went out, but appeared again on the other side of a clump of underbush fairly distinctly. I made a short cut for it and the next news was I was in a heap, on a lot of spikes, some fifteen feet or so below ground level, at the bottom of a bag-shaped game pit.

It is at these times that you realise the blessings of a good thick skirt. Had I paid heed to the advice of many people in England, who ought to have known better, and did not do it themselves, and adopted masculine garments, I should have been spiked to the bone, and done for. Whereas, save for a good many bruises, here I was with the fulness of my skirt tucked under me, sitting on nine ebony spikes some twelve inches long, in comparative comfort, howling lustily to be hauled out. The Duke came along first, and looked down at me. I said, 'Get a bush-rope and haul me out.' He grunted and sat down on a log. The Passenger came next, and he looked down. 'You kill?' says he. 'Not much,' says I; 'get a bush-rope and haul me out.' 'No fit,' says he, and sat down on the log. Presently, however, Kiva and Wiki came up, and Wiki went and selected the one and only bush-rope suitable to haul an English lady of my exact complexion, age and size, out of that one particular pit.

EDITH WHARTON
(1862–1937)

American novelist. She published more than forty books – novels, stories, essays, travel books and memoirs – and was a perceptive chronicler of New York society. In 1910 she settled in France, travelling widely in Europe. On visiting Morocco in 1917, and discovering that there was no guide-book to the country, she promptly wrote one, the wonderfully evocative *In Morocco* (1920).

The souks of Marrakesh

Dark, fierce and fanatical are these narrow *souks* of Marrakech. They are mere mud lanes roofed with rushes, as in South Tunisia and Timbuctoo, and the crowds swarming in them are so dense that it is hardly possible, at certain hours, to approach the tiny raised kennels where the merchants sit like idols among their wares. One feels at once that something more than the thought of bargaining – dear as this is to the African heart – animates these incessantly moving throngs. The *souks* of Marrakech seem, more than any others, the central organ of a native life that extends far beyond the city walls into secret clefts of the mountains and far-off oases where plots are hatched and holy wars fomented – farther still, to yellow deserts whence Negroes are secretly brought across the Atlas to that inmost recess of the bazaar where the ancient traffic in flesh and blood still surreptitiously goes on.

All these many threads of the native life, woven of greed and lust, of fetishism and fear and blind hate of the stranger, form, in the *souks*, a thick network in which at times one's feet seem literally to stumble. Fanatics in sheepskins glowering from the guarded thresholds of the mosques, fierce tribesmen with inlaid arms in their belts and the fighters' tufts of wiry hair escaping from camel's-hair turbans, mad Negroes standing stark naked in niches of the walls and pouring down Soudanese incantations upon the fascinated crowd, consumptive Jews with pathos and cunning in their large eyes and smiling lips, lusty slave-girls with earthen oil-jars resting against swaying hips, almond-eyed boys leading fat merchants by the hand, and bare-legged Berber women, tattooed and insolently gay, trading their striped blankets, or bags of dried roses and irises, for sugar, tea, or Manchester cottons – from all these hundreds of unknown and unknowable people, bound together by secret affinities, or intriguing against each other with secret hate, there emanated an atmosphere of mystery and menace more stifling than the smell of camels and spices and black bodies and smoking fry which hangs like a fog under the close roofing of the *souks*.

COLETTE
(1873–1954)

French novelist. A reluctant traveller – she preferred the beauties of her beloved France – Colette was invited to Morocco in 1926 and fell in love with North Africa.

A Moroccan luncheon

'Azil!'

A silken scarf, modelled like a Parisian hat, revealed nothing of her hair. Azil was young and zealous and did not allow herself to smile. Her soft cheeks and bare round arms captured the blue from without whenever she passed the bay-window opening on to the sea. Azil mirrored the blue of the sky, the green of foliage; from each ear a glass pendant swung to its own bluish reflection on her strong neck. Azil was beautiful like a polished jar, beautiful like a young seal, beautiful like any well-treated, well-fed, sixteen-year-old slave.

She had already placed before us pale girdle-cakes soaked in sugared butter and sprinkled with almonds; pigeons bathed in succulent juice with green olives, chick-peas melting in flour, sweet onions; chickens buried under fresh beans with wrinkled skins and lemon cooked and re-cooked and reduced to a savoury purée. We had also had mutton, and mutton again, and once more; mutton stuffed with fennel, mutton with cumin and courgettes, mutton with twenty spices; and an exquisite diversion – girdle-cakes flaky to the limit of flakiness, rendered transparent, concealing a soft nugget of minced fowl, sugared and flavoured with nutmeg. . . .

Ceaselessly Azil fetched and carried the red bowls. The spring vegetables took pride of place – broad beans, asparagus, new peas in a pot decorated with orange-trees, artichokes round as roses; small turnips, marrows and carrots appeared under swelling yellow enamel, with whole eggs broken over the dish a quarter of an hour before serving. Finally came couscous, at once soft and granular – couscous, discreet harbinger of desert and fruit – couscous with a surrounding rampart, a small fortress, of sweet onions and muscat grapes swollen to the sweating-point, couscous and bowls of barely soured buttermilk. We lifted our heads, we began to look at the sea, beyond an abyss of greenery tumbling to the shore.

They have vagabond, noble, disinterested souls who commit themselves to a motionless siesta on divans stuffed with fine wool and contemplate the Mediterranean through half-closed eyes. Already we can hear the water simmering in the bowls of the samovar. Faithful to tradition, our host rises to prepare the green mint tea. And if, simultaneously, we all turn to watch Azil of the black and pink feet, it is not because she seems more beautiful as she runs unburdened, it is because she is bringing to our host – oh, that odour that touches the throat with an iced finger, which plumbs the depths of the lungs, tells of snow and subtle pepper, wakens the spirits and deludes thirst! – a green bunch of crinkled mint.

EVELYN WAUGH
(1903–1966)

English novelist. Between 1928 and 1937 Waugh had 'no fixed home and no possessions which would not conveniently go on a porter's barrow'. He travelled widely, writing four travel books during this period. In 1929, a 'tourist' rather than a 'traveller', he embarked on a pleasure cruise on a Norwegian ship of 'almost glacial cleanliness'. By the time she arrived in Port Said, Waugh had struck up a friendship with a Cambridge solicitor. Together, armed with 'life-preservers of lead, leather and whale-bone', they went out for a night on the town.

Port Said, 1929

As we progressed the houses became more and more tumble-down and the street more narrow. We were on the outskirts of the small Sudanese quarter where a really primitive life is led. Then suddenly we came into a rough, highly lighted square with two or three solid stucco-fronted houses and some waiting taxis. One side was open to the black, shallow waters of the lake, and was fringed with the masts of the little fishing-boats. Two or three girls in bedraggled European evening dress seized hold of us and dragged us to the most highly lighted of the buildings; this had 'Maison Dorée' painted across its front, and the girls cried, 'Gol'-'ouse, gol'-'ouse,' 'Vair good, vair clean.' It did not seem either very good or very clean to me. We sat in a little room full of Oriental decorations and drank some beer with the young ladies. Madame joined us, a handsome Marseillaise in a green silk embroidered frock; she cannot have been more than forty, and was most friendly and amusing. Four or five other young ladies came in, all more or less white; they sat very close together on the divan and drank beer, making laudably little effort to engage our attention. None of them could talk any English, except, 'Cheerioh, Mr American.' I do not know what their nationality was. Jewesses, Armenians, or Greeks, I suppose. They cost 50 piastres each, Madame said. These were all European ladies. The other, neighbouring houses, were full of Arabs – horrible, dirty places, she said. Some of the ladies took off their frocks and did a little dance, singing a song which sounded like ta-ra-ra-boom-de-ay. There was a jolly-sounding party going on upstairs, with a concertina and glass-breaking, but Madame would not let us go up. Then we paid for our drinks and went out.

Then we went next door to a vastly more plebeian house called Les Folies Bergères, kept by a gross old Arab woman who talked very little French and no English. She had a licence for eight girls, but I do not think hers was a regular establishment. On our arrival a boy was sent out into the streets, and he brought back half a dozen or so Arab girls, all very stout and ugly and carelessly daubed with powder and paint. All round were the little alleys where the freelance prostitutes lived. These were one-roomed huts like bathing cabins. The women who were not engaged sat at their open doors sewing industriously, and between stitches looking up and calling for custom; many had their prices chalked on the door-posts – 25 piastres in some cases, but usually less. Inside iron bedsteads were visible, and hanging banners worked with the crests of British regiments.

On our way back we came upon another gaily illuminated building called Maison Chabanais. We went in, and were surprised to encounter Madame and all her young ladies from the Maison Dorée. It was, in fact, her back door. Sometimes, she explained, gentlemen went away unsatisfied, determined to find another house, then as often as not they found the way round to the other side, and the less observant ones never discovered their mistake.

In 1930, on his way to the coronation of Haile Selassie in Addis Ababa, Waugh docked at Djibouti, where he put up at the Hotel des Arcades. The proprietress, he remarks, had the 'peculiar good fortune to subsist upon the inadequacies of the Franco-Ethiopian railway service, for no one voluntarily spends long in Djibouti.'

A tour of the town, Djibouti, October 1930

This fact, sufficiently clear from our earliest impression, became clearer when, after luncheon, the rain having stopped, we drove for a tour of the town. We bumped and rocked along in a one-horse cab through pools of steaming mud. The streets, described by the official guidebook as 'elegant and smiling,' were mere stretches of waste-land between blocks of houses. These, in the European quarter, were mostly built on the same plan as the hotel, arcaded and decaying.

'They look as though they might fall down any minute,' remarked my companion as we drove past one more than usually dissolute block of offices, and while we looked they actually did begin to fall. Great flakes of stucco crumbled from the front; a brick or two, toppling from the coping, splashed into the mud below. Some scared Indian clerks scampered into the open, a Greek in shirt-sleeves appeared from the house opposite, a group of half-naked natives rose from their haunches and, still scouring their teeth with sticks of wood, gazed apprehensively about them. Our driver pointed excitedly with his whip and admonished us in Somali. It had been an earthquake which, in the more sensible motion of the cab, had escaped our notice.

GRAHAM GREENE
(1904–   )

English novelist. In 1935 he travelled on foot through 350 miles of forest in Liberia, visiting places where no white man had been seen in living memory. He returned to West Africa during the war to work in intelligence.

Freetown, Sierra Leone, in the mid-1930s

Freetown, the capital of Sierra Leone, at first was just an impression of heat and damp; the mist streamed along the lower streets and lay over the roofs like smoke. Nature, conventionally grand, rising in tree-covered hills above the sea and the town, a dull uninteresting green, was powerless to carry off the shabby town. One could see the Anglican cathedral, laterite bricks and tin with a square tower, a Norman church built in the nineteenth century, sticking up out of the early morning fog. There was no doubt at all that one was back in home waters. Among the swarm of Kru boats round the ship the *Princess Marina* with its freshly painted name was prominent. '*Princess Marina*,' the half-naked owner kept on calling. 'Sweetest boat on the coast.'

Tin roofs and peeling posters and broken windows in the public library and wooden stores, Freetown had a Bret Harte air without the excitement, the saloons, the revolver shots or the horses. There was only one horse in the whole city, and it was pointed out to me by the proprietor of the Grand Hotel, a thin piebald beast pulled down the main street like a mule. There had been other horses from time to time, but they had all died. Where there wasn't a tin shed there were huge hoardings covered with last year's Poppy Day posters (the date was January the fifteenth). On the roofs the vultures sat nuzzling under their wings with horrible tiny undeveloped heads; they squatted in the gardens like turkeys; I could count seven out of my bedroom window. When they moved from one perch to another they gave no sensation of anything so aerial as flight; they seemed to hop across the street, borne up just high enough by the flap-flap of their dusty wings.

This was an English capital city; England had planted this town, the tin shacks and the Remembrance Day posters, and had then withdrawn up the hillside to smart bungalows, with wide windows and electric fans and perfect service. Every call one paid on a white man cost ten shillings in taxi fares, for the railway to Hill Station no longer ran. They had planted their seedy civilisation and then escaped from it as far as they could.

SIR CECIL BEATON
(1904–1980)

English photographer, designer, traveller and diarist.

An evening with the Rolling Stones, Marrakesh, March 1967

On the Tuesday evening I came down to dinner very late, and, to my surprise, sitting in the hotel lobby, discovered Mick Jagger and a sleepy looking band of gipsies. . . .

It was a strange group. The three 'Stones': Brian Jones, with his girlfriend, beatnik-dressed Anita Pallenberg – dirty white face, dirty blackened eyes, dirty canary drops of hair, barbaric jewelry – Keith Richard in eighteenth-century suit, long black velvet coat and the tightest pants; and, of course, Mick Jagger, together with hangers-on, chauffeurs, and Americans.

I didn't want to give the impression that I was only interested in Mick, but it happened that we sat next to one another as he drank a Vodka Collins and smoked with pointed finger held high. His skin is chicken-breast white and of a fine quality. He has an inborn elegance. He talked of native music; he had heard a local tribe play pipes like those used in Hungary and Scotland. He liked Indian music too. He said he would like to go to Kashmir and to Afghanistan, in fact to get right away from England, which he considered had become a police state, with harassment and interference. Recently twenty policemen had invaded the house of his drummer in the country looking for dope. The newspapers had published completely false accounts. He was going to sue the *News of the World*. He maintained that he had done nothing to deprave the youth of the country. Here in Morocco people were not curious or bad-mannered. He liked people that were permissive.

By degrees the shy aloofness of the gang broke down. We got into two cars; the Bentley I was in had been driven from Brian Jones's house in Swiss Cottage to here, and the driver was a bit tired. The car was filled with pop-art cushions, scarlet fur rugs, and sex magazines. Immediately the most tremendous volume of pop music boomed in the region of the back of my neck. Mick and Brian responded rhythmically and the girl leant forward and screamed in whispers that she had just played a murderess in a film that was to be shown at the Cannes Festival.

We went to a Moroccan restaurant – tiles, banquettes, women dancers. Mick considered the style of decoration gave little opportunity of expression to the artist. He is very gentle, and with perfect manners. He indicated that I should follow his example and eat the chicken in my fingers. It was tender and good. He has much appreciation, and his small, albino-fringed eyes notice everything. 'How different and more real this place is to Tangier – the women more rustic, heavy, lumpy, but their music very Spanish and their dancing too.' He has an analytical slant and compares everything he is seeing here with earlier impressions in other countries. . . .

By the time we reached the hotel it was three o'clock and my bedtime, but they were quite happy to go on. Never a yawn and they had been up since five o'clock this morning.

It is a way of life very different from mine and I enjoyed being jerked out of myself. Mick listened to pop records for a couple of hours, and was then so tired that he went to sleep without taking off his clothes. He woke at eight, undressed and got into bed to sleep for another couple of hours.

At eleven o'clock he appeared at the swimming pool. I could not believe it was the same person walking towards us. The very strong sun, reflected from the white ground, made his face look a white, podgy, shapeless mess; eyes very small, nose very pink and spreading, hair sandy dark. His figure, his hands and arms were incredibly feminine.

None of them was willing to talk except in spasms. No one could make up their minds what to do, or when.

. . . Their wardrobe is extensive. Mick showed me the rows of brocade coats. Everything is shoddy, poorly made, the seams burst. Keith himself had sewn his trousers, lavender and dull rose, with a band of badly stitched leather dividing the two colours.

Brian, at the pool, appears in white pants with a huge black square applied on to the back. It is very smart, in spite of the fact that the seams are giving way. But with such marvellously flat, tight, compact figures as they have, with no buttocks or stomach, almost anything looks well on them.

GEOFFREY GORER
(1905–   )

English writer. In 1934 he went to West Africa with Feral
Banga, a famous black dancer, to study traditional black
dances. Their journey took them from Dakar to Senegal,
Guinea, the Ivory Coast, Dahomey, the Gold Coast and
Nigeria.

The women fetishers of Dahomey

In an area which was certainly less than a hundred square feet there
were more than a dozen women. They were all dressed alike with a
cap of purple net from which hung long strings threaded with
cowries falling to the breast, so thick that they completely hid the
face. Across the otherwise naked torso were slings of cowries and
purple beads; they had ordinary skirts and anklets of cowries. They
were all in very deep trance and completely motionless; all the
actions of everyday life, feeding, washing and so on, had to be done
for them. They were no longer themselves; they were filled with the
power of the fetish. They could no longer speak; only by a certain
ritual could the priest make them talk, and then it was no longer the
woman but the fetish itself talking through its agent in its own
language. In the present instance the women were to be in this state
for three weeks, during which, except for ceremonies, they could
not go out of the hut or see the light. The wonderworkers are in this
state permanently; if a man is completely filled with the fetish he
performs no ordinary actions and never sees the light, nor does he
eat any solid food. These wonderworkers are few and live in the
most deserted places; their powers can be controlled because they
can work only through the agency of a normally conscious priest.

To call these entranced women out of the hut an elaborate
ceremonial is necessary. They can move only to the sound of a
special tomtom; when this starts playing the chief fetish priest
kneels by the entrance and shakes a rattle while he invokes the fetish
with prayers; the other fetishers present prostrate themselves and
repeat the prayers, rubbing their hands together. After some time
the tomtoms become louder and the fetishers shriek; one of the
women has shown her mask at the door. A cockerel is immediately

fetched; its legs and wings are broken and its tongue pulled out; its beak is stuffed with special leaves and it is held by its legs; a drop of the blood is let fall on each of the woman's big toes; she comes out and with head downcast starts dancing feverishly, swinging her shoulders with a force which would tire an ordinary person in a few minutes. After the first several more are called out with the same ceremonial; not all that are in the hut, for that can only be left completely empty at the greatest ceremonies. The women dance in a vague circle, but like blind people; they have to be continually guided to prevent them knocking themselves against the buildings. Before they can return to the fetish hut they have to be purified; they are led on to a special mat where their hands and feet are laved in holy water, after which another chicken is mutilated in the same cruel fashion and a drop of blood is allowed to fall from its beak on their thumbs and big toes. They are led back to the hut with prayers and rattles; they enter it backwards, creeping on all fours. This is the essential basis of fetish worship; the body is used as a vessel to be filled with the divine force, no less holy because the owner of the body is unaware of what occurs.

SIR LAURENS
VAN DER POST
(1906–   )

South African writer, farmer and traveller. He has made a number of expeditions into little-known parts of Africa, exploring the Kalahari Desert and Mount Mlanje and the Nyika Plateau in Malawi.

Nyika Plateau

There was no wind any more. There was no cloud or mist in the sky. I have never known such stillness. The only sound was the sound of one's blood murmuring like a far sea in one's ears: and that serene land and its beauty, and the level golden sunlight seemed to have established such a close, delicate, tender communion with us that the murmur in my ears seemed also like a sound from without; it was like a breathing of the grasses, a rustle of the last shower of daylight, or the swish of the silk of evening across the purple slopes.

Suddenly Karramba touched my arm. We could hardly believe

our eyes. A very big male leopard, bronze, his back charged with sunset gold, was walking along the slope above the pool on the far side about fifty yards away. He was walking as if he did not have a fear or care in the world, like an old gentleman with his hands behind his back, taking the evening air in his own private garden. When he was about twelve yards from the pool, he started walking around in circles examining the ground with great attention. Then he settled slowly into the grass, like a destroyer sinking into the sea, bow first, and suddenly disappeared from our view. It was rather uncanny. One minute he was magnificently there on the bare slope and the next he was gone from our view. . . .

We waited attentively. About five minutes passed: not a sound anywhere, except this remote music of all our being. I was lying with my ear close to the ground when I heard a new sound that made my heart beat faster: it was the drumming of hooves far away. It was a lovely, urgent, wild, barbaric sound. It was getting louder and coming straight for us. I caught a glimpse of Michael's face, shining with excitement. The drumming of the hooves came towards us from somewhere behind the far slope, like a great Pacific comber, like a charge of Napoleon's cavalry at Waterloo, and then out of the midst of this drumming, this surf of sound, there was thrown up like a call on a silver trumpet, or the voice of an emperor born to command, a loud, clear neigh. It was one of the most beautiful sounds I have ever heard, and it established itself in all my senses like the far silver fountain that I had once seen a great blue whale throw up on a South Atlantic horizon after a storm. Now, as the sun tinted the horizon, the wave of sound rose towering into the air and then crashed down on to the summit of the slope opposite us. A troop of about forty zebra, running as if they had never known walking, the rhythm of their speed moving in waves across their shining flanks, charged over the crest and made for the pool where the leopard lay.

I wondered how it was going to end. I could not believe a leopard would attack such a lusty group of zebra, although I had never seen a leopard behave quite as this one did, so frankly, so openly. At that very moment, the leader of the troop with his mane streaming from him like the strands of the Mistral itself, stopped dead. At one minute he must have been going at thirty-five miles an hour, at the next he stopped without a slither in his tracks, two fountains of steam shooting out of dilated nostrils.

The rest of the group stopped with him. Had they seen the leopard or seen us? For about five minutes we saw a group of zebra, not fifty yards away, in earnest consultation. I saw Michael raise his gun and then put it down again. He had, I knew, to kill one zebra because it was his duty to examine them for parasites. I saw him take aim several times but always he put his gun down again.

Meanwhile the consultation went on, soundlessly and ceaselessly. Some invisible, some electric exchange of meaning was going on between those vivid creatures on the darkening slope. They looked so heraldic, like unicorns who had just had their horns pared. They had beautifully marked golden skins, with black blazonings. For five minutes they stood, their steaming heads close together, and then somewhere in the magnetic depths of themselves, their meaning fused and became one. They whirled swiftly round and charged back over the crest straight into the dying day and we did not see them again.

'I am sorry,' Michael said to me, breathing hard: 'I am sorry but I just could not shoot: they were beautiful.'

'I am glad you didn't,' I answered.

PETER MAYNE
(1908–)

English writer and traveller.

The language of love in Marrakesh

On my way across the Djema'a el-Fna for an evening aperitif I was stopped by a Moor I have often seen at the café but to whom I have never spoken. He is obviously a respected person, and I have remarked that he gets served promptly by all the *garçons*. I have also remarked that he arrives at the café on a bicycle which has two little 'driving-mirrors'. These are fastened on the handlebars and I believe he uses them more for looking at himself in, than to warn him of traffic coming up behind, because they are both tipped up into his face. He is rather a handsome fellow, as well as respected. Anyway, this time he greeted me as if we met regularly. I begin to manage the standard greetings fairly fluently now, unreeling my 'no-harms' and 'peace-on-you's' with quite an air. He suggested that we share the expenses of a lady wrapped in a *hāik* who was hurrying not very fast across the *place* in the opposite direction.

'Do you think . . . ?' I began, as best I could in Arabic.

He said: 'You want or you don't want?'

I started to say that I must look at my watch and consider my engagements for the evening, but by now the lady was hurrying back again at about the same speed and the man said urgently:

'You will pay her two parts and I will pay one part. Yes? I shall ask her?'

'Do you know her?' I inquired, still anxious to gain time. The lady was quite near now.

'No,' he said. 'But I will ask her.'

I said: 'I would like to see her properly first.' She was completely covered by her *hāik* and I am not one who can judge from a pair of thick ankles. She looked like any other woman would look wrapped up in a cloth bundle. There was nothing to indicate her business at this hour and place that I could see.

'Why?' he demanded.

'Well, because . . .' But by this time the lady was several yards beyond us again.

'You are as nothing!' the man cried angrily and hurried after her.

JOHN HILLABY
(1917–   )

English writer and naturalist. One of the world's great walkers. His journeys, on foot and often alone, have taken him through Africa, across Europe from the North Sea to the Mediterranean, and from Land's End to John O'Groats. Early in the 1960s he walked through Kenya to Lake Rudolf, the Jade Sea.

The very essence of treacle

Wrapped up in three cotton vests at the bottom of my medicine chest I kept a little wireless set, made in Japan and extraordinarily efficient at picking up three, and almost only three, types of music. Europe and North America seemed to transmit almost nothing but rock-and-roll, augmented by peculiarly British Early Morning and Workers' Playtime type of bands. Whatever the repertoire the *dumpty dumpty* ditties were delivered at exactly the same tempo, *encore et encore, ad nauseam.* A twist of the dial brought in the wail of Islam, costive and insistent in North Africa but enriched in the Sudan by full-throated recitations from the *Qu'ran.* From Nairobi, the coast, and all points east came the cheerful, irregular songs of India in Gujuratic and Hindi, to me the most attractive oriental sounds of all.

One night, high above the Chalbi, I went to bed early, intent on hearing a retransmission of a Festival Hall concert in London, due to begin at half-past nine. I tuned in to the short wave and turned the volume down to a mere breath of sound to dampen either a quiz programme or a spelling bee. The radio twittered on the floor about a yard from my ear and I fell asleep.

Shortly before midnight I awoke to find the blades of four spears outlined against the sky. The shafts were held by four young Samburu who were kneeling with their heads bent down over the radio. They were listening to the whine of a late-night dance band. Softly, I asked them if they liked it. They ran away. Calling them back I repeated the question. Was it good? Did they like the noise? In a phrase which I treasure, one of them said it was *asali kabissa;* the very essence of treacle.

GEOFFREY MOORHOUSE
(1931–   )

English writer and traveller. In October 1972 he set off from Chinguetti in Mauritania to cross the continent to the Nile, by way of Timbuktu, a journey never before attempted by a European. In March 1973, having crossed 2000 miles of the Sahara, 300 of them on foot after the last of his camels had died, he reached Tamanrasset and was forced to give up.

Nothing but pain

At a little after three o'clock we prepared to start under a moon that was something from fantasy. Never in my life had I seen it looming as large as when it topped the horizon. It seemed to fill a quarter of the heavens, a full circle which itself was encircled by a colossal and golden penumbra. It was a moon from a children's picture book, with the colour of a Gloucester cheese. There was a sleepy farewell salute from the bundle of blankets nearby as we set off. It was unlikely that we should see the three again, with a four-hour start, in conditions ideal for a night march. There was not a breath of wind, though it was excessively cold. Even with my howli muffled thickly between chin and eyes under a bare head, my face was numb for hours, as well as hands and feet. Had I been snowballing in an English winter, I could scarcely have been colder. In this condition we attacked the dunes and it was heavy work, head-hauling the beasts one at a time up the steeper slopes, the brown bull and the broken-toothed white frequently falling to their knees. Dawn found us on the gravel reg again, and all day we plodded across its flat and featureless surface, blistered now as fiercely by the sun as we had been frozen by night under the moon.

Slumped that evening against the unloaded baggage, I was beyond responding to the sunset. On days without number I had been revived by the magical half hour of the sun's decline: most beautiful of all were those evenings when the horizon glowed with green, yellow and blood-red rays, in which the very thin crescent of a new moon rose a trifle above the ground before slipping back again in pursuit of the sun, without the strength yet to climb into the sky. On this evening the colours stained some wisps of high, stratospheric cloud that a remote wind was unravelling towards the west. But I was too weary to delight in it.

I awoke at 3.30, shivering in spite of a great blaze of grass that Ibrahim had started beside us; its light leapt and flickered upon the four camels, which we had couched on the spot before going to sleep. There was a stiffness in my body that came not from the cold nor yet from long exertions, but seemed to issue now from the deepest fibres of my being in a translated protest of the soul at the very thought of movement. I felt as though I were inhabiting a spent and useless contraption of tissue and bone which no longer had any relevance to me and what I really was. Was this, I wondered, why the mystics came to the desert: to be so alienated from their own flesh, at a distance that was beyond repugnance, that they might dwell, without alternative, upon and within the boundaries of the spirit? . . . .

There was nothing but pain in this desert, for human beings and animals alike. Life was pain. Only in death was there relief.

PATRICK MARNHAM
(1943–   )

English writer and traveller. He has travelled extensively in Africa, India, the Middle East and South America. In 1976 he toured West Africa to write a report on the Nomads of the Sahel for the Minority Rights Group.

Traffic jams African-style

Almost all the cars in Africa are to be found in or around African cities, and in Lagos the traffic jams last all day. For hours and hours every morning the traffic attempting to reach the centre of the city sits motionless, festooned in delicate patterns across the marshes and townships and plains surrounding it, now looping over and back onto itself as it follows the filigree of six-lane highways which enterprising German engineers have sold to the government, but which lead eventually to the impassable alleyways of the colonial settlement. This is getting to work.

Later in the day there is going home. The same bus lines, but now in the heat and filth of the city afternoon. The same traffic jam, day after day.

The slowness of the traffic is so predictable that a sizeable part of the city's commerce takes place by the side of the road, in just such a leisurely manner as was possible before cars were invented. All along the looping overpasses there are peddlers with full trays. One can buy car accessories, toys for bored children, immersion heaters, tool kits, toothpaste, patent medicine, clothing, cassettes, jewelry, oranges, or pornographic home movies. As one sits there in the back of a rusting twenty-year-old sedan, half-asphyxiated by the gas fumes, life takes on a dying pace which overwhelms the Northern sense of purpose. The signs on the grimy buildings seem less and less plausible, 'Right Time Hotel – Barristers and Solicitors Within,' 'Motherless Babies Home,' 'School of Dental Hygiene,' 'Mukky Cuts – Butcher'; when the traffic does move, the car behind promptly rams the old sedan. . . .

For most of the people who work in the city, the bus is the only means of transport, and the jams are not the only hazard. In Nairobi the bus crews work for rival companies, and they earn more money if they carry more passengers, so they race each other from one bus stop to the next. Sometimes rival buses, having raced side by side down a stretch of road, reach a crowd of passengers at the same time. The conductor and driver then fight each other, armed with crankshafts and wrenches and knives, to decide whose bus shall be filled to the point where any further passengers would fall off. In Kenya a single bus crash resulted in the death of ten passengers and the injuring of ninety-two others. After such a crash the police do not expect to interview the driver. If he is able to, he runs away and hides for some days. You have to wait to overcome the universal shock of a road accident before you realize that the survivors are not gathered around the injured people, assisting them, but are gathered around the driver (having left the bodies strewn all over the road) and are beating him to death.

EUROPE

ATLANTIC

OCEAN

NORTH
SEA

BALTIC SEA

Moscow

R Dvina

London

Hanover
Berlin

Warsaw

BAY OF
BISCAY

Paris

Lyon

A L P S

Vienna

R Danube

BLACK SEA

Lisbon

Madrid

Pyrenees

Venice

Istanbul
(Constantinople)

Rome
Naples

MEDITERRANEAN

MALTA

SEA

Athens

HANNIBAL
(247–182 BC)

Carthaginian general. Commander of the Carthaginian army in the Second Punic War (218–201 BC). After capturing Sagunto in Valencia, despite heroic resistance by its inhabitants, he invaded Italy, crossing the Pennine Alps with an army of 40,000 men and defeating the Romans at Trasimene (217 BC) and Cannae (216). In 203 he returned to Carthage to defend it against the Romans and was defeated at Zama the following year. Hannibal committed suicide in Asia Minor to avoid extradition by the Romans. His invasion of Italy was described by the Greek historian Polybius.

The crossing of the Alps, 218 BC

... They at length reached a place where it was impossible for either the elephants or the pack-animals to pass owing to the extreme narrowness of the path, a previous landslip having carried away about one and a half stades of the face of the mountain and a further landslip having recently occurred, and here the soldiers once more became disheartened and discouraged. The Carthaginian general at first thought of avoiding the difficult part by a detour, but as a fresh fall of snow made progress impossible he had to abandon this project. ...

Hannibal encamped on the ridge, sweeping it clear of snow, and next set the soldiers to work to build up the path along the cliff, a most toilsome task. In one day he had made a passage sufficiently wide for the pack-train and horses; so he at once took these across and encamping on ground free of snow, sent them out to pasture, and then took the Numidians in relays to work at building up the path, so that with great difficulty in three days he managed to get the elephants across, but in a wretched condition from hunger; for the summits of the Alps and the parts near the top of the passes are all quite treeless and bare owing to the snow lying there continuously both winter and summer, but the slopes half-way up on both sides are grassy and wooded and on the whole inhabitable.

Hannibal having now got all his forces together continued the descent, and in three days' march from the precipice just described reached flat country. He had lost many of his men by the hands of the enemy in the crossing of rivers and on the march in general, and the precipices and difficulties of the Alps had cost him not only many men, but a far greater number of horses and sumpter-animals. The whole march from New Carthage had taken him five months, and he had spent fifteen days in crossing the Alps, and now, when he thus boldly descended into the plain of the Po and the territory of the Insubres, his surviving forces numbered twelve thousand African and eight thousand Iberian foot, and not more than six thousand horse in all, as he himself states in the inscription on the column at Lacinium relating to the number of his forces.

LUITPRAND OF CREMONA
(fl. AD 946)

Italian diplomat. In 946 he went to Constantinople as the ambassador of King Berengarius II of Italy. He was received in the Magnaura Palace by the Emperor, Constantine Porphyrogenitus, seated on the legendary Throne of Solomon, which had been constructed in the reign of the Emperor Theophilus (AD 829–842).

The throne of Solomon

Constantine, as much on account of the Spanish ambassadors who had then recently arrived, as for myself and Luitfred, received us with the following ceremonial. A gilt bronze tree was before the Emperor, and its branches were covered with various kinds of gilt birds, each one of which sang according to its kind. The throne was so artfully contrived that while at one moment it was on the ground, at the next it was off it, and anon it was seen high up in the air. The foot of the throne, which was of great size, and made I know not whether of bronze or wood, had great gilt lions guarding it. I was brought into the presence of the Emperor supporting myself on the shoulders of two eunuchs. As soon as I appeared, the lions roared and the birds sang according to their various kinds. I felt no terror, however, nor was I moved with astonishment, for I had made inquiry concerning all these things of one who knew all about them. Having worshipped (the Emperor) for the third time by a full-length prostration, I raised my head, and whereas I had seen him in the first place seated a little higher up than the floor, I now saw him dressed in other robes, and seated near the ceiling of the room.

BENVENUTO CELLINI
(1500–1571)

Italian sculptor, gold and silver smith and engraver. His patrons included two popes, Clement VII and Paul III and King Francis I of France. A Florentine of a violent and homicidal disposition, he was the most skilful metalworker of his day.

Horrid revenge on an innkeeper near Chioggia

A few days afterwards we set out on our return to Florence. We lay one night at a place on this side Chioggia, on the left hand as you go toward Ferrara. Here the host insisted upon being paid before we went to bed, and in his own way; and when I observed that it was the custom everywhere else to pay in the morning, he answered: 'I insist on being paid overnight, and in my own way.' I retorted that men who wanted everything their own way ought to make a world after their own fashion, since things were differently managed here. Our host told me not to go on bothering his brains, because he was determined to do as he had said. Tribolo stood trembling with fear, and nudged me to keep quiet, lest they should do something worse to us; so we paid them in the way they wanted, and afterwards we retired to rest. We had, I must admit, the most capital beds, new in every particular, and as clean as they could be. Nevertheless I did not get one wink of sleep, because I kept on thinking how I could revenge myself. At one time it came into my head to set fire to his house; at another to cut the throats of four fine horses which he had in the stable; I saw well enough that it was easy for me to do all this; but I could not see how it was easy to secure myself and my companion. At last I resolved to put my things and my comrade's on board the boat; and so I did. When the towing-horses had been harnessed to the cable, I ordered the people not to stir before I returned, for I had left a pair of slippers in my bedroom. Accordingly I went back to the inn and called our host, who told me he had nothing to do with us, and that we might go to Jericho. There was a ragged stable-boy about, half asleep, who . . . asked me for a tip, and I gave him a few Venetian coppers, and told him to make the barge man wait till I had found my slippers and returned. I went upstairs, took out a little knife as sharp as a razor, and cut the four beds that I found there into ribbons. I had the satisfaction of knowing I had done a damage of more than fifty crowns. Then I ran down to the boat with some pieces of the bed-covers in my pouch, and bade the bargee start at once without delay. We had not gone far before my gossip Tribolo said that he had left behind some little straps belonging to his carpet-bag, and that he must be allowed to go back for them. I answered that he need not take thought for a pair of little straps, since I could make him as many big ones as he liked. He told me I was always joking, but that he must really go back for his straps. Then he began ordering the bargee to stop, while I kept ordering him to go on. Meanwhile I informed my friend what kind of trick I had played our host, and showed him specimens of the bed-covers and other things, which threw him into such a quaking fright that he roared out to the bargee: 'On with you, on with you, as quick as you can!' and never thought himself quite safe until we reached the gates of Florence.

When we arrived there, Tribolo said: 'Let us bind our swords up, for the love of God; and play me no more of your games, I beg; for all this while I've felt as though my guts were in the saucepan.' I made answer: 'Gossip Tribolo, you need not tie your sword up, for you have never loosed it.'

GEORGE TURBEVILLE
(1540?–1610?)

English poet. A member of an ancient Dorset family, the D'Urbervilles of Thomas Hardy's *Tess*. In 1568 he went to Moscow as secretary to the English ambassador, Thomas Randolph. From there he sent a series of letters, written in verse, to his friends in London.

Among the Russes

I left my native soile, full like a retchlesse man,
And unacquainted of the coast, among the Russes ran:
A people passing rude, to vices vile inclinde,
Folke fit to be of Bacchus traine, so quaffing is their kinde.

Drinke is their whole desire, the pot is all their pride,
The sobrest head doth once a day stand needfull of a guide.
If he to banket bid his friends, he will not shrinke
On them at dinner to bestow a douzen kindes of drinke:
Such licour as they have, and as the countrey gives,
But chiefly two, one called Kvas, whereby the Mousike lives.
Small ware and waterlike, but somewhat tart in taste,
The rest is Mead of honie made, wherewith their lips they baste.
And if he goe unto his neighbour as a guest,
He cares for litle meate, if so his drinke be of the best. . . .

GILES FLETCHER
(1549?–1611)

English diplomat and poet. In 1588 he led an embassy to
Russia, where he was subjected to a variety of indignities
but succeeded in negotiating various concessions on be-
half of English merchants. His book on Russia, *Of the
Russe Common Wealth* (1591), was suppressed by Lord
Burghley at the request of the East Coast merchants, who
feared that it might give offence to the tsar.

Russians in the bath

The Russe because that he is used to both these extremities of heat
and of cold, can beare them both a great deale more patiently, then
strangers can doe. You shall see them sometimes (to season their
bodies) come out of their bathstoves all on a froth, and fuming as
hoat almost as a pigge at a spit, and presently to leape into the river
starke naked, or to powre cold water all over their bodies, and that
in the coldest of all the winter time. The women to mende the bad
hue of their skinnes, use to paint their faces with white and red
colours, so visibly, that every man may perceive it. Which is made
no matter, because it is common and liked well by their husbands:
who make their wives and daughters as ordinarie allowance to buy
them colours to paint their faces withall, and delight themselves
much to see them of fowle women to become such faire images. This
parcheth the skinne, and helpeth to deforme them when their
painting is of.

OTTAVIANO BON
(1551–1622)

Venetian *bailo* (diplomatic agent) to the Sublime Porte, the court of the Ottoman sultans in Constantinople, between 1604 and 1607.

Sultan Ahmet I chooses a bedfellow

... If he should require one of them for his pleasure or to watch them at play or hear their music, he makes known his desire to the Head Kadin, who immediately sends for the girls who seem to her to be the most beautiful in every respect and arranges them in a line from one end of the room to the other. She then brings in the King, who passes before them once or twice, and according to his pleasure fixes his eyes on the one who attracts him most, and as he leaves throws one of his handkerchiefs into her hand, expressing the desire to sleep the night with her. She, having this good fortune, makes up as well as she can and, coached and perfumed by the Kadin, sleeps the night with the King in the Royal chamber in the women's apartments, which is always kept ready for such an event. And while they are sleeping the night the Kadin arranges for some old Moorish women, who take it in turn to stay in the room for two or three hours at a time. There are always two torches burning there, one at the door of the room, where one of the old women is, and the other at the foot of the bed; and they change without making a sound, so that the King is not disturbed in any way. On rising in the morning the King changes all his clothes, leaving the girl those he was wearing with all the money that was in the purses: then, going to his other rooms, he sends her a present of clothes, jewels, and money in accordance with the satisfaction and pleasure received. The same procedure holds good for all the others who take his fancy, lasting longer with one than with another according to the pleasure and affection he feels for her. And she who becomes pregnant is at once called Cassachi Sultan – that is to say, Queen Sultana – and if she bears a son its arrival is heralded with the greatest festivities.

THOMAS CORYATE
(1577?–1617)

English traveller. Son of the rector of Odcombe, Somerset, he became a licensed buffoon at the court of James I. His appearance was comic: 'He carried folly in his very face,' according to a contemporary. In 1608 he travelled through Europe, walking 1975 miles and visiting forty-five cities. His account of the journey – *Coryats Crudities. Hastily gobled up in Five Moneths Travells in France, Savoy, Italy, Rhetia comonly called the Grisons Country, Helvetia alias Switzerland, some parts of high Germany, and the Netherlands; Newly digested in the hungry aire of Odcombe in the County of Somerset, and now dispersed to the nourishment of the travelling Members of this Kingdome* – was for a long time the only handbook for continental travellers. When he returned from his 'gobling', Coryate hung the shoes in which he had walked from Venice to Odcombe in the church there, where they remained until the beginning of the eighteenth century. A second journey, begun in 1612, took him through Constantinople, Greece, Asia Minor, Egypt, the Holy Land and Persia to India, where he died in 1617.

A nice-looking gallows

A little on this side Paris, even at the towns end, there is the fayrest Gallowes that ever I saw, built upon a little hillocke called Mount Falcon, which consisteth of fourteene fair pillars of free-stone: this gallowes was made in the time of the Guisian massacre, to hang the Admiral of France Chatillion, who was a Protestant, Anno Dom. 1572.

Three ostriches at Fontainebleau

I saw there three Ostriches, called in Latin Struthiocameli, which are such birds that (as Historians doe write of them) will eate yron, as a key, or a horse shoe; one male and two female. Their neckes are much longer than Cranes, and pilled, having none or little feathers about them. They advance themselves much higher than the tallest man that ever I saw. Also their feete and legs, which are wonderfull long, are pilled and bare: and their thighes together with their hinder parts are not only bare, but also seeme very raw and redde, as if they had taken some hurt, but indeed they are naturally so. Their heads are covered all with small stubbed feathers: their eies great and black: their beakes short and sharp: their feete cloven, not unlike to a hoofe, and their nailes formed in that manner, that I have read they will take up stones with them, and throw at their enimies that pursue them, and sometimes hurt them. The feathers of their wings and tailes, but especially of their tailes are very soft and fine. In respect whereof they are much used in the fannes of Gentlewomen. The Authors do write that it is a very foolish bird: for whereas hee doth sometimes hide his necke behind a bush, he thinks that no body sees him, though indeede he be seene of every one. Also he is said to be so forgetfull, that as soone as he hath laid his egges, he hath cleane forgotten them till his young ones are hatched.

WILLIAM LITHGOW
(1582–1645)

Scottish traveller. Born in Lanark, where he was known as 'Cut-lugged Willie', four brothers having cut off his ears after finding him with their sister. Lithgow claimed to have walked over 36,000 miles in Europe, Asia and Africa during 1610–29. His other journeys included London to Edinburgh on foot. A contemporary of Coryate, but more accident-prone – assailed in Libya, beset in Moldavia, tortured on the rack by the Inquisition in Malaga – he was the author of *The Totall Discourse, of Rare Adventures, and painfull Peregrinations of long nineteene yeares travayles* (1632).

Beset in Moldavia, 1616

... Now having left this Religious Country [Transylvania], and crossing the North passage of the Hils, called the Borean Berger, or North mountaine, I entred in Moldovia; where for my welcome in the midst of a border-Wood, I was beset with six murderers, Hungarians and Moldavians: where having with many prayers saved my life, they robbed mee of threescore Hungar Duccats of gold, and all my Turkish clothes, leaving me stark naked; save onely they returned to me my Patents, Papers, and Seales.

This done, and for their better security, they caryed mee a little out of the way, and bound my naked body fast about the middle to an Oaken tree, with wooden ropes, and my armes backward so likewise: swearing to me, that if I cryed for helpe, or marred them of their designes before the Sun set, they would turne backe and kill me; promising then to set me free.

But night come, and I forgotten, was left here in a trembling feare, for Wolves and wild Boares till the morrow; where at last by Gods providence I was relieved in the morning by a company of Heards: who clothing me with an old long coat of theirs, and refreshing me with meat; one of them caryed me five leagues unto the Lord of the ground, the Baron of Starhulds a Moldavian Protestant, with whom I stayed fifteene dayes: And was more than repaired of all my losses, by his owne bounty, and Noble Kinsmen, his neighbouring friends, and would not suffer mee to goe any further in the Countrey, because of the Turkes jealousie over strangers.

Thomas Dallam
(fl. 1599–1615)

English organ-builder; built organs for Worcester Cathedral, 1613, and King's College, Cambridge, 1615. In 1599 he took an organ to Sultan Mehmed III in Constantinople, a gift from Queen Elizabeth I. Whilst there he looked into the Harem at Topkapi through a wall grating, one of the few ever to do so and live to tell the tale.

'That sighte did please me wondrous well'

When he [a black eunuch] had showed me many other thinges which I wondered at, than crossinge throughe a litle squar courte paved with marble, he poynted me to goo to a graite in a wale, but made me a sine that he myghte not goo thether him selfe. When I came to the grait the wale was verrie thicke, and graited on bothe the sides with iron verrie strongly; but through that graite I did se thirtie of the Grand Sinyor's Concobines that weare playinge with a bale in another courte. At the firste sighte of them I thoughte they had bene yonge men, but when I saw the hare of their heades hange doone on their backes, platted together with a tasle of smale pearle hanginge in the lower end of it, and by other plaine tokens, I did know them to be women, and verrie prettie ones in deede.

Theie wore upon theire heades nothinge bute a little capp of clothe of goulde, which did but cover the crowne of her heade; no bandes a boute their neckes, nor anythinge but faire cheans of pearle and a juell hanginge on their breste, and juels in their ears; their coats weare like a souldier's mandilyon [cloak], som of reed sattan and som of blew, and som of other collors, and grded like a lace of contraire collor; they wore britchis of scamatie, a fine clothe made of coton woll, as whyte as snow and as fine as lane [muslin]; for I could desarne the skin of their thies throughe it. These britchis cam doone to their mydlege; som of them did weare fine cordevan buskins, and som had their leges naked, with a goulde ringe on the smale of her legg; on her foute a velvett panttoble [high shoe] 4 or 5 inches hie. I stood so longe loukinge upon them that he which had showed me all this kindnes began to be verrie angrie with me. He made a wrye mouthe, and stamped with his foute to make me give over looking; the which I was verrie lothe to dow, for that sighte did please me wondrous well.

JOHN EVELYN
(1620–1706)

English diarist. Between 1643 and 1647 he made a grand tour of France, Italy and Switzerland, *en route* marrying the daughter of the English ambassador in Paris. His journeys are described in his famous *Diaries*.

A visit to the galleys at Marseilles, 1644

We went then to visit the galleys, being about twenty-five in number; the *capitaine* of the Galley Royal gave us most courteous entertainment in his cabin, the slaves in the interim playing both loud and soft music very rarely. Then he showed us how he commanded their motions with a nod, and his whistle making them row out. The spectacle was to me new and strange, to see so many hundreds of miserable naked persons, their heads being shaven close, and having only high red bonnets, a pair of coarse canvas drawers, their whole backs and legs naked, doubly chained about their middle and legs, in couples, and made fast to their seats, and all commanded in a trice by an imperious and cruel seaman. One Turk amongst the rest he much favoured, who waited on him in his cabin, but with no other dress than the rest, and a chain locked about his leg, but not coupled. This galley was richly carved and gilded, and most of the rest were very beautiful. After bestowing something on the slaves, the *capitaine* sent a band of them to give us music at dinner where we lodged. I was amazed to contemplate how these miserable caitiffs lie in their galley crowded together; yet there was hardly one but had some occupation, by which, as leisure and calms permitted, they got some little money, insomuch as some of them have, after many years of cruel servitude, been able to purchase their liberty. The rising-forward and falling-back at their oar, is a miserable spectacle, and the noise of their chains, with the roaring of the beaten waters, has something of strange and fearful in it to one unaccustomed to it. They are ruled and chastised by strokes on their backs and soles of their feet, on the least disorder, and without the least humanity, yet are they cheerful and full of knavery.

MADAME DE SÉVIGNÉ
(1626–1696)

French woman of letters. Marie de Rabutin-Chantal, Marquise de Sévigné, left a correspondence of over 1500 letters, most of which were written to her daughter, the Comtesse de Grignan. Brilliant, acute and delightful, they are a revealing chronicle of social life during the reign of Louis XIV.

Taking the waters, Vichy, 4 June 1676

At length I have finished douching and exuding; in one week I have lost over thirty pints of water, and believe myself to be immune from the rheumatics for the rest of my life. There is little doubt the cure is a painful one, but a wonderful moment dawns at last when, empty and renewed, one sits relishing a cup of fresh chicken broth which joy is not to be despised, indeed I rank it very high: this is an adorable place. . . .

Tomorrow I take a mild dose, drink the waters for another week, and the trick is done. My knees are as good as cured, I still cannot close my hands; but using me as a bundle of soiled linen had proved a highly successful operation. We have here an old Madame Barois, who stutters as a result of apoplexy. I am sorry for her, but seeing she is most ill-favoured, no longer young though she decks herself out in absurd little double-crowned hats, falls in love after twenty-two years of widowhood with a M. de Barois on whom she showers her wealth and who, if you please, openly loves another and stoutly refuses to sleep with her for more than a quarter of an hour, and that only to consolidate his gains ... (a long-winded sentence) – one finds it difficult to keep one's hands off her and not spit in her face.

We are advised Madame de Pecquigny has also arrived or is expected. She is the Cumæan Sibyl, and wishes to be cured of her sixty-six years which she resents; this place is becoming a mad-house.

JAMES DRUMMOND
(1648–1716)

Fourth Earl of Perth. Scottish nobleman. Appointed Chancellor of Scotland, 1684. A member of the Stuart party and a Catholic convert, he took ship for France after James II's deposition, but, disguised in women's clothes, was intercepted by fishermen in the Firth of Forth and imprisoned. Exiled, he went first to Rome and then to James's court at St Germain. He is described by a biographer as a cruel man and proud, but as telling a story 'very prettily'.

Shrove Thursday, Venice, 1695

On Shrove Thursday a bull is beheaded by a butcher chosen by his fellows for that feat, and if he does it well in presence of the Doge and all the Senate is treated *in senerissimo*, feasted, and has the best musick at supper that can be. He I saw do it did it cleverly at one blow, and did not seem to strain neither. The Doge's guards conducted him to and from the place, and a firework is sett on fire in fair daylight. A fellow is drawn up on a flying rope, such as mountebanks use, in a ship about the bigness of a gondola (which is a very long small boat), and all the way he fires gunns and throws grenads amongst the people, but they are only paper ones. Then he flies down from the top of St. Mark's steeple, where he had left his gondola. This steeple is disjointed from the church 70 or 80 paces. And thus they divert the people here to amuse them and keep them from framing conceits of government and religion, such as our giddy people frame to themselves and make themselves the scorn and reproach of mankind. . . .

Lady Mary Wortley Montagu
(1689–1762)

English writer, best known for her letters. The daughter of the first Duke of Kingston, she eloped at the age of twenty-three with Edward Wortley Montagu. When he was appointed ambassador to Turkey in 1716, she accompanied him to the Sublime Porte.

The Turkish bath at Sophia

. . . I must not omit what I saw remarkable at Sophia, one of the most beautiful towns in the Turkish empire, and famous for its hot baths, that are resorted to both for diversion and health. I stopped here one day on purpose to see them. Designing to go *incognito*, I hired a Turkish coach. These voitures are not at all like ours. . . . They are covered all over with scarlet cloth, lined with silk, and very often richly embroidered and fringed. This covering entirely hides the persons in them, but may be thrown back at pleasure, and the ladies peep through the lattices. . . .

In one of these covered waggons, I went to the bagnio about ten o'clock. It was already full of women. . . . I was in my travelling habit, which is a riding dress, and certainly appeared very extraordinary to them. Yet there was not one of them that shewed the least surprise or impertinent curiosity, but received me with all the obliging civility possible. I know no European court where the ladies would have behaved themselves in so polite a manner to a stranger. I believe in the whole there were two hundred women, and yet none of those disdainful smiles, or satiric whispers, that never fail in our assemblies when anybody appears that is not dressed exactly in the fashion. They repeated over and over to me, '*Uzelle, pék uzelle,*' which is nothing but Charming, very charming.

The first sofas were covered with cushions and rich carpets, on which sat the ladies; and on the second, their slaves behind them, but without any distinction of rank in their dress, all being in the state of nature, that is, in plain English, stark naked, without any beauty or defect concealed. Yet there was not the least wanton smile or immodest gesture among them. They walked and moved with the same majestic grace which Milton describes of our general mother. There were many amongst them as exactly proportioned as ever any goddess was drawn by the pencil of Guido or Titian – and most of their skins shiningly white, only adorned by their beautiful hair divided into many tresses, hanging on their shoulders, braided either with pearl or ribbon, perfectly representing the figures of the Graces.

I was here convinced of the truth of a reflection I had often made, that if it was the fashion to go naked, the face would be hardly observed. I perceived that the ladies with the finest skins and most delicate shapes had the greatest share of my admiration, though their faces were sometimes less beautiful than those of their companions. To tell you the truth, I had the wickedness enough to wish secretly that Mr Jervas could have been there invisible. I fancy it would have very much improved his art to see so many fine women naked, in different postures, some in conversation, some working, others drinking coffee or sherbert, and many negligently lying on their cushions, while their slaves (generally pretty girls of seventeen or eighteen) were employed in braiding their hair in several pretty fancies. In short, it is the women's coffee-house, where all the news of the town is told, scandal invented, etc. . . . The lady that seemed most considerable among them entreated me to sit by her, and would fain have undressed me for the bath. I excused myself with difficulty. They being all so earnest in persuading me, I was at last forced to open my shirt, and shew them my stays; which satisfied them very well for, I saw, they believed I was so locked up in that machine that it was not in my own power to open it, which contrivance they attributed to my husband.

HENRY FIELDING
(1707–1754)

English novelist, dramatist and magistrate. After a successful double career as a novelist – *Joseph Andrews* (1742), *Tom Jones* (1749), *Amelia* (1751) – and as justice of the peace for Westminster and then Middlesex, Fielding's health deteriorated and he resigned his office in 1753. The next year, in an attempt to regain his health, he left Rotherhithe on a voyage to Lisbon. He died after two months in the city and was buried in the English cemetery. His *Journal of a Voyage to Lisbon*, which is as humorous as it is courageous, was published posthumously.

A dying man sets off for Lisbon, 26 June 1754

To go on board the ship it was necessary first to go into a boat; a matter of no small difficulty, as I had no use of my limbs, and was to be carried by men, who tho' sufficiently strong for their burden, were, like Archimedes, puzzled to find a steady footing. Of this, as few of my readers have not gone into wherries on the Thames, they will easily be able to form to themselves an idea. However, by the assistance of my friend Mr Welch, whom I never think or speak of but with love and esteem, I conquered this difficulty, as I did afterwards that of ascending the ship, into which I was hoisted with more ease by a chair lifted with pullies. I was soon seated in a great chair in the cabin, to refresh myself after a fatigue which had been more intolerable, in a quarter of a mile's passage from my couch to the ship, than I had before undergone in a land-journey of twelve miles, which I had travelled with the utmost expedition.

This latter fatigue was, perhaps, somewhat heightened by an indignation which I could not prevent arising in my mind. I think, upon my entrance into the boat, I presented a spectacle of the highest horror. The total loss of limbs was apparent to all who saw me, and my face contained marks of a most diseased state, if not of death itself. Indeed so ghastly was my countenance, that timorous women with child had abstained from my house, for fear of the ill consequences of looking at me. In this condition, I ran the gauntlope, (so, I think I may justly call it) through rows of sailors and watermen, few of whom failed of paying their compliments to me, by all manner of insults and jests on my misery. No man who knew me will think I conceived any personal resentment at this behaviour; but it was a lively picture of that cruelty and inhumanity, in the nature of men, which I have often contemplated with concern; and which leads the mind into a train of very uncomfortable and melancholy thoughts.

Arriving at the nastiest city in the world, August 1754

About seven in the evening I got into a chaise on shore, and was driven through the nastiest city in the world, tho' at the same time one of the most populous, to a kind of coffee-house, which is very pleasantly situated on the brow of a hill, about a mile from the city, and hath a very fine prospect of the river Tajo from Lisbon to the sea.

Here we regaled ourselves with a good supper, for which we were as well charged, as if the bill had been made on the Bath road, between Newbury and London.

And now we could joyfully say,

'Egressi optata Troes potiuntur aren.'
['The Trojans having disembarked take possession of the longed-for shore.']

Therefore in the words of Horace,

'——hic finis chartæq; viæq;'
['Here is the end of the map; and of the road.']

LAURENCE STERNE
(1713–1768)

Anglo-Irish novelist. Born at Clonmel in Tipperary. Ordained in 1738, he was parson of Sutton, Yorkshire, until 1759. In that year he began his great novel, *Tristram Shandy*; the first volume was published in 1760 and Sterne contracted to supply a fresh volume every remaining year of his life. In 1762 he began the journey through France and Italy immortalized in *A Sentimental Journey* (1768).

A case of delicacy – an adventure in Savoy

'Twas a wet and tempestuous night: so that by the delay, and that together, the Voiturin found himself obliged to keep up five miles short of his stage at a little decent kind of an inn by the road-side.

I forthwith took possession of my bed-chamber, got a good fire, order'd supper; and was thanking Heaven it was no worse, when a voiture arrived with a lady in it and her servant-maid.

As there was no other bed-chamber in the house, the hostess, without much nicety, led them into mine, telling them, as she usher'd them in, that there was nobody in it but an English gentleman; that there were two good beds in it, and a closet within the room which held another. . . .

The lady was a Piedmontese of about thirty, with a glow of health in her cheeks. The maid was a Lyonoise of twenty, and as brisk and lively a French girl as ever moved. There were difficulties every way – and the obstacle of the stone in the road, which brought us into the distress, great as it appeared whilst the peasants were removing it, was but a pebble to what lay in our ways now. I have only to add, that it did not lessen the weight which hung upon our spirits, that we were both too delicate to communicate what we felt to each other upon the occasion.

We sat down to supper; and had we not had more generous wine to it than a little inn in Savoy could have furnish'd, our tongues had been tied up, till necessity herself had set them at liberty, but the lady having a few bottles of Burgundy in her voiture, sent down her Fille de Chambre for a couple of them; so that by the time supper was over, and we were left alone, we felt ourselves inspired with a strength of mind sufficient to talk, at least, without reserve upon our situation. We turn'd it every way, and debated and considered it in all kind of lights in the course of a two hours' negotiation; at the end of which the articles were settled finally betwixt us, and stipulated for in form and manner of a treaty of peace – and I believe with as much religion and good faith on both sides, as in any treaty which has yet had the honour of being handed down to posterity.

They were as follow:

First. As the right of the bed-chamber is in Monsieur, and he thinking the bed next to the fire to be the warmest, he insists upon the concession on the lady's side of taking up with it.

Granted, on the part of Madame; with a proviso: that as the curtains on that bed are of a flimsey transparent cotton, and appear likewise too scanty to draw close, that the Fille de Chambre shall fasten up the opening, either by corking pins, or needle and thread, in such manner as shall be deem'd a sufficient barrier on the side of Monsieur.

2dly. It is required on the part of Madame, that Monsieur shall lie the whole night through in his robe de chambre.

Rejected: inasmuch as Monsieur is not worth a robe de chambre; he having nothing in his portmanteau but six shirts and a black silk pair of breeches.

The mentioning the silk pair of breeches made an entire change of the article, for the breeches were accepted as an equivalent for the robe de chambre; and so it was stipulated and agreed upon, that I should lie in my black silk breeches all night.

3dly. It was insisted upon, and stipulated for by the lady, that after Monsieur was got to bed, and the candle and fire extinguished, that Monsieur should not speak one single word the whole night.

Granted; provided Monsieur's saying his prayers might not be deem'd an infraction of the treaty.

There was but one point forgot in this treaty, and that was the manner in which the lady and myself should be obliged to undress and get to bed. There was one way of doing it, and that I leave to the reader to devise; protesting as I do, that if it is not the most delicate in nature, 'tis the fault of his own imagination – against which this is not my first complaint.

Now when we were got to bed, whether it was the novelty of the situation, or what it was, I know not; but so it was, I could not shut my eyes; I tried this side and that, and turn'd and turn'd again, till a full hour after midnight; when Nature and patience both wearing out, O my God! said I.

You have broke the treaty, Monsieur, said the lady, who had no more sleep than myself. I begg'd a thousand pardons, but insisted it was no more than an ejaculation. She maintain'd 'twas an entire infraction of the treaty. I maintain'd it was provided for in the clause of the third article.

The lady would by no means give up the point, though she weaken'd her barrier by it; for in the warmth of the dispute, I could hear two or three corking pins fall out of the curtain to the ground.

Upon my word and honour, Madame, said I, stretching my arm out of bed by way of asseveration——

(I was going to have added, that I would not have trespass'd against the remotest idea of decorum for the world)——

But the Fille de Chambre hearing there were words between us, and fearing that hostilities would ensue in course, had crept silently out of her closet, and it being totally dark, had stolen so close to our beds, that she had got herself into the narrow passage which separated them, and had advanced so far up as to be in a line betwixt her mistress and me——

So that when I stretch'd out my hand, I caught hold of the Fille de Chambre's——

THOMAS GRAY
(1716–1771)

English poet, best known for his 'Elegy Written in a Country Churchyard'. In 1739 he set out on a Grand Tour of the Continent with Horace Walpole, with whom he had been at Eton. They quarreled in Italy and Gray returned home in 1741. Three years later the friends were reconciled, but Gray lived a secluded life thereafter.

Versailles, May 1739

Well! and is this the great front of Versailles? What a huge heap of littleness! it is composed, as it were, of three courts, all open to the eye at once, and gradually diminishing till you come to the royal apartments, which on this side present but half a dozen windows and a balcony. This last is all that can be called a front, for the rest is only great wings. The hue of all this mass is black, dirty red, and yellow; the first proceeding from stone changed by age; the second, from a mixture of brick; and the last, from a profusion of tarnished gilding. You cannot see a more disagreeable tout-ensemble; and, to finish the matter, it is all stuck over in many places with small busts of a tawny hue between every window.

Extracts from an outline for a Book of Travels

Proposals for printing by Subscription, in

THIS LARGE
LETTER

The Travels of T: G: GENT: which will consist of the following Particulars.

CHAP: I:

The Author arrives at Dover; his conversation with the Mayor of that Corporation; sets out in the Pacquet-Boat, grows very sick; the Author spews, a very minute account of all the circumstances thereof: his arrival at Calais; how the inhabitants of that country speak French, & are said to be all Papishes; the Author's reflexions thereupon.

2.

How they feed him with Soupe, & what Soupe is. how he meets with a Capucin; & what a Capucin is. how they shut him up in a Post-Chaise, & send him to Paris; he goes wondring along dureing 6 days; & how there are Trees, & Houses just as in England. arrives at Paris without knowing it.

3.

Full account of the river Seine, & of the various animals & plants its borders produce. Description of the little Creature, called an Abbé, its parts, & their uses; with the reasons, why they will not live in England, & the methods, that have been used to propagate them there. a Cut of the Inside of a Nunnery; it's Structure, wonderfully adapted to the use of the animals, that inhabit it: a short account of them, how they propagate without the help of a Male, & how they eat up their own young ones, like Cats, and Rabbets. supposed to have both Sexes in themselves, like a Snail. . . .

4.

Goes to the Opera; grand Orchestra of Humstrums, Bagpipes, Salt-boxes, Tabours, & Pipes. Anatomy on a French Ear, shewing the formation of it to be entirely different from that of an English one, & that Sounds have a directly contrary effect upon one & the other. . . .

5.

The Author takes unto him a Taylour. his Character. how he covers him with Silk, & Fringe, & widens his figure with buckram a yard on each side; Wastcoat, & Breeches so strait, he can neither breath, nor walk. how the Barber curls him en Bequille, & à la negligee, & ties a vast Solitaire about his Neck; how the Milliner lengthens his ruffles to his finger's ends, & sticks his two arms into a Muff. how he cannot stir, & how they cut him in proportion to his Clothes.

6.

He is carried to Versailles; despises it infinitely. a dissertation upon Taste. goes to an Installation in the Chappel-royal. enter the King, & 50 Fiddlers Solus. Kettle-Drums, & Trumpets, Queens, & Dauphins, Princesses, & Cardinals, Incense, & the Mass. Old Knights, makeing Curtsies; Holy-Ghosts, & Fiery-tongues.

7.

Goes into the Country to Rheims in Champagne. stays there 3 Months, what he did there (he must beg the reader's pardon, but) he has really forgot.

8.

Proceeds to Lyons. Vastness of that City. Can't see the Streets for houses. how rich it is, & how much it stinks. Poem upon the Confluence of the Rhône, & the Saône, by a friend of the Author's; very pretty!

9.

Makes a journey into Savoy, & in his way visits the Grande Chartreuse; he is set astride upon a Mule's back, & begins to climb up the Mountain. Rocks & Torrents beneath; Pine-trees, & Snows above; horrours, & terrours on all sides. the Author dies of the Fright.

10.

He goes to Geneva. his mortal antipathy to a Presbyterian, & the cure for it. returns to Lyons. gets a surfeit with eating Ortolans, & Lampreys; is advised to go into Italy for the benefit of the air. . . .

11.

Sets out the latter end of November to cross the Alps. he is devoured by a Wolf, & how it is to be devoured by a Wolf. the 7th day he comes to the foot of Mount Cenis. how he is wrap'd up in Bear Skins, & Beaver-Skins, Boots on his legs, Caps on his head, Muffs on his hands, & Taffety over his eyes; he is placed on a Bier, & is carried to heaven by the savages blindfold. how he lights among a certain fat nation, call'd Clouds; how they are always in a Sweat, & never speak, but they fart. how they flock about him, & think him very odd for not doing so too. he falls flump into Italy.

12.

Arrives at Turin; goes to Genoa, & from thence to Placentia; crosses the River Trebia: the Ghost of Hannibal appears to him; & what it, & he, say upon the occasion. locked out of Parma in a cold winter's night: the author by an ingenious stratagem gains admittance. despises that City, & proceeds through Reggio to Modena. how the Duke, & Dutchess lye over their own Stables, & go every night to a vile Italian Comedy. despises them, & it; & proceeds to Bologna.

13.

Enters into the Dominions of the Pope o' Rome. meets the Devil, & what he says on the occasion. very publick, & scandalous doings between the Vines & the Elm-trees, & how the Olive-trees are shock'd thereupon. Author longs for Bologna-Sausages, & Hams; & how he grows as fat as a Hog. . . .

15.

Arrival at Florence. is of opinion, that the Venus of Medicis is a modern performance, & that a very indifferent one, & much inferiour to the K: Charles at Charing-Cross. Account of the City, & Manners of the Inhabitants. a learned Dissertation on the true Situation of Gomorrah. . . .

And here will end the first part of these instructive & entertaining Voyages. the Subscribers are to pay 20 Guineas; 19 down, & the remainder upon delivery of the book. N:B: A few are printed on the softest Royal Brown Paper for the use of the Curious.

HORACE WALPOLE
(1717–1797)

English writer, collector, wit and traveller. Youngest son of Sir Robert Walpole, he became fourth Earl of Orford in 1791. In 1747 he acquired Strawberry Hill, a country house on the Thames at Twickenham, where he built a pseudo-Gothic castle and established a printing press. His works include *The Castle of Otranto* (1765) and 36 volumes of letters. The extracts that follow are from letters to Richard West.

Wolf snatches dog, November 1739

We were eight days in coming hither from Lyons; the four last in crossing the Alps. Such uncouth rocks, and such uncomely inhabitants! My dear West, I hope I shall never see them again! At the foot of Mount Cenis we were obliged to quit our chaise, which was taken all to pieces and loaded on mules; and we were carried in low arm-chairs on poles, swathed in beaver bonnets, beaver gloves, beaver stockings, muffs, and bear-skins. When we came to the top, behold the snows fallen! and such quantities, and conducted by such heavy clouds that hung glouting, that I thought we could never have waded through them. The descent is two leagues, but steep and rough as O **** father's face, over which, you know, the devil walked with hobnails in his shoes. But the dexterity and nimbleness of the mountaineers are inconceivable: they run with you down steeps and frozen precipices, where no man, as men are now, could possibly walk. We had twelve men and nine mules to carry us, our servants, and baggage, and were above five hours in this agreeable jaunt! The day before, I had a cruel accident, and so extraordinary an one, that it seems to touch upon the traveller. I had brought with me a little black spaniel of King Charles's breed; but the prettiest, fattest, dearest creature! I had let it out of the chaise for the air, and it was waddling along close to the head of the horses, on the top of the highest Alps, by the side of a wood of firs. There darted out a young wolf, seized poor dear Tory by the throat, and, before we could possibly prevent it, sprung up the side of the rock and carried him off. The postilion jumped off and struck at him with his whip, but in vain. I saw it and screamed, but in vain; for the road was so narrow, that the servants that were behind could not get by the chaise to shoot him. What is the extraordinary part is, that it was but two o'clock, and broad sunshine. It was shocking to see anything one loved run away with to so horrid a death.

Chilly in Italy, March 1740

In Italy they seem to have found out how hot their climate is, but not how cold; for there are scarce any chimneys, and most of the apartments painted in fresco; so that one has the additional horror of freezing with imaginary marble. The men hang little earthen pans of coals upon their wrists, and the women have portable stoves under their petticoats to warm their nakedness, and carry silver shovels in their pockets, with which their Cicisbeos stir them — Hush! by them, I mean their stoves.

Rome in decay, April 1740

I am very glad that I see Rome while it yet exists; before a great number of years are elapsed, I question whether it will be worth seeing. Between the ignorance and poverty of the present Romans, every thing is neglected and falling to decay; the villas are entirely out of repair, and the palaces so ill kept, that half the pictures are spoiled by damp. At the villa Ludovisi is a large oracular head of red marble, colossal, and with vast foramina for the eyes and mouth: — the man that showed the palace said it was *un ritratto della famiglia?* The Cardinal Corsini has so thoroughly pushed on the misery of Rome by impoverishing it, that there is no money but paper to be seen. He is reckoned to have amassed three millions of crowns. You may judge of the affluence the nobility live in, when I assure you, that what the chief princes allow for their own eating is a testoon a day; eighteenpence: there are some extend their expense to five pauls, or half a crown: Cardinal Albani is called extravagant for laying out ten pauls for his dinner and supper. You may imagine they never have any entertainments: so far from it, they never have any company. The princesses and duchesses particularly lead the dismallest of lives. Being the posterity of popes, though of worse families than the ancient nobility, they expect greater respect than my ladies the countesses and marquises will pay them; consequently they consort not, but mope in a vast palace with two miserable tapers, and two or three monsignori, whom they are forced to court and humour, that they may not be entirely deserted. Sundays they do issue forth in a vast unwieldy coach to the Corso.

In short, child, after sunset one passes one's time here very ill; and if I did not wish for you in the mornings, it would be no compliment to tell you that I do in the evening. Lord! how many English I could change for you, and yet buy you wondrous cheap! And then French and Germans I could fling into the bargain by dozens. Nations swarm here. You will have a great fat French cardinal garnished with thirty abbés roll into the area of St. Peter's, gape, turn short, and talk of the chapel of Versailles. I heard one of them say t'other day, he had been at the *Capitale*. One asked of course how he liked it – *Ah! il y a assez de belles choses.*

PHILIP THICKNESSE
(1719–1792)

English traveller and soldier. Cantakerous and eccentric, he spent his life writing, travelling and quarrelling. He 'discovered' Gainsborough and was his patron for twenty years until their friendship was shattered by the inevitable row. In 1775 he travelled through France and Spain, accompanied by his daughters, his wife (who broke into song at every opportunity), his spaniel, Mrs Thicknesse's parakeet (who flew freely above the coach) and Jocko the monkey, who rode postillion, dressed in a special livery and a hat with a pigtail attached.

A dish of delicate spinach

POST-HOUSE, ST. GEORGE, six leagues from LYONS.
I am particular in dating this letter, in hopes that every English traveller may avoid the place I write from, by either stopping short, or going beyond it; as it is the only house of reception for travellers in the village, and the worst I have met with in my whole journey. . . . As a specimen of French auberge cookery, I cannot help serving up a dish of spinage to you, as it was served to me at this house. We came in early in the afternoon, and while I was in the

court-yard I saw a flat basket stand upon the ground, the bottom of which was covered with boiled spinage; and as my dog, and several others in the yard, had often put their noses into it, I concluded it was put down for *their* food, not *mine*, till I saw a dirty girl patting it up into round balls; and two children, the eldest not above three years old, slavering in, and playing with it, one of whom, *to lose no time*, was performing *an office* that none could *do for her*. I asked the maid what she was about, and what it was she was so preparing! for I began to think I had been mistaken, till she told me it was spinage; – 'not for me, I hope,' said I, – '*oui, pour vous et le monde.*' I then forbad her bringing any to table; and putting the little girl *off her centre*, by an angry push, made her almost as dirty as the spinage; and I could perceive her mother, the hostess, and some French travellers who were near, looked upon me as a brute for *disturbing la pauvre enfant*; nevertheless, with my *entrée* came up a dish of this *delicate spinage*, with which I made the girl a very pretty *Chapeau Anglois*, for I turned it, dish and all, upon her head.

TOBIAS SMOLLETT
(1721–1771)

Scottish novelist and surgeon. In 1740 he sailed with the British fleet to the West Indies as surgeon's mate. Returning to London in 1744 with a rich Jamaican wife, he practised for a while as a surgeon before beginning his literary career. As well as writing his own novels, *Roderick Random*, *Peregrine Pickle* and *Humphrey Clinker*, he also translated *Don Quixote* into English. From 1763–5 he travelled in France and Italy, taking a jaundiced view of what he saw ('I was much disappointed at sight of the Pantheon, which . . . looks like a huge cockpit open at the top') and setting it down for our delectation in *Travels through France and Italy* (1766).

A temple of Cloacina at Nimes

Provence is a pleasant country, well cultivated; but the inns are not so good here as in Languedoc, and few of them are provided with a certain convenience which an English traveller can very ill dispense with. Those you find are generally on the tops of houses, exceedingly nasty; and so much exposed to the weather, that a valetudinarian cannot use them without hazard of his life. At Nismes in Languedoc, where we found the temple of Cloacina in a most shocking condition, the servant maid told me her mistress had caused it to be made on purpose for the English travellers; but now she was very sorry for what she had done, as all the French who frequented her house, instead of using the seat, left their offerings on the floor, which she was obliged to have cleaned three or four times a day. This is a degree of beastliness, which would appear detestable even in the capital of North Britain.

Gallic faith in the efficacy of bouillon

A *bouillon* is an universal remedy among the good people of France; insomuch, that they have no idea of any persons dying, after having swallowed *un bon bouillon*. One of the English gentlemen, who were robbed and murdered about thirty years ago, between Calais and Boulogne, being brought to the post-house of Boulogne, with some signs of life, this remedy was immediately administered. 'What surprises me greatly,' said the postmaster, speaking of this melancholy story to a friend of mine, two years after it happened, 'I made an excellent *bouillon*, and poured it down his throat with my own hands, and yet he did not recover.' Now, in all probability, this *bouillon* it was that stopped his breath. When I was a very young man, I remember to have seen a person suffocated by such impertinent officiousness.

EDWARD GIBBON
(1737–1794)

English historian, author of *The History of the Decline and Fall of the Roman Empire*. He had no formal education, but read omnivorously; at the age of fifteen he went to Oxford, but was forced to leave because of his conversion to Roman Catholicism. In 1753 his father sent him to Lausanne, where he was reconverted to Protestantism and fell in love with Suzanne Curchod, the penniless daughter of a pastor. When his father refused to consent to their marriage, Gibbon 'sighed as a lover' but 'obeyed as a son'. On a visit to Rome in 1764 he conceived the

idea of his great book. Personally unprepossessing –
under five foot in height, fat and always extravagantly
dressed – he was a figure of ridicule among his contem-
poraries.

Preparations for a Transalpine expedition

. . . Many hours were lost in dissipation, many more were employed
in literary labour. In the country, Horace and Virgil, Juvenal and
Ovid, were my assiduous companions: but, in town, I formed and
executed a plan of study for the use of my Transalpine expedition:
the topography of old Rome, the ancient geography of Italy, and the
science of medals. 1. I diligently read, almost always with a pen in
my hand, the elaborate treatises of Nardini, Donatus, etc., which fill
the fourth volume of the *Roman Antiquities* of Grævius. 2. I next
undertook and finished the *Italia Antiqua* of Cluverius, a learned
native of Prussia, who had measured, on foot, every spot, and has
compiled and digested every passage of the ancient writers. These
passages in Greek or Latin authors I perused in the text of Cluverius,
in two folio volumes: but I separately read the descriptions of Italy
by Strabo, Pliny, and Pomponius Mela, the Catalogues of the epic
poets, the Itineraries of Wesseling's Antoninus, and the coasting
voyage of Rutilius Numatianus; and I studied two kindred subjects
in the *Mesures Itinéraires* of d'Anville, and the copious work of
Bergier, *Histoire des grands Chemins de l'Empire Romain*. From
these materials I formed a table of roads and distances reduced to
our English measure; filled a folio commonplace-book with my
collections and remarks on the geography of Italy; and inserted in
my journal many long and learned notes on the insulæ and popu-
lousness of Rome, the social war, the passage of the Alps by
Hannibal, etc. 3. After glancing my eye over Addison's agreeable
dialogues, I more seriously read the great work of Ezechiel
Spanheim, *de Præstantiâ et Usû Numismatum*, and applied with
him the medals of the kings and emperors, the families and colonies,
to the illustration of ancient history. And thus was I armed for my
Italian journey.

JAMES BOSWELL
(1740–1795)

Scottish man of letters, friend and biographer of Samuel
Johnson. The son of a distinguished judge, he studied law
and was admitted to the bar in 1766. On a trip to London
in 1763 he met Dr Johnson and determined on a literary
career, although he practised law all his life. In the same
year he set out on an extensive tour of the Continent.

Is it come to this?

I set out upon my travels with a kind of gloom upon my mind. My
enthusiastic love of London made me leave it with a heavy heart. It
might not have been the case had I been setting out on an immediate
tour through the gay regions of Italy and France. But to comply with
my father's inclinations I had agreed to pass my first winter at
Utrecht, a Dutch university town of which I had received the most
disagreeable prepossessions. Mr Samuel Johnson honoured me
with his company to Harwich, where he saw me embark and set sail
from Britain. I was sick and filled with a crowd of different ideas.
But we had a good passage, and landed on Sunday the 7 of August,
at twelve at noon. I shall not be tedious with particulars, but give
you the great lines of my story.... I arrived at Utrecht on a
Saturday evening. I went to the Nouveau Château d'Anvers. I was
shown up to a high bedroom with old furniture, where I had to sit
and be fed by myself. At every hour the bells of the great tower
played a dreary psalm tune. A deep melancholy seized upon me. I
groaned with the idea of living all winter in so shocking a place. I
thought myself old and wretched and forlorn. I was worse and
worse next day. All the horrid ideas that you can imagine, recurred
upon me. I was quite unemployed and had not a soul to speak to but
the clerk of the English meeting, who could do me no good. I sunk
quite into despair. I thought that at length the time was come that I
should grow mad. I actually believed myself so. I went out to the
streets, and even in public could not refrain from groaning and
weeping bitterly. I said always, 'Poor Boswell! is it come to this?
Miserable wretch that I am! what shall I do?' – O my friend, pause
here a little and figure to yourself what I endured. I took general

speculative view of things; all seemed full of darkness and woe. Tortured in this manner, I determined to leave Utrecht, and next day returned to Rotterdam in a condition that I shudder to recollect. . . .

A closet in Potsdam

To punish my extravagant rodomontading, and to bring up my affairs and compose my spirit, I had sitten up all night. Grievous was it to the flesh till seven in the morning, when my blood took a fine flow. I was quite drunk with brisk spirits, and about eight, in came a woman with a basket of chocolate to sell. I toyed with her and found she was with child. Oho! a safe piece. Into my closet. 'Habs er ein Man?' 'Ja, in den Gards bei Potsdam.' To bed directly. In a minute – over. I rose cool and astonished, half angry, half laughing. I sent her off. Bless me, have I now committed adultery? Stay, a soldier's wife is no wife. Should I now torment myself with speculations on sin, and on losing in one morning the merit of a year's chastity? No: this is womanish.

LADY ANNA MILLER
(1741–1781)

English verse writer. Born Miss Riggs, she was heiress to a large fortune. Her *Letters from Italy* were published anonymously in 1776. Four years later, on a visit to Bath, Fanny Burney wrote: 'Nothing here is more tonish than to visit Lady Miller. She is a round, plump, coarse-looking dame of about forty, and while all her aim is to appear the elegant woman of fashion, all her success is to seem an ordinary woman in very common life, with fine clothes on.'

Venetian ladies and their Cavalieri Serventi
c. 1770

The custom of *Cavalieri Serventi* prevails universally here: this usage would appear in a proper light, and take off a great part of the odium thrown upon the Italians, if the *Cavalieri Serventi* were called husbands; for the real husband, or beloved friend, of a Venetian lady (often for life), is the *Cicisbeo*. The husband married in Church is the choice of her friends, not by any means of the lady. . . .

The Venetian ladies have a gay manner of dressing their heads, which becomes them extremely when young, but appears very absurd when age has furrowed over their fine skins, and brought them almost to the ground. I felt a shock at first sight of a tottering old pair I saw enter a coffee-house the other evening; they were both shaking with the palsy, leant upon each other, and supported themselves by a crutch-stick; they were bent almost double by the weight of years and infirmities, yet the lady's head was dressed with great care; a little rose-coloured hat, nicely trimmed with blond, was stuck just above her right ear, and over her left was a small mat of artificial flowers; her few grey hairs behind were tied with ribbon, but so thinly scattered over her forehead, that large patches of her shrivelled skin appeared between the parting curls; the *Cavaliere* was not dressed in the same style, all his elegance consisted in an abundance of wig which flowed upon his shoulders. I enquired who this venerable couple were, and learnt, that the gentleman had been the faithful *Cavaliere* of the same lady above forty years; that they had regularly frequented the Place of St. Mark and the coffee-houses, and with the most steady constancy had loved each other, till age and disease were conducting them hand in hand together to the grave.

ARTHUR YOUNG
(1741–1820)

English agriculturist. He made three visits to France in
1787, 1788 and 1789 and was an eyewitness of the
Revolution. On one visit his mare, on whom he had
ridden 3700 miles, went blind; Young brought her back
to England, not having the heart to sell her in France.

On French cooking

Of their cookery, there is but one opinion; for every man in Europe,
that can afford a great table, either keeps a French cook, or one
instructed in the same manner. That it is far beyond our own, I have
no doubt in asserting. We have about half-a-dozen real English
dishes, that exceed anything, in my opinion, to be met with in
France; by English dishes I mean, a turbot and lobster sauce; ham
and chicken; turtle; a haunch of venison; a turkey and oysters; and
after these, there is an end of an English table. It is an idle prejudice,
to class roast beef among them; for there is not better beef in the
world than at Paris. Large handsome pieces were almost constantly
on the considerable tables I have dined at. The variety given by their
cooks, to the same thing, is astonishing; they dress an hundred
dishes in an hundred different ways, and most of them excellent;
and all sorts of vegetables have a savouriness and flavour, from rich
sauces, that are absolutely wanted to our greens boiled in water.
This variety is not striking, in the comparison of a great table in
France with another in England; but it is manifest in an instant,
between the tables of a French and English family of small fortune.
The English dinner, of a joint of meat and a pudding, as it is called,
or *pot luck*, with a neighbour, is bad luck in England; the same
fortune in France gives, by means of cookery only, at least four
dishes to one among us, and spreads a small table incomparably
better.

JOHANN WOLFGANG VON GOETHE
(1749–1832)

German poet, novelist and dramatist. A few days after his thirty-seventh birthday he set off for Italy, where he visited Venice, Florence and Naples. He kept a journal of his travels and wrote many letters; it was on these sources that he based his *Italiensche Reise* (*Italian Journey*, 1816), one of the great travel books of all time.

Venice through the eyes of the artist,
October 1786

My old gift of seeing the world with the eyes of that artist, whose pictures have most recently made an impression on me, has occasioned me some peculiar reflections. It is evident that the eye forms itself by the objects, which, from youth up, it is accustomed to look upon, and so the Venetian artist must see all things in a clearer and brighter light than other men. We, whose eye when out of doors, falls on a dingy soil, which, when not muddy, is dusty, – and which, always colourless, gives a sombre hue to the reflected rays, or at home spend our lives in close, narrow rooms, can never attain to such a cheerful view of nature.

As I floated down the lagunes in the full sunshine, and observed how the figures of the gondoliers in their motley costume, and as they rowed, lightly moving above the sides of the gondola, stood out from the bright green surface and against the blue sky, I caught the best and freshest type possible of the Venetian school. The sunshine brought out the local colours with dazzling brilliancy, and the shades even were so luminous, that, comparatively, they in their turn might serve as lights. And the same may be said of the reflection from the sea-green water. All was painted 'chiaro nell chiaro,' so that foamy waves and lightning flashes were necessary to give it a grand finish.

Lady Hamilton, Caserta, March 1787

If in Rome one can readily set oneself to study, here one can do nothing but live. You forget yourself and the world; and to me it is a strange feeling to go about with people who think of nothing but enjoying themselves. Sir William Hamilton, who still resides here as ambassador from England, has at length, after his long love of art, and long study, discovered the most perfect of admirers of nature and art in a beautiful young woman. She lives with him: an English woman of about twenty years old. She is very handsome and of a beautiful figure. The old knight has made for her a Greek costume, which becomes her extremely. Dressed in this, and letting her hair loose, and taking a couple of shawls, she exhibits every possible variety of posture, expression, and look, so that at the last the spectator almost fancies it is a dream. One beholds here in perfection, in movement, in ravishing variety, all that the greatest of artists have rejoiced to be able to produce. Standing, kneeling, sitting, lying down, grave or sad, playful, exulting, repentant, wanton, menacing, anxious — all mental states follow rapidly one after another. With wonderful taste she suits the folding of her veil to each expression, and with the same handkerchief makes every kind of head-dress. The old knight holds the light for her, and enters into the exhibition with his whole soul. He thinks he can discern in her a resemblance to all the most famous antiques, all the beautiful profiles on Sicilian coins — aye, of the Apollo Belvedore itself. This much at any rate is certain — the entertainment is unique. We spent two evenings on it with thorough enjoyment. To-day Tischbein is engaged in painting her. . . .

Hamilton is a person of universal taste, and after having wandered through the whole realm of creation, has found rest at last in a most beautiful wife, a masterpiece of the great artist — Nature.

WILLIAM BECKFORD
(1760–1844)

English writer, author of *Vathek*. Son of a Lord Mayor of London with immense possessions in the West Indies, Beckford travelled extensively on the Continent and bought Gibbon's library at Lausanne. He turned the family mansion at Fonthill, Wiltshire, into an extravagant Gothic castle with a tower three hundred feet high, which subsequently fell down and was rebuilt. In 1822 he disposed of Fonthill and its contents for £330,000. When he died he had an income of £80,000 a year, having started life with £100,000 a year and a million pounds in hand.

A feather from the wings of the Archangel Gabriel, the Escurial, near Madrid, 1787

The prior, who is not easily pleased, seemed to have suspicions that the seriousness of my demeanour was not entirely orthodox; I overheard him saying to Roxas, 'Shall I show him the Angel's feather? you know we do not display this our most-valued, incomparable relic to everybody, nor unless upon special occasions.' – 'The occasion is sufficiently special,' answered my partial friend; 'the letters I brought to you are your warrant, and I beseech your reverence to let us look at this gift of heaven, which I am extremely anxious myself to adore and venerate.'

Forth stalked the prior, and drawing out from a remarkably large cabinet an equally capacious sliding shelf – (the source, I conjecture, of the potent odour I complained of) – displayed lying stretched out upon a quilted silken mattress, the most glorious specimen of plumage ever beheld in terrestrial regions – a feather from the wing of the Archangel Gabriel, full three feet long, and of a blushing hue more soft and delicate than that of the loveliest rose.

MICHAEL KELLY
(1762–1826)

Irish singer, actor and composer. The son of Dublin wine merchant, he sang at the court theatre in Vienna, where he became a friend of Mozart. In 1786 he sang in the first performance of *The Marriage of Figaro*. Later he tried to sell music and wine from the same shop, with unfortunate results.

The miracle of San Gennaro, Naples, 1779

I went . . . to visit the miracle of St Gennaro or Januario, in the Cathedral; the King and Queen [Ferdinand IV and Maria Carolina], in state, attended his saintship. There were two immense orchestras erected in the church, and all good professors, vocal and instrumental, were engaged to perform upon these occasions. The Archbishop prays, or appears to pray, while the Te Deum is sung. He then displays a phial, which contains the congealed blood of St Gennaro; towards this he holds up a large wax taper, that the people may perceive it is congealed. The miracle consists, as everybody knows, in this blood dissolving before the congregation, and is supposed to be performed by the saint himself. As soon as it is liquefied, the Archbishop roars lustily, 'the miracle is accomplished!' The Te Deum is again sung, and the whole congregation prostrate themselves before the altar of the saint with gratitude and devotion, and every face beams with delight.

On one of these miraculous days, I witnessed a ludicrous scene. It happened by some accident, that the Archbishop could not make the miracle work. The Lazzaroni and old women loudly called on the Virgin for assistance. 'Dear Virgin Mary! Blessed Madonna! Pray use your influence with St Gennaro! Pray induce him to work the miracle! Do we not love him? Do we not worship him?' But when they found the Saint inexorable, they changed their note, and seemed resolved to abuse him into compliance. They all at once cried out, 'Porco di St Gennaro!' – 'You pig of a Saint!' – 'Barone maladetto!' – 'You cursed rascal!' – 'Cane faccia gialutta!' – 'You yellow-faced dog!' In the midst of this, the blood (thanks to the heat of the Archbishop's hand) dissolved. They again threw themselves on their knees, and tearing their hair, (the old ladies particularly), with streaming eyes, cried, 'Oh! most holy Saint, forgive us this once, and never more will we doubt your goodness!'

EDWARD DANIEL CLARKE
(1769–1822)

English antiquary and mineralogist. Between 1790 and 1801 he travelled extensively in Britain, Europe and the Near East, acting as tutor to the sons of gentlemen. The most prodigious of these journeys was undertaken in the company of John Marten Cripps. It took them through Scandinavia and Southern Russia (in the company of T. R. Malthus, the political economist) to Constantinople, then on to the Troad, where Clarke identified the site of Novum Ilium. They then went on to Palestine, Egypt and Greece, where Clarke succeeded in carrying off – with the aid of 'a rope of twisted herbs', some large nails, several long poles, an axe and a six-inch saw – a colossal two-ton statue dating from the third or fourth century BC. The ship transporting it to England was wrecked off Beachy Head, but the statue was saved.

Alarming the Lapps with a balloon, c. 1799

It was not until the evening that the tempest had sufficiently subsided to admit of another attempt with the balloon. By this time, some of the *Lapps* had left *Enontekis*: and as it was perceived that more were moving towards the shore, to embark in their boats, we sent to them, saying, that we would now launch it, if they would remain aloof, and not interfere with the preparations necessary for that purpose. Upon this, they all returned. Our *Swedish* interpreter ascended the roof of one of their little store-houses with a pole, from the end of which the balloon was suspended: others held out the sides: a large ball of cotton, well steeped in *alcohol*, was then fastened below the centre of the hoop, with fine wire; and being kindled by means of a spunge held at the end of a deal splinter, the two ignited balls were kept burning together for some time, to expedite the rarefaction of the air within the balloon, which, becoming rapidly distended, soon began to float. The pole above being then removed, and the lighted spunge withdrawn, the volant

orb rose majestically into the atmosphere, to the great astonishment, and evidently to the dismay, of all the *Lapps*; for their
rein-deer taking fright, scampered off in all directions, followed by
their owners, who were not a whit less alarmed themselves. The
balloon, after soaring over the source of the *Muonio* descended into
the Lake, where, rolling about upon the surface of the water, we
expected to see it presently immersed; but, to our surprise, notwithstanding all the moisture it had imbibed, it rose again to a considerable height, and then fell. When this exhibition was over, which, for
reasons we could not explain, gave rather uneasiness, than pleasure,
to the *Laplanders*, we hoisted the large *kite* we had made for Mr
Grape's children; at sight of which, the *Lapps* were beyond measure
delighted. Both old and young, men, women, and children, all were
alike transported, expressing their joy by capering and squeaking,
each coming in his turn to lay hold upon the string: when, finding
that it was pulled by the *kite*, they burst into loud fits of laughter,
and would have remained the whole night amused by the sight it
afforded. Even the worthy Pastor himself said it should be carefully
preserved; as it would be useful to him to use as a signal for calling
the *Lapps* together, when he might wish to bring them to his house.
Having succeeded much more to the satisfaction of the *Lapps* with
our *kite* than with our *balloon*, they began to kiss our hands, and
were willing to grant us any favour. The rest of the night, therefore,
was past in mirth and rejoicing: we had races in sledges, drawn by
rein-deer over the smooth grass; and amused ourselves by riding
upon the backs of these animals; being always outstripped by the
Lapps, who were as much delighted with our awkwardness as we
were with the strange gestures and manners of this very singular
people.

Marriage customs among the Calmuks on the shores of the Black Sea, c. 1800

Calmuck women ride better than the men. A male *Calmuck* on
horseback looks as if he was intoxicated, and likely to fall off every
instant, although he never loses his seat: but the women sit with
more ease, and ride with extraordinary skill. The ceremony of
marriage among the *Calmucks* is performed on horseback. A girl is
first mounted, who rides off in full speed. Her lover pursues: if he
overtake her, she becomes his wife, and the marriage is consum-
mated upon the spot: after this she returns with him to his tent. But

it sometimes happens that the woman does not wish to marry the person by whom she is pursued: in this case she will not suffer him to overtake her. We were assured that no instance occurs of a *Calmuck* girl being thus caught, unless she have a partiality for her pursuer. If she dislike him, she rides, to use the language of English sportsmen, '*neck or nothing*,' until she has completely effected her escape, or until the pursuer's horse becomes exhausted, leaving her at liberty to return, and to be afterwards chased by some more-favoured admirer.

WILLIAM HAZLITT
(1778–1830)

English critic and essayist. Of somewhat untidy appearance, he had the habit of falling frequently and passionately in love. In 1824–5 he visited France, Italy and Switzerland, returning to England by way of the Rhine and Holland. Although delicate-looking, Hazlitt could walk fifty miles in a day and was a good fives player.

Paris, 1824

Paris is a beast of a city to be in – to those who cannot get out of it. Rousseau said well, that all the time he was in it, he was only trying how he should leave it. . . . Fancy yourself in London with the footpath taken away, so that you are forced to walk along the middle of the streets with a dirty gutter running through them, fighting your way through coaches, waggons, and hand-carts trundled along by large mastiff-dogs, with the houses twice as high, greasy holes for shop-windows, and piles of wood, green-stalls, and wheelbarrows placed at the doors, and the contents of wash-hand basins pouring out of a dozen stories – fancy all this and worse and, with a change of scene, you are in Paris. The continual panic in which the passenger is kept, the alarm and the escape from it, the anger and the laughter at it, must have an effect on the Parisian character, and tend to make it the whiffling, skittish, snappish, volatile, inconsequential, unmeaning thing it is.

STENDHAL
(1783–1842)

Pseudonym of Marie Henri Beyle. French novelist. He grew up in Grenoble, hating his father and the bourgeois atmosphere of the provinces. Gaining a place in the ministry of war, he went to Italy for the first time in 1800, as a dragoon in Napoleon's army. Having served the Emperor again in the disastrous Russian campaign of 1812, he returned to Italy in 1814 and lived there for six years, beginning the literary career that was to produce his masterpieces, *Le Rouge et le Noir* (1831) and *La Chartreuse de Parme* (1839).

An encounter at Terracina, 1817

We halted in Terracina; and there, in that sumptuous hostelry erected by Pius VI, we were invited to take supper with a party of travellers newly arrived out of Naples. Gathered about the table, I observed some seven or eight persons, amongst whom, in particular, my eyes lighted upon a fair-haired young man, of some five or six-and-twenty years of age, astonishingly handsome in spite of a slight touch of baldness. I pressed him for news of Naples, and in particular, of music in that city: he answered my curiosity with answers that were clear-cut, brilliant and humorous. I enquired of him whether, when I reached Naples, I might still hope to see Rossini's *Otello*. I pursued the topic, asserting that, in my opinion, Rossini was the bright hope of the Italian school; that he was the only living composer who had true genius as his birthright. At this point I noticed that my man seemed faintly embarrassed, while his companions were grinning openly. To cut a long story short, this *was* Rossini.

BENJAMIN ROBERT
HAYDON
(1786–1846)

English historical painter, whose autobiographical writings compensate for his indifferent paintings. Twice imprisoned for debt, quarrelsome and often on the edge of madness, he eventually committed suicide. His journals, which filled twenty-six volumes, 'bulky, parchment-bound, ledger-like folios', record his tragic life.

The allies in Paris after the fall of Bonaparte, 1814

In the middle of the day the Rue St. Honoré was the most wonderful sight. Don Cossack chiefs loosely clothed and moving as their horses moved, with all the bendings of their bodies visible at every motion; the half-clothed savage Cossack horseman, his belt stuck full of pistols and watches and hatches, crouched up on a little ragged-maned, dirty-looking, ill-bred, half-white, shaggy pony; the Russian Imperial guardsmen pinched in at the waist like a wasp, striding along like a giant, with an air of victory that made every Frenchman curse within his teeth as he passed him; the English officer, with his boyish face and broad shoulders; the heavy Austrian; the natty Prussian, and now and then a Bashkir Tartar, in the ancient Phrygian cap, with bow and arrows and chain armour, gazing about him from his horse in the midst of black-eyed grisettes, Jews, Turks and Christians from all countries in Europe and Asia. It was a pageant that kept one staring, musing and bewildered from morning till night.

GEORGE GORDON, LORD BYRON
(1788–1824)

English poet. With his good looks, his lameness (he had a club foot) and his flamboyant style of living, not to mention his turbulent relationships with women, Byron was a legend in his own time. In 1809 he made a grand tour of Spain, Portugal, Italy and the Balkans. Seven years later, the scandal of his supposed relationship with his half-sister Augusta Leigh breaking around him, he left England for good. He went first to Switzerland, before settling in Venice in 1817. He died in Greece in 1824 during the War of Independence.

A visit to Ali Pasha, the bloodthirsty governor of Albania – from a letter to his mother from Prevesa, November 1809

I rode out on the vizier's horses, and saw the palaces of himself and grandsons: they are splendid, but too much ornamented with silk and gold. I then went over the mountains through Zitza, a village with a Greek monastery (where I slept on my return), in the most beautiful situation (always excepting Cintra, in Portugal) I ever beheld. In nine days I reached Tepaleen. Our journey was much prolonged by the torrents that had fallen from the mountains, and intersected the roads. I shall never forget the singular scene on entering Tepaleen at five in the afternoon, as the sun was going down. It brought to my mind (with some change of *dress*, however) Scott's description of Branksome Castle in his *Lay*, and the feudal system. The Albanians, in their dresses, (the most magnificent in the world, consisting of a long *white kilt*, gold-worked cloak, crimson velvet gold-laced jacket and waistcoat, silver-mounted pistols and daggers,) the Tartars with their high caps, the Turks in their vast pelisses and turbans, the soldiers and black slaves with the horses, the former in groups in an immense large open gallery in front of the palace, the latter placed in a kind of cloister below it, two hundred steeds ready caparisoned to move in a moment, couriers entering or passing out with despatches, the kettle-drums beating, boys calling the hour from the minaret of the mosque, altogether, with the singular appearance of the building itself, formed a new and delightful spectacle to a stranger. . . .

The next day I was introduced to Ali Pacha. I was dressed in a full suit of staff uniform, with a very magnificent sabre, etc. The vizier receivd me in a large room paved with marble; a fountain was playing in the centre; the apartment was surrounded by scarlet ottomans. He received me standing, a wonderful compliment from a Mussulman, and made me sit down on his right hand. I have a Greek interpreter for general use, but a physician of Ali's named Femlario, who understands Latin, acted for me on this occasion. His first question was, why, at so early an age, I left my country? – (the Turks have no idea of travelling for amusement). He then said, the English minister, Captain Leake, had told him I was of a great family, and desired his respects to my mother; which I now, in the name of Ali Pacha, present to you. He said he was certain I was a man of birth, because I had small ears, curling hair, and little white hands, and expressed himself pleased with my appearance and garb. He told me to consider him as a father whilst I was in Turkey, and said he looked on me as his son. Indeed, he treated me like a child, sending me almonds and sugared sherbet, fruit and sweetmeats, twenty times a day. He begged me to visit him often, and at night, when he was at leisure. I then, after coffee and pipes, retired for the first time. I saw him thrice afterwards. It is singular that the Turks, who have no hereditary dignities, and few great families, except the Sultans, pay so much respect to birth; for I found my pedigree more regarded than my title.

His highness is sixty years old, very fat, and not tall, but with a fine face, light blue eyes, and a white beard; his manner is very kind, and at the same time he possesses that dignity which I find universal amongst the Turks. He has the appearance of anything but his real character, for he is a remorseless tyrant, guilty of the most horrible cruelties, very brave, and so good a general, that they call him the Mahometan Buonaparte.

PERCY BYSSHE SHELLEY
(1792–1822)

English poet. In 1818 he left England to settle in Italy. He visited Lord Byron in Venice and went to Naples, Rome, Leghorn (Livorno), Florence, Pisa and Lerici (in 1822), producing the great body of his work during these travels. He drowned in July 1822 while sailing in the Bay of Spezia.

Rome – from a letter to Thomas Love Peacock from Naples, December 1818

I have seen the ruins of Rome, the Vatican, St. Peter's, and all the miracles of ancient and modern art contained in that majestic city. The impression of it exceeds anything I have ever experienced in my travels. . . . We visited the Forum and the ruins of the Coliseum every day. The Coliseum is unlike any work of human hands I ever saw before. It is of enormous height and circuit, and the arches built of massy stones are piled on one another, and jut into the blue air, shattered into the forms of overhanging rocks. It has been changed by time into the image of an amphitheatre of rocky hills overgrown by the wild olive, the myrtle, and the fig-tree, and threaded by little paths, which wind among its ruined stairs and immeasurable galleries. . . . The interior is all ruin. I can scarcely believe that when encrusted with Dorian marble and ornamented by columns of Egyptian granite, its effect could have been so sublime and so impressive as in its present state. It is open to the sky, and it was the clear and sunny weather of the end of November in this climate when we visited it, day after day. . . .

In Rome, at least in the first enthusiasm of your recognition of ancient time, you see nothing of the Italians. The nature of the city assists the delusion, for its vast and antique walls describe a circumference of sixteen miles, and thus the population is thinly scattered over this space, nearly as great as London. Wide wild fields are enclosed within it, and there are grassy lanes and copses winding among the ruins, and a great green hill, lonely and bare, which overhangs the Tiber. The gardens of the modern palaces are like wild woods of cedar, and cypress, and pine, and the neglected walks are overgrown with weeds. The English burying-place is a green slope near the walls, under the pyramidal tomb of Cestius, and is, I think, the most beautiful and solemn cemetery I ever beheld. To see the sun shining on its bright grass, fresh, when we first visited it, with the autumnal dews, and hear the whispering of the wind among the leaves of the trees which have overgrown the tomb of Cestius, and the soil which is stirring in the sun-warm earth, and to mark the tombs, mostly of women and young people who were buried there, one might, if one were to die, desire the sleep they seem to sleep. Such is the human mind, and so it peoples with its wishes vacancy and oblivion.

ASTOLPHE, MARQUIS DE CUSTINE
(1793–1857)

French writer and traveller. Both his father and grand-father were guillotined in the Reign of Terror, shortly after his birth. He travelled in England, Scotland, Switzerland, Spain and Russia, about which he wrote a remarkably perceptive account.

The treatment of travellers in Russia, 1839

Russian hospitality is so hedged around with formalities as to render life unpleasant to the most favoured strangers. It is a civil pretext for restraining the movements of the traveller, and for limiting the freedom of his observations . . . the observer can inspect nothing without a guide; never being alone, he has the greater difficulty in forming his judgement upon his own spontaneous impressions . . . Would you see the curiosities of a palace, they give you a chamberlain, with whom you are obliged to view everything, and, indiscriminately, to admire all that he admires; a camp – an officer, sometimes a general officer, accompanies you; . . . a school, or any other public institution, the director or the inspector must be previously apprised of your visit, and you find him, under arms, prepared to brave your examination; if an edifice, the architect himself leads you over the whole building, and explains to you all that you do not care to know, in order to avoid informing you on points which you would take interest in knowing. . . . In this manner they tyrannise over us in pretending to do us honour. Such is the fate of privileged travellers. As to those who are not privileged, they see nothing at all.

RICHARD FORD
(1796–1858)

English travel-writer. Author of *Handbook for Travellers in Spain* (1845) and *Gatherings from Spain* (1846), two of the best books ever written about the country and its people.

Thirst

Then, when the heavens and earth are on fire, and the sun drinks up rivers at one draught, when one burnt sienna tone pervades the tawny ground, and the green herb is shrivelled up into black gunpowder, and the rare pale ashy olive-trees are blanched into the livery of the desert; then, when the heat and harshness make even the salamander muleteers swear doubly as they toil along like demons in an ignited salitrose dust – then, indeed, will an Englishman discover that he is made of the same material, only drier, and learn to estimate water; but a good thirst is too serious an evil, too bordering on suffering, to be made, like an appetite, a matter of congratulation; for when all fluids evaporate, and the blood thickens into currant jelly, and the nerves tighten up into the catgut of an overstrung fiddle, getting attuned to the porcupinal irritability of the tension of the mind, how the parched soul sighs for the comfort of a Scotch mist, and fondly turns back to the uvula-relaxing damps of Devon! – then, in the blackhole-like thirst of the wilderness, every mummy hag rushing from a reed hut, with a porous cup of brackish water, is changed by the mirage into a Hebe, bearing the nectar of the immortals. . . .

GEORGE BORROW
(1803–1881)

English writer and traveller. From 1835 to 1840 he travelled extensively in Spain as a salesman for the British and Foreign Bible Society. His adventures were exciting, sometimes gruesome, in a country in the throes of civil war. He was imprisoned for selling the gypsies his new translation of the Gospels in their own language, Calé. Borrow went to Spain only because, on his way from China – where he had been peddling his Manchu translation of the New Testament – he was refused permission to go to Tibet to convert the Dalai Lama.

A Catalan gentleman converses with a lady at Medina del Campo

We experienced some difficulty in obtaining admission into the posada, which was chiefly occupied by Catalans from Valladolid. These people not only brought with them their merchandise but their wives and children. Some of them appeared to be people of the worst description: there was one in particular, a burly savage-looking fellow, of about forty, whose conduct was atrocious; he sat with his wife, or perhaps concubine, at the door of a room which opened upon the court; he was continually venting horrible and obscene oaths, both in Spanish and Catalan. The woman was remarkably handsome, but robust, and seemingly as savage as himself; her conversation likewise was as frightful as his own. Both seemed to be under the influence of an incomprehensible fury. At last, upon some observation from the woman, he started up, and drawing a long knife from his girdle, stabbed at her naked bosom; she, however, interposed the palm of her hand, which was much cut. He stood for a moment viewing the blood trickling upon the ground, whilst she held up her wounded hand, then with an astounding oath he hurried up the court to the Plaza. I went up to the woman and said, 'What is the cause of this? I hope the ruffian has not seriously injured you.' She turned her countenance upon me with the glance of a demon, and at last with a sneer of contempt exclaimed, '*Caráls que es eso?* Cannot a Catalan gentleman be conversing with his lady upon their own private affairs without being interrupted by you?'

JULIA PARDOE
(1806–1862)

English writer. A prolific author – she published a volume
of poems when she was only fourteen – she accompanied
her father, Major Thomas Pardoe, to Constantinople in
1835. She produced two fine books on the city, *The City
of the Sultan and Domestic Manners of the Turks* (1837)
and *The Beauties of the Bosphorus* (1839).

Fountain of the Asian Sweet Waters

The Valley of Guiuk-Suy, charmingly situated about mid-way of the
Bosphorus, and called by Europeans the Asian Sweet Waters, owes
its charm and its popularity ... to the circumstance of its being
intersected by a pretty stream of fresh water, which, after flowing
along under the shadows of tall and leafy trees, finally mingles its
pigmy ripples with the swifter waves of the channel. The Anadoli
Hissari, or Castle of Asia, stands upon its margin, and painfully
recalls the mind to the darker and sterner realities of life; or the
visitor to Guiuk-Suy might fancy himself in Arcadia, so lovely is the
locality. . . .

All ranks alike frequent this sweet and balmy spot. The Sultanas
move along in quiet stateliness over the greensward in their gilded
arabas, drawn by oxen glittering with foil, and covered with
awnings of velvet, heavy with gold embroidery and fringes; the light
carriages of the Pashas' harems roll rapidly past, decorated with
flashing draperies, the horses gaily caparisoned, and the young
beauties within pillowed on satins and velvets, and frequently
screened by shawls of immense value; while the wives of many of
the Beys, the Effendis, and the Emirs, leave their arabas, and seated
on Persian carpets under the leafy canopy of the superb maple-trees
which abound in the valley, amuse themselves for hours, the elder
ladies with their pipes, and the younger ones with their hand-
mirrors; greetings innumerable take place on all sides; and the
itinerant confectioners and water-venders reap a rich harvest.

The Fountain of Guiuk-Suy stands in the midst of a double
avenue of trees, which fringe the border of the Bosphorus. It is built
of delicate white marble, is extremely elegant in design, and elabor-

ately ornamented with arabesques. The spot which it adorns is a point of reunion for the fair idlers of the valley, when the evening breeze upon the channel renders this portion of the glen more cool and delicious than that in which they pass the earlier hours of the day; and is only separated from it by the stream already named, which is traversed by a heavy wooden bridge.

The whole *coup-d'œil* is charming; slaves hurry hither and thither, carrying water from the fountain to their respective mistresses, in covered crystal goblets, or vases of wrought silver. Fruit-merchants pass and repass with amber-coloured grapes and golden melons; Sclavonian musicians collect a crowd about them, which disperses the next moment to throng round a gang of Bedouin tumblers; serudjhes gallop over the soft grass in pursuit of their employers; carriages come and go noiselessly along the turf at the beck of their fair occupants; a fleet of caïques dance upon the ripple, ready to convey a portion of the revellers to their homes on the European shore; and the beams of the bright sun fall full on the turretted towers of the Castle of Europe, on the opposite side of the channel, touching them with gold, and contrasting yet more powerfully their long and graceful shadows upon the water.

ALEXANDER KINGLAKE
(1809–1891)

English historian and author of the classic *Eothen* (see p. 60).

Night in the great Servian Forest

. . . Night closed in as we entered the great Servian forest. Through this our road was to last for more than a hundred miles. Endless and endless now on either side the tall oaks closed in their ranks, and stood gloomily lowering over us, as grim as an army of giants with a thousand years' pay in arrear. One strived, with listening ear, to catch some tidings of that forest-world within – some stirring of beasts, some night-bird's scream; but all was quite hushed, except the voice of the cicalas that peopled every bough, and filled the depths of the forest through and through with one same hum everlasting – more stilling than very silence.

At first our way was in darkness, but after a while the moon got up, and touched the glittering arms and tawny faces of our men with light so pale and mystic, that the watchful Tatar felt bound to look out for demons, and take proper means for keeping them off. Forthwith he determined that the duty of frightening away our ghostly enemies, like every other troublesome work, should fall upon the poor Suridgees; they accordingly lifted up their voices, and burst upon the dreaded stillness of the forest with shrieks and dismal howls. These precautions were kept up incessantly, and were followed by the most complete success, for not one demon came near us.

Long before midnight we reached the hamlet in which we were to rest for the night; it was made up of about a dozen clay huts standing upon a small tract of ground hardly won from the forest. The peasants living there spoke a Slavonic dialect, and Mysseri's knowledge of the Russian tongue enabled him to talk with them freely. We took up our quarters in a square room with white walls and an earthen floor, quite bare of furniture and utterly void of women. They told us, however, that these Servian villagers lived in happy abundance, but that they were careful to conceal their riches, as well as their wives.

The burdens unstrapped from the pack-saddles very quickly furnished our den: a couple of quilts spread upon the floor with a carpet-bag at the head of each, became capital sofas; portmanteaus, and hat-boxes, and writing-cases, and books, and maps, and gleaming arms, soon lay strewed around us in pleasant confusion. Mysseri's canteen, too, began to yield up its treasures, but we relied upon finding some provisions in the village. At first the natives declared that their hens were mere old maids, and all their cows unmarried; but our Tatar swore such a grand sonorous oath, and fingered the hilt of his yataghan with such persuasive touch, that the land soon flowed with milk, and mountains of eggs arose.

And soon there was tea before us, with all its welcome fragrance; and as we reclined on the floor we found that a portmanteau was just the right height for a table. The duty of candlesticks was ably performed by a couple of intelligent natives: the rest of the villagers stood by the open doorway at the lower end of the room, and watched our banquet with grave and devout attention.

Robert Curzon
(1810–1873)

English traveller, collector of manuscripts and diplomat. Fourteenth Baron de la Zouche. In 1833 he began his travels in search of ancient manuscripts, which were in imminent danger of being used as firelighters in the monasteries of Egypt, Palestine, Greece and what was then Albania, where he made some hair-raising ascents to the rock monasteries of the Meteora.

The library of the Monastery of Caracalla, Mount Athos, c. 1833

The library I found to be a dark closet near the entrance of the church; it had been locked up for many years, but the agoumenos made no difficulty in breaking the old-fashioned padlock by which the door was fastened. I found upon the ground and upon some broken-down shelves about four or five hundred volumes, chiefly printed books; but amongst them, every now and then, I stumbled upon a manuscript: of these there were about thirty on vellum and fifty or sixty on paper. I picked up a single loose leaf of very ancient uncial Greek characters, part of the Gospel of St. Matthew, written in small square letters and of small quarto size. I searched in vain for the volume to which this leaf belonged.

As I had found it impossible to purchase any manuscripts at St. Laura, I feared that the same would be the case in other monasteries; however, I made bold to ask for this single leaf as a thing of small value.

'Certainly!' said the agoumenos: 'what do you want it for?'

My servant suggested that, perhaps, it might be useful to cover some jam pots or vases of preserves which I had at home.

'Oh!' said the agoumenos, 'take some more;' and, without more ado, he seized upon an unfortunate thick quarto manuscript of the Acts and Epistles, and drawing out a knife cut out an inch thickness of leaves at the end before I could stop him. It proved to be the Apocalypse, which concluded the volume, but which is rarely found in early Greek manuscripts of the Acts: it was of the eleventh century. I ought, perhaps, to have slain the *tomecide* for his dreadful act of profanation, but his generosity reconciled me to his guilt, so I pocketed the Apocalypse, and asked him if he would sell me any of the other books, as he did not appear to set any particular value upon them.

'Malista, certainly,' he replied; 'how many will you have? They are of no use to me, and as I am in want of money to complete my buildings, I shall be very glad to turn them to some account.'

EDWARD LEAR
(1812–1888)

English artist and author of nonsense poems and limericks. In 1848–9 he travelled through Greece and Albania, suffering the hospitality of the Turkish rulers. In Shköder he was treated to a dinner of fifty courses in apparently random order: 'the richest pastry came immediately after dressed fish and was succeeded by beef, honey, and cakes; pears and peaches; crabs, ham, boiled mutton, chocolate cake, garlic and fowl. . . .'

An exhausting evening with the Bey of Króia, Albania, September 1848

. . . On my letter of introduction being sent in to the Bey, I was almost instantly asked into his room of reception – a three-windowed, square chamber (excellent, according to the standard of Turkish ornament, taste, and proportion) – where, in a corner of the raised divan sat Ali, Bey of Króia – a lad of eighteen or nineteen, dressed in the usual blue frock-coat now adopted by Turkish nobles or officers. A file of kilted and armed retainers were soon ordered to marshal me into a room where I was to sleep, and the little Bey seemed greatly pleased with the fun of doing hospitality to so novel a creature as a Frank. . . . It was not easy to shake off the attentions of ten full-dressed Albanian servants, who stood in much expectation, till, finding I was about to take off my shoes, they made a rush at me . . . and showed such marks of disappointment at not being allowed to make themselves useful that I was obliged to tell Giorgio to explain that we Franks were not used to assistance every moment of our lives and that I should think it obliging of them if they would leave me in peace. After changing my dress, the Bey sent to say that supper should be served in an hour, he having eaten at sunset, and in the meantime he would be glad of my society; so I took my place on the sofa by the little gentleman's side, and Giorgio, sitting on the ground, acted as interpreter. At first Ali Bey said little, but soon became immensely loquacious, asking numerous questions about Stamboul and a few about Franks in general – the different species of whom he was not very well informed. At length, when the conversation was flagging, he was moved to discourse about ships that went without sails and coaches that were impelled without horses; and to please him I drew a steamboat and a railway carriage; on which he asked if they made any noise; and I replied by imitating both the inventions in question in the best manner I could think of – 'Tik-tok, tik-tok, tik-tok, tokka, tokka, tokka, tokka, tokka-tok' (crescendo), and 'Squish-squash, squish-squash, squish-squash, thump-bump,' – for the land and sea engines respectively – a noisy novelty, which so intensely delighted Ali Bey that he fairly threw himself back on the divan and laughed as I never saw Turk laugh before.

The woes of Thessaly, May 1849

The woes of Thessaly continued. In the middle of the night, the roof of Seid Efféndi's house being slight, a restless stork put one of his legs through the crevice and could not extricate it; whereon ensued much kicking and screams, and at the summons came half the storks in Thessaly, and all night long the uproar was portentous. Four very wet jackdaws also came down the chimney and hopped over me and about the room till dawn.

JOHN RUSKIN
(1819–1900)

English critic and social theorist. He was educated by his wealthy, evangelical parents, who intended that he should become a priest. In 1833 they took him on the first of many tours of Europe. His works, notably *The Stones of Venice* (1851–3), established him as the arbiter of artistic taste in England for many years. His later works of social theory contained many proposals that have

since been put into effect, among them old age pensions
and state education.

First view of the Alps, from Schaffhausen, at the age of fourteen

We must have still spent some time in town-seeing, for it was
drawing towards sunset when we got up to some sort of garden
promenade – west of the town, I believe; and high above the Rhine,
so as to command the open country across it to the south and west.
At which open country of low undulation, far into blue, – gazing as
at one of our own distances from Malvern of Worcestershire, or
Dorking of Kent, – suddenly – behold – beyond!

There was no thought in any of us for a moment of their being
clouds. They were clear as crystal, sharp on the pure horizon sky,
and already tinged with rose by the sinking sun. Infinitely beyond all
that we had ever thought or dreamed, – the seen walls of lost Eden
could not have been more beautiful to us; not more awful, round
heaven, the walls of sacred Death.

It is not possible to imagine, in any time of the world, a more
blessed entrance into life, for a child of such a temperament as mine.
True, the temperament belonged to the age: a very few years, –
within the hundred, – before that, no child could have been born to
care for mountains, or for the men that lived among them, in that
way. Till Rousseau's time, there had been no 'sentimental' love of
nature; and till Scott's, no such apprehensive love of 'all sorts and
conditions of men,' not in the soul merely, but in the flesh. St.
Bernard of La Fontaine, looking out to Mont Blanc with his child's
eyes, sees above Mont Blanc the Madonna; St. Bernard of Talloires,
not the Lake of Annecy, but the dead between Martigny and Aosta.
But for me, the Alps and their people were alike beautiful in their
snow, and their humanity; and I wanted, neither for them nor
myself, sight of any thrones in heaven but the rocks, or any of spirits
in heaven but the clouds.

JOHN MACGREGOR
(1825–1892)

Scottish philanthropist and traveller, known as 'Rob Roy' MacGregor. He was the first to enjoy the pleasure of canoeing as a pastime, and to popularize it in Britain. His first *Rob Roy* was a canoe built of oak and covered with cedar, 15 feet long; in it he travelled through Europe by river, canal and lake in 1855. In 1866 he canoed in Germany and Scandinavia, and in 1868 through the Suez Canal and into the Red Sea.

Launching the Rob Roy on the Danube, 1855

By dusk I marched into Donaueschingen, and on crossing the little bridge saw at once I could begin the Danube from its very source, for there were at least three inches of water in the middle of the stream. . . .

From near the little bridge, on August 28, while the singer *sol-faed* excessively, and shouted 'hochs' and farewells to the English 'flagge', and the landlord bowed, and the populace stared, the *Rob Roy* shot off like an arrow on a river delightfully new. At first the Danube is a few feet broad, but it soon enlarges, and the streams of a great plain quickly bring its volume to that of the Thames at Henley. The quiet, dark Donau winds about then in slow serpentine smoothness for hours in a level mead, with waving sedge on the banks and silken sleepy weeds in the water. Here the long-necked, long-winged, long-legged heron, that seems to have forgotten to get a body, flocks by scores with various ducks, while pretty painted butterflies float on the sunbeams, and fierce-looking dragonflies simmer in the air.

Soon the hills on either side have houses and old castles, and then wood, and lastly rock; and with these, mingling the bold, the wild, and the sylvan, there begins a grand panorama of river beauties to be unrolled for days and days. Few rivers I have seen surpass this upper Danube. The wood is so thick, the rocks so quaint and high and varied, the water so clear, and the grass so green. Winding here and turning there, and rushing fast down this reach and paddling slow along that, with each minute a fresh view, the mind is ever on the *qui vive*, or the boat will go bump on a bank, crash on a rock, or plunge into a tree full of gnats and spiders. It is exciting to direct a camel over the sandy desert when you have lost your fellow-travellers, and to guide a horse in trackless wilds alone; but the pleasure of paddling a canoe down a rapid, high-banked and unknown river is far more exhilarating than these. Part of this pleasure flows from the mere sense of rapid motion. In going down a swift reach of the river there is the same sensation about one's midriff that is felt when one goes forward smoothly on a lofty rope swing.

EARL OF DUFFERIN
(1826–1902)

English diplomat and administrator, born Frederick Temple Hamilton-Temple Blackwood. Ambassador to St Petersburg and Constantinople, and Governor-General of both Canada and India. An enthusiastic yachtsman, he undertook adventurous voyages in his yacht *Foam*. In 1854, while sailing in the Baltic, he took part in the siege of Bomarsund, displaying great coolness. In 1855 he made a voyage to Iceland, Jan Mayen Island and Spitsbergen.

The intoxicating hospitality of Count Trampe, Governor of Iceland, June 1856

Yesterday – no, the day before – in fact I forget the date of the day – I don't believe it had one – all I know is, I have not been in bed since – we dined at the Governor's – though dinner is too modest a term to apply to the entertainment.

The invitation was for four o'clock, and at half-past three we pulled ashore in the gig; I, innocent that I was, in a well-fitting white waistcoat. . . .

. . . As soon as the door was opened, Count Trampe tucked me under his arm – two other gentlemen did the same to my two companions – and we streamed into the dining-room. The table was very prettily arranged with flowers, plate, and a forest of glasses. Fitzgerald and I were placed on either side of our host, the other guests, in due order, beyond. On my left sat the Rector, and opposite, next to Fitz, the chief physician of the island. Then began a series of transactions of which I have no distinct recollection; in fact, the events of the next five hours recur to me in as great disarray as reappear the vestiges of a country that has been disfigured by some deluge. . . .

I gather . . . from evidence – internal and otherwise – that the dinner was excellent, and that we were helped in Benjamite proportions; but as before the soup was finished I was already hard at work hob-nobbing with my two neighbours, it is not to be expected I should remember the bill of fare.

With the peculiar manners used in Scandinavian skoal-drinking I was already well acquainted. In the nice conduct of a wine-glass I knew that I excelled, and having an hereditary horror of heel-taps, I prepared with a firm heart to respond to the friendly provocations of my host. I only wish you could have seen how his kind face beamed with approval when I chinked my first bumper against his, and having emptied it at a draught, turned it towards him bottom upwards, with the orthodox twist. Soon, however, things began to look more serious even than I had expected. I knew well that to refuse a toast, or to half empty your glass, was considered churlish. I had come determined to accept my host's hospitality as cordially as it was offered. I was willing, at a pinch, to *payer de ma personne*; should he not be content with seeing me *at* his table, I was ready, if need were, to remain *under* it; but at the rate we were then going it seemed probable this consummation would take place before the second course: so, after having exchanged a dozen rounds of sherry and champagne with my two neighbours, I pretended not to observe that my glass had been refilled; and, like the sea-captain, who, slipping from between his two opponents, left them to blaze away at each other the long night through, withdrew from the combat. But it would not do; with untasted bumpers, and dejected faces, they politely waited until I should give the signal for a renewal of *host*ilities, as they well deserved to be called. Then there came over me a horrid wicked feeling. What if I should endeavour to floor the Governor, and so literally turn the tables on him! It is true I had lived for five-and-twenty years without touching wine; but was not I my great-grandfather's great-grandson, and an Irish peer to boot? Were there not traditions, too, on the other side of the house, of casks of claret brought up into the dining-room, the door locked, and the key thrown out of the window? With such antecedents to sustain me, I ought to be able to hold my own against the staunchest toper in Iceland! So, with a devil glittering in my left eye, I winked defiance right and left, and away we went at it again for another five-and-forty minutes. At last their fire slackened: I had partially quelled both the Governor and the Rector, and still survived. It is true I did not feel comfortable; but it was in the neighbourhood of my waistcoat, not my head, I suffered. . . .

Still the neck of the banquet was broken – Fitzgerald's chair was not yet empty – could we hold out perhaps a quarter of an hour longer, our reputation was established; guess then my horror, when the Doctor, shouting his favourite dogma, by way of battle-cry, 'Si trigintis guttis, morbum curare velis, erras,' gave the signal for an unexpected onslaught, and the twenty guests poured down on me in succession. I really thought I should have run away from the house; but the true family blood, I suppose, began to show itself, and with a calmness almost frightful, I received them one by one.

After this began the public toasts.

Although up to this time I had kept a certain portion of my wits about me, the subsequent hours of the entertainment became thenceforth enveloped in a dreamy mystery. I can perfectly recall the look of the sheaf of glasses that stood before me, six in number; I could draw the pattern of each; I remember feeling a lazy wonder they should always be full, though I did nothing but empty them, and at last solved the phenomenon by concluding I had become a kind of Danaid, whose punishment, not whose sentence, had been reversed: then suddenly I felt as if I were disembodied – a distant spectator of my own performances, and of the feast at which my person remained seated. The voices of my host, of the Rector, of the Chief Justice, became thin and low, as though they reached me through a whispering tube; and when I rose to speak, it was as to an audience in another sphere, and in a language of another state of being: yet, however unintelligible to myself, I must have been in some sort understood, for at the end of each sentence, cheers, faint as the roar of waters on a far-off strand, floated towards me; and if I am to believe a report of the proceedings subsequently shown us, I must have become polyglot in my cups. According to that report it seems the Governor threw off (I wonder he did not do something else) with the Queen's health in French: to which I responded in the same language. Then the Rector, in English, proposed my health – under the circumstances a cruel mockery – but to which, ill as I was, I responded very gallantly by drinking to the *beaux yeux* of the Countess. Then somebody else drank success to Great Britain, and I see it was followed by really a very learned discourse by Lord D., in honour of the ancient Icelanders; during which he alluded to their discovery of America, and Columbus' visit. Then came a couple of speeches in Icelandic, after which the Bishop, in a magnificent Latin oration of some twenty minutes, a second time proposes my health; to which, utterly at my wits' end, I had the audacity to reply in the same language.

MARK TWAIN
(1835–1910)

Pseudonym of Samuel Langhorne Clemens. American novelist and humorous writer. He worked first as a printer, then as a pilot on the Mississippi, then as a silver miner in Nevada, before becoming a journalist. In 1867 he visited Europe and the Near East to gather material for *The Innocents Abroad* (1869), which sold 125,000 copies in the first three years after publication.

Tsar Alexander II and his family at Yalta

At the appointed time we drove out three miles, and assembled in the handsome garden in front of the Emperor's palace.

We formed a circle under the trees before the door, and in a few minutes the imperial family came out bowing and smiling, and stood in our midst. A number of great dignitaries of the Empire, in undress uniforms, came with them. With every bow, his Majesty said a word of welcome. I copy these speeches. There is character in them – Russian character – which is politeness itself, the genuine article. The French are polite, but it is often mere ceremonious politeness. A Russian imbues his polite things with a heartiness that compels belief in their sincerity. As I was saying, the Czar punctuated his speeches with bows: 'Good morning – I am glad to see you – I am gratified – I am delighted – I am happy to receive you!' All took off their hats, and the Consul inflicted the address on him. He bore it with unflinching fortitude, then took the rusty-looking document and handed it to some great officer or other, to be filed away among the archives of Russia – in the stove. He thanked us for the address, and said he was very pleased to see us, especially as such friendly relations existed between Russia and the United States. The Empress said the Americans were favourites in Russia, and she hoped the Russians were similarly regarded in America. These were all the speeches that were made, and I recommend them to parties who present policemen with gold watches, as models of brevity and point. After this the Empress went and talked sociably (for an Empress) with various ladies around the cricle; several gentlemen entered into a disjointed conversation with the Emperor; the Dukes and Princes, Admirals and Maid of Honour dropped into free-and-easy chat with first one and then another of our party, and whoever chose stepped forward and spoke with the modest little Grand Duchess Marie, the Czar's daughter. She is fourteen years old, light-haired, blue-eyed, unassuming and pretty. Everybody talks English.

A strange new sensation is a rare thing in this humdrum life, and I had it here. It seemed strange – stranger than I can tell – to think that the central figure in the cluster of men and women, chatting here under the trees like the most ordinary individual in the land, was a man who could open his lips and ships would fly through the waves, couriers would hurry from village to village, a hundred telegraphs would flash the word to the four corners of the Empire that stretches over a seventh part of the habitable globe, and a countless multitude of men would spring to do his bidding. I had a sort of vague desire to examine his hands and see if they were of flesh and blood, like other men's. Here was a man who could do this wonderful thing, and yet if I chose I could knock him down. If I could have stolen his coat, I would have done it. When I meet a man like that, I want something to remember him by.

As a general thing, we have been shown through palaces by some plush-legged filagreed flunkey or other, who charged a franc for it; but after talking with the company half-an-hour, the Emperor of Russia and his family conducted us through all their mansion themselves. They made no charge. They seemed to take a real pleasure in it.

We spent half-an-hour idling through the palace, admiring the cosy apartments and the rich but eminently home-like appointments of the place, and then the Imperial family bade our party a kind good-bye, and proceeded to count the spoons.

FREDERICK BURNABY
(1842–1885)

English traveller and soldier. Huge, with a thin, piercing voice, Burnaby was reckoned to be one of the strongest men in Europe (he could hold a pony under his arm). In the 1860s and 70s he travelled in Central and South America, Spain, Tangier and Russia. In 1875 he rode to Khiva on horseback, his account of the journey bringing him wide fame. In 1882 he crossed the Channel in a balloon. He died in the Sudan, on the expedition to relieve Khartoum.

'Je suis Anglais; no passport' – at the Russian frontier, December 1875

It was not a pleasant thing to be kept waiting in a cold room for at least three-quarters of an hour, whilst some spectacled officials suspiciously conned each passport. The Russian secretary himself was not at all impressed with the wisdom of his Government in still adhering to this system, which is so especially invented to annoy travellers. 'What nonsense it is,' he remarked; 'the greater scoundrel a man is the greater certainty of his passport being in the most perfect order. Whenever I go to France, and am asked for my passport, I avoid the difficulty by saying, 'Je suis Anglais; no passport;' and the officials, taking me for an Englishman, do not bother me, or make me show it. . . .

The customs examination was easily got through. The only part of my luggage which puzzled the *douane* officer was the sleeping-bag. He smelt it suspiciously, the waterproof cloth having a strong odour. 'What is it for?' 'To sleep in.' He put his nose down again, and apparently uncertain in his own mind as to what course to pursue, called for another official, who desired me to unroll it. 'And you sleep in that big bag?' was the question. 'Yes.' 'What extraordinary people the English are!' observed the man who had inspected my passport, and *sotto voce*, 'he must be mad;' when the other bystanders drew back a little, thinking that possibly I was dangerous as well.

W. H. MALLOCK
(1849–1923)

English writer. After leaving Oxford he enjoyed immediate success and became part of fashionable society, 'a mode of life which to the end of his days he appreciated and enjoyed' (*DNB*).

A piece of the true cross

Our own part of the ship was not invaded by anybody, except one solitary figure. He was a man in European dress, with wistful eyes and a fine Hellenic face. Advancing to us with dignity, he asked us if we would buy what he called 'special photographs'. 'Be off,' said one of my friends. 'Take the beastly things away.' 'Not beastly,' he said gently, 'academic.' Then opening a leather case which he carried, he produced from its depths some polished cubes of olive-wood, and with no change of manner except an increased gravity. 'Perhaps,' he went on, 'you would like a piece of the true Cross.'

ROBERT LOUIS STEVENSON
(1850–1894)

Scottish novelist, poet and essayist. Although he struggled all his life against TB, he was an extensive traveller. He canoed in France and Belgium in 1876, travelled through the Cévennes in South-East France with a donkey in 1878 and on an emigrant ship to the USA in 1879. In 1889 he set out for the South Seas, settling in Samoa, where he died and was buried high on Mount Vaea.

Camping in the Cévennes

At last black trees began to show upon my left, and, suddenly crossing the road, made a cave of unmitigated blackness right in front. I call it a cave without exaggeration; to pass below that arch of leaves was like entering a dungeon. I felt about until my hand encountered a stout branch, and to this I tied Modestine, a haggard, drenched, desponding donkey. Then I lowered my pack, laid it along the wall on the margin of the road, and unbuckled the straps. I knew well enough where the lantern was; but where were the candles? I groped and groped among the tumbled articles, and, while I was thus groping, suddenly I touched the spirit lamp. Salvation! This would serve my turn as well. The wind roared unwearyingly among the trees; I could hear the boughs tossing and the leaves churning through half a mile of forest; yet the scene of my encampment was not only as black as the pit, but admirably sheltered. At the second match the wick caught flame. The light was both livid and shifting; but it cut me off from the universe, and doubled the darkness of the surrounding night.

I tied Modestine more conveniently for herself, and broke up half the black bread for her supper, reserving the other half against the morning. Then I gathered what I should want within reach, took off my wet boots and gaiters, which I wrapped in my waterproof, arranged my knapsack for a pillow under the flap of my sleeping-bag, insinuated my limbs into the interior, and buckled myself in like a *bambina*. I opened a tin of Bologna sausage and broke a cake of chocolate, and that was all I had to eat. It may sound offensive, but I ate them together, bite by bite, by way of bread and meat. All I had to wash down this revolting mixture was neat brandy; a revolting beverage in itself. But I was rare and hungry; ate well, and smoked one of the best cigarettes in my experience. Then I put a stone in my straw hat, pulled the flap of my fur cap over my neck and eyes, put my revolver ready to my hand, and snuggled well down among the sheepskins.

THOMAS STEVENS
(b. 1855)

American traveller (by bicycle). On 22 April 1884 he left San Francisco on a penny-farthing bicycle with a fifty-inch front wheel. Having crossed the Sierra Nevada, the Rockies and the Great Plains, he sailed to Germany and proceeded to pedal through Austria, Hungary, the Balkans, Persia, Afghanistan, India, Singapore, China and Japan, arriving at Yokohama on 17 December 1886. He had ridden 13,500 miles. On his return a dinner in his honour was given by the Massachusetts Bicycle Club.

A spot of bother in Adrianople, Turkey

At eleven o'clock I decide to make a start, I and the bicycle being the focus of attraction for a most undignified mob as I trundle through the muddy streets toward the suburbs. Arriving at a street where it is possible to mount and ride for a short distance, I do this in the hope of satisfying the curiosity of the crowd, and being permitted to leave the city in comparative peace and privacy; but the hope proves a vain one, for only the respectable portion of the crowd disperses, leaving me, solitary and alone, among a howling mob of the rag, tag, and bobtail of Adrianople, who follow noisily along vociferously yelling for me to '*bin! bin!*' (mount, mount), and '*chu! chu!*' (ride, ride) along the really unridable streets. This is the worst crowd I have encountered on the entire journey across two continents, and, arriving at a street where the prospect ahead looks comparatively promising, I mount, and wheel forward with a view of outdistancing them if possible; but a ride of over a hundred yards without dismounting would be an exceptional performance in Adrianople after a rain, and I soon find that I have made a mistake in attempting it, for, as I mount, the mob grows fairly wild and riotous with excitement, flinging their red fezes at the wheels, rushing up behind and giving the bicycle smart pushes forward, in their eagerness to see it go faster, and more than one stone comes bounding along the street, wantonly flung by some young savage unable to contain himself. I quickly decide upon allaying the excitement by dismounting, and trundling until the mobs gets tired of following, whatever the distance.

This movement scarcely meets with the approval of the unruly crowd, however, and several come forward and exhibit ten-para pieces as an inducement for me to ride again, while overgrown gamins swarm around me, and, straddling the middle and index fingers of their right hands over their left, to illustrate and emphasize their meaning, they clamorously cry, '*bin! bin! chu! chu! monsieur! chu! chu!*'

C. E. MONTAGUE
(1867–1928)

English novelist, essayist and journalist. He joined the
Manchester Guardian in 1890 and was one of the most
brilliant journalists of his time.

The Swiss

The Swiss are inspired hotel-keepers. Some centuries since, when
the stranger strayed into one of their valleys, their simple forefathers
would kill him and share out the little money he might have about
him. Now they know better. They keep him alive and writing
cheques.

JOHN FOSTER FRASER
(*fl.* 1896–1899)

English traveller. In 1896, with two companions, he
bicycled 19,237 miles around the world. Although they
'had never been scalped, or had hooks through our
spines; never been tortured, or had our eyes gouged;
never been rescued after living for a fortnight on our
shoes', Fraser's account of their adventures is a classic.

Germany – its smells and its music

A thick-moustached and lager-blown constable stopped us when
we treadled into Cologne. We had no official number on our
machines, and therefore had to walk through the town. We found it
maintained loyally its reputation for odours. Coleridge described it
as a place with 'seven-and-twenty smells, all well-defined and
genuine stinks.' Coleridge was right. Still, smells apart, I enjoyed the
ramble through the gloomy lanes, endeavouring to discover how
many truly authentic and original makers of the renowned Eau-de-
Cologne there are. When I reached the round dozen I abandoned the
search.

Two days were spent running by the side of the legendary Rhine from Cologne to Mayence – two days of constant joy, with a panorama perpetually unfolding before our eyes. Two nights – with Sunday in between – we halted at Mayence. Each evening we visited the Stadthalle Garten, and, with other idlers, sipped our wine, while the band played classic music. Yes, classical – Beethoven and Wagner, Schubert and Liszt and Gounod!

'Ah! these Germans are musical,' I thought; 'they know good music. They're not always wanting to be tickled by music-hall airs like Londoners. It's refreshing to get the real thing, not hackneyed.'

Just then the band struck up the intermezzo from *Cavalleria Rusticana*. Next they started at 'The Man that Broke the Bank at Monte Carlo,' and by the time I reached the gate they were drivelling about 'Daisy Bell'!

NORMAN DOUGLAS
(1868–1952)

English writer. He entered the Foreign Office in 1893, but resigned three years later and bought a villa in Posilipo. In 1904 he moved to Capri, an island he made famous in his novel *South Wind* (1917). He was the author of three remarkable travel books, *Siren Land* (1911), *Fountains in the Sand* (1912) and *Old Calabria* (1915).

The women of San Giovanni

It will not take you long to discover that the chief objects of interest in San Giovanni are the women. Many Calabrian villages still possess their distinctive costumes – Marcellinara and Cimigliano are celebrated in this respect – but it would be difficult to find anywhere an equal number of handsome women on such a restricted space. In olden days it was dangerous to approach these attractive and mirthful creatures; they were jealously guarded by brothers and husbands. But the brothers and husbands, thank God, are now in America and you may be as friendly with them as ever you please, provided you confine your serious attentions to not more than two or three. Secrecy in such matters is out of the question, as with the Arabs; there is too much gossip, and too little coyness about what is natural; your friendships are openly recognized, and tacitly approved. The priests do not interfere; their hands are full.

To see these women at their best one must choose a Sunday or a feast-day; one must go, moreover, to the favourite fountain of Santa Lucia, which lies on the hill-side and irrigates some patches of corn and vegetables. Their natural charms are enhanced by elaborate and tasteful golden ornaments, and by a pretty mode of dressing the hair, two curls of which are worn hanging down before their ears with an irresistible seductive air. Their features are regular; eyes black or deep gentian blue; complexion pale; movements and attitudes impressed with a stamp of rare distinction. Even the great-grandmothers have a certain austere dignity – sinewy, indestructible old witches, with tawny hide and eyes that glow like lamps.

And yet San Giovanni is as dirty as can well be; it has the accumulated filth of the Eastern town, while lacking all its glowing tints or harmonious outlines. We are disposed to associate squalor with certain artistic effects, but it may be said of this and many other Calabrian places that they have solved the problem how to be ineffably squalid without becoming in the least picturesque.

ROSE MACAULAY
(1884?–1958)

English writer. Author of twenty-three novels, including *The Towers of Trebizond* (1956), and a series of delightful travel books which inspire the reader to embark instantly for foreign climes.

Sybaris, Southern Italy

To enjoy the ruins of Sybaris ... destroyed and drowned two thousand four hundred and sixty years ago, and now lying buried deep in rich river mud, requires not only imagination but a little knowledge of what Sybaris was like when it was to be seen. That opulent ancient city, once the capital of Magna Graecia, once so happy in its vast prosperity and elegance, was destroyed by its rival Croton, and drowned by the diversion of the river Cratis over its razed temples and courts, theatres, streets and baths, and lies fathoms deep beneath the marshy plain, sunk without trace. . . . No trace of its ruins remains above ground; no one is certain of the site. We know nothing of ruined Sybaris; all the records are of the city in its rich florescence, that scented, delicate hot-house bloom of luxury. It is on this Sybaris that we muse as we stand above the sunk city preserved in river mud, the city whose broken temples must resemble those of her daughter city, Paestum; her marble baths and great fora perhaps surpass any others in beauty. The sense of grandiose ruin is sharpened by the dreams we have of those who inhabited there; those Sybaritish Achaean Greeks, the envy and derision of their neighbours, a legend down the centuries that followed their dispersal, with their exquisite meals, their silken garments, their prolonged matutinal slumbers that must not be disturbed by cocks, their horses that caprioled and danced to music, their wanton pleasure-seeking that has made of them for twenty-six centuries a legend, 'those prodigious prodigals and mad Sybaritical spendthrifts', as Robert Burton sourly called them – imagining those sunk and viewless ruins of their city, we can see them still, strolling languidly about their wrecked streets, carefully shaded from the sun, followed by pet dwarfs and leading costly little dogs from Malta, saying to their friends, 'You must dine with me a year from to-day' (so great an occasion was a Sybarite dinner), turning away their eyes in distaste (or even swooning) if they saw a labourer at work, going to the baths leading slaves in chains, in order to punish them if the water should prove too hot or too little perfumed, lying on beds of rose petals, complaining in anguish if any were crumpled, discussing new and exquisite sauces for fish (for in this matter of sauces they were excessively ingenious, bestowing especial rewards on those who invented anything recherché, such as roe pickled in brine and soaked in oil and sweet wine, which was, it seems, something like anchovy sauce), crowning with gold crowns those who were judged to have given the most sumptuous public dinners. Reclining on the turf so far above the lost city, we can almost see those marble-pillared arcades and courts where elegant Sybarites drank together (women, too, for this happy and admirable people practised sex equality in pleasure, shocking their less advanced neighbours such as the sour puritan Pythagorean citizens of Croton who barbarously destroyed them in the end.) There the magnificent city lies, wrecked and drowned, but safe from quarrying, protected these thousands of years by river mud and earth, as Pompeii and Herculaneum by ashes and lava; its fallen columns lying lovely and intact, its buildings worthy of the greatest and richest city of Greater Greece; its temples were perhaps as huge as Selinunte, huger than Paestum. A complete civilization lies beneath our feet as we tread the marshy ground through which the Cratis winds. What sculptures, lavish in beauty, decorate this city; what baths, what plumbing, what heating, what beds! None of those hard bedsteads used by those of Herculaneum; the beds of the Sybarites would have, we may be sure, beneath the withered rose petals (potpourri by now) admirable springs. When Sybarites visited Sparta, the hard benches they had to sit on at meals, and the frugal food, caused them to exclaim that they no longer wondered at the courage of these people in battle, for what regret could attend the leaving of so harsh a life, so different from that of Sybaris, where, lapped in rose-leaves and silken sheets, Sybarites lay late in exquisite chambers?

D. H. LAWRENCE
(1885–1930)

English novelist, poet and essayist. In 1912 he went abroad for the first time, eloping to the Continent with his future wife, Frieda von Richtofen. He lived for a time in Germany, in the Isar Valley, before migrating to Austria and then to Lake Garda in Italy. From September 1913 until June 1914 he lived at Lerici. After the war Lawrence had a nomadic life, living in Europe, Ceylon, the United States and Mexico.

A letter from Lerici – to Edward Garnett, September 1913

I am so happy with the place we have at last discovered, I must write smack off to tell you. It is perfect. There is a little tiny bay half-shut in by rocks, and smothered by olive woods that slope down swiftly. Then there is one pink, flat, fisherman's house. Then there is the villino of Ettore Gambrosier, a four-roomed pink cottage among vine gardens, just over the water and under the olive woods. There, D.V., is my next home. It is exquisite. One gets by rail from Genoa or from Parma to Spezia, by steamer across the gulf to Lerici, and by rowing boat round the headlands to Fiascherino, where is the villino which is to be mine. It is L60 a month – 60 lire, that is – furnished – and 25 lire for the woman who does all the work and washing and sleeps in Tellaro, the fishing village twenty minutes off; in all, 85 francs a month. You run out of the gate into the sea, which washes among the rocks at the mouth of the bay. The garden is all vines and fig trees, and great woods on the hills all round. Now you will come and see us – and so will Constanza Davidovna – she promised – she would be so happy. Yellow crocuses are out, wild. The Mediterranean washes softly and nicely, with just a bit of white against the rocks. Figs and grapes are ripe. You will come and see us – and David too – it is a perfect place for him. Think, we can sit round the open chimney in the kitchen at night, and burn olive wood, and hear the sea washing. I want to go to-morrow. But the proprietor remains in possession still another eight days, for the crops. I feel I can't wait: Though this is a delicious hotel – 6 francs a day pension, jolly good food, wine and all included – a big bedroom with a balcony just over the sea, very beautiful. But I want to go to my villino.

WALTER STARKIE
(1894–1976)

Irish writer. An expert on Romance languages, he made several journeys, on foot and living with gypsies, through Italy, Spain, Dalmatia and Albania. From 1940–1954 he was Director of the British Institute in Madrid.

The great botafumeiro at Santiago de Compostela in north-western Spain

In the dim distance the main altar was a blaze of lights, and an apotheosis of baroque ornamentation with its twisted lamps. Salomonic columns, chubby angels, scrolls, escutcheons and riding high above the Churrugueresque extravaganza the 'Moor-slayer' in full panoply. Even the venerable thirteenth-century stone statue of the Apostle was so bedizened with shells and scrolls and precious stones that he looked like a heathen idol. The procession of cardinals, archbishops and bishops in their red and purple vestments and gold and silver mitres attended by the canons of the cathedral, who used to be called cardinals, and the colourful sequence of the Generalissimo and his suite, the ministers and distinguished foreign guests, was imposing and it became a pageant of sound as well as colour, for the vast choirs on both sides of the main altar responded to each other in strophe and antistrophe, while the organ pealed triumphantly. I could see the acolytes in black and scarlet gather below in the crossing of the cathedral, and by a rope over a pulley they pulled down a great hook called the *alcachofa* or 'artichoke,' to which they fixed the *botafumeiro*, the gigantic silver censer, after the incense had been ignited. The seven men then pulled the ropes, raising the great censer off the floor. At first it moved slowly and it seemed as if it was being pushed by the men from one to the other as in a game, but then it began to gather momentum rhythmically and the men disappeared into the crowd as it mounted higher and higher while flames and trailing clouds of fragrant incense became, as it were, the emanations of the soaring music from the choirs and the organ. It swept exultantly above the galleries to the very roof of the basilica and then rushed vertiginously down like a flaming meteor just above the heads of the watchful multitude. Meanwhile the organ rang out and I heard the choir and the massed pilgrims' voices singing the mediæval hymn of Santiago from the *Codex* of Pope Calixtus and towards the end of the hymn the flights of the monster censer became gradually slower and shorter, as its breath grew fainter, until at last it sank lifeless to earth, whereupon it was seized with amazing skill and rapidity by its custodian dressed in scarlet wool and his assistants, who bore it away to its lair in the library of the chapter house.

SIR VICTOR PRITCHETT
(1900–   )

English writer, critic, scholar and traveller. He began his working life in the leather trade in London at the age of sixteen, then worked in the glue trade in Paris. In the 1920s he was a newspaper correspondent in Spain and Ireland.

Castile – where Spain begins

Spain begins after Miranda de Ebro, where one sees the last big river of silver water and the last rain-washed, glass-enclosed balconies of the north. The train begins its climb on to the tableland of Castile, which occupies the centre of the country and which stretches east and west from Portugal to the mountains above Valencia and from the Ebro to the Andalusian valleys. . . . Nine months of winter, three of hell, is the proverbial description of Castilian weather, the weather of half of Spain: a dry climate of fine air under a brassy sun, where the cold wind is wicked and penetrating, a continual snake-fang flicker against the nostrils. Castile is a steppe. Its landscape is the pocked and cratered surface of the moon.

Dust and yellow earth have begun; the grass, if there are patches of it, is wire, the trees only mark the roads, there are no others, and the roads, too, are rare. It is steppe, not desert, a steppe variegated only by wilderness. And there appear those strange flat-topped hills of the country. A half-mile long, perhaps, and anything from 400 to 450 feet high, they have been planed off at the summit and are water-hollowed in their flanks. They are as pale as china clay. Half a dozen of these dry hills would be a curiosity, like the Wiltshire barrows, but these mesetas stretch in their hundreds, miles deep like some geometry written on the land by wind and drought, an immense, wearying encampment. Some are pocked with tufts of grass: here and there some peasant has tried to cultivate a lower slope, but the water clearly drains off them and most of them are bare. No house or village is on them; they are the ghosts of nature and they pass in pointless fantasy.

These hills bleach the country and, in the heat, the air trembles over them. Their moment is the evening. When the sun goes down they are transfigured, for first they fall into lavender pools of shadow, then into deep blue and at last violet. For a moment or two the sight is weird and beautiful; then it becomes ghastly, for they take on the colour of bruised bodies, the corpse colour of those dead Christs the Spanish painters like to paint with the realism of the mortuary, the sick skin of the wrung-out stomachs and malodorous mouths of El Greco's saints. The Spanish painters have dipped their brushes into the death-palette of the steppe, and that night change is one of the frightening sights of Europe.

CYRIL CONNOLLY
(1903–1974)

English writer, critic and editor. In 1940 he founded the literary journal *Horizon* and edited it for nine years. In 1948, under the pseudonym 'Palinurus' he published *The Unquiet Grave*, a remarkably evocative work that recalls his travels between the wars.

Autumn in Paris

With the first leaves being swept up in the square, the first misty morning, the first yellowing of the planes, I remember Paris and all the excitement of looking for autumn lodgings in a hotel. Streets round the Rue de l'Université, Rue Jacob, Rue de Bourgogne and Rue de Beaune, with their hotel signs and entrances and their concierges walled in by steamer-trunks. Stuffy salons full of novels by Edith Wharton, purple wall-paper which later we grow to hate as we lie in bed with grippe, chintz screens round the bidets, high grey panelling with cupboards four inches deep. . . .

Route Nationale

Peeling off the kilometres to the tune of 'Blue Skies', sizzling down the long black liquid reaches of Nationale Sept, the plane trees going sha-sha-sha through the open window, the windscreen yellowing with crushed midges, she with the Michelin beside me, a handkerchief binding her hair. . . .

Cannes

Back-streets of Cannes: tuberoses in the window, book-shops over the railway bridge which we comb for old memoirs and detective stories, while the cushions of the car deflate in the afternoon sun. *Petit Marseillais, Eclaireur de Nice:* head-lines about the Spanish war soaked in sun-bathing oil, torn maps, wet bathing-dresses wrapped in towels, – and now we bring home memoirs, detective stories, tuberoses, round the dangerous corner of the Rue d'Antibes and down the coast road by the milky evening sea.

EVELYN WAUGH
(1903–1966)

English novelist. (See p. 87).

Etna at sunset

I do not think I shall ever forget the sight of Etna at sunset; the mountain almost invisible in a blur of pastel grey, glowing on the top and then repeating its shape, as though reflected, in a wisp of grey smoke, with the whole horizon behind radiant with pink light, fading gently into a pastel grey sky. Nothing I have ever seen in Art or Nature was quite so revolting.

SIR CECIL BEATON
(1904–1980)

English photographer, designer, traveller and diarist.

A night out in Budapest, 1936

By the time we staggered to our beds at dawn, we felt as though we'd already spent a week sightseeing and living in Budapest. Many impressions had been gathered. A letter of introduction provided us with a willing escort, who promptly guided two eager foreigners and showed them every aspect of night life. We ate Hungarian food in enormous quantities including a kind of salmon-trout from Lake Balaton. Gypsy orchestras serenaded us. In the huge inferno-nightclub *Arizona*, spectacle vyed with spectacle. There were revolving dance floors and a cabaret that went on from ten o'clock until three in the morning. The walls had breathing shells; balconies suddenly shot ceilingwards on the trunk of a palm tree; stars flashed and chorus girls, suspended by their teeth, twirled at the ends of ropes. To Miss Arizona, once a beauty and now the singer-wife of the proprietor, were allotted the big 'production numbers'. Her entrances were spectacular accompanied by every variety of dog, or riding an elephant.

A luncheon at Vienne

We were foolish and greedy to try and arrive in time for luncheon at what is generally considered to be the best restaurant in France: La Pyramide at Vienne. The heat was almost too great for such a long dose of motoring. The result was that we wondered, as we opened the iron gate and walked up a curving gravel path, if we were not too late and exhausted to do justice to the famous cuisine. Monsieur Point had had the idea of naming a small, but superb, restaurant after the neighbouring eighteenth-century obelisk commemorating the retreat of the Egyptians in battle with the Romans. Soon after he opened, the word went round, and gourmets from over all France made their tracks to La Pyramide.

At the mere sight of the pyramids of butter, and the basket of breads, toasts and biscuits, our juices began to flow, and curiosity was feverish by the time the first course was presented on a silver tray decorated with a large vase of mixed anemones. The dish consisted of pale rose-colour *pâté*, truffle-dotted, embedded in a sponge cake. How could this miracle be achieved? But this mystery is only one of Monsieur Point's secrets, and the *Pâté Erioche* proved to be an unbelievable delicacy, the richness of the *pâté* contrasting with the dry lightness of the sponge. A turbot in champagne sauce was served on a tray decorated with other flowers; in fact, each item of our enormous meal was served to the accompaniment of new floral delights. The turbot savoured to the accompaniment of an excellent dry white Bordeaux, evaporated lightly on the tongue in a haze of the most delicate scent. Now, on a dish displaying a small Roman chariot of tiny garden flowers with its wheels set in the sauce, came the *pièce de résistance* in the form of a duck cooked in sauerkraut: the dark sauce and the flesh of the bird was of an unimaginable richness. The accompanying wine was a Côtes du Rhône *rouge*.

When our oxygen seemed to be running low, the palate was titillated by a display of home-made ice-creams in different flavours. Alongside was another tray of doll-like pots, each containing a vanilla cream or chocolate mousse. As if Pelion had not long ago been piled upon Ossa, another treat of the day was presented: a special *gâteau* – today's being flavoured with a coffee cream, of a light, but richly succulent consistency. By now the meal could be considered at an end, yet here was the serious matter of the *petits fours* – a jewel-like selection of bright and shining colours. Then came the '*digestives*', made on the premises. If you should acquiesce to the invitation of the wine waiter, wearing a green baize apron, his heavy hand pours with such prodigality and lavishness that you would imagine he was offering you a libation of water. Before you can cry 'Whoa!' your glass is filled from a vast bottle (labelled in pretty, faded handwriting) in which a whole golden William pear has been submerged to scent the liqueur.

As we left La Pyramide the final gesture of service was shown by a waiter opening, for our comfort, the door to the lavatory.

ROBERT BYRON
(1905–1941)

English traveller, art critic and historian. After leaving Oxford he travelled extensively, first in Europe and then in Asia. His best and best-known book is *The Road to Oxiana* (1937).

A visit to Lenin's Tomb, 1930

In the midst of this tall, dim interior, sheeted with sombre, close-grained stones, the mummy lay on a tall pedestal sheltered by an inverted cradle of plate-glass, and brightly lit. Below, in pairs at either end, stood four sentries. We lengthened into single file. Mounting a flight of steps, I took my view and, in virtue of the atmosphere, paid my homage. Round the walls, I noticed, ran a frieze of vitreous scarlet lightning.

Lenin must have been a very small man. He rests on a bed of dun-coloured draperies, which engulf his legs with the tasteful negligence of a modiste's window. His upper part wears a khaki jacket buttoned at the neck. The finely modelled hands and features are of waxen texture, like the petals of a magnolia flower. The beard and moustache turn from straw-colour to brown, a fact which caused Bernard Shaw more surprise (so he told me) than anything else in his self-patented Russian Elysium. One might have said: A nice little man, fond of his grandchildren, and given to pruning his trees. I wondered whether a countenance so placid and benign was not really made of wax. For rumour insists that the sewers of the Kremlin recently overflowed into the shrine, to the detriment of its keepsake. But when I got outside, I had not walked a hundred yards before I met an old man with features, beard, and expression exactly similar to those I had just examined. So that there need be nothing inherently false about the present appearance of the relic.

GEORGE MILLAR
(1910–   )

English journalist, soldier, sailor, writer and farmer. Taken prisoner in Italy in 1943, he escaped while being transported to Germany and reached Spain. In 1944 he parachuted into France to work with the Maquis.

Crossing the Pyrenees beyond Perpignan, December 1943

At the corner of a ploughed field I was introduced to the man who was to lead us into Spain. He was a willowy, bronzed creature with a thin line of moustache on his upper lip. His large eyes stuck out prominently from his thin face. There were hollows in the backs of his hands where the skin sagged between the bones.

He bade us put on *espadrilles*. (Enough of these rope-soled canvas shoes for all of us had been brought by the Americans from Paris.) I kept on my half-boots, for their rubber soles made no noise, and from experience I knew that espadrilles, probably the most comfortable shoes on earth, could play hell with one's feet on a long walk. . . .

The guide whispered injunctions in halting French.

'Complete silence ... never smoke unless I tell you yes ... follow in single file ... avoid rattling stones or cracking branches ... lie down if I do ... run if I do ... don't separate if we meet a German patrol ... just run after me into the darkness ... if the Germans shoot and wound one the others must not stop, run on ... there is much walking to-night. ....'

'How much?'

'Forty-five kilometres [28 miles] and six rivers to cross.'

... At last we came out on the plateau. It looked unnatural, like the face of the moon. The bitter wind swept across it, bludgeoning us forward, stabbing us forward. The guide nudged me and pointed to a hillock at the far edge of the plateau.

'Keep that on your left hand,' he said. 'It marks the Spanish frontier. But you must make them run across here. We're in full view. It's not far. Look. Only 300 metres.'

He and the other Spaniard began to run away in front of us.

'Run!' I shouted. 'That's the frontier.'

The Trapper and Fritz ran on. Charlie stumbled after them. A wild exaltation gripped me, filled me, maddened me.

'Just 300 yards now, Charlie,' I shouted at him. 'Run with me.'

'I can't.'

'Run! Run! Run!'

I took him by the hand and pulled him. The pair of us broke into a shambling trot. I pulled and the wind pushed. Charlie responded. Our speed increased. We crossed the plateau; and suddenly we were running away with ourselves as we dropped over the edge of the plateau – into Spain.

SIR FITZROY MACLEAN
(1911–   )

Scottish diplomat, soldier, traveller and Member of Parliament.

Leaving the Gare du Nord for Moscow, 1937

Slowly gathering speed, the long train pulled out of the Gare du Nord. The friends who had come to see me off waved and started to turn away; the coaches jolted as they passed over the points, and the bottles of mineral water by the window clinked gently one against the other. Soon we had left the dingy grey suburbs of Paris behind us and were running smoothly through the rainswept landscape of northern France. Night was falling and in my compartment it was nearly dark. I did not switch on the light at once, but sat looking out at the muddy fields and dripping woods. . . .

I was twenty-five. But, already, I was beginning to get a little set in my ways; perhaps, I reflected in my rare moments of introspection, even a little smug. There were those pin-striped suits from Scholte; those blue and white shirts from Beale and Inman with their starched collars; those neat, well-cleaned shoes from Lobb; the dark red carnation that came every morning from the florist in the Faubourg Saint Honoré. After breakfast, a brief walk under the trees in the Champs Elysées. Or sometimes a ride among the leafy avenues of the Bois. Then the daily, not disagreeable task of drafting telegrams and dispatches, on thick, blue laid paper, in a style and a handwriting which, I flattered myself, both discreetly reflected a classical education. Occasional telephone calls. Occasional visits to the Quai d'Orsay: the smell of bees-wax in the passages; the rather fusty smell of the cluttered, steam-heated offices; *comment allez-vous, cher collègue?* Luncheon at a restaurant or at somebody's house: politics and people. Afterwards, a pleasant feeling of reple-tion. Then, more telegrams, more dispatches, more telephone calls till dinner time. A bath. A drink. And then all the different lights and colours and smells and noises of Paris at night. Big official dinner parties, with white ties and decorations. Small private dinner parties with black ties and that particular type of general conversation at which the French excel. The best-dressed women, the best food, the best wine, the best brandy in the world. Parties in restaurants. Parties in night clubs. The Théâtre de Dix Heures, the chansonniers: jokes about politics and sex. The Bal Tabarin: the rattle and bang of the can-can; the plump thighs of the dancers in their long black silk stockings. Week after week; month after month. An agreeable existence, but one that, if prolonged unduly, seemed bound to lead to chronic liver trouble, if to nothing worse.

I have always relished contrasts, and what more complete contrast could there be after Paris than Moscow? I had seen something of the West. Now I wanted to see the East.

WILLIAM SANSOM
(1912–   )

English writer and traveller.

The siesta

Now everything is dead. Pale brown dogs lie like a death of bones in the cactus shade. A horse lies sprawled like a huge hare. The trees and the grasses, wood-engraved, seem to pause under a great silencing weight from above – even the vegetable, hungriest of lives, knows a waiting suspense. It is the Panic hour, when the goats take on a knowing human look – and what Greek maiden would not have been startled by the two cunning eyes of old bearded biglip cutting at her from the ilex shade, what myths might not have been begun? – the hour of heavy windless light and wide suspense when ancient shepherds felt the imminence of Nature taking Form and Henry James brought out his sunny ghosts to play, a time allied to terror; when every black-cut shadow cloaks an unseen standing figure, when each motionless bush holds the breath of its leaves for what might burst through and awfully stand revealed. Only the carapaced, inward insect perforates the silence – the cicada sounds its resonant chapels, and giant bees extend their tongues to lick the sleeping honey; the mantis, falsely, stands as stiff as all siesta. A fool cock may crow out a single note of strutting nerves – but that is all. The rest is silence; heavy, hot and huge.

And on the bed? What cool quiet shade in the watered light of jalousie and curtain, of rattan Spanish blind and striped Venetian shutter. There is such burning power outside that each infusion holds a luminescence of its own, as though phosphorus was laid there, original light powdered on the shutters and diffused in green reflection round the room. No sleep at first, the pillow white and cool, the one light-weary fly exhausting the circuit of the walls to drop and buzz itself to death on the tiled floor; and as relaxation takes its course, sheets kicked away and body naked for the shadow's cooling touch, cool as the tiled floor – then what calligraphies astound the walls. What memories come back – for this is the nearest we will ever get to those long-lost hours of childhood's afternoon rest, even to earlier silk-fringed moments in the pram.

Lawrence Durrell
(1912–   )

English novelist and poet. Describing himself as 'one of the world's expatriates', he has travelled widely and currently lives in France. His books include *The Alexandria Quartet* (1957–60).

Landscape with olive trees, Corfu, 1938

The olive-gathering is an all-weather business; in the blinding February storms you hear the little hard berries dropping to the ground, and, if you happen to be standing on high ground looking southward you can see the visible track of the north wind as it strikes the valley, turning the olive trees inside out – so that they change from green to silver and back to green. Under the shelter of archway and wall the woman stoop in circles steadily filling their hampers while the rain rattles like small-shot in the leaves about them and the first thirsty wild flowers stir in the cold ground under their feet.

But the olive-tree has hardly suited its internal economy to its position, for its attenuated white flowering commences in April, just when it is most occupied with the ripening of its fruit: so that if its previous year's blossom has been prolific, it has hardly the strength to blossom again. Its crop is irregular, and the lean years for the harvesters are very lean indeed. Bread and oil as a diet hardly leaves any margin for thrift.

After the first pressing in the mill-bed the men come with their wide-mouthed baskets and gather up the magma, piling its greyish mass into a wooden press; the pony, whose efforts at the millstone are now no longer necessary, is unharnessed and turned loose in the paddock. Taking up the long wooden lever, the men begin to screw at the pulp, helping the oil away if the weather is cold, by pouring boiling water upon it. As the pressure becomes stronger, they fasten a rope to a sort of primitive windlass, and give the creaking structure their whole weight. It is like the birth of something in the gloom of the great magazine; their groans echo through the cypress floors of the house. The windlass creaks. The fowls cluck nervously about the feet of the men. Appreciatively sitting in the great fireplace with the light playing upon his beard, the abbot of the local monastery lends moral support as he sips his glass of wine. . . .

The whole Mediterranean – the sculptures, the palms, the gold beads, the bearded heroes, the wine, the ideas, the ships, the moonlight, the winged gorgons, the bronze men, the philosophers – all of it seems to rise in the sour, pungent taste of these black olives between the teeth. A taste older than meat, older than wine. A taste as old as cold water.

PATRICK LEIGH FERMOR
(1915–   )

English traveller, soldier and writer. In 1933, at the age of eighteen, he walked from Holland to Constantinople, a journey which took one and a half years and which he describes in part in *A Time of Gifts* (1977). Altogether he spent four years travelling in Central Europe, the Balkans and Greece. During the war he spent two years in German-occupied Crete, organizing the resistance forces and planning the kidnapping of the German commander, General Kreipe. After the war he travelled in the Caribbean, a journey that produced *The Traveller's Tree*, one of the great classics of post-war travel writing.

At the foothills of the White Mountains

Now and then one finds oneself, in the dilettante fashion of one of Marie Antoinette's ladies-in-waiting, helping in some pleasant and unexacting task: gathering olives onto spread blankets in late autumn, after beating fruit from the branches with long rods of bamboo; picking grapes into baskets, shelling peas or occasionally, in late summer, helping to tread the grapes. I remember one such occasion in Crete, in a cobbled and leafy yard in the village of Vaphé at the foothills of the White Mountains. First we spread deep layers of thyme branches at the bottom of a stone vat which stood breast-high like a giant Roman sarcophagus; then a troop of girls hoisted their heavy baskets and tipped in tangled cataracts of white and black grapes. The treading itself is considered a young man's job. The first three, of which I was one, had their long mountain boots pulled off; buckets of water were sloshed over grimy shanks and breeches rolled above the knee. 'A pity to wash off the dirt,' croaked the old men that always gather on such occasions. 'You'll spoil the taste.' This chestnut – which I imagine to have existed for several millennia – evoked its ritual laughter while we climbed on the edge and jumped down on the resilient mattress of grapes. Scores of skins exploded and the juice squirted between our toes. . . . In a minute or two a mauve-pink trickle crossed the stone lip of the spout, and dripped into the waiting tub; the trickle broadened, the drops became a stream and curved into a splashing arc. . . . We were handed glasses of the sweet juice which already – or was this imagination? – had a corrupt and ghostly tang of fermentation. When the stream slackened, the manhood of the treaders, shuffling calf-deep in a tangled slush by now and purple to the groin, was jovially impugned. . . . For days the sweet heady smell of the must hangs over the village. All is sticky to the touch, purple splashes and handprints on the whitewash and spilt red rivulets between the cobbles and the clouds of flies suggest a massacre. Meanwhile, in the dark crypts of the houses, in huge grooved Minoan amphorae, the must grumbles and hits out and fills the house with unnerving fumes and a bubbling noise like the rumour of plots, a dark conspiracy of whispers. For as long as this vaulted collusion lasts, a mood of swooning and Dionysiac laxity roves the air.

EDITH TEMPLETON
(1916–   )

English writer. Born and educated in Prague, she is the author of *The Surprise of Cremona* (1954), a witty and sharply original account of 'one woman's adventures in Cremona, Oarma, Mantua, Ravenna, Urbino and Arezzo'.

Parma Cathedral

To-day is my birthday. 'Would you like a whole carafe of wine?' I ask myself, tenderly. Yes, I would.

And now to the cathedral. I fortify myself with another glance into the guide-book. The guide-book calls it 'impressive'. The word 'impressive' is always a bad sign. It means that the guide-book writer has scraped the bottom of the barrel, for want of other words. An impression can be good or bad; so it lets him off nicely.

As soon as I enter the cathedral square I get a shock of revulsion. Talk of functional. I did not know that the twelfth century could produce anything quite so beastly.

This is what must have happened, I think, as I gaze at the inordinately high front rising in a stepped-up outline, reminiscent of the stepped-up gables of the old warehouses on the Trave in Lübeck. The citizens of Parma thought they must have a cathedral because all the other towns had one, too. The architect they commissioned for the work did not believe in God in the way most people believed in God at the time. I imagine he thought of God as a sort of mathematical formula, in the manner of early Greek philosophers, like: 'God has the shape of a spiral, winding higher and higher but always returning upon itself'; or: 'God is his own prisoner' or: 'the essence of God is geometry.' Anyway, something utterly cheerless like that.

Besides, he was not really interested in God at all. Also, he had no time for saints and angels. He would have much rather built a factory, but there was no demand for factories in those days. So he got down to it and made a design straight up and narrow and coming to a point at the top, the plainest pattern he could think of. At the time it was fashionable to have little arched colonnades strung like galleries round the walls, supporting exactly nothing. So he stuck those on, saying, 'Thank you for nothing', and framed the stepped-up top with them as well, till it ends in a point. It was also fashionable in those days to put stone lions in front of the portal, guarding the steps leading inside, and, therefore, he shoved in a couple of lions, and very bad-tempered beasts they are, too, and constipated-looking. Thus the Parmesans did not get a cathedral but a factory for praying, a storehouse for absolutions, and a distribution centre for the spreading of the glory of God.

I step inside – I might just as well. But how beautiful it is. Every inch of wall is covered with paintings, and the ribs of the vault are banded thickly in gilt. In the cupola above the choir there are frescoes by Correggio and I stand there like the ox in front of the gate. They look wonderful. That is to say, they make you feel as though you were asked: 'Would you like some of this cake?' and you would reply: 'I'd love a slice. It looks wonderful.' In other words, the Correggio paintings look wonderfully promising, and I am sure that they would look wonderful if I could see them properly. . . .

For a while I fight against the crick in my neck and gaze into Correggio's exceedingly pleasant heaven, sky-pink, sky-blue, and clouded white, with cherubs strewing flowers in all directions. It is a rendering of the Assumption, and seems deliciously lively.

On the high altar there is a row of Baroque candlesticks, gigantic and wrought of silver, resting on scrolled three-legged supports. It is a sight which would warm the heart of any Mayfair interior decorator. It is a pleasant surprise to see them just for once in their proper place and being used for what they were meant to be used, instead of seeing them deprived of their lily-white tapers, wired for electricity, over-hatted with a lampshade, and shedding light on a stock-broker's evenings.

JAN MORRIS
(1926–   )

Welsh writer and traveller. As James Morris, she worked as a journalist on *The Times*, taking part in the 1953 expedition to Everest. She has travelled and written about almost every part of the world and her books on Venice and Oxford have become classics.

Warsaw in the 1960s

Seen across the hours from a hotel window in the depths of winter, Warsaw could only be Warsaw, for nowhere else on the face of the earth breathes quite the same fusion of atmosphere. Room 221 in the Bristol Hotel is heavily but quite cosily Victorian, with a wicker mat hung in incongruous ornamentation on one wall and a bright if unadventurous abstract on another. Outside the door two dear old pudgy housemaids sit habitually on the floor in white caps, aprons, and carpet slippers, sibilantly gossiping, and down the corridor the immense glass lift, like a cage for a phoenix, slides in magnificent lurches to the foyer, its voyagers slipping a few zlotys to the operator as they leave. There is a violent smell of cooking on the landing, and downstairs you may just hear the tapping of a progressive American playwright's typewriter – he spent last evening with a group of eminent sociologists, and is busy working up his notes.

It is a fusty, old-fashioned, plush but mournful hostelry: but outside the window Warsaw is nothing if not spacious. The sky is grey, immense, and unmistakably Central European. The snow lies thick and sullen on the broad streets. Down the hill only a thin winding stream of water forces a way through the frozen Vistula. The air, to a visitor from England, seems slightly perfumed with petrol and boiled potatoes, but feels nevertheless like country air, blown out of forests and endless plains and Carpathian ravines; and when you first lean from your window in the icy morning you will hear the clatter of horses' hooves and the triumphant crow of a cold but irrepressible cock. Below you then the first citizens of the morning intermittently appear: an elderly lady with a jolly black dog, a covey of merry school-children, entrancing high-boned faces peering through their fur hoods like fox cubs through the bushes. Long carts full of snow go by, with a column of big lorries, and even an antique barouche trundles with creaks and squeaks towards its cab-rank; and presently Warsaw is wide awake, the sun is wanly shining, and the observer in Room 221 can watch the world of the Poles pass by.

COLIN THUBRON
(1939–   )

English writer and traveller. He began his travels in Asia and North Africa, then wrote five books about the Middle East. His best-known book, *Among the Russians* (1983), is an account of a lone, ten-thousand-mile journey through modern Russia in an old Morris Marina car and of his encounters with ordinary Russians.

Mushroom-hunting

To the Russians the wild mushroom has a peculiar mystique, and these expeditions lie somewhere between sport and ritual. They mingle the country-love of an English blackberry hunt with the delicate discrimination of the blossom-viewing Japanese. If Russia's national tree is the silver birch, then her national plant is this magic fungus, burgeoning in the forest shadows. . . .

'Mushroom-hunting . . . I wish I could express it to you.'

Volodya's face became filled with this obscure national excitement. 'It's like this. You get into the forests and you know instinctively if the conditions are right for them. You can sense it. It gives you a strange thrill. Perhaps the grass is growing at the right thickness, or there's the right amount of sun. You can even smell them. You just know that here there'll be mushrooms' – he spoke the word 'mushrooms' in a priestly hush – 'so you go forward in the shadows, or in a light clearing perhaps, and there they are, under the birches!' He reached out in tender abstraction and plucked a ghostly handful from the air. 'Have you ever sniffed mushrooms? The poisonous ones smell bitter, but the good ones – you'll remember that fragrance for ever!'

He went on to talk about the different kinds and qualities of mushroom, and how they grew and where to find them – delicate white mushrooms with umbrellaed hats, which bred in the pine forests; red, strong-tasting birch-mushrooms with whitish stems and feverish black specks; the yellow 'little foxes', which grew in huddles all together; and the sticky, dark-tipped mushroom called 'butter-covered', delicate and sweet. Then there was the *apyata* which multiplied on shrubs – 'you can pick a whole bough of them!' – and at last, in late autumn, came a beautiful green-capped mushroom which it was sacrilege to fry. All these mushrooms, he said, might be boiled in salt and pepper, laced with garlic and onions, and the red ones fried in butter and cut into bits until they appeared to have shrunk into nothing, then gobbled down with vodka all winter.

We sat on the verge for a little longer, talking of disconnected things. He was going to Brest, and I to Smolensk, and it was futile to pretend that we would ever meet again. This evanescence haunted all my friendships here. Their intimacy was a momentary triumph over the prejudice and fear which had warped us all our lives; but it could never be repeated.

Volodya clasped my hand in parting, and suddenly said: 'Isn't it all ridiculous – I mean propaganda, war. Really I don't understand.' He stared at where we'd been sitting – an orphaned circle of crushed grass. 'If only I were head of the Politburo, and you were President of America, we'd sign eternal peace at once' – he smiled sadly – 'and go mushroom-picking together!'

I never again equated the Russian system with the Russian people.

GREAT BRITAIN
AND IRELAND

PYTHEAS
(*fl.* 325–285 BC)

Greek navigator, astronomer and geographer. He visited Britain *c.* 310 BC, circumnavigating the country. Describing it as 'triangular in shape like Sicily, with three unequal sides', he reckoned its perimeter to be 42,500 stades, or 4670 miles, about twice what it in fact is. In the course of this voyage he visited 'Thule', six days to the north of Britain, around which 'there is neither sea nor air, but a mixture like sea-lung, in which earth and air are suspended'.

Far removed from the knavishness of modern man

The inhabitants of Britain are said to be sprung from the soil and to preserve a primitive style of life. They make use of chariots in war, such as the ancient Greek heroes are reputed to have employed in the Trojan War; and their habitations are rough-and-ready, being for the most part constructed of wattles or logs. They harvest their grain crops by cutting off the ears without the haulms and stowing them in covered granges; from these they pull out the oldest and prepare them for food. They are simple in their habits, and far removed from the cunning and knavishness of modern man. Their diet is inexpensive and quite different from the luxury that is born of wealth. The island is thickly populated, and has an extremely chilly climate, as one would expect in a sub-Arctic region. It has many kings and potentates, who live for the most part in a state of mutual peace.

STRABO
(b. *c.* 63 BC, d. after AD 21)

Greek geographer, historian and philosopher. Although a great traveller in the Mediterranean lands, he never visited Britain. He derived much of his information from the works of Caesar.

On the Irish

Besides some small islands round about Britain, there is also a large island, Ierne, which stretches parallel to Britain on the north, its breadth being greater than its length. Concerning this island I have nothing certain to tell, except that its inhabitants are more savage than the Britons, since they are man-eaters as well as heavy eaters, and since, further, they count it an honourable thing, when their fathers die, to devour them, and openly to have intercourse, not only with the other women, but also with their mothers and sisters; but I am saying this only with the understanding that I have no trustworthy witnesses for it; and yet, as for the matter of man-eating, that is said to be a custom of the Scythians also, and, in cases of necessity forced by sieges, the Celti, the Iberians, and several other peoples are said to have practised it.

GIRALDUS CAMBRENSIS
(*c.* 1145–1223)

Welsh priest and historian, also known as Gerald of Wales. Court chaplain to Henry II, in 1188 he accompanied Baldwin, the Archbishop of Canterbury, on a preaching tour of Wales to gain support for the Third Crusade.

Two extraordinary lakes

I must not fail to tell you about the mountains which are called Eryri by the Welsh and by the English Snowdon, that is the Snow Mountains. . . .

At the very top of these mountains two lakes are to be found, each of them remarkable in its own way. One has a floating island, which moves about and is often driven to the opposite side by the force of the winds. Shepherds are amazed to see the flocks which are feeding there carried off to distant parts of the lake. . . . The second lake has a remarkable and almost unique property. It abounds in three different kinds of fish, eels, trout and perch, and all of them have only one eye, the right one being there but not the left. If the careful reader asks me the cause of such a remarkable phenomenon, I can only answer that I do not know. It is worth noticing that in Scotland, too, in two different places, one to the east and one to the west, the fish called mullet are found in the sea with only one eye. They lack the left eye but have the right one.

A very remarkable eagle

There is a remarkable eagle which lives in the mountains of Snowdonia. Every fifth feast-day, it perches on a particular stone, hoping to satiate its hunger with the bodies of dead men, for on that day it thinks that war will break out. The stone on which it takes its stand has a hole pierced nearly through it, for it is there that the eagle cleans and sharpens its beak. An eagle is said to know the place where it can find its prey, but not the time. A raven knows the time, but not the place.

The mice of Ynys Lannog (Priestholm)

Close to Anglesey and almost adjoining it, there is a small island inhabited by hermits, who live in the service of God by the labour of their hands. They are remarkable in that, should they have ever quarrelled with each other for reasons of human frailty, a species of small mice, which abound on the island, consume most of their food and drink, and befoul the rest. As soon as their argument is over, the plague of mice disappears immediately. . . . In Welsh this island is called Ynys Lannog, which means Priests' Island, because so many of the Saints have been buried there. No women are ever allowed on the island.

JOHN LELAND
(*c.* 1506–1552)

English antiquary. Successively chaplain and librarian to Henry VIII, in 1533 he was appointed king's antiquary, 'an office which had neither predecessor nor successor'. His task was to travel the country searching out antiquities, and between 1534 and 1543 he visited 'almost every bay, river, lake, mountain, valley, moor, heath, wood, city, castle, manor-house, monastery and college in the land'. Leland intended to write a book entitled *History and Antiquities*, but the work overtaxed his brain and in 1550 he became incurably insane.

Taking the waters at Bath

There be 2. springes of whote wather in the west south west part of the towne. Whereof the bigger is caullid the Crosse Bath, bycause it hath a cross erectid in the midle of it. This bath is much frequentid of people deseasid with lepre, pokkes, scabbes, and great aches, and is temperate and pleasant, having a 11. or 12. arches of stone in the sides for men to stonde under yn tyme of reyne.

Many be holp by this bathe from scabbes and aches.

The other bathe is a 2. hunderith foote of, and is lesse in cumpace withyn the waulle then the other, having but 7. arches yn the waulle. This is caullid the Hote Bathe; for at cumming into it men think that it wold scald the flesch at the first, but after that the flesch ys warmid it is more tolerable and pleasaunt.

EMANUEL VAN METEREN
(d. 1612)

Dutch merchant. In 1575 he travelled through England and Ireland with his cousin, Abraham Ortelius, the geographer. In 1583 he was appointed Dutch Consul for England.

Like all islanders, of a weak and tender nature

The English are a clever, handsome, and well-made people, but, like all islanders, of a weak and tender nature. . . .

The people are bold, courageous, ardent, and cruel in war, fiery in attack, and having little fear of death; they are not vindictive, but very inconstant, rash, vain-glorious, light, and deceiving, and very suspicious, especially of foreigners, whom they despise. They are full of courtly and affected manners and words, which they take for gentility, civility, and wisdom. They are eloquent and very hospitable; they feed well and delicately, and eat a great deal of meat; and as the Germans pass the bounds of sobriety in drinking, these do the same in eating. . . .

The people are not so laborious and industrious as the Netherlanders or French, as they lead for the most part an indolent life like the Spaniards; the most toilsome, difficult, and skilful works are chiefly performed by foreigners, as among the idle Spaniards. They have a great many sheep which bear fine wool, of which for these 200 years they have learnt to make fine cloth. They keep many lazy servants, and also many wild animals for their pleasure, rather than trouble themselves to cultivate the land. The island which they inhabit is very large, and abounds with fish; they have likewise the best harbours in Christendom. They are also rich in ships; nevertheless they do not catch as many fish as they require, so that they are obliged to buy more from their neighbours.

. . . The women there are entirely in the power of their husbands except for their lives, yet they are not kept so strictly as they are in Spain or elsewhere. Nor are they shut up, but they have the free management of the house or housekeeping, after the fashion of those of the Netherlands and others their neighbours. They go to market to buy what they like best to eat. They are well-dressed, fond of taking it easy, and commonly leave the care of household matters and drudgery to their servants. They sit before their doors, decked out in fine clothes, in order to see and be seen by the passers-by.

FYNES MORYSON
(1566–1617)

English traveller. In 1589, having had 'a great desire to see foreign countries' since his 'tender youth', he obtained a licence to travel, but did not set off until 1591 when he embarked on six years of incessant wandering in Europe. In Prague he dreamt of his father's death the day it occurred. In 1596 he visited the Holy Land, the Levant and Constantinople. Two years later he began to travel nearer home, in England, Scotland, and later in Ireland, where he helped to suppress the rebellion of the second Earl of Tyrone, Hugh O'Neill. Moryson was interested in the minutiae of travel – the inns he stayed in, food and drink, what things cost, the clothes people wore – which makes his *Itinerary* such a fascinating source of mundane information about his times.

On the diet of the Scots

My self was at a Knights house, who had many servants to attend him, that brought in his meate with their heads covered with blew caps, the Table being more then halfe furnished with great platters of porredge, each having a little peece of sodden meate; And when the Table was served, the servants did sit downe with us, but the upper messe in steede of porredge, had a Pullet with some prunes in the broth. And I observed no Art of Cookery, or furniture of Household stuffe, but rather rude neglect of both, though my selfe and my companion, sent from the Governour of Barwicke about bordering affaires, were entertained after their best manner. . . .

The Scots living then in factions, used to keepe many followers, and so consumed their revenew of victuals, living in some want of money. They vulgarly eate harth Cakes of Oates, but in Cities have also wheaten bread, which for the most part was bought by Courtiers, Gentlemen, and the best sort of Citizens.

An uncomplimentary view of the Irish, c. 1605

The wild and (as I may say) meere Irish, inhabiting many and large Provinces, are barbarous and most filthy in their diet. They skum the seething pot with an handfull of straw, and straine their milke taken from the Cow through a like handfull of straw, none of the cleanest, and so clense, or rather more defile the pot and milke. They devoure great morsels of beefe unsalted, and they eat commonly Swines flesh, seldom mutton, and all these pieces of flesh, as also the intralles of beasts unwashed, they seeth in a hollow tree, lapped in a raw Cowes hide, and so set over the fier, and therewith swallow whole lumps of filthy butter. Yea (which is more contrary to nature) they will feede on Horses dying of themselves, not only upon small want of flesh, but even for pleasure. . . .

Neither have they any Beere made of Malt and Hoppes, nor yet any Ale, no, not the chiefe Lords, except it be very rarely: but they drinke Milke like Nectar, warmed with a stone first cast into the fier, or else Beefe-broath mingled with milke: but when they come to any Market Towne, to sell a Cow or a Horse, they never returne home, till they have drunke the price in Spanish Wine (which they call the King of Spaines Daughter), or an Irish Usqueboagh, and till they have out-slept two or three daies drunkennesse. And not onely the common sort, but even the Lords and their wives, the more they want this drinke at home, the more they swallow it when they come to it, till they be as drunke as beggers.

Many of these wilde Irish eate no flesh, but that which dyes of disease or otherwise of it selfe, neither can it scape them for stinking. They desire no broath, nor have any use of a spoone. They can neither seeth Artichokes, nor eate them when they are sodden. It is strange and ridiculous, but most true, that some of our carriage Horses falling into their hands, when they found Sope and Starch, carried for the use of our Laundresses, they thinking them to bee some dainty meates, did eate them greedily, and when they stuck in their teeth, cursed bitterly the gluttony of us English churles, for so they terme us.

PETER MUNDY
(*fl.* 1600–1667)

English traveller. Beginning his career as a cabin-boy, he travelled extensively in Europe and the East, visiting India, China, Japan, Russia and many other countries. Indefatigable and curious about everything, he embellished his journal with lively drawings of various curiosities seen on his travels. In 1639 he made a 'Petty Progresse through some part of England and Wales'.

Summing up

7 things wherein England may bee said to excell. . . .
Imprimis, above all a peaceable and quiett enjoying off Gods true Religion.

Secondly, a temperate ayre and healthy Climate, taken one with another.

Thirdly, our aboundance and plenty off whatt Most usefull For the liffe off Man, especially in these Northerne parts, as Corne, woolle, Flesh, Fish, Tynne, Iron, lead, Seacole, etts., with all which our owne land is not only sufficiently served, butt Many Countries and Nationes Farre and Neare are supplied From us.

Fourthly, our Sciences and discipline For the well ordring off our peace att home and prevention of our enemies abroad, *viz.*, our two Famous universities off Oxfford and Cambridge etts. greatt schooles (Nurseries off learning both divine and humaine) For the Former. Then, For the latter, our well ordred Martiall companies, *viz.*, Trayned band, Artillery gardein, Military yard, due and tymely Musters all the land over, with our beacons in convenient places throughoutt the kingdome. This For the shoare. For the Sea: The Kings Navy Royall, with a Number off tall warlike Merchantts shippes, sodainly [immediately] ready For service off their King and Country.

Fifftly, For Trafficke and discoveries, *viz.*, soe many encorporated companies off Merchantts For Forraigne trade who employ their study and Meanes For the Encreas therof by adventuring their goodes and sending Fleetes and shippes into Most parts off the knowne world.

Sixtly, For excellencies off art. Among the rest St Paules great Church For the land and the greatt shippe *Royall Soveraigne* For the Sea, Not to bee paralelled in the world beeside, the Former For greattnesse and Cost, the latter, if not For greatnesse, yett For Cost and ex[q]uisite art in worckmanshippe; Allsoe in Westminster Abby, the like on the rossetts [rosettes, sculptured ornaments] off the Chappell and the Art and Richesse on the Monuments of Marble etts. Costly stones. London Bridge beeffore it was Fired. The Royall Exchange; the pretty contrived confformable shoppes over the Burse or New Exchange Moore Feilds; Sir Nicholas Caries gardein by London. All these in and aboutt the Citty.

Then Salisburies high and spiry steeple all of hewen stone, 133 yards, or 399 Foote, From the toppe off the Crosse to the ground; the Earle of Pembrokes pretty gardein by Wilton Near Salisbury; Stonehenge by Amesbury; the high square tower att Glocester with the church and whispring place therein; all our Cathedrall Churches in generall, as Salisbury, etts.; Our sweet and artificiall ringuing off tuneable bells. Thus much For the Artificiall.

Then For Naturall wonders. Mayneambar Stone, 8 Miles From Penrin in Cornewall, which I have More then once Mooved with one hand, waying by computation 11 or 12 tonnes, soe equally is it placed and poized naturally on a lesser.

The Hawthorne tree by Glacenbury [Glastonbury], Flowrishing in Winter.

The hotte and Medicinable springs off water att the Bathe.

The incredible sentt off our bloudhounds and hunting dogges, hardly to bee beeleived, were itt nott soe common to bee seene.

The Invincible courage off our Mastives and Fighting Cockes, Mayneteyning their duell oftentymes till death.

Off all these former Native blessings, excellencies, etts., my selffe am wittnesse and doe testifie thatt in all places thatt I have yett bin, scarce any one off them can be equalled. . . .

By report allsoe, there are Fountaines off Salt water Farre uppe in the land, wherwith they make very white salt; others thatt convert wood into stone. And if wee make bould with Scotland, there are Ilands in certaine lakes said to Floate and drive to and Fro with the winde with cattle and trees on them. Allsoe a Fowle to breed off trees, growing out off them as Fruite outt off others, which I partly beeleive, having heard itt conffirmed by some; butt it is to bee understood they are such trees as lie within the wash off the sea, a certaine shell Fish growing thereon, as oysters on rockes, or barnacles on shippes sides, which in tyme open, the yong Fowle droppe outt, groweth bigger, Flyeth abroad, and by the Country people are called Clawgeese. This requires Farther triall.

MARTIN MARTIN
(c. 1655–1719)

Scottish writer. Born on the Isle of Skye, he travelled extensively in the Western Islands of Scotland and in May 1697 sailed to St Kilda in an open boat. Reading Martin's *A Description of the Western Islands*, Dr Johnson remarked, 'No man now writes so ill as Martin's account of the Hebrides is written' – but this did not deter him from visiting Scotland himself with Martin's book in his baggage.

An inhabitant of St Kilda visits Glasgow in the early eighteenth century

Upon his arrival at Glasgow, he was like one that had dropt from the Clouds into a new World, whose Language, Habit, &c. were in all respects new to him: he never imagin'd that such big Houses of Stone were made with hands; and for the Pavements of the Streets, he thought it must needs be altogether Natural; for he could not believe that Men would be at the pains to beat stones into the ground to walk upon. He stood dumb at the door of his Lodging with the greatest admiration; and when he saw a Coach and two Horses, he thought it to be a little House they were drawing at their Tail, with Men in it; but he condemn'd the Coach-man for a Fool to sit so uneasy, for he thought it safer to sit on the horses back. The Mechanism of the Coach-Wheel, and its running about, was the greatest of all his Wonders.

When he went through the Streets, he desired to have one to lead him by the hand. Thomas Ross a merchant, and others, that took the diversion to carry him through the Town, ask'd his Opinion of the high Church? He answer'd, that it was a large Rock, yet there were some in St. Kilda much higher, but that these were the best Caves he ever saw. . . .

When he saw the Womens feet, he judged them to be of another shape than those of the Men, because of the different shape of their

Shoes. He did not approve of the heels of Shoes worn by Men or Women; and when he observ'd Horses with shoes on their Feet, and fastned with Iron Nails, he could not forbear laughing, and thought it the most ridiculous thing that ever fell under his Observation. He long'd to see his Native Country again, and passionately wish'd it were blessed with Ale, Brandy, Tobacco and Iron, as Glasgow was.

DANIEL DEFOE
(1660?–1731)

English writer. Author of *Robinson Crusoe, Moll Flanders* and *A Journal of the Plague Year*. Imprisoned in 1703 for writing a satire, *The Shortest Way with the Dissenters*, he was rescued by the Tory leader Robert Harley and subsequently acted as a confidential agent of the government, reporting the state of opinion in all parts of Britain. The results of these journeys he later gathered and refined into a book, *A Tour through the Whole Island of Great Britain* (1724–6).

The treacherous decoy ducks of the Lincolnshire Fens

The art of taking the fowls, and especially of breeding up a set of creatures, call'd decoy ducks, to entice and then betray their fellow-ducks into the several decoys, is very admirable indeed, and deserves a description; tho' 'tis not very easy to describe it, take it in as few words as I can.

The decoy ducks are first naturalised to the place, for they are hatch'd and bred up in the decoy ponds: There are in the ponds certain places where they are constantly fed, and where being made tame, they are used to come even to the decoy man's hand for their food.

When they fly abroad, or, as might be said, are sent abroad, they go none knows where; but 'tis believ'd by some they fly quite over the seas in Holland and Germany; There they meet with others of their acquaintance, that is to say, of their own kind, where sorting with them, and observing how poorly they live, how all the rivers are frozen up, and the lands cover'd with snow, and that they are almost starv'd, they fail not to let them know, (in language that they make one another understand) that in England, from whence they came, the case is quite alter'd; that the English ducks live much better than they do in those cold climates; that they have open lakes, and sea shores full of food, the tides flowing freely into every creek; that they have also within the land, large lakes, refreshing springs of water, open ponds, covered and secured from human eyes, with large rows of grown trees and impenetrable groves; that the lands are full of food, the stubbles yielding constant supplies of corn, left by the negligent husbandmen, as it were on purpose for their use, that 'tis not once in a wild duck's age, that they have any long frosts or deep snows, and that when they have, yet the sea is never frozen, or the shores void of food; and that if they will please but to go with them into England, they shall share with them in all these good things.

By these representations, made in their own duck language, (or by whatever other arts which we know not) they draw together a vast number of the fowls, and, in a word, kidnap them from their own country; for being once brought out of their knowledge, they follow the decoys, as a dog follows the huntsman; and 'tis frequent to see these subtle creatures return with a vast flight of fowls with them, or at their heels, as we may say, after the said decoy ducks have been absent several weeks together.

When they have brought them over, the first thing they do is to settle with them in the decoy ponds, to which they (the decoy ducks) belong: Here they chatter and gabble to them, in their own language, as if they were telling them, that these are the ponds they told them of, and here they should soon see how well they should live, how secure and how safe a retreat they had here.

When the decoy-men perceive they are come, and that they are gathering and encreasing, they fail not to go secretly to the pond's side, I say secretly, and under the cover which they have made with reeds, so that they cannot be seen, where they throw over the reeds handfuls of corn, in shallow places, such where the decoy ducks are usually fed, and where they are sure to come for it, and to bring their new guests with them for their entertainment.

This they do for two or three days together, and no harm follows, 'till throwing in this bait one time in an open wide place, another time in another open wide place, the third time it is thrown in a narrower place; that is to say, where the trees, which hang over the water and the banks, stand nearer, and then in another yet narrower, where the said trees are overhead like an arbour, though at a good hight from the water.

Here the boughs are so artfully managed, that a large net is spread near the tops of the trees among the branches, and fasten'd to hoops which reach from side to side: This is so high and so wide, and the room is so much below, and the water so open, that the fowls do not perceive the net above them at all.

Here the decoy-man keeping unseen, behind the hedges of reeds, which are made perfectly close, goes forward, throwing corn over the reeds into the water; the decoy ducks greedily fall upon it, and calling their foreign guests, seem to tell them, that now they may find their words good, and how well the ducks live in England; so inviting or rather wheedling them forward, 'till by degrees they are all gotten under the arch or sweep of the net, which is on the trees, and which by degrees, imperceptibly to them, declines lower and lower, and also narrower and narrower, 'till at the farther end it comes to a point like a purse; though this farther end is quite out of sight, and perhaps two or three hundred yards from the first entrance.

When the whole quantity are thus greedily following the leading ducks or decoys, and feeding plentifully as they go; and the decoy-man sees they are all within the arch of the net, and so far within as not to be able to escape, on a sudden a dog, which 'till then he keeps close by him, and who is perfectly taught his business, rushes from behind the reeds, and jumps into the water, swimming directly after the ducks, and (terribly to them) barking as he swims.

Immediately the ducks (frighted to the last degree) rise upon the wing to make their escape, but to their great surprize, are beaten down again by the arched net, which is over their heads: Being then forced into the water, they necessarily swim forward, for fear of that terrible creature the dog; and thus they crowd on, 'till by degrees the net growing lower and narrower, as is said, they are hurried to the very farther end, where another decoy-man stands ready to receive them, and who takes them out alive with his hands.

As for the traytors, that drew the poor ducks into this snare, they are taught to rise but a little way, and so not reaching to the net, they fly back to the ponds, and make their escape; or else, being used to the decoy-man, they go to him fearless, and are taken out as the rest; but instead of being kill'd with them, are strok'd, made much of, and put into a little pond just by him, and fed and made much of for their services.

CELIA FIENNES
(1662–1741)

English traveller. The daughter of a Cromwellian co-lonel, and an ardent nonconformist, between 1685 and 1710 she rode on horseback through every county in England. Her account of her journeys is a unique record of English social life at the end of the seventeenth century.

'Clouted creame' at St Austell, Cornwall, 1698

Well to pass on I went over some little heath ground, but mostly lanes and those stony and dirty 3 mile and halfe to Parr [Par]; here I ferry'd over againe, not but when the tyde is out you may ford it; thence I went over the heath and commons by the tinn mines, 3 miles and halfe to St. Austins [St Austell] which is a little Market town where I lay, but their houses are like barnes up to the top of the house; here was a pretty good dineing-roome and chamber within it, and very neate country women; my Landlady brought me one of the West Country tarts, this was the first I met with, though I had asked for them in many places in Sommerset and Devonshire, its an apple pye with a custard all on the top, its the most acceptable entertainment that could be made me; they scald their creame and milk in most parts of those countrys and so its a sort of clouted creame as we call it, with a little sugar, and soe put on the top of the apple pye; I was much pleased with my supper tho' not with the custome of the country, which is a universall smoaking both men women and children have all their pipes of tobacco in their mouths and soe sit round the fire smoaking, which was not delightful to me when I went down to talke with my Landlady for information of any matter and customs amongst them; I must say they are as comely sort of women as I have seen any where tho' in ordinary dress, good black eyes and crafty enough and very neate.

On the way to Land's End

Pensands [Penzance] is rightly named being all sands about it . . . it looks soe snugg and warme and truely it needs shelter haveing the sea on the other side and little or no fewell: turff and furse and ferne;

they have little or noe wood and noe coale which differences it from Darbyshire. . . . The Lands End is 10 mile farther, pretty good way but much up hills and down, pretty steep and narrow lanes, but its not shelter'd with trees or hedg rows this being rather desart and like the Peake Country in Darbyshire, dry stone walls and hills full of stones; but it is in most places better land and yeilds good corne both wheate barley and oates and some rhye; about 2 mile from Lands End I came in sight of the maine ocean on both sides, the south and north sea, and soe rode in its view till I saw them joyn'd at the poynt, and saw the Island of Sily [Scilly] which is 7 leagues off Lands End; they tell me that in a cleer day those in the Island can discern the people on the maine as they goe up the hill to Church, they can describe their clothes; this Church and little parish which is called Church town is about a mile from the poynt, the houses are but poor cottages like barns to look on, much like those in Scotland – but to doe my own Country its right the inside of their little cottages are clean and plaister'd, and such as you might comfortably eate and drink there, and for curiosity sake I dranck there, and met with very good bottled ale.

César de Saussure
(b. 1705)

Swiss traveller. In 1725 he left Lausanne and travelled for eleven years. In England between 1725 and 1730, he wrote regular letters home, which were circulated between at least 200 people in Berne, Geneva and Lausanne, including Voltaire. When he left England he accompanied Lord Kinnoull, the British Ambassador, to Constantinople, later becoming first secretary of the British Embassy there.

Lord Mayor's Day – a danger to foreigners

You cannot imagine the quantity of people there are at the windows, balconies, and in the streets to see the pageant pass. The Lord Mayor's Day is a great holiday in the City. The populace on that day is particularly insolent and rowdy, turning into lawless freedom the great liberty it enjoys. At these times it is almost dangerous for an honest man, and more particularly for a foreigner, if at all well dressed, to walk in the streets, for he runs a great risk of being insulted by the vulgar populace, which is the most cursed brood in existence. He is sure of not only being jeered at and being bespattered with mud, but as likely as not dead dogs and cats will be thrown at him, for the mob makes a provision beforehand of these playthings, so that they may amuse themselves with them on the great day. If the stranger were to get angry, his treatment would be all the worse. The best thing to be done on these occasions is not to run the risk of mixing with the crowd; but, should you desire to do so from curiosity, you had better dress yourself as simply as possible in the English fashion, and trust to pass unnoticed. I daresay it would interest you to hear of the style and the way Englishmen usually dress. They do not trouble themselves about dress, but leave that to their womenfolk. When the people see a well-dressed person in the streets, especially if he is wearing a braided coat, a plume in his hat, or his hair tied in a bow, he will, without doubt, be called 'French dog' twenty times perhaps before he reaches his destination. This name is the more common, and evidently, according to popular idea the greatest and most forcible insult that can be given to any man, and it is applied indifferently to all foreigners, French or otherwise.

JAMES BOSWELL
(1740–1795)

Scottish man of letters, friend and biographer of Samuel Johnson. (See p. 133.) In 1773 he accompanied Dr Johnson – who ten years previously had expressed the opinion that 'the noblest prospect a Scotsman ever sees is the high road that leads him to England' – on a tour of Scotland.

The evening effluvia of Edinburgh

Mr. Johnson and I walked arm-in-arm up the High Street to my house in James's Court; it was a dusky night; I could not prevent his being assailed by the evening effluvia of Edinburgh. I heard a late baronet of some distinction in the political world in the beginning of the present reign observe that 'walking the streets of Edinburgh at night was pretty perilous and a good deal odoriferous.' The peril is much abated by the care which the magistrates have taken to enforce the city laws against throwing foul water from the windows; but, from the structure of the houses in the old town, which consist of many storeys in each of which a different family lives, and there being no covered sewers, the odour still continues. A zealous Scotsman would have wished Mr. Johnson to be without one of his five senses upon this occasion. As we marched slowly along, he grumbled in my ear, 'I smell you in the dark!'

Dr Johnson loses his walking-stick on the sparsely-wooded island of Mull

He was more out of humour today than he has been in the course of our tour, being fretted to find that his little horse could scarcely support his weight; and having suffered a loss, which, though small in itself, was of some consequence to him while travelling the rugged steeps of Mull, where he was at times obliged to walk. The loss that I allude to was that of the large oak-stick, which, as I formerly mentioned, he had brought with him from London. It was of great use to him in our wild peregrination; for, ever since his last illness in 1766, he has had a weakness in his knees, and has not been able to walk easily. It had too the properties of a measure, for one nail was driven into it at the length of a foot, another at that of a yard. In return for the services it had done him, he said this morning he would make a present of it to some museum, but he little thought he was so soon to lose it. As he preferred riding with a switch, it was entrusted to a fellow to be delivered to our baggage-man, who followed us at some distance; but we never saw it more. I could not persuade him out of a suspicion that it had been stolen. 'No, no, my friend,' said he, 'it is not to be expected that any man in Mull who has got it will part with it. Consider, sir, the value of such a *piece of timber* here!'

A hut on the banks of Loch Ness

A good way up the Loch, I perceived a little hut with an oldish woman at the door of it. I knew it would be a scene for Mr. Johnson. So I spoke of it. 'Let's go in,' said he. So we dismounted, and we and our guides went in. It was a wretched little hovel, of earth only, I think; and for a window had just a hole which was stopped with a piece of turf which could be taken out to let in light. In the middle of the room (or space which we entered) was a fire of peat, the smoke going out at a hole in the roof. She had a pot upon it with goat's flesh boiling. She had at one end, under the same roof but divided with a kind of partition made of wands, a pen or fold in which we saw a good many kids.

Mr. Johnson asked me where she slept. I asked one of the guides, who asked her in Erse. She spoke with a kind of high tone. He told us she was afraid we wanted to go to bed to her. This coquetry, or whatever it may be called, of so wretched a like being was truly ludicrous. Mr. Johnson and I afterwards made merry upon it. I said it was he who alarmed the poor woman's virtue. 'No, sir,' said he. 'She'll say, "There came a wicked young fellow, a wild young dog, who I believe would have ravished me had there not been with him a grave old gentleman who repressed him. But when he gets out of the sight of his tutor, I'll warrant you he'll spare no woman he meets, young or old."' 'No,' said I. 'She'll say, "There was a terrible ruffian who would have forced me, had it not been for a gentle, mild-looking youth, who, I take it, was an angel."'

JAMES WOODFORDE
(1740–1803)

English clergyman. From 1758 until October 1802, less than three months before he died, Parson Woodforde kept a diary of his life as a curate in Oxford and Somerset and then as vicar of Weston Longville, Norfolk. A mine of information about rural life and often very funny, it has deservedly become a classic.

A coach ride to Bath in 1793

JUNE 28, FRIDAY. We got up about 4 o'clock this morning and at 5 got into the Bath Coach from the Angel and set off for Bath. Briton on the top of the Coach. The Coach carries only 4 inside Passengers. We had a very fat Woman with a Dog and many band boxes, which much incommoded us, and also a poor sickly good kind of a Man that went with us. We breakfasted at Maidenhead on Coffee & Tea. For Strawberries at Maidenhead pd. o. 1. o. For our breakfasts pd. o. 2. o. We were very near meeting with an Accident in Reading, passing a Waggon, but thank God we got by safe and well. It was owing to the Coachman. As we went out of Reading we met a Regiment of Soldiers, some Militia going into Reading. At Reading there were two young Gentlemen by name Jolliffe that got up on the top of the Coach, being going home from School for the Vacation. I remembered their Father at Winchester School. We dined at the Pelican Inn, Speanham Land. The young Gentlemen dined with us, I franked them. Their Father lives about 10 Miles beyond Bath. For our Dinners, Coachman &c. pd. abt. 14. o. Paid at Speenham Land for extra Luggage abt. 4. o. About 10 o'clock this Evening, thank God, we got safe and well to Bath, to the White Hart Inn, where we supped & slept – a very noble Inn. Found our Friends Mr. and Mrs. Pounsett & Daughter at Bath, at Lodgings in the Orange-Grove, at one Roubelles, all tolerably well. Mr. Pounsett better for being at Bath. They were very glad to see us. For Extraordinaries on the road to day pd. abt. 2. 6. As soon as the young Jolliffes got to Bath, they hired a Chaise immediately & set off for home. The fat Lady that came with us, supped with us. It was rather late before we got to bed. We were very happy to find that our friends were not gone from Bath. We are to have Lodgings to Morrow in the same house with them.

CARL PHILIP MORITZ
(1757–1793)

German traveller. In 1782 he visited England, writing a
vivid account of his travels. Four years later he went to
Italy, where he met Goethe in Rome.

Leicester to Northampton by coach: a prospect of certain death

... This ride from Leicester to Northampton, I shall remember as
long as I live.

The coach drove from the yard through a part of the house. The
inside passengers got in, in the yard; but we on the outside were
obliged to clamber up in the public street, because we should have
had no room for our heads to pass under the gateway.

My companions on the top of the coach were a farmer, a young
man very decently dressed, and a black-a-moor. The getting up
alone was at the risk of one's life; and when I was up, I was obliged
to sit just at the corner of the coach, with nothing to hold by but a
sort of little handle fastened on the side. I sat nearest the wheel, and
the moment that we set off, I fancied that I saw certain death await
me. All I could do, was to take still faster hold of the handle, and to
be more and more careful to preserve my balance.

The machine now rolled along with prodigious rapidity, over
the stones through the town, and every moment we seemed to fly
into the air; so that it was almost a miracle that we still stuck to the
coach, and did not fall. We seemed to be thus on the wing, and to fly,
as often as we passed through a village, or went down a hill.

At last the being continually in fear of my life became insupportable, and as we were going up a hill, and consequently proceeding
rather slower than usual, I crept from the top of the coach, and got
snug into the basket.

'O, sir, sir, you will be shaken to death!' said the black; but I
flattered myself he exaggerated the unpleasantness of my post.

As long as we went up hill, it was easy and pleasant. And, having
had little or no sleep the night before, I was almost asleep among the
trunks and the packages; but how was the case altered when we
came to go down hill, then all the trunks and parcels began, as it

were, to dance around me, and every thing in the basket seemed to be alive; and I every moment received from them such violent blows, that I thought my last hour was come. . . . I was obliged to suffer this torture nearly an hour, till we came to another hill again, when quite shaken to pieces, and badly bruised, I again crept to the top of the coach, and took possession of my former seat. . . .

We at last reached Northampton, where I immediately went to bed, and have slept almost till noon. Tomorrow morning I intend to continue my journey to London in some other stage-coach.

WILLIAM COBBETT
(1763–1835)

English journalist and reformer. He was the son of a farm labourer from Farnham, Surrey, a county he later described as having 'some of the worst lands, not only in England, but in the world'. Outspoken, radical (his journal *The Political Register* had an enormous influence), he twice had to flee to America to evade prosecution. His *Rural Rides* (1830) is a classic account of the situation of the rural poor and a vivid portrait of the English countryside.

'That villainous hole': Cricklade, Wiltshire, 1821

I passed through that villainous hole, Cricklade, about two hours ago; and, certainly, a more rascally looking place I never set my eyes on. I wished to avoid it, but could get along no other way. All along here the land is a whitish stiff loam upon a bed of soft stone, which is found at various distances from the surface, sometimes two feet and sometimes ten. Here and there a field is fenced with this stone, laid together in walls without mortar or earth. All the houses and out-houses are made of it, and even covered with the thinnest of it formed into tiles. The stiles in the fields are made of large flags of this stone, and the gaps in the hedges are stopped with them. – There is very little wood all along here. The labourers seems miserably poor. Their dwellings are little better than pig-beds, and their looks indicate that their food is not nearly equal to that of a pig. Their wretched hovels are stuck upon little bits of ground *on the road side*, where the space has been wider than the road demanded. In many places they have not two rods to a hovel, it seems as if they had been swept off the fields by a hurricane, and had dropped and found shelter under the banks on the road side! Yesterday morning was a sharp frost; and this had set the poor creatures to digging up their little plats of potatoes. In my whole life I never saw human wretchedness equal to this: no, not even amongst the free negroes in America, who, on an average, do not work one day out of four. And this is *prosperity*, is it? These, O Pitt! are the fruits of thy hellish system! However, this *Wiltshire* is a horrible county. This is the county that the *Gallon-loaf* man belongs to. The land all along here is good. Fine fields, and pastures all around; and yet the cultivators of those fields so miserable!

FRANÇOIS DE LA ROCHEFOUCAULD
(1765–1848)

French soldier and politician. De la Rochefoucauld was sent to England in 1784 at the age of eighteen to further his education. The place chosen for his stay was Bury St Edmunds in Suffolk, on the grounds that there the rainfall was low and the English pure. With his brother and a friend, he rented a house in Bury, and throughout his stay in England he kept notes of the people and places and customs of the inhabitants.

A day at an English country house

Throughout England it is the custom to breakfast together, the meal resembling a dinner or supper in France. The commonest breakfast-hour is 9 o'clock and by that time the ladies are fully dressed with their hair properly done for the day. Breakfast consists of tea and bread and butter in various forms. In the houses of the rich you have coffee, chocolate and so on. The morning newspapers are on the table and those who want to do so, read them during breakfast, so that the conversation is not of a lively nature. At 10 o'clock or 10.30 each member of the party goes off on his own pursuit – hunting, fishing, or walking. So the day passes till 4 o'clock, but at 4 o'clock precisely you must present yourself in the drawing-room with a great deal more ceremony than we are accustomed to in France. This sudden change of social manners is quite astonishing and I was deeply struck by it. In the morning you come down in riding-boots and a shabby coat, you sit where you like, you behave exactly as if you were by yourself, no one takes any notice of you, and it is all extremely comfortable. But in the evening, unless you have just arrived, you must be well-washed and well-groomed. The standard of politeness is uncomfortably high – strangers go first into the dining-room and sit near the hostess and are served in seniority in accordance with a rigid etiquette. In fact for the first few days I was tempted to think that it was done for a joke. . . .

After the sweets, you are given water in small bowls of very clean glass in order to rinse out your mouth – a custom which strikes me as extremely unfortunate. . . . This ceremony over, the cloth is removed and you behold the most beautiful table that it is possible to see. It is indeed remarkable that the English are so much given to the use of mahogany. . . . After the removal of the cloth, the table is covered with all kinds of wine. . . .

At this point all the servants disappear. The ladies drink a glass or two of wine and at the end of half an hour all go out together. It is then that real enjoyment begins – there is not an Englishman who is not supremely happy at this particular moment. One proceeds to drink – sometimes in an alarming measure. . . .

Sometimes conversation becomes extremely free upon highly indecent topics – complete licence is allowed and I have come to the conclusion that the English do not associate the same ideas with certain words that we do. Very often I have heard things mentioned in good society which would be in the grossest taste in France.

HSIEH CH'ING-KAO
(1765–1822)

Chinese sailor. At the age of eighteen he boarded a foreign trading ship and spent the next fourteen years visiting the major ports of Europe, America and Asia. When he was thirty-one he went blind and returned to China. There, two years before he died, he was visited by a young friend who noted down the illiterate sailor's impressions of the West.

Lun-lun

England is located southwest [*sic*] of France and could be reached by sailing north from St. Helena for about two months. . . . Near the sea is Lun-lun [London], which is one of the largest cities in the country. In this city is a fine system of waterworks. From the river, which flows through the city, water is raised by means of revolving wheels, installed at three different places, and poured into pipes which carry it to all parts of the city. Anyone desirous of securing water would just have to lay a pipe between his house and the water mains, and water would be available. The water tax for each family is calculated on the number of persons in that family.

Men and women all wear white ordinarily; for mourning, however, black is used. The army wears a red uniform. Women wear long dresses that sweep the floor, with the upper part tight and the lower part loose. At the waist is a tight belt with a buckle. Whenever there is a celebration of festive occasion, then some young and beautiful girls would be asked to sing and dance to the accompaniment of music. Girls of rich and noble families start to learn these arts when they are very young.

LOUIS SIMOND
(1767–1831)

French traveller. Simond was born in France but had lived in the USA for more than twenty years before his arrival in England in 1809 for a two-year visit. His *Journal* was written in English. He had an English wife and owed to her his 'introduction [to] a greater share of domestic intimacy than foreigners usually enjoy in England'.

An English dinner – the unavoidable consequences of drinking

There are some customs here not quite consistent with that scrupulous delicacy on which the English pique themselves. Towards the end of dinner, and before the ladies retire, bowls of coloured glass full of water are placed before each person. All (women as well as men) stoop over it, sucking up some of the water, and returning it, perhaps more than once, and, with a spitting and washing sort of noise, quite charming, – the operation frequently assisted by a finger elegantly thrust into the mouth! This done, and the hands dipped also, the napkins, and sometimes the table-cloth, are used to wipe hand and mouth. This, however, is nothing to what I am going to relate. Drinking much and long leads to unavoidable consequences. Will it be credited, that, in a corner of the very dining-room, there is a certain convenient piece of furniture, to be used by any body who wants it. The operation is performed very deliberately and undisguisedly, as a matter of course, and occasions no interruption of the conversation. I once took the liberty to ask why this convenient article was not placed out of the room, in some adjoining closet; and was answered, that, in former times, when good fellowship was more strictly enforced than in these degenerate days, it had been found that men of weak heads or stomachs took advantage of the opportunity to make their escape shamefully, before they were quite drunk; and that it was to guard against such an enormity that this nice expedient had been invented.

The ladies of Llangollen

Near Llangollen, where we dined, is the residence of two ladies, whose names are identified with the vale, Lady E. Butler and Miss Ponsonby; and after having informed ourselves of the etiquette of the place, we dispatched a note requesting permission to see the grounds, announcing ourselves, in hopes of strengthening our claim, as American travellers. The ladies, however, were cruel, and answered, 'it was not convenient to permit the place to be seen that day.' The landlady, who had overheard some words of French spoken among us, observed that the ladies were fond of the French language, and that, if we had petitioned in French, we should have been admitted. The hint came too late. . . .

. . . French readers may wish to learn something of these ladies. Their story is understood to be, that with birth, beauty, and fortune, they embraced, in the prime of their youths, half a century ago, the romantic idea of consecrating the remainder of their lives to pure friendship, far from the world, its vanities, its pleasures, and its pains; and, literally running away from their families in Ireland, with a faithful woman-servant, lately dead, they hid themselves in this then profound solitude, where they have lived ever since. . . . Llangollen is, like all the little old towns of this and all countries, a hideous object.

JACQUES LOUIS DE BOUGRENET, CHEVALIER DE LA TOCNAYE
(fl. 1792–1798)

French cavalry officer. He came to England in 1792, fleeing the Revolution. A tour of England and a two-year stay in Scotland produced his *Promenade dans La Grande Bretagne* (1795). He then decided to travel in Ireland, walking the length and breadth of the country in 1796–7, carrying his possessions in three bundles slung across his shoulder. His account of the journey, translated as *A Frenchman's Walk through Ireland* (1798), is a fascinating account of Ireland just before the 1798 Rebellion.

A French traveller's equipment

At Limerick I was obliged entirely to renew my wardrobe, which at the time of my departure from Dublin consisted only of my clothes and what could be contained in two silk stockings from which I had cut the feet. Although my baggage was inconsiderable, I wanted for nothing, and had the means of appearing in society as well dressed as others.

For the information of future travellers on foot, it is my pleasure here to give details of my complete equipment.

A powder bag made out of a woman's glove.
A razor.
Thread.
Needles.
Scissors.
A comb, carried in one of a pair of dress shoes.
A pair of silk stockings.
Breeches, fine enough to be, when folded, not bigger than a fist.
Two very fine shirts.
Three cravats.
Three handkerchiefs.
The clothes in which I travelled.

The sundries I divided in three, two lots going into the silk stockings which served as bags, the third packet contained my shoes. I had six pockets: in three of them were stowed the packets, as described, when I was about to enter a house of consequence; but as this packing would be very inconvenient while walking, I was accustomed, on the road, to tie my three packets in a handkerchief and carry the load over my shoulder at the end of my sword-stick, on which I had grafted an umbrella which excited, everywhere, curiosity, and made the girls laugh – I can't tell why. The remaining pockets were reserved for letters, my pocket-book, and ordinary uses.

The persons who received me, and whose offers of linen I always refused, were much astonished to see me reappear in the drawing-room in silk stockings and powder, as if I had travelled with considerable baggage at my ease, and in a fine carriage.

Surprises in Galway

Crossing the beautiful bay of Galway I came to the town of same name. It is situated between a great lake and the sea without deriving much advantage from one or other. The river leaving the lake a quarter mile from the sea flows like a torrent, no effort has been made to construct a canal, and the port is outside the town.

One is surprised, on entering Galway, to see the disposition of the streets, and especially the placing of the houses, which is different from that in other Irish towns. Almost every one has the gable turned to the street, and has a *porte cochère*, such as is found in old towns on the Continent. Galway was built, they say, by the Spanish, to whom it belonged. . . .

This city had formerly an extensive commerce, but it is much decayed in recent times. Efforts are needed for the encouragement of industry, and it is desirable that some means should be adopted to make beggars work, and prevent lunatics from running about the streets.

A wine merchant gave me, in good faith, an explanation of the decay of commerce. 'Before France knew how to make wine,' said he, 'we made it here.' 'What,' said I, 'I never heard that you grew grapes at Galway.' 'Oh, we never did,' he replied, 'but in France the wine was simply juice of the grape, and we brought it to Galway to make it drinkable. Unfortunately, the Bordeaux merchants can prepare it now as well as we did, and that has cut the feet from under us.'

DOROTHY WORDSWORTH
(1771–1855)

English diarist, sister of William Wordsworth. She lived
with her brother for much of his life and her diary entries
provided inspiration for many of his poems. In 1803 she
accompanied him and Coleridge on a walking tour in
Scotland. Coleridge dropped out at early stage of the
journey, possibly because the Wordsworths had discovered his dependence on opium.

A ferryman's hut on the shores of Loch Katrine, Perthshire, 27 August 1803

We caroused our cups of coffee, laughing like children at the strange
atmosphere in which we were: the smoke came in gusts, and spread
along the walls and above our heads in the chimney, where the hens
were roosting like light clouds in the sky. We laughed and laughed
again, in spite of the smarting of our eyes, yet had a quieter pleasure
in observing the beauty of the beams and rafters gleaming between
the clouds of smoke. They had been crusted over and varnished by
many winters, till, where the firelight fell upon them, they were as
glossy as black rocks on a sunny day cased in ice. When we had
eaten our supper we sate about half an hour, and I think I had never
felt so deeply the blessing of a hospitable welcome and a warm fire.
When I went to bed, the mistress, desiring me to 'go ben,' attended
me with a candle, and assured me that the bed was dry, though not
'sic as I had been used to.' . . .

The walls of the whole house were of stone unplastered. It
consisted of three apartments – the cow-house at one end, the
kitchen or house in the middle, and the spence at the other end. The
rooms were divided, not up to the rigging, but only to the beginning
of the roof, so that there was a free passage for light and smoke from
one end of the house to the other.

I went to bed some time before the family. The door was shut
between us, and they had a bright fire, which I could not see; but the
light it sent up among the varnished rafters and beams, which
crossed each other in almost as intricate and fantastic a manner as I
have seen the underboughs of a large bench-tree withered by the
depth of the shade above, produced the most beautiful effect that

can be conceived. It was like what I should suppose an underground cave or temple to be, with a dripping or moist roof, and the moonlight entering in upon it by some means or other, and yet the colours were more like melted gems. I lay looking up till the light of the fire faded away, and the man and his wife and child had crept into their bed at the other end of the room. I did not sleep much, but passed a comfortable night, for my bed, though hard, was warm and clean: the unusualness of my situation prevented me from sleeping. I could hear the waves beat against the shore of the lake; a little 'syke' close to the door made a much louder noise; and when I sate up in my bed I could see the lake through an open window-place at the bed's head. Add to this, it rained all night.

Prince Hermann Pückler-Muskau
(1785–1871)

German prince. Handsome, dashing and brave, he was a great traveller, a gifted writer and a talented landscape gardener. He travelled throughout Europe, the Near East, and Africa and, according to his first biographer, had more loves than Don Juan and Solomon put together. In 1817 he married Lucie, Countess of Pappenheim, but immediately ran through her fortune improving his estate (he planted more than a million trees during their engagement alone). The only solution to their financial ruin was to divorce and for Pückler-Muskau to seek a new heiress. The divorce was made absolute in 1826 and in the autumn of that year he set off for London. During his two-year stay he wrote to Lucie almost every day. He did not find a wife, but the publication of these letters, suitably edited, brought him literary fame.

An audience with King George IV, December 1826

I ought to have begun by telling you that I was presented to the King today, at a great Levée. – I give it you as a proof of the extraordinary voluntary seclusion of the present sovereign, that our Secretary of Legation was presented with me *for the first time*, though he has been here in that capacity for two years. His Majesty has a very good memory. He immediately recollected my former visit to England, though he mistook the date of it by several years. I took occasion to make my compliments to him on the extraordinary embellishment of London since that time, which indeed is to be ascribed in great measure to him. After a gracious reply, I passed on, and placed myself in a convenient station for seeing the whole spectacle. It was odd enough.

The King, on account of the feeble state of his health, remained seated; – the company marched past him in a line; each made his bow, was addressed or not, and then either placed himself in the row on the other side of the room, or quitted it. All those who had received any appointment kneeled down before the king and kissed his hand, at which the American Minister, near whom I had accidentally placed myself, made a rather satirical face. The clergymen and lawyers in their black gowns and white powdered wigs, short and long, had a most whimsical masquerading appearance. One of them was the object of an almost universal ill-suppressed laugh. This personage had kneeled to be 'knighted,' as the English call it, and in this posture, with the long fleece on his head, looked exactly like a sheep at the slaughter-block. His Majesty signed to the great Field Marshal to give him his sword. For the first time, perhaps, the great warrior could not draw the sword from the scabbard; he pulled and pulled, – all in vain. The king waiting with outstretched arm; the Duke vainly pulling with all his might; the unhappy martyr prostrate in silent resignation, as if expecting his end, and the whole brilliant Court standing around in anxious expectation: – it was a group worthy of Gilray's pencil. At length the state weapon started like a flash of lightning from its sheath. His Majesty grasped it impatiently, – indeed his arm was probably weary and benumbed with being so long extended, – so that the sword, instead of alighting on a new knight, fell on an old wig, which for a moment enveloped king and subject in a cloud of powder.

The living skeleton and the fattest woman in the world, London, July 1827

On my way home I passed a booth where a man was calling out that here were the famous German dwarf and his three dwarf children; the living skeleton; and, to conclude, the fattest girl that ever was seen. I paid my shilling, and went in. After waiting a quarter of an hour, till five other spectators arrived, the curtain was drawn up, and the most impertinent 'charlatanerie' exhibited that ever I witnessed. The living skeleton was a very ordinary-sized man, not much thinner than I. As an excuse for our disappointment, we were assured that when he arrived from France he was a skeleton, but that since he had eaten good English beef steaks, it had been found impossible to check his tendency to corpulence.

The fattest woman in the world was a perfect pendant to the skeleton. She was not fatter than the Queen of Virginia Water.

GEORGE BORROW
(1803–1881)

English writer and traveller. (See p. 151.) During the summer and autumn of 1854 he went on a walking tour of Wales, where, accompanied as he was by his wife and stepdaughter, 'he found it impossible to indulge his bohemian proclivities'.

A man and his mort on the way to Llangedwin

After an hour's walking I overtook two people, a man and a woman laden with baskets, which hung around them on every side. The man was a young fellow of about eight-and-twenty, with a round face, fair flaxen hair, and rings in his ears; the female was a blooming buxom lass of about eighteen. After giving them the sele of the day, I asked them if they were English.

'Aye, aye, master,' said the man; 'we are English.'

'Where do you come from?' said I.

'From Wrexham,' said the man.

'I thought Wrexham was in Wales,' said I.

'If it be,' said the man, 'the people are not Welsh; a man is not a horse because he happens to be born in a stable.'

'Is that young woman your wife?' said I.

'Yes,' said he, 'after a fashion' – and then he leered at the lass, and she leered at him.

'Do you attend any place of worship?' said I.

'A great many, master!'

'What place do you chiefly attend?' said I.

'The Chequers, master!'

'Do they preach the best sermons there?' said I.

'No, master! but they sells the best ale there.'

'Do you worship ale?' said I.

'Yes, master; I worships ale.'

'Anything else?' said I.

'Yes, master! I and my mort worships something besides good ale; don't we, Sue?' and then he leered at the mort, who leered at him, and both made odd motions backwards and forwards, causing the baskets which hung around them to creak and rustle, and uttering loud shouts of laughter, which roused the echoes of the neighbouring hills.

FANNY KEMBLE
(1809–1893)

English actress and writer. A member of a renowned family actors (Sarah Siddons was her aunt), she went to America in 1833 and married a Georgian plantation-owner. They separated in 1846 and she returned to England. Her biographer describes her as having 'a sparkling, saucy, and rather boisterous individuality' and a string of elderly admirers, including Macaulay, Long-fellow, and Edward Fitzgerald, translator of *The Rubaiyat of Omar Khayyam*. She was twenty-one when she travelled on the Liverpool–Manchester Railway, which was opened in 1830. The promoters had offered a prize for the most efficient locomotive, which was won by Stephenson's Rocket. Miss Kemble may well have been the first woman to travel by train.

A trip on Stephenson's Rocket, August 1830

My father knew several of the gentlemen most deeply interested in the undertaking [the Liverpool-Manchester railway], and Stephenson having proposed a trial trip as far as the fifteen-mile viaduct, they, with infinite kindness, invited him and permitted me to accompany them; allowing me, moreover, the place which I felt to be one of supreme honour, by the side of Stephenson. . . . He was a rather stern-featured man, with a dark and deeply-marked countenance; his speech was strongly inflected with his native Northumbrian accent. . . .

. . . We were introduced to the little engine which was to drag us along the rails. . . . This snorting little animal, which I felt rather inclined to pat, was then harnessed to our carriage, and, Mr. Stephenson having taken me on the bench of the engine with him, we started at about ten miles an hour. The steam-horse being ill-adapted for going up and down hill, the road was kept at a certain level, and appeared sometimes to sink below the surface of the earth, and sometimes to rise above it. Almost at starting it was cut through the solid rock, which formed a wall on either side of it, about sixty feet high. You can't imagine how strange it seemed to be journeying on thus, without any visible cause of progress other than the magical machine, with its flying white breath and rhythmical, unvarying pace. . . . We were to go only fifteen miles, that distance being sufficient to show the speed of the engine. . . . After proceeding through this rocky defile, we presently found ourselves raised upon embankments ten or twelve feet high; we then came to a moss, or swamp, of considerable extent, on which no human foot could tread without sinking, and yet it bore the road which bore us. This had been the great stumbling-block in the minds of the committee of the House of Commons; but Mr. Stephenson has succeeded in overcoming it. . . .

We had now come fifteen miles, and stopped where the road traversed a wide and deep valley. Stephenson made me alight and led me down to the bottom of this ravine, over which, in order to keep his road level, he has thrown a magnificent viaduct of nine arches, the middle one of which is seventy feet high, through which we saw the whole of this beautiful little valley. . . . We then rejoined the rest of the party, and the engine having received its supply of water, the carriage was placed behind it, for it cannot turn, and was set off at its utmost speed, thirty-five miles an hour, swifter than a bird flies (for they tried the experiment with a snipe). You cannot conceive what that sensation of cutting the air was; the motion is as smooth as possible, too. I could either have read or written.

***

WILLIAM MAKEPEACE THACKERAY
(1811–1863)

English novelist. (See p. 64.) In 1842 he visited Ireland, where, once he had survived the horrors of the Irish packet, he thoroughly enjoyed himself.

Killarney Races

By this time we are got upon the course, which is really one of the most beautiful spots that ever was seen: the lake and mountains lying along two sides of it, and of course visible from all. They were busy putting up the hurdles when we arrived: stiff bars and poles, four feet from the ground, with furze-bushes over them. The grand stand was already full; along the hedges sat thousands of the people, sitting at their case doing nothing, and happy as kings. A daguerreotype would have been of great service to have taken their portraits, and I never saw a vast multitude of heads and attitudes so picturesque and lively. The sun lighted up the whole course and the lakes with amazing brightness, though behind the former lay a huge rack of the darkest clouds, against which the cornfields and meadows shone in the brightest green and gold, and a row of white tents was quite dazzling.

There was a brightness and intelligence about this immense Irish crowd, which I don't remember to have seen in an English one. The women in their blue cloaks, with red smiling faces peering from one end, and bare feet from the other, had seated themselves in all sort of pretty attitudes of cheerful contemplation; and the men, who are accustomed to lie about, were doing so now with all their might – sprawling on the banks, with as much ease and variety as club-room loungers on their soft cushions – or squatted leisurely among the green potatoes. The sight of so much happy laziness did one good to look on. Nor did the honest fellows seem to weary of this amusement. Hours passed on, and the gentlefolks (judging from our party) began to grow somewhat weary; but the finest peasantry in Europe never budged from their posts, and continued to indulge in greetings, indolence, and conversation.

ALEXANDER HERZEN
(1812–1870)

Russian philosopher and writer. In 1847 he emigrated to Paris, where he was active during the 1848 revolution. From 1852–1864 he lived in London, where his house became a meeting-place for emigrés of all nationalities.

On the need to travel

Ten years ago, as I was going through the Haymarket late one cold, raw winter evening, I came upon a Negro, a lad of seventeen; he was barefooted and without a shirt, and on the whole rather undressed for the tropics than dressed for London. Shivering all over, with his teeth chattering, he asked me for alms. Two days later I met him again, and then again and again. Eventually I got into conversation with him. He spoke a broken Anglo-Spanish, but it was not hard to understand the sense of his words.

'You are young and strong,' I said to him, 'why don't you look for work?'

'No one will give it me.'

'Why is that?'

'I know no one who would give me a character.'

'Where do you come from?'

'From a ship.'

'What ship?'

'A Spanish one; the captain beat me a lot, so I left.'

'What were you doing on board the ship?'

'Everything: brushed the clothes, washed up, did the cabins.'

'What do you mean to do?'

'I don't know.'

'But you will die of cold and hunger, you know, or anyhow you will certainly get a fever.'

'What am I to do?' said the Negro in despair, looking at me and shivering all over with cold.

Well, I thought, here goes. It is not the first stupid thing I've done in my life.

'Come with me. I'll give you clothes and a corner to sleep in; you shall sweep my rooms, light the fires and stay as long as you like, if you behave quietly and properly. *Si no – no.*'

The Negro jumped for joy.

Within a week he was fatter, and gaily did the work of four. In this way he spent six months with us; then one evening he appeared before my door, stood a little while in silence and then said to me:

'I have come to say good-bye.'

'How's that?'

'It's enough for now: I am going.'

'Has anybody been nasty to you?'

'No, indeed, I am pleased with everyone.'

'Then where are you going?'

'To a ship.'

'What for?'

'I am dreadfully sick of it, I can't stand it, I shall do a mischief if I stay. I need the sea. I will go away and come back again, but for now it is enough.'

I made an effort to stop him; he stayed on for three days, and then announced for the second time it was beyond his powers, that he must go away, that 'for now it is enough'.

That was in the spring. In the autumn he turned up once more, tropically divested, and again I clothed him; but he soon began playing various nasty tricks, and even threatened to kill me, so I was obliged to turn him away.

These last facts are irrelevant, but the point is that I completely share the Negro's outlook. After living a long time in one place and in the same rut, I feel that for a certain time *it is enough*, that I must refresh myself with other horizons and other faces . . . and at the same time must retire into myself, strange as that sounds. The superficial distractions of the journey do not interfere.

There are people who prefer to get away *inwardly*, some with the help of a powerful imagination and an ability to abstract themselves from their surroundings (for this a special endowment is needed, bordering on genius and insanity), some with the help of opium or alcohol. Russians, for instance, will have a drinking-bout for a week or two, and then go back to their homes and duties. I prefer shifting my whole body to shifting my brain, and going round the world to letting my head go round.

Perhaps it is because I have a bad head after too much to drink.

ALPHONSE ESQUIROS
(1814–1876)

French writer and politician. Author of an extraordinary book entitled *The English at Home* in which he explores, *inter alia*, the relationship between geology and national character.

The Celtic rats of Wapping

The old Celtic race has left in Great Britain another representative we might hardly expect: it is the rat. I was walking one night with a Scotch naturalist in Wapping, that poorest, most ill-famed, ugliest, oldest, and yet most picturesque part of London. Here you see docks, suffrance wharfs, sail, anchor, and rope factories; sailors of every country and colour lodge in equivocal houses in narrow streets; a muddy pavement, crushed by the wheels, sees every day the riches of a universe passing by on heavy carts. We went down Wapping Old Stairs, celebrated in sailors' songs; the moon shed a sickly light over the Thames, and, except the voice of the river, all was silent. On the muddy worn steps we witnessed a fight between two rats of different size and colour, and the weaker of the adversaries was killed by the stronger ere we had time to interfere. My friend gave vent to a sigh. 'Poor Briton!' he exclaimed, 'such is your fate. Everywhere you succumb to the assaults of invaders. But a short time longer and the naturalist will seek you in vain on the surface of your native isles!' He then explained to me that there were two sorts of rats in England – the black and the brown: the brown rat, so the tradition runs, came from Germany in the vessel that brought a new dynasty – the House of Hanover. This intruder, the Hanoverian rat, has gradually destroyed the native, or old Celtic rat, which can only be met with in some remote parts of England, and at Wapping.

231

QUEEN VICTORIA
(1819–1901)

Queen of Great Britain and Ireland and Empress of India. In 1840 she married Prince Albert of Saxe-Coburg-Gotha and he became the dominant influence in her life. Victoria travelled widely in Europe, but never went further afield because she was a bad sailor. She saw comparatively little of England (indeed in some counties which she had never visited at all she was known as 'the Great Unseen'), but often toured the Scottish Highlands when staying at Balmoral.

The inn at Dalwhinnie: no pudding and no fun, 8 October 1861

It became cold and windy with occasional rain. At length, and not till a quarter to nine, we reached the inn of Dalwhinnie – 29 miles from where we had left our ponies, – which stands by itself, away from any village. Here, again, there were a few people assembled, and I thought they knew us; but it seems they did not, and it was only when we arrived that one of the maids recognised me. She had seen me at Aberdeen and Edinburgh. We went upstairs: the inn was much larger than at Fettercairn, but not nearly so nice and cheerful; there was a drawing-room and a dining-room, and we had a very good-sized bedroom. Albert had a dressing-room of equal size. Mary Andrews (who was very useful and efficient) and Lady Churchill's maid had a room together, every one being in the house, but unfortunately there was hardly anything to eat, and there was only tea, and two miserable starved Highland chickens, without any potatoes! No pudding, and no *fun*; no little maid (the two there not wishing to come in), nor our two people – who were wet and drying our and their things – to wait on us! It was not a nice supper, and the evening was wet. As it was late we soon retired to rest.

Mary and Maxted (Lady Churchill's maid) had been dining below with Grant, Brown, and Stewart (who came, the same as last time, with the maids) in the 'commercial room' at the foot of the stairs. They had only the remnants of our two starved chickens!

BAYARD TAYLOR
(1825–1878)

American journalist and poet. He travelled widely in
Europe, Africa and the Far East, in 1844–6 walking
through England, France, Germany and Italy. His translation of Goethe's *Faust* earned him the appointment of
US Minister to Germany in 1878.

An American in a London fog,
c. 1844

London has the advantage of one of the most gloomy atmospheres
in the world. During this opening spring weather, no light and
scarcely any warmth can penetrate the dull, yellowish-gray mist,
which incessantly hangs over the city. Sometimes at noon we have
for an hour or two a sickly gleam of sunshine, but it is soon
swallowed up by the smoke and drizzling fog. The people carry
umbrellas at all times, for the rain seems to drop spontaneously out
of the very air, without waiting for the usual preparation of a
gathering cloud . . . A few days ago we had a real fog – a specimen of
November weather, as the people said. If November wears such a
mantle, London, during that sober month, must furnish a good idea
of the gloom of Hades. The streets were wrapped in a veil of dense
mist, a dirty yellow color, as if the air had suddenly grown thick and
mouldy. The houses on the opposite sides of the street were
invisible, and the gas-lamps, lighted in the shops, burned with a
white and ghastly flame. Carriages ran together in the streets, and I
was kept constantly on the look-out, lest someone should come
suddenly out of the cloud around me, and we should meet with a
shock like that of the two knights at a tournament. As I stood in the
centre of Trafalgar Square, with every object invisible around me, it
reminded me, (hoping the comparison will not be accepted in every
particular) of Satan resting in the middle of Chaos. The weather
sometimes continues thus for whole days together.

HIPPOLYTE TAINE
(1828–1893)

French critic, philosopher and historian. Taine visited England three times, in 1859, 1862 and 1871, making detailed notes that were later gathered into a book.

Carried away by Blenheim Palace

In the course of another trip I saw Blenheim Castle, near Woodstock, property of the Duke of Marlborough. It is a sort of Louvre, and was given by the nation to the great general, the first duke. . . . The apartments contain paintings by Reynolds, five or six large Van Dyck portraits, a Raphael Madonna and ten Rubens in which sensuality, passion, boldness and genius pour out a whole river of splendours and enormities. Two of these are Bacchanals: a colossal female faun has thrown herself down on the ground and sits stooped above her dropping dugs, and her two young, lying on their backs and glued to her nipples, are sucking avidly, the whole a great jumble of palpitating flesh; above, the dark torso of Silenus throws into relief the dazzling whiteness of a strapping, hoydenish, writhing nymph; nearby is another Silenus, bronzed and enormous, laughing a drunkard's laugh, dancing with all his heart and might so that his paunch is bouncing about, while a beautiful young woman, resting on her hip, displays the long, undulating lines of side and breasts. I would not dare to describe the third picture, the most vivid of all, of a sublime grossness, the very sap and flower of irrepressible passionate sensuality, the whole poetry of drunkenness unrestrained and bestial satiety; the title, *Lot and his two daughters*. But I am forgetting myself; these memories, like a gust of warm air, have made me digress.

A Manchester brothel

Next, to a brothel. One of the policemen told us that the girls are recruited chiefly among the mill-girls. They sat in a low room downstairs and were not at all *décolletées*. Several of them were very thin and their ignoble faces had become, as it were, like those of savages. Next to a greasy mulatto woman I noticed a young girl with a pretty, delicate, intelligent face, thoughtfully bent towards the red glow of the fire. The month is July but this fire is necessary of an evening. It was the same in thieves' public houses; we saw twenty or thirty of these dens, and there was always a heaped-up fire of red-hot coal to do the cooking and dry the washing. The men sit about playing dominoes and smoking; when we came in they said nothing but all raised bright, motionless eyes, the eyes of a beast of prey, and stared at us. The crude gas-light is horrible, playing upon such faces.

. . . I felt I was in a nightmare, or in a story by 'Edgar Poe'. The gas-light cannot overcome the shadows in that heavy, stifling air full of unfamiliar exhalations. Nothing could be more frightening than that black darkness shot through with vacillating fingers of brightness. The symmetrical streets seem like the corpses of streets laid out side by side and for ever still. Here and there one sees wretched women trailing their faded finery, wearing their professional smile: and as they pass you are tempted to draw away, as from a haunting spectre, a soul in agony.

HENRY JAMES
(1843–1916)

American novelist and critic. He travelled widely in America and Europe before settling in London in 1876. He became a British citizen in 1915.

St James's Park – the salon of the slums

If the Green Park is familiar, there is still less of the exclusive in its pendant, as one may call it – for it literally hangs from the other, down the hill – the remnant of the former garden of the queer, shabby old palace whose black, inelegant face stares up St James's Street. This popular resort has a great deal of character, but I am free to confess that much of its character comes from its nearness to the Westminster slums. It is a park of intimacy, and perhaps the most democratic corner of London, in spite of its being in the royal and military quarter and close to all kinds of stateliness. There are few hours of the day when a thousand smutty children are not sprawling over it, and the unemployed lie thick on the grass and cover the benches with a brotherhood of greasy corduroys. If the London parks are the drawing-rooms and clubs of the poor – that is, of those poor (I admit it cuts down the number) who live near enough to them to reach them – these particular grass-plots and alleys may be said to constitute the very *salon* of the slums.

Derby Day

The course at Epsom is in itself very pretty, and disposed by nature herself in sympathetic prevision of the sporting passion. It is something like the crater of a volcano without the mountain. The outer rim is the course proper; the space within it is a vast, shallow, grassy concavity in which vehicles are drawn up and beasts tethered and in which the greater part of the multitude – the mountebanks, the betting-men and the myriad hangers-on of the scene – are congregated. The outer margin of the uplifted rim in question is occupied by the grand stand, the small stands, the paddock. The day was exceptionally beautiful; the charming sky was spotted over with little idle-looking, loafing, irresponsible clouds; the Epsom Downs went swelling away as greenly as in a coloured sporting-print, and the wooded uplands, in the middle distance, looked as innocent and pastoral as if they had never seen a policeman or a rowdy. The crowd that spread itself over this immense expanse was as rich representation of human life off its guard as one need see. One's first fate after arriving, if one is perched upon a coach, is to see the coach guided, by means best known to the coachman himself, through the tremendous press of vehicles and pedestrians, introduced into a precinct roped off and guarded from intrusion save under payment of a fee, and then drawn up alongside of the course, as nearly as possible opposite the grand stand and the winning-post. Here you have only to stand up in your place – on tiptoe, it is true, and with a good deal of stretching – to see the race fairly well. But I hasten to add that seeing the race is indifferent entertainment. In the first place you *don't* see it, and in the second – to be Irish on the occasion of a frolic – you perceive it to be not much worth the seeing. It may be fine in quality, but in quantity it is inappreciable. The horses and their jockeys first go dandling and cantering along the course to the starting-point, looking as insubstantial as sifted sunbeams. Then there is a long wait, during which, of the sixty thousand people present (my figures are imaginary), thirty thousand declare positively that they have started, and thirty thousand as positively deny it. Then the whole sixty thousand are suddenly resolved into unanimity by the sight of a dozen small jockey-heads whizzing along a very distant sky-line. In a shorter space of time than it takes me to write it, the whole thing is before you, and for the instant it is anything but beautiful. A dozen furiously revolving arms – pink, green, orange, scarlet, white – whacking the flanks of as many straining steeds; a glimpse of this, and the spectacle is over. The spectacle, however, is of course an infinitesimally small part of the purpose of Epsom and the interest of the Derby. The finer vibration resides presumably in having money on the affair.

EDITH WHARTON
(1862–1937)

American novelist. (See p. 84.) In 1913 she settled in France, and thereafter travelled widely in Europe. She was a close friend of another American expatriate, Henry James.

Henry the navigator

James, who was a frequent companion on our English motor-trips, was firmly convinced that, because he lived in England and our chauffeur (an American) did not, it was necessary that the latter should be guided by him through the intricacies of the English countryside. Signposts were rare in England in those days, and for many years afterwards. . . .

It chanced however that Charles Cook, our faithful and skilful driver, was a born path-finder, while James's sense of direction was non-existent, or rather actively but always erroneously alert; and the consequences of his intervention were always bewildering and sometimes extremely fatiguing. . . .

The most absurd of these episodes occurred on another rainy evening when James and I chanced to arrive at Windsor long after dark. We must have been driven by a strange chauffeur – perhaps

Cook was on holiday; at any rate, having fallen into the lazy habit of trusting him to know the way, I found myself at a loss to direct his substitute to the King's Road. While I was hesitating and peering out into the darkness James spied an ancient doddering man who had stopped in the rain to gaze at us. 'Wait a moment, my dear – I'll ask him where we are'; and leaning out he signalled to the spectator.

'My good man, if you'll be good enough to come here, please; a little nearer – so,' and as the old man came up: 'My friend, to put it to you in two words, this lady and I have just arrived here from *Slough*; that is to say, to be more strictly accurate, we have recently *passed through* Slough on our way here, having actually motored to Windsor from Rye, which was our point of departure; and the darkness having overtaken us, we should be much obliged if you would tell us where we now are in relation, say, to the High Street, which, as you of course know, leads to the Castle, after leaving on the left hand the turn down to the railway station.'

I was not surprised to have this extraordinary appeal met by silence, and a dazed expression on the old wrinkled face at the window; nor to have James go on: 'In short' (his invariable prelude to a fresh series of explanatory ramifications), 'in short, my good man, what I want to put to you in a word is this: supposing we have already (as I have reason to think we have) driven past the turn down to the railway station (which in that case, by the way, would probably not have been on our left hand, but on our right) where are we now in relation to . . .'

'Oh, please,' I interrupted, feeling myself utterly unable to sit through another parenthesis, 'do ask him where the King's Road is.'

'Ah –? The King's Road? Just so! Quite right! Can you, as a matter of fact, my good man, tell us where, in relation to our present position, the King's Road exactly *is*?'

'Ye're in it', said the aged face at the window.

NIKOS KAZANTZAKIS
(1883–1957)

Greek novelist, poet, dramatist and traveller. Born in Crete, he studied in Paris and spent four years in Germany and Italy. He spent most of the years 1920–40 travelling, and was in England during the early days of World War II. Kazantzakis's books include *Zorba the Greek* and *The Odyssey: A Modern Sequel*, at 33,333 lines possibly the longest poem ever written.

A royal sacrament in wartime

Another day, in London. The railway station hummed with people. The King, First Gentleman of the Empire, was returning from Canada today. The English people love official processions, medieval costumes, wigs, lords' ermines, the antiquated gold royal coaches driving their King to Westminster for the opening of Parliament, the heavy keys handed by the Lord Mayor to the King as he enters the City. . . .

The train arrived. The King appeared, smiling, slender, slightly weary. All the Englishmen thundered and waved their arms and opened their mouths to sing. Some sang the royal anthem, others sang gay, simple little tunes. And a few of them chanted psalms from the Gospels. There was no slavish uniformity here. Everyone was expressing his joy, but freely, in his own separate way. In England the masses manage to save their independence and individual dignity from getting completely drowned. They are no herd, dully and monolithically following a slogan. They know how to take the same slogan and adapt it to a completely different entity. They bestow a nuance of freedom upon necessity, and they chant religious hymns or gay songs or national anthems, each group with its own spirit, to welcome back their King.

I was standing in a corner of the railway station, listening – a hubbub as in a beehive. Occasionally in springtime, there are throngs of bees buzzing mournfully, when they are left orphaned, without their queen. Then suddenly they bring back their queen and at once the buzzing changes its tone, becoming a rich, joyous, profound song, so profound that we forget the way the song had begun, and we too seem to be singing inside ourselves, as though welcoming some age-old hope. . . .

The moment the King mounted his carriage, all the people began running along behind him, singing as they went. All their faces became suffused with a curious glint of royal purple, a curious Royal Communion! I did not join the procession. I just stood there avidly observing this extraordinary Royal 'sacrament.'

'You're a foreigner? You don't want to join in? You're not singing?' an old man asked me, as he rushed by on his way to join the crowd.

'No,' I answered, 'I don't want to join. I'm not singing. I am a foreigner.'

'Well, if you stay long here in England,' he laughed, 'you'll turn royalist too!'

I shuddered.

KAREL CAPEK
(1890–1938)

Czech novelist, dramatist and essayist. The son of a country doctor, he studied philosophy in Prague, Berlin and Paris. He worked as a journalist throughout his life and travelled extensively in Europe, writing a series of idiosyncratic travel books.

At Madame Tussaud's

Madame Tussaud's is a museum of famous people, or rather of their wax-effigies. The Royal Family is there (also King Alphonso, somewhat moth-eaten). Mr. MacDonald's Ministry, French Presidents, Dickens and Kipling, marshals, Mademoiselle Lenglen, famous murderers of last century and souvenirs of Napoleon, such as his socks, belt and hat; then in a place of dishonour Kaiser Wilhelm and Franz Josef, still looking spruce for his age. Before one particularly effective effigy of a gentleman in a top-hat I stopped and looked into the catalogue to see who it was; suddenly the gentleman with the top-hat moved and walked away; it was awful. After a while two young ladies looked into the catalogue to see whom I represented. At Madame Tussaud's I made a somewhat unpleasant discovery: either I am quite incapable of reading human faces, or else physiognomies are deceptive. So for example I was at first sight attracted by a seated gentleman with a goatee beard, No. 12. In the catalogue I found: '12. Thomas Neill Cream, hanged in 1892. Poisoned Matilda Glover with strychnine. He was also found guilty of murdering three other women.' Really, his face is very suspicious. No. 13, Franz Müller, murdered Mr. Briggs in the train. H'm. No. 20, a clean-shaven gentleman, of almost worthy appearance: Arthur Devereux, hanged 1905, known as the 'trunk murderer,' because he hid the corpses of his victims in trunks. Horrid. No. 21 – no, this worthy priest cannot be 'Mrs. Dyer, the Reading baby murderess.' I now perceive that I have confused the pages of the catalogue, and I am compelled to correct my impressions: the seated gentleman, No. 12, is merely Bernard Shaw; No. 13 is Louis Blériot, and No. 20 is simply Guglielmo Marconi.

Never again will I judge people by their faces.

A Czech view of the English

Every Englishman wears a mackintosh, and has a cap on his head and a newspaper in his hand. As for the Englishwoman, she carries a mackintosh or a tennis racket. Nature here has a propensity for unusual shagginess, excrescences, woolliness, spikiness, and all kinds of hair; English horses, for example, have regular tufts and tassels of hair on their legs, and English dogs are nothing more nor less than absurd bundles of forelocks. Only the English lawn and the English gentleman are shaved every day. . . .

. . . . Here the people always manage to help each other, but they never have anything to say to each other, except about the weather. That is probably why Englishmen have invented all games, and why they do not speak during their games. . . .

It is perhaps through sheer taciturnity that the English swallow half of every word, and then the second half they somehow squash; so it is difficult to understand them. I used to travel every day to Ladbroke Grove; the conductor would come and I would say: 'Ledbruk Grröv.' '. . . ?? Eh?' 'Ledbhuk Ghöv!' '. . . ??? Eh?' 'Hevhuv Hev!' 'Aa, Hevhuv Hov!' The conductor would rejoice and give me a ticket to Ladbroke Grove. I shall never learn this as long as I live.

H. V. MORTON
(1892–1979)

English travel writer and journalist. Author of a series of best-selling travel books. Some, such as *In Search of England* (1927), now have a remarkable period flavour.

Lobster tea in Dorset

In Christchurch, near the Priory, is a short, narrow street full of tea-shops. It is so full of tea-shops that several charming waitresses and proprietresses – for this street seems entirely a feminine endeavour – picket the doors and say with a smile, if you appear to linger bunwards, 'Oh, wouldn't you like some tea?' And you think, 'Oh, probably I would!' and so you become deflected from the Priory. Goodness alone knows how many religious pilgrims have been lured to repletion in this street of the sirens.

I was walking on with a soul full of Norman transepts when a maiden stood before me and looked. She had the greyest eyes.

'Would you,' she said, 'like a lobster?'

I observed her closely and realized that she was serious. Behind her lay in negligent attitudes dozens of lobsters on a table among roses. It was 4.30 p.m. It had never occurred to me that people eat lobster at tea-time. In fact, there is to my mind something almost indecent about it. I was so embarrassed that I said 'Yes', whereupon, giving me no time to repent, in the manner of women, she picked up a big scarlet brute and disappeared, leaving me to slink miserably to a chintz chair, with a clammy foreboding of great evil.

'Tea?' she asked.

I made a feeble protest, but she assured me that China tea 'goes' with lobster. I wanted to ask whether this experiment had ever been tried before by man, but I was given no time. When the shell was empty some devil entered into me and urged me to reply 'Yes' to everything this girl said (and she was a good talker), with the result that basins of Dorset cream, pots of jam, puffy cakes oozing sweetness, ramparts of buns and crisp rolls became piled up behind the rose-bowl. The only thing I missed at this tea-party was the Mad Hatter.

The place where London ends – the Bath Road, Middlesex, in the 1920s

Of course, no living man has seen London. London has ceased to be visible since Stuart days. It was then possible for the last time in history to stand among the water meadows at Westminster and to see London riding on Ludgate Hill escorted by her church towers and spires. Plantagenet London must have been the best of all the Londons for the purpose of a farewell speech: a city behind its wall, something definite to see and to address. To-day, even if you climb to the dome of St. Paul's you see not London the City State but London the labyrinth. The nearest approach to a real view of London is that from the tower of Southwark Cathedral or, better still, from a boat on the Thames at night when darkness lends an ancient enchantment to the roof lines.

However, a man contemplating a farewell address to London finds that all enthusiasm has evaporated by the time he reaches the Place Where London Ends.

Now London ends at a public-house.

Outside the public-house stood an old man wearing silver side-whiskers and a peevish expression which suggested to me that some one had promised to stand him a drink in '85 and had never turned up.

'Hallo,' I said to him, but he looked the other way and spat rudely.

In a line with the public-house were new shops. In a field some way off the high road were scared-looking, pink and white villas, each one possessing a bald garden and a brand-new galvanized dustbin at the back door. Wives as new as the gardens and the houses busied about their work and took frequent peeps through the front windows to make sure that the baby was still on the safe side of the garden fence. The most significant item on the landscape was an empty omnibus standing in a weary attitude opposite the public-house. There were London names on the indicator board, but they seemed as unlikely as the Italian names on the French expresses at Calais.

The history of London is the moving on of that red omnibus another mile along the road; more pink and white houses; more shops; more wives; more babies.

'Good morning,' said I to the ancient man.

'Straight on,' he replied.

'Good morning,' I ventured again.

'About seven miles,' he retorted.

I felt that we were going to be great friends.

'Will you have a drink?' I asked.

Even this failed to bring us together, so I went right into his silver side-whiskers and shouted 'Beer!' whereon he sprang smartly to attention and walked into the bar. By shouting slightly to the right of his left ear I found myself in touch with a personality not only charming but also interesting.

CYRIL CONNOLLY
(1903–1974)

English writer, critic and editor. (See p. 177.)

Angoisse des Gares

Angoisse des Gares: A particularly violent form of Angst. Bad when we meet someone at the station, much worse when we are seeing them off; not present when departing oneself, but unbearable when arriving in London, if only from a day in Brighton. Since all Angst is identical, we may learn something from these station-fears: Arrival-Angst is closely connected with guilt, with the dread of something terrible having happened during our absence. Death of parents. Entry of bailiffs. Flight of loved one. Sensations worse at arriving in the evening than the morning, and much worse at Victoria and Waterloo than at Paddington. Partly this is due to my having gone abroad every vacation and, therefore, to returning to London with guilt-feelings about having spent all my money, or not written to parents, and to endless worry over work and debts. . . . Much of our anxiety is caused by the horror of London itself; of its hideous entrails as seen from the southern approaches, its high cost of living, its embodiment of ugly and unnatural urban existence. When living in France, I began to feel the same way about Paris, though it has none of the same associations. I deduce, therefore, that though it is wrong for us to live and work in great cities, it is also wrong to live away from them *without working*. Angst begins at Reading (for Paddington), Brookwood, the London Necropolis (for Waterloo), the tunnels through the North Downs (for Victoria), or even in

Paris, when we see the grisly English faces homeward bound at the Gare du Nord. First-class or third makes no difference. 'They' will get you, Palinurus, 'they' aren't taken in.

HEINRICH BÖLL
(1917–1985)

German novelist. Winner of the Nobel Prize for literature in 1972. In the mid-1950s he visited Ireland, keeping and later publishing a journal of his impressions.

Drumcliff churchyard

As the train entered Sligo it was still raining; kisses were exchanged under umbrellas, tears were wept under umbrellas; a taxi driver was asleep over his steering wheel, his head resting on his folded arms; I woke him up; he was one of those pleasant people who wake up with a smile.

'Where to?' he asked.

'To Drumcliff churchyard.'

'But nobody lives there.'

'Maybe,' I said, 'but I'd like to go there.'

'And back?'

'Yes.'

'All right.'

We drove through puddles, empty streets; in the twilight I looked through an open window at a piano; the music looked as if the dust on it must be an inch thick. A barber was standing in his doorway, snipping with his scissors as if he wanted to cut off threads of rain; at the entrance to a movie a girl was putting on fresh lipstick, children with prayer books under their arms ran through the rain, an old woman shouted across the street to an old man: 'Howya, Paddy?' and the old man shouted back: 'I'm all right – with the help of God and His most blessed Mother.'

'Are you quite sure,' the driver asked me, 'you really want to go to Drumcliff churchyard?'

'Quite sure,' I said.

The hills round about were covered with faded ferns like the wet hair of an aging red-haired woman, two grim rocks guarded the entrance to this little bay: 'Benbulbin and Knocknarea,' said the driver, as if he were introducing me to two distant relations he didn't much care about.

'There,' said the driver, pointing to where a church tower reared up in the mist; rooks were flying round the tower, clouds of rooks, and from a distance they looked like black snowflakes. 'I think,' said the driver, 'you must be looking for the old battlefield.'

'No,' I said, 'I've never heard of any battle.'

'In 561,' he began in a guide's mild tone of voice, 'a battle was fought here which was the only one ever fought in all the world on account of a copyright.'

I shook my head as I looked at him.

'It's really true,' he said; 'the followers of St. Columba had copied a psalter belonging to St. Finian, and there was a battle between the followers of St. Finian and the followers of St. Columba. Three thousand dead – but the king decided the quarrel; he said: "As the calf belongs to every cow, so the copy belongs to every book." You're sure you don't want to see the battlefield?'

'No,' I said, 'I'm looking for a grave.'

'Oh yes,' he said. 'Yeats, that's right – then I expect you want to go to Innisfree too.'

'I don't know yet,' I said; 'wait here, please.'

Rooks flew up from the old gravestones, circled cawing around the old church tower. Yeats' grave was wet, the stone was cold, and the lines which Yeats had had inscribed on his gravestone were as cold as the ice needles that had been shot at me from Swift's tomb: 'Cast a cold eye on life, on death. Horseman, pass by!' I looked up; were the rooks enchanted swans? They cawed mockingly at me, fluttered around the church tower. The ferns lay flat on the surrounding hills, beaten down by the rain, rust-colored and withered. I felt cold.

'Drive on,' I said to the driver.

'On to Innisfree then?'

'No,' I said, 'back to the station.'

Rocks in the mist, the lonely church, encircled by fluttering rooks, and three thousand miles of water beyond Yeats' grave. Not a swan to be seen.

JOHN HILLABY
(1917–   )

English writer and naturalist. (See p. 97.) Among his epic journeys on foot was one from Land's End to John O'Groats.

A boxer's remedy for a walker's pains

In a Bristol hotel the next morning I thought the walk had come to an end. Overworked calf muscles seemed to have gone on strike. They had seized up. Despite hot baths and amateurish attempts at massage, I could scarcely walk for more than a few paces without wincing.

A long-distance telephone call to an old friend in the medical business confirmed what I knew: that I needed rest; that I should take things easy. I would be advised, he said, to get some professional attention, locally. It could be serious. I shouldn't fool around with myself. And so on.

All very well, this, but though my legs were in poor shape, somewhere else inside a hound still leaped, barking, anxious to get off the chain. Still, if I had to rest . . . I lay back on the bed and rang for the Manager, determined to squeeze the last star of luxury out of that hotel.

The Manager recommended the personal attention of his chef and offered to send up Paddy, the head porter, who at one time had apparently been something of what is called a professor in the boxing game. He reckoned that if anyone could get a man to his feet it was Paddy.

The consultation had about it the atmosphere of almost forgotten visits to the regimental medical officer. No formality. No speeches. A brief examination and then an almost oracular pronouncement.

Paddy looked me up and down. With something near affection he stroked the pink, swollen muscles with his forefinger, and sighed. Was he, I wondered, about to recommend a masseur, faradic baths, an ambulance? Not a bit of it.

'What you want, sir,' he said, 'is *exercise*.'

NEAR ASIA

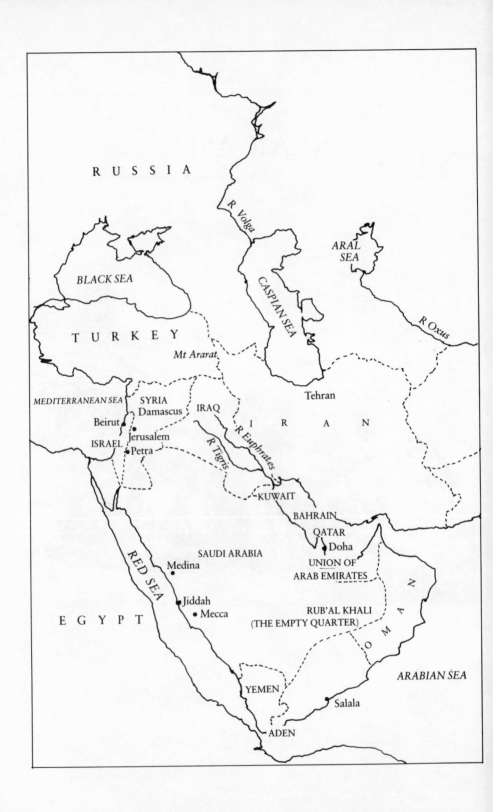

XENOPHON
(430?–355? BC)

Greek historian. He joined the 'Ten Thousand', the
Greek force fighting for Cyrus of Persia against his
brother Artaxerxes. When Cyrus was killed at the Battle
of Cunaxa the Greek mercenaries found that the river-
crossings leading to the Royal Persian Road by which
they intended to return to the Mediterranean were held
by hostile Kurds. It was decided to force a way north-
wards through the mountains of Kurdistan and Armenia,
and this they did, passing to the west of Lake Van and
crossing the upper waters of the Euphrates, 'wetting
themselves to the navel'. There they were exposed to the
full fury of winter on the high Armenian plateau.

The retreat of the Ten Thousand

Meanwhile they were being followed by the enemy, some of whom
had banded together and were seizing such of the pack animals as
lacked the strength to go on, and fighting over them with one
another. Some of the soldiers likewise were falling behind – those
whose eyes had been blinded by the snow, or whose toes had rotted
off by reason of the cold. It was a protection to the eyes against the
snow if a man marched with something black in front of them, and a
protection to the feet if one kept moving and never quiet, and if he
took off his shoes for the night; but in all cases where men slept with
their shoes on, the straps sunk into their flesh and the shoes froze on
their feet; for what they were wearing, since their old shoes had
given out, were brogues made of freshly flayed ox-hides. . . .

The houses here were underground, with a mouth like that of a
well, but spacious below; and while entrances were tunnelled down
for the beasts of burden, the human inhabitants descended by a
ladder. In the houses were goats, sheep, cattle, fowls, and their
young; and all the animals were reared and took their fodder there
in the houses. Here were also wheat, barley, and beans, and
barley-wine in large bowls. Floating on the top of this drink were
the barley-grains and in it were straws, some larger and others
smaller, without joints; and when one was thirsty, he had to take
these straws into his mouth and suck. It was an extremely strong

drink unless one diluted it with water, and extremely good when one was used to it.

Xenophon made the chief man of this village his guest at dinner and bade him be of good cheer, telling him that he should not be deprived of his children, and that before they went away they would fill his house with provisions by way of reward in case he should prove to have given the army good guidance until they should reach another tribe. He promised to do this, and in a spirit of kindliness told them where there was wine buried. For that night, then, all Xenophon's soldiers, in this village where they were thus separately quartered, went to bed amid an abundance of everything, keeping the village chief under guard and his children all together within sight.

On the next day Xenophon took the village chief and set out to visit Cheirisophus; whenever he passed a village, he would turn aside to visit the troops quartered there, and everywhere he found them faring sumptuously and in fine spirits. . . .

. . . When they reached Cheirisophus, they found his troops also feasting in their quarters, crowned with wreaths of hay and served by Armenian boys in their strange, foreign dress; and they were showing the boys what to do by signs, as if they were deaf and dumb.

As soon as Cheirisophus and Xenophon had exchanged warm greetings, they together asked the village chief, through their Persian-speaking interpreter, what this land was. He replied that it was Armenia.

ST PAUL
(d. AD 64 or 67)

Jewish tent-maker who was converted to Christianity on the road to Damascus in AD 33. He undertook many missionary journeys to convert the Gentiles. In AD 57 he went to Jerusalem, but he was arrested for provoking a riot, held prisoner for two years, then sent under guard to Rome. The journey was not without incident.

Shipwrecked on Malta, AD 59–60

And when it was day, they knew not the land: but they discovered a certain creek with a shore, into the which they were minded, if it were possible, to thrust in the ship. And when they had taken up the anchors, they committed themselves unto the sea, and loosed the rudder bands, and hoisted up the mainsail to the wind, and made toward shore. And falling into a place where two seas met, they ran the ship aground; and the forepart stuck fast, and remained unmoveable, but the hinder part was broken with the violence of the waves. And the soldiers' counsel was to kill the prisoners, lest any of them should swim out, and escape. But the centurion, willing to save Paul, kept them from their purpose; and commanded that they which could swim should cast themselves first into the sea, and get to land: and the rest, some on boards, and some on broken pieces of the ship. And so it came to pass, that they escaped all safe to land.

And when they were escaped, then they knew that the island was called Melita. And the barbarous people showed us no little kindness: for they kindled a fire, and received us every one, because of the present rain, and because of the cold.

And when Paul had gathered a bundle of sticks, and laid them on the fire, there came a viper out of the heat, and fastened on his hand. And when the barbarians saw the venomous beast hang on his hand, they said among themselves, No doubt this man is a murderer, whom, though he hath escaped the sea, yet vengeance suffereth not to live. And he shook off the beast into the fire, and felt no harm. Howbeit they looked when he should have swollen, or fallen down dead suddenly: but after they had looked a great while, and saw no harm come to him, they changed their minds, and said that he was a god.

In the same quarters were possessions of the chief man of the island, whose name was Publius; who received us, and lodged us three days courteously. And it came to pass, that the father of Publius lay sick of a fever and of a bloody flux: to whom Paul entered in, and prayed, and laid his hands on him, and healed him. So when this was done, others also, which had diseases in the island, came, and were healed: who also honoured us with many honours; and when we departed, they laded us with such things as were necessary.

And after three months we departed in a ship of Alexandria, which had wintered in the isle, whose sign was Castor and Pollux. And landing at Syracuse, we tarried there three days. And from thence we fetched a compass, and came to Rhegium: and after one day the south wind blew, and we came the next day to Puteoli: where we found brethren, and were desired to tarry with them seven days: and so we went toward Rome. And from thence, when the brethren heard of us, they came to meet us as far as Appii Forum, and The Three Taverns: whom when Paul saw, he thanked God, and took courage.

ST WILLIBALD
(700?–786)

English monk. At the age of twenty-two he set off on a pilgrimage to Rome with his brother Wunebald and his father Richard. Richard died en route to Rome and Willibald went on to visit the Holy Land. His journey lasted ten years, including two years in Constantinople. He then spent ten years in the monastery at Monte Cassino, before answering a call from his uncle, St Boniface, to assist him in his missionary labours in Germany. There he built a monastery at Eichstatt, where he died. The story of his travels, entitled *Vita seu Hodoeporicon Sancti Willibaldi*, he dictated to a German nun.

Calvary, AD 724

From there he came on to Jerusalem, to the place where the Lord's Holy Cross was found. That place is called 'The Place of Calvary' and there is now a church there: in earlier times it was outside Jerusalem, but Helena put the place inside Jerusalem when she found the Cross. Now there are three wooden crosses standing there outside the church, on the east of it near the wall, to commemorate the Holy Cross of the Lord, and those of the others who were crucified with him. Nowadays they are not indoors, inside the church, but stand out of doors under a roof outside the church. And near there is the garden in which was the Saviour's tomb. The tomb had been carved out of rock, and the rock stands up out of the ground: at the bottom it is square, but it is pointed on top. The tomb is now surmounted by a cross, and there is now a remarkable building over it. On the east of the tomb, in the actual rock, a door has been made, through which people enter the tomb for prayer. And inside there is a shelf on which the Lord's body lay. Fifteen golden bowls stand on the shelf. They are filled with oil, and burn day and night. The shelf on which the Lord's body lay is inside the rock of the tomb on the north side, that is, on the right side as one enters the tomb to pray. And there also, in front of the tomb door, lies a large square stone, like the original stone which the angel rolled away from the tomb door.

ODORIC OF PORDENONE
(1274?–1331)

Italian friar. A Franciscan, he was one of the great missionary travellers. In 1316 he set out on a journey to the East that lasted fourteen years and during which he baptized some 10,000 people. He was the first European to mention Sumatra, and the first to describe the use of the blowpipe by the aboriginal tribesmen of the East Indies, the use of cormorants for fishing in China and the Chinese customs of growing the fingernails and binding women's feet. He returned to Padua in 1330, where he wrote his memoirs.

Travelling to Trebizond with 4000 partridges

First, then, going with the galleys from Venice, I crossed over the Greater Sea, and so passed to TREBIZOND, which was of old called Pontus. This city is situated passing well, and is a haven for the Persians, Medes, and all the people on the further side of the sea. And in this country I saw a very pretty sight which I am the more bold to tell, because many persons with whom I have spoken in Venice assure me that they have seen the like. I beheld a certain man taking about with him more than four thousand partridges. For as the man went along the ground, the partridges followed him flying in the air. These partridges he was then taking to a certain castle which is called ZEGANA, distant three days' journey from Trebizond, where they dig copper and crystal. And the way with these partridges was this, that whenever the man wanted to lie down or go to sleep, they all gathered about him like chickens about a hen. And in this manner he took them along to Trebizond, to the palace of the emperor; and he, when they were thus brought before him, took as many partridges as he desired; but the rest of them the man led back to the place whence he had first brought them.

LUDOVICO DI VARTHEMA
(fl. 1505)

Italian traveller. A native of Bologna, he was inspired to travel by sheer curiosity. In April 1503 he reached Damascus, where he enrolled himself in the Mameluke escort to the great Haj (pilgrim) caravan to Mecca. To do this he had, ostensibly at least, to become a Muslim. (Mamelukes were originally Turkish slaves who had been freed by their owners and formed the bodyguard of the reigning sultan.) In this capacity he became the second non-Muslim to visit the Holy City (the first was Pedro de Covilhao, presumed to have reached Mecca in 1492).

The haphazard love-life of the Mamelukes

The said Mamelukes, when they go about the city [Damascus], are always in companies of two or three, as it would be a great disgrace if they went alone. If they accidentally meet two or three ladies, they possess this privilege, or if they do not possess it they take it: they go to lay in wait for these ladies in certain places like great inns, which are called Chano, and as the said ladies pass before the door each Mameluke takes his lady by the hand, draws her in, and does what he will with her. But the lady resists being known, because they all wear the face covered, so that they know us, but we do not know them. The Mameluke says to her, that he wishes to know who she is, and she replies: 'Brother, is it not enough that you do with me what you will, without desiring to know who I am?' and she entreats him so much that he lets her go. And sometimes they think that they take the daughter of the lord, when in fact they take their own wives; and this has happened while I was there. . . .

At Mecca, Varthema deserted from the Mamelukes and joined a caravan bound for Jiddah on the Red Sea, where he took ship for Aden. There he was seized as a Christian spy and sent inland to Rada', where he was interrogated by the Sultan. The 160-mile journey took eight days, and Varthema was incommoded by eighteen pounds of leg irons. 'In my time,' he wrote, 'he had 15,000 or 16,000 men in chains.' The Sultan, who was on the point of departing for a war, threw him into prison, where he found himself in an even more perilous situation.

A lustful queen

In the said palace of the city there was one of the three wives of the Sultan, who remained there with twelve or thirteen very beautiful damsels, whose colour was more near to black than otherwise. This queen was very kind to me. I and my companion and a Moor, being all three in prison here, we arranged that one of us should pretend to be mad, in order the better to assist one another. Finally, the lot fell upon me to be mad. Having then taken this enterprise upon myself, it behoved me to do such things as were natural to madmen. Truly, I never found myself so wearied or so exhausted as during the first three days that I feigned madness. The reason was that I had constantly behind me fifty or sixty little children, who threw stones at me, and I threw stones at them. They cried out: 'Iami iasion Iami ianun;' that is to say: 'Madman.' And I had my shirt constantly full of stones, and acted like a madman. The queen was always at her window with her damsels, and remained there from morning till evening to see me and talk with me; and I, being mocked by many men and merchants, taking off my shirt, went, quite naked as I was, before the queen, who took the greatest delight in seeing me, and would not let me leave her, and gave me good and sound food to eat, so that I gained my point. . . .

The first night ensuing, the queen came to visit me with five or six of her damsels, and began to examine me, and I began to give her to understand by degrees that I was not mad. She, being a clever woman, saw that I was not at all mad, and began to make much of me; ordered a good bed after their fashion to be given me, and sent me plenty of good food. The following day she had prepared for me a bath according to their custom, with many perfumes, and continued these caresses for twelve days. Afterwards, she began to come down to visit me every night at three or four o'clock, and always brought me good things to eat. Entering where I was, she called me 'Iunus tale inte iohan,' that is, 'Lodovico, come here, are you hungry?' And I replied: 'E vualla,' that is, 'Yes,' for the hunger which was to come; and I rose on my feet and went to her in my shirt. And she said: 'Leis leis camis foch,' that is, 'Not in that manner, take off your shirt.' I replied: 'Iaseti ane maomigenon de lain,' which is, 'O, madam, I am not mad now.' She answered me: 'Vualla ane arf in te habedenin te migenon inte mafdunia metalon,' that is, 'By God, I know well that thou never wast mad, on the contrary, that thou art the best witted man that ever was seen.' In order to please her I took off my shirt, and held it before me for modesty's sake, and thus she kept me before her for two hours, contemplating me as though I had been a nymph. . . . She wept continually and sighed, passing her hands over me all the while, and promising me that, as soon as the Sultan returned, she would make him take off my irons. On the next night the queen came to me with two of her damsels and brought me some good food to eat, and said to me: 'Tale Iunus,' that is, 'Come here, Lodovico;' 'Ane igi andech,' I replied. 'Leis setti ane mochaet ich fio,' that is, said the queen, 'Lodovico, would you like that I should come and stay a little while with you.' I answered: 'No; that it was quite enough that I was in chains, without her causing me to have my head cut off.'

> *After being fed by the Sultan's wife for twenty days on 'eggs, hens, pigeons, pepper, cinnamon, cloves, and nutmegs', Varthema fell into a feigned trance. On coming out of it, he persuaded the Sultan's wife that, while in the trance, he made a promise to God that he would visit a certain holy man in Aden in order to be cured of the affliction. She had him released and provided him with camels and money for the journey.*

GEFFREY DUCKET
(fl. 1568–1574*)*

English agent of the Muscovy Company.

On the inadvisability of addressing the Great Sophy as the Great Sophy

The king of Persia (whom here we call the great Sophy) is not there so called, but is called the Shaugh. It were there dangerous to cal him by the name of Sophy, because that Sophy in the Persian tongue, is a begger, & it were as much as to call him, The great begger. . . . The king hath not come out of the compasse of his owne house in 33. or 34. yeeres, whereof the cause is not knowen, but as they say, it is upon a superstition of certaine prophesies to which they are greatly addicted: he is now about 80. yeeres of age, and very lusty. And to keepe him the more lusty, he hath 4. wives alwayes, and about 300.

concubines, and once in the yeere he hath all the faire maidens and wives that may be found a great way about brought unto him, whom he diligently peruseth, feeling them in all parts, taking such as he liketh, and putting away some of them which he hath kept before, & with them that he putteth away, he gratifieth some such as hath done him the best service. And if hee chance to take any man's wife, her husband is very glad thereof, and in recompense of her, oftentimes he giveth the husband one of his old store, whom he thankfully receiveth.

Of Persian women and Persian oil

When a merchant or traveller commeth to any towne where he entendeth to tary any time, he hireth a woman, or somtimes 2. or 3. during his abode there. And when he commeth to an other towne, he doeth the like in the same also: for there they use to put out their women to hire, as wee do here hackney horses.

There is a very great river which runneth through the plaine of Javat, which falleth into the Caspian sea, by a towne called Bachu, neere unto which towne is a strange thing to behold. For there issueth out of the ground a marveilous quantitie of oile, which oile they fetch from the uttermost bounds of all Persia: it serveth all the countrey to burne in their houses.

This oyle is blacke, and is called Nefte: they use to cary it throughout all the Countrey upon kine & asses, of which you shall oftentimes meet with foure or five hundred in a company. There is also by the said towne of Bachu another kind of oyle which is white and very precious: and is supposed to be the same that here is called Petroleum. There is also not far from Shamaky, a thing like unto tarre, and issueth out of the ground, whereof we have made the proofe, that in our ships it serveth well in the stead of tarre.

JOHANN LUDWIG BURCKHARDT
(1784–1817)

Swiss traveller. (See p. 46.) In 1812, disguised as a Muslim pilgrim, he was the first European to set eyes on the city of Petra, the ancient rock city in present-day Jordan. Two years later, having failed to reach Massawa in Ethiopia by way of the Nubian Desert, he crossed the Red Sea to Jiddah. From there he went inland to Ta'if, south-east of Mecca, where the Viceroy of Egypt, Mehemet Ali, who knew of Burkhardt by reputation, arranged for him to be pronounced not only a Muslim but an extremely devout and well-informed one. He thus became the first, and probably the last, non-Muslim to visit Mecca openly and in safety.

An infidel at Petra, 22 August 1812

Near the west end of Wady Mousa are the remains of a stately edifice, of which part of the wall is still standing; the inhabitants call it Kaszr Bent Faraoun, or the palace of Pharaoh's daughter. In my way I had entered several sepulchres, to the surprise of my guide, but when he saw me turn out of the footpath towards the Kaszr, he exclaimed: 'I see now clearly that you are an infidel, who have some particular business amongst the ruins of the city of your forefathers; but depend upon it that we shall not suffer you to take out a single para of all the treasures hidden therein, for they are in our territory, and belong to us.' I replied that it was mere curiosity, which prompted me to look at the ancient works, and that I had no other view in coming here, than to sacrifice to Haroun; but he was not easily persuaded, and I did not think it prudent to irritate him by too close an inspection of the palace, as it might have led him to declare, on our return, his belief that I had found treasures, which might have led to a search of my person and to the detection of my journal, which would most certainly have been taken from me, as a book of magic. It is very unfortunate for European travellers that the idea of treasures being hidden in ancient edifices is so strongly rooted in the minds of the Arabs and Turks; nor are they satisfied with watching all the stranger's steps; they believe that it is sufficient for a true magician to have seen and observed the spot where treasures are hidden (of which he is supposed to be already informed by the old books of the infidels who lived on the spot) in order to be able afterwards, at his ease, to command the guardian of the treasure to set the whole before him. It was of no avail to tell them to follow me and see whether I searched for money. Their reply was, 'of course you will not dare to take it out before us, but we know that if you are a skilful magician you will order it to follow you through the air to whatever place you please.' If the traveller takes the dimensions of a building or a column, they are persuaded that it is a magical proceeding. Even the most liberal minded Turks of Syria reason in the same manner, and the more travellers they see, the stronger is their conviction that their object is to search for treasures, 'Maou delayl', 'he has indications of treasure with him,' is an expression I have heard a hundred times.

ALEXANDER KINGLAKE
(1809–1891)

English historian and author of the classic *Eothen*. (See p. 60.)

Two Englishmen in a desert –
en route from Jerusalem to Cairo, 1835

I can understand the sort of amazement of the orientals at the scantiness of the retinue with which an Englishman passes the Desert, for I was somewhat struck myself when I saw one of my countrymen making his way across the wilderness in this simple style. At first there was a mere moving speck in the horizon; my party of course became all alive with excitement, and there were many surmises. Soon it appeared that three laden camels were approaching, and that two of them carried riders. In a little while we saw that one of the riders wore the European dress, and at last the travellers were pronounced to be an English gentleman and his servant; by their side there were a couple of Arabs on foot; and this, if I rightly remember was the whole party. . . .

This Englishman, as I afterwards found, was a military man returning to his country from India, and crossing the Desert at this part in order to go through Palestine. As for me, I had come pretty straight from England, and so here we met in the wilderness at about half-way from our respective starting-points. As we approached each other, it became with me a question whether we should speak. I thought it likely that the stranger would accost me, and in the event of his doing so, I was quite ready to be as sociable and chatty as I could be according to my nature; but still I could not think of anything particular that I had to say to him. Of course, among civilised people the not having anything to say is no excuse at all for not speaking; but I was shy and indolent, and I felt no great wish to stop and talk like a morning visitor in the midst of those broad solitudes. The traveller perhaps felt as I did, for, except that we lifted our hands to our caps, and waved our arms in courtesy, we passed each other quite as distantly as if we had passed in Pall Mall. Our attendants, however, were not to be cheated of the delight that they felt in speaking to new listeners and hearing fresh voices once more. The masters, therefore, had no sooner passed each other, than their respective servants quietly stopped and entered into conversation. As soon as my camel found that her companions were not following her, she caught the social feeling and refused to go on. I felt the absurdity of the situation, and determined to accost the stranger, if only to avoid the awkwardness of remaining stuck fast in the Desert whilst our servants were amusing themselves. When with this intent I turned round my camel, I found that the gallant officer had passed me by about thirty or forty yards, and was exactly in the same predicament as myself. I put my now willing camel in motion and rode up towards the stranger: seeing this he followed my example, and came forward to meet me. He was the first to speak. Too courteous to address me, as if he admitted the possibility of my wishing to accost him from any feeling of mere sociability or civilian-like love of vain talk, he at once attributed my advances to a laudable wish of acquiring statistical information; and accordingly, when we got within speaking distance, he said, 'I daresay you wish to know how the plague is going on at Cairo?' and then he went on to say he regretted that his information did not enable him to give me in numbers a perfectly accurate statement of the daily deaths. He afterwards talked pleasantly enough upon other and less ghastly subjects. I thought him manly and intelligent – a worthy one of the few thousand strong Englishmen to whom the empire of India is committed.

Sir Richard Francis Burton
(1821–1890)

English explorer. (See p. 76.) In July 1853, having been circumcised for the purpose and disguised as an Indian-born Afghan doctor, he set sail from Suez in a pilgrim ship bound for Yenbo (Yanbu). His aim – which he failed to accomplish – was to cross the Arabian Peninsula in a direct line from Medina to Muscat or diagonally from Mecca to Makallah on the Indian Ocean. From Yenbo he travelled to Medina, the burial place of the Prophet, Muhammad. On 31 August he set off with a caravan for Mecca. There he took part in the Ramy, the ceremony in the course of which pilgrims throw seven stones at stone pillars at the place where the Devil was driven away by stones by Abraham, Hagar and Ishmael.

Cleaning the Prophet's tomb at Medina

The eunuchs (guardians of the tomb) positively declare that no one ever approaches the tomb, and that he who ventured to do so would at once be blinded by the supernatural light. Moreover the historians of El Medinah all quote certain visions of the Prophet, directing his tomb to be cleared of dust that had fallen upon it from above, in which case some man celebrated for piety and purity was *let through a hole in the roof*, by cords, with directions to wipe it with his beard.

The view through the Prophet's window

Shaykh Hamid, after wrenching a beggar or two from my shoulders, then permitted me to draw near the little window called the Apostle's, and to look in. Here my proceedings were watched with suspicious eyes. The Persians have sometimes managed to pollute the part near Abu Bakr's and Omar's graves by tossing through the aperture what is externally a handsome shawl intended as a present for the tomb. After straining my eyes for a time, I saw a curtain, or rather hangings, with three inscriptions in large gold letters, informing readers that behind them lie Allah's Apostle and the first two Caliphs.

The exact place of Mohammed's tomb is moreover distinguished by a large pearl rosary, and a peculiar ornament, the celebrated *Kaukab-al-Durri*, or constellation of pearls, suspended to the curtain breast-high. This is described to be a 'brilliant star set in diamonds and pearls,' placed in the dark in order that man's eye may be able to bear its splendours: the vulgar believe it to be a 'jewel of the jewels of Paradise.' To me it greatly resembled the round glass stoppers used for the humbler sort of decanters; but . . . I never saw it quite near enough to judge fairly, and I did not think fit to pay an exorbitant sum for the pleasure of entering the inner passage of the baldaquin.

On Mecca

. . . Those who find danger the salt of pleasure may visit Meccah; but if asked whether the results justify the risk, I should reply in the negative.

CHARLES MONTAGU DOUGHTY
(1843–1926)

English traveller and poet. Perhaps the greatest of all Arabian explorers, he set off in November 1876 with the Haj caravan from Damascus to Mecca. He left it at Meda'in Salih and began the wanderings that took him, at the same speed as the Bedouin in whose encampments he lived, to Tayma, then east to Boreida and south-west to Jiddah. Often in great danger and suffering dreadful privations, his journey lasted for more than one and a half years. Doughty's account, *Travels in Arabia Deserta* (1888), written in elaborately archaic prose which deters many readers, is a masterpiece.

Summer days in the wilderness

Now longwhile our black booths had been built upon the sandy stretches, lying before the swelling white Nefûd side: the lofty coast of Irnàn in front, whose cragged breaches, where is any footing for small herbs nourished of this barren atmosphere, are the harbour of wild goats, which never drink. The summer's night at end, the sun stands up as a crown of hostile flames from that huge covert of inhospitable sandstone bergs; the desert day dawns not little and little, but it is noontide in an hour. The sun, entering as a tyrant upon the waste landscape, darts upon us a torment of fiery beams, not to be remitted till the far-off evening. – No matins here of birds; not a rock partridge-cock, calling with blithesome chuckle over the extreme waterless desolation. Grave is that giddy heat upon the crown of the head; the ears tingle with a flickering shrillness, a subtle crepitation it seems, in the glassiness of this sun-stricken nature: the hot sand-blink is in the eyes, and there is little refreshment to find in the tent's shelter; the worsted booths leak to this fiery rain of sunny light. Mountains looming like dry bones through the thin air, stand far around about us: the savage flank of Ybba Moghrair, the high spire and ruinous stacks of el-Jebâl Chebàd, the coast of Helwàn! Herds of the weak nomad camels waver dispersedly, seeking pasture in the midst of this hollow fainting country, where but lately the swarming locusts have fretted every green thing. This silent air burning about us, we endure breathless till the assr: when the dazing Arabs in the tents revive after their heavy hours. The lingering day draws down to the sun-setting; the herdsmen, weary of the sun, come again with the cattle, to taste in their menzils the first sweetness of mirth and repose. – The day is done, and there rises the nightly freshness of this purest mountain air: and then to the cheerful song and the cup at the common fire. The moon rises ruddy from that solemn obscurity of jebel like a mighty beacon: – and the morrow will be as this day, days deadly drowned in the sun of the summer wilderness.

EDWARD GRANVILLE
BROWNE
(1862–1926)

English Orientalist and scholar of Persian. In 1887–8 he
lived in Persia, later writing a classic account of his stay,
A Year Amongst the Persians (1893).

Difficulties with the local dialect on the way from
Teheran to Isfahan in 1888

I now for the first time realised the difficulty of obtaining precise
information from uneducated people with regard to their language.
In particular, it was most difficult to get them to give me the
different parts of the verbs. I would ask, for example, 'How would
you say, "I am ill"?' They gave me a sentence which I wrote down.
Then I asked, 'Now, what is "thou art ill"?' They repeated the same
sentence. 'That can't be right,' I said; 'they can't both be the same.'
'Yes, that is right,' they answered; 'if we want to say "thou art ill"
we say just what we have told you.' 'Well, but suppose you were ill
yourself what would you say?' 'Oh, then we should say so-and-so.'
This readiness in misapprehending one's meaning and reversing
what one had said gave rise to one class of difficulties. Another class
arose from the extreme simplicity of the people. For instance, after
asking them the words for a number of common objects in their
language, I asked, 'And what do you call "city"?' 'Káshán,' they
replied. 'Nonsense!' I said, 'Káshán is the name of a particular city:
what do you call cities in general?' 'No,' they said, 'it is quite right:
in Persian you say "*shahr mi-ravam*," "I am going to the city": we
say "*Káshán mi-ravam*": it is all the same.' It was useless to argue,
or to point out that there were many other cities in the world besides
Káshán: to these simple-minded folk Káshán remained 'the city' *par
excellence*, and they could not see what one wanted with any other.
Finally I had to give up the struggle in despair, and to this day I do
not know whether the Kohrúdí dialect possesses a general term for
'city' or not.

The Antidote

My eye was now so painful that I determined to cover it with a bandage, which at once called the attention of my guests to its condition. They all expressed the greatest concern, and Ustá Akbar begged me to allow him to try a remedy which he had never known to fail. In this request he was so importunate that at last I most foolishly consented. Thereupon he went out into the garden and gathered some leaves from the hollyhock or other similar plant, with which he soon returned. Then he called for an egg, broke it into a cup, removed the yolk, leaving only the white, and bade me lie down on the floor on my back, and, if possible, keep the inflamed eye open. Then he poured the white of the egg over the eye, covered it up with the leaves, and entreated me to remain still as long as I could, that the treatment might work. It did work: in two or three minutes the pain became so acute that I could bear it no longer, and called for warm water to wash away the horrid mess which half-blinded me. Ustá Akbar remonstrated, but I told him that the remedy was worse than the disease.

'Ah,' said he, 'it is clear that I have made a mistake. When you told me that you had been bathing your eye in iced water, I assumed that this cold was the cause of the affection, and so applied a hot remedy. Now it is evident that it is due not to cold but to heat, so that a cold remedy should be applied. And I know one which will not disappoint you.'

'Thank you,' I rejoined, 'if it is anything like the last I should prefer to have nothing to do with it.'

'It is nothing like the last,' he answered. 'What I would suggest is that you should smoke a pipe of opium. That is a cold drug most potent in the treatment of hot maladies, and of its efficacy you cannot but have heard.'

Opium! There was something fascinating about the idea. The action on the mental functions exercised by narcotic drugs had always possessed for me a special interest, and though the extremely unpleasant results of an experiment on the subjective effects of *Cannabis Indica* (Indian hemp) which I had tried while a student at St Bartholomew's Hospital had somewhat cooled my enthusiasm for this sort of research, the remembrance of that dreadful evening when Time and Space seemed merging in confused chaos, and my very personality appeared to be undergoing disintegration, had now sufficiently lost its vividness to make me not unwilling to court some fresh experience of this kind. So, after a few moments' reflection, I signified my willingness to try Ustá Akbar's new cure; and ten minutes later my whole being was permeated with that glow of tranquil beatitude, conscious of itself, nay, almost exultant in its own peaceful serenity, which constitutes the fatal charm of what the Persians call *par excellence* 'the Antidote' (*tiryák*).

DAVID GEORGE HOGARTH
(1862–1927)

English archaeologist, scholar and traveller. Between 1915–18 he was Director of the Arab Bureau in Cairo and in this capacity was one of the architects of the Arab Revolt. Keeper of the Ashmolean Museum in Oxford, 1908–27.

Eastern hospitality as demonstrated by some Yuruk nomads at Patara in South-West Turkey

The ruins of Pátara lie round its silted harbour, which is become a reedy morass. A fortress of the Byzantine age has been the last permanent habitation; and along the broken crenellations of its walls we followed clumsily the soft-shod feet of an agile Yuruk boy. It was no holiday ramble. The wall was a mere *arête* between inky depths to left and a slimy jungle to right; it was often broken and always unsafe, and over its rottenest parts passage had to be forced through clumps of rank vegetation. We made slow progress, marked by the splashing of loose stones into the pool and the scurrying of its myriad gruesome tenants, and when we had struggled to dry land, near the sand-choked ruin of the Theatre, it was high time to seek some lodging for the night.

Far up the marsh the cry of a goatherd driving his flock to higher ground sounded faintly amid a responsive jangle of gathering bells; and loud in our ears sang the first mosquitoes of sundown. What pests must rise from that rotting slough of a summer night, making a camp intolerable, even on the heights above! But in chill April weather one might hope to pass the dark hours well enough. We made for the pine-log shelter and the three black booths, and finding the first full of dung, wherein fleas and ticks unnumbered lay in wait, sent our Greek ahead to parley with the Yuruks. This was a tactical mistake. Hospitality, even in the East, is more often enforced by public opinion than offered out of the fulness of the heart. . . .

The Greek came back to say that we were among bad men, and had best go back to Kalamáki, night though it was. But we had no mind to remount our jaded beasts and stumble for four hours over that execrable path, and the Yuruks looked honest folk enough. So doing last what we should have done first, we walked straightway into the largest tent and sat down by the ashes of its hearth. No one showed surprise. We were within our social right by the code, and the owner had no choice but to follow and speak the customary words of welcome. But suspicion clouded his simple mind, and we had to go through that exasperating Ollendorfian dialogue, which, in one language or another, must be held on arrival wherever men have been taught by long experience to conceal their substance.

'Have you barley for our beasts?'

'We have no barley.'

'But we give money.' (*Chins jerked and tongues clicked to imply incredulity and denial.*)

'Well – have you chopped straw?'

'There is none, Wallah!'

'Good – nor eggs?'

'We have no eggs.' (*Abundance in the next camp.*)

'Nor milk?'

'To-day, none.' (*Yesterday and to-morrow, never to-day.*)

'Nor butter, nor bread, nor anything?'

'Not anything, by the head of God!'

'But these fowls, they are barren?'

'Ai-i! they lay eggs, God be praised!'

'And those nanny-goats, they are all dry?'

'Wallah! They make milk.'

'Then, by God's will, we stay. Quick! barley, milk, eggs! We stay.'

Should an Eastern depart from his indifferent reserve and greet you cordially at first sight, beware of him. He meditates some particular motive of self-interest.

Haggling for a Hittite stela at the dirty town of Bor in Anatolia

Bor is a dirty town, three miles distant from the site of the very ancient and royal city of Tyana; whence had been brought (to be lodged, alas! in the house of a Greek virago) part of a Hittite *stela*. It bore a broken relief of a head, crowned with a kingly tiara, and a long incised inscription in the linear Hittite hieroglyphic character, of which, at that time, only one other example was known. Its existence was discovered by Mr. Ramsay in 1882, but then the owner would allow no impression to be taken, and frustrated all attempts to make a careful copy. Returning four years later, the discoverer could obtain neither permission to see it, nor even information of its whereabouts. We resolved to make another and last effort in 1890, and took up our quarters in the *khan* at Bor.

The Greek woman had found no purchaser in ten years, and was not averse now to reopen negotiations. We soon had news of the 'black stone', and the same afternoon a guide led us through narrow streets and up a closed courtyard to a barn, where in a dark hole in the mud floor lay the treasure. Deputing a go-between to open negotiations for purchase, we took advantage of the diversion and the owner's apparent graciousness to set to work with pencil and note-book. In a moment the Greek had leapt on to the stone, spreading herself like a hen on a sitting of eggs, whilst a crowd of friends bustled to her assistance. Under such circumstances it was impossible to copy an inscription in an unknown character; so we had no resource but to bargain. The Greek demanded five hundred liras; we consulted and made a handsome offer of five for immediate possession. She collapsed in her son's arms, and recognizing that the ice was broken, we went away.

All the evening the go-betweens came and went. Next morning our caravan was ordered to start, and the price came down to forty liras. When the horses were yoked to the baggage-waggon, the market fell to thirty: as the waggon rumbled out before us under the *khan* gate, the figure was twenty-five; with my foot in the stirrup I was asked for twenty-two, and riding out for twenty. Doubtless we could have got the stone for less, but we were pressed for time, and it was worth more than twenty liras. So the bargain was struck and the stone lifted into our waggon. Needless to say, we could not hope to carry off so well-known a treasure under the very eyes of the local Governor, unless prepared to pay more in *bakshish* than in purchase, and, once we had impressions and copies, the stone itself might as well be placed in the Imperial Museum at Stambul. Making, therefore, an ostentatious virtue of necessity, we conveyed it ten miles to Nigdeh, and lodged it there in trust for His Majesty the Sultan. The excitement was immense, and we became the observed of all the town. Strolling that night in the dark over the crowded roof of the *khan*, I heard that certain Franks had tried to escape with a stone worth 10,000 liras, but had been arrested by the police and forced to disgorge. Officials themselves deprecated such wasteful generosity; and a Government secretary approached us privately next day with a kind suggestion that, if our difficulty related to the conveyance of the stone to the coast, he could arrange that we should be robbed of it outside the town, and for a slight consideration recover it at the port. Gratefully and regretfully we declined.

GERTRUDE BELL
(1868–1926)

English traveller, writer, mountaineer, archaeologist and member of the British Secret Service. From 1899 she travelled extensively in Persia, Anatolia and Syria, one of her most enterprising journeys being a fourteen-day crossing of the Syrian Desert in 1911. Indefatigable and courageous, it was of Gertrude Bell that an Arab chief is said to have remarked, 'And if this is one of their women! Allah, what must their men be like!'

Gardens in the Persian desert, June 1892

Well in this country the men wear flowing robes of green and white and brown, the women lift the veil of a Raphael Madonna to look at you as you pass; wherever there is water a luxuriant vegetation springs up and where there is not there is nothing but stone and desert. Oh the desert round Teheran! miles and miles of it with nothing, *nothing* growing; ringed in with bleak bare mountains snow crowned and furrowed with the deep courses of torrents. I never knew what desert was till I came here; it is a very wonderful thing to see; and suddenly in the middle of it all, out of nothing, out of a little cold water, springs up a garden. Such a garden! trees, fountains, tanks, roses and a house in it, the houses which we heard of in fairy tales when we were little: inlaid with tiny slabs of looking-glass in lovely patterns, blue tiled, carpeted, echoing with the sound of running water and fountains. Here sits the enchanted prince, solemn, dignified, clothed in long robes. He comes down to meet you as you enter, his house is yours, his garden is yours, better still his tea and fruit are yours, so are his kalyans (but *I* think kalyans are a horrid form of smoke, they taste to me of charcoal and paint and nothing else.) By the grace of God your slave hopes that the health of your nobility is well? It is very well out of his great kindness. Will your magnificence carry itself on to this cushion? Your magnificence sits down and spends ten minutes in bandying florid compliments through an interpreter while ices are served and coffee, after which you ride home refreshed, charmed, and with many blessings on your fortunate head. And all the time your host was probably a perfect stranger into whose privacy you had forced yourself in this unblushing way. Ah, we have no hospitality in the west and no manners. I felt ashamed almost before the beggars in the street – they wear their rags with a better grace than I my most becoming habit, and *the* veils of the commonest women (now the veil is the touchstone on which to try a woman's toilette) are far better put on than mine. A veil should fall from the top of your head to the soles of your feet, of that I feel convinced, and it should not be transparent.

Say, is it not rather refreshing to the spirit to lie in a hammock strung between the plane trees of a Persian garden and read the poems of Hafiz – in the original mark you! – out of a book curiously bound in stamped leather which you have bought in the bazaars. That is how I spend my mornings here; a stream murmurs past me which Zoroastrian gardeners guide with long handled spades into tiny sluices leading into the flower beds all around. The dictionary which is also in my hammock is not perhaps so poetic as the other attributes – let us hide it under our muslin petticoats!

This also is pleasant: to come in at 7 o'clock in the morning after a two hours' ride, hot and dusty, and find one's cold bath waiting for one scented with delicious rose water, and after it an excellent and longed for breakfast spread in a tent in the garden.

T. E. LAWRENCE
(1888–1935)

English adventurer, soldier and scholar. After visiting the
Middle East as an archaeologist, he joined the intelligence section of the British Army in Egypt when war
broke out in 1914. In 1916 he became one of the leaders
of the Arab Revolt. In 1919 he started to write a book
about his Arabian adventures, but lost most of the manuscript. He had to rewrite it without help from his notes,
which he had destroyed. Finally published commercially
in 1935, *The Seven Pillars of Wisdom* is deservedly a
classic.

The streets of Jiddah

The style of architecture was like crazy Elizabethan half-timber
work, in the elaborate Cheshire fashion, but gone gimcrack to an
incredible degree. House-fronts were fretted, pierced and pargetted
till they looked as though cut out of cardboard for a romantic
stage-setting. Every storey jutted, every window leaned one way or
other; often the very walls sloped. It was like a dead city, so clean
underfoot, and so quiet. Its winding, even streets were floored with
damp sand solidified by time and as silent to the tread as any carpet.
The lattices and wall-returns deadened all reverberation of voice.
There were no carts, nor any streets wide enough for carts, no shod
animals, no bustle anywhere. Everything was hushed, strained, even
furtive. The doors of houses shut softly as we passed. There were no
loud dogs, no crying children: indeed, except in the bazaar, still half
asleep, there were few wayfarers of any kind; and the rare people we
did meet, all thin, and as it were wasted by disease, with scarred,
hairless faces and screwed-up eyes, slipped past us quickly and
cautiously, not looking at us. Their skimp, white robes, shaven polls
with little skull-caps, red cotton shoulder-shawls, and bare feet
were so same as to be almost a uniform.

The atmosphere was oppressive, deadly. There seemed no life in
it. It was not burning hot, but held a moisture and sense of great age
and exhaustion such as seemed to belong to no other place: not a
passion of smells like Smyrna, Naples or Marseilles, but a feeling of
long use, of the exhalations of many people, of continued bath-heat

and sweat. One would say that for years Jidda had not been swept through by a firm breeze: that its streets kept their air from year's end to year's end, from the day they were built for so long as the houses should endure. There was nothing in the bazaars to buy.

'Lord, I am gone blind'

We were riding for Rumm, the northern water of the Beni Atiyeh: a place which stirred my thought, as even the unsentimental Howeitat had told me it was lovely. The morrow would be new with our entry to it: but very early, while the stars were yet shining, I was roused by Aid, the humble Harithi Sherif accompanying us. He crept to me, and said in a chilled voice, 'Lord, I am gone blind'. I made him lie down, and felt that he shivered as if cold; but all he could tell me was that in the night, waking up, there had been no sight, only pain in his eyes. The sun-blink had burned them out.

BERTRAM THOMAS
(1892–1950)

English explorer. In the winter of 1930–1 Thomas, a former political officer in the Middle East, made the first crossing of the Rub'al Khali, 'The Abode of Emptiness', the last great unexplored region of Arabia. He landed at Salala on the coast of Oman and set off northward with a party of Rashid Bedouin who had sworn loyalty to him. Their destination was Doha, on the Persian Gulf, which they reached after an epic journey of sixty-seven days.

An Arab in Erewhon, Rub'al Khali,
January 1931

My electric torch was a source of wonderment to my companions. 'Could a strayed or stolen camel be tracked on a dark night with it?' that was the crucial question. The first Badu to place his hand over the lighted end discovered that there was practically no heat, and brought the miracle to the notice of his companions. They all followed suit and when, instead of feeling heat they saw the red hue of blood and shadowy finger-bones, they burst out in astonished cries – 'There is no god but God. Surely the Sahib's tribe must be a wonderful people?' It was idle for me to declare that I had not made the torch, for did we not make still more marvellous works – rifles and ammunition!

'Who makes rifles?' asked one Badu, fondling his own.

'The Infidels,' said another without looking up.

'No,' I corrected them, 'we are Believers.'

'And if we came to your country, Sahib, would you be our *rabia* [representative of a tribe whose presence with strangers ensures their protection] so that none should harm us?'

'There is no need for a *rabia* in my country.'

'But,' said Hamad, 'if one should slay me and you were my *rabia* what would you do?'

'But none would slay you. Nobody may carry arms in my country.'

'What a place!' I felt them to be thinking, 'fit only for women and slaves!'

'And should we get camel's milk to drink?'

'We have no camels,' I returned apologetically, for I knew I should get few marks for this.

'Then what have you got? Sheep? Cows?'

'Yes, sheep and cows,' I said, 'but we make ships and rifles and all manner of things from the iron of the earth.'

'True,' interjected Shaikh Salih with a sophisticated air, 'I've heard a Mansuri from Abu Dhabi say that one day a Nasrani came to the shaikh and told him that in his country a bar of iron like this,' and he flourished his camel stick, 'would make five rifles.'

Chorus of Badawin: 'There is no god but God.'

One picked up the torch again. 'It is heavy,' he said. 'God! it's heavy,' said another, as he took it out of his comrade's hand.

Salih: 'They are not an easy people' (*i.e.* not a weak tribe whose members could be treated as inferiors).

'Inside the torch is *guwa*' – strength – (a word they reverence) 'more potent than bullets, and such that it kills men,' I said.

'But why kill them?'

'Only bad men,' I returned – 'murderers.'

'Yes, and very right too – "an eye for an eye and a tooth for a tooth" – 'tis God's Law.'

'But have you no blood-money?'

'None,' I said.

'Then the murdered man's brother or cousin does not profit a single dollar.'

'Not a single dollar,' I repeated, conscious that I was scoring very few marks again.

'But have you no sanctuary?'

'No, our shaikh is strong, and no one would dare to give a murderer sanctuary.'

'But with us,' said Salih, 'sanctuary is honoured, unless there is shame in the murder, such for instance as a *rabia* who has betrayed his companion. What good man is there,' he continued, looking round his companions, 'who would withhold sanctuary from one who had killed his enemy?'

Chorus of Badawin: 'Yes, by God!'

'Which direction is your country, Sahib?' said one of them after a pause.

I pointed with my riding cane in a north-westerly direction.

'How far is it away?'

'*Hol* – a year's march, from Ramadhan to Ramadhan,' I said, 'at our pace.'

Chorus of Badawin: 'There is no god but God.'

'And which direction is it from Mecca?' interposed Salih, one of the few South Arabian Badawin I knew who had made the Pilgrimage.

I pointed as before, perhaps a shade more northerly.

'And how far is it from there?'

'Almost as far as it is from here.'

Chorus: 'There is no god but God.'

'Then it is beyond the sea, Sahib?'

'Yes,' I said, 'beyond the sea.'

'And what is there beyond it?'

'The sea again,' I said.

'Where is the Sea of Barlimul?' said Talib. 'I think you must mean the Sea of Barlimul.' He turned to tell his companions that there the world ended. Beyond was nothing. It was the seventh and last sea – *Allahu 'Alim!*

DAME FREYA STARK
(1893–   )

English traveller and writer. One of the most remarkable travellers of the age, she made her first journey (to the Middle East) in 1928, her latest (to Nepal) in 1981.

The days of 'Ashura, Kuwait

All through the ten days of 'Ashura the Shi'as in Islam mourn for the death of Husain, until the slow mounting tide of their grief reaches its climax with the last processions, and the slain body itself is carried under a blood-stained sheet through wailing crowds, where the red headdress of the Sunni is well advised not to make itself conspicuous. All is represented, every incident of the fatal day of Kerbela; and the procession stops at intervals to act one episode or other in a little clearing of the crowd. One can hear it coming from far away by the thud of the beaters beating their naked chests, a mighty sound like the beating of carpets; or see the blood pour down the backs of those who acquire merit with flails made of knotted chains with which they lacerate their shoulders, bared for the purpose: and when the body itself comes, headless (the man's head is hidden in a box and a small boy with a fan walks beside it to prevent suffocation), its two feet sticking out of the bloody drapery, the truncated neck of a sheep protruding at the other end, a dagger cunningly stuck above each shoulder into the cloth – when this comes heaving through the crowd, there is such a passion of anger and sorrow, such a wailing of women from the roofs, such glances of repulsion towards the foreigner who happens to be looking on, that it is quite understandable that the civilized governments of the East are now doing all they can to discourage this expression of religion in favour of forms more liturgical. . . .

Before the excitement of this climax had subsided we left our places, climbed to our roof, and came away, for curious glances had already been cast towards us. And as we walked back, closely veiled through the dusty street, I thought, not of this violence of passion, but of the august ritual of our own cathedrals, aethereal and remote; and wondered in what similarity of instinct, what selfsame desire to express the inexpressible in visible shape, this too had had its birth. On the last day of the 'Ashura the Persian children in Kuwait are taken to the Mulla, who passes a knife under their chin in sign of sacrifice or dedication; from mythology to religion, from religion to mysticism, the great truths pass: and it is well now and then to see them in those simple forms that belong to our first awakening in this world, so that we may not forget the brotherhood of men.

The East

The *inscrutability* of the East is, indeed, I believe a myth . . . the ordinary inhabitant is incomprehensible merely to people who never trouble to have anything much to do with him.

EVELYN WAUGH
(1903–1966)

English novelist. (See p. 87.)

Not like English boys – the Aden scout troop in 1930

One unifying influence among the diverse cultures of the Crater was the Aden troop of Boy Scouts. It is true that Arabs cannot be induced to serve in the same patrol with Jews, but it is a remarkable enough spectacle to see the two races sitting amicably on opposite sides of a camp-fire, singing their songs in turn and occasionally joining each other in chorus. The scoutmaster, an English commercial agent, invited me to attend one of these meetings.

The quarters were a disused sergeants' mess and the former barrack square. My friend was chiefly responsible for the Arab patrol, the Jews having an independent organization. As I approached, rather late, I saw the latter drilling in their own quarter of the parade ground – a squad of lengthy, sallow boys in very smart uniforms furnished with every possible accessory by the benefaction of a still-wealthy local merchant. The Arabs – with the exception of one resplendent little Persian, for 'Arab' in this connexion was held to include all Gentiles, Somali, Arab, and Mohammedan Indians – were less luxuriously equipped. There were also far fewer of them. This was explained by the fact that two of the second-class scouts were just at that time celebrating marriages.

Tests were in progress for the tenderfoot and other badges. The acquiring of various badges is a matter of primary concern in the Aden troop. Some of the children had their arms well covered with decorations. 'We generally let them pass after the third or fourth attempt,' the scoutmaster explained. 'It discourages them to fail too often.'

Two or three figures crouching against corners of masonry were engaged on lighting fires. This had to be done with two matches; they had been provided by their mothers with horrible messes of food in tin cans, which they intended to warm up and consume. I believe this qualified them for a cookery medal. 'Of course, it isn't like dealing with English boys,' said the scoutmaster; 'if one isn't pretty sharp they put paraffin on the sticks.'

The scoutmaster kept the matchbox, which was very quickly depleted. Breathless little creatures kept running up. 'Please, sahib, no burn. Please more matches.' Then we would walk across, scatter the assembled sticks and tinder, and watch them built up again. It was not a long process. A match was then struck, plunged into the centre of the little pile, and instantly extinguished. The second match followed. 'Please, sahib, no burn.' Then the business began again. Occasionally crows of delight would arise and we were hastily summoned to see a real conflagration. Now and then a sheet of flame would go up very suddenly, accompanied by a column of black smoke. 'Oil,' said the scoutmaster, and that fire would be disqualified.

Later a Somali boy presented himself for examination in scout law. He knew it all by heart perfectly. 'First scoot law a scoot's honour iss to be trust second scoot law . . .' et cetera, in one breath.

'Very good, Abdul. Now tell me what does "thrifty" mean?'
'Trifty min?'
'Yes, what do you mean, when you say a scout is thrifty?'
'I min a scoot hass no money.'
'Well, that's more or less right. What does "clean" mean?'
'Clin min?'
'You said just now a scout is clean in thought, word, and deed.'
'Yis, scoot iss clin.'
'Well, what do you mean by that?'
'I min tought, worden deed.'
'Yes, well, what do you *mean* by clean?'
Both parties in this dialogue seemed to be losing confidence in the other's intelligence.

'I min the tenth scoot law.'

A pause during which the boy stood first on one black leg, then on the other, gazing patiently into the sun.

'All right, Abdul. That'll do.'

'Pass, sahib?'

'Yes, yes.'

An enormous smile broke across his small face, and away he went capering across the parade ground, kicking up dust over the fire-makers and laughing with pleasure.

'Of course, it isn't quite like dealing with English boys,' said the scoutmaster again.

ROBERT BYRON
(1905–1941)

English traveller, art critic and historian. Author of *The Road to Oxiana*. (See p. 180.)

An encounter in the Church of the Holy Sepulchre, Jerusalem

Set in this radiant environment, the Church of the Holy Sepulchre appears the meanest of churches. Its darkness seems darker than it is, its architecture worse, its cult more degraded. The visitor is in conflict with himself. To pretend to detachment is supercilious; to pretend to reverence, hypocritical. The choice lies between them. Yet for me that choice has been averted. I met a friend in the doorway, and it was he who showed me how to cope with the Holy Places.

My friend was a black-robed monk, wearing short beard, long hair, and a tall cylindrical hat.

'Hail,' said I in Greek. 'You come from Mount Athos?'

'I do,' he replied, 'from the monastery of Docheiariou. My name is Gabriel.' . . .

We were now in a broad circular chamber as high as a cathedral, whose shallow dome was supported on a ring of massive piers. In the middle of the empty floor stood the shrine, a miniature church resembling an old-fashioned railway engine.

'When were you last on Mount Athos?' asked Gabriel.

'In 1927.'

'I remember. You came to Docheiariou.'

'Yes. And how is my friend Synesios?'

'Very well. But he's too young yet to be an Elder. Come in here.'

I found myself in a small marble chamber, carved in the Turkish baroque style. The way to the inner sanctuary as blocked by three kneeling Franciscans.

'Whom else do you know at Docheiariou?'

'I know Frankfort. Is he well?'

'Frankfort?'

'Frankfort, Synesios's cat.'

'Ah! his cat. . . . Don't mind those men; they're Catholics. It's a black cat –'

'Yes, and jumps.'

'I know. Now here we are. Mind your head.'

Stepping through the Franciscans as though they were nettles, Gabriel dived into a hole three feet high, from which came a bright light. I followed. The inner chamber was about seven feet square. At a low slab of stone knelt a Frenchwoman in ecstasy. By her side stood another Greek monk.

'This gentleman has been to Mount Athos,' announced Gabriel to his crony, who shook hands with me across the body of the Frenchwoman. 'It was six years ago and he remembers Synesios's cat. . . . This is the Tomb' – pointing to the slab of stone – 'I shall be in here all day tomorrow. You must come and see me. There's not much room, is there? Let's go out. Now I'll show you the other places. This red stone is where they washed the body. Four of the lamps are Greek, the others Catholic and Armenian. Calvary's upstairs. Ask your friend to come up. This is the Greek part, that the Catholic. But these are Catholics at the Greek altar, because Calvary was there. Look at the inscription over the cross. It's in real diamonds and was given by the Tsar. And look at this image. Catholics come and give these things to her.'

Gabriel pointed to a glass case. Inside I beheld a wax Virgin, draped in a pawnbroker's stock of chains, watches, and pendants.

'My friend here is a Catholic,' I informed Gabriel maliciously.

'Oh, is he? And what are you? Protestant? Or nothing at all?'

'I think I shall be Orthodox while I'm here.'

'I shall tell God that. You see these two holes? They put Christ in them, one leg in each.'

'But is that in the Bible?'

'Of course it's in the Bible. This cave is the place of the Skull. That's where the earthquake split the rock. My mother in Samos had thirteen children. Now only my brother in America, my sister in Constantinople, and myself are left. That there is Nicodemus's tomb, and that the tomb of Joseph of Arimathaea.'

'And what are the two little tombs?'

'They're for the children of Joseph of Arimathaea.'

'I thought Joseph of Arimathaea was buried in England.'

Gabriel smiled, as though to say 'Tell that to the marines'.

'Here,' he continued, 'is a picture of Alexander the Great visiting Jerusalem, and being received by one of the prophets – I can't remember which.'

'But did Alexander ever visit Jerusalem?'

'Certainly. I only tell you the truth.'

'I'm sorry. I thought it might be a legend.'

We emerged at last into the daylight.

'If you come and see me the day after tomorrow, I shall be out of the Tomb again. I come out at eleven, after being in all night.'

'But won't you want to sleep?'

'No. I don't like sleeping.'

WILFRED THESIGER
(1910–   )

English soldier, writer, photographer and explorer. In the immediate post-war years he made two crossings of the Empty Quarter (the Rub'al Khali), the first since Thomas's in 1930–1. Thesiger's first crossing was made from Salala in 1946–7; he assembled a party of Bait Kathir, men who had never seen or even heard of Englishmen and who spoke a difficult Arabic dialect, to take him to the edge of the sands at Mughshin, north of Dhufar. The actual crossing was made with four Rashdi, members of the same tribe who had accompanied Thomas. His second crossing, in 1948, was made through the Western Sands from the Manwakh Well, north of Hadhramaut, again with Rashid Bedouin. Sixteen days after setting out, they reached their first water at Hassi in Jabal Tuwaiq, on the north side of the Rub'al Khali, having narrowly missed the two parties sent out by the Governor of Jauf to kill them. At Sulaiyil they were imprisoned and only released after the personal intervention of the King of Saudi Arabia and his adviser St John Philby. From here the gigantic return journey was made by way of the Jabrin oasis to the east, and from there to Abu Dhabi on the Trucial Coast.

The great dunes beyond the Last Bitter Watering Place, Khaur bin Atarit, November 1946

What were we going to do if we could not get the camels over it? I knew that we could not go any farther to the east, for al Auf had told me that the quicksands of Umm al Samim were in that direction. To the west the easier sands of Dakaka, where Thomas had crossed, were more than two hundred miles away. We had no margin, and could not afford to lengthen our journey. Our water was already dangerously short, and even more urgent than our own needs were those of the camels, which would collapse unless they were watered soon. We *must* get them over this monstrous dune, if necessary by unloading them and carrying the loads to the top. But what was on the other side? How many more of these dunes were there ahead of us? If we turned back now we might reach Mughshin, but I knew that once we crossed this dune the camels would be too tired and thirsty to get back even to Ghanim. Then I thought of Sultan and the others who had deserted us, and of their triumph if we gave up and returned defeated. Looking again at the dune ahead I noticed that al Auf was coming back. A shadow fell across the sand beside me. I glanced up and bin Kabina stood there. He smiled, said 'Salam alaikum', and sat down. Urgently I turned to him and asked, 'Will we ever get the camels over that?' He pushed the hair back from his forehead, looked thoughtfully at the slopes above us, and answered, 'It is very steep but al Auf will find a way. He is a Rashid; he is not like these Bait Kathir.' Unconcernedly he then took the bolt out of his rifle and began to clean it with the hem of his shirt, while he asked me if all the English used the same kind of rifle.

When al Auf approached we went over to the others. Mab-khaut's camel had lain down; the rest of them stood where we had left them, which was a bad sign. Ordinarily they would have roamed off at once to look for food. Al Auf smiled at me as he came up but said nothing, and no one questioned him. Noticing that my camel's load was unbalanced he heaved up the saddle-bag from one side, and then picking up with his toes the camel-stick which he had dropped, he went over to this own camel, caught hold of its head-rope, said 'Come on', and led us forward.

The closing door

I knew that I had made my last journey in the Empty Quarter and that a phase in my life had ended. Here in the desert I had found all that I asked; I knew that I should never find it again. But it was not only this personal sorrow that distressed me. I realized that the Bedu with whom I had lived and travelled, and in whose company I had found contentment, were doomed. Some people maintain that they will be better off when they have exchanged the hardship and poverty of the desert for the security of a materialistic world. This I do not believe. I shall always remember how often I was humbled by those illiterate herdsmen who possessed, in so much greater measure than I, generosity and courage, endurance, patience and light-hearted gallantry. Among no other people have I ever felt the same sense of personal inadequacy.

On the last evening, as bin Kabina and bin Ghabaisha were tying up the few things they had bought, Codrai said, looking at the two small bundles, 'It is rather pathetic that this is all they have.' I understood what he meant; I had often felt the same. Yet I knew that for them the danger lay, not in the hardship of their lives, but in the boredom and frustration they would feel when they renounced it. The tragedy was that the choice would not be theirs; economic forces beyond their control would eventually drive them into the towns to hang about street corners as 'unskilled labour'.

The lorry arrived after breakfast. We embraced for the last time. I said, 'Go in peace', and they answered together, 'Remain in the safe keeping of God, Umbarak.' Then they scrambled up on to a pile of petrol drums beside a Palestinian refugee in oil-stained dungarees. A few minutes later they were out of sight round a corner. I was glad when Codrai took me to the aerodrome at Sharja. As the plane climbed over the town and swung out above the sea I knew how it felt to go into exile.

GEOFFREY BIBBY
(1917–   )

English archaeologist. In 1953 he went to Bahrain to search for the 'lost civilization' of Dilmun, which had dominated the trade routes between Mesopotamia and the Indus Valley between 3000 and 500 BC.

Sherd-hunting with Sheikh Sulman, ruler of Bahrain, 1954

Thus when one day we topped a ridge and saw, some hundred yards away, a small building with several cars and trucks parked nearby we felt it only polite to turn back and continue our search for flint on the near side of the slope. But the Arab of the desert has sharper eyes than we, and a few minutes later a tall Arab strode down to us and told us that His Highness wished to see us. Approaching, we found Sheikh Sulman sitting on a carpet spread on the sand in front of the building, flanked by his bodyguard, who all appeared at first glance to be fierce-eyed, with jutting aggressive beards and rifles held suspiciously loosely. But the sheikh seemed to have no objection at all to being interrupted in his hunting by a couple of European trespassers. He bade us be seated, called for coffee, and asked us, in halting English, what we had found. We showed him our flints, and tried to convince him that they were in fact fashioned by man. He was unconvinced, but responded by sending a servant to unearth from a dusty corner of the hunting lodge several large fossil shells that he said had been found in the neighbourhood. And then he offered to take us to see the places in the south of the island where, by tradition, there had been villages, before the water supply gave out. He crooked a finger, and the long black limousine parked beside the lodge purred up behind us. We were motioned into the broad rear seat and Sheikh Sulman climbed in and wedged himself between us. The driver and an escort, bearing the sheikh's sporting rifle as well as his own Lee Enfield, took their places in front, and we drove south. Looking back I saw two large covered trucks pull away and follow us.

The south end of Bahrain narrows to a point, and distances in the southern part of the island are therefore not long. After twenty minutes' cruising on cushioned springs over trackless country that would have chattered our teeth in our station-car and must have given the occupants of the trucks behind something to think about, we turned down a valley to a couple of palm-trees and a well. There were no ruins of houses to be seen, but for perhaps two hundred yards in every direction from the well the ground was littered with potsherds. I picked up a piece of typical blue-and-white glazed Ming china, such as I used to collect on my free afternoons in and around the Portuguese fort on the north coast of the island. 'From the time of the Portuguese,' I said impressively.

It had never occurred to Sheikh Sulman that a site could be dated otherwise than by written records, and he turned the sherd over and back, looking for the date inscribed on it. 'Where is the writing?' he asked. I explained, haltingly, that there was no writing, but that pottery like this was made in China four hundred years ago and could only have been brought here by the Portuguese. Sheikh Sulman grasped the principle of dating sites by surface indications with the instantaneous comprehension that one hopes for and rarely finds in first-year archaeology students. For the next half-hour he and P.V. and I quartered the site, picking up representative sherds of every type of pottery visible, meeting occasionally to compare notes and sherds and to speculate on the possibility of any of our collection being from before the Portuguese. I often saw Sheikh Sulman in later years, until his death in 1962, at official functions and receptions, or on visits to our excavations, but he has never impressed me as much as on that afternoon when, with his red-and-blue ankle-length *abba* flapping in the wind and with an almost boyish smile on his fiercely bearded face, he brought handfuls of potsherds for our inspection. Not a few kings have been archaeologists of repute, and, given the training, I am sure Sheikh Sulman would have been a worthy addition to their number.

All that afternoon we drove from site to site collecting sherds, and each time we returned to the car we found the carpet rolled out beside it and the cook, who rode in one of the trucks, standing by with freshly brewed coffee in the brass coffee-pot. We would sit for ten minutes through the ritual three cups, eating sweet biscuits or sticky *halwa*, and then board the car again. The bodyguard and the falconers would climb into their truck, the servants and the cook would whisk away the carpet and the coffee cups and get into the other truck, and the cavalcade would start off again. The sun was setting, and it was time for the evening prayer, when we got back to the hunting lodge. We said our farewells, took our bags of pot-sherds, entered our own, distinctly shabby-looking, station-car and pressed the self-starter. Nothing happened. The sheikh, who had turned to Mecca to begin his *rakāt*, looked over his shoulder, and snapped his fingers. The escort, the falconers, even the cook, got behind us and pushed. After ten yards the motor fired and we drove away over the ridge. Sheikh Sulman was already back at his devotions.

DERVLA MURPHY
(1931–   )

Intrepid Irish traveller, mostly in Asia and Ethiopia, mostly on bicycles or with quadrupeds, or on local transport.

A lone female cyclist deals with a randy Kurd on the Turkish-Iranian frontier, 1963

An ancient Jewish legend says that the Kurds are descended from four hundred virgins who were deflowered by devils while on their way to King Solomon's court and my own experiences in both Turkish and Persian Azerbaijan prompt me to accept this genealogy as an historic fact.

At Dogubayzit, the last little town en route to the Persian frontier-post, I stayed in the local doss-house, where my bedroom was a tiny box leading off the wide loft which accommodated the majority of the 'Otel's patrons. This room had a flimsy door, without any fastening, and there was no movable piece of furniture which could have been placed against it as a security measure. The squalid bedding was inhabited by a host of energetic fleas, but their attentions were wasted on me and within minutes of retiring I was sound asleep.

Some hours later I awoke to find myself bereft of bedding and to see a six-foot, scantily-clad Kurd bending over me in the moonlight. My gun was beneath the pillow and one shot fired at the ceiling concluded the matter. I felt afterwards that my suitor had shown up rather badly; a more ardent admirer, of his physique, could probably have disarmed me without much difficulty.

As a result of the loud report and my visitor's rapid retreat there was a stirring of many bodies on the floor outside my room and a few sleepy mutterings – then quiet.

PAUL THEROUX
(1941–   )

American novelist and traveller. He has lived in Africa, Singapore and London, writing memorable fiction about each of these places, *The Great Railway Bazaar*, his account of a journey around the world by train, was one of the most popular travel books of recent years.

On the Lake Van express from Haydarpasa, c. 1973

The German-speaking Turk described the rest of the train as *schmoozy* and made a face. But it was only in the schmoozy part that English was spoken. There, one saw tall fellows with pigtails and braids, and short-haired girls who, lingering near their boyfriends, had the look of pouting catamites. Gaunt wild-haired boys with shoulder bags and sunburned noses stood rocking in the corridors, and everyone had dirty feet. They grew filthier and more fatigued-looking as I moved down the cars, and at the very front of the train they might have passed for the unfortunate distant relatives of the much cleaner Turks who shared their compartments, munching bread, combing food out of their mustaches, and burping their babies. On the whole, the hippies ignored the Turks; they played guitars and harmonicas, held hands, and organized card games. Some simply lay on their seats lengthwise, hogging half the compartment, and humped under the astonished eyes of Turkish women who sat staring in dark *yashmaks*, their hands clasped between their knees. Occasionally, I saw an amorous pair leave their compartment hand in hand to go copulate in a toilet.

Most were on their way to India and Nepal, because

The wildest dreams of Kew are the facts of Khatmandhu,
And the crimes of Clapham chaste in Martaban.

But the majority of them, going for the first time, had that look of frozen apprehension that is the mask on the face of an escapee.

Indeed, I had no doubt that the teen-aged girls who made up the bulk of these loose tribal groups would eventually appear on the notice boards of American consulates in Asia, in blurred snapshots or retouched high-school graduation pictures: MISSING PERSON and HAVE YOU SEEN THIS GIRL? These initiates had leaders who were instantly recognizable by the way they dressed: the faded dervish outfit, the ragged shoulder bag, the jewelry – earrings, amulets, bracelets, necklaces. Status derived solely from experience, and it was possible to tell from the ornaments alone – that jangling in the corridor – whose experience had made him the leader of his particular group. All in all, a social order familiar to the average Masai tribesman.

I tried to find out where they were going. It was not easy. They seldom ate in the dining car; they often slept; they were not allowed in the fastness of the Turks' de luxe. Some stood by the windows in the corridor, in the trancelike state the Turkish landscape induces in travelers. I sidled up to them and asked them their plans. One did not even turn around. He was a man of about thirty-five, with dusty hair, a T-shirt that read 'Moto-Guzzi,' and a small gold earring in the lobe of his ear. I surmised that he had sold his motorcycle for a ticket to India. He held the windowsill and stared at the empty reddish yellow flatlands. In reply to my question he said softly, 'Pondicherry.'

'The ashram?' Auroville, a kind of spiritual Levittown dedicated to the memory of Sri Aurobindo and at that time ruled over by his ninety-year-old French mistress (the 'Mother'), is located near Pondicherry, in South India.

'Yes. I want to stay there as long as possible.'

'How long?'

'Years.' He regarded a passing village and nodded. 'If they let me.'

It was the tone of a man who tells you, with a mixture of piety and arrogance, that he has a vocation. But Moto-Guzzi had a wife and children in California. Interesting: he had fled his children and some of the girls in his group had fled their parents.

Another fellow sat on the steps of the bogie, dangling his feet in the wind. He was eating an apple. I asked him where he was going. 'Maybe try Nepal,' he said. He took a bite of the apple. 'Maybe Ceylon, if it's happening there.' He took another bite. The apple was like the globe he was calmly apportioning to himself, as small, bright, and accessible. He poised his very white teeth and bit again. 'Maybe Bali.' He was chewing. 'Maybe go to Australia.' He took a last bite and winged the apple into the dust. 'What are you, writing a book?'

JONATHAN RABAN
(1942–   )

English writer, critic and traveller. In 1977, curious about the Arabs who were settling around him in London, he made a long journey through contemporary Arabia.

Doha, Quatar

I asked him what changes he'd seen in the country since he first came.

'I'm afraid,' said Mr Moon, 'that I'm rather an unobservant man. I've only really noticed one thing – the flyover.'

I went out to look at the place for myself. It was at that moment in the evening when the low sun goes squashy in the Gulf and coats everything with a soft thick light the colour of broom. It gilded the wailing six-lane highway. It gilded the sandy roadside where I walked. It gilded the long trail of garbage – the crushed Pepsi cans, discarded Frigidaires, torn chunks of motor tyre, cardboard boxes, broken fan-belts lying in the dust like snakes, the building rubble, polystyrene packing-blocks, and a rather long-dead goat. So many cars had been junked at the side of the road, and reared, rusting, on their axles, that it seemed legitimate to wonder whether people here threw Pepsi cans out of cars or cars out of Pepsi cans. There were ruins, but they were not picturesque: squalid little rectangles of mud whose walls had fallen out, leaving a pathetic detritus in view – a few stained and ripped cushions, a child's graffito, a wrecked tricycle. A very pregnant, yellow, vulpine bitch – a degenerate descendant of the Saluki family – bared its teeth at me from the heap of rubbish which it was defending; and a rat the size of a domestic cat ambled coolly through a pile of fluttering multi-coloured rags.

It looked more like the scene of a recent civil war than a utopian city-state. Yet there was something about it which I recognized – the careless absentmindedness of the very rich. No one leaves more squalor in his wake than a passing millionaire: some hireling will clear up the mess afterwards, and to be tidy is to reveal a streak of mean thrift. Really lavish waste is one of the most certain of all signs of wealth. The man who can afford to create stinking eyesores, then negligently turn his back on them, is displaying his money just as arrogantly as the man who furnishes his house with solid gold doorknobs and diamond-crusted coffee tables. In a poor country the junked cars would have been either stripped or restored; the Frigidaires lovingly salvaged; even the cardboard boxes would have been dragged away to make improvised dwellings. Here they were simply litter – the overspill of some vast and smelly garbage bag. As the corpulent rats had evidently discovered, this was a handsome treasury of filth.

Down over the hump of Mr Moon's flyover I could see the bits of the city that one was supposed to notice. They looked as if a rich man had been making a hobby of them. The national museum was a castellated wedding-cake, creamy and toothsome in the sunset. The Qatar Monetary Agency was a giant gold ingot, its tinted windows taking their colour from the hammered sea. Around the harbour-front, the Corniche looped in a wide sweep past the moored yachts, the fishing dhows, cranes, container trucks and ships' funnels. It was, if one squinted a little and held one's nose, a lovely little golden city on the sea; and as the fairy-lights came up on the minarets, Doha gleamed and twinkled as prettily as if it had quite forgotten where it was and had mistaken the Gulf for the Riviera. The word 'Corniche' alone, of course, assisted in the illusion; it tried to nudge one into remembering that other city on a bay, where Regine's, the Casino and the Royal Palace glitter in a tideless mirror of sewage and suntan oil.

MIDDLE ASIA

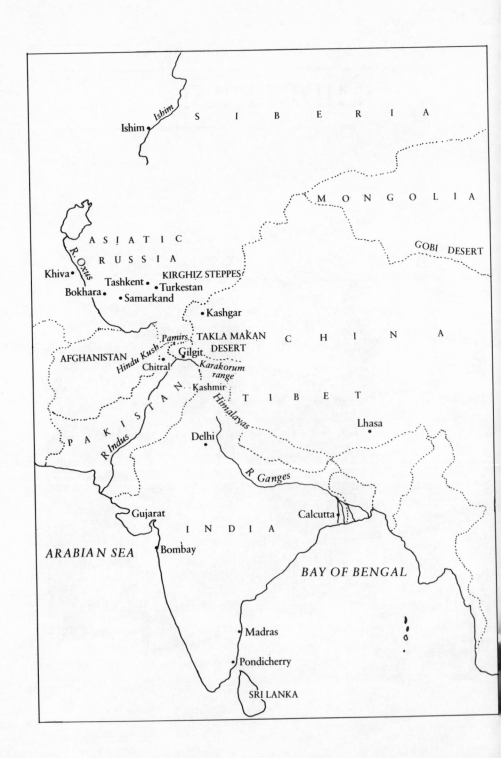

ALEXANDER THE GREAT
(356–323 BC)

Macedonian king. In 334 BC he crossed the Hellespont, defeated a Persian army and went on to conquer the entire Persian Empire. He then marched through present-day Afghanistan into northern India, where, having over-run the Punjab, his men would go no further. Alexander's address to his officers on the banks of the Hyphasis (the Sutlej) was recorded by the second-century Greek historian Arrian.

Knowing when to stop, 326 BC

'I observe, gentlemen, that when I lead you on a new venture you no longer follow me with your old spirit. I have asked you to meet me that we may come to a decision together: are we, upon my advice, to go forward, or, upon yours, to turn back?

'. . . For a man who *is* a man, work, in my belief, if it is directed to noble ends, has no object beyond itself; none the less, if any of you wish to know what limit may be set to this particular campaign, let me tell you that the area of country still ahead of us, from here to the Ganges and the Eastern ocean is comparatively small. You will undoubtedly find that this ocean is connected with the Myrcanian Sea [the Caspian], for the great Stream of Ocean encircles the earth. Moreover I shall prove to you, my friends, that the Indian and Persian Gulfs and the Myrcanian Sea are all three connected and continuous. Our ships will sail round from the Persian Gulf to Libya as far as the Pillars of Hercules, whence all Libya to the eastward will soon be ours, and all Asia too, and to this empire there will be no boundaries but what God Himself has made for the whole world. . . .'

When Alexander ended there was a long silence.

The officers present were not willing to accept what he had said, yet no one liked to risk an unprepared reply. Several times Alexander invited comment, should any wish to give it and genuinely hold different views from those he had expressed; but in spite of his invitation nothing was said until at last Coenus, son of Polemocrates, plucked up his courage to speak.

Which he did, at some length, ending with the words 'Sir, if there is one thing above all others a successful man like you should know, it is *when to stop.*'

NEARCHUS
(*fl.* 325 BC)

Macedonian general. In 325, having decided to leave India, Alexander the Great built a fleet in the Indus to transport part of his army home. Nearchus was placed in command, and the ships sailed up the Persian coast, rejoining Alexander in Susa. Nearchus' account of the voyage appears in Arrian's *Indica*.

Ichthyopagi (fish-eaters) on the Makran coast of Baluchistan, 325 BC

They eat them raw, just as they take them from the water, that is, the more tender kinds; the larger ones, which are tougher, they dry in the sun till they are quite sere and then pound them and make a flour and bread of them; others even make cakes of this flour. Even their flocks are fed on the fish, dried; for the country has no meadows and produces no grass. They collect also in many places crabs and oysters and shell-fish. There are natural salts in the country; from these they make oil. Those of them who inhabit the desert parts of their country, treeless as it is and with no cultivated parts, find all their sustenance in the fish; but a few of them sow part of their district, using the corn as a relish to the fish, for the fish form their bread. The richest among them have built huts; they collect the bones of any large fish which the sea casts up, and use them in place of beams. Doors they make from any flat bones which they can pick up. But the greater part of them, and the poorer sort, have huts made from the fishes' backbones.

MEGASTHENES
(*fl.* 300 BC)

Greek writer. Friend and companion of Seleucus Nicator (the first member of a great royal dynasty which at the height of its power ruled over an area extending from Thrace to India), who sent him to India as ambassador to King Chandragupta at Pataliputra on the Ganges (near present-day Patna).

The care of the king's person

... The care of the king's person is committed to women, who also are purchased from their parents; and the body-guards and the rest of the military force are stationed outside the gates. And a woman who kills a king when he is drunk receives as her reward the privilege of consorting with his successor; and their children succeed to the throne. Again, the king does not sleep in daytime; and even at night he is forced to change his bed from time to time because of the plots against him. Among the non-military departures he makes from his palace, one is that to the courts, where he spends the whole day hearing cases to the end, none the less even if the hour comes for the care of his person. This care of his person consists of his being rubbed with sticks of wood, for while he is hearing the cases through, he is also rubbed by four men who stand around him and rub him.

ODORIC OF PORDENONE
(1274?–1331)

Italian friar. One of the great missionary travellers. (See p. 255.) His massive fourteen-year journey took him through India and China to Tibet; he was the first European to give an account of Lhasa.

A certain great kingdom called Tibet

Quitting this province I came to a certain great kingdom called TIBET, which is on the confines of India Proper, and is subject to the Great Khan. They have in it great plenty of bread and wine as anywhere in the world. The folk of that country dwell in tents made of black felt. But the chief and royal city is all built with walls of black and white, and all its streets are very well paved.

In this city no one shall dare to shed the blood of any, whether man or beast, for the reverence they bear a certain idol which is there worshipped. In that city dwelleth the *Abassi*, i.e. in their tongue the Pope, who is the head of all the idolaters, and who has the disposal of all their benefices such as they are after their manner.

And the fashions of this kingdom are thus. The women have their hair plaited in more than one hundred tresses, and they have a couple of tusks as long as those of wild boars. And another fashion they have in this country is this. Suppose such an one's father to die, then the son will say, 'I desire to pay respect to my father's memory' and so he calls together all the priests and monks and players in the country round, and likewise all the neighbours and kinsfolk. And they carry the body into the country with great rejoicings. And they have a great table in readiness, upon which the priests cut off the head, and then this is presented to the son. And the son and all the company raise a chant and make many prayers for the dead. Then the priests cut the whole of the body to pieces, and when they have done so they go up again to the city with the whole company, praying for him as they go. After this the eagles and vultures come down from the mountains and every one takes his morsel and carries it away. Then all the company shout aloud, saying, 'Behold! the man is a saint! For the angels of God come and carry him to Paradise.' And in this way the son deems himself to be honoured in no small degree, seeing that his father is borne off in this creditable manner by the angels. And so he takes his father's head, and straightway cooks it and eats it; and of the skull he maketh a goblet, from which he and all of the family always drink devoutly to the memory of the deceased father. And they say that by acting in this way they show their great respect for their father. And many other preposterous and abominable customs have they.

MARCO POLO
(1254?–1324?)

Venetian merchant and traveller. In 1271, at the age of seventeen, Marco Polo set off from Venice for China with his father and uncle (who had already made the great journey). Their route was by way of Hormuz at the mouth of the Persian Gulf, the Hindu Kush in what is now Afghanistan, the Pamirs, Kashgar, Yarkand and the Gobi Desert. In 1275 they reached Cambaluc (Peking), where they remained for sixteen years at the court of Kublai Khan. Marco became one of the Mongol emperor's advisers and travelled extensively in the Far East on various missions. In 1292 the travellers left China, arriving back at Venice in 1295. Marco joined the Venetian forces fighting the Genoans and was taken prisoner.

During his two-year captivity he dictated an account of his travels.

Crossing the Gobi Desert, c. 1274

The length of this Desert is so great that 'tis said it would take a year and more to ride from one end of it to the other. And here, where its breadth is least, it takes a month to cross it. 'Tis all composed of hills and valleys of sand, and not a thing to eat is to be found on it. But after riding for a day and a night you find fresh water, enough mayhap for some 50 or 100 persons with their beasts, but not for more. And all across the Desert you will find water in like manner, that is to say, in some 28 places altogether you will find good water, but in no great quantity; and in four places also you find brackish water.

Beasts there are none; for there is nought for them to eat. But there is a marvellous thing related of this Desert, which is that when travellers are on the move by night, and one of them chances to lag behind or to fall asleep or the like, when he tries to gain his company again he will hear spirits talking, and will suppose them to be his comrades. Sometimes the spirits will call him by name; and thus shall a traveller ofttimes be led astray so that he never finds his party. And in this way many have perished. Sometimes the stray travellers will hear as it were the tramp and hum of a great cavalcade of people away from the real line of road, and taking this to be their own company they will follow the sound; and when day breaks they find that a cheat has been put on them and that they are in an ill plight. Even in the day-time one hears those spirits talking. And sometimes you shall hear the sound of a variety of musical instruments, and still more commonly the sound of drums. Hence in making this journey 'tis customary for travellers to keep close together. All the animals too have bells at their necks, so that they cannot easily get astray. And at sleeping-time a signal is put up to show the direction of the next march.

So thus it is that the Desert is crossed.

IBN BATTUTA
(1304–1377)

Arab traveller. (See p. 32.)

Delhi depopulated by the excesses of Sultan Tughlag, c. 1340

One of the gravest charges against the sultan is that of compelling the inhabitants of Delhi to leave the town. The reason for this was that they used to write missives reviling and insulting him, seal them and inscribe them, 'By the hand of the Master of the World, none but he may read this.' They then threw them into the audience-hall at night, and when the sultan broke the seal he found them full of insults and abuse. He decided to lay Delhi in ruins, and having bought from all the inhabitants their houses and dwellings and paid them the price of them, he commanded them to move to Dawlat Ábád. They refused, and his herald was sent to proclaim that no person should remain in the city after three nights. The majority complied with the order, but some of them hid in the houses. The sultan ordered a search to be made for any persons remaining in the town, and his slaves found two men in the streets, one a cripple and the other blind. They were brought before him and he gave orders that the cripple should be flung from a mangonel and the blind man dragged from Delhi to Dawlat Ábád, a distance of forty days' journey [700 miles]. He fell to pieces on the road and all of him that reached Dawlat Ábád was his leg. When the sultan did this, every person left the town, abandoning furniture and possessions, and the city remained utterly deserted. A person in whom I have confidence told me that the sultan mounted one night to the roof of his palace and looked out over Delhi, where there was neither fire nor smoke nor lamp, and said 'Now my mind is tranquil and my wrath appeased.' Afterwards he wrote to the inhabitants of the other cities commanding them to move to Delhi to repopulate it. The result was only to ruin their cities and leave Delhi still unpopulated, because of its immensity, for it is one of the greatest cities in the world. It was in this state that we found it on our arrival, empty and unpopulated, save for a few inhabitants.

GONZALEZ DE CLAVIJO
(d. 1412)

Spanish nobleman. In 1403 he was sent with an embassy
to the court of Timur Leng (Tamerlane) at Samarkand.
Timur, who was near the end of his life, had in his time
conquered the area between the Caspian and the Black
Sea, Delhi, Aleppo and Baghdad; he was now planning
the invasion of China. Clavijo's journey was accomplished at breakneck speed, travelling by way of Trebizond, thanks to the excellent communications system
that existed in the Mongol domains. When he arrived at
Samarkand, which he described as being 'rather larger
than Seville', Clavijo found a multitude of 150,000 people assembled for the wedding of Timur's eleven-year-old
son Ulug Beg. The ambassadors, who had brought costly
gifts (the Egyptian ambassador brought nine ostriches
and a giraffe), found themselves in a dream world. Twenty thousand tents had been pitched for the occasion, some
of them capable of holding 10,000 people, one of the
smaller ones being partially lined with sable.

Caño, chief wife of Timur, arrives at a feast

On Monday, the 13th of October, Timour Beg gave a feast, and sent
for the ambassadors. . . . On this day there were many games,
played in various ways, and the elephants which the lord had, were
painted green and red, with their castles, and they were made to
exhibit their performances. The noise made by the drums, during
these games, was so great that it was quite wonderful; and near the
pavilion, where the lord sat, there were many performing jugglers.

There were three hundred jars of wine placed before the lord, on
the ground; and there were also large skins full of cream, into which
the attendants put loaves of sugar, and mixed it up; and this was
what they drank on that day. When the people were all arranged in
order round the wall which encircled the pavilion, Caño, the chief
wife of the lord, came forth to be present at the feast. She had on a
robe of red silk, trimmed with gold lace, which was long and
flowing, but without sleeves, or any opening, except one to admit
the head, and two arm holes. It had no waist, and fifteen ladies held
up the skirts of it, to enable her to walk. She had so much white lead

on her face, that it looked like paper; and this is put on to protect it from the sun, for when they travel in winter or summer, all great ladies put this on their faces. She had a thin veil over her face, and a crested head dress of red cloth, which hung some way down the back. This crest was very high, and was covered with large pearls, rubies, emeralds, and other precious stones, and it was embroidered with gold lace, on the top of which there was a circlet of gold, set with pearls. On the top of all there was a little castle, on which were three very large and brilliant rubies, surmounted by a tall plume of white feathers. One of these feathers hung down as low as the eyes, and they were secured by golden threads; and, as she moved, they waved to and fro.

Her hair, which was very black, hung down over her shoulders, and they value black hair much more than any other colour. She was accompanied by three hundred ladies, and an awning was carried over Caño, supported by a lance which was borne by a man. It was made of white silk, in the form of the top of a round tent, and held over her, to protect her from the sun.

THOMAS CORYATE
(1577?–1617)

English traveller. (See p. 111.) In 1612, on the second of his great journeys, he set off overland for India. There he stayed at the court of the Mogul, Jahangir.

'My journey betwixt Jerusalem and this Moguls Court'

I spent in my journey betwixt Jerusalem and this Moguls court 15 moneths and odde daies; all which way I traversed afoot, but with divers paire of shooes, having beene such a propateticke (I will not call my selfe peripatetick, because you know it signifieth one that maketh a perambulation about a place, περιπατεῖν signifying to walk about), that is, a walker forward on foote, as I doubt whether you ever heard of the like in your life; for the totall way betwixt Jerusalem and the Moguls court containeth two thousand and seaven hundred English miles. My whole perambulation of this Asia the Greater is like to bee a passage of almost six thousande miles, by that time that in my returne backe thorough Persia, afterward also by Babylon and Ninivie, I shall come to Cairo in Egypt, and from that downe the Nylus to Alexandria, there to be one daie (by Gods helpe) imbarqued for Christendome; a verie immense dimension of ground. . . .

You may remember to relate this unto your friends that I will now mention as a matter verie memorable: I spent in my ten moneths travels betwixt Aleppo and the Moguls court but three pounds sterling, yet fared reasonable well everie daie; victuals beeing so cheape in some countries where I travelled, that I oftentimes lived competentlie for a pennie sterling a day. Yet of that three pound I was cousened of no lesse then ten shillings sterling by certaine lewd Christians of the Armenian nation; so that indeed I spent but fiftie shillings in my ten moneths travailes.

PIETRO DELLA VALLE
(1586–1652)

Italian traveller. He sailed from Venice in 1614, spent a year in Constantinople, then travelled in Egypt, the Holy Land, Arabia, Persia and India, returning to Italy in 1626.

A bird hospital at Cambay in Gujarat

The people of *Cambaia* are most part Gentiles; and here, more than elsewhere, their vain superstitions are observed with rigor. Wherefore we, who came particularly to see these things the same day of our arrival, after we had din'd and rested a while, caus'd ourselves to be conducted to see a famous Hospital of Birds of all sorts, which for being sick, lame, depriv'd of their mates, or otherwise needing food and care, are kept and tended there with diligence; as also the men who take care of them are maintain'd by the publick alms; the Indian Gentiles, who, with *Pythagoras* and the ancient *Ægyptians* (the first Authors of this opinion according to *Herodotus*) believe in the Transmigration of Souls, not onely from Man to Man, but also from Man to brute beast, conceiving it no less a work of Charity to do good to beasts then to Men. The House of this Hospital is small, a little room sufficing for many Birds: yet I saw it full of Birds of all sorts which need tendance, as Cocks, Hens, Pigeons, Peacocks, Ducks and small Birds, which during their being lame, or sick, or mateless, are kept here, but being recover'd and in good plight, if they be wild they are let go at liberty; if domestick they are given to some pious person who keeps them in his House. The most curious thing I saw in this place were certain little Mice, who being found Orphans without Sire or Dam to tend them, were put into this Hospital, and a venerable Old Man with a white Beard, keeping them in a box amongst Cotton, very diligently tended them with his spectacles on his nose, giving them milk to eat with a bird's feather, because they were so little that as yet they could eat nothing else; and, as he told us, he intended when they were grown up to let them go free whither they pleas'd.

EDWARD TERRY
(1590–1660)

English cleric. In 1615 he sailed to India as chaplain to the East India Company's fleet. On arrival he was appointed chaplain to Sir Thomas Roe, ambassador to the court of the Mogul, Jahangir. In 1617, with four other Englishmen (who were bearing gifts to the Emperor), he travelled to his camp at Mandoa.

The death of Thomas Coryate, 1617

O what pains this poor man took to make himself a subject for present and after discourse; being troubled at nothing for the present, unless with the fear of not living to reap that fruit he was so ambitious of in all his undertakings. And certainly he was surprized with some such thoughts and fears (for so he told us afterwards), when upon a time, he being at Mandoa with us, and there standing in a room against a stone pillar, where the Embassadour was and myself present with them, upon a sudden he fell into such a swoon that we had very much ado to recover him out of it. But at last come to himself, he told us that some sad thoughts had immediately before presented themselves to his fancy, which (as he conceived) put him into that distemper; like Fannius in Martial: *Ne moriare mori*, to prevent death by dying. For he told us that there were great expectations in England of the large accounts he should give of his travels after his return home; and that he was now shortly to leave us, and he being at present not very well, if he should dye in the way toward Surat, whither he was now intended to go (which place he had not as yet seen), he might be buried in obscurity and none of his friends ever know what became of him, he travelling now, as he usually did, alone. Upon which my Lord willed him to stay longer with us; but he thankfully refused that offer, and turned his face presently after towards Surat, which was then about three hundred miles distant from us. And he lived to come safely thither; but there being over-kindly used by some of the English, who gave him sack which they had brought from England; he calling for it as soon as he first heard of it, and crying: Sack, sack; is there such a thing as sack? I pray give me some sack; and drinking of it, though, I conceive, moderately (for he was a very temperate man), it increased his flux which he had then upon him. And this caused him within a few daies, after his very tedious and troublesome travels (for he went most on foot) at this place to come to his journies end; for here he overtook Death in the month of December 1617, and was buried (as aforesaid) under a little monument, like one of those are usually made in our church-yards.

ALEXANDER VON HUMBOLDT
(1769–1859)

German naturalist and traveller. Between 1799 and 1804 he explored Central and South America, tracing the course of the Orinoco River and the sources of the Amazon, a journey that made him famous throughout Europe. In 1829 he set off for Russia and Siberia, making a 9700-mile journey in less than six months with the help of Tsar Nicholas I, who provided him with 12,244 post horses. His fame and the Tsar's patronage did not, however, stretch as far as Ishim in Siberia, where he was kept under constant surveillance by the prefect of police, who, after a few days, felt compelled to write to the Governor-General of the Province.

Ishim endangered

Your Excellency,

A few days ago there arrived here a German of shortish stature, insignificant appearance, fussy and bearing a letter of introduction from Your Excellency to me. I accordingly received him politely;

but I must say that I find him suspicious, and even dangerous. I disliked him from the first.

He talks too much and despised my hospitality. He pays no attention to the leading officials of the town and associates with Poles and other political criminals. I take the liberty of informing Your Excellency that his intercourse with political criminals does not escape my vigilance. On one occasion he proceeded with them to a hill overlooking the town. They took a box with them and got out of it a long tube which we all took for a gun. After fastening it to three feet they pointed it down on the town and one after another examined whether it was properly sighted. This was evidently a great danger for the town which is built entirely of wood; so I sent a detachment of troops with loaded rifles to watch the German on the hill. If the treacherous machinations of this man justify my suspicions, we shall be ready to give our lives for the Tsar and Holy Russia. I send this despatch to Your Excellency by special messenger.

THOMAS MANNING
(1772–1840)

English scholar and traveller. After exhausting the intricacies of Greek, Latin and mathematics, he sought a new challenge for his formidable intelligence: Chinese. Having learnt the language he sailed for China in 1806. From there he went via India to Tibet, disguised as a Chinese. After a long and eventful journey he arrived in Lhasa in December 1811. Eccentric, paranoid, 'the first Chinese scholar in Europe' (according to an obituarist), he was also renowned for his beard, which by 1815 reached his waist.

Lhasa

If the Palace [the Potala] exceeded my expectations, the town fell far short of them. There is nothing striking, nothing pleasant in its appearance. The habitations are begrimed with smut and dirt. The avenues are full of dogs, some growling and gnawing bits of hide which lie about in profusion, and emit a charnel house smell; others limping and looking livid; others ulcerated; others starved and dying, pecked at by ravens; some dead and preyed upon. In short, everything seems mean and gloomy, and excites the idea of something unreal. Even the mirth and laughter of the inhabitants I thought dreamy and ghostly. The dreaminess, no doubt, was in my mind, but I could never get rid of the idea; it strengthened upon me afterwards.

JOSEPH WOLFF
(1795–1862)

German clergyman, missionary and traveller. The son of a Bavarian rabbi, he converted to Catholicism at the age of eleven, was expelled from home and arrived at Prague in 1812 having attended twelve different academies and monasteries. He went on to Rome, where he met the pope before being thrown out for heresy in 1818. The next year he arrived in England, where he converted to the Church of England and joined the Society for Promoting Christian Knowledge amongst the Jews. During the 1820s he carried his message to the Jewish communities of the eastern Mediterranean, Mesopotamia, Persia and Central Asia, making few converts and courting appalling dangers. In 1838, having married Lady Georgiana Walpole, he settled down as vicar of High Hoyland, Yorkshire. But not for long: 1844 found him in Bukhara, in worse danger than ever. Wolff had travelled there to discover the fate of two British officers, Colonel Stoddart and Captain Conolly, who were being held hostage by the emir, Nasrullah Khan. By the time he arrived the officers were already dead, having been thrown into a pit infested with vermin and reptiles and subsequently beheaded.

A narrow escape

The day following, a mullah came, and asked me, in his majesty's name, whether I would turn Mussulman. I replied, 'Tell the king, NEVER – NEVER – NEVER!' He asked me, 'Have you not a more polite answer for the King?' I said 'I beg you to tell his majesty, that you asked me whether I had not a more polite answer for his majesty, and I said, "Decidedly not."'

A few hours after the executioner came – the same who had put to death Stoddart and Conolly – and said, 'Joseph Wolff, to thee it shall happen as it did to Stoddart and Conolly', and made a sign at my throat with his hand. I prepared for death, and carried opium about with me, that, in case my throat should be cut, I might not feel the pain. However, at last I cast away the opium, and prayed, and wrote in my Bibles these words:

> My Dearest Georgiana and Henry,
> I have loved both of you unto death.
> Your affectionate husband and father,
> J. Wolff.

But that very same day, Abbas Kouli Khan sent word to the Ameer, that he had received a letter for his majesty from Muhammed Shah. The Ameer send word that Abbas Kouli Khan should send the letter by the Shekhawl; but Abbas Kouli Khan replied, that he had received orders from his court to deliver the letter in person. The Ameer sent word again that he should send the letter; but Abbas Kouli Khan protested against it, when his majesty at last consented to his coming to the palace. Abbas Kouli Khan delivered the letter to the Ameer; after having perused it he said, 'Well, I make a present to you of Joseph Wolff: he may go with you.'

EMILY EDEN
(1797–1869)

English novelist and traveller. A famous political hostess and friend of Lord Melbourne, she accompanied her brother George, second Earl of Auckland, to India when he was made Governor-General in 1835. Arriving in March 1836, she spent six years there. In 1837 Lord Auckland and an entourage of 12,000 people, 850 camels, 140 elephants and hundreds of horses and bullocks left Calcutta for a tour of the Upper Provinces.

On the march with the Governor-General,
November 1837

Mohun ke Serai.

We made our first march. The bugle sounds at half-past five to wake us, though the camels perform that ceremony rather earlier, and we set off at six as the clock strikes, for as nobody is allowed to precede the Governor-General, it would be hard upon the camp if we were inexact. The comfort of that rule is inexpressible, as we escape all dust that way. G. and F., with Captain N. and Captain M., went in the carriage towards Chumar, and I went with Captain J., Captain D., and W. the regular route, each on our elephant half way, and the other half on horseback.

It is very pleasant and cool at that time, really nice weather, and we had a short march – only seven miles and a half. It seems somehow wicked to move 12,000 people with their tents, elephants, camels, horses, trunks, &c., for so little, but there is no help for it. There were a great many robberies in the camp last night. Mrs. A. saw a man on his hands and knees creeping through her tent, but she called out, and he ran away without taking anything. Mr. B. says, when he and his wife were encamped last year on this spot, which is famous for thieves, they lost everything, even the shawl that was on the bed, and the clothes Mrs. B. had left out for the morning wear, and he had to sew her up in a blanket, and drive her to Benares for fresh things. W. and I went out on the elephant in search of a sketch in the afternoon. . . .

Tamarhabad, Friday, Nov. 24.

We marched ten miles to-day. These moves are the most amusing part of the journey; besides the odd native groups, our friends catch us up in their *déshabille* – Mrs. A. carrying the baby in an open carriage; Mrs. C. with hers fast asleep in a tonjaun; Miss H. on the top of an elephant, pacifying the big boy of the A.'s; Captain D. riding on in a suit of dust-coloured canvas, with a coal-heaver's hat, going as hard as he can, to see that the tent is ready for his wife; Mrs. B. carrying Mr. B.'s pet cat in her palanquin carriage, with her ayah opposite guarding the parroquet from the cat. Then Giles comes bounding by, in fact, run away with, but apologises for passing us when we arrive, by saying he was going on to take care that tea was ready for us. Then we overtake Captain D.'s dogs, all walking with red great coats on – our dogs all wear coats in the morning; then Chance's servant stalking along, with a great stick in one hand, a shawl draped over his livery, and Chance's nose peeping from under the shawl. F.'s pets travel in her cart.

JOHN WOOD
(1811–1871)

English naval officer and geographer. He entered the East India Company's naval service in 1826, and captained one of the first ships that sailed the Indus River after it was opened for commerce in 1835.

The cost of setting up a married household at Jurm in Badakshan, in 1838

The domestic arrangements of these people are as simple as with other mountaineers. Whilst we were at Jerm a neighbour of Hussein's was married. This gave us an opportunity of learning at what outlay the peasantry of this secluded region can commence housekeeping. I will state the articles separately. The first and largest item is –

	Tangas.	Rupees.
The purchase of a wife	0	25
Bedding	0	6
Antimony for the lady's eyes	3	
An iron boiler	0	2
A wooden bowl and spoons	3	
Flour-sieve	2	
Drinking bowl	1	
Table-cloth	2	
Dresser	2	
Knife for cutting beans	3	
Wooden ladle	1	
Frying pan	6	
A wooden pitcher	2	
Stone lamp	4	
Iron girdle for baking	2	
Culinary and other utensils	31 or	1½
Carried forward		34½

Brought forward		34½
Lutta, or head covering	10	
Kurta, or shirt	40	
Pajamah, or trousers	20	
Kufsh, or shoes	20	
Wife's wardrobe	90	or 4½
Lallah, or turban	6	
Takun	2	
Chukmum, or cloak	40	
Chamboor, or shoes	10	
Jurab, or stockings	6	
Kummer for the waist	40	
Pajamah	10	
Karid, or long sword	40	
Tufungh, or matchlock	200	
Matchlock furniture	22	
Husband's wardrobe and equipment	376	or 18¾

57¾,
or 5*l*. 14*s*. sterling.

EVARISTE REGIS HUC
(1813–1860)

French Lazarist missionary. In 1844 Father Huc and a
fellow missionary, Father Gabet, disguised themselves as
lamas and set off from China to Tibet. On the way they
passed through the great imperial forest, teeming with
tigers, panthers, bears and wolves, crossed a blistering
desert, and lived with Mongols and Tartars before
reaching the Koko Nor lake, where they waited until
October 1855 before joining the great ambassadorial
caravan to Lhasa. They reached the city in January 1846,
but despite getting on well with the Regent, were expelled
after a stay of only two months.

Death visits the caravan – en route to Lhasa from the Koko Nor

More than forty men of the caravan were abandoned still living, in the desert, without the slightest possibility of our aiding them. They were carried on horseback and on camelback so long as any hope remained, but when they could no longer eat, or speak, or hold themselves up, they were left on the way-side. The general body of the caravan could not stay to nurse them, in a barren desert, where there was hourly danger of wild beasts, of robbers, and, worse than all, of a deficiency of food. Yet, it was a fearful spectacle to see these dying men abandoned on the road! As a last token of sympathy, we placed beside each, a wooden cup and a small bag of barleymeal, and then the caravan mournfully proceeded on its way. As soon as the last straggler had passed on, the crows and vultures that incessantly hovered above the caravan, would pounce down upon the unhappy creatures who retained just enough of life to feel themselves torn and mangled by these birds of prey.

The Regent observes a louse through a microscope, Lhasa, January 1846

While adjusting [the microscope] we tried to give our auditor, as well as we could, some notions of optics, but seeing that the theory did not excite much enthusiasm, we proceeded at once to the practice. We asked if one of the company would be so good as to procure us a louse. The article was easier to find than a butterfly. A noble Lama, secretary to his excellency the First Kalon, had merely to put his hand under his silk dress to his armpit, and an extremely vigorous louse was at our disposition. We seized it by the sides with our nippers, but the Lama forthwith opposed this proceeding, and insisted upon putting a stop to the experiment, on the ground that we were going to cause the death of a living being. 'Do not be afraid,' we said, 'your louse is only taken by the skin; besides, he seems strong enough to get over the pressure, even were it greater.' . . .

We continued the experiment, and fixed in the glass the poor little beast, that struggled, with all its might, at the extremity of the nippers. We then requested the Regent to apply his right eye, shutting his left, to the glass at the top of the machine. 'Tsong-Kaba!' exclaimed the Regent, 'the louse is as big as a rat.' After looking at it for a moment, he raised his head and hid his face with both hands, saying, it was a horrible to look at. He tried to dissuade the other from examining it; but his influence failed to make any impression. Everyone, in his turn, looked through the microscope, and started back with cries of horror. Then the secretary, seeing that his little animal scarcely moved, advanced a claim in its favour. We removed the nippers, and let the louse fall into the hands of its owner. But, alas! the poor victim did not move. The Regent said, laughingly, to his secretary, 'I think your louse is unwell; go and see if you can get it to take some physic, otherwise it will not recover.'

No one wishing to see other living creatures, we continued the entertainment, by passing a small collection of microscopical pictures before the eyes of the spectators. Every one was charmed and exclaimed with admiration, 'What prodigious capacity the French have!' The Regent told us, 'Your railways and your aeriel ships no longer astonish me so much: men who can invent such a machine as that, are capable of anything.'

LUCY ATKINSON
(fl. 1849–1853)

English governess and traveller. In the late 1830s she went to St Petersburg to be the governess of the daughter of a Russian general. In 1847 she met Thomas Witlam Atkinson, an English architect and painter, whom she subsequently married. Two years later they began a series of journeys through Siberia, southwards to the Kirghiz steppes, and to the borders of China, in the course of which they covered 39,500 miles. It was on one of these journeys, in the Kirghiz steppes, that Mrs Atkinson's son Atalan was born.

A true Briton revolts against swaddling

I do not believe I have told you about their wishing to swaddle the child. When first my boy was born they wished to swaddle him, but I assured them it was not customary in England. A few days afterwards, my friend seemed so much to urge the necessity of the swaddling system, that, to give her satisfaction, I consented to its being done, only that I had no knowledge of anything of the kind; so forthwith she commenced with stroking down the arms and legs; then she began binding him, but he very shortly showed her that he was a true Briton, and was not going to stand any such treatment, for he fought bravely, so much so that the bandaging was given up. Looking innocently into my face, she exclaimed, 'How very odd! I could not have believed it, had I not seen it; what a difference there is between English and Russian children! This proves to me they are not accustomed to swaddling.'

MRS R. M. COOPLAND
(fl. 1857)

English wife of the chaplain at Gwalior in central India. When Indian troops mutinied in June 1857 her husband, George Coopland, was murdered, and she and other ladies from the garrison were forced to make their escape.

A lady's escape from Gwalior

The palace was surrounded by a crowd of horsemen, soldiers and natives, all most insolent in their manner to us, calling out 'your Raj is over now.' The Maharajah refused to see us. . . . Why were we so heartlessly treated by him, when he had been so kind to Major Macpherson and his party, even lending them carriages and a guard, and facilitating their escape in every way? . . . Perhaps he thought that helpless women could never be of any use to him. This is a mystery that no one can explain to the Rajah's credit. We felt it keenly, to be thus driven from his palace gate with contempt.

We proceeded on our way, the people yelling and shouting after us, and we expecting every instant to be stopped and torn out of our carriage and given up to be killed by them; for nothing could exceed their savage looks and language. . . .

A chuprassi [messenger] of the Rajah's took the carriage from us, and made us get out and wait by the road side till he sent us two or three native carts; they were miserable things without springs, had no covers to protect us from the sun, and were drawn by wretchedly weak bullocks. . . .

We had now almost lost the power of thinking and acting, for we had been from nine the preceding evening without food, water, or rest; and our minds were on the rack, tortured by grief and suspense. Here we were, about eight miserable women, alone and unprotected, without food or proper clothing, exhausted by fatigue, and not knowing what to do; some had no shoes or covering for their heads. At last Muza said we had better get into our carts and push on; for the natives of the Lushkur, hearing we were here, would follow and kill us. The bullocks went very slowly, and we could not make them move faster. The sensation of horror and helplessness oppressed us like a nightmare: for all this time we were only a few miles from Gwalior, and could even hear the shouting and crying there.

Mrs. Campbell having broken one of the bottles of beer, we had each drank a little, which greatly refreshed us.

We toiled slowly onwards the whole of that long, hot afternoon; the dust rising in clouds, and the hot wind parching us. The men who drove the bullocks could hardly make them move. We mixed a few drops of the camphor-water with the water Muza occasionally brought us from the wells we passed, and found it support us a little. . . .

. . . We were then obliged to get out of the carts, and lie on the ground, in the middle of a dusty road, huddled together, whilst the villagers collected to stare at us: they even brought torches to aid their scrutiny, as it was now getting dark. . . . The natives were very insolent; they looked at us all in succession, and said, 'Well, they are not worth a pice each'; but to Mrs. Campbell they said, 'You are worth an anna': they said she was (burra kubsoorut) very handsome. She was a very beautiful woman, and had formerly been called the 'Rose of Gibraltar,' when she was there with her father. They pulled aside her chudda, with which she tried to conceal her face, and said, 'We will look at you.' At last, worn out with fatigue, we slept, and the next morning (Wednesday) continued our journey. . . .

. . . On the other side [of the River Chumbul], we entered a small chowki near the river bank, into which we were followed by at least twenty horrid savage-looking men, armed with rusty old matchlocks and tulwahs. I shall never forget the expression of their faces; we could see well now, as it was light, and we were neither agitated nor excited, many of us having almost lost all longing for life. We sat here for more than an hour, surrounded by these men, who every now and then drew out their tulwahs, and slowly polished them with their fingers, seeming to whet and sharpen them. They watched us closely: one man especially, with only one eye, and that had a horrid basilisk expression in it, watched me the whole time. They appeared to consult how they should kill us, and I kept thinking what a dreadful death they would put us to with their rusty weapons: a bullet would have been a merciful death in comparison. They would occasionally leave us, and then return, as if purposely keeping us in suspense. . . .

Muza now said we had better walk on a little way, till he could procure us some more carts; so we walked on under the burning sun, our wet clothes clinging to us. Some of the women had no shoes or stockings; and one tore off pieces of her dress to wrap round her bleeding feet. Mrs. Kirke and Mrs. Campbell, who had no bonnets, put part of their dresses over their heads, to protect them from the burning rays of the sun. Mrs. Gilbert could hardly walk; but some of the women helped her along, and others carried the children. At last Mrs. Quick fell down in an apoplectic fit, and became black in the face; some of the ladies kindly stayed with her, but in a quarter of an hour she died. The natives crowded round, laughing at her immense size, and mocked her. We asked them to bury her; but I don't know whether they did, as we left her body lying on the road.

We sat for a long time waiting for carts, in a lane with high banks on each side, which sheltered us a little from the sun; at last, to our great delight, a native mounted policeman, riding Captain Campbell's own 'Blacky,' came up and told us that Captain Campbell was at the first dak bungalow from Agra; not daring to come any further, and uncertain if we had escaped, with food.

The man then rode off to ask the Rajah of Dholepore for some carts for us. It seemed strange to see this man, and hear him speak so kindly to us. He alone remained faithful when all the other mounted policemen afterwards mutinied at Agra.

ARMINIUS VÁMBÉRY
(1832–1913)

Hungarian scholar and traveller. At the age of twenty-five he went to Constantinople, where he spent six years studying languages and dialects and becoming a Turk in all but name. In 1863, after waiting at the Turkish Embassy in Teheran for eight months before a suitable caravan appeared, he joined one made up of pilgrims returning from Mecca to Eastern Turkestan. He travelled disguised as a dervish, crossing the Caspian Sea and the terrifying Kara Kum, the Black Sands, on the way to Khiva. Vámbéry left the caravan at Samarkand, having several times come within an inch of being exposed as an impostor, and eventually returned to Teheran.

The Black Sands: the place where men perish

Then we had had rain water; but here there was not a single source that could be turned to account. With unutterable regret our eyes rested on the Oxus, that became more and more remote, and shone doubly beautiful in the last beams of the departing sun. Even the camels, who before we started had drunk abundantly, kept their eyes so full of expression for a long, long time turned in the same direction! . . .

Our morning station bore the charming appellation of Adam-kyrylgan (which means 'the place where men perish'), and one needed only to cast a look at the horizon to convince himself how appropriate is that name. Let the reader picture to himself a sea of sand, extending as far as eye can reach, on one side formed into high hills, like waves, lashed into that position by the furious storm; on the other side, again, like the smooth waters of a still lake, merely rippled by the west wind. Not a bird visible in the air, not a worm or beetle upon the earth; traces of nothing but departed life, in the bleaching bones of man or beast that has perished, collected by every passer-by in a heap, to serve to guide the march of future travellers! . . .

We passed three days in the sandy parts of the desert. We had now to gain the firm plain, and come in sight of the Khalata mountain, that stretches away toward the north. Unhappily, disappointment again awaited us. Our beasts were incapable of further exertion, and we passed a fourth day in the sand. I had still left about six glasses of water in my leathern bottle. These I drank drop by drop, suffering, of course, terribly from thirst. Greatly alarmed to find that my tongue began to turn a little black in the centre, I immediately drank off at a draught half of my remaining store, thinking so to save my life; but, oh! the burning sensation, followed by headache, became more violent towards the morning of the fifth day, and when we could just distinguish, about mid-day, the Khalata mountains from the clouds that surrounded them, I felt my strength gradually abandon me. . . .

I was no longer able to dismount without assistance; they laid me upon the ground; a fearful fire seemed to burn my entrails; my headache reduced me almost to a state of stupefaction. My pen is too feeble to furnish even a slight sketch of the martyrdom that thirst occasions; I think that no death can be more painful. Although I have found myself able to nerve myself to face all other perils, here I felt quite broken. I thought, indeed, that I had reached the end of my life. Towards midnight we started, I fell asleep, and on awaking in the morning found myself in a mud hut, surrounded by people with long beards; in these I immediately recognised children of 'Iran.' They said to me: 'Shuma ki Hadji nistid' (You, certainly, are no Hadji). I had no strength to reply. They at first gave me something warm to drink, and a little afterwards some sour milk, mixed with water and salt, called here 'Airan:' that gave me strength and set me up again.

HARI RAM
(*fl.* 1871–1873)

Indian surveyor and secret agent. In 1871 he set off on a secret mission from Darjeeling as one of the 'pundits' (in Hindi, 'learned experts') who were recruited to carry out survey work beyond the frontiers of India for the Great Trigonometrical Survey – work which would have been impossible for Europeans to achieve. The names of these gallant men, who counted their paces as they walked, never appeared in their reports, only initials. In the course of this, his first journey, Hari Ram encircled Everest and made the important discovery that the watershed of the Himalayas was 'far behind or north of the lofty peaks that are visible from Hindustan'.

The path down the Bhotia Kosi River in Nepal

Between Nilam and Listi Bhansār he followed the general course of the Bhotia Kosi river [one of the principal affluents of the Sun Kosi] and though it is but some twenty-five miles direct distance between the two places, the explorer had to cross the Bhotia river fifteen times, by means of three iron suspension and eleven wooden bridges, each from twenty-four to sixty paces in length. At one place the river ran in a gigantic chasm, the sides of which were so close to one another that a bridge of twenty-four paces was sufficient to

span it. This was just below or south of the village of Choksum.
Near the bridge the precipices were so impracticable that the path
had of necessity to be supported on iron pegs let into the face of
rock, the path being formed by bars of iron and slabs of stone
stretching from peg to peg and covered with earth. This extraordinary path is in no place more than eighteen inches and often not more
than nine inches in width and is carried for more than one-third of a
mile (775 paces) along the face of the cliff, at some 1500 feet above
the river, which could be seen roaring below in its narrow bed. The
explorer, who has seen much difficult ground in the Himalaya, says
he never in his life met with anything to equal this bit of path. . . .

FREDERICK BURNABY
(1842–1885)

English traveller and soldier. Author of *A Ride to Khiva*.
(See p. 165.)

'*We manage things better in Khiva*', *January 1876*

'Which do you like best, your horse or your wife?' inquired the man.

'That depends upon the woman,' I replied; and the guide, here
joining in the conversation, said in England they do not buy or sell
their wives, and that I was not a married man.

'What! you have not got a wife?'

'No; how could I travel if I had one?'

'Why, you might leave her behind, and lock her up, as our
merchants do with their wives when they go on a journey.'

'In my country the women are never locked up.'

'What a marvel!' said the man; 'and how can you trust them? Is
it not dangerous to expose them to so much temptation? They are
poor weak creatures and easily led. But if one of them is unfaithful
to her husband, what does he do?'

'He goes to our moullah, whom we call a judge, and obtains a
divorce, and marries some one else.'

'What! you mean to say he does not cut the woman's throat?'

'No; he would very likely be hanged himself if he did.'

'What a country!' said the host; 'we manage things better in
Khiva.'

319

Eating a horse on the north bank of the Oxus, January 1876

My faithful follower now whispered in my ear, 'We are to have a great feast to-night. The guide's brother-in-law has a horse which is not very well. The animal is to be killed directly, and we are to eat him.' Later on, an enormous cauldron was suspended from a tripod across the fire. A heap of fagots was piled upon the embers, and a dense smoke filled the tent. Large pieces of the unfortunate quadruped were now thrown into the pot by the guide's wife, who officiated as cook. The host and the rest of the party superintended the operations with the greatest interest.

'Will there be anything else to eat?' I inquired.

'No,' was the answer of my surprised Tartar. 'What more would you have? We might eat two sheep at a time; but a horse – no. There will, perhaps, be enough left for breakfast, praise be to God for His bounty!' and the little man, opening his mouth from ear to ear, licked his lips in anticipation of the banquet.

SIR GEORGE SCOTT ROBERTSON
(1852–1916)

English administrator in India. Political agent in Gilgit. In 1890–91 he made a long journey in Kafiristan, until then an almost completely unexplored region between Chitral and Afghanistan, walled in by mountains. At that time the Kafirs were living in an almost pristine state of paganism, and Robertson was the last foreigner to observe them before their forcible conversion to Islam in 1895. From then on Kafiristan, 'the Land of the Unbelievers', was to be known as Nuristan, 'the Country of Light'.

Tree-climbing Kafir girls

Girls from their earliest days run wild, and climb and practise gymnastics just as boys do in other countries. A boy comes to a stranger to be petted, a girl goes into shy contortions at a distance, or climbs trees or the wooden framework of the dance-houses.

Women also climb trees with facility. I have passed under a large mulberry tree, and found it tenanted with matronly figures literally grazing on the fruit. It is astounding how big and old-looking many of the Presun girls are before they attain the cap which marks maturity.

Immoral Kafir women

Young women are very immoral, not because their natural average disposition is either better or worse than that of women of other tribes and races, but because public opinion is all in favour of what may be called 'gallantry.' When a woman is discovered in an intrigue, a great outcry is made, and the neighbours rush to the scene with much laughter. A goat is sent for on the spot for a peace-making feast between the gallant and the husband. Of course the neighbours also partake of the feast; the husband and wife both look very happy, and so does every one else, except the lover, who has to pay for the goat.

The attributes of a manly character

In the Kafir's opinion, a really fine manly character, what he emphatically calls a 'good' man, must possess the following attributes: – He must be a successful homicide, a good hill-man, ever ready to quarrel, and of an amorous disposition. If he is also a good dancer, a good shot with bow and arrow or matchlock, and a good 'aluts' or stone-quoit player, so much the better. These qualities constitute a fine man; but to be really influential in the tribe, an individual must be also rich.

GEORGE NATHANIEL CURZON
(1859–1925)

Marquess Curzon of Kedleston. English statesman. Viceroy of India from 1898–1905; Foreign Secretary, 1919–24. 'A most superior person' (as he was described by an anonymous member of Balliol College, Oxford, in the 1870s), he made enormous, adventurous journeys, principally in Asia between 1887 and 1894.

The gloom and grandeur of Central Asia – from a train on the Trans-Caspian Railway, 1888

In these solitudes, the traveller may realise in all its sweep the mingled gloom and grandeur of Central Asian scenery. Throughout the still night the fire-horse, as the natives have sometimes christened it, races onward, panting audibly, gutturally, and shaking a mane of sparks and smoke. Itself and its riders are all alone. No token or sound of life greets eye or ear; no outline redeems the level sameness of the dim horizon; no shadows fall upon the staring plain. The moon shines with dreary coldness from the hollow dome, and a profound and tearful solitude seems to brood over the desert. The returning sunlight scarcely dissipates the impression of sadness, of desolate and hopeless decay, of a continent and life sunk in a mortal swoon. The traveller feels like a wanderer at night in some desecrated graveyard, amid crumbling tombstones and half-obliterated mounds. A cemetery, not of hundreds of years but of thousands, not of families or tribes but of nations and empires, lies outspread around him: and ever and anon, in falling tower or shattered arch, he stumbles upon some poor unearthed skeleton of the past.

An audience with Abdur Rahman Khan, the Amir of Afghanistan, 1894

'When I come to England and to London and am received by the Queen, shall I tell you what I will do?'

'Yes, Your Highness, I shall be glad to hear.'

'I understand that there is in London a great Hall that is known as Westminster Hall. Is not that so?'

'It is.'

'There are also in London two Mejilises [i.e. Houses of Parliament]. One is called the House of Lords and the other is called the House of Commons?'

'It is so.'

'When I came to London, I shall be received in Westminster Hall. The Queen will be seated on her throne at the end of the Hall, and the Royal Family will be around her; and on either side of the Hall will be placed the two Mejilises – the House of Lords on the right, and the House of Commons on the left. Is not that the case?'

'It is not our usual plan; but will Your Highness proceed?'

'I shall enter the Hall, and the Lords will rise on the right, and the

Commons will rise on the left to greet me, and I shall advance between them up the Hall to the dais, where will be seated the Queen upon her throne. And she will rise and will say to me, "What has your Majesty come from Kabul to say?" And how then shall I reply?'

'I am sure I do not know.'

'I shall reply: "I will say nothing" – and the Queen will then ask me why I refuse to say anything; and I shall answer: "Send for Roberts. I decline to speak until Roberts comes." And then they will send for Roberts, and there will be a pause until Roberts comes, and when Roberts has come and is standing before the Queen and the two Mejilises, then will I speak.'

'And what will Your Highness say?'

'I shall tell them how Roberts paid thousands of rupees to obtain false witness at Kabul and that he slew thousands of my innocent people, and I shall ask that Roberts be punished, and when Roberts has been punished, then will I speak.'

ANTON CHEKHOV
(1860–1904)

Russian dramatist and story-writer. In 1890, already suffering from the tuberculosis that would eventually kill him, he made a gruelling journey through Siberia to the prison colony of Sakhalin off the Pacific coast.

On the road through Siberia, 14 May 1890

I left Tyumen on May the third after a stop of two or three days in Ekaterinburg, which I applied to the repair of my coughing and haemorrhoidal personage. Both post and private drivers make the trans-Siberian trip. I elected to use the latter, as it was all the same to me. They put your humble servant into a vehicle resembling a little wicker basket and off we drove with a pair of horses. You sit in the basket, and look out upon God's earth like a bird in a cage, without a thought on your mind. . . .

Travelling is a cold business. I am wearing my sheepskin jacket. I don't mind my body, that's all right, but my feet are always freezing. I wrap them in my leather coat but it doesn't help. I am wearing two pairs of trousers. Well, you go on and on. Road signs flash by, ponds, little birch groves. . . . Now we drive past a group of new settlers, then a file of prisoners. . . . We've met tramps with pots on their backs; these gentlemen promenade all over the Siberian plain without hindrance. On occasion they will murder a poor old woman to obtain her skirt for leg puttees; or they will tear off the tin numbers from the road signs, on the chance they may find them useful; another time they will bash in the head of a passing beggar or knock out the eyes of one of their own banished brotherhood, but they won't touch people in vehicles. On the whole, as far as robbery is concerned, travelling hereabouts is absolutely safe. From Tyumen to Tomsk neither the drivers of the post coaches nor the independent drivers can recall anything ever having been stolen from a traveller; when you get to a station, you leave your things outside; when you ask whether they won't be stolen you get a smile in reply. It is not good form to mention burglaries and murders on the road.

SIR FRANCIS YOUNGHUSBAND
(1863–1942)

English explorer, soldier, diplomat and mystic. In 1886 he explored Manchuria. The following year he spent seven months travelling from Peking to India, travelling more than 1250 miles through the Gobi Desert and crossing the Karakoram range by the Mustagh Pass (c. 18,000 feet).

The virtue of holding one's tongue

It was nearly midday when we reached the top of the pass. . . . There was nothing but a sheer precipice, and those first few moments on the summit of the Mustagh Pass were full of intense anxiety to me. If we could but get over, the crowning success of my expedition would be gained. But the thing seemed to me simply an impossibility. I had had no experience of Alpine climbing, and I had no ice-axes or other mountaineering appliances with me. I had not even any proper boots. All I had for footgear were some native boots of soft leather, without nails and without heels – mere leather stockings, in fact – which gave no sort of grip upon an icy surface. . . .

What, however, saved our party was my holding my tongue. I kept quite silent as I looked over the pass, and waited to hear what the men had to say about it. They meanwhile were looking at me, and, imagining that an Englishman never went back from an enterprise he had once started on, took it as a matter of course that, as I gave no order to go back, I meant go on. So they set about their preparations for the descent. We had brought an ordinary pickaxe with us, and Wali went on ahead with this, while the rest of us followed one by one behind him, each hanging on to a rope tied round Wali's waist to support him in case he slipped while hewing steps across the ice-slope. This slope was of hard ice, very steep, and, thirty yards or so below the line we took, ended in an ice-fall, which again terminated far beneath in the head of a glacier at the foot of the pass. Wali with his pickaxe hewed a way step by step across the ice-slopes, so as to reach the rocky cliff by which we should have to descend on to the glacier below. We slowly edged across the slope after him, but it was hard to keep cool and steady. From where we stood we could see nothing over the end of the slope but the glacier many hundreds of feet below us. Some of the men were so little nervous that they kicked the fragments of ice hewed out by Wali down the slope, and laughed as they saw them hop down it and with one last bound disappear altogether. But an almost sickening feeling came on me as I watched this, for we were standing on a slope as steep as the roof of a house. We had no ice-axes with which to anchor ourselves or give us support; and though I tied handker-chiefs, and the men bits of leather and cloth, round the insteps of our smooth native boots, to give us a little grip on the slippery ice, I could not help feeling that if any one of us had lost his foothold, the rest of us would never have been able to hold him up with the rope, and that in all likelihood the whole party would have been carried away and plunged into the abyss below. Outwardly I kept as cool and cheerful as I could, but inwardly I shuddered at each fresh step I took. . . .

At last, just as the sun set, we reached the glacier at the foot of the pass. We were in safety once more. The tension was over, and the last and greatest obstacle in my journey had been surmounted. Those moments when I stood at the foot of the pass are long to be remembered by me – moments of intense relief, and of deep gratitude for the success that had been granted. Such feelings as mine were now cannot be described in words, but they are known to every one who has had his heart set on one great object and has accomplished it. I took one last look at the pass, never before or since seen by a European, and then we started away down the glacier to find some bare spot on which to lay our rugs and rest.

SVEN HEDIN
(1869–1952)

Swedish geographer and explorer. By the time he was twenty-two, he had already crossed the Elburz Mountains, travelled through Persia on horseback, and visited Bukhara, Samarkand and Kashgar. He promptly planned a second expedition, his aim being 'to conquer all Asia, from west to east'. The journey was an epic. Hedin reached Tashkent after a frightful journey through the Siberian winter, crossed the Pamirs, climbed 20,000 feet up Mount Mustagh-ata, and on 23 April 1894 reached the edge of the Takla Makan Desert, east of Kashgar. The crossing was a nightmare, only Hedin and one of his companions surviving. But even this experience did not deter him: he went on to cross not only the Takla Makan again, but also the Ordos and the Gobi Deserts. In the course of his journey he 'covered a distance greater than that from Pole to Pole' and mapped out 10,500 kilometres, 'equivalent to one-fourth the circumference of the earth'.

The valley of the shadow – crossing the Takla Makan Desert

May 1st. The night was cold; the thermometer fell to 35°9 Fahr. (2°2 C.), the lowest reading we had during the twenty-six days we were crossing the desert. But the atmosphere was pure, and the stars glittered with incomparable brilliancy. The morning dawned calm and gloriously bright – not a speck of cloud in the sky, not a breath of wind on the tops of the dunes. No sooner had the sun risen than it began to be warm. . . . All the previous day I had not tasted a drop of water. But suffering the extreme tortures of thirst, I ventured to swallow about a tumblerful of the horrible and abominable concoction which the Chinese call brandy, stuff that we carried to burn in our Primus cooking-stove. It burned my throat like oil of vitriol. . . . In the still atmosphere the funereal camels' bells rang out clearer than ever before. We had left three graves behind us. How many more were we destined to leave by the side of our track? The funeral procession was rapidly approaching the churchyard. . . .

Was there *no* means of imparting moisture to our bodies before we left this hateful spot – even though it were only a moistening of the lips and throat? We were all suffering incredible agonies of thirst, the men more than I. My eyes chanced to fall upon the cock that still remained alive. He was walking about amongst the camels with all the gravity of his kind. Why not tap and drink his blood? One of the men made an incision in the animal's neck. The blood trickled out slowly, and in small quantity. It was not enough; we wanted more. Yet another innocent life must be sacrificed. But the men hesitated a long time before they could bring themselves to slaughter our docile travelling-companion, the sheep, which had followed us through every danger with the fidelity of a dog. But I told them, it was to save our own lives, which might be prolonged a little if we drank the sheep's blood. . . .

May 4th. . . . Kasim [the only other man still alive] was sinking fast. He was incapable of digging a hole in the sand to lie in; and, as he was also unable to cover me with cool sand, I suffered terribly from the heat. All day long we never spoke a word. Indeed, what was there we could talk about? Our thoughts were the same, our apprehensions the same. The fact is we really could not talk; we could only whisper or hiss out our words.

May 5th. . . . Still we toiled on for life – bare life. Then imagine our surprise, our amazement, when on the long sloping surface of a dune we perceived human footsteps imprinted in the sand! . . .

We followed up the trail till we came to the top of a dune, where the sand was driven together in a hard compact mass, and the footprints could be more distinctly made out.

Kasim dropped on his knees; then cried in a scarcely audible voice, 'They are our own footsteps!'

May 7th. . . . Shortly before five o'clock we came to a *darah* (strictly speaking, valley) or depression in the sand, and I soon arrived at the conclusion, that it was a former bed of the river. Numerous poplars grew in its lowest part. There must be water not very far below them. Once more we seized the spade; but we had not strength enough to dig. We were forced to struggle on again towards the east.

We travelled at first across a belt of low, barren sand. But at half-past five we entered the thick, continuous forest. . . .

. . . I called upon Kasim to come with me to the water. But he was beaten at last. He shook his head, and with a gesture of despair, signed to me to go on alone, drink, and bring back water to him. Otherwise he would just die where he lay. . . .

I now changed my course to due south-east. Why so? Why did I not keep on towards the east, as I had always done hitherto? I do not know. Perhaps the moon bewitched me; for she showed her silver crescent in that quarter of the heavens and shed down a dim, pale blue illumination over the silent scene. Leaning on the spade-shaft, I plodded away at a steady pace in a straight line towards the south-east, as though I were being led by an unseen, but irresistible, hand. At intervals I was seized by a traitorous desire to sleep, and was obliged to stop and rest. My pulse was excessively weak; I could scarcely discern its beats. I had to steel myself by the strongest effort of will to prevent myself from dropping off to sleep. I was afraid that if I did go off, I should never waken again. I walked with my eyes riveted upon the moon, and kept expecting to see its silver belt glittering on the dark waters of the stream. But no such sight met my eyes. The whole of the east quarter was enshrouded in the cold night mist.

After going about a mile and a half, I was at length able to distinguish the dark line of the forest on the right bank of the river. It gradually became more distinct as I advanced. There was a thicket of bushes and reeds; a poplar blown down by the wind lay across a deep hole in the river-bed. I was only a few yards from the bank when a wild-duck, alarmed by my approach, flew up and away as swift as an arrow. I heard a splash, and in the next moment I stood on the brink of a little pool filled with fresh, cool water – beautiful water!

It would be vain for me to try to describe the feelings which now overpowered me. They may be imagined; they cannot be described.

ALEXANDRA DAVID-NEEL
(1869–1968)

French explorer. She made a series of extraordinary journeys in Central Asia. At the age of fifty-five she disguised herself as a Tibetan beggar woman and was the first European woman to enter Lhasa.

The lung-gom-pa runners of Tibet

Under the collective term of *lung-gom* Tibetans include a large number of practices which combine mental concentration with various breathing gymnastics and aim at different results either spiritual or physical. . . .

Though the effects ascribed to *lung-gom* training vary considerably, the term *lung-gom* is especially used for a kind of training which is said to develop uncommon nimbleness and especially enables its adepts to take extraordinarily long tramps with amazing rapidity. . . . It should be explained that the feat expected from the *lung-gom-pa* is one of wonderful endurance rather than of momentary extreme fleetness. In this case, the performance does not consist in racing at full speed over a short distance as is done in our sporting matches, but of tramping at a rapid pace and without stopping during several successive days and nights. . . .

I met the first *lung-gom-pa* in the Chang thang of Northern Tibet.

Towards the end of the afternoon, Yongden, our servants and I were riding leisurely across a wide tableland, when I noticed, far away in front of us, a moving black spot which my field-glasses showed to be a man. I felt astonished. Meetings are not frequent in that region, for the last ten days we had not seen a human being. Moreover, men on foot and alone do not, as a rule, wander in these immense solitudes. Who could the strange traveller be?

. . . As I continued to observe him through the glasses, I noticed that the man proceeded at an unusual gait and, especially, with an extraordinary swiftness. Though, with the naked eyes, my men could hardly see anything but a black speck moving over the grassy ground, they too were not long in remarking the quickness of its advance. I handed them the glasses and one of them, having observed the traveller for a while, muttered:

'*Lama lung-gom-pa chig da.*' (It looks like a lama *lung-gom-pa.*) . . .

The man continued to advance towards us and his curious speed became more and more evident. What was to be done if he really was a *lung-gom-pa*? I wanted to observe him at close quarters, I also wished to have a talk with him, to put him some questions, to photograph him. . . . I wanted many things. But at the very first words I said about it, the man who had recognized him as a lama *lung-gom-pa* exclaimed:

'Your Reverence will not stop the lama, nor speak to him. This would certainly kill him. These lamas when travelling must not break their meditation. The god who is in them escapes if they cease to repeat the *ngags*, and when thus leaving them before the proper time, he shakes them so hard that they die.' . . .

By that time he had nearly reached us; I could clearly see his perfectly calm impassive face and wide-open eyes with their gaze fixed on some invisible far-distant object situated somewhere high up in space. The man did not run. He seemed to lift himself from the ground, proceeding by leaps. It looked as if he had been endowed with the elasticity of a ball and rebounded each time his feet touched the ground. His steps had the regularity of a pendulum. He wore the usual monastic robe and toga, both rather ragged. His left hand gripped a fold of the toga and was half hidden under the cloth. The right held a *phurba* (magic dagger). His right arm moved slightly at each step as if leaning on a stick, just as though the *phurba*, whose pointed extremity was far above the ground, had touched it and were actually a support.

My servants dismounted and bowed their heads to the ground as the lama passed before us, but he went his way apparently unaware of our presence. . . .

We followed him for about two miles and then he left the track, climbed a steep slope and disappeared in the mountain range that edged the steppe. Riders could not follow that way and our observations came to an end. We could only turn back and continue our journey.

FREDERICK M. BAILEY
(1882–1967)

English soldier, explorer and naturalist. In 1913, with another officer, Captain H. T. Morshead, he went on foot from India to Tibet in order to determine the course of the Brahmaputra River. In the course of the expedition Bailey discovered the blue poppy that bears his name, *Meconopsis Baileyi*. In 1919 he succeeded in getting himself recruited into the counter-intelligence department of the Bolshevik Secret Service at Tashkent; his task was to seek out a British spy named Bailey.

An assignation with immortality near Lunang, July 1913

Five miles after leaving Tongkyuk bridge we came to a single house among fields, and just beyond that there were some grassy meadows covered in Alpine flowers, on which I caught a number of butterflies.

In describing these meadows, I find myself in a quandary. I have attempted throughout this book to present things as they appeared to me at the time, making quite clear the few occasions when I intrude information gained at a subsequent date. In this aim I have been assisted by the diaries which I wrote at the time. But at this point I realise the inadequacy of my method.

I realise that for every one person who may be interested in the story of this journey, there are ten thousand or more who are interested in the blue poppy, described in seedsman's catalogues as *Meconopsis Baileyi*, which is today so easy to buy and so rewarding to grow. If I am to perpetuate my name at all, my best chance is as the discoverer of the blue poppy; and in gratitude, I feel that I ought to write of the emotions which were stirred by the first sight of that wonderful turquoise blue flower with its wonderful golden centre.

Yet when I consult my diary, written in Lunang on the evening of July 10th, 1913, after riding for sixteen and a half miles on a very uncomfortable Tibetan saddle, I find the following entry.

Among the flowers were blue poppies I had not seen before and purple iris and primulas. There was also a good deal of aconite.

What a pedestrian way to record one's assignation with the immortality of a seedsman's catalogue! Not even a sentence to itself.

J. R. ACKERLEY
(1896–1967)

English writer and critic. In 1923, on the recommendation of his friend E. M. Forster, he went to India for five months to serve as private secretary to the Maharajah of Chhokrapur. *Hindoo Holiday* (1932), Ackerley's journal of his experiences, is one of the most delightful books ever written about India.

The Maharajah hopes for a mongoose

This morning His Highness took me out for a drive in one of his cars. He knows no more about cars than I do, and chooses them by the appeal of their names. So he bought a 'Sunbeam.' It would surely be a very pretty car; but it seemed much the same as any other, and he was equally disappointed by a 'Moon.' He asked me to-day what his next car should be, for two of the four he already has are getting very old, and I suggested a 'Buick,' which was the only make I could call to mind; but after pronouncing the word two or three times with evident disfavour, and making it sound like a sneeze, he did not refer to the matter again. He was wearing a purple overcoat, of European cut, lined with pink; the yellow spots down the collapsed bridge of his nose had been renewed; he had not shaved. A travelling-rug was draped about his knees, and over the top of his green and gold bonnet and beneath his chin a bright red woollen muffler was bound.

It is the last day of the old year, and he said he was extremely anxious to see a mongoose, for a mongoose is a very good omen; so we passed slowly along the Deori road in search of one, while he fired rapid questions at me regarding my circumstances, nodding briefly at my answers but never taking his eyes off the landscape.

How many members were there of my family? Was I the only son? Did I have to support the family? Oh, not while my father lived? And what was my father's business? And his income? And was he old? How old? Was he strong? Did he move, like His Highness himself, stiffly, with difficulty? And so on, to the object of them all – Would I stay with him and be tutor to his son (now aged two) when he should be old enough to need one, and be also his private secretary, and even, later on, his Prime Minister? Would I stay with him for – sixteen years? I said I didn't know if I would, postponing a definite refusal by saying I could hardly be expected yet to know my own mind. Meanwhile, no mongoose having been observed, he had ordered the chauffeur to turn the car off the road, and we were now rocking and bumping over the open country among stones and bushes; but the only life I could see were large black-faced monkeys scampering off with their babies clinging to their stomachs.

'Look!' I said, pointing suddenly. 'What's that?'

'Where? Where?' he cried, following my direction anxiously.

Then he leaned back abruptly in the car, and turned his face away.

'A jackal; a very bad omen,' he said gloomily, and then began to shake with laughter.

'Am I very silly?' he asked, with pathetic charm.

'I should like to see a mongoose myself,' I replied.

Ella Maillart
(1903–)

Swiss explorer, writer, actress, athlete and intrepid traveller. Captain of the Swiss women's hockey team, she also represented her country at sailing and skiing. In 1932 she travelled alone in Russian Turkestan. Two years later she went to Manchoukuo, returning overland to India (with Peter Fleming) in 1935.

A Kirghiz dinner, Turkestan, 1932

The old mother takes some of the broth in a ladle, pours it into a bowl, and tastes. Is it strong enough? She passes it to the head man, who considers it satisfactory. Then a child takes a jug of warm water from near the fire and goes round, pouring it on our hands. These latter are held well forward to make sure the water falls into the zone of dead ashes. Then a towel is passed round, the state of which had better be left undescribed, and a light cloth is unfolded in front of the seat of honour to serve as the tablecloth.

Then from the cauldron out comes the liver, which is cut into slices, in addition to chunks of fat – all their sheep have fat tails – and the table is laid. The meal is eaten with the fingers, by making small sandwiches of liver and fat which are plunged into a bowl containing salt passed from hand to hand. The delicate flavour is delicious: I would willingly have made it my main sustenance.

The woman then takes the pieces of meat from the cauldron and begins to sort them out, the head and joints going into a wooden platter, which is passed to Auguste, who is still too ill to be able to eat any. Whereupon our host takes up the head, gouges the eyes out, and eats the points of the ears on the end of his knife. After this the platter is passed to us. The meat is delicious, and comes away of itself from the bone, so tender and succulent, that even when we are full we go on energetically chewing for the pleasure of having the feel of the firm, sweet-tasting flesh in our mouths.

When I come to a stop at last, my knife, cheeks, and all ten fingers swimming in grease, I begin to observe my Kirghiz neighbours. They are still eating, slowly and scrupulously; masticating the very tendons even. One would think they had not had a decent meal for ages. But, as Karutz writes, 'To realize how they give themselves up to the pleasure of eating, one must have witnessed it oneself. Anybody who wants to know how the mounds composed of the débris of past feasts built themselves up in prehistoric caves, needs only to eat one sheep among the Kirghiz people. He will then realize what a "clean sweep" really means. Only then will he divine the zeal, the understanding, and success with which a mutton bone can be handled, the persistent and ingenious art with which it can be gnawed, scraped, bitten, crushed, broken, sucked; and how without the aid of the least instrument it can be scraped so irreproachably clean.'

When the guests have finished, the dish is passed to the other men, then to the children, and finally to the women.

Thus a child can be seen to pass a practically gnawed-clean bone to his father. The gesture might seem ironic, but quite the contrary, for the marrow is considered a great delicacy, and the father sucks mightily away.

The fragments of meat that have come away in the cooking have been put on one side. Now two boys take them, and seizing the meat firmly between the thumb and left forefinger, so that it projects slightly beyond the hand, begin rapidly slicing and, cutting towards themselves, make a hash of it. The fat is treated in the same way, after which a little of the boiling broth is added, and the third course goes round, the 'bish barmak.'

We each help ourselves, filling our bowls, and this, too, is eaten with the fingers, and that needs courage, for if one attempts to grasp the mixture, it is so greasy that it slips away at once, and it is impossible to get a decent mouthful. The Kirghiz are wonderful, for with one hand they take up a handful of the hash, gather it in their palms, and neatly compress it in their shut fingers; then, at the very moment they open their mouths, the fingers are released, so that the food is carried into the lips and sucked up in one breath, leaving the hand absolutely clean.

Try it! It's a trick worthy of a conjuror.

Neighbours keep coming in, depositing their goloshes to one side of the doorway before squatting down, and odd relics of the feast are presented to them. For the last course a bowl of broth goes round again, very greasy and hot, because it comes straight out of the cauldron. It does one good. Though I have filled up in every meaning of the term, I drink the velvety, fragrant liquid with delight.

The cloth containing the débris is then gathered up, water is poured over our hands, and the same towel is called into service again. Instinctively I have used the rich white fat that has solidified on my hands to grease my shoes, and lo and behold! our host does the same.

Then everyone stretches out, takes a siesta, and breaks wind. How Matkerim is still able to swallow a few more bowls of koumiss is a mystery to me.

PETER FLEMING
(1907–1971)

English traveller, soldier, writer and journalist. During the 1930s he travelled in Brazil, China, Japan and Mongolia, writing a series of immensely popular books about his adventures.

Crossing the Mintaka Pass with Ella ('Kini') Maillart, 1935

A little further on we sighted it: the Mintaka Pass, the Pass of a Thousand Ibex, 15,600 feet above sea-level. A rough zig-zag track led up to it, climbing painfully the steep and rock-strewn wall of the valley. We had come to the extremest boundary of China.

Snow began to fall as we attacked the pass. The tired ponies came up very slowly, the Turkis stabbing them in the nose and changing the loads repeatedly. I left the sorry hugger-mugger of the caravan and walked on ahead, leading Cloud; the altitude affected me very little and I enjoyed the climb. Here and there beside the track the bones of horses lay whitening, and with a sudden stab of pity I remembered Slalom, standing groggily with his head hanging and his feet apart, just as we had left him; I would have given a lot to know that he was still alive. A flight of snow-partridges swept past and disappeared round a corner; two little birds like redstarts chattered thinly among the rocks. The falling snow made a veil which half shut out the world, the valley sprawling below me and the jagged peaks above; so that small things close at hand took on a kind of intimacy, a new importance. There was no sound at all save the chink of the stallion's hooves on rock and an occasional faint wail of execration from the struggling Turkis beneath me.

About half-way up the track was inexplicably decorated with a fragment of *The Times* newspaper, and I took this for a good omen. Now I could see that the head of the pass was marked by four or five little pillars of close-piled stones. I was suddenly aware that this was an Occasion. In less than an hour our ambitions would be realized; the forlorn hope would have come off. In less than an hour we should be in India.

When I reached the top I found a stone shelter for mail-runners standing in a twisting gully of screes whose turns shut out the prospect ahead of me; the stallion and I were on British-Indian soil, a somewhat metaphorical commodity among these rocks. I sat down on the threshold of the hut and smoked a pipe, feeling sleepy and complacent. Snow was still falling; Cloud shivered and nudged me with his nose, trying to point out that this was a poor sort of place to halt.

Half an hour later, heralded by the raucous objurgations of the Turkis, the caravan came plunging into sight over the lip of the pass; Kini reported a gruelling climb, and most of the ponies were in a bad way. It was getting late and we pushed on without delay — over the screes, into an awkward wilderness of boulders, across a patch of soggy ground, and out on to a little rocky platform whence we looked, for the first time, into India.

The snow had drawn off. Below us a glacier sprawled, grey and white, in the shadowed bottom of a gigantic pit. Opposite, wearing their wisps of cloud superbly, two towering snow-peaks were refulgent in the last of the sunlight. It was a sight to take your breath away.

'So far I like India,' said Kini.

HEINRICH HARRER
(1912–   )

Austrian mountaineer. In 1938 he was one of the Austro-German party that made the first ascent of the north face of the Eiger. In 1939 he went to the Himalayas to climb Nanga Parbat in Kashmir and was interned by the British when war broke out. In August 1944 he escaped and, with Peter Aufschnaiter, another mountaineer, made the gruelling journey across the Changthang plateau to Lhasa. Harrer stayed in the Tibetan capital for five years, eventually becoming the tutor and confidant of the four-teen-year-old Dalai Lama.

The Dalai Lama's procession

We heard the blare of copper horns and trumpets. The procession approached. The murmurs of the crowd were hushed and a reverent silence reigned, for the head of the column was in sight. A host of serving monks formed the vanguard. With them they carried the God-King's personal effects done up in bundles, each bundle wrapped in a yellow silk cloth. . . .

Soon we saw the God-King's favourite birds being carried by in their cages. Now and then a parrot called out a welcoming word in Tibetan, which the faithful crowd received with rapturous sighs as a personal message from their God. At an interval behind the servants came monks with banners decorated with texts. Next came a band of mounted musicians wearing brightly coloured, old-fashioned garb and playing old-fashioned instruments, from which they produced curious, whimpering sounds. After them followed an army of monks of the Tsedrung order, also on horseback and marshalled in order of rank. Behind them grooms led the favourite horses of the Dalai Lama, splendidly caparisoned. Their bridles were yellow and their bits and saddles of pure gold.

Then came a flock of high dignitaries and senior members of the God-King's household, the latter all monks with the rank of abbot. These are the only persons, except his parents and brothers and sisters, who have the right of speech with the Dalai Lama. Alongside them marched the tall figures of the bodyguard – huge fellows chosen for their size and strength. I was told that none of them is under six feet six inches in height and one of them measures eight feet. Their padded shoulders make them look even more formidable and they carry long whips in their hands. The only sound to be heard came from them as in deep bass voices they called on the crowd to make way and take off their hats. . . .

And now approached the yellow, silk-lined palanquin of the Living Buddha, gleaming like gold in the sunlight. The bearers were six-and-thirty men in green silk cloaks, wearing red plate-shaped caps. A monk was holding a huge iridescent sunshade made of peacock's feathers over the palanquin. The whole scene was a feast for the eyes – a picture revived from a long-forgotten fairy-tale of the Orient.

Round us all heads were bowed in deep obeisance and no one dared to raise his eyes. Aufschnaiter and I must have been noticeable with our heads only slightly bent. We absolutely had to see the Dalai Lama! And there he was – bowing to us with a smile behind the glass front of his sedan-chair. His finely cut features were full of charm and dignity, but his smile was that of a boy, and we guessed that he, too, was curious to see us. . . .

Deep in contemplation of the spectacle I suddenly heard the sound of familiar music. Yes – no mistake about it, the British National Anthem! The band of the bodyguard had taken up its station halfway along the route, and the Royal Chair must just have come up to them. So, to honour the God, they played 'God Save the Queen.' I have generally heard it better played but it has never caused me such bewilderment. I learned later that the bandmaster had been trained in the Indian Army. He had noticed that this air played an important part at all ceremonies, so he brought the music back with him. It has been set to Tibetan words but I have never heard them sung. The brass band finished the anthem creditably with the exception of a few wrong notes by the trumpets due to the rarefied air, and then the pipers of the police band played a selection of Scottish airs.

Eric Newby
(1919–   )

English traveller and writer.

Meeting an explorer in the Hindu Kush, 1956

We crossed the river by a bridge, went up through the village of Shāhnaiz and downhill towards the Lower Panjshir.

'Look,' said Hugh, 'it must be Thesiger.'

Coming towards us out of the great gorge where the river thundered was a small caravan like our own. He named an English explorer, a remarkable throwback to the Victorian era, a fluent speaker of Arabic, a very brave man, who has twice crossed the Empty Quarter and, apart from a few weeks every year, has passed his entire life among primitive peoples.

We had been on the march for a month. We were all rather jaded; the horses were galled because the drivers were careless of them, and their ribs stood out because they had been in places only fit for mules and forded innumerable torrents filled with slippery rocks as big as footballs; the drivers had run out of tobacco and were pining for their wives; there was no more sugar to put in the tea, no more jam, no more cigarettes and I was reading *The Hound of the Baskervilles* for the third time; all of us suffered from a persistent dysentery. The ecstatic sensations we had experienced at a higher altitude were beginning to wear off. It was not a particularly gay party. . . .

[Thesiger's] party consisted of two villainous-looking tribesmen dressed like royal mourners in long overcoats reaching to the ankles; a shivering Tajik cook, to whom some strange mutation had given bright red hair, unsuitably dressed for Central Asia in crippling pointed brown shoes and natty socks supported by suspenders, but no trousers; the interpreter, a gloomy-looking middle-class Afghan in a coma of fatigue, wearing dark glasses, a double-breasted lounge suit and an American hat with stitching all over it; and Thesiger himself, a great, long-striding crag of a man, with an outcrop for a nose and bushy eyebrows, forty-five years old and as hard as nails, in an old tweed jacket of the sort worn by Eton boys, a pair of thin grey cotton trousers, rope-soled Persian slippers and a woollen cap comforter.

'Turn round,' he said, 'you'll stay the night with us. We're going to kill some chickens.' . . .

Soon we were sitting on a carpet under some mulberry trees, surrounded by the entire population, with all Thesiger's belongings piled up behind us. . . .

The chickens were produced. They were very old; in the half-light they looked like pterodactyls.

'Are they expensive?'

'The Power of Britain never grows less,' said the headman, lying superbly.

'That means they are very expensive,' said the interpreter, rousing himself.

Soon the cook was back, semaphoring desperately.

'Speak up, can't understand a thing. You want sugar? Why don't you say so?' He produced a large bunch of keys, like a housekeeper in some stately home. All that evening he was opening and shutting boxes so that I had tantalising glimpses of the contents of an explorer's luggage – a telescope, a string vest, the *Charterhouse of Parma, Du Côté de Chez Swann*, some fish-hooks and the 1/1000000 map of Afghanistan – not like mine, a sodden pulp, but neatly dissected, mounted between marbled boards.

'That cook's going to die,' said Thesiger; 'hasn't got a coat and look at his feet. We're nine thousand feet if we're an inch here. How high's the Chamar Pass?' We told him 16,000 feet. 'Get yourself a coat and boots, do you hear?' he shouted in the direction of the camp fire.

After two hours the chicken arrived; they were like elastic, only the rice and gravy were delicious. Famished, we wrestled with the bones in the darkness.

'England's going to pot,' said Thesiger, as Hugh and I lay smoking the interpreter's King Size cigarettes, the first for a fortnight. 'Look at this shirt, I've only had it three years, now it's splitting. Same with tailors; Gull and Croke made me a pair of whipcord trousers to go to the Atlas Mountains. Sixteen guineas – wore a hole in them in a fortnight. Bought half a dozen shotguns to give to my headmen, well-known make, twenty guineas apiece, absolute rubbish.'

He began to tell me about his Arabs.

'I give them powders for worms and that sort of thing.' I asked him about surgery. 'I take off fingers and there's a lot of surgery to be done; they're frightened of their own doctors because they're not clean.'

'Do you do it? Cutting off fingers?'

'Hundreds of them,' he said dreamily, for it was very late. 'Lord, yes. Why, the other day I took out an eye. I enjoyed that.

'Let's turn in,' he said.

The ground was like iron with sharp rocks sticking up out of it. We started to blow up our air-beds. 'God, you must be a couple of pansies,' said Thesiger.

ROGER ST MARTIN O'TOOLE
(*fl.* 1960s)

American traveller. A Korean war veteran who used his gratuity to travel round the world in order to study women at close quarters.

Looping the loop in India

It is two and a half hours by jet from permissive Siam to puritanical India. Pan Am's Flight No. 1 Around the World leaves Bangkok at two in the morning and flies due north-west over Burma and the Bay of Bengal into the heart of the world's largest democracy. When the moon is full, you can see the silver summits of the Himalayas edging the horizon on the starboard side. . . .

Across the aisle was an American doctor on his way to India for consultations as a 'sterilization expert'. Twinkling behind rimless glasses, he looked like a mad scientist in the comic strips. He showed me a large plastic loop.

'Can you guess what it is?' he asked.

I couldn't.

'Contraceptive,' he said. 'Intra-uterine. I invented it. It's the answer to India's problem,' he added complacently, as though India had but one.

I stared at the loop in disbelief; it was a rather large affair.

'I know what you're thinking,' twinkled the doctor, 'but it's not for human beings. It's for cows.'

He twirled the loop like a miniature lasso.

'You just insert it like that into the uterus,' he said, 'and the cow cannot conceive.'

'There are nearly two hundred million sacred cows in India,' he continued, 'wandering around, uncared for, perfectly useless.'

'What is that you are saying, sir?' said an owlish, dark-skinned gentleman next to him. He spoke in the precise, lilting, school-masterish English of the educated Indian. 'Are you saying that the cow is a useless animal? Is that what you are contending?'

'I am speaking of your surplus cows,' the doctor said amiably.

'If you are introducing that device into the cow, then there will be no more cows. Isn't it?' said the Indian.

'Right,' said the doctor.

'Oh, sir,' said the Indian. 'I am afraid you are misunderstanding the nature of my country. If you are extinguishing our cows, then who will be pulling the bullock carts? Who will be ploughing the rice fields? If you want to have oxen, the only place you will be getting them is from cows. Isn't it?'

'Now hold on a minute,' the doctor said. 'I'm not planning to introduce the loop into *all* the cows of India.'

But this did not reassure that owlish Brahman. His dark eyes shone with religious conviction as he recited a veritable bovine litany.

'You are reproaching us for our sacred cows,' he said. 'Why should they not be sacred? Only consider what they are giving to us – butter, *ghee*, milk, curds, transportation, traction, building blocks, and fuel. If there is no cow dung, what is the village housewife using to cook the dinner with? Pray answer me that.

'Then the cow is also giving us medicine,' he said.

'Medicine?' I asked.

'Yes,' he replied. 'The urine. A few drops – it is very good for the system.'

'Internally?' I asked.

The doctor was staring desperately at the ceiling; I think the magnitude of his mission had just swept over him.

'Internally, yes,' said the Indian. 'You would be surprised at what it is curing.'

I decided then and there that nothing about chaste, priapic, splendid, squalid, gorgeous, filthy, tragic, comic India would sur-prise me.

FAR ASIA

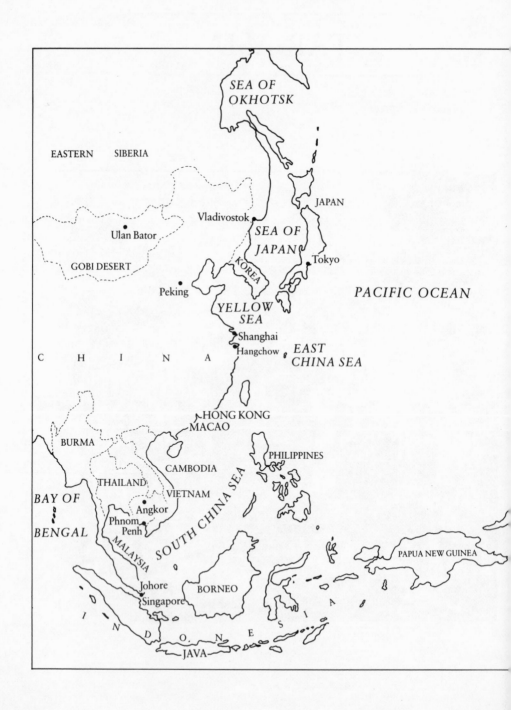

FA-HSIEN
(fl. AD 399–414)

Chinese Buddhist monk. One of the greatest of the travelling monks. In 399 he set out on a fifteen-year journey to India to study the sacred Buddhist texts at their sources.

Fa-Hsien returns to China, AD 414

. . . After sailing day and night for twelve days, they reached the shore on the south of mount Lâo [on the Shantung promontory] on the borders of the prefecture of Ch'ang-kwang, and immediately got good water and vegetables. They had passed through many perils and hardships, and had been in a state of anxious apprehension for many days together; and now suddenly arriving at this shore, and seeing those (well-known) vegetables, the lei and kwoh, they knew indeed that it was the land of Han.

HSUAN-TSANG
(AD 600?–649)

Chinese Buddhist monk. In 629 he set off from China to 'travel to the countries of the west in order to question the wise men on the points that were troubling his mind'. His route to India took him by way of the Barkol Tagh and Tien Shan mountains, through the Hindu Kush and the Khyber Pass to India. His journey lasted fifteen years and he returned with a great chariot drawn by twenty horses and loaded with more than 700 religious books and relics. He spent the rest of his life compiling the *Ta-T'ang-Si Yu-Ki* (Memoirs on Western Countries); it has been estimated that the wordage translated in the last five years of Hsuan-tsang's life was 84 times that of the Bible.

When he set off on his epic journey to India, there was an imperial rescript forbidding anyone to go abroad. Hsuan-tsang evaded the authorities and left Chang-an on an old horse reputed to have crossed the Gobi Desert fifteen times. His troubles began on the way to the Chinese watch-towers on the western borders of Sink-iang.

Mirages on the way to the first watch-tower

And now, alone and deserted, he traversed the sandy waste; his only means of observing the way being the heaps of bones and the horse-dung, and so on; thus slowly and cautiously advancing, he suddenly saw a body of troops, amounting to several hundreds, covering the sandy plain; sometimes they advanced and sometimes they halted. The soldiers were clad in fur and felt. And now the appearance of camels and horses, and the glittering of standards and lances met his view; then suddenly fresh forms and figures changing into a thousand shapes appeared, sometimes at an immense distance and then close at hand, and then they dissolved into nothing.

The Master of the Law when he first beheld the sight thought they were robbers, but when he saw them come near and vanish, he knew that they were the hallucinations of demons. Again, he heard in the void sounds of voices crying out: 'Do not fear! do not fear!' On this he composed himself, and having pushed on eighty *li* or so, he saw the first watch-tower. Fearing lest the lookouts should see him, he concealed himself in a hollow of sand until night; then going on west of the tower, he saw the water; and going down, he drank and washed his hands. Then as he was filling his water-vessel with water an arrow whistled past him and just grazed his knee, and in a moment another arrow. Knowing then that he was discovered, he cried with a loud voice: 'I am a priest come from the capital, do not shoot me!' Then he led his horse towards the tower, whilst the men on guard opening the gate, came out; after looking at him they saw that he was indeed a priest, and so they entered in together to see the commander of the guard-house, whose name was Wang-siang. Wang, having ordered the fire to be well lit up for the purpose of inspecting the Master, said: 'This is no priest of our country of Ho-si, he is indeed one from the capital:' then he asked him about his object in travelling.

GIOVANNI DE PIANO
CARPINI
(c. 1180–1252)

Italian monk and ambassador. In 1245 Carpini, the provincial of the Franciscan order at Cologne, was sent by Pope Innocent IV with letters to the 'King and People of the Tartars', exhorting them to 'avert their onslaughts on Christendom through fear of divine wraths'. On 22 July 1246, after a series of forced marches across the Mongolian plateau, Carpini's party reached the encampment near Karakoram of Guyuk, son of Ogadei, who was about to be elected Great Khan. They stayed until November, observing the festivities, then set off home. The return journey was even more arduous and the Great Khan's reply to the Pope, which Carpini delivered in November 1247, was hardly encouraging: '. . . you must come yourself at the head of all your kings and prove to Us your fealty and allegiance, And if you disregard the command of God and disobey Our instructions, We shall look upon you as Our enemy. Whoever recognizes and submits to the Son of God and Lord of the World, the Great Khan, will be saved, whoever refuses submission will be wiped out.'

A problem of translation

. . . The Emperor sent for us, giving us to understand by Chingay his chief Secretary, that wee should write downe our messages & affaires, and should deliver them unto him. Which thing we performed accordingly. After many daies he called for us againe, demanding whether there were any with our Lord the Pope, which understood the Russian, the Sarracen, or the Tartarian language? To whom we answered, that we had none of those letters or languages. Howbeit, that there were certaine Saracens in the land, but inhabiting a great distance from our Lord the Pope. And wee saide, that wee thought it most expedient, that when they had written their mindes in the Tartarian language, and had interpreted the meaning therof unto us, we should diligently translate it into our own tongue, and so deliver both the letter and the translation thereof unto our Lord the Pope. Then departed they from us, and

347

went unto the Emperour. And after the day of S. Martine, we were called for againe. . . . Then Kadac principal agent for the whole empire, and Chingay, and Bala, with divers other Scribes, came unto us, and interpreted the letter word for word. And having written it in Latine, they caused us to interprete unto them eche sentence, to wit if we had erred in any word. And when both letters were written, they made us to reade them over twise more, least we should have mistaken ought. For they said unto us: Take heed that ye understand all things throughly, for if you should not understand the whole matter aright, it might breed some inconvenience.

WILLIAM OF RUBRUCK
(1215–1270)

Flemish Franciscan monk. In 1253 he was sent with another Franciscan, Bartholomew of Cremona, to the court of the Great Khan, Mangu, at Karakoram, as the emissary of King Louis IX of France. When he arrived, after a seven-month journey, he was astonished to find French jewellers, Armenian priests and Chinese merchants among the Khan's entourage. He left a detailed account of the Mongols and their customs.

An audience with Mangu Khan

On the Octave of the Innocents [3rd January, 1254] we were taken to court . . . and, as it was the Nativity, we began to sing:

> 'A solis ortus cardine
> Et usque terre limitem
> Christum canamus principem
> Natum Maria virgine.'

When we had sung this hymn, they searched our legs and breasts and arms to see if we had knives upon us. They had the interpreter examined, and made him leave his belt and knife in the custody of a door-keeper. Then we entered, and there was a bench in the entry with *cosmos*, and near by it they made the interpreter stand. They made us, however, sit down on a bench near the ladies. The house was all covered inside with cloth of gold, and there was a fire of briars and wormwood roots – which grow here to great size – and of cattle dung, in a grate in the centre of the dwelling. He (Mangu) was seated on a couch, and was dressed in a skin spotted and glossy, like a seal's skin. He is a little man, of medium height, aged forty-five years, and a young wife sat beside him; and a very ugly, full-grown girl called Cirina, with other children sat on a couch after them. This dwelling had belonged to a certain Christian lady, whom he had much loved, and of whom he had had this girl. Afterwards he had taken this young wife, but the girl was the mistress of all this *ordu*, which had been her mother's.

He had us asked what we wanted to drink, wine or *terracina*, which is rice wine (*cervisia*), or *caracosmos*, which is clarified mare's milk, or *bal*, which is honey mead. For in winter they make use of these four kinds of drinks. I replied: My lord, we are not men who seek to satisfy our fancies about drinks; whatever pleases you will suit us.' So he had us given of the rice drink, which was clear and flavoured like white wine, and of which I tasted a little out of respect for him, but for our misfortune our interpreter was standing by the butlers, who gave him so much to drink, that he was drunk in a short time . . . and Mangu himself appeared to me tipsy. . . .

Then Mangu held out toward me the staff on which he leaned, saying, 'Fear not.' I, smiling, said in an undertone, 'If I had been afraid I should not have come here.'

Marco Polo
(1254?–1324?)

Venetian merchant and traveller. (See p. 298.)

Kublai Khan and his concubines

THE personal appearance of the Great Kaan, Lord of Lords, whose name is Cublay, is such as I shall now tell you. He is of a good stature, neither tall nor short, but of a middle height. He has a becoming amount of flesh, and is very shapely in all his limbs. His complexion is white and red, the eyes black and fine, the nose well formed and well set on. He has four wives, whom he retains permanently as his legitimate consorts. . . . He has also a great number of concubines, and I will tell you how he obtains them.

You must know that there is a tribe of Tartars called UNGRAT, who are noted for their beauty. Now every year an hundred of the most beautiful maidens of this tribe are sent to the Great Kaan, who commits them to the charge of certain elderly ladies dwelling in his palace. And these old ladies make the girls sleep with them, in order to ascertain if they have sweet breath and do not snore, and are sound in all their limbs. Then such of them as are of approved beauty, and are good and sound in all respects, are appointed to attend on the Emperor by turns. Thus six of these damsels take their turn for three days and nights, and wait on him when he is in his chamber and when he is in his bed, to serve him in any way, and to be entirely at his orders. At the end of the three days and nights they are relieved by the other six. And so throughout the year, there are reliefs of maidens by six and six, changing every three days and nights.

156,000 suits

Now you must know that the Great Kaan hath set apart 12,000 of his men who are distinguished by the name of *Keshican*, as I have told you before; and on each of these 12,000 Barons he bestows thirteen changes of raiment, which are all different from one another: I mean that in one set the 12,000 are all of one colour; the next 12,000 of another colour, and so on; so that they are of thirteen different colours. These robes are garnished with gems and pearls and other precious things in a very rich and costly manner. And along with each of these changes of raiment, *i.e.* 13 times in the year, he bestows on each of those 12,000 Barons a fine golden girdle of great richness and value, and likewise a pair of boots of *Camut*, that is to say of *Borgal*, curiously wrought with silver thread; insomuch that when they are clothed in these dresses every man of them looks like a king! And there is an established order as to which dress is to be worn at each of those thirteen feasts. The Emperor himself also has his thirteen suits corresponding to those of his Barons; in *colour*, I mean (though his are grander, richer, and costlier), so that he is always arrayed in the same colour as his Barons, who are, as it were, his comrades. And you may see that all this costs an amount which it is scarcely possible to calculate.

ODORIC OF PORDENONE
(1274–1331)

Italian friar. (See p. 255.)

An unusual zoo at Cansai (Hangchow)

This is the royal city in which the king of Manzi formerly dwelt. And four of our friars that were in that city had converted a man that was in authority there, in whose house I was entertained. And he said to me one day: '*Atha* (which is to say *Father*) wilt thou come and see the place?' And when I said that I would willingly go, we got into a boat, and went to a certain great monastery of the people of the country which was called THEBE. And he called to him one of their monks, saying: 'Seest here this *Franki Rabban*? (which meaneth this Frank monk). He cometh from where the sun sets, and goeth now to Cambalech to pray for the life of the great Khan. Show him therefore, prithee, something worth seeing, so that if he get back to his own country he may be able to say, "I have seen such and such strange things in Cansai!"' And the monk replied that he would do so with pleasure.

So he took two great buckets full of scraps from the table, and opening the door of a certain shrubbery which was there we went therein. Now in this shrubbery there is a little hill covered with pleasant trees and all full of grottoes. And as we stood there he took a gong, and began to beat upon it, and at the sound a multitude of animals of divers kinds began to come down from the hill, such as apes, monkeys, and many other animals having faces like men, to the number of some three thousand and took up their places round about him in regular ranks. And when they were thus ranged round about him, he put down the vessels before them and fed them as fast as he was able. And when they had been fed he began again to beat the gong, and all returned to their retreats. So I, laughing heartily, began to say: 'Tell me, prithee, what this meaneth?' And he answered: 'These animals be the souls of gentlemen, which we feed in this fashion for the love of God!' But quoth I: 'No souls be these, but brute beasts of sundry kinds.' And he said: 'No, forsooth, they be nought else but the souls of gentlemen. For if a man be noble his soul entereth the form of some one of these noble animals; but the souls of boors enter the forms of baser animals and dwell therein!' And say what I list against it, nought else would he believe.

IBN BATTUTA
(1304–1377)

Arab traveller. (See p. 32.)

A declaration of affection for the Sultan of Mul-Jawa

While this sultan was sitting in audience, I saw a man with a knife in his hand resembling a book-binders' tool. He put this knife to his own neck, and delivered a long speech which I did not understand, then gripped it with both hands and cut his own throat. So sharp was the knife and so strong his grip that his head fell to the ground. I was amazed at his action. The sultan said to me, 'Does anyone do this in your country?' I replied 'I have never seen such a thing.' Then he laughed and said 'These are our slaves, who kill themselves for love of us.' He gave orders that the body should be carried away and burned, and the sultan's lieutenants, the officers of state, the troops, and the citizens went out to his cremation. The sultan assigned a large pension to his children, wife, and brothers, and they were held in high esteem because of this act. One of those present at this audience told me that the speech made by the man was a declaration of his affection for the sultan, and that he was slaying himself for love of him, as his father had slain himself for love of the sultan's father, and his grandfather for love of the sultan's grandfather. Thereafter I withdrew from the audience.

MA HUAN
(*fl.* 1416–1435)

Chinese naval secretary and interpreter. Between 1405 and 1433 the Chinese emperor sent seven expeditions to explore the 'Western Oceans'. All were commanded by Cheng Ho, the 'Three Jewel Eunuch'. The expeditions, which were on the grand scale, carrying as many as 37,000 troops and vast amounts of gold and other treasures, went as far as Africa. Ma Huan, who like Cheng Ho was a Muslim from Yunnan, accompanied the eunuch on several of the voyages, visiting twenty Asian countries.

The country of Hsien-lo (Thailand)

It is their custom that all affairs are managed by their wives; both the king of the country and the common people, if they have matters which require thought and deliberation – punishments light and heavy, all trading transactions great and small – they all follow the decisions of their wives, [for] the mental capacity of the wives certainly exceeds that of the men.

If a married woman is very intimate with one of our men from the Central Country, wine and food are provided, and they drink and sit and sleep together. The husband is quite calm and takes no exception to it; indeed he says 'My wife is beautiful and the man from the Central Country is delighted with her'. The men dress the hair in a chignon, and use a white head-cloth to bind round the head [and] on the body they wear a long gown. The women also pin up the hair in a chignon, and wear a long gown.

When a man has attained his twentieth year, they take the skin which surrounds the *membrum virile*, and with a fine knife shaped like [the leaf of] an onion they open it up and insert a dozen tin beads inside the skin; [then] they close it up and protect it with medicinal herbs. The man waits till the opening of the wound is healed; then he goes out and walks about. The [beads] look like a cluster of grapes. There is indeed a class of men who arrange this operation; they specialize in inserting and soldering these beads for people; [and] they do it as a profession.

If it is the king of the country or a great chief or a wealthy man [who has the operation], then they use gold to make hollow beads, inside which a grain of sand is placed, and they are inserted [in the *membrum virile*]; when the man walks about, they make a tinkling sound, and this is regarded as beautiful. The men who have no beads inserted are people of the lower classes. This is a most curious thing.

LUDOVICO DI VARTHEMA
(fl. 1505)

Italian traveller. (See p. 256.)

Recycling the dead in Java, c. 1507

The people in this island who eat flesh, when their fathers become so old that they can no longer do any work, their children or relations set them up in the market-place for sale, and those who purchase them kill them and eat them cooked. And if any young man should be attacked by any great sickness, and that it should appear to the skilful that he might die of it, the father or the brother of the sick man kills him, and they do not wait for him to die. And when they have killed him they sell him to others to be eaten. We, being astonished at such a thing, some merchants of the country said to us: 'O you poor Persians, why do you leave such charming flesh to be eaten by the worms?' My companion hearing this immediately exclaimed: 'Quick, quick, let us go to our ship, for these people shall never more come near me on land.'

ANONYMOUS ENGLISHMAN
(16th century)

The Japanese

The inhabitants shewe a notable witte, and an incredible pacience in sufferinge, labour, and sorowes. They take greate and diligent care lest, either in worde or deede, they shoulde shewe either feare, or dulnesse of mynde, and lest they should make any man (whosoever he be) partaker of their trowbles and wantes. They covet exceedinglye honour and prayse; and povertie with them bringeth no dammage to the nobilitie of bloude. They suffer not the least injurie in the worlde to passe unrevenged. For gravitie and curtesie they gyve not place to the Spainardes. They are generally affable and full of compliments. They are very punctuall in the entertayning of strangers, of whom they will curiously inquyre even tryfles of forreyne people, as of their manners, and such like thinges. They will as soone lose a limbe as omit one ceremonie in welcoming a friend. They use to give and receive the cup at one the other hands, and before the master of the house begins to drinke, hee will proffer the cup to every one of his guests, making shew to have them to begin. Fish, rootes, and rice, are their common junkets, and if they chance to kill a hen, ducke, or pigge, which is but seldome, they will not like churles eat it alone; but their friendes shall be surely partakers of it. The most parte of them that dwell in cyties can write and reade. They only studie martiall feates and are delighted in armes. They are far from all avarice, and for that cause detest both dice and all other playe which is for gayne.

The people be fayre and verye comely of shape. The marchantes, althoughe very riche and wealthye, yet nothing accompted of there; those that are of nobilite are greatly esteemed althoughe they be never so poore. Both men and women goe bareheaded without any difference, bothe in the sunne and rayne. They wash theyre yonge children in rivers as sone as they are borne, and when they are weaned they are taken out of their mothers sight, and are exercised in huntinge and armes. When theyre children once come to four-teene yeares oulde, they wear sword and dagger, and as they be taught, do revenge the least injurye that is offred them. . . .

They have strong wine and rack distill'd of ryce, of which they will sometimes drinke largely, especially at their feasts and meet-ings, and being moved to anger, or wrath, in the heate of their drinke, you may as soone perswade tygres to patience and quietnes-se as them, so obstinate and willfull they are in the furie of their impatience. As concernynge another drinke, they take great delighte in water mingled with a certeine powder which is very pretiouse, which they call CHIA.

MATSUO BASHO
(1644–1694)

Japanese poet and traveller, a master of the seventeen-syllable poem known as *haiku*.

The narrow road to the deep north

Days and months are travellers of eternity. So are the years that pass by. Those who steer a boat across the sea, or drive a horse over the earth till they succumb to the weight of years, spend every minute of their lives travelling. There are a great number of ancients, too, who died on the road. I myself have been tempted for a long time by the cloud-moving wind – filled with a strong desire to wander.

It was only towards the end of last autumn that I returned from rambling along the coast. I barely had time to sweep the cobwebs from my broken house on the River Sumida before the New Year, but no sooner had the spring mist begun to rise over the field than I wanted to be on the road again to cross the barrier-gate of Shiraka-wa in due time. The gods seemed to have possessed my soul and turned it inside out, and roadside images seemed to invite me from every corner, so that it was impossible for me to stay idle at home. Even while I was getting ready, mending my torn trousers, tying a new strap to my hat, and applying *moxa* to my legs to strengthen them, I was already dreaming of the full moon rising over the islands of Matsushima.

ENGELBERT KAEMPFER
(1651–1716)

German doctor. In 1683 he travelled with the Swedish ambassador to Persia, and there joined the fleet of the Dutch East India Company, which was cruising in the Persian Gulf. In 1690 he set out from Batavia to Japan as physician to the Company's annual embassy to the Japanese Emperor.

The train of a Japanese prince, 1692

It is a sight exceedingly curious and worthy of admiration, to see all the persons, who compose the numerous train of a great prince, the pike-bearers only, the Norimon-men and Liverymen excepted, clad in black silk, marching in an elegant order, with a decent becoming gravity, and keeping so profound a silence, that not the least noise is to be heard, save what must necessarily arise from the motion and rushing of their habits, and the trampling of the horses and men. On the other hand it appears ridiculous to an European, to see all the Pike bearers and Norimon-men, with their cloaths tuck'd up above their waste, exposing their naked backs to the spectator's view, having only their privities cover'd with a piece of cloath. What appears still more odd and whimsical, is to see the Pages, Pikebearers, Umbrello and hat-bearers, Fassanbak or chestbearers, and all the footmen in liveries, affect a strange mimic march or dance, when they pass through some remarkable Town, or Borough, or by the train of another Prince or Lord. Every step they make, they draw up one foot quite to their back, in the mean time stretching out the arm on the opposite side as far as they can, and putting themselves in such a posture, as if they had a mind to swim through the air. Mean while the pikes, hats, umbrello's, Fassanbacks, boxes, baskets, and what ever else they carry, are danced and toss'd about in a very singular manner, answering the motion of their bodies. The Norimon-men have their sleeves tied with a string, as near the shoulders as possible, and leave their arms naked. They carry the pole of the Norimon either upon their shoulders, or else upon the palm of the hand, holding it up above their heads. Whilst they hold it up with one arm, they stretch out the other, putting the hand into a horizontal posture, whereby, and by their short deliberate steps and stiff knees, they affect a ridiculous fear and circumspection.

The poisonous Blower Fish

People that by some long and tedious sickness are grown weary of their lives, or are otherwise under miserable Circumstances, frequently chuse this poisonous Fish, instead of a knife or halter, to make away with themselves. A Neighbour of my Servant at Nangasaki being so strongly infected with the Pox, that his nose was ready to drop off, resolv'd to take this Meal, in order to get rid at once both of his life and distemper. Accordingly he bought a good quantity of this poisonous Fish, cut it into pieces, boil'd it, and in order as he thought, to make the poison still stronger, he took soot from the thatch'd roof of his house, and mix'd it with the rest. After dinner he laid himself down to die, and soon falling mortally sick, he brought up not only the poison he had taken, but a large quantity of viscid, sharp, nasty matter, probably not the least cause of his distemper, and by this means found life and health, in what he sought for death, for he recover'd and was well afterwards.

ISABELLA BIRD
(1831–1904)

English traveller. When young she suffered from a spinal complaint (which plagued her for the rest of her life) and in 1854 was sent on a convalescent sea voyage to Canada and the United States. Her account of the journey was published to great success, but it was another twenty years before she began to travel in earnest. It is easier to enumerate the places she did not visit than those she did. In 1873 her first major expedition took her to Australia, New Zealand, Hawaii and the Rocky Mountains. In 1877 she travelled to Japan, Hong Kong, China and Malaya. On her return she married Dr John Bishop, but as he himself admitted, he had 'only one formidable rival in Isabella's heart, and that is the high Table Land of Central Asia'. When he died in 1886, Isabella did an intensive course in nursing and set off hot-foot for Tibet. In 1890 she was a member of a 'military-geographical' mission to Persia, making what even she described as 'an awful journey' from Baghdad to Teheran. From there she travelled on through Kurdistan and Armenia to Trebizond on the coast of the Black Sea. Between 1894 and 1897 she was back in the Far East, covering 8000 miles in China alone and founding hospitals in Korea and China and an orphanage in Japan. Her last journey before her death in 1904 was to Africa, a continent she had previously avoided because she felt that the climate would disagree with her.

A public lunch in Yusowa, Japan

Yusowa is a specially objectionable-looking place. I took my lunch – a wretched meal of a tasteless white curd made from beans, with some condensed milk added to it – in a yard, and the people crowded in hundreds to the gate, and those behind, being unable to see me, got ladders and climbed on the adjacent roofs, where they remained till one of the roofs gave way with a loud crash, and precipitated about fifty men, women, and children into the room below, which fortunately was vacant. Nobody screamed – a noteworthy fact – and the casualties were only a few bruises. Four policemen then appeared and demanded my passport, as if I were responsible for the accident, and failing, like all others, to read a particular word upon it, they asked me what I was travelling for, and on being told 'to learn about the country,' they asked if I was making a map! Having satisfied their curiosity they disappeared, and the crowd surged up again in fuller force. The Transport Agent begged them to go away, but they said they might never see such a sight again! One old peasant said he would go away if he were told whether 'the sight' were a man or a woman, and, on the agent asking if that were any business of his, he said he should like to tell at home what he had seen, which awoke my sympathy at once, and I told Ito to tell them that a Japanese horse galloping night and day without ceasing would take 5½ weeks to reach my country – a statement which he is using lavishly as I go along.

Nikolai Mikailovich
Prejevalsky
(1839–1888)

Russian explorer and soldier. In 1870 Lieutenant-Colonel Prejevalsky was sent by the Imperial Geographical Society of St Petersburg to explore Southern Mongolia. Two years later he went to Tibet, returning across the Gobi Desert to Urga in 1873. Travelling with a single companion, Michail Alexandrovich Pyltseff, he covered 7000 miles in three years, half of which were over previously unexplored territory. One of the greatest of all explorers in Central Asia and China, he was also the discoverer of Prejevalsky's Horse.

Chilly nights on the Mongolian Plateau

The thermometer at sunrise descended to $-32.7°$ Cent. $(-26°$ Fahr.); and the frost was often accompanied by strong winds and sleet. All this happened in the very place where in summer we had $37°$ Cent. ($98°$ Fahr.) of heat. . . .

My companion, still weak and shaken in health, was obliged to sit on horseback day after day, wrapt in a sheepskin cloak. We, who usually went on foot, did not feel the cold so much whilst on the march; but in camp the severity of the winter was felt by us all with a vengeance. How well I remember the purple glow of the setting sun in the west, and the cold blue shades of night stealing over the eastern sky. We would then unload our camels and pitch our tent, after first clearing away the snow, which was certainly not deep although dry and fine as dust. Then came the very important question of fuel, and one of the Cossacks usually rode forward to the nearest Mongol yurta to buy argols [lumps of dung] if we had not already laid in a supply. . . . Once, at our wits' end for fuel, we were obliged to cut up a saddle in order to boil a little tea, and had to content ourselves with this frugal supper after a march of 23 miles in severe cold and snow-storm!

When a fire was lighted inside our tent the warmth was sufficient at all events for that part of the body which was immediately turned towards the hearth; but the smoke irritated the eyes, and when aggravated by dust became almost unbearable. In winter the steam from the open soup-kettle completely filled our tent, reminding us of a Russian bath, only that of course the temperature was very different. Boiled meat became quite cold before we had time to eat it, and the hands and mouth were covered with a layer of grease which had to be scraped off with a knife. And in the stearine candle that lighted us at supper-time, the part close to the wick would burn down so low, that we had from time to time to break off the outer shell, which remained unaffected by the flame.

For the night we piled round the tent all the packs and closed the entrance as tightly as possible, but notwithstanding all these precautions the temperature inside our dwelling was very little warmer than out of doors, as we kept up no fire after supper-time until morning. We all slept under fur cloaks or sheepskin coverings, generally undressing to sleep more comfortably. While asleep we were warm enough, because our whole bodies, head and all, were under the coverings, and we sometimes added felts over all. My companion slept with Faust [their dog], and was very glad of such a bedfellow. Hardly a night passed quietly. Prowling wolves often frightened our camels and horses, and the Mongol or Chinese dogs would occasionally enter the tent to steal meat, generally paying the penalty of their lives for such unceremonious behaviour. After such an episode, how long it was before he whose turn it had been to quiet the startled camels, or to shoot the wolf or thieving dog, could get his blood a little warm again!

THOMAS STEVENS
(b. 1855)

American traveller. (See p. 167.) In 1884–6 he went round the world on a penny-farthing bicycle.

Lugging a bicycle through a gorge on the Pi-Kiang River, China, 1886

A few miles above Chin-yuen the river enters a rocky gorge, and the marvellous beauty of the scenery rivets me to the spot in wondering contemplation for an hour. It is the same picture of rocky mountains, blue water, junks, bridges, temples, and people, one sometimes sees on sets of chinaware. Never was water so intensely blue, or sand so dazzlingly white, as the Pi-kiang at the entrance to this gorge this sunny morning; on its sky-blue bosom float junks and sampans, their curious sails appearing and disappearing around a bend in the cañon. The brown battlemented cliffs are relieved by scattering pines, and in the interstices by dense thickets of bamboo; temples, pagodas, and a village complete a scene that will be long remembered as one of the loveliest bits of scenery the whole world round. The scene is pre-eminently characteristic, and after seeing it, one no longer misunderstands the Chinaman who persists in thinking his country the great middle kingdom of landscape beauty and sunshine, compared to which all others are 'regions of mist and snow.'

Across the creeks which occasionally join issue with the river, are erected frail and wabbly bamboo foot-rails; some of these are evidently private enterprises, as an ancient Celestial is usually on hand for the collection of tiny toll. Narrow bridges, rude steps cut in the face of the cliffs, trails along narrow ledges, over rocky ridges, down across gulches, and anon through loose shale on ticklishly sloping banks, characterize the passage through the cañon. The sun is broiling hot, and my knee swollen and painful. It is barely possible to crawl along at a snail's pace by keeping my game leg stiff; bending the knee is attended with agony. Frequent rests are necessary, and an examination reveals my knee badly inflamed.

Hours are consumed in scrambling for three or four miles up and down steps, and over the most abominable course a bicycle was ever dragged, carried, up-ended and lugged over.

BEATRIX BULSTRODE
(fl. 1913)

English traveller. An extremely resourceful lady, she travelled through Mongolia on the eve of the First World War with an equally fire-eating companion, Edward Manico Gull, whom she subsequently married.

Men encoffined for life at Urga, 1913

Few, if any, Europeans other than Russians have seen the inside of this Mongol prison; and truly the dungeons at Urga beggar description. . . .

Passing on to the interior, we came upon a heavy wooden chest, some 4 to 4½ feet long by 2½ feet deep, iron-bound and secured by two strong padlocks. To our horror we discovered that it contained a man – one might have imagined that a wild beast to be sent by train was temporarily imprisoned therein! But a man! The hole in the side was of sufficient size to enable the prisoner to thrust out his manacled hands. This also provided the sole means of ventilation. But this unfortunate creature was well off compared with the others we saw subsequently. At least he was breathing in the open air. The dungeons, we were told, were so full that this prisoner had to remain outside. While we were discussing his pitiable lot, clank, clank, went the great bars and bolts, and the gaoler had opened the double doors leading into the first dungeon. There must have been from twenty to thirty coffins in this, some piled on the tops of the others, and the atmosphere was absolutely putrid. The two Mongol officials, whose general tone I cannot say impressed us very favourably, now very ostentatiously held their long sleeves over their noses, accustomed to smells though they were. One imagines that there may have been some means of cleaning out the coffins from underneath as is the case in cages in a menagerie, for it was most strongly impressed upon us that never under any circumstances whatsoever are the prisoners allowed to come out except for execution or – rarely – to be set free. The majority are in for life sentences.

MILDRED CABLE
(1878–1952)
and
FRANCESCA FRENCH
(1871–1960)

English missionaries. Two adventurous, formidable women who, with Francesca French's sister Eva, made up the 'Trio' of missionaries who ran a girls' school in Hwochow, China. In 1923 they received permission to preach to the nomadic tribes of the Gobi Desert and for the next fifteen years they travelled huge distances through this fearsome wilderness, crossing the Desert five times. The first Christians to go to the region since the sixth century, they were driven out in 1936, during the Sino-Japanese War, and returned to England.

The robbers' den

Every wayfarer fears this gorge through the mountains. The overhanging rocks tower threateningly, the road twists treacherously, and every sound echoes through the narrow defile to within hidden caverns where robbers may lurk, watching for defenceless caravans.

The most frightening feature was neither the loneliness nor the stark desolation, but the sinister look of that inn dug-out. All day there had been no sign of human life until a thin spiral of blue smoke curling out from between rocks showed that someone was close at hand. This must be the inn, for there was only one well within many miles.

The entrance was hard to find, for great boulders blocked the way. Then, from behind a crag, an evil-looking man appeared and, seeing us, half turned and called backward to some unseen person.

'Can we have a drink of water here?' was my request.

'Come inside,' was the answer, and the man turned and led me to the entrance of his cave-dwelling. Behind the rock was a narrow passage between two boulders, and he bent to enter a low doorway.

Three steps down, and I was in a kitchen built between rock walls. The chimney from which the smoke came was a natural exit, the fireplace was made of big stones, and a nondescript woman hovered near the hearth and stirred the pot. My first feeling was of fear at being entirely at the mercy of these people, then a strange sound asserted itself. It was the weirdest thing, a lilting voice which rose and fell on a sliding scale of quarter-tones. It seemed like a chant of Koranic magic, and was difficult to locate among those rock recesses. What sort of people were these among whom we had fallen? What could possibly be the occupation of this mysterious and terrifying household? One thing was certain, I determined that nothing should keep us there for the night. We would drink our tea, eat our morsel of bread and then away. These people were capable of any evil, and the sinister aspect of their living-place was a symbol of the cruel intentions of their hearts. 'Don't unhitch the beasts, we shall push on farther,' was the order given to the carter.

We did not pass this way again until several years later, when Turkestan was in rebellion and this thieves' kitchen was known to be the haunt of a nefarious band. This time we were obliged to stay the night, and prayed that a special angel guard might be on duty while we slept through the hours of darkness. The angel of the Lord truly encamped around us, no harm befell us, and we left again in peace, but twenty-four hours later there was murder in that place. News filtered slowly from the desolate ravine, but when the crime became known a squad of soldiers was sent to investigate and to punish the criminals. They never caught them, for when the soldiers got there the caves were all deserted and the terrible robber-band had vanished into deeper fastnesses, where even the desert rangers could not venture to pursue them.

SIR OSBERT SITWELL
(1892–1969)

English man of letters. Always on the look-out for new
aesthetic experiences, he travelled widely in Europe and
the Far East. As a writer his finest achievement was his
five-volume autobiography, *Left Hand, Right Hand.*

Angkor Thom, the ancient capital of the Khmers, Cambodia, c. 1937

From this height, too, it is possible to descry the towers of Angkor
Thom, in the depths of the forest, and even, here and there, the lines
of its walls. . . . Below, scattered thickly under the above the
mammoth trees, in that deranged, visionary world of Piranesi's,
stand gates and walls and water-basins, niches and sanctuaries,
sculptured islands lying on pools, terraces with a frieze of elephants
cut out of the stone that supports them, magnificent staircases,
flying on wings from one level to another, and descending to
nothing, causeways across moats and canals from which, in the
passage of centuries, the water has receded (assuming new and
unexpected positions a little distance off), leaving the channels
choked with water-flowers of such luxuriant beauty that, each time
you see them, they take your breath away, while birds as gorgeous
in their plumage as ever was the Queen of Sheba in her attire, stalk
round the edge of marsh or pool or wade deep among the blossoms.
From the exuberance of the vegetation, out of the festoons and
wreaths trailing from the trees, appear roofs and shattered cornices,
fallen stone beams of enormous size, great stones, like boulders,
jutting out at insane, because purposeless, angles, carved heads of
men and lions, horses and serpents, colossal statues on their splin-
tered plinths, round the bodies of which have wound the long,
snake-like coils of some parasitic tropical plant. Crowned with
high, pointed tiaras, dancers extend their fingers in the significant
gestures of Cambodian ballet from mossy walls under cascades of
green leaves or sprays of flowers, and blossoms grow, too, from
their pagoda-shaped head-dresses and from the round caps of the
comedians and acrobats. The walls of whole towns and monasteries
now form park-like enclosures: in them the fangs of the gigantic

roots of a tree clamp together the sagging door of a sanctuary, or the immense trunk itself has split, to reveal the image of Rama, or some bas-relief of ancient triumph, while, in contrary process, the roots of other trees are disrupting a cloister, so that a man's bones appear beneath a stone slab. Nature and art are engaged everywhere in ferocious battle, or merge in wild and inextricable confusion. Trees sprout like antlers from the heads of gods; lions and gryphons, as though they were alive, peer through the fluttering screens of leaves. The prone image of the Buddha is being gradually raised from the ground by the force of the plants beneath his weight, and near by a stone Siva, destroyer and creator, is, in his turn, being destroyed by his creations.

JOHN MORRIS
(1895–1980)

English traveller, academic and broadcaster. He travelled extensively in Central Asia, Tibet, Bhutan, Africa and the Far East, and took part in two Everest expeditions. Between 1938 and 1942 he was Professor of English Literature at Keio University in Japan, leaving to become Head of the Far Eastern Service of the BBC. From 1952–8 he was Controller of the Third Programme.

Mount Fuji

. . . It is seen at its best from the sea at dawn. At such times it seems to tower over everything, its perfect snow-capped cone, a purplish green in the light of early morning, seeming to be suspended in the sky. The beauty of Fuji is due to the simplicity of its outlines and the fact that it stands alone; from wherever one views it there is little to distract the eye.

The ascent of the mountain does not call for even the most elementary skill in mountaineering. There is a path, rough it is true, right to the summit, up which it would be possible to ride a motor-cycle, while to a horseman the journey would not present the slightest difficulty. The road, however, is littered with advertisements, broken bottles, the remains of food and human excreta; and at every stage the weary traveller is importuned by begging priests who spend the summer months in the various shrines situated on the mountain slopes. I made the pilgrimage with a party of my students, and we spent the afternoon and evening of a broiling August day toiling upwards over the gritty lava of which the mountain is composed. We slept the night at a hut about three-quarters of the way up and arrived on the summit, in company with several thousand other people, shortly before dawn. The view from the top was astounding: over a maze of still, dark lakes and valleys we looked out right across the Pacific, the line of the coast faintly visible, like a meandering smear brushed in with purple ink. We stayed there only long enough to see the rising sun dissipate the miracle, and then slid down over the grit again, reaching Tokyo in the evening. I wish, however, that I had not climbed Mount Fuji; never again was I able quite to capture the feeling of pristine beauty that it undoubtedly gives until such time as one actually sets foot upon its slopes. But then, as one of my Japanese friends was fond of saying, Fuji is only a 'seeing' mountain; it was never meant to be climbed. The Japanese, however, have a saying that there are two kinds of fool: those who have never climbed Mount Fuji, and those who have climbed it more than once.

S. J. Perelman
(1904–1979)

American writer and humorist.

Johore – the rubber treatment

There are other vignettes of Johore sharply etched on the memory – our afternoon with the elderly sister of the Sultan, the Tengku Ampuan, a woman of surpassing grace and distinction; the colorful tattoo put on by the Welsh Fusiliers, quite patently to remind the natives that the British lion still had claws; the reckless profusion of orchids on everyone's dinner table, worth hundreds of dollars by New York mid-winter standards; and most unforgettable of all, our visit to a rubber estate. There ought to be some kind of insurance policy available whereby the traveler could protect himself against visiting a rubber estate. Unless your name is Harvey Firestone, it is doubtful whether the sight of twelve thousand acres of future hot-water bottles will affect you as the Grecian urn did Keats.

PETER FLEMING
(1907–1971)

English traveller, soldier, writer and journalist. (See p. 335.)

A crash on the Trans-Siberian railway, 1933

There was a frightful jarring, followed by a crash. . . .

I sat up in my berth. From the rack high above me my heaviest suitcase, metal-bound, was cannonaded down, catching me with fearful force on either knee-cap. I was somehow not particularly surprised. This is the end of the world, I thought, and in addition they have broken both my legs. I had a vague sense of injustice.

My little world was tilted drunkenly. The window showed me nothing except a few square yards of goodish grazing, of which it offered an oblique bird's eye view. Larks were singing somewhere. It was six o'clock. I began to dress. I now felt very much annoyed.

But I climbed out of the carriage into a refreshingly spectacular world, and the annoyance passed. The Trans-Siberian Express sprawled foolishly down the embankment. The mail van and the dining-car, which had been in front, lay on their sides at the bottom. Behind them the five sleeping-cars, headed by my own, were disposed in attitudes which became less and less grotesque until you got to the last, which had remained, primly, on the rails. Fifty yards down the line the engine, which had parted company with the train, was dug in, snorting, on top of the embankment. It had a truculent and naughty look; it was defiantly conscious of indiscretion. . . .

. . . There she lay, in the middle of a wide green plain: the crack train, the Trans-Siberian Luxury Express. For more than a week she had bullied us. She had knocked us about when we tried to clean our teeth, she had jogged our elbows when we wrote, and when we read she had made the print dance tiresomely before our eyes. Her whistle had arbitrarily curtailed our frenzied excursions on the wayside platforms. Her windows we might not open on account of the dust, and when closed they had proved a perpetual attraction to small, sabotaging boys with stones. She had annoyed us in a hundred little ways: by spilling tea in our laps, by running out of butter, by regulating her life in accordance with Moscow time, now six hours behind the sun. She had been our prison, our Little Ease. We had not liked her.

Now she was down and out. We left her lying there, a broken, buckled toy, a thick black worm without a head, awkwardly twisted: a thing of no use, above which larks sang in an empty plain.

If I know Russia, she is lying there still.

NORMAN LEWIS
(1914–   )

English novelist and travel-writer. He has travelled in most parts of the world – Spain, Italy, the Balkans, Arabia, Mexico, Africa, the Far East – and written some of the finest travel books of our time. In 1950 he travelled through Vietnam, Laos and Cambodia; his account of that journey, *A Dragon Apparent* (1951), is a picture of a civilization on the brink of destruction.

The Moïs – the 'wild men' of Indo-China

The non-scientific visitor appears to be most impressed by the innumerable rituals with which the Moïs surround their existence. The most onerous of these are concerned with death. Those which are associated with good health are the least important and tend to be quite perfunctory because to die of sickness is a sign of the spirits' favour and ensures a comfortable hereafter in the bowels of the earth. Doctor Jouin had the greatest difficulty in persuading the Moïs to accept any kind of medical treatment, as they pointed out to him that he wanted to deprive them of the chance of a 'good' death, exposing them therefore, when cured, to the possibility of a 'bad' death by accident or violence. Such a 'bad' death condemns the ghost to wander in eternal wretchedness in the heavens.

Lepers are regarded as having been born under a lucky star, as they do no work, are fed by the tribe and are certain of an exemplary end.

The death rites, on the contrary, are prolonged over two years and are so costly that a single death may exhaust the equivalent of the village income for one month, whereas an epidemic, by causing it to use up in sacrifices the whole of its reserves, is certain to bring starvation in its train.

In arranging their ceremonies the Moïs pay great attention to the type of death the defunct has suffered. There are specially complicated and expensive rites for those who have died from various kinds of violence, who have died in a foreign country, have disappeared and are presumed dead, for young children, lunatics and, of course, for women dead in childbirth who are believed to turn into revengeful demons. The village is surrounded by open tombs, the occupants of which are 'fed' daily and kept informed of all family affairs.

From the sheer multiplicity of the rites, all of which require alcoholic consumption, the intriguing side-issue emerges that respectability and drunkenness are allied. The upright man gives evidence of his ritual adequacy by being drunk as often as possible, he is respected by all for his piety, a pattern held up to youth. The words *nam lu* uttered in grave welcome to the stranger in a Moï village, and meaning let us get drunk together, have all the exhortatory value of an invitation to common prayer. Moï villages are said to be one of the few places in the world where the domestic animals, dogs, pigs and hens, having fed in the fermented mash from the sacred jars, are to be seen in a state of helpless intoxication. Conviviality is the rule; a norm of polite conduct. Passers-by are begged to join in Moï orgies of eating and drinking and it is bad taste – that is offensive to the spirits – to eat or drink less than is provided by the fearsome liberality of the hosts. To prevent any possibility of the visitor's unwittingly commiting this kind of discourtesy, or remaining in a state of disreputable sobriety, an attendant squats at his side keeping a careful check on his consumption and ensuring that he drinks at least the minimum measure of three cow's horns.

A Vietnamese banquet

Vietnamese cooking, like most aspects of Vietnamese culture, has been strongly influenced by the Chinese. By comparison it is provincial, lacking the range and the formidable ingenuity of the Pekinese and Cantonese cuisines. But there are a few specialities which have been evolved with a great deal of dietetic insight. The best known of these is *Cha Gió*, with which we were served as an entrée. *Chà Gió* consists fundamentally of very small, highly spiced meat-rolls, which are transferred easily enough with chopsticks from the dish to one's plate. But this is nothing more than a preliminary operation, and many dexterous manipulations follow. Two or three kinds of vegetable leaves are provided as salad, plus minute spring-onions. A leaf of each kind is picked up and – this is not so easy – placed in superimposition on one's plate and garnished with an onion, ready to receive the meat roll in the middle. And now comes the operation calling for natural skill, or years of practice, since the leaves must be wrapped neatly round the narrow cylinder of mincemeat. The *Chà-Gió*, now fully prepared, is lifted with the chopsticks and dowsed in the saucer of *nuóc-mâm* at the side of one's plate, from which, according to Mr. Houghton-Broderick, an odour resembling that of tiger's urine arises. The total operation takes the non-expert several minutes and involves as many contretemps as one would expect. On this occasion, the Europeans soon gave up the struggle, throwing dignity to the winds, and dabbled happily with their fingers. A spirit of comradeship was noticeable, a democratic kinship born in an atmosphere of common endeavour, frustration and ridicule.

When travelling I make a sincere effort to throw overboard all prejudices concerning food. Consequently after a brief period of struggle I had already come to terms with *nuóc-mâm*, about which almost every writer on Indo-China since the first Jesuit has grumbled so consistently. I felt indeed that I had taken the first steps towards connoisseurship, and it was in this spirit that I congratulated the Governor on his supply which was the colour of pale honey, thickish and of obvious excellence. *Nuóc-mâm* is produced by the fermentation of juices exuded by layers of fish subjected to pressure between layers of salt. The best result as in viniculture is produced by the first drawing-off, before artificial pressure is applied, and there are three or more subsequent pressings with consequent deteriorations in quality. First *crus* are allowed to mature like brandy, improving steadily with age. The Governor told me that he thought his stock, which he had inherited, was over a hundred years old. All the fierce ammoniacal exhalations were long since spent, and what remained was not more than a whiff of mellow corruption. Taking a grain of cooked rice, he deposited it on the golden surface, where it remained supported by the tension – an infallible test of quality, he said.

After the *Chà Gió* came a flux of delicacies, designed undoubtedly to provoke curiosity and admiration and to provide the excuse for enormously prolonged dalliance at the table, rather than to appease gross appetites. The Vietnamese picked judiciously at the breasts of lacquered pigeons, the sliced coxcombs and the tiny diaphanous fish, while the Europeans ate with barbarian forthrightness, finding their chopsticks useful to illustrate with fine flourishes – since shop-talk had crept in – the feints, the encirclements, the annihilation. The Governor had been presented with a remarkable lighter, an unwieldy engine, which commanded admiration by producing flame in some quite unexpected way. How this was done, I have forgotten, but I know that it was not by friction on a flint. Throughout the meal he could hardly bear to put this away and fiddled continually with it between the courses, while his guests stuffed themselves with the rare meats he hardly touched. For me there was an allegory in this scene.

OLIVER STATLER
(1915–   )

American scholar and traveller. He first went to Japan in 1947. In 1968 and again in 1971 he performed the annual thousand-mile long pilgrimage around the Japanese island of Shikoku, birthplace of Kōbō Daishi (774–835), the founder of Shingon Buddhism. On their journey, the pilgrims visit eighty-eight temples.

Dinner at the twenty-fifth temple

It was late afternoon when we reached Temple Twenty-five. It looked like rain and I was ready to stop. Also I was hungry for vegetables, our recent diet having consisted of not much but rice, and so at a shop in the town I had bought large bunches of spinach and carrots. The priest who appeared several moments after we rang the bell was brusque, it seemed to me. He summoned a much younger priest and departed. After the usual discussion necessary to establish that I did not require Western food, the young man said that we could stay and accepted my purchases. The food at the temple was vegetarian, he remarked; there was no objection to preparing vegetables. He showed us to an upstairs room.

I was concerned that the head priest was going to be uncooperative about talking with us, so I asked Mizuno to press for an interview soon. The request was shunted aside with word that we were about to be served tea. A second appeal was smothered in the announcement that our bath was ready. After bathing I changed to fresh underclothes and felt better.

We were shown then to a downstairs room overlooking a little garden with a pool containing orange and white carp. The head priest appeared, now the soul of cordiality. He made tea for us himself and he talked freely and knowledgeably about his temple. I could not have asked for more.

Then, in the same handsome room, came dinner. There were my spinach and carrots, beautifully prepared, but all kinds of other vegetables too: bamboo sprouts, tender fernlike shoots, and other things I cannot name. There was a huge bowl of red-ripe tomatoes and chopped cabbage – a salad never looked so good. There was *sashimi* of tuna, uncooked, fresh from the sea a few hundred yards away. And as a final blow to vegetarianism there was *tataki*, my first taste of one of the great dishes of Japan, a special food of Tosa. The young priest – we knew by then that he was the head priest's adopted son and son-in-law – sat and chatted with us as we ate. He explained how tataki is prepared. A filet from a choice bonito is lightly toasted over a fire; there are differing opinions about what should fuel the fire, he said, but he held with those purists who insist that it must be pine needles. While being delicately browned but by no means cooked, it is beaten with straws to imbue the flavor of the fragrant smoke (beaten with straws – rather like being tickled to death). It is served in a special soy sauce laced with garlic. I am afraid I ate immoderately. Dessert was sliced apples and summer oranges which the young man peeled and sectioned for us.

JAMES KIRKUP
(1923–   )

English poet, scholar, playwright and traveller. He has
taught at universities in England, Sweden, Spain,
Malaysia and Japan. Among his recreations is 'standing
in shafts of moonlight'.

The smells of Japan

I knew at last, as I walked the winter streets of Osaka, that I was
back in Japan, because of the peculiarly delightful fragrance of the
air. Just as one knows one is in France from the smells of Gitanes,
coffee, chestnuts, beer and garlic, so one knows one is in Japan from
the mingled aromas of bath-fumes, woodsmoke, Peace and Ikoi
cigarettes, hot soy sauce, dried fish, pickles and seaweed. But the
most typical fragrance of all, and one uniquely Japanese, is that of
pomade: the crisp, clear air of winter was drugged with the scent of
rich, black, pomaded hair. It is spiced too with the clean, fresh smell
of Japanese bodies, savoury with the breath of peppery rice crackers
wrapped in seaweed, laced with hot saké and the sweet tang of boot
polish rising from the rows of shoe-shiners kneeling on bits of old
tatami matting along the edges of the pavements, where their little
tin braziers were odorous with burning *sushi* (fish) and *o-bento*
boxes – the disposable wood-shaving lunchboxes of Japan. All this
had haunted my nostrils ever since I had left Japan just over a year
ago, and now came back to me like a remembered dream perfectly
realized. At every step I was wafted along on waves of this delicious
mixture of erotic aromas.

Despite their worried early morning faces, Osaka people are
among the cheeriest in Japan, and they are also the most money
conscious. The usual greeting in Osaka is not 'How are you?' but
'How much money are you making?'

GAVIN YOUNG
(1928–   )

English writer, traveller and journalist. He has lived with
the Marsh Arabs of southern Iraq and the people of the
plains and mountains of south-western Arabia. In 1979
he sailed from Greece to China, travelling by whatever
waterborne transport he could find. On the journey
home, described in *Slow Boats Home* (1985), he not only
rounded the Horn, but landed on it too.

Rush hour in Shanghai

When it was time to go, Wei Kuen and Shun Ling wrapped scarves
round their necks in the doorway.

We groped our way down the ramshackle stairs into the blackness of the street, and it was like lowering ourselves into an icy
flood. Shanghai was blacked out like wartime London and it was
rush hour. A solid, pushing, human mass filled the pavements;
people in dark blue tunics barely seen, identical shapes advancing
silently, dark against the darkness.

I was suddenly frightened that I might get separated from Wei
Kuen. He could be swept away from me very easily – and what
then? I was utterly incapable of telling any of these blue-uniformed
shapes where I wanted to go to. Claustrophobia! Alone in China's
largest city, a freezing night coming on, inadequately clothed,
deprived of speech. . . . For once I was grateful that I towered above
the Chinese. Thanks to that I managed, with difficulty, to keep Wei
Kuen in sight or in touch; time and again my desperate handholds
on his arm were torn away by the press. I could see his face, a pale
buoy bobbing in and out of an ocean of inky waves, straining to
keep me in sight. I saw reflected in it my own anxiety.

In the main thoroughfare the crowds surged round a bus stop
like breakers round a rock. Buses came and went, but again and
again the human turbulence swept me away from their doors. At
last a likely one wallowed up – but stopped a hundred yards down
the road. We fought our way towards it. 'Ha!' – Wei Kuen reached
the door as it closed, banged on it with his fists and pointed to me.
The door opened and I leaped in. 'Tell him where I go,' I yelled to
Wei Kuen, but the door snapped shut sharply, blotting him out.

Would I ever see him again? The bus moved jerkily away. My arms were pinned by mufflered strangers, and to avoid my head banging the low roof I was obliged to stand stooped like an old heron. I could imagine what a ludicrous sight I was, and suddenly I wanted to giggle. 'Mysterious disappearance of. . . . Last seen running for a bus in Shanghai.' I could see the headline now.

Someone tugged at my anorak. A woman had moved aside on her bench, pressing aginst her neighbour to make a tiny space for me. I squeezed in between her and a dark-skinned soldier with the narrowest slit eyes I've ever seen. His gaze for the next twenty minutes never left my face. It was as if he had dislocated his neck into a permanent eyes-right.

Much later the bus pulled up on the Bund, and of course now my semi-panic shamed me. The conductor patted my arm, and in a moment the warmth and light of the Peace Hotel washed over me.

I went to the bar and asked the barman for a Panda Cocktail.

'Panda, good,' he said, smiling encouragingly as I drank.

'Same again,' I said.

Whenever I heard the 'Chinese masses' mentioned in future, I would remember this hectic evening in the Shanghai blackout.

REDMOND O'HANLON
(1947–   )

English naturalist, critic and traveller. In 1983 he and the poet James Fenton, after rudimentary instruction by the SAS, made an intrepid expedition into the heart of Borneo. O'Hanlon's account of their journey will surely join the ranks of the travel classics.

Fishing on the Baleh River

. . . After a burning swig all round from the arak rice-brandy five-gallon converted petrol-can, Dana, Leon and Inghai, drawing their parangs from their carved wooden scabbards, set off to cut down the saplings for our pole-beds; and I decided it was time that James and I taught them how to fish to maximum effect, like Englishmen. But first a little practice would be necessary.

Withdrawing quietly behind a massive jumble of boulders, well out of sight, I unpacked our precious cargo. Two new extendable rods, the toughest in town. A hundred yards of heavy line. A heavy bag of assorted lead weights. A termite's nest of swivels. A thorn-bush of hooks. Fifty different spinners, their spoons flashing in the sun, all shapes and all sizes for every kind of fish in every sort of inland water.

'The trouble is,' said James, flicking a rod handle and watching the sections telescope out into the blue beyond, 'my elder brother was the fisherman. That was his thing, you see, he filled that role. So I had to pretend it was a bore; and I never learned.'

'What? You never fished?'

'No. Never. What about you?'

'Well, *my* elder brother went fishing.'

'So you can't either?'

'Not exactly. Not with a rod. I used to go mackerel fishing with a line. All over the place.'

'Mackerel fishing! Now you tell me!' said James, looking really quite agitated and frightening a bright orange damsel-fly off his hat. 'Still,' he said, calming down, 'if *they* could do it it can't be that diffy, can it?'

'Of course not – you just stick the spinner and swivels and weights on that end and swing it through the air.'

The heat was unbearable. The fiddling was insupportable. The gut got tangled; the hooks stuck in our fingers; the knot diagram would have given Baden-Powell a blood clot in the brain. We did it all and forgot the nasty little weights. But eventually we were ready to kill fish.

'The SAS say it's simpler to stick in a hand-grenade.'

'They're right,' said James.

'But the Major said all you had to do was hang your dick in the river and pull it out with fish on it.'

'Why don't you stick your dick in the river?' said James.

Standing firm and straight, James cast the spinner into the river. It landed in the water straight down at the end of the rod. Clunk. James pulled. The line snapped. We went through the whole nasty rigmarole again, with fresh swivels, weights and spinner.

'Try again. Throw it a little further.'

James reached right back and then swung the rod forwards and sideways as if he was axeing a tree.

At that very moment, it seemed, the Borneo banded hornet, *Vesta tropica*, sunk its sting into my right buttock.

377

'Jesus!' I said.

It was huge and jointed, this hornet, flashing red and silver in the sun.

'You are hooked up,' said James matter-of-factly. 'You have a spinner in your bum.'

There was a weird, gurgling, jungle-sound behind us. Dana, Leon and Inghai were leaning against the boulders. The Iban, when they decide that something is really funny, and know that they are going to laugh for a long time, lie down first.

Dana, Leon and Inghai lay down.

'You should try it with harpoon!' shrieked Leon, helpless.

NORTH AMERICA

ALASKA

Mackenzie R

HUDSON BAY

St John's
NEWFOUNDLAND

Gaspé Peninsula

R
o
c
k
y

G
R
E
A
T

M
t
s

P
L
A
I
N
S

St Laurence River

MAINE

Quebec

Nova Scotia

Lake Superior

Montreal

Boston

Columbia R

OREGON

N & S
DAKOTA

Niagara Falls

Pierre

L Michigan

PENN
SYLVANIA

New York

Chicago

OHIO

Philadelphia

Salt Lake
• City

Sacramento

R
M
i
s
s
o
u
r
i

Indianapolis

San Francisco

CALIFORNIA

R Colorado

COLORADO

St Louis

VIRGINIA

Roanoke I

Grand
Canyon

MISSOURI

N & S
CAROLINA

ATLANTIC

Los Angeles

R
M
i
s
s
i
s
s
i
p
p
i

GEORGIA

Cape Fear

OCEAN

Jacksonville

PACIFIC

M
E
X
I
C
O

FLORIDA

OCEAN

Galveston

Tampa

Appalachee
Bay

GULF OF MEXICO

CARIBBEAN SEA

Leif Ericsson
(fl. 999–1002)

Norse discoverer of America. The son of Eric the Red, he spent his youth in Greenland and in 999 visited Norway where he was converted to Christianity and commissioned by King Olaf I to carry the faith to Greenland. In c. 1002 he set out on a voyage to the lands in the West.

Vinland

There was now great talk of discovering new countries. Leif, the son of Erik the Red of Brattahlid, went to see Bjarni Herjolfsson and bought his ship from him, and engaged a crew of thirty-five. . . .

They made their ship ready and put out to sea. The first landfall they made was the country that Bjarni had sighted last. They sailed right up to the shore and cast anchor, then lowered a boat and landed. There was no grass to be seen, and the hinterland was covered with great glaciers, and between glaciers and shore the land was like one great slab of rock. It seemed to them a worthless country.

Then Leif said, 'Now we have done better than Bjarni where this country is concerned – we at least have set foot on it. I shall give this country a name and call it *Helluland*.'

They returned to their ship and put to sea, and sighted a second land. Once again they sailed right up to it and cast anchor, lowered a boat and went ashore. This country was flat and wooded, with white sandy beaches wherever they went; and the land sloped gently down to the sea.

Leif said, 'This country shall be named after its natural resources: it shall be called *Markland*.'

They hurried back to their ship as quickly as possible and sailed away to sea in a north-east wind for two days until they sighted land again. They sailed towards it and came to an island which lay to the north of it.

They went ashore and looked about them. The weather was fine. There was dew on the grass, and the first thing they did was to get some of it on their hands and put it to their lips, and to them it seemed the sweetest thing they had ever tasted. Then they went back to their ship and sailed into the sound that lay between the island

and the headland jutting out to the north.

They steered a westerly course round the headland. There were extensive shallows there and at low tide their ship was left high and dry, with the sea almost out of sight. But they were so impatient to land that they could not bear to wait for the rising tide to float the ship; they ran ashore to a place where a river flowed out of a lake. As soon as the tide had refloated the ship they took a boat and rowed out to it and brought it up the river into the lake, where they anchored it. They carried their hammocks ashore and put up booths. Then they decided to winter there, and built some large houses.

There was no lack of salmon in the river or the lake, bigger salmon than they had ever seen. The country seemed to them so kind that no winter fodder would be needed for livestock: there was never any frost all winter and the grass hardly withered at all.

In this country, night and day were of more even length than in either Greenland or Iceland: on the shortest day of the year, the sun was already up by 9 a.m., and did not set until after 3 p.m.

One evening news came that someone was missing: it was Tyrkir the Southerner. Leif was very displeased at this, for Tyrkir had been with the family for a long time, and when Leif was a child had been devoted to him. Leif rebuked his men severely, and got ready to make a search with twelve men.

They had gone only a short distance from the houses when Tyrkir came walking towards them, and they gave him a warm welcome. Leif quickly realized that Tyrkir was in excellent humour.

Tyrkir had a prominent forehead and shifty eyes, and not much more of a face besides; he was short and puny-looking but very clever with his hands.

Leif said to him, 'Why are you so late, foster-father? How did you get separated from your companions?'

At first Tyrkir spoke for a long time in German, rolling his eyes in all directions and pulling faces, and no one could understand what he was saying. After a while he spoke in Icelandic.

'I did not go much farther than you,' he said. 'I have some news. I found vines and grapes.'

'Is that true, foster-father?' asked Leif.

'Of course it is true,' he replied. 'Where I was born there were plenty of vines and grapes.'

They slept for the rest of the night, and next morning Leif said to his men, 'Now we have two tasks on our hands. On alternate days we must gather grapes and cut vines, and then fell trees, to make a cargo for my ship.'

This was done. It is said that the tow-boat was filled with grapes. They took on a full cargo of timber; and in the spring they made ready to leave and sailed away. Leif named the country after its natural qualities and called it *Vinland*.

CHRISTOPHER COLUMBUS
(1451–1506)

Italian navigator and explorer, in the service of Spain. He sailed from Spain on 3 August 1492 and made his first landfall in the New World on 12 October. The country he had discovered was a small island in the Bahamas; Columbus, who believed it to lie off the coast of Asia, named it San Salvador. Even before the Europeans landed, the natives, who called the island Guanahani, had gathered to meet them.

First contact

I, in order that they might feel great amity towards us, because I knew that they were a people to be delivered and converted to our holy faith rather by love than by force, gave to some among them some red caps and some glass beads, which they hung round their necks, and many other things of little value. At this they were greatly pleased and became so entirely our friends that it was a wonder to see. Afterwards they came swimming to the ships' boats, where we were, and brought us parrots and cotton thread in balls, and spears and many other things, and we exchanged for them other things, such as small glass beads and hawks' bells, which we gave to them. In fact, they took all and gave all, such as they had, with good will, but it seemed to me that they were a people very deficient in everything. They all go naked as their mothers bore them, and the women also, although I saw only one very young girl. And all those whom I did see were youths, so that I did not see one who was over thirty years of age; they were very well built, with very handsome bodies and very good faces. Their hair is coarse almost like the hairs of a horse's tail and short; they wear their hair down over their eyebrows, except for a few strands behind, which they wear long and never cut. Some of them are painted black, and they are the colour of the people of the Canaries, neither black nor white, and some of them are painted white and some red and some in any colour that they find. Some of them paint their faces, some their whole bodies, some only the eyes, and some only the nose. They do not bear arms or know them, for I showed to them swords and they took them by the blade and cut themselves through ignorance. They have no iron. Their spears are certain reeds, without iron, and some of these have a fish tooth at the end, while others are pointed in various ways. They are all generally fairly tall, good looking and well proportioned. I saw some who bore marks of wounds on their bodies, and I made signs to them to ask how this came about, and they indicated to me that people came from other islands, which are near, and wished to capture them, and they defended themselves. And I believed and still believe that they come here from the mainland to take them for slaves. They should be good servants and of quick intelligence, since I see that they very soon say all that is said to them, and I believe that they would easily be made Christians, for it appeared to me that they had no creed. Our Lord willing, at the time of my departure I will bring back six of them to Your Highnesses, that they may learn to talk. I saw no beast of any kind in this island, except parrots.

GIOVANNI DA VERRAZANO
(c. 1480–1527)

Florentine navigator. Having left Madeira in March 1524, he reached Cape Fear, North Carolina, in March. On 17 April he anchored in the Narrows now spanned by the Verrazano Bridge at the entrance to New York Harbour, 'a very pleasant place'. He returned home via Maine, Novia Scotia and Newfoundland, reaching Dieppe on 8 July. If the Indians of North America were not always friendly to Verrazano and his men, those of the West Indies were distinctly unfriendly: on a second voyage a few years later Verrazano was captured, killed and possibly eaten.

The Indians of Virginia or Maryland conduct an examination

Sending ashore by swimming one of our young sailors carrying to them some trinkets, such as little bells, mirrors, and other favours, and being approached within 4 fathoms of them, throwing the goods to them and wishing to turn back he was so tossed by the waves that almost half dead he was carried to the edge of the shore. Which having been seen, the people of the land ran immediately to him: taking him by the head, legs and arms, they carried him some distance away. Where, the youth, seeing himself carried in such way, stricken with terror, uttered very loud cries, which they did similarly in their language, showing him that he should not fear. After that, having placed him on the ground in the sun at the foot of a little hill, they performed great acts of admiration, regarding the whiteness of his flesh, examining him from head to foot. Taking off his shirt and hose, leaving him nude, they made a very large fire near him, placing him near the heat. Which having been seen, the sailors who had remained in the small boat, full of fear, as is their custom in every new case, thought that they wanted to roast him for food. His strength recovered, having remained with them awhile, he showed by signs that he desired to return to the ship; who, with the greatest kindness, holding him always close with various embraces, accompanied him as far as the sea, and in order to assure him more, extending themselves on a high hill, stood to watch him until he was in the boat. Which young man learned of this people that they are thus: of dark colour like the others, the flesh more lustrous, of medium stature, the face more clear-cut, much more delicate of body and other members, of much less strength and even of intelligence. He saw nothing else.

JACQUES CARTIER
(1491–1557)

French navigator and explorer. In 1534 he discovered the mouth of the St Lawrence River, landing on the Gaspé Peninsula to take possession for France. A year later he returned and sailed up the St Lawrence as far as Hochelaga, the Huron city that is the site of present-day Montreal.

The Hurons

This tribe has no belief in God that amounts to anything; for they believe in a god they call *Cudouagny*, and maintain that he often holds intercourse with them and tells them what the weather will be like. They also say that when he gets angry with them, he throws dust in their eyes. They believe furthermore that when they die they go to the stars and descend on the horizon like the stars. Next, that they go off to beautiful green fields covered with fine trees, flowers and luscious fruits. After they had explained these things to us, we showed them their error and informed them that their *Cudouagny* was a wicked spirit who deceived them, and that there is but one God, Who is in Heaven, Who gives us everything we need and is the Creator of all things and that in Him alone we should believe. Also that one must receive baptism or perish in hell. . . .

These people live with almost everything in common, much like the Brazilians. They go clothed in beasts' skins, and rather miserably. In winter they wear leggings and moccasins made of skins, and in summer they go barefoot. They maintain the order of marriage except that the men take two or three wives. On the death of their husband the wives never marry again, but wear mourning all their lives by dyeing their faces black with brayed charcoal and grease as thick as the back of a knife-blade; and by this one knows they are widows. They have another very bad custom connected with their daughters who as soon as they reach the age of puberty are all placed in a brothel open to every one, until the girls have made a match. We saw this with our own eyes; for we discovered wigwams as full of these girls as is a boys' school with boys in France. And furthermore betting, after their fashion, takes place in these wigwams in which they stake all they own, even to the covering of their privy parts. They are by no means a laborious people and work the soil with short bits of wood about half a sword in length. With these they hoe their corn which they call *ozisy*, in size as large as a pea. Corn of a similar kind grows in considerable quantities in Brazil. They have also a considerable quantity of melons, cucumbers, pumpkins, pease and beans of various colours and unlike our own. Furthermore they have a plant, of which a large supply is collected in summer for the winter's consumption. They hold it in high esteem, though the men alone make use of it in the following manner. After drying it in the sun, they carry it about their necks in a small skin pouch in lieu of a bag, together with a hollow bit of stone or wood. Then at frequent intervals they crumble this plant into powder, which they place in one of the openings of the hollow instrument, and laying a live coal on top, suck at the other end to such an extent, that they fill their bodies so full of smoke, that it streams out of their mouths and nostrils as from a chimney. They say it keeps them warm and in good health, and never go about without these things. We made a trial of this smoke. When it is in one's mouth, one would think one had taken powdered pepper, it is so hot. . . . Both the men, women and children are more indifferent to the cold than beasts; for in the coldest weather we experienced, and it was extraordinary severe, they would come to our ships every day across the ice and snow, the majority of them almost stark naked, which seems incredible unless one has seen them.

PETRO DE CASTANEDA
(fl. 1540)

Spanish Conquistador and explorer. A member of Francisco Vasquez de Coronado's great expedition from the Gulf of California to the plains of Kansas, 1540–42. Members of de Coronado's party were the first white men to see the Grand Canyon of the Colorado River; desperate for water, they were unable to reach it.

The Conquistadors see their first bison

. . . There was not one of the horses that did not take flight when he saw them first, for they have a narrow, short face, the brow two palms across from eye to eye, the eyes sticking out at the side, so that, when they are running, they can see who is following them. They have very long beards, like goats, and when they are running they throw their heads back with the beard dragging on the ground. There is a sort of girdle round the middle of the body. The hair is very woolly, like a sheep's, very fine, and in front of the girdle the hair is very long and rough like a lion's. They have a great hump, larger than a camel's. The horns are short and thick, so that they are not seen much above the hair. In May they change the hair in the middle of the body for a down, which makes perfect lions of them. They rub against the small trees in the little ravines to shed their hair, and they continue this until only the down is left, as a snake changes his skin. They have a short tail, with a bunch of hair at the end. When they run, they carry it erect like a scorpion. It is worth noticing that the little calves are red and just like ours, but they change their colour and appearance with time and age.

Another strange thing was that all the bulls that were killed had their left ears slit, although these were whole when young. The reason for this was a puzzle that could not be guessed.

PHILIP AMADAS
(1550–1618)

English navigator. With another sea captain, Arthur Barlowe, he was sent by Sir Walter Raleigh in 1584 to explore the North American coast. In July they reached Roanoke Island, now part of North Carolina.

The Discovery of Virginia

. . . We viewed the land about us, being, whereas we first landed, very sandie and low towards the waters side, but so full of grapes, as the very beating and surge of the Sea overflowed them, of which we found such plentie, as well there as in all places else, both on the sand and on the greene soile on the hills, as in the plaines, as well on every little shrubbe, as also climing towardes the tops of high Cedars, that I thinke in all the world the like abundance is not to be found: and my selfe having seene those parts of Europe that most abound, find such difference as were incredible to be written. . . .

This Island had many goodly woodes full of Deere, Conies, Hares, and Fowle, even in the middest of Summer in incredible abundance. The woodes are not such as you finde in Bohemia, Moscovia, or Hercynia, barren and fruitles, but the highest and reddest Cedars of the world. . . . We remained by the side of this Island two whole dayes before we saw any people of the Countrey: the third day we espied one small boate rowing towardes us having in it three persons: this boat came to the Island side, foure har-quebuz-shot from our shippes, and there two of the people remaining, the third came along the shoreside towards us, and wee being then all within boord, he walked up and downe upon the point of the land next unto us: then the Master and the Pilot of the Admirall, Simon Ferdinando, and the Captaine Philip Amadas, my selfe, and others rowed to the land, whose comming this fellow attended, never making any shewe of feare or doubt. And after he had spoken of many things not understood by us, we brought him with his owne good liking, aboord the ships, and gave him a shirt, a hat & some other things, and made him taste of our wine, and our meat, which he liked very wel: and after having viewed both barks, he departed, and went to his owne boat againe, which hee had left in a little Cove or Creeke adjoyning: assoone as hee was two bow shoot into the water, he fell to fishing, and in lesse then halfe an houre, he had laden his boate as deepe, as it could swimme, with which hee came againe to the point of the lande, and there he devided his fish in two parts, pointing one part to the ship, and the other to the pinnesse: which, after he had (as much as he might) requited the former benefites received, departed out of our sight.

The next day there came unto us divers boates, and in one of them the Kings brother, accompanied with fortie or fiftie men, very handsome and goodly people, and in their behaviour as mannerly and civill as any of Europe. His name was Granganimeo, and the king is called Wingina, the countrey Wingandacoa, and now by her Majestie Virginia.

JOHN WHITE
(fl. 1585–93)

English artist, cartographer and colonist in Virginia. In 1585 he was among the first colonists to settle on Roanoke Island, following Amadas' and Barlowe's enthusiastic report. Despite the dreadful hardships undergone by the colonists, White developed a passion for Virginia and did all he could to promote the settlement. In 1587 he returned to England to organize urgent supplies for the colonists, but a series of misfortunes (among them the Spanish Armada) delayed his return. It was not until 17 August 1590 that he again set foot on Roanoke Island. The fate of the colonists remains a mystery.

The lost colony

... Our boates and all things fitted againe, we put off from
Hatorask, being the number of 19 persons in both boates: but
before we could get to the place, where our planters were left, it was
so exceeding darke, that we overshot the place a quarter of a mile:
there we espied towards the North end of the Iland the light of a
great fire thorow the woods, to the which we presently rowed: when
wee came right over against it, we let fall our Grapnel neere the
shore, & sounded with a trumpet a Call, & afterwards many
familiar English tunes of Songs, and called to them friendly; But we
had no answere, we therefore landed at day-breake, and comming
to the fire, we found the grasse & sundry rotten trees burning about
the place. From hence we went thorow the woods to that part of the
Iland directly over against Dasamongwepeuk, & from thence we
returned by the water side, round about the Northpoint of the Iland,
untill we came to the place where I left our Colony in the yeere 1586.
In all this way we saw in the sand the print of the Salvages feet of 2 or
3 sorts troaden that night, and as we entred up the sandy banke
upon a tree, in the very browe thereof were curiously carved these
faire Romane letters C R O: which letters presently we knew to
signifie the place, where I should find the planters seated, according
to a secret token agreed upon betweene them & me at my last
departure from them, which was, that in any wayes they should not
faile to write or carve on the trees or posts of the dores the name of
the place where they should be seated; for at my comming away
they were prepared to remove from Roanoak 50 miles into the
maine. . . . Therefore at my departure from them in Anno 1587 I
willed them that if they should happen to be distressed in any of
these places, that then they should carve the letters or name, a
Crosse ✠ in this forme, but we found no suche signe of distresse.
And having well considered of this, we passed toward the place
where they were left in sundry houses, but we found the houses
taken downe, and the place very strongly enclosed with a high
palisado of great trees, with cortynes and Flankers very Fort-like,
and one of the chiefe trees or postes at the right side of the entrance
had the barke taken off, and 5. foote from the grounde in fayre
Capitall letters was graven CROATOAN without any crosse or sign
of distresse; this done we entred in to the palisado, where we found
many barres of Iron, two pigges of Lead, foure yron fowlers, Iron
sacker-shotte, and such like heavie things, throwen here and there,

almost overgrowen with grasse and weedes. . . .

Presently Captaine Cooke and I went to the place, which was in the ende of an olde trench, made two yeers past by Captaine Amadas: wheere wee found five Chests, that had been carefully hidden of the Planters, and of the same chests three were my owne, and about the place many of my things spoyled and broken, and my bookes torne from the covers, the frames of some of my pictures and Mappes rotten and spoyled with rayne, and my armour almost eaten through with rust; this could bee no other but the deede of the Savages our enemies at Dasamongwepeuk, who had watched the departure of our men to Croatoan; and assone as they were departed, digged up every place where they suspected any thing to be buried: but although it much grieved me to see such spoyle of my goods, yet on the other side I greatly joyed that I had safely found a certaine token of their safe being at Croatoan, which is the place where Manteo was borne, and the Savages of the Iland our friends.

JOHN SMITH
(1580–1631)

English soldier of fortune, explorer and colonist in America. His life was adventurous in the extreme: in 1601–2 he fought against the Turks in Transylvania and Hungary, was captured, sold into slavery and taken to Constantinople, where a young Turkish lady fell in love with him. She sent him to her brother, a pasha, who treated him so cruelly that Smith killed him and made his escape. In 1606 he sailed for Virginia and was appointed a member of the governing council of Jamestown, the first permanent English settlement in America. In December 1607 he was captured by the Indians and only released, according to his own version, by the intervention of the Indian princess Pocahontas. In October 1609, having been badly injured in an explosion, he returned to England.

Powhatan and Pocahontas, Virginia, January 1608

At last they brought him to *Meronocomoco*, where was *Powhatan* their Emperor. Here more than two hundred of those grim Courtiers stood wondering at him, as he had beene a monster; till *Powhatan* and his trayne had put themselves in their greatest braveries. Before a fire upon a seat like a bedsted, he sat covered with a great robe, made of *Rarowcun* skinnes, and all the tayles hanging by. On either hand did sit a young wench of 16 or 18 yeares, and along on each side the house, two rowes of men, and behind them as many women, with all their heads and shoulders painted red: many of their heads bedecked with the white downe of Birds; but every one with something: and a great chayne of white beads about their necks.

At his entrance before the King, all the people gave a great shout. The Queene of *Appamatuck* was appointed to bring him water to wash his hands, and another brought him a bunch of feathers, in stead of a Towell to dry them: having feasted him after their best barbarous manner they could, a long consultation was held, but the conclusion was, two great stones were brought before *Powhatan*: then as many as could layd hands on him, dragged him to them, and thereon laid his head, and being ready with their clubs, to beate out his braines, *Pocahontas* the Kings dearest daughter, when no intreaty could prevaile, got his head in her armes, and laid her owne upon his to save him from death: whereat the Emperour was contented he should live to make him hatchets, and her bells, beads, and copper; for they thought him aswell of all occupations as themselves. For the King himselfe will make his owne robes, shooes, bowes, arrowes, pots; plant, hunt, or doe any thing so well as the rest. . . .

Two days after, *Powhatan* having disguised himselfe in the most fearefullest manner he could, caused Captain *Smith* to be brought forth to a great house in the woods, and there upon a mat by the fire to be left alone. Not long after from behinde a mat that divided the house, was made the most dolefullest noyse he ever heard; then *Powhatan* more like a devill then a man, with some two hundred more as blacke as himselfe, came unto him and told him now they were friends, and presently he should goe to *Iames* towne, to send him two great gunnes, and a gryndstone, for which he would give him the Country of *Capahowosick* and for ever esteeme him as his sonne *Nantaquoud*.

CLAUDE JEAN
ALLOUEZ, S.J.
(1622–1689)

French Jesuit Missionary in Canada and the American Midwest.

On the way into the Outaouac (Ottawa) Country,
August 1665

No sooner had I embarked than he [an Indian] put a paddle in my hand, urging me to use it and assuring me it was an honourable employment, and one worthy of a great captain. I willingly took the paddle and, offering up to God this labour in atonement for my sins and to hasten those poor savages' conversion, I imagined myself a malefactor sentenced to the galleys; and, although I became entirely exhausted, yet God gave me sufficient strength to paddle all day long, and often a good part of the night. But this application did not prevent my being commonly the object of their contempt and the butt of their jokes; for, however much I exerted myself, I accomplished nothing in comparison with them, their bodies being large and strong and perfectly adapted to such labours. The slight esteem in which they held me caused them to steal from me every article of my wardrobe that they could; and I had much difficulty in retaining my hat, the wide rim of which seemed to them peculiarly fitted for defence against the excessive heat of the sun. And when evening came, as my pilot took away a bit of blanket that I had to serve him as a pillow, he forced me to pass the night without any covering but the foliage of some tree.

When hunger is added to these discomforts it is a severe hardship, but one that soon teaches a man to find a relish in the bitterest roots and the most putrid meat. God was pleased to make me suffer from hunger, on Fridays especially, for which I heartily thank him.

We were forced to accustom ourselves to eat a certain moss growing upon the rocks. It is a sort of shell-shaped leaf which is always covered with caterpillars and spiders; and which, on being boiled, furnishes an insipid soup, black and viscous, that rather serves to ward off death than to impart life.

One morning we found a stag that had been dead four or five days. It was a lucky accident for poor starvelings. I was given a piece of it, and, although its offensive odour deterred some from eating any, hunger made me take my share; but my mouth had a putrid taste, in consequence, until the next day.

Amid all these hardships, whenever we came to any rapids I carried as heavy burdens as I could; but I often succumbed under them, and that made our savages laugh and mock me, saying they must call a child to carry me and my burden. Our good God did not forsake me utterly on these occasions, but often wrought on some of the men so that, touched with compassion, they would, without saying anything, relieve me of my *chapelle* [group of sacred vessels for celebration of the mass] or of some other burden, and would help me to journey a little more at my ease.

It sometimes happened that, after we had carried our loads and plied our paddles all day long, and even two or three hours into the night, we went supperless to bed on the ground or on some rock, to begin over again the next day with the same labours. But everywhere the Divine Providence mingled some little sweetness and relief with our fatigue. . . .

HANNAH SWARTON
(*fl.* 1690)

American settler. She was captured by the Indians in Maine in May 1690.

Up and down the wilderness

I was taken by the *Indians* when *Casco* Fort was taken. My Husband being slain, and four Children taken with me. The Eldest of my Sons they kill'd, about two Months after I was taken, and the rest scatter'd from me. I was now left a Widow, and as bereav'd of my Children; though I had them alive, yet it was very seldom that I could see 'em. . . . We had no Corn or Bread; but sometimes *Groundnuts, Acorns, Purslain, Hogweed*, Weeds, Roots, and sometimes *Dogs Flesh*, but not sufficient to satisfie Hunger with these; having but little at a time. We had no Success at hunting save that one Bear was killed, which I had part of; and a very small part of a

Turtle I had another time, and once an *Indian* gave me a piece of a *Moose's* Liver, which was a sweet Morsel to me; and *Fish* if we could catch it. Thus I continued with them, hurry'd up and down the Wilderness, from May 20, till the middle of *February*; carrying continually a great Burden in our Travels; and I must go their Pace, or else be killed presently; and yet was pinch'd with Cold for want of Cloathing, being put by them into an *Indian* Dress, with a sleight Blanket, no Stockins, and but one pair of *Indian* Shooes, and of their Leather Stockins for the Winter: My Feet were pricked with sharp Stones and prickly Bushes sometimes, and other times pinch'd with Snow, Cold, and Ice, that I travell'd upon, ready to be frozen, and faint for want of Food; so that many times I thought I could go no further, but must lie down, and if they would kill me, let 'em kill me. Yet then the Lord did so renew my Strength, that I went on still further as my Master would have me, and held out with them. Though many English were taken, and I was brought to some of 'em at times, while we were about *Casco Bay* and *Kennebeck River*, yet at *Norridgawock* we were separated, and no *English* were in our Company, but one *John York* and my self, who were both almost starv'd for Want; and yet told, that if we could not hold up to travel with them, they would kill us. And accordingly *John York* growing weak by his Wants, they killed him, and threatned me with the like. One time my *Indian* Mistress and I, were left alone, while the rest went to look for *Eels*; and they left us no Food from *Sabbath-day* Morning till the next *Saturday*; save that we had a *Bladder* (of Moose I think) which was well fill'd with Maggots, and we boild it, and drank the Broth; but the Bladder was so tough we could not eat it. . . .

My *Indian* Mistress was one that had been bred by the *English* at *Black-Point*, and now married to a *Canada Indian*, and turned Papist; and she would say, *That had the* English *been as careful to instruct her in our Religion as the* French *were, to instruct her in theirs, she might have been of our Religion:* and she would say, *That God delivered us into their Hands to punish us for our Sins*; And this I knew was true as to my self.

JOHN LAWSON
(d. 1711)

Scottish explorer. He arrived in America in 1700 and travelled approximately 1000 miles through unexplored parts of the Carolinas, living on terms of intimacy with various local tribes. In 1711 he was captured and tortured to death by the Tuscarora Indians.

The Indian women of North Carolina

As for the Indian Women which now happen in my Way, when young, and at Maturity, they are as fine shaped Creatures, (take them generally,) as any in the Universe. They are of a tawny Complexion, their Eyes very brisk and amorous, their Smiles afford the finest Composure a Face can possess, their Hands are of the finest Make, with small, long Fingers, and as soft as their Cheeks, and their whole Bodies of a smooth Nature. They are not so uncouth or unlikely as we suppose them, nor are they Strangers or not Proficients in the soft Passion. They are, most of them, mercenary, except the married Women, who sometimes bestow their Favours also to some or other, in their Husband's Absence; for which they never ask any Reward. As for the Report, that they are never found unconstant, like the Europeans, it is wholly false; for were the old World and the new one put into a Pair of Scales (in point of constancy) it would be a hard Matter to discern which was the heavier. As for the Trading Girls, which are those designed to get Money by their Natural Parts, these are discernable by the Cut of their Hair; their tonsure differing from all others of that Nation, who are not of their Profession, which Method is intended to prevent Mistakes; for the Savages of America are desirous (if possible) to keep their Wives to themselves, as well as those in other Parts of the World. When any Addresses are made to one of these Girls, she immediately acquaints her Parents therewith, and they tell the King of it, (provided he that courts her be a Stranger) his Majesty commonly being the principal Bawd of the Nation he rules over, and there seldom being any of these Winchester-Weddings agreed on without his Royal Consent. He likewise advises her what Bargain to make, and if it happens to be an Indian Trader that wants a Bed-fellow and has got Rum to sell, be sure the King must have a large Dram for a Fee to confirm the Match. These Indians that are of the elder sort, when any such Question is put to them, will debate the Matter amongst themselves with all the Sobriety and Seriousness imaginable, every one of the Girl's Relations arguing the Advantage or Detriment that may ensue such a Night's Encounter; all which is done with as much Steadiness and Reality as if it was the greatest Concern in the World, and not so much as one Person shall be seen to smile, so long as the Debate holds, making no Difference betwixt an Agreement of this Nature and a Bargain of any other. If they comply with the Men's Desire, then a particular Bed is provided for them, either in a Cabin by themselves or else all the young people turn out to another Lodging, that they may not spoil Sport, and if the old People are in the same Cabin along with them all Night, they lie as unconcerned as if they were so many Logs of Wood.

PETER KALM
(1716–1779)

Swedish naturalist and botanist. In 1748 he was sent by Linnaeus on a botanizing trip to America, travelling in New York and Canada over the next three years. His *Travels into North America* was translated into English in 1772 despite the misgivings of the translator about Kalm's 'unfavourable bias' against the English.

The difference between the ladies of Quebec and those of Montreal, 1749

There are some difference between the ladies of *Quebec*, and those of *Montreal*; those of the last place seemed to be generally handsomer than those of the former. Their behaviour likewise seemed to me to be somewhat too free at *Quebec*, and of a more becoming modesty at *Montreal*. The ladies at *Quebec*, especially the unmarried ones, are not very industrious. A girl of eighteen is reckoned very poorly off, if she cannot enumerate at least twenty lovers. These young ladies, especially those of a higher rank, get up at seven, and dress till nine, drinking their coffee at the same time. When they are dressed, they place themselves near a window that opens into the street, take up some needle-work, and sew a stitch now and then; but turn their eyes into the street most of the time. When a young fellow comes in, whither they are acquainted with him or not, they immediately lay aside their work, sit down by him, and begin to chat, laugh, joke, and invent *double-entendres*; and this is reckoned being very witty. In this manner they frequently pass the whole day, leaving their mothers to do all the business in the house. In *Montreal*, the girls are not quite so volatile, but more industrious. They are always at their needle-work, or doing some necessary business in the house. They are likewise chearful and content; and nobody can say that they want either wit, or charms. Their fault is that they think too well of themselves. However, the daughters of people of all ranks, without exception, go to market, and carry home what they have bought. They rise as soon, and go to bed as late, as any of the people in the house. I have been assured, that, in general, their fortunes are not considerable; which are rendered still more scarce by the number of children, and the small revenues in a house. The girls at *Montreal* are very much displeased that those at *Quebec* get husbands sooner than they. The reason of this is, that many young gentlemen who come over from *France* with the ships, are captivated by the ladies at *Quebec*, and marry them; but as these gentlemen seldom go up to *Montreal*, the girls there are not often so happy as those of the former place.

WILLIAM BARTRAM
(1739–1823)

American traveller and naturalist. Son of the famous botanist John Bartram, whom he accompanied in 1765–6 in exploring the St John's River in Florida by canoe. His *Travels* (1791) was immensely popular in America and Europe.

Alligators fishing in the St John's River

It was by this time dusk, and the alligators had nearly ceased their roar, when I was again alarmed by a tumultuous noise that seemed to be in my harbor and therefore engaged my immediate attention. Returning to my camp, I found it undisturbed and then continued on to the extreme point of the promontory, where I saw a scene, new and surprising, which at first threw my senses into such a tumult, that it was some time before I could comprehend what was the matter. However, I soon accounted for the prodigious assemblage of crocodiles at this place, which exceeded everything of the kind I had ever heard of. . . .

. . . The river (in this place), from shore to shore and perhaps near half a mile above and below me, appeared to be one solid bank of fish of various kinds, pushing through to his narrow pass of St. Juan's into the little lake on their return down the river, and . . . the alligators were in such incredible numbers and so close together from shore to shore that it would have been easy to have walked across on their heads, had the animals been harmless. What expressions can sufficiently declare the shocking scene that for some minutes continued, whilst this mighty army of fish were forcing the pass? During this attempt, thousands, I may say hundreds of thousands, of them were caught and swallowed by the devouring alligators. I have seen an alligator take up out of the water several great fish at a time, and just squeeze them betwixt his jaws, while the tails of the great trout flapped about his eyes and lips, ere he had swallowed them. The horrid noise of their closing jaws, their plunging amidst the broken banks of fish and rising with their prey some feet upright above the water, the floods of water and blood rushing out of their mouths, and the clouds of vapor issuing from their wide nostrils were truly frightful. This scene continued at intervals during the night, as the fish came to the pass. After this sight, shocking and tremendous as it was, I found myself somewhat easier and more reconciled to my situation; being convinced that their extraordinary assemblage here was owing to the annual feast of fish; and that they were so well employed in their own element that I had little occasion to fear their paying me a visit.

ALEXANDER HENRY
(1739–1824)

American fur trader. In June 1763 he was captured by the Chippewa Indians in a surprise attack on Fort Michilimackinac, of which he was one of the few survivors. A Chippewa chief adopted him as a brother and he was released the following year. In 1776 he attempted to reach the Rocky Mountains, but got only as far as the Great Plains.

A *fatal game of baggatiway at Fort Michilimackinac,*
5 June 1763

The morning was sultry. A Chipeway came to tell me that his nation was going to play at *bag'gat'iway*, with the Saes or Saäkies, another Indian nation, for a high wager. He invited me to witness the sport, adding that the commandant was to be there and would bet on the side of the Chipeways. In consequence of this information, I went to the commandant and expostulated with him a little, representing that the Indians might possibly have some sinister end in view; but the commandant only smiled at my suspicions.

Baggatiway, called by the Canadians *le jeu de la crosse* [lacrosse], is played with a bat and ball. The bat is about four feet in length, curved, and terminating in a sort of racket. Two posts are planted in the ground at a considerable distance from each other, as a mile or more. Each party has its post, and the game consists in throwing the ball up to the post of the adversary. The ball, at the beginning, is placed in the middle of the course, and each party endeavors as well to throw the ball out of the direction of its own post as into that of the adversary's.

I did not go myself to see the match which was now to be played without the fort because, there being a canoe prepared to depart on the following day for Montréal, I employed myself in writing letters to my friends; and even when a fellow trader, Mr. Tracy, happened to call upon me, saying that another canoe had just arrived from Détroit and proposing that I should go with him to the beach to inquire the news, it so happened that I still remained to finish my letters, promising to follow Mr. Tracy in the course of a few minutes. Mr. Tracy had not gone more than twenty paces from my door when I heard an Indian war cry and a noise of general confusion.

Going instantly to my window, I saw a crowd of Indians within the fort, furiously cutting down and scalping every Englishman they found. . . .

John Gottlieb Ernestus Heckewelder
(1743–1823)

Moravian missionary. Born in England, he settled in
Pennsylvania in 1754 and spent years working with the
Pennsylvania Indians who had been removed to Ohio. He
wrote numerous accounts of Indian life.

Travelling Indians on the Muskingum River, Ohio, 1777

Some travelling Indians having in the year 1777, put their horses
over night to pasture in my little meadow, at Gnadenhutten on the
Muskingum, I called on them in the morning to learn why they had
done so. I endeavoured to make them sensible of the injury they had
done me, especially as I intended to mow the meadow in a day or
two. Having finished my complaint, one of them replied: 'My
friend, it seems you lay claim to the grass my horses have eaten,
because you had enclosed it with a fence: now tell me, who caused
the grass to grow? Can *you* make the grass grow? I think not, and no
body can except the great Mannitto. He it is who causes it to grow
both for my horses and for yours! See, friend! the grass which grows
out of the earth is common to all; the game in the woods is common
to all. Say, did you ever eat venison and bear's meat? – 'Yes, very
often.' – Well, and did you ever hear me or any other Indian
complain about that? No; then be not disturbed at my horses having
eaten only once, of what you call *your* grass, though the grass my
horses did eat, in like manner as the meat you did eat, was given to
the Indians by the Great Spirit. Besides, if you will but consider, you
will find that my horses did not eat *all* your grass. For friendship's
sake, however, I shall never put my horses in your meadow again.'

MÉDERIC LOUIS ÉLIE
MOREAU DE SAINT-MÉRY
(1750–1819)

French lawyer and politician. Born in Martinique, he became a judge in Santa Domingo before returning to Paris where he was briefly president of the Paris commune. When Robespierre came to power he fled to America, where from 1794 to 1798 he worked as a shipping clerk, a printer and a bookseller in Norfolk, New York and Philadelphia. He returned to France in 1798 and resumed his political career.

A Frenchman's view of American women

American girls are pretty, and their eyes are alive with expression; but their complexions are wan, bad teeth spoil the appearance of their mouths, and there is also something disagreeable about the length of their legs. In general, however, they are of good height, are graceful, and, in enumerating their charms, one must not forget the shapeliness of their breasts. . . .

But these girls soon become pale, and an indisposition which is reckoned among the most unfavorable for the maintenance of the freshness of youth is very common among them. They have thin hair and bad teeth, and are given to nervous illnesses. The elements which embellish beauty, or rather which compose and order it, are not often bestowed by the graces. Finally, they are charming, adorable at fifteen, dried up at twenty-three, old at thirty-five, decrepit at forty or fifty.

SIR ALEXANDER
MACKENZIE
(1764–1820)

Scottish fur-trader and explorer. In 1779 he entered a Toronto fur-trading company and later spent some years at Fort Chipewyan, at the head of Lake Athabasca in Alberta, trading with the Chippewas. In June 1789, together with a small party of Canadians and Indians, travelling in birch bark canoes, he set off from Fort Chipewyan to explore the unknown country to the north-west. On 15 July they reached the Arctic Ocean at the mouth of the Mackenzie River. After a journey of 2990 miles and 102 days, he returned to Fort Chipewyan. In 1792 he made a second expedition, this time with a Scot named Mackay, six voyageurs and two Indians, following the Peace River to the west. In the spring of 1793 they crossed the Great Divide and descended the Fraser and Bella Coola Rivers, eventually reaching the Pacific, the first men to cross the continent since Cabeca de Vaca in 1536. Knighted in 1802, he returned to Scotland shortly afterwards.

Indian physicians hard at work to counteract the effect of Turlington's Balsam, Bella Coola River, 19 July 1793

At an early hour this morning I was again visited by the chief, in company with his son. The former complained of a pain in his breast; to relieve his suffering, I gave him a few drops of Turlington's Balsam on a piece of sugar; and I was rather surprised to see him take it without the least hesitation. When he had taken my medicine, he requested me to follow him, and conducted me to a shed, where several people were assembled around a sick man, who was another of his sons. They immediately uncovered him, and shewed me a violent ulcer in the small of his back, in the foulest state that can be imagined. One of his knees was also afflicted in the same manner. This unhappy man was reduced to a skeleton, and, from his appearance, was drawing near to the end of his pains. . . . He was in such a dangerous state that I thought it prudent to yield no further to the importunities than to give the sick person a few drops of Turlington's Balsam in some water. . . . On my return I found the native physicians busy in practising their skill and art on the patient. They blew on him, and then whistled; at times they pressed their extended fingers, with all their strength on his stomach; they also put their fore fingers doubled into his mouth, and spouted water from their own with great violence into his face. To support these operations the wretched sufferer was held up in a sitting posture; and when they were concluded, he was laid down and covered with a new robe made of the skins of the lynx. I had observed that his belly and breast were covered with scars, and I understood that they were caused by a custom prevalent among them, of applying pieces of lighted touch wood to their flesh, in order to relieve pain or demonstrate their courage. He was now placed on a broad plank, and carried by six men into the woods, where I was invited to accompany them. I could not conjecture what would be the end of this ceremony, particularly as I saw one man carry fire, another an axe, and a third dry wood. I was, indeed, disposed to suspect that, as it was their custom to burn the dead, they intended to relieve the poor man from his pain, and perform the last sad duty of surviving affection. When they had advanced a short distance into the wood, they laid him upon a clear spot, and kindled a fire against his back, when the physician began to scarify the ulcer with a very blunt instrument, the cruel pain of which operation the patient bore with incredible resolution. The scene afflicted me and I left it.

MERIWETHER LEWIS
(1774–1809) and
WILLIAM CLARK
(1770–1838)

American explorers and army officers. Lewis was private secretary to President Thomas Jefferson, who had long considered sending an expedition to explore the American West. When Congress approved the plan in 1803, Jefferson appointed Lewis to lead the expedition and he chose Clark as his fellow commander. The two men were given a detailed 'draught of instructions' by the President. The expedition set off from St Louis in May 1804 and spent the first winter at Fort Mandan, North Dakota. In 1805 they reached the Missouri River and followed the branch they named the Jefferson as far as they could. They then crossed the Rockies and followed the Snake and Columbia Rivers to the Pacific, where they spent the second winter. In March 1806 they set out on the return journey, finally arriving back at St Louis on 23 September 1806. Lewis was subsequently appointed Governor of Louisiana. In 1809, believing himself to be under suspicion of having mismanaged public funds, he set off for Washington, but was either murdered or committed suicide on the way. Clark became Governor of Missouri and superintendent of Indian affairs.

'The object of your mission . . .' – Jefferson's instructions,
20 June, 1803

The object of your mission is to explore the Missouri river, and such principal streams of it, as, by its course and communication with the waters of the Pacific ocean, whether the Columbia, Oregan [*sic*], Colorado, or any other river, may offer the most direct and practicable water-communication across the continent, for the purposes of commerce. . . .

Your observations are to be taken with great pains and accuracy; to be entered distinctly and intelligibly for others as well as yourself; to comprehend all the elements necessary, with the aid of the usual tables, to fix the latitude and longitude of the places at which they were taken. . . . Several copies of these, as well as of your other notes, should be made at leisure times, and put into the care of the most trustworthy of your attendants to guard, by multiplying them against the accidental losses to which they will be exposed. A further guard would be, that one of these copies be on the cuticular membranes of the paper-birch, as less liable to injury from damp than common paper. . . .

In all your intercourse with the natives, treat them in the most friendly and conciliatory manner which their own conduct will admit; allay all jealousies as to the object of your journey; satisfy them of its innocence; make them acquainted with the position, extent, character, peaceable and commercial dispositions of the United States; of our wish to be neighborly, friendly, and useful to them, and of our dispositions to a commercial intercourse with them; confer with them on the points most convenient as mutual emporiums, and the articles of most desirable interchange for them and us. . . .

On your arrival on that coast, endeavor to learn if there be any port within your reach frequented by the sea vessels of any nation, and to send two of your trusty people back by sea, in such way as shall appear practicable, with a copy of your notes; and should you be of opinion that the return of your party by the way they went will be imminently dangerous, then ship the whole, and return by sea, by the way either of Cape Horn, or the Cape of Good Hope, as you shall be able. As you will be without money, clothes, or provisions, you must endeavor to use the credit of the United States to obtain them; for which purpose open letters of credit shall be furnished you, authorizing you to draw on the Executive of the United States, or any of its officers, in any part of the world, in which draughts can be disposed of and to apply with our recommendations to the consuls, agents, merchants, or citizens of any nation with which we have intercourse, assuring them in our name that any aids they may furnish you shall be honorably repaid, and on demand. Our consuls, Thomas Hewes, at Batavia in Java, William Buchanan in the Isles of France and Bourbon, and John Elmslie at the Cape of Good Hope, will be able to supply your necessities by draughts on us.

Should you find it safe to return by the way you go, after sending two of your party round by sea, or with your whole party, if no conveyance by sea can be found, do so. . . .

To provide, on the accident of your death, against anarchy, dispersion, and the consequent danger to your party, and total failure of the enterprise, you are hereby authorized, by any instrument signed and written in your own hand, to name the person among them who shall succeed to the command on your decease, and by like instruments to change the nomination, from time to time, as further experience of the characters accompanying you shall point out superior fitness.

Given under my hand at the City of Washington, this twentieth day of June, 1803.

THOMAS JEFFERSON
President of the United States of America.

'Not a painted white man'
– Fort Mandan, 9 March 1805

The morning cloudy and cool, the wind from the north. The grand chief of the Minnetarees, who is called by the French Le Borgne, from his having but one eye, came down for the first time to the fort. He was received with much attention, two guns being fired in honor of his arrival; the curiosities were exhibited to him, and as he said that he had not received the presents which we had sent to him on his arrival, we again gave him a flag, a medal, shirt, arm-braces, and the presents usual on such occasions, with all which he was much pleased. In the course of the conversation, the chief observed that some foolish young men of his nation had told him there was a person among us who was quite black, and he wished to know if it could be true. We assured him that it was true, and sent for York [Clark's Negro servant]. Le Borgne was very much surprised at his appearance, examined him closely, and spit on his finger and rubbed the skin in order to wash off the paint; nor was it until the negro uncovered his head and showed his short hair, that Le Borgne could be persuaded that he was not a painted white man.

The river straddled and God thanked – the expedition reaches the Great Divide of the Rocky Mountains at Lemhi Pass, 12 August 1805

They then continued through the low bottom, along the main stream, near the foot of the mountains on their right. For the first five miles, the valley continues toward the southwest, being from two to three miles in width; then the main stream, which had received two small branches from the left in the valley, turned abruptly to the west through a narrow bottom between the mountains. The road was still plain, and, as it led them directly on toward the mountain, the stream gradually became smaller, till, after going two miles, it had so greatly diminished in width that one of the men, in a fit of enthusiasm, with one foot on each side of the river thanked God that he had lived to bestride the Missouri. As they went along their hopes of soon seeing the Columbia [*i.e.*, the Pacific watershed] arose almost to painful anxiety, when after four miles from the last abrupt turn of the river, they reached a small gap formed by the high mountains, which recede on each side, leaving room for the Indian road. From the foot of one of the lowest of these mountains, which rises with a gentle ascent of about half a mile, issues the remotest water of the Missouri.

They had now reached the hidden sources of that river, which had never yet been seen by civilized man. As they quenched their thirst at the chaste and icy fountain – as they sat down by the brink of that little rivulet, which yielded its distant and modest tribute to the parent ocean – they felt themselves rewarded for all their labors and all their difficulties.

JANET SCHAW
(fl. 1776)

Scottish 'Lady of Quality'. In 1774–6 she visited the West Indies, North Carolina and Portugal.

The coast of North Carolina, 1775

At last America is in my view; a dreary waste of white barren sand, and melancholy, nodding pines. In the course of many miles, no cheerful cottage has blest my eyes. All seems dreary, savage and desert; and was it for this that such sums of money, such streams of British blood have been lavished away? Oh, thou dear land, how dearly hast thou purchased this habitation for bears and wolves. Dearly has it been purchased, and at a price far dearer still it will be kept. My heart dies within me, while I view it.

An uncomplimentary view of American colonists on the eve of the War of Independence, 1775

. . . But tho' I may say what I formerly did of the West India Islands, that nature holds out to them everything that can contribute to conveniency, or tempt to luxury, yet the inhabitants resist both, and if they can raise as much corn and pork, as to subsist them in the most slovenly manner, they ask no more; and as a very small proportion of their time serves for that purpose, the rest is spent in sauntering thro' the woods with a gun or sitting under a rustic shade, drinking New England rum made into grog, the most shocking liquor you can imagine. By this manner of living, their blood is spoil'd and rendered thin beyond all proportion, so that it is constantly on the fret like bad small beer, and hence the constant slow fevers that wear down their constitutions, relax their nerves and enfeeble the whole frame. Their appearance is in every respect the reverse of that which gives the idea of strength and vigour, and for which the British peasantry are so remarkable. They are tall and lean, with short waists and long limbs, sallow complexions and languid eyes, when not inflamed by spirits. Their feet are flat, their joints loose and their walk uneven. These I speak of are only the peasantry of this country, as hitherto I have seen nothing else, but I make no doubt when I come to see the better sort, they will be far from this description. For tho' there is a most disgusting equality, yet I hope to find an American gentleman a very different creature from an American clown. Heaven forefend else.

John Frederick Reichel
(fl. 1780)

German Moravian bishop. In 1752, the Moravians, an evangelical Christian sect from Germany, established a settlement at Salem, North Carolina. Fifteen years later Bishop Reichel was sent out from Saxony to 'give comfort and counsel to the Brethren' in America. His diary of the journey from Lititz, Pennsylvania, to Salem conveys the hardships and the joys of many such emigrants to America.

Led by the Saviour

[*June 8, 1780*] We crossed a bridge over the little Roanoke, a small but very deep stream, and passed Charlotte Court-House. We had rain until nearly noon when it cleared somewhat. But as we finished lunch there came a thunder storm with strong wind and pouring rain. We crept into and under the wagons and so protected ourselves from the rain. In the afternoon it was clear, and we crossed marshy ground on a corduroy road half a mile long, to drive over which would certainly be good medecine for a hypocondriac. We spent the night in a pretty open green spot, where we ate the first Journey-Cakes with a good appetite. It was a very cool night.

The 9. In the morning we crossed a bridge all full of holes, and were grateful to the Saviour for our safety as we considered the very apparent danger. We also passed safely through the deep bottom as we neared Stanton River and across its ford whose steep approaches gave the teamsters much trouble. It took eight horses to pull Conrad's wagon out, and that with difficulty. On the farther bank we stopped at noon, and nine miles beyond made our night's camp.

The 10. The roads were very bad. Steep hills washed by the heavy rains alternated with deep bottoms and swampy places. Everything fell out of the wagons. Here we made a new arrangement. B[rothe]r. and S[iste]r. Neilsen and Br. and Sr. Aust rode double on two of the horses, and Sr. Reichel rode for the first time alone, the rest went afoot. We thanked the dear Lord that everything went through without accident, and that Sr. Nielsen was not hurt when she fell from her horse. Noon was spent at the high Bannister Bridge. We had trouble in getting water enough from a muddy spring. Our night camp was half a mile from Old Halifax, 100 miles from Salem.

The 11. When we were in Old Halifax we asked about this famous town and received the information, 'You are in the very city.' (This is only an application of an old story.) There are only a couple of houses here. Sr. Reichel had a headache to-day, but was better in the afternoon. At noon as she lay on a bed in the shade a hog jumped over her because the dog was after it, and that cured her. (This creature is far too familiar in Virginia, and must be forcibly driven away.) The heat was great, and we had storms every day. We made nineteen miles to-day, and camped by Lynch's Tavern.

The 12. Yesterday afternoon and this morning the road was so hilly, rough and washed by the rains, that we might well thank the Saviour that we had no accident. Br. Jeppe Nielsen was so weak to-day that he could not ride and had to stay in the wagon most of the time. Hauser was made happy by the arrival of his men, Jac. Stotz and Sam. Strubb of Bethanian, who came to help him, and as one of the wheel horses to Conrad's wagon was quite worn out one of theirs was put in its place. We stopped for noon at the Sandy River. Toward evening a heavy storm broke, and we were soaked.

The 13. A miserable road, ruts filled with sand by the rain, stony, hilly, and full of holes. Hauser nearly had a bad accident with his horses and wagon, for as they were going down a steep hill the breast chain broke and the near horse was thrown under the wheel; but the driver saw it in time and the horse escaped serious injury, being only scratched on crupper and one foot. The hand of the Lord protected us that we did not have a terrible misfortune. This morning we crossed the Carolina line, and our noon rest was for the first time on Carolina soil.

The 15. We rose early and took up our journey with joy, crossing the Dan River safely, and reaching the Brethren in Salem about six in the evening, thankful to the Saviour Who had guided and led us like children, and had given us to feel His peace and presence throughout the entire way. We were welcomed with trombones, which played 'Euren Eingang segen Gott.'

FRANCES TROLLOPE
(1780–1863)

English novelist, mother of Anthony Trollope. In 1827 she and her husband emigrated to Cincinnati, where they opened a fancy goods store. It was not a success and they returned to England. Her account of her travels, *The Domestic Manners of the Americans* (1832), sold very well in England but did less well in the United States, no doubt because much of it was extremely uncomplimentary.

Slaves in the Southern States

I observed everywhere throughout the slave States that all articles which can be taken and consumed are constantly locked up, and in large families, where the extent of the establishment multiplies the number of the keys, these are deposited in a basket, and consigned to the care of a little negress, who is constantly seen following her mistress's steps with this basket on her arm, and this, not only that the keys may be always at hand, but because, should they be out of sight one moment, that moment would infallibly be employed for the purposes of plunder. It seemed to me in this instance, as in many others, that the close personal attendance of these sable shadows must be very annoying; but whenever I mentioned it, I was assured that no such feeling existed, and that use rendered them almost unconscious of their presence.

I had, indeed, frequent opportunities of observing this habitual indifference to the presence of their slaves. They talk of them, of their condition, of their conduct, exactly as if they were incapable of hearing. I once saw a young lady, who, when seated at table between a male and a female, was induced by her modesty to intrude on the chair of her female neighbour to avoid the indelicacy of touching the elbow of *a man*. I once saw this very young lady lacing her stays with the most perfect composure before a negro footman. A Virginian gentleman told me that ever since he had married, he had been accustomed to have a negro girl sleep in the same chamber with himself and his wife. I asked for what purpose this nocturnal attendance was necessary? 'Good heaven!' was the reply, 'if I wanted a glass of water during the night, what would become of me?'

FANNY KEMBLE
(1809–1893)

English actress and writer. (See p. 226.) She went to America in 1833 and enjoyed a brilliant success on the stage. In 1834 she married Pierce Butler, owner of a plantation in Georgia. She left her husband in 1846 and returned to England, but later went back to the United States and lived in Massachusetts.

Broadway in 1832

... After walking nearly a mile up Broadway, we came to Canal Street: it is broader and finer than any I have yet seen in New York; and at one end of it, a Christian church, copied from some Pagan temple or other, looked exceedingly well, in the full flood of silver light that streamed from heaven. There were many temptations to look around, but the flags were so horribly broken and out of order, that to do so was to run the risk of breaking one's neck: – this is very bad. The street was very much thronged, and I thought the crowd a more civil and orderly one, than an English crowd. The men did not jostle or push one another, or tread upon one's feet, or kick down one's shoe heels, or crush one's bonnet into one's face, or turn it round upon one's head, all which I have seen done in London streets. There is this to be said: this crowd was abroad merely for pleasure, sauntering along, which is a thing never seen in London; the proportion of idle loungers who frequent the streets there being very inconsiderable, when compared with the number of people going on business through the town. I observed that the young men to-night invariably made room for the women to pass, and many of them, as they drew near us, took the segar from their mouth, which I thought especially courteous. They were all smoking, to a man, except those who were spitting, which helped to remind me of Paris, to which the whole place bore a slight resemblance. The shops appear to me to make no show whatever, and will not bear a comparison with the brilliant display of the Parisian streets, or the rich magnificence of our own, in that respect. The women dress very much, and very much like French women gone mad; they all of them seem to me to walk horribly ill, as if they wore tight shoes.

JOHN CHARLES FREMONT
(1813–1890)

American explorer, soldier and politician. The last of the great explorers of the interior of America, a man who 'made the unknown countries known'. In 1842, with Kit Carson as guide, he led an expedition from Missouri to the Rocky Mountains. The next year, again with Carson, and dragging a twelve-pound brass howitzer to deter hostile Indians, he followed the Arkansas and Platte Rivers to the Great Salt Lake, then crossed the Sierra Nevada to California. His enthusiastic reports created enormous interest in the West. In 1856 he was Republican candidate for the presidency and 1878 was appointed governor of Arizona Territory.

The highest humblebee – on the summit of Snow Peak in the Rocky Mountains, 15 August 1842

During our morning's ascent we had met no sign of animal life, except the small sparrowlike bird already mentioned. A stillness the most profound and a terrible solitude forced themselves constantly on the mind as the great features of the place. Here, on the summit, where the stillness was absolute, unbroken by any sound, and the solitude complete, we thought ourselves beyond the region of animated life; but while we were sitting on the rock, a solitary bee (*Bombus*, the humblebee) came winging his flight from the eastern valley, and lit on the knee of one of the men.

It was a strange place, the icy rock and the highest peak of the Rocky Mountains, for a lover of warm sunshine and flowers; and we pleased ourselves with the idea that he was the first of his species to cross the mountain barrier – a solitary pioneer to foretell the advance of civilization. I believe that a moment's thought would have made us let him continue his way unharmed; but we carried out the law of this country, where all animated nature seems at war, and, seizing him immediately, put him in at least a fit place – in the leaves of a large book, among the flowers we had collected on our way. The barometer stood at 18.293, the attached thermometer at 44°; giving for the elevation of this summit thirteen thousand five hundred and seventy feet above the Gulf of Mexico, which may be called the highest flight of the bee. It is certainly the highest known flight of that insect.

G. D. WARBURTON
(1816–1857)

Irish soldier and writer. An officer in the Royal Artillery, he was badly wounded in Spain. In 1844 he went to Canada, writing a very successful book on the country called *Hochelaga* (1846). In 1857 he was elected to Parliament, but his new responsibilities were too much for him. He began to suffer so badly from 'severe pains and attacks of indigestion' that he chose the ultimate cure and shot himself through the head.

St John's, Newfoundland – the fishiest capital in the world

In trying to describe St. John's there is some difficulty in applying to it an adjective sufficiently distinctive and appropriate. We find other cities coupled with epithets which at once give their predominant characteristic: London the richest, Paris the gayest, St. Petersburg the coldest. In one respect the chief town of Newfoundland has, I believe, no rival: we may therefore call it the fishiest of modern capitals. Round a great part of the harbour are sheds, acres in extent, roofed with cod split in half, laid on like slates, drying in the sun, or rather the air, for there is not much of the former to depend upon. Those ships, bearing nearly every flag in the world, are laden with cod; those stout weatherly boats crowding up to the wharves have just now returned from fishing for cod; those few scant fields of cultivation, with lean crops coaxed out of the barren soil, are manured with cod; those grim, snug-looking wooden houses, their handsome furniture, the piano and the musical skill of the young lady who plays it, the satin gown of the mother, the gold chain of the father, are all paid for in cod; the breezes from the shore, soft and warm on this bright August day, are rich not with the odours of a thousand flowers but of a thousand cod. Earth, sea and air are alike pervaded with this wonderful fish. There is only one place which appears to be kept sacred from its intrusion, and strange to say that is the dinner table. An observation made on its absence from that apparently appropriate position excited as much astonishment as if I had made a remark to a Northumberland squire that he had not a head-dish of Newcastle coals.

HENRY DAVID THOREAU
(1817–1862)

American essayist, poet, naturalist and social critic. In 1845, wanting to live alone in harmony with nature, he retired to a small cabin on the banks of Walden Pond, near Concord, Massachusetts. From his journal he distilled *Walden* (1854), his masterpiece.

Making camp in the Maine Woods, 1857

We generally told the Indian that we would stop at the first suitable place, so that he might be on the lookout for it. Having observed a clear, hard, and flat beach to land on, free from mud, and from stones which would injure the canoe, one would run up the bank to see if there were open and level space enough for the camp between the trees, or if it could be easily cleared, preferring at the same time a cool place, on account of insects. Sometimes we paddled a mile or more before finding one to our minds, for where the shore was suitable, the bank would often be too steep, or else too low and grassy, and therefore mosquitoey. We then took out the baggage and drew up the canoe, sometimes turning it over on shore for safety. The Indian cut a path to the spot we had selected, which was usually within two or three rods of the water, and we carried up our baggage.

One, perhaps, takes canoe-birch bark, always at hand, and dead dry wood or bark, and kindles a fire five or six feet in front of where we intend to lie. It matters not, commonly, on which side this is, because there is little or no wind in so dense a wood at that season; and then he gets a kettle of water from the river, and takes out the pork, bread, coffee, etc., from their several packages. Another, meanwhile, having the axe, cuts down the nearest dead rock-maple or other dry hard wood, collecting several large logs to last through the night, also a green stake, with a notch or fork to it, which is slanted over the fire, perhaps resting on a rock or forked stake, to hang the kettle on, and two forked stakes and a pole for the tent.

The third man pitches the tent, cuts a dozen or more pins with his knife, usually of moose-wood, the common underwood, to fasten it down with, and then collects an armful or two of fir-twigs, arbor-vitæ, spruce, or hemlock, whichever is at hand, and makes the bed, beginning at either end, and laying the twigs wrong side up, in regular rows, covering the stub ends of the last row; first, however, filling the hollows, if there are any, with coarser material. Wrangel says that his guides in Siberia first strewed a quantity of dry brushwood on the ground, and then cedar twigs on that.

Commonly, by the time the bed is made, or within fifteen or twenty minutes, the water boils, the pork is fried, and supper is ready. We eat this sitting on the ground, or a stump, if there is any, around a large piece of birch-bark for a table, each holding a dipper in one hand and a piece of ship-bread or fried pork in the other, frequently making a pass with his hand, or thrusting his head into the smoke, to avoid the mosquitoes.

Next, pipes are lit by those who smoke, and veils are donned by those who have them, and we hastily examine and dry our plants, anoint our faces and hands, and go to bed, – and – the mosquitoes. Though you have nothing to do but see the country, there's rarely any time to spare, hardly enough to examine a plant, before the night or drowsiness is upon you.

Such was the ordinary experience.

FRANCIS PARKMAN
(1823–1893)

American historian and traveller. After leaving Harvard in 1844 'with "Injuns" on the brain', he decided to study the American wilderness. Two years later, with his cousin Quincy A. Shaw, he travelled from Boston to Independence, Missouri. From there they picked up the Oregon Trail, passing several months with a band of Sioux Indians and mixing with the hunters, trappers and frontiersmen. One of America's most distinguished historians, he was the first literary figure to understand the character and motives of the North American Indians.

Notes from the old Oregon Trail, 1846

May 24th. We have struck upon the old Oregon Trail, just beyond the Big Blue, about seven days from the Platte. The waggons we saw were part of an emigrant party. . . . They encamped about a mile from us behind a swell in the prairie. The Capt. paid them a visit, and reported that the women were damned ugly. . . .

May 26th. Nooned on Black Walnut Creek. Put Pond. in harness. Afternoon, not well – sat slouching on horse, indulging in an epicurian reverie – intensely hot – dreamed of a cool mountain spring, in a forest country – two bottles of Champagne cooling in it, and cut-glass tumblers, full of the sparkling liquor. A wide expanse of perfectly flat prairie – rode over it hour after hour – saw wolves – and where they had dug up a recent grave. . . .

May 27th. Among the Sioux, a species of penance, or act to secure the favor of the manito[u], is to fasten a buffalo's skull to a hole through the sinews of the back, and to run until it tears out – or rots away. . . .

May 28th. Wolves all night. Camped on Little Blue. Saw wolves and two antelopes in the morning. Grave of a child 4 yrs. old – May 1845.

. . . Immense masses of blue, lurid clouds in the west shadowed the green prairie, and the sun glared through purple and crimson. As we drew near the valley of the stream, a furious wind, presaging a storm, struck us. We galloped down in the face of it – horses snorting with fear. . . .

June 3rd. . . . We saw several buffalo in a distant ravine, who scented us and began to ascend the hills in Indian file, appearing and disappearing in the gorges. Presently more and more appeared, but all, getting wind of us, got in motion. Henry's blood was up. We spurred along through ravines, and getting to leeward, managed to approach one little herd of cows. I held the horses – Henry crept over the hill and fired. I saw the buffalo come running down the hollow, and soon perceived that we had shot one. Skinned and cut her up, and then saw another herd, at which Henry again fired and brought down another cow. By the time we had finished dissecting her, a devil of a cold, penetrating, driving storm of sleet came upon us, and as, with the meat at our saddles, we rode from the hills and over the prairie to find the camp, we were well drenched. An infernal storm – temperature about 32°.

June 6th. Emigrants' cattle all driven off by wolves for many miles – their guard having fallen asleep. This detained us; and Q. and I, with Henry, went off to run buffalo. Rode 6 miles – saw a herd of bulls and several of cows – set after the former full-drive. Could not bring

Pond. close up – wounded, but killed none. Q. shot one. Got separated from the others – rode for hours westwardly over the prairie – saw the hills dotted with thousands of buffalo. Antelopes, prairie-dogs – burrowing owls – wild geese – wolves, etc.

July 3rd. Tunica's village here at last. Bull Bear and several of his brothers came yesterday. . . .

An old man sent to invite us to a dog-feast – the dish was placed before us – we eat what we wished – then took away what we thought proper, and passed the rest to our host and his family, who had looked on meanwhile.

The old joker, who kept up a constant stream of raillery – especially about the women, declaring in their presence that he had lain with them, at which they laughed, without the slightest inclination to blush. Reynal says, and indeed it is very observable, that *anything* may be said without making a girl blush; but that liberties cannot be taken with a young girl's person without exciting her shame.

[Sept.] 21st. Camped at Dragoon Creek, after travelling 21 miles. Met waggons. 'Whar ye from? Californy?' 'No.' 'Santy Fee?' 'No, the Mountains.' 'What yer been doing thar? Tradin'?' 'No.' 'Trappin'?' 'No.' 'Huntin'?' 'No.' 'Emigratin'?' 'No.' 'What *have* ye been doing then, God damn ye?' (Very loud, as we were by this time almost out of hearing.)

[Sept.] 26th. . . . Soon began to see Shawnee farms. A beautiful country; the foliage just touched with the hues of autumn. Neat houses – fields of corn and grain – pastures with cattle – and a glorious day after the dreary rain of yesterday – combined to make the ride agreeable. Saw the Shawnee mission – passed the borders of the forest country where in place of the blossoms of last spring was now hanging fruit hardly less fragrant – and at length saw Westport. . . . Sold off our outfit, and in the afternoon rode to Kansas. . . .

ALONZO DELANO
(*fl.* 1849)

American merchant and traveller. Having been advised by his doctor that a journey across the plains would benefit his health, he set off from St Joseph, Missouri, for California in 1849. It was the height of the Gold Rush and Delano intended to sell goods to the miners.

The inventive genius of the emigrant, the valley of the Sacramento, September 1849

We were now in the valley of plenty. Our poor teeth, which had been laboring on the filelike consistency of pilot bread, had now a respite, in the agreeable task of masticating from the 'flesh pots' of California.

As we determined to lay over during the day, our wagon master, Traverse, concluded to butcher an ox, and the hungry Arabs of our train were regaled with a feast of dead kine. Feeling an aristocratic longing for a rich beef steak, I determined to have one. There was not a particle of fat in the steak to make gravy, nor was there a slice of bacon to be had to fry it with, and the flesh was as dry and as hard as a bone. But a nice broiled steak, with a plenty of gravy, I would have – and I had it. The inventive genius of an emigrant is almost constantly called forth on the plains, and so in my case, I laid a nice cut on the coals, which, instead of broiling, only burnt and carbonized like a piece of wood, and when one side was turned to cinder, I whopped it over to make charcoal of the other. To make butter gravy, I melted a stearin candle, which I poured over the delicious tit-bit, and, smacking my lips, sat down to my feast, the envy of several lookers-on. I sopped the first mouthful in the nice looking gravy, and put it between my teeth, when the gravy cooled almost instantly, and the roof of my mouth and my teeth were coated all over with a covering like hard beeswax, making mastication next to impossible.

'How does it go?' asked one.

'O, first rate,' said I, struggling to get the hard, dry morsel down my throat; and cutting another piece, which was free from the delicious gravy, 'Come, try it,' said I; 'I have more than I can eat (which was true). You are welcome to it.' The envious, hungry soul sat down and, putting a large piece between his teeth, after rolling it about in his mouth awhile, deliberately spit it out, saying, with an oath, that

'Chips and beeswax are hard fare, even for a starving man.'

Ah, how hard words and want of sentiment will steal over one's better nature on the plains. As for the rest of the steak, we left it to choke the wolves.

GEORGE AUGUSTUS SALA
(1828–1896)

English writer and journalist. He went to America in December 1863 and stayed for a year, travelling all over a country then racked by civil war. His book, *My Diary in America in the Midst of War* (1865), is marvellously vivid, outspoken and cussed as Sala praises or – more usually – berates America and her people.

Niagara Falls

These then were the famous Falls I had come so far to see; – 144 rods wide, 158 feet high, 1500 millions of cubic feet of water tumbling over a wall or rock every minute, a column of spray 200 – some say 300 – feet in altitude. Well, I confess that as I stood staring, there came over me a sensation of bitter disappointment. And was this all? You who have seen the field of Waterloo, who have seen the Pyramids, who have seen St. Peter's, bear with me. Was this all? There was a great deal of water, a great deal of foam, a great deal of spray, and a thundering noise. This *was* all, abating the snow where I stood and the black river beneath. These were the Falls of Niagara. *They looked comparatively small, and the water looked dingy.* Where was the grand effect – the light and shade? There was, it is true, a considerable amount of effervescence; but the foaminess of the Falls, together with the tinge of tawny yellow in the troubled waters, only reminded me of so much unattainable soda and sherry, and made me feel thirstier than ever.

FREDERICK WHYMPER
(*fl.* 1866–1868)

An Englishman who went to Alaska in 1866 to take part in the Alaska Survey, which was carried out just before the United States bought Alaska from Russia for $7,200,000 in October 1867.

'But the weather was lovely . . .' – on the north bank of the Yukon, December 1866

The windows of our room were of seal gut, and, as the days were now about two hours in length, our light inside was none of the best. We slept wrapped up in fur-lined blankets and skins on a platform raised about two feet above the floor, which latter we had caulked with moss and covered with straw and skins. Even then, although our room was generally warm enough, the floor was sometimes intensely cold. I once hung up some damp cloth to dry; near the rafters it steamed; within a foot of the ground it froze firmly, with long icicles hanging therefrom. The air near the floor has shown a temperature of + 4° when the upper part of the room was + 60° or + 65° Fahr. . . .

The effect of intense cold on our stores in the magazine was a very interesting study; our fried apples were a mass of rock and had to be smashed up with an axe, our molasses formed a thick black paste, and no knife we had would cut a slice of ham from the bone till it was well thawed in our warmer room. Our preserved meats would, with a continuation of those times, have been preserved forever and would have made, as Kane says, excellent 'canister shot.' After purchasing grouse or hares from the Indians, they would remain, uneaten, for a month or longer period in as good condition as ever, and there was no fear of their getting too 'high' in that climate.

Our coldest day for the whole season occurred in December. On the 26th of November the thermometer fell suddenly from the comparatively moderate temperature of + 2° to − 18°, and continued lowering steadily – day by day – till it reached (on the 5th December) − 58° Fahr., or *ninety degrees below freezing*. But the weather was lovely; no wind blew or snow fell during the whole time, and we did not feel the cold as much as at many other times.

Strong meat and drink at Plover Bay, August 1867

Whilst stopping in Plover Bay some of our men found a keg of specimens preserved in alcohol belonging to one of our Smithsonian collectors. Having had a long abstinence from exhilarating drinks, the temptation was too much for them, and they proceeded to broach the contents. After they had imbibed to their hearts' content and become 'visibly affected thereby,' they thought it a pity to waste the remaining contents of the barrel, and, feeling hungry, went on to eat the lizards, snakes, and fish which had been put up for a rather different purpose! Science was avenged in the result, nor do I think they will ever repeat the experiment. . . .

ISABELLA BIRD
(1831–1904)

English traveller. (See p. 358.) She made her first visit to America in 1854, travelling through Novia Scotia, up the St Lawrence, around the Great Lakes and as far west as Chicago. In 1873, when she was forty-two, she went to Colorado, where she met Rocky Mountain Jim, 'a man who any woman might love, but who no sane woman would marry'.

The Rock Island Line, 1854

On we flew to the West, the land of Wild Indians and buffaloes, on the narrow rims of metal with which this 'great people' is girdling the earth. Evening succeeded noon, and twilight to the blaze of a summer day; the yellow sun sank cloudless behind the waves of the rolling prairie, yet still we hurried on, only stopping our headlong course to take in wood and water at some nameless stations. When the sun set, it set behind the prairie waves. I was oblivious of any changes during the night, and at rosy dawn an ocean of long green grass encircled us round. Still on – belts of timber diversify the prospect – we rush into a thick wood, and, emerging from it, arrive at Rock Island, an unfinished-looking settlement, which might bear the name of the Desert City, situated at the confluence of the Rock River and Mississippi. We stop at a little wharf, where waits a little steamer of uncouth construction; we step in, a steam-whistle breaks the silence of that dewy dawn, and at a very rapid rate we run between high wooded bluffs, down a turbid stream, whirling in rapid eddies. We steam for three miles, and land at a clearing containing the small settlement of Davenport. We had come down the Mississippi, mightiest of rivers! half a mile wide seventeen hundred miles from its mouth, and were in the *far West*. Wagons with white tilts, thick-hided oxen with heavy yokes, mettlesome steeds with high peaked saddles, picketed to stumps of trees, lashing away the flies with their tails; emigrants on blue boxes, wondering if this were the El Dorado of their dreams; arms, accoutrements, and baggage surrounded the house or shed where we were to breakfast. Most of our companions were bound for Nebraska, Oregon, and Utah, the most distant districts of which they would scarcely reach with their slow-paced animals for four months; exposed in the meantime to the attacks of the Sioux, Comanches, and Blackfeet.

There, in a long wooden shed with blackened rafters and an earthen floor, we breakfasted, at seven o'clock, on johnny-cake, squirrels, buffalo-hump, dampers, and buckwheat, tea and corn spirit, with a crowd of emigrants, hunters, and adventurers; and soon after re-embarked for Rock Island, our little steamer with difficulty stemming the mighty tide of the Father of Rivers. The machinery, such as it was, was very visible, the boiler patched in several places, and steam escaped in different directions. I asked the captain if he were not in the habit of 'sitting upon the safety-valve', but he stoutly denied the charge. At eight we left Rock Island, and, turning my unwilling steps eastward from the land of adventure and romance, we entered the cars for Chicago.

Rock Mountain Jim – on the way to Estes Park, Colorado, 1873

Roused by the growling of the dog, his owner came out, a broad, thickset man, about the middle height, with an old cap on his head, and wearing a grey hunting-suit much the worse for wear (almost falling to pieces, in fact), a digger's scarf knotted round his waist, a knife in his belt, and 'a bosom friend', a revolver, sticking out of the breast-pocket of his coat; his feet, which were very small, were bare, except for some dilapidated moccasins made of horse hide. The marvel was how his clothes hung together, and on him. The scarf round his waist must have had something to do with it. His face was remarkable. He is a man about 45, and must have been strikingly handsome. He has large grey-blue eyes, deeply set, with well-marked eyebrows, a handsome aquiline nose, and a very handsome mouth. His face was smooth shaven except for a dense moustache and imperial. Tawny hair, in thin uncared-for curls, fell from under his hunter's cap and over his collar. One eye was entirely gone, and the loss made one side of the face repulsive, while the other might have been modelled in marble. 'Desperado' was written in large letters all over him. I almost repented of having sought his acquaintance.

His first impulse was to swear at the dog, but on seeing a lady he contented himself with kicking him, and coming up to me he raised his cap, showing as he did so a magnificently formed brow and head, and in a cultured tone of voice asked if there were anything he could do for me? I asked for some water, and he brought some in a battered tin, gracefully apologizing for not having anything more presentable. We entered into conversation, and as he spoke I forgot both his reputation and appearance, for his manner was that of a chivalrous gentleman, his accent refined, and his language easy and elegant. I inquired about some beavers' paws which were drying, and in a moment they hung on the horn of my saddle. Apropos of the wild animals of the region, he told me that the loss of his eye was owing to a recent encounter with a grizzly bear, which after giving him a death hug, tearing him all over, breaking his arm and scratching out his eye, had left him for dead. As we rode away, for the sun was sinking, he said, courteously, 'You are not an American. I know from your voice that you are a countrywoman of mine. I hope you will allow me the pleasure of calling on you.'

JOHN WESLEY POWELL
(1834–1902)

American geologist and ethnologist. Despite losing an arm at the Battle of Shiloh in the Civil War, in 1869 Powell led the first party to navigate the 280-mile-long Grand Canyon of the Colorado River.

Powell spends an evening on the Rio Virgen with some Shi-vwhit Indians who have killed three of his men

I wish to learn about their cañons and mountains, and about themselves, to tell other men at home; and that I want to take pictures of everything, and show them to my friends. All this occupied much time, and the matter and manner made a deep impression.

Then their chief replies: 'Your talk is good, and we believe what you say. We believe in Jacob, and look upon you as a father. When you are hungry, you may have our game. You may gather our sweet fruits. We will give you food when you come to our land. We will show you the springs, and you may drink; the water is good. We will be friends, and when you come we will be glad. We will tell the Indians who live on the other side of the great river that we have seen *Ka'-pu-rats* [Arm Off], and he is the Indians' friend. We will tell them he is Jacob's friend. We are very poor. Look at our women and children; they are naked. We have no horses; we climb the rocks, and our feet are sore. We live among rocks, and they yield little food and many thorns. When the cold moons come, our children are hungry. We have not much to give; you must not think us mean. You are wise; we have heard you tell strange things. We are ignorant. Last year we killed three white men. Bad men said they were our enemies. They told great lies. We thought them true. We were mad; it made us big fools. We are very sorry. Do not think of them, it is done; let us be friends. We are ignorant – like little children in understanding compared with you. When we do wrong, do not get mad, and be like children too.

'When white men kill our people, we kill them. Then they kill more of us. It is not good. We hear that the white men are a great number. When they stop killing us, there will be no Indian left to bury the dead.'

R. M. BALLANTYNE
(1835–1894)

Scottish writer. At the age of sixteen he was apprenticed as a clerk in the Hudson's Bay Company and went out to Rupert Land, where he spent six years trading with the Indians. On these experiences he based his first book, *Hudson's Bay* (1848). In 1855 it was suggested he should write a book for boys; the result – *Snowflakes and Sunbeams, or the Young Fur Traders* – was a success and for the rest of his life Ballantyne 'lived by making story books for young folks'.

Crossing Lake Superior, 1845

On one occasion, after having been ashore for two days, the wind moderated in the afternoon and we determined to proceed if possible. The sun set gloriously, giving promise of fine weather. The sky was clear and cloudless and the lake calm. For an hour or so the men sang as they paddled, but as the shades of evening fell they ceased; and as it was getting rather chilly I wrapped myself in my green blanket (which served me for a boat-cloak as well as a bed) and soon fell fast asleep. How long I slept I know not, but when I awoke the regular rapid hiss of the paddles struck upon my ear, and upon throwing off the blanket the first thing that met my eye was the dark sky spangled with the most gorgeous and brilliant stars I ever beheld. The whole scene indeed was one of the most magnificent and awful that can be imagined. On our left hand rose tremendous precipices and cliffs, around the bottom and among the caverns of which the black waters of the lake curled quietly (for a most deathlike unearthly calm prevailed), sending forth a faint hollow murmur as of distant waters which ended at long intervals in a slow melancholy cadence. Before and behind us abrupt craggy islands rose from the water, assuming every imaginable and unimaginable shape in the uncertain light; while on the right the eye ranged over the inky lake till it was lost in thick darkness. A thin transparent night-fog added to the mystical appearance of the scene, upon which I looked with mingled feelings of wonder and awe. The only distinct sound that could be heard was the measured sound of the paddles which the men plied in silence, as if unwilling to break the stillness of the night.

Suddenly the guide uttered in a hoarse whisper. '*A terre!*', startling the sleepy men and rendering the succeeding silence still more impressive. The canoe glided noiselessly through a maze of narrow passages among the tall cliffs and grounded on a stony beach. Everything was then carried up and the tents pitched in the dark as no wood could be conveniently found for the purpose of making a fire; and without taking any supper or even breaking the solemn silence of the night, we spread our beds as we best could upon the round stones (some of which were larger than a man's foot) and sank into repose.

JOHN MUIR
(1838–1914)

American wanderer, naturalist and inventer. Born in Scotland, he went to the USA in 1849. In 1867 after being nearly blinded in an accident in a factory at Indianapolis, he set off to walk to the Gulf of Mexico, a journey of a thousand miles. Muir also travelled in Alaska (where he discovered the glacier that bears his name), Russia, India and Australia.

Among the tombs, Bonaventure, Georgia

I was very thirsty after walking so long in the muggy heat, a distance of three or four miles from the city, to get to this graveyard. A dull, sluggish, coffee-colored stream flows under the road just outside the graveyard garden park, from which I managed to get a drink after breaking a way down to the water through a dense fringe of bushes, daring the snakes and alligators in the dark. Thus refreshed I entered the weird and beautiful abode of the dead.

All the avenue where I walked was in shadow, but an exposed tombstone frequently shone out in startling whiteness on either hand, and thickets of sparkleberry bushes gleamed like heaps of crystals. Not a breath of air moved the gray moss, and the great black arms of the trees met overhead and covered the avenue. But the canopy was fissured by many a netted seam and leafy-edged opening, through which the moonlight sifted in auroral rays, broidering the blackness in silvery light. Though tired, I sauntered a while enchanted, then lay down under one of the great Oaks. I found a little mound that served for a pillow, placed my plant-press and bag beside me and rested fairly well, though somewhat disturbed by large prickly-footed beetles creeping across my hands and face, and by a lot of hungry stinging mosquitoes.

When I awoke, the sun was up and all Nature was rejoicing. Some birds had discovered me as an intruder, and were making a great ado in interesting language and gestures. I heard the screaming of the bald eagles, and of some strange waders in the rushes. I heard the hum of Savannah with the long jarring hallos of negroes far away. On rising I found that my head had been resting on a grave, and though my sleep had not been quite so sound as that of the person below, I awoke refreshed, and looking about me, the morning sunbeams pouring through the Oaks and gardens dripping with dew, the beauty displayed was so glorious and exhilarating that hunger and care seemed only a dream.

BRUCE SIBERTS
(1868–1952)

American rancher. 'At the age of twenty-two,' Siberts writes, 'I beat it out to the Black Hills to make my fortune . . . and finally became a cattle and horse rancher. I have done a lot of bad things in my life, but I never did stoop to sheep ranching.' *Nothing but Prairie and Sky*, his account of his nomadic life on the range in South Dakota, is a marvellous evocation of what frontier life was really like.

Fort Pierre, South Dakota

Here I was at the Medicine Creek Russian colony sixty miles from Pierre and 150 miles from my log mansion on Plum Creek. There were no ranches between the settlements, and I had a badly spoiled, unbroke mare and twenty-six big and little cattle worth $400. Being my first venture, these cows seemed to me as valuable as all the gold in the Black Hills. From one of the Russians I got two loaves of bread and a dozen hard-boiled eggs for a quarter and started out. The mare did not want to leave her old haunts and would rear and fall back, so I had to lead her or risk being killed or crippled out in this no man's land. In the first two days I ate the bread and eggs, and the next day I lived on plums. Fort Pierre looked good to me that afternoon at four. I turned the cattle loose in a grassy spot, put my nag in a feed barn, and after a double order of beefsteak I felt better.

There did not seem to be any loafing place around except saloons, so I went into a joint behind a false front. It was a dirty place lined with loafers sitting on beer kegs. I told the tough-looking bartender that I wanted a glass of beer. While he fiddled around drawing it from a keg, one of the bar flies come up, friendly like, asked me how things were in the country. I tasted the beer. It was warm. The bartender asked my 'friend' what he wanted, and he said whiskey sour. Four others lined up at the bar. He took their order.

They watched me. I knew I was getting the works so I laid a silver dollar on the bar. He looked at me rather hard, said it was $1.60. The first bar fly asked me for a loan of two dollars, said he felt lucky and wanted to try the monte game in the back part. I wanted to get out of the place so I slid another dollar across the bar. The bartender put it in the till and looked out the window, rather bored it seemed to me. I saw it was my play and said, 'How about the change?' He looked out into the street, walked slowly to the till and got the change, and laid it on the back of the bar near the back room entrance. I started out pretty mad. He called out, 'Get your change.' I told him, 'Keep it. You need it worse than I do.' Their mouths flopped open, but no one made a move. Saloons then and now are good places to keep out of.

I went across the street to a store and bought four cans of tomatoes and some other lunch stuff, put it in a sack, went to the barn for my nag, and rode out of town. I drove the cattle up Bad River about three miles and while they stood in the water, I had a bath and washed my clothes. That night as I lay on some buffalo grass trying to sleep I cussed my 'friends' at the saloon in Fort Pierre. I was out two dollars but had got a lot of experience. The rounders in Fort Pierre were always willing to divide, that is, take half of all one would give them. There were a few good people in Fort Pierre. Some argued there were fifteen or eighteen, but others said that estimate was too high.

W. H. DAVIES
(1871–1940)

Welsh poet, writer and wanderer. Leaving school at an early age, he lived for a number of years as a peddler and hobo in the USA. His book, *The Autobiography of a Super-Tramp* (1908), has become a classic.

How to live well on the eastern seaboard in the 1890s

I shall never forget the happy summer months I spent with Brum at the seaside. Some of the rich merchants there could not spare more than a month or six weeks from business, but, thanks be to Providence, the whole summer was at our disposal. If we grew tired of one town or, as more often the case, the town grew tired of us, we would saunter leisurely to the next one and again pitch our camp; so on, from place to place, during the summer months. We moved freely among the visitors, who apparently held us in great respect, for they did not address us familiarly, but contented themselves with staring at a distance. We lay across their runs on the sands and their paths in the woods; we monopolised their nooks in the rocks and took possession of caves, and not a murmur heard, except from the sea, which of a certainty could not be laid to our account. No doubt detectives were in these places, but they were on the look out for pickpockets, burglars and swindlers; and, seeing that neither the visitors nor the boarding house keepers made any complaint, these detectives did not think it worth while to arrest tramps; for there was no promotion to be had by doing so. 'Ah,' I said to Brum, as we sat in a shady place, eating a large custard pudding from a boarding house, using for the purpose two self-made spoons of wood – 'Ah, we would not be so pleasantly occupied as tramps in England. We would there receive tickets for soup; soup that could be taken without spoons; no pleasant picking of the teeth after eating; no sign of a pea, onion or carrot; no sign of anything except flies.' Two-thirds of a large custard pudding between two of us, and if there was one fault to be found with it, it was its being made with too many eggs. Even Brum was surprised at his success on this occasion. 'Although,' as he said, 'she being a fat lady, I expected something unusual.' Brum had a great admiration for fat women; not so much, I believe, as his particular type of beauty, but for the good natured qualities he claimed corpulence denoted. 'How can you expect those skinny creatures to sympathise with another when they half starve their own bodies? he asked. He often descanted on the excellencies of the fat, to the detriment of the thin, and I never yet heard another beggar disagree with him.

ANDY ADAMS
(n.d.)

American cowboy.

A dry drive across the Great Plains

Holding the herd this third night required all hands. Only a few men at a time were allowed to go into camp and eat, for the herd refused even to lie down. What few cattle attempted to rest were prevented by the more restless ones. By spells they would mill, until riders were sent through the herd at break-neck pace to break up the groups. . . . As the horses were loose for the night, we could not start them on the trail until daybreak gave us a change of mounts, so we lost the early start of the morning before.

Good cloudy weather would have saved us, but in its stead was a sultry morning without a breath of air, which bespoke another day of sizzling heat. We had not been on the trail over two hours before the heat became almost unbearable to man and beast. Had it not been for the condition of the herd, all might yet have gone well; but over three days had now elapsed without water for the cattle, and they became feverish and ungovernable. The lead cattle turned back several times, wandering aimlessly in any direction, and it was with considerable difficulty that the herd could be held on the trail. The rear overtook the lead, and the cattle lost all semblance of a trail herd. Our horses were fresh, however, and after about two hours' work, we once more got the herd strung out in trailing fashion; but before a mile had been covered, the leaders again turned, and the cattle congregated into a mass of unmanageable animals, milling and lowing in their fever and thirst. . . . No sooner was the milling stopped than they would surge hither and yon, sometimes half a mile, as ungovernable as the waves of an ocean. After wasting several hours in this manner, they finally turned back over the trail, and the utmost efforts of every man in the outfit failed to check them. We threw our ropes in their faces, and when this failed, we resorted to shooting; but in defiance of the fusillade and the smoke they walked sullenly through the line of horsemen across their front. Six-shooters were discharged so close to the leaders' faces as to singe their hair, yet, under a noonday sun, they disregarded this and every other device to turn them, and passed wholly out of our control. In a number of instances wild steers deliberately walked against our horses, and then for the first time a fact dawned on us that chilled the marrow in our bones – *the herd was going blind*.

CHIEF BUFFALO CHILD LONG LANCE
(*fl.* 1890–1928)

American Indian chief. A chief of the Blackfoot tribe of the far North-West of the United States, restless nomads who travelled incessantly from the Missouri River in Montana to the Peace River country eight hundred miles to the north. Long Lance enlisted in the Canadian Army in 1914 and fought as a sniper and raider in the trenches of Flanders.

Meeting the white man

We travelled along the Namaka until we came to the foothills of the Rockies, and here we came upon the Suksiseoketuk Indians – the Rocky Mountain Band of Assiniboines – whose hunting-grounds were up there in the foothill country. Their chief, Chief Travels-Against-The-Wind, asked us who we were. Our chief said:

'We are roving *Seeha-sapa* from the plains, whose only enemy is the *Okotoks Isahpo* – the Rock Band of Crows.'

'*Ha-h! Neena-washtay – washtaydo. Amba wastaytch, See-ha-sapa!* – Oh! Very good – exceptionally good. Howdy do Blackfeet,' said the Suksiseoketuk chief.

Then he told our chief to tell his tribesmen to get off their ponies and sit down and he would have the Suksiseoketuk women make us some of the white man's *minne-seeha* – 'black water', or tea. And the chief said that while we were drinking of it he would tell us about the white man.

We had never had tea before, and we youngsters did not like it; it was bitter. The chief said that the Hudson's Bay Company had traded it for some of their skins – and they seemed to like this tea. Our old people liked it, too.

But we boys were very interested in what the chief told us about the white man. He told us to beware of his food; as it would make our teeth come out. He told us about the bread and the sweets which the white man ate, and he pulled up his upper lip and said:

'*Wambadahka* – Behold – my teeth are good, and so are the teeth of all our old people; but behold,' he said, walking over to a young boy and pulling up his lip, 'behold, these teeth of the young people are not good – too much white man's food. Our people, like yours, never used to die until they were over a hundred years old. Now, since we started to eat that white man's food we are sick all of the time. We keep getting worse and soon it will kill us all.'

And then the chief reached up and took hold of a shock of his hair at the top of his head, and he said:

'*Payheeh* – hair – the white man has none of this on top of his head. The crown of his head is as slick as the nose of a buffalo. Every time the Indian eats he wipes grease into his hair. White man wash it all out with bad medicine – soap – take all grease out and make all of his hair drop off. Swap your buffalo robes for the white man's blankets and gunpowder, but take not of his food,' said the chief, 'nor of his "bad medicine" for washing your hair.'

The next day we started north, accompanied by fifty of the Suksiseoketuk warriors. We travelled for six days, keeping always to the edge of the foothills. On the sixth day the Suksiseoketuks told us to pitch our camp at a point we had reached late in the afternoon, and they would send over a messenger to tell the white people at the trading post that we were there to see them.

After we had pitched our camp, several of our warriors went out to see if they could find some otter, which were plentiful in that part of the northland. While they were out they came upon a cabin, and they saw six long-haired people with light skin, going in and out of his place. Our warriors sat down and watched them and tried to figure out what they were; they had never seen any people like them before. They were not Indians and they were not white men; so one of our warriors, Big Darkness, said that they must be the white man's woman – their wives – white women! They had never seen any white women before; so they all agreed that that must be what they were.

But when they came back to camp and told the others about it, another of our warriors, Sun Calf, who had seen the women, changed his mind and said that he did not believe they were white women after all; they were 'some other kind of people', he said.

This started an argument which became so heated that our chief was afraid that it would lead to a fight. So he said the best way to settle the dispute was for the two warriors to put up a bet, and then go over and capture one of the 'strange beings' and bring it back, and the camp would decide what they were.

The men led out five ponies each and bet them on their respective beliefs. And when darkness came ten of our warriors, including Big Darkness and Sun Calf, crept over to the shack and overpowered one of the 'strange beings' and brought it back.

When they returned to our camp, we were waiting around a big fire singing, so that the disturbance would not attract the trading post. They led a very scared-looking 'being' to the edge of the fire, and Big Darkness exclaimed to the throng:

'Now look. Is it not a woman?'

Half of the tribe believed that it was a woman, and the other half said that it was not. The confusion of the argument which followed grew so noisy that it awoke some of the Suksiseoketuk warriors who had their camp about a hundred yards away, and they came over to see what was going on.

They stopped and listened for a moment, and then they began to laugh. They laughed for a long time before they would tell us what they were laughing at. And then one of them said:

'Inexperienced Blackfeet! It is neither a white woman nor any kind on being that you have ever seen before. It is a man from across the *Minne-Tonka*,' and he waved his arm towards the Pacific Ocean.

It was a Chinaman! One of the Chinese employed as cooks by some white prospectors.

HENRY MILLER
(1891–1980)

American novelist. In 1940, having lived for many years in Europe, Miller returned to his homeland, 'not with the intention of remaining in the bosom of the family but of wandering forth again, perhaps never to return.' His account of his journeys through America, *The Air-Conditioned Nightmare* (1947), is a coruscating view of the country and its people.

A soiree in Hollywood

My first evening in Hollywood. It was so typical that I almost thought it had been arranged for me. It was by sheer chance, however, that I found myself rolling up to the home of a millionaire in a handsome black Packard. I had been invited to dinner by a perfect stranger. I didn't even know my host's name. Nor do I know it now.

The first thing which struck me, on being introduced all around, was that I was in the presence of wealthy people, people who were bored to death and who were all, including the octogenarians, already three sheets to the wind. The host and hostess seemed to take pleasure in acting as bar-tenders. It was hard to follow the conversation because everybody was talking at cross-purposes. The important thing was to get an edge on before sitting down to the table. One old geezer who had recently recovered from a horrible automobile accident was having his fifth old-fashioned – he was proud of the fact, proud that he could swill it like a youngster even though he was still partially crippled. Everyone thought he was a marvel. . . .

The old geezer who was still tottering about handed me a highball. I tried to tell him that I didn't want any but he insisted that I take it anyway. He wanted to have a word with me, he said, winking at me as though he had something very confidential to impart.

'My name is Harrison,' he said. 'H-a-r-r-i-s-o-n,' spelling it out as if it were a difficult name to remember.

'Now what is your name, may I ask?'

'My name is Miller M-i-l-l-e-r,' I answered, spelling it out in Morse for him.

'Miller! Why, that's a very easy name to remember. We had a druggist on our block by that name. Of course. *Miller*. Yes, a very common name.'

'So it is,' I said.

'And what are you doing out here, Mr Miller? You're a stranger, I take it?'

'Yes,' I said, 'I'm just a visitor.'

'You're in business, are you?'

'No, hardly. I'm just visiting California.'

'I see. Well, where do you come from – the Middle West?'

'No, from New York.'

'From New York City? Or from up-state?'

'From the city.'

'And have you been here very long?'

'No, just a few hours.'

'A few hours? My, my . . . well, that's interesting. And will you be staying long, Mr Miller?'

'I don't know. It depends.'

'I see. Depends on how you like it here, is that it?'

'Yes, exactly.'

'Well, it's a grand part of the world, I can tell you that. No place like California, I always say. Of course I'm not a native. But I've been out here almost thirty years now. Wonderful climate. And wonderful people, too.'

'I suppose so,' I said, just to string him along. I was curious to see how long the idiot would keep up his infernal nonsense.

'You're not in business you say?'

'No, I'm not.'

'On a vacation, is that it?'

'No, not precisely. I'm an ornithologist, you see.'

'A what? Well, that's interesting.'

'*Very,*' I said, with great solemnity.

'Then you may be staying with us for a while, is that it?'

'That's hard to say. I may stay a week and I may stay a year. It all depends. Depends on what specimens I find.'

'I see. Interesting work, no doubt.'

'*Very!*'

'Have you ever been to California before, Mr Miller?'

'Yes, twenty-five years ago.'

'Well, well, is that so? *Twenty-five years ago!* And now you're back again.'

'Yes, back again.'

'Were you doing the same thing when you were here before?'

'You mean ornithology?'

'Yes, that's it.'

'No, I was digging ditches then.'

'Digging ditches? You mean you were – *digging ditches*?'

'Yes, that's it, Mr Harrison. It was either dig ditches or starve to death.'

'Well, I'm glad you don't have to dig ditches any more. It's not much fun – *digging ditches*, is it?'

'No, especially if the ground is hard. Or if your back is weak. Or vice versa. Or let's say your mother had just been put in the mad house and the alarm goes off too soon.'

'I beg your pardon! *What did you say'?*

'If things are not just right, I said. You know what I mean – bunions, lumbago, scrofula. It's different now, of course. I have my birds and other pets. Mornings I used to watch the sun rise. Then I would saddle the jackasses – I had two and the other fellow had three . . .'

'This was in California, Mr Miller?'

'Yes, twenty-five years ago. I had just done a stretch in San Quentin . . .'

'San Quentin?'

'Yes, attempted suicide. I was really gaga but that didn't make any difference to them. You see, when my father set the house afire one of the horses kicked me in the temple. I used to get fainting fits and then after a time I got homicidal spells and finally I became suicidal. Of course I didn't know that the revolver was loaded. I took a pot-shot at my sister, just for fun, and luckily I missed her. I tried to explain it to the judge but he wouldn't listen to me. I never carry a revolver any more. If I have to defend myself I use a jack-knife. The best thing, of course, is to use your knee . . .'

'Excuse me, Mr Miller, I have to speak to Mrs So-and-so a moment. Very interesting what you say. *Very interesting indeed.* We must talk some more. Excuse me just a moment. . . .'

JOHN GUNTHER
(1901–1970)

American journalist and writer. Between 1944 and 1946 he travelled all over America, gathering facts and impressions for his *Inside USA*, 'a circumnavigation of the greatest, craziest, most dangerous, least stable, most spectacular, least grown-up, and most powerful and magnificent nation ever known'.

New York City in the late 1940s

New York City has more trees (2,400,000) than houses, and it makes 18,200,000 telephone calls a day, of which about 125,000 are wrong numbers. Its rate of divorces is the lowest of any big American city, less than a tenth of that of Baltimore for instance, and even less than that in the surrounding countryside. One of its hotels, built largely over railway tracks, has an assessed valuation of $22,500,000 (there are 124 buildings valued at more than a million dollars in Manhattan alone), and it is probably the only city in the world that still maintains sheriff's juries and has five district attorneys.

New York City has such admirable institutions as the New School for Social Research, the Council on Foreign Relations, Cooper Union, the Museum of Modern Art, and the Century Association. It has 17 billion dollars' worth of real estate, and a black market in illegitimate babies. It has 492 playgrounds, more than 11,000 restaurants, 2,800 churches, and the largest store in the world, Macy's, which wrote 40,328,836 sales checks in 1944, and serves more than 150,000 customers a day. It has the Great White Way, bad manners, 33,000 schoolteachers (average pay $3,803), and 500 boy gangs.

New York makes three-quarters of all the fur coats in the country, and its slang and mode of speech can change hour by hour. It has New York University, a wholly private institution which is the second largest university in the country, with 13,800 Jews in its student body, 12,000 Protestants, and 7,200 Catholics, and a great municipal institution, the City College of the College of the City of New York, one of four famous city colleges. In New York people drink 14 million gallons of hard liquor a year, and smoke about 20 billion cigarettes. It has 301,850 dogs, and one of its unsolved murders is the political assassination of Carlo Tresca.

New York has 9,371 taxis and more than 700 parks. Its budget runs to $175,000,000 for education alone, and it drinks 3,500,000 quarts of milk a day. The average New York family (in normal times) moves once every eighteen months, and more than 2,200,000 New Yorkers belong to the Associated Hospital Service. New York has a birth every five minutes, and a marriage every seven. It has 'more Norwegian-born citizens than Tromsoe and Narvik put together,' and only one railroad, the New York Central, has the perpetual right to enter it by land. It has 22,000 soda fountains, and 112 tons of soot fall per square mile every month, which is why your face is dirty.

JOHN STEINBECK
(1902–1968)

American novelist. Author of *The Grapes of Wrath* (1939) and *Of Mice and Men* (1937); awarded the Nobel Prize for Literature in 1962. At the age of fifty-eight, he discovered that 'I did not know my own country' and set out in pick-up truck on a journey through thirty-four states, travelling over 10,000 miles. His only companion was Charley, 'an old French gentleman poodle'. . . .

Trying to leave town

It rained in New York State, the Empire State, rained cold and pitiless, as the highway signwriters would put it. Indeed, the dismal downpour made my intended visit to Niagara Falls seem redundant. I was then hopelessly lost in the streets of a small but endless town in the neighbourhood of Medina, I think. I pulled to the side of the street and got out my book of road maps. But to find where you are going, you must know where you are, and I didn't. The windows of the cab were tightly closed and opaque with streaming rain. My car radio played softly. Suddenly there was a knock on the window, the door was wrenched open, and a man slipped into the seat beside me. The man was quite red of face, quite whisky of breath. His trousers were held up by red braces over the long, grey underwear that covered his chest.

'Turn that damn thing off,' he said, and then turned off my radio himself. 'My daughter saw you out the window,' he continued. 'Thought you was in trouble.' He looked at my maps. 'Throw those things away. Now, where is it you want to go?'

I don't know why it is a man can't answer such a question with the truth. The truth was that I had turned off the big highway 104 and into the smaller roads because the traffic was heavy and passing vehicles threw sheets of water on my windshield. I wanted to go to Niagara Falls. Why couldn't I have admitted it? I looked down at my map and said, 'I'm trying to get to Erie, Pennsylvania.'

'Good,' he said. 'Now, throw those maps away. Now you turn around, go two traffic lights, that'll bring you to Egg Street. Turn left there and about two hundred yards on Egg turn right at an angle. That's a twisty kind of street and you'll come to an overpass, but don't take it. You turn left there and it will curve around like this – see? Like this.' His hand made a curving motion. 'Now, when the curve straightens out you'll come to three branching roads. There's a big red house on the left-hand branch so you don't take that, you take the right-hand branch. Now, have you got that so far?'

'Sure,' I said. 'That's easy.'

'Well repeat it back so I'll know you're going right.'

I had stopped listening at the curving road. I said, 'Maybe you better tell me again.'

'I thought so. Turn around and go two traffic lights to Egg Street, turn left for two hundred yards and turn right at an angle on a twisty street till you come to an overpass but don't take it.'

'That clears it up for me,' I said quickly. 'I sure do thank you for helping me out.'

'Hell,' he said, 'I ain't even got you out of town yet.'

SIR CECIL BEATON
(1904–1980)

English photographer, designer, traveller and diarist.

An invitation to Xanadu from Randolph Hearst, December 1930

The sun poured down with theatrical brilliance on tons of white marble and white stone. There seemed to be a thousand marble statues, pedestals, urns. The flowers were unreal in their ordered profusion. Hearst stood smiling at the top of one of the many flights of garden steps. . . .

We went outdoors and toured the formal terraces, then wandered in the vast garden. Some of the statues, I noted with surprise, were not up to scratch, even cheapjack. Perhaps it was by intent; we'd been so overpowered by Donatellos and Della Robbias that it made the place come alive to see a nymph with bobbed hair eating an apple, or three very obviously Victorian graces playing together.

Inside the cathedral-like assembly-room the party now gathered, all bemoaning the non-arrival of their bags. Some stood in awe at the grandeur of their surroundings. Those who didn't, the tough blondes and nonentities, had been here before. Blasé, they made efforts to explain what certain pieces were, where they came from and their date. This aesthetic assessment ended in shrieks of ribaldry. In fact, Eileen Percy was already making whoopee, rushing about with a sword she had picked up for an impromptu bacchanale.

The lunch table looked like a scene in some epic film about the lives of the Caesars. A never-ending length of table was literally covered with food – bottles of pickled fruits of all descriptions, chutneys, olives, onions, squares of every kind of cheese, bowls of fresh fruit. Purple glass goblets, vivid hanging banners and urns of poinsettias completed a Lucullan sight. The food turned out to be as good as it looked. I gobbled away, while the blondes became increasingly hilarious as they planned a cockeyed New Year's Eve.

Trunks arrived. I retired to shave and put on entirely new clothes. In doing so, I lingered too long. Feeling spick and span, I came down from my Jacobean magnificence to join the party but could find no one. Every guest had disappeared.

JACK KEROUAC
(1922–1969)

American novelist and traveller. Figurehead of the beat generation, his novel *On the Road* inspired a generation to take to the highways. Although published as fiction, it was basically a mythologized version of his own experience.

A quiet drive with Dean Moriarty

THE car belonged to a tall, thin fag who was on his way home to Kansas and wore dark glasses and drove with extreme care; the car was what Dean called a 'fag Plymouth'; it had no pickup and no real power. 'Effeminate car!' whispered Dean in my ear. There were two other passengers, a couple, typical half-way tourist who wanted to stop and sleep everywhere. The first stop would have to be Sacramento, which wasn't even the faintest beginning of the trip to Denver. . . .

We left Sacramento at dawn and were crossing the Nevada desert by noon, after a hurling passage of the Sierras that made the fag and the tourists cling to each other in the back seat. We were in front, we took over. Dean was happy again. All he needed was a wheel in his hand and four on the road. He talked about how bad a driver Old Bull Lee was and to demonstrate – 'Whenever a huge big truck like that one coming loomed into sight it would take Bull infinite time to spot it, 'cause he couldn't see, man, he can't *see*.' He rubbed his eyes furiously to show. 'And I'd say, "Whoop, look out, Bull, a truck", and he'd say, "Eh? what's that you say, Dean?" "Truck! truck!" and at the *very* last *moment* he would go right up to the truck like this –' And Dean hurled the Plymouth head-on at the truck roaring our way, wobbled and hovered in front of it a moment, the truck driver's face growing grey before our eyes, the people in the back seat subsiding in gasps of horror, and swung away at the last moment. 'Like that, you see, exactly like that, how bad he was.' I wasn't scared at all; I knew Dean. The people in the back seat were speechless. In fact they were afraid to complain: God knew what Dean would do, they thought, if they should ever complain. He balled right across the desert in this manner, demonstrating various ways of how not to drive, how his father used to drive jalopies, how great drivers made curves, how bad drivers hove over too far in the beginning and had to scramble at the curve's end, and so on. It was a hot, sunny afternoon. Reno, Battle Mountain, Elko, all the towns along the Nevada road, shot by one after another, and at dusk we were in the Salt Lake flats with the lights of Salt Lake City infinitesimally glimmering almost a hundred miles across the mirage of the flats, twice showing, above and below the curve of the earth, one clear, one dim. I told Dean that the thing that bound us all together in this world was invisible, and to prove it pointed to long lines of telephone poles that curved off out of sight over the bend of a hundred miles of salt. His floppy bandage, all dirty now, shuddered in the air, his face was a light. 'Oh yes, man, dear God, yes, yes!' Suddenly he stopped the car and collapsed. I turned and saw him huddled in the corner of the seat, sleeping. His face was down on his good hand, and the bandaged hand automatically and dutifully remained in the air.

The people in the back seat sighed with relief. I heard them whispering mutiny. 'We can't let him drive any more, he's absolutely crazy, they must have let him out of an asylum or something.'

I rose to Dean's defence and leaned back to talk to them. 'He's not crazy, he'll be all right, and don't worry about his driving, he's the best in the world.'

'I just can't stand it,' said the girl in a suppressed, hysterical whisper. I sat back and enjoyed nightfall on the desert and waited for poorchild Angel Dean to wake up again. We were on a hill overlooking Salt Lake City's neat patterns of light and he opened his eyes to the place in this spectral world where he was born, unnamed and bedraggled, years ago.

'Sal, Sal, look, this is where I was born, think of it! People change, they eat meals year after year and change with every meal. EE! Look!' He was so excited it made me cry. Where would it all lead? The tourists insisted on driving the car the rest of the way to Denver. Okay, we didn't care. We sat in the back and talked. But they got too tired in the morning and Dean took the wheel in the eastern Colorado desert at Craig. We had spent almost the entire night crawling cautiously over Strawberry Pass in Utah and lost a lot of time. They went to sleep. Dean headed pellmell for the mighty wall of Berthoud Pass that stood a hundred miles ahead on the roof of the world, a tremendous Gibraltarian door shrouded in clouds. He took Berthoud Pass like a June bug – same as at Tehachapi, cutting off the motor and floating it, passing everybody and never halting the rhythmic advance that the mountains themselves intended, till we overlooked the great hot plain of Denver again – and Dean was home.

It was with a great deal of silly relief that these people let us off the car at the corner of 27th and Federal. Our battered suitcases were piled on the sidewalk again; we had longer ways to go. But no matter, the road is life.

Norman Levine
(1924–   )

Canadian novelist. In 1949 he left Canada to live in
Europe; a few years later, like Henry Miller, he decided to
return to his homeland, and like Miller he wrote an
extraordinary travel book about his journeys through the
country.

The treatment, Montreal

The room was deserted. The barman looked bored. A figure whom I
hadn't noticed before came over to where I was sitting with a glass
in his hand: grey hair, crew cut, overweight, bow tie, rimless glasses.
He looked too much of a type that one sees but does not notice.

'You don't look well,' he said.

'I don't feel well.'

'Have you had the treatment?'

I held up my glass with brandy in it.

'No, not that. I've got something better. Follow me.'

I followed him to the bar. He told me to face the narrow wall
which was hidden in shadow to the left of the bar. 'Closer,' he said.
'It won't bite you.'

I waited. I didn't know what to expect. Then lights went on and
the wall, a few inches from my face, was lit up with enormous
breasts, nipples, buttocks, legs, shaved groins.

'Pretty good,' he smiled.

'Pretty good,' I said.

I returned to my seat. He followed.

'I've got something else that helps to give me a pick-up when I
feel down. And if you don't mind my saying so you look pretty
down to me.'

He brought out a black pen, pulled off the handle; inside the
glass tube, in some liquid, was a nude rubber girl about two inches
long. He tilted the pen as if it was a seesaw and the girl opened and
closed her legs. Then from his coat pocket he took out a nutcracker;
the two handles were made out of wood and shaped as a pair of
girl's legs. He took out a hazel nut and put it between the legs and
gave the cracker to me. 'Go on crack it! It's no good just holding it.
You gotta crack it; you'll feel better.'

HOOD RIVER BLACKIE
(1926–   )

American hobo, born Ralph Goodings.

Running away

Then came 1940. I was a big kid for 14, standing about five foot ten and weighing 160 pounds. Everyone said I looked 18. In the early part of 1940, after some family troubles, I ran away from home.

I guess it was only natural that I take to the rails, but my first ride in a boxcar was a terrifying thing. I swear, if that train had stopped I would have gotten off it and gone right back home. But after a few hours, I saw it wasn't going to jump the tracks. I also noticed a strange feeling coming over me, a kind of pleasant swelling sensation in my chest that I now know was freedom.

About a week later I piled off the freight at the little California desert town of Mecca. I had a bedroll, a packsack, and a few dollars I had been saving to buy an old car. If anyone who reads this ever gets to Mecca, or if you live there, walk over to the tracks and look at the big tamarisk tree located at the southern edge of the town on the west side of the tracks. Under this tree on a hot September day in 1940, I met Tex Medders. Tex was probably the finest human being I've ever known. He looked rather frail to me at five foot seven and 135 pounds, sitting on a rusty five-gallon can watching a stew cook over a small fire. I can close my eyes now and still see his old face and the merry twinkle in his faded blue eyes. . . .

It didn't take him long to get the story of my running away out of me, and to my surprise he tried to talk me into going back home and getting an education. By dark, though, I guess it had become apparent to him that I never would go home again, for all at once he looked across the fire at me and said, 'Kid, let's you and me head up north to Oregon and pick some apples.' I can still see the shadows of the fire flickering on his face. Never had I felt such happiness. At last I was going to be a hobo and travel with these strange wanderers.

And so started our 25-year journey across America. Tex showed me the land and taught me to survive along the rails, and I learned a lot. I learned that when I came into Chicago on the Rock Island from Denver, I had to get off out at the Blue Island icing station and catch the Indiana Harbor Belt line, which went around Chicago and crossed 30 railroads. This way I could catch whichever road I wanted. I learned that the Union Pacific branched at Borie Junction west of Cheyenne, Wyoming, and that the left branch went to Denver and the right one to Pocatello, Idaho. I learned that there was a 'bull school' (for training railroad police) at Cheyenne, making it a very 'hot' town for hoboes.

I learned that the mosquitoes were bad along the Yellowstone River at Livingston, Montana, and that I didn't like the hobo jungle under the willows along the Milwaukee main line. . . .

Whistles

Never has man produced a more lonely sound than the whistle of a steam locomotive. It was a sad sound that seemed to say to each of us who heard it: 'Come with me and I'll show you America. Follow me all the days of your life, and as you lie down to die, you'll pray with your last breath to follow me once again.' Whistles had that effect on a lot of us, and I've seen many a man get up and catch a train out in the night when he had no intention of leaving until morning.

JOHN MCPHEE
(1931–   )

American writer. *The Survival of the Bark Canoe*, one of seventeen books by John McPhee, is the story of the building of birch-bark canoes and of a 150-mile expedition through the Maine woods in those graceful survivors of a prehistoric technology.

Up Allagash Stream, north-eastern Maine, with a bark canoe

Allagash Stream, the highest reach of the river, drops to the head of Chamberlain Lake from the west-northwest. Recrossing the isthmus carry, we go in the morning to the mouth of the stream. By noon, we are literally in the water. As it pours toward us, it is too shallow to be paddled, too shallow to be poled. There is nothing to do but frog it – get out of the canoes and walk them up the current. If it is this shallow here, it is not in all likelihood going to get any deeper as we go along; therefore, as the map informs us, the best we can hope for is a seven-mile walk in the water.

Alternative routes are, for various reasons, less attractive, and do not include Allagash Lake, whose remoteness is written in its approaches: from the east, seven miles' sloshing up a rocky stream; from the west, a portage of three miles, by far the longest in the Allagash woods. So we drag the canoes – in two, three inches of water, jumping, bubbling, rushing at us. We lift them at the gunwales to reduce the draw. Now and again, we slide and fall on rock shelves covered with algae. In pools, we go in to the hips, to the chest, all the way. The cool water feels good coming on. It feels good rushing around the ankles. It feels good closing overhead. I would prefer to frog fifty miles up a forest stream than paddle ten against a big lake head wind.

Often, if it necessary to heave rocks aside to create a channel wide enough for the canoes. On many of the rocks are heavy streaks of paint or aluminium left by hundreds of canoes that have come banging down this river in varying levels of water under the care of people who did not give a damn what they hit. What comes home once more at the sight of those aluminum covered rocks is the world of difference in the way we feel towards our canoes, and it is the central pleasure of this trip: we care so much about them. We scrape a little, too, and it can't be helped. *Tant pis*, as Henri says. Bark leaves no marks behind. Warren, leading, voraciously sculpts the river – kicking stones aside, lifting rocks so large they appear to be ledges and stuffing them into the banks. Then he hauls the canoe up the freeways he has made. Henri walks behind with a rope in his hand. It is tied to the stern, which he moves from side to side, as if the canoe were a horse on a halter.

The stream is a white-water primer, for it is flowing much like a riverine rapid, which is what it is, scaled down. All in miniature, the haystacks, the standing waves, the souse holes, the eddies, the satin-water pillows are here, and usually there is a place to go – a *fil d'eau* – that is deeper and better than anywhere else. One learns to read the stream. After four hours, we have gone two miles.

Henri remarks that he is now hungry enough to eat a moose, and wouldn't mind trying if one were to appear. . . .

A windfall fir lies across the stream now and stops us altogether, but Henri unsheathes his axe and sends flotillas of chips down the current. The log drops into the water. We shove it out of the way.

The air is chill. The sky, all but unnoticed by us, has clouded over, and the afternoon is almost gone. Even Henri is ready to stop.

JOHNATHAN RABAN
(1942–)

English writer, critic and traveller. In 1979 he sailed down the Mississippi from Minneapolis to New Orleans in a small boat with an outboard motor. At Memphis he – and his boat – hitched a ride on one of the giant towboats that ply the river.

A bad night on the Mississippi

In the pilot house, Mac had taken over the nightwatch. He was the grandfather of the boat. His mottled face, dentures and spectacles made him look as if he might be more in place sitting by a fire in his slippers instead of pushing 9000 tons of ammonia through a filthy night on the river.

There were flashes of sheet lightning ahead. The searchlights rested on fog banks as thick and hard-edged as clouds seen from above on a high-altitude flight.

'Shoot,' said Mac, then 'shit', then 'shoot' again.

The river was now only legible in the bright copper-coloured picture on the radar screen. The lights picked out little cattle-ponds of water in the gaps between the fog. The hostile weather had made the strangely tender quality of the talk over the radio even tenderer.

'Now you come in here real close with me, Cap.'

'I'm tight with you, now. Okay?'

'That's fine and dandy.'

The captains enquired after each other's wives and children. Everyone was just called 'Cap' over the radio. People had made close friends with familiar voices without ever knowing the names of their owners. 'Cap' was enough. If your name was 'Cap' you were a buddy.

One might have been far out at sea, with nothing but pillars of ochreous fog and narrow, winding tracks of water. Then, suddenly, just a few yards ahead of the leading barges, there would be trees, a caving cliff of riverbank, a rock revetment. Once, the black wedge of a barge came nuzzling out of the fog a hundred feet or so to port.

'Hey, Cap!' called Mac over the radio. 'You're running so goddam close, you want me to spit in your engine room?'

'Sorry, Cap. I got you now. Hey, what you got in them fancy barges, for god's sakes?'

'*Pison*,' Mac said with an air of grand smugness. '*Moneyer*.'

'Shit, Cap – I coulda cut you half in two.'

'That's just what I was thinking. Have a good trip, now.'

'You too, Cap. And don't go letting that 'monia out all over the river. This goddam fog's bad enough for my sonofabitch lungs.'

The further south we went, the more the fog thickened. Our lights made a low tunnel into which Mac fed the tow-fleet inch by inch.

'I done enjoying just about as much of this as I can stand,' he said. 'Times like this, I think if I was at home they'd never get me out again. Shoot.' The tow was going on a sideways slide. 'Rat's-ass-eddy.' We straightened up again. 'I wouldn't want to wish this on my worst enemy, not on a night like this.'

All down the river, the tow-fleets were laying up inshore. Mac, too, gave in eventually. He sent the four bargemen and deckhands forward, where they disappeared into the fog and turned into more voices on the radio. I watched the radar screen. The river made a slow turn round 180 degrees, and the leading barges touched the bank with a grind and a bump. As Mac eased the towboat in on the current, the searchlight-beam travelled along the levee and lit up a herd of grazing deer. They looked like silver paper cut-outs. For a moment they were quite still, mesmerised by the light, then they scattered into the forest.

With the engines off, one could listen to the river. As it scoured the hulls of the barges and sluiced past our stern, it sounded as if it was breathing heavily in its sleep, making a continuous line of Z's. Mac was brewing coffee in the percolator.

'Well, now you've seen what a bad night on the river's like. They don't come much worse than this.'

He had been working on the Mississippi since 1937, when he had started to run tugs round Memphis harbour. There were still steamboats then and Mac could remember them lining the wharf, packed solid with bales of cotton.

"They say now they was the good old days. Seems to me that, taken all around, they was bad days, mostly. I never saw too much romance in 'em.'

CENTRAL AND SOUTH AMERICA and THE CARIBBEAN

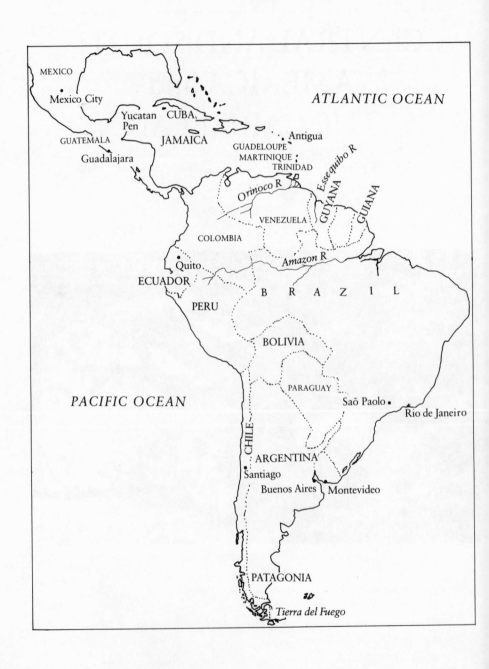

AMERIGO VESPUCCI
(1454–1512)

Florentine navigator, after whom America was named. On the basis of letters written by him, Vespucci has been credited with four separate voyages, but two of them are suspect. On the first, he is supposed to have set out from Cadiz in May 1497, sailed first to the Canaries and then after twenty-seven days to 'a coast that we thought to be that of a continent', possibly the shore of Campeche Bay, the innermost part of the Gulf of Mexico. From here he may have followed the southern seaboard of North America, doubled Cape Sable at the tip of Florida and reached Cape Hatteras on the coast of North Carolina. Whether this voyage was genuine may never be known, but with its mention of hammocks Vespucci's letter (written in 1504) seems to be describing the Indians of either Yucatan or Mexico.

Neither Moors nor Jews

The manner of their living is very barbarous, because they do not eat at fixed times, but as often as they please. And it matters little to them that they should be seized with a desire to eat at midnight rather than by day, for at all times they eat. . . . They sleep in certain nets made of cotton, very big, and hung in the air. And although this their way of sleeping may appear uncomfortable, I say that it is a soft way to sleep; because it was very frequently our lot to sleep in them, and we slept better in them than in quilts. They are people neat and clean of person, owing to the constant washing they practise. When, begging your pardon, they evacuate the bowels, they do everything to avoid being seen; and just as in this they are clean and modest, the more dirty and shameless are they in making water (both men and women). . . . They are not very jealous, and are libidinous beyond measure, and the women far more than the men. . . . They are so heartless and cruel that, if they become angry with their husbands, they immediately resort to a trick whereby they kill the child within the womb, and a miscarriage is brought about, and for this reason they kill a great many babies. They are women of pleasing person, very well proportioned, so that one does not see on their bodies any ill-formed feature or limb. And although

453

they go about utterly naked, they are fleshy women, and that part of their privies which he who has not seen them would think to see is invisible. . . . They showed themselves very desirous of copulating with us Christians. While among these people we did not learn that they had any religion. They can be termed neither Moors nor Jews; and they are worse than heathen; because we did not see that they offered any sacrifice, nor yet did they have [any] house of prayer. I deem their manner of life to be Epicurean. Their dwellings are in common, and their houses built after the fashion of huts, but stoutly wrought and constructed out of very large trees and thatched with palm leaves, safe against tempests and winds, and in some places of such breadth and length that in a single house we found there were 600 souls; and we saw towns of only thirteen houses where there were 4,000 souls. . . . Their wealth consists of feathers of many-hued birds, or of little rosaries which they make out of fish bones, or of white or green stones which they stick through cheeks, lips, and ears, and of many other things to which we attach no value.

FERDINAND MAGELLAN
(c. 1480–1521)

Portuguese navigator in the service of Spain. He commanded an expedition of five ships that set out in September 1519 to sail to the Moluccas by way of a passage to the West. As well as the hazards of bad weather and high seas, Magellan had to contend with mutiny, the loss of ships, men and stores, and scurvy. In March 1521 he reached the Philippines, and was killed in a pointless skirmish with the natives. The survivors went on, eighteen of the original complement of 237 men returning to Spain in September 1522. They were the first men to circumnavigate the world. A first-hand account of the voyage was made by Antonio Pigafetta.

Giants at Port St Julian, Patagonia

. . . One day, without anyone expecting it, we saw a giant, who was on the shore of the sea, quite naked, and was dancing and leaping, and singing, and whilst singing he put the sand and dust on his head. . . . He was so tall that the tallest of us only came up to his waist; however he was well built. He had a large face, painted red all round, and his eyes also were painted yellow around them, and he had two hearts painted on his cheeks; he had but little hair on his head, and it was painted white. When he was brought before the captain he was clothed with the skin of a certain beast, which skin was very skilfully sewed. This beast has its head and ears of the size of a mule, and the neck and body of the fashion of a camel, the legs of a deer, and the tail like that of a horse, and it neighs like a horse. There is a great quantity of these animals in the same place. . . . The captain caused food and drink to be given to this giant, then they showed him some things, amongst others, a steel mirror. When the giant saw his likeness in it, he was greatly terrified, leaping backwards, and made three or four of our men fall down. . . . One of the companions of this giant, who would never come to the ship, on seeing the other coming back with our people, came forward and ran to where the other giants dwelled. These came one after the other all naked, and began to leap and sing, raising one finger to heaven, and showing to our people a certain white powder made of the roots of herbs, which they kept in earthen pots, and they made signs that they lived on that, and that they had nothing else to eat than this powder. . . . Their wives came after them laden like donkeys, and carried their goods. The women are not as tall as the men, but they are very sufficiently large. When we saw them we were all amazed and astonished, for they had the breasts half an ell long, and had their faces painted, and were dressed like the men. But they wore a small skin before them to cover themselves. They brought with them four of those little beasts of which they make their clothing, and they led them with a cord in the manner of dogs coupled together.

A cure for stomach-ache and some possible causes

When these giants have a stomach-ache, instead of taking medicine they put down their throats an arrow about two feet long; then they vomit a green bile mixed with blood: and the reason why they throw up this green matter is because they sometimes eat thistles. . . . Two giants that we had in the ship ate a large basketful of biscuit, and rats without skinning them, and they drank half a bucket of water at each time.

BERNAL DIAZ DE CASTILLO
(c. 1492–1581)

Spanish Conquistador. He served in the New World under various commanders before joining Hernan Cortes in 1519 on his expedition into Mexico. In November the Spaniards arrived at the Aztec capital of Tenochtitlan and were welcomed by Montezuma, the emperor.

Dinner at Montezuma's, November 1519

His cooks had upwards of thirty different ways of dressing meats, and they had earthen vessels so contrived as to keep them always hot. For the table of Montezuma himself, above three hundred dishes were dressed, and for his guards, above a thousand. Before dinner, Montezuma would sometimes go out and inspect the preparations, and his officers would point out to him which were the best, and explained of what birds and flesh they were composed; and of those he would eat. But this was more for amusement than any thing else. It is said that at times the flesh of young children was dressed for him; but the ordinary meats were, domestic fowls, pheasants, geese, partridges, quails, venison, Indian hogs, pigeons, hares, and rabbits, with many other animals and birds peculiar to the country. This is certain; that after Cortes had spoken to him relative to the dressing human flesh, it was not practised in his palace. At his meals, in the cold weather, a number of torches of the bark of a wood which makes no smoke and has an aromatic smell, were lighted, and that they should not throw too much heat, screens, ornamented with gold, and painted with figures of idols, were placed before them. Montezuma was seated on a low throne, or chair, at a table proportioned to the height of his seat. The table was covered with white cloths and napkins, and four beautiful women presented him with water for his hands, in vessels which they call Xicales, with other vessels under them like plates, to catch the water; they also presented him with towels. Then, two other women brought small cakes of bread, and when the king began to eat, a large screen of wood, gilt, was placed before him, so that people should not during that time see him. The women having retired to a little distance, four ancient lords stood by the throne, to whom Montezuma from time to time spoke or addressed questions, and as a mark of particular favour, gave to each of them a plate of that which he was eating. I was told that these old lords, who were his near relations, were also counsellors and judges. The plates which Montezuma presented to them, they received with high respect, eating what was in them without taking their eyes off the ground. He was served on earthenware of Cholula, red and black. While the king was at table, no one of his guards, or in the vicinity of his apartment, dared for their lives make any noise. Fruit of all the kinds that the country produced was laid before him; he eat very little, but from time to time, a liquor prepared from cocoa, and of a stimulative, or corroborative quality, as we were told, was presented to him in golden cups. We could not at that time see if he drank it or not, but I observed a number of jars, above fifty, brought in, filled with foaming chocolate, of which he took some, which the women presented to him. At different intervals during the time of dinner, there entered certain Indians, humpbacked, very deformed, and ugly, who played tricks of buffoonery, and others who they said were jesters. There was also a company of singers and dancers, who afforded Montezuma much entertainment. To these he ordered the vases of chocolate to be distributed. The four female attendants then took away the cloths, and again with much respect presented him with water to wash his hands, during which time Montezuma conversed with the four old noblemen formerly mentioned, after which they took their leave with many ceremonies. One thing I forgot, and no wonder, to mention in its place, and that is, that during the time Montezuma was at dinner, two very beautiful women were busily employed making small cakes with eggs and other things mixed therein. These were delicately white, and when made they presented them to him on plates covered with napkins. Also another kind of bread was brought to him in long loaves, and plates of cakes resembling wafers. After he had dined, they presented to him three little canes highly ornamented, containing liquid amber, mixed with an herb they call tobacco; and when he had sufficiently viewed and heard the singers, dancers, and buffoons, he took a little of the smoke of one of these canes, and then laid himself down to sleep; and thus his principal meal concluded.

HANS STADE OF HESSE
(*fl.* 1547–1555)

German sailor. In 1547 he was captured by the Tupinamba people of Eastern Brazil.

'How my two masters came to me and told me that they had presented me to one of their friends, who was to keep me and kill me, when I was to be eaten.'

The two above-mentioned who had taken me said, 'Now will the women lead thee out to the Aprasse:' this word I understood not then, but it means dancing. Thus they dragged me along with the ropes, which were round my neck, from out of the huts on to an open place. Then came all the women who were in the seven huts, and seized hold of me, and the men went away. Several of the women led me along by the arms, and several of the ropes which were bound round my neck, so roughly and rightly that I could hardly breathe. In this manner they went along with me, and I knew not what they intended doing to me, upon which I remembered the sufferings of our Lord Jesus Christ, and how he suffered innocently at the hands of the vile Jews, whereby I consoled myself and became more resigned. Then they brought me before the huts of the king, who was called Vratinge Wasu, which means in German, the Great White Bird. Before his huts lay a heap of freshly dug earth, whither they led me and sat me down thereon, and some held me, when I thought nothing else but that they would dispatch me at once. I looked round for the Iwara Pemme, wherewith they club men, and asked whether they were going to kill me then, when they answered, 'not yet.' Upon which a woman came from out of the crowd towards me, holding a fragment of a crystal, set in a thing like a bent ring, and with this same piece of crystal shaved off my eyebrows, and would also have cut the beard from my chin, but this I would not suffer, and said, that they should kill me with my beard. Then they replied, that for the present they would not kill me, and left me my beard. But after some days they cut it off with a pair of scissors, which the Frenchmen had given them.

Hans Stade survived 'long misery, peril of life and body', and after five years returned to the Grand Duchy of Hesse.

FRANCIS FLETCHER
(fl. 1577–1580)

English clergyman. Chaplain on board Sir Francis Drake's ship the *Pelican* during his voyage around the world in 1577–80.

A sleeping Spaniard on the coast of Peru

As we sayled along, continually searching for fresh water, we came to a place called *Tarapaca*, and landing there we lighted on a Spaniard who lay asleepe, and had lying by him 13 barres of silver, waighing in all about 4000 Spanish duccatts: we would not (could wee have chosen) have awaked him of his nappe: but seeing we, against our wills, did him that injury, we freed him of his charge, which otherwise perhaps would have kept him waking, and so left him to take out (if it pleased him) the other part of his sleepe in more security. . . .

SIR WALTER RALEIGH
(1554?–1618)

English soldier, sailor, explorer and courtier. As a soldier, he fought in France and Ireland. When he returned to England in 1581 he became a favourite of Queen Elizabeth I and was active in promoting colonization in Virginia. In 1595, having fallen out of favour with the Queen, he embarked on an expedition to find the legendary city of El Dorado. With his fellow adventurer Laurence Kemys, he penetrated 300 miles up the Orinoco River into the interior of Guiana.

Going up the Orinoco

Our old Pilot of the *Ciawani* . . . told us, that if we would enter a branch of a river on the right hand with our barge and wherries, and leave the *Galley* at ancor the while in the great river, he would bring us to a towne of the *Arwacas* where we should find store of bread, hens, fish, and of the countrey wine, and perswaded us that departing from the *Galley* at noone, we might returne ere night. . . . But when it grew towardes night, and we demaunding where the place was, he tolde us but fower reaches more: when we had rowed fower and fower, we saw no signe, and our poore water men even hart broken, and tired, were ready to give up the ghost; for we had now come from the *Galley* neer forty miles.

At the last we determined to hang the Pilot, and if we had well knowen the way backe againe by night, he had surely gone, but our owne necessities pleaded sufficiently for his safetie: for it was as darke as pitch, and the river began so to narrow it selfe, and the trees to hang over from side to side, as we were driven with arming swordes to cut a passage thorow those branches that covered the water. We were very desirous to finde this towne hoping of a feast, bicause we made but a short breakfast aboord the *Galley* in the morning, and it was now eight a clock at night, and our stomacks began to gnaw apace: but whether it was best to returne or go on, we began to doubt, suspecting treason in the Pilot more and more: but the poore olde Indian ever assured us that it was but a little farther, and but this one turning, and that turning, and at last about one a clocke after midnight we saw a light, and rowing towards it, we heard the dogs of the village. When wee landed we found few people, for the Lord of that place was gone with divers *Canoas* above 400 miles of, upon a journey towards the head of *Orenoque* to trade for gold, and to buy women of the *Canibals*, who afterward unfortunately passed by us as we rode at an ancor in the port of *Morequito* in the dark of night, and yet came so neer us, as his *Canoas* grated against our barges: he left one of his companie at the port of *Morequito*, by whom we understood that he had brought thirty yoong woomen, divers plates of gold, and had great store of fine peeces of cotton cloth, and cotton beds. In his house we had good store of bread, fish, hens, and Indian drinke, and so rested that night. . . .

. . . Upon this river there were great store of fowle, and of many sorts: we saw in it divers sorts of strange fishes, and of marvellous bignes, but for *Lagartos* [alligators] it exceeded, for there were thousands of those uglie serpents, and the people call it for the abundance of them the river of *Lagartos*, in their language. I had a *Negro* a very proper yoong fellow, that leaping out of the *Galley* to swim in the mouth of this river, was in all our sights taken and devoured with one of those *Lagartos*. . . .

JOHN CHILTON
(fl. 1561–1585)

English sailor. He went to Spain in 1561 and lived there for seven years. Between 1568 and 1585 he travelled in New Spain (Mexico) and the West Indies.

'Thanke God thou art leane': nearly eaten by cannibals, Mexico, 1569

The next day in the morning we passed over the river in a canoa; and being on the other side, I went my selfe before alone: and by reason there met many wayes traled by the wilde beasts, I lost my way, and so travelled thorow a great wood about two leagues: and at length fell into the hands of certaine wilde Indians, which were there in certaine cottages made of straw; who seeing me, came out to the number of twenty of them, with their bowes and arrowes, and spake unto mee in their language, which I understood not: and so I made signes unto them to helpe mee from my horse; which they did by commandement of their lord, which was there with them; and lighted downe. They caried me under one of their cottages, and layed me upon a mat on the ground: and perceiving that I could not understand them, they brought unto mee a little Indian wench of Mexico, of fifteene or sixteene yeeres of age, whom they comman-ded to aske me in her language from whence I came, and for what intent I was come among them: for (sayth she) doest thou not know Christian, how that these people will kill and eat thee? To whom I answered, let them doe with me what they will; heere now I am. Shee replied, saying, thou mayest thanke God thou art leane; for they feare thou hast the pocks; otherwise they would eate thee. So I presented to the king a little wine which I had with me in a bottle; which he esteemed above any treasure: for for wine they will sell their wives and children. Afterwards the wench asked me what I would have, and whether I would eat any thing. I answered that I desired a little water to drinke, for that the countrey is very hote. . . . Having now bene conversant with them about three or foure houres, they bid her aske me if I would goe my way. I answered her, that I desired nothing els.

MILES PHILIPS
(fl. 1568–1582)

English sailor. In 1568 he sailed with Sir John Hawkins from the west coast of Africa to the West Indies, carrying a cargo of slaves. Captured and imprisoned by the Spanish, he was eventually taken to Mexico to face the rigours of the Inquisition. After being in captivity for '15 or 16 yeres', he was 'delivered from their bloody hands, and returned into his owne Countrey' in 1582.

The cruel judgement of the Inquisition, Mexico, 1574

... From time to time we were called upon to confesse, and about the space of 3 moneths before they proceeded to their severe judgement, we were al rackt, and some enforced to utter that against themselves, which afterwards cost them their lives. And thus having gotten from our owne mouthes matter sufficient for them to proceed in judgement against us, they caused a large scaffold to be made in the middest of the market place in Mexico right over against the head church, & 14 or 15 daies before the day of their judgement, with the sound of a trumpet, and the noise of their Attabalies, which are a kind of drummes, they did assemble the people in all parts of the citie: before whom it was then solemnely proclaimed, that whosoever would upon such a day repaire to the market place, they should heare the sentence of the holy Inquisition against the English heretikes, Lutherans, and also see the same put in execution. Which being done, and the time approching of this cruell judgement, the night before they came to the prison where we were, with certaine officers of that holy hellish house, bringing with them certaine fooles coats which they had prepared for us, being called in their language S. Benitos, which coats were made of yellow cotten & red crosses upon them, both before & behind: they were so busied in putting on their coats about us, and bringing us out into a large yard, and placing and pointing us in what order we should go to the scaffold or place of judgement upon the morrow, that they did not once suffer us to sleepe all that night long. The next morning being come, there was given to every one of us for our breakfast a cup of wine, and a slice of bread fried in honie, and so about eight of the clocke in the morning, we set foorth of the prison, every man alone in his yellow coat, and a rope about his necke, and a great greene Waxe candle in his hand unlighted, having a Spaniard appointed to goe upon either side of every one of us: and so marching in this order and maner toward the scaffold in the market place, which was a bow shoot distant or thereabouts, we found a great assembly of people all the way, and such a throng, that certain of the Inquisitors officers on horseback were constrained to make way, and so comming to the scaffold, we went up by a paire of stayres, and found seates readie made and prepared for us to sit downe on, every man in order as he should be called to receive his judgement. We being thus set downe as we were appointed, present-ly the Inquisitors came up another paire of staires, and the Viceroy and all the chiefe Justices with them. When they were set downe and placed under the cloth of estate agreeing to their degrees and calling, then came up also a great number of Friers, white, blacke and gray, about the number of 300 persons, they being set in the places for them appointed. Then was there a solemne Oyes made, and silence commanded, and then presently beganne their severe and cruell judgement.

The first man that was called was one Roger the chiefe Armour-er of the Jesus, and hee had judgement to have three hundred stripes on horsebacke, and after condemned to the gallies as a slave for 10 yeeres.

After him were called John Gray, John Browne, John Rider, John Moone, James Collier, and one Thomas Browne: these were adjudged to have 200 stripes on horsebacke, and after to be committed to the gallies for the space of 8 yeeres.

Then was called John Keyes, and was adjudged to have 100 stripes on horsebacke, and condemned to serve in the gallies for the space of 6. yeeres.

Then were severally called the number of 53 one after another, and every man had his severall judgement, some to have 200 stripes on horsebacke, and some 100, and condemned for slaves to the gallies, some for 6 yeeres, some for 8 and some for 10.

And then was I Miles Philips called, and was adjudged to serve in a monasterie for 5 yeeres, without any stripes, and to weare a fooles coat, or S. Benito, during all that time.

SAMUEL FRITZ
(1654–1724)

German Jesuit missionary. Father Fritz spent thirty-seven years (1686–1723) among the primitive tribes of the Amazon valley. Much of his energy was devoted to protecting the Indians from Portuguese slave-traders.

Three unpleasant months with the Jurimaguas of the Maranon River, c. 1689

Meanwhile, as I was staying in this Jurimagua village, already almost wholly inundated, in a shelter on a roof made of the bark of trees, I fell sick of most violent attacks of fever and of dropsy that began in the feet with other complaints principally caused by worms. I was obliged to remain day and night for the space of well-nigh three months shut up in this shelter without being able to stir. In the daytime I felt somewhat easier, but the nights in unutterable burnings, as the river though it was passing but a handbreadth from the bed was out of reach of my mouth, and in sleeplessness, caused not only by my infirmities, but also from the gruntings of the crocodiles or lizards that all night long were roving round the village, beasts of horrible deformity. One night one of them entered my canoe, whose prow stood within the house, so that if it had advanced, it would have made an end of my boy and of myself, as there was no possibility of escape.

Besides the lizards so many rats made their way into my dwelling-place, and so hungry, that they gnawed even my spoon and my plate and the haft of my knife and ate up the little food I had for my sustenance. Almost all the people of the village began to take themselves off in search of dry ground and forest fruits to escape starvation, since their store of food, that is the Mandioca, was buried beneath the water, and I for my sustenance was reduced to obtaining at times by fishing a few little fish, and to begging for some plantains, which it was necessary to send for lower down, and to fetch from the Aysuares.

Remarkable is the fact, that I at this time found out in this village of the Jurimaguas, which is that in a revelry that they were making, I, from the ranch where I was lying, heard a flute played, that caused me so great terror, that I could not endure its sound. When they left off playing that flute I asked what it meant, and they answered me, that they were playing in this manner, to Guaricaya, that was the Devil, who from the time of their ancestors came in visible form, and took up his abode in their villages; and they always made him a house apart from the village within the forest, and there they brought him drink and the sick that he might cure them. Finally enquiring with what kind of face and form he came, the chief, named Mativa, answered, 'Father I could not describe it, only that it is horrible, and when he comes all the women with their little ones flee, only the grown-up men remain, and then the Devil takes a whip that for this purpose we keep provided with a leather lash made of the hide of a Sea-Cow, and he flogs us on the breast until much blood is drawn.'

JANET SCHAW
(fl. 1776)

Scottish 'Lady of Quality'. In 1774–6 she visited the West Indies, North Carolina and Portugal.

Slaves at Mount Misery, Antigua, c. 1774

The negroes who are still in troops are sorted so as to match each other in size and strength. Every ten negroes have a driver, who walks behind them, holding in his hand a short whip and a long one. You will too easily guess the use of these weapons; a circumstance of all other the most horrid. They are naked, male and female, down to the girdle, and you constantly observe where the application has been made. But however dreadful this must appear to the humane European, I will do the Creoles the justice to say, they would be averse to it as we are, could it be avoided, which has often been tried to no purpose. When one comes to be better acquainted with the nature of the negroes, the horror of it must wear off. It is the suffering of the human mind that constitutes the greatest misery of punishment, but with them it is merely corporeal. As to the brutes it inflicts no wound on their mind, whose natures seem made to bear it, and whose sufferings are not attended with shame or pain beyond the present moment. When they are regularly ranged, each has a little basket, which he carries up the hill filled with manure and returns with a load of canes to the mill. They go up at a trot, and return at a gallop, and did you not know the cruel necessity of this alertness, you would believe them the merriest people in the world.

ALEXANDER VON HUMBOLDT
(1769–1859)

German naturalist and traveller. (See p. 305.) Between 1799 and 1804 he explored Central and South America, tracing the course of the Orinoco River and the sources of the Amazon.

The insect life of the Orinoco, Altures Rapids, April 1800

It is impossible not to be constantly disturbed by the mosquitoes, zancudos, jejenes, and tempraneros, that cover the face and hands, pierce the clothes with their long needle-forming suckers, and getting into the mouth and nostrils, cause coughing and sneezing whenever any attempt is made to speak in the open air. . . . What appeared to us very remarkable is that at different hours of the day you are stung by distinct species. From half past six in the morning till five at night the air is filled with a tiny biting fly called jejen. An hour before sunset the tempraneros, a species of small gnat, take their place. Their presence scarcely lasts an hour and a half; they disappear between six and seven in the evening, or, as they say here, after the Angelus. After a few minutes' repose, you feel yourself stung by zancudos, another species of gnat with very long legs. The zancudos, the proboscis of which contains a sharp-pointed sucker, causes the most acute pain, and a swelling that remains for several weeks. . . .

It is neither the dangers of navigating in small boats, nor the savage Indians, nor the serpents, crocodiles or jaguars, that make Spaniards dread a voyage on the Orinoco; it is as they say with simplicity, 'el sudar y las moscas' (the sweat and the flies).

The insouciance of the inhabitants of Quito, in the shadow of the Pichincha volcano, Ecuador, 1802

The town breathed an atmosphere of luxury and voluptuousness, and perhaps nowhere is there a population so entirely given up to the pursuit of pleasure. Thus can man accustom himself to sleep in peace on the brink of a precipice.

CHARLES WATERTON
(1782–1865)

English naturalist. The splendidly eccentric descendant of an ancient Catholic family. In 1817 he climbed the lightning conductor on the top of St Peter's, Rome, and followed up this feat by standing on one leg on the head of an angel at the Castello di Sant'Angelo. Between 1812 and 1824 he made several journeys into the interior of Guiana, by way of the Demerara and Essequibo Rivers. As a naturalist, he had an original approach – 'I went expressly to look for wild beasts and, having found them, it would have been impossible for me to have refrained from coming into actual contact with them' – and it was on his third expedition, on the Essequibo, that he had his famous encounter with a cayman, the crocodile of tropical America.

Riding a cayman, Guiana, 1820

The day was now declining apace, and the Indian had made his instrument to take the cayman. It was very simple. There were four pieces of tough, hard wood a foot long, and about as thick as your little finger, and barbed at both ends; they were tied round the end of the rope in such a manner that if you conceive the rope to be an arrow, these four sticks would form the arrow's head; so that one end of the four united sticks answered to the point of the arrow-head, while the other end of the sticks expanded at equal distances round the rope. . . . Now it is evident that, if the cayman swallowed this (the other end of the rope, which was thirty yards long, being fastened to a tree), the more he pulled the faster the barbs would stick into his stomach. This wooden hook, if you may so call it, was well-baited with the flesh of the acouri, and the entrails were twisted round the rope for about a foot above it. . . .

The Indian then took the empty shell of a land-tortoise and gave it some heavy blows with an axe. I asked why he did that. He said it was to let the cayman hear that something was going on. In fact, the Indian meant it as the cayman's dinner-bell. . . .

About half-past five in the morning the Indian stole off silently to take a look at the bait. On arriving at the place he set up a tremendous shout. We all jumped out of our hammocks and ran to him. The Indians got there before me, for they had no clothes to put on, and I lost two minutes in looking for my trousers and in slipping into them.

We found a cayman ten feet and a half long fast to the end of the rope. Nothing now remained to do but to get him out of the water without injuring his scales. . . .

. . . I now walked up and down the sand, revolving a dozen projects in my head. The canoe was at a considerable distance, and I ordered the people to bring it round to the place where we were. The mast was eight feet long, and not much thicker than my wrist. I took it out of the canoe and wrapped the sail round the end of it. Now it appeared clear to me that, if I went down upon one knee and held the mast in the same position as the soldier holds his bayonet when rushing to the charge, I could force it down the cayman's throat should he come open-mouthed at me. When this was told to the Indians they brightened up, and said they would help me to pull him out of the river. . . .

. . . I now took the mast of the canoe in my hand (the sail being tied round the end of the mast) and sunk down upon one knee, about four yards from the water's edge, determining to thrust it down his throat in case he gave me an opportunity. I certainly felt somewhat uncomfortable in this situation, and I thought of Cerberus on the other side of the Styx ferry. The people pulled the cayman to the surface; he plunged furiously as soon as he arrived in these upper regions, and immediately went below again on their slackening the rope. I saw enough not to fall in love at first sight. I now told them we would run all risks and have him on land immediately. They pulled again, and out he came – 'monstrum, horrendum, informe.' This was an interesting moment. I kept my position firmly, with my eye fixed steadfast on him.

By the time the cayman was within two yards of me I saw he was in a state of fear and perturbation. I instantly dropped the mast, sprung up and jumped on his back, turning half round as I vaulted, so that I gained my seat with my face in a right position. I immediately seized his fore-legs, and by main force twisted them on his back; thus they served me for a bridle.

He now seemed to have recovered from his surprise, and probably fancying himself in hostile company he began to plunge furiously, and lashed the sand with his long and powerful tail. I was out of reach of the strokes of it by being near his head. He continued to plunge and strike and made my seat very uncomfortable. It must have been a fine sight for an unoccupied spectator. . . .

. . . The people now dragged us above forty yards on the sand: it was the first and last time I was ever on a cayman's back. Should it be asked how I managed to keep my seat, I would answer, I hunted some years with Lord Darlington's fox-hounds. . . .

The cayman has no grinders; his teeth are entirely made for snatch and swallow: there are thirty-two in each jaw. Perhaps no animal in existence bears more decided marks in his countenance of cruelty and malice than the cayman. He is the scourge and terror of all the large rivers in South America near the line.

HENRY NELSON
COLERIDGE
(1798–1843)

English traveller. In 1825, in an attempt to cure his rheumatism, he spent six months in the West Indies, visiting each of the islands in turn. The attempt succeeded: he returned to England 'derheumatized'.

The West Indian ball

I like a ball in the West Indies better than in England. True it is that you perspire, but then you have not to undergo the triumph of superior frigidity in your partner; she perspires in precise analogy with yourself, lifts and relifts the cambric toties quoties, as the Papists say, whiles ever doth the orient humor burst forth at intervals upon her ivory cheek, and gravitate in emulous contrafluence with your own. Windows, doors and jalousies are all thrown open to the breezes of night; flowers and evergreens give life and verdancy to the walls, and the golden moon or diamond stars gleam through the many openings with that rich and sleepy splendor which good men will see hereafter in Paradise. It is my advice not to drink much; restrain yourself till twelve o'clock or so, and then eat some cold meat and absorb a pint of porter cup, which is perfectly innoxious to the system, and more restorative to the animal spirits than punch, wine or sangaree. Above all do not be persuaded to swallow any washy tea; it gives neither strength or vivacity, but rather impairs both, and makes you excessively uncomfortable.

MADAME CALDERON
DE LA BARCA
(1804–1882)

Scottish traveller. Born Frances Erskine Inglis in Edinburgh, she emigrated when young to America, where in 1838 she married Don Angel Calderon de la Barca. In the same year he was appointed Spanish Minister to Mexico, and in October 1839 they set sail from New York to Vera Cruz, via Cuba. The letters Madame Calderon de la Barca wrote from Mexico during her two-year stay were published in 1843 as *Life in Mexico*; they provide a vivid and often marvellously funny portrait of the country. Don Angel later became Foreign Minister of Sapin; when he died in 1861 his wife became tutor to the Infanta Isabella and was eventually created a Marquesa.

A journey by coach

We climbed into the coach, which was so crowded that we could but just turn our heads to groan an adieu to our friends. The coach rattled off through the streets, dashed through the Alameda, and gradually we began to shake down, and, by a little arrangement of cloaks and sarapes, to be less crowded. A *padre* with a very Indian complexion sat between K—— and me, and a horrible, long, lean, bird-like female, with immense red goggle-eyes, coal-black teeth, fingers like claws, a great goitre, and drinking brandy at intervals, sat opposite to us. There were also various men buried in their sarapes. Satisfied with a cursory inspection of our companions, I addressed myself to *Blackwood's Magazine*, but the road which leads towards the Desierto, and which we before passed on horseback, is dreadful, and the mules could scarcely drag the loaded coach up the steep hills. We were thrown into ruts, horribly jolted, and sometimes obliged to get out, which would not have been disagreeable but for the necessity of getting in again. The day and the country were beautiful, but impossible to enjoy either in a shut coach. We were rather thankful when the wheels, sticking in a deep rut, we were forced to descend, and walk forwards for some time. We had before seen the view from these heights, but the effect never was more striking than at this moment. The old city with her towers, lakes, and volcanoes, lay bathed in the bright sunshine. Not a cloud was in the sky – not an exhalation rose from the lake – not a shadow was on the mountains. All was bright and glittering, and flooded in the morning light; while in contrast rose to the left the dark, pine-covered crags, behind which the Desierto lies.

At Santa Fé we changed horses, and found there an escort which had been ordered for us by General Tornel; a necessary precaution in these robber-haunted roads. We stopped to breakfast at *Quajimalpa*, where the inn is kept by a Frenchman, who is said to be making a large fortune, which he deserves for the good breakfast he had prepared for us. . . .

After leaving this inn, situated in a country formed of heaps of lava and volcanic rocks, the landscape becomes more beautiful and wooded. It is, however, dangerous, on account of the shelter which the wooded mountains afford to the knights of the road, and to whose predilection for these wild solitudes, the number of crosses bore witness. In a woody defile there is a small clear space called 'Las Cruces,' where several wooden crosses point out the site of the famous battle between the curate Hidalgo and the Spanish General Truxillo. An object really in keeping with the wild scenery, was the head of the celebrated robber *Maldonado*, nailed to the pine-tree beneath which he committed his last murder. It is now quite black, and grins there, a warning to his comrades and an encouragement to travellers. From the age of ten to that of fifty, he followed the honourable profession of free-trader, when he expiated his crimes. The padre who was in the coach with us, told us that he heard his last confession. That grinning skull was once the head of a man, and an ugly one too, they say; but stranger still it is to think, that that man was once a baby, and sat on his mother's knee, and that his mother may have been pleased to see him cut his *first tooth*. If she could but see his teeth now!

The famous fleas of Valladolid

I ought not to omit, in talking of the natural productions of Valladolid, to mention that it is famous for *fleas*. We had been alarmed by the miraculous stories related to us of these vivacious animals, and were rejoiced to find ourselves in a house, from which, by dint of extreme care, they are banished. But in the inns and inferior houses they are said to be a perfect pestilence, sometimes literally walking away with a piece of matting upon the floor, and covering the walls in myriads. The nuns, it is said, are or were in the habit of harnessing them to little carriages, and of showing them off by other ingenious devices.

JOHN LLOYD STEPHENS
(1805–1852)

American writer and traveller. He travelled widely in Europe, the Middle East and Central America. In 1839 Stephens, and his companion the English artist Frederick Catherwood, after travelling through the dense, fever-ridden jungles of Honduras, discovered the lost Mayan city of Copán. The city was completely overgrown. Its courtyard, with fourteen intricately carved stone idols, masterpieces of Mayan art; its tiered walls; its pyramids; its immense ball court in which the Mayans played the disagreeable game called Pok-Ta-Pok (the losing side were sometimes slaughtered) – all were buried under vast masses of vegetation. The travellers did not even have an axe. The only cutting instruments were some machetes wielded by listless Indians. But what Stephens did manage to find under the vegetation convinced him that he must return without delay with proper tools and live on the site. The six thousand acres of forest in which the city stood was held by a local man on a lease that had three years to run. Stephens promptly bought the unexpired portion.

Exploring the ruins of Copán

It is impossible to describe the interest with which I explored these ruins. The ground was entirely new; there were no guidebooks or guides; the whole was a virgin soil. We could not see ten yards before us, and never knew what we should stumble upon next. At one time we stopped to cut away branches and vines, which concealed the face of a monument, and dig around and bring to light a fragment, a sculptured corner of which protruded from the earth. I leaned over with breathless anxiety while the Indians worked, and an eye, an ear, a foot, or a hand was disentombed; and when the machete rang against the chiseled stone, I pushed the Indians away and cleared out the loose earth with my hands. The beauty of the sculpture, the solemn stillness of the woods disturbed only by the scrambling of monkeys and the chattering of parrots, the desolation of the city, and the mystery that hung over it, all created an interest higher, if possible, than I had ever felt among the ruins of the Old World. After several hours' absence I returned to Mr. Catherwood and reported upward of fifty objects to be copied.

I found him not so well pleased as I had expected with my report. Standing with his feet in the mud, he was drawing with his gloves on to protect his hands from the mosquitoes. As we feared, the designs were so intricate and complicated, the subjects so entirely new and unintelligible that he was having great difficulty in drawing. He had made several attempts both with the camera lucida and without, but failed to satisfy himself or even me, who was less severe in criticism. The idol seemed to defy his art; two monkeys on a tree on one side appeared to be laughing at him, and I felt discouraged and despondent. In fact, I made up my mind with a pang of regret that we must abandon the idea of carrying away any materials for antiquarian speculation, and must be content with having seen them ourselves. Of that satisfaction nothing could deprive us.

Buying an old city

The reader is perhaps curious to know how old cities sell in Central America. Like other articles of trade, they are regulated by the quantity in the market and the demand; but, not being staple articles like cotton and indigo, they were held at fancy prices, and at that time were dull of sale. I paid fifty dollars for Copán. There was never any difficulty about price. I offered that sum, for which Don José María thought me only a fool; if I had offered more, he would probably have considered me something worse.

CHARLES DARWIN
(1809–1882)

English naturalist. After studying medicine at Edinburgh and for the priesthood at Cambridge, he was appointed official naturalist on the *Beagle* in 1831 and set off on a five-year voyage to chart the coast of South America. Darwin's discoveries on this journey were the first stage in his formulation of the theory of evolution.

Natives of Tierra del Fuego, December 1832

While going one day on shore near Wollaston Island, we pulled alongside a canoe with six Fuegians. These were the most abject and miserable creatures I anywhere beheld. On the east coast the natives, as we have seen, have guanaco cloaks, and on the west, they possess seal-skins. Amongst these central tribes the men generally have an otter-skin, or some small scrap about as large as a pocket-handkerchief, which is barely sufficient to cover their backs as low down as their loins. It is laced across the breast by strings, and according as the wind blows, it is shifted from side to side. But these Fuegians in the canoe were quite naked, and even one full-grown woman was absolutely so. It was raining heavily, and the fresh water, together with the spray, trickled down her body. In another harbour not far distant, a woman, who was suckling a recently-born child, came one day alongside the vessel, and remained there out of mere curiosity, whilst the sleet fell and thawed on her naked bosom, and on the skin of her naked baby! These poor wretches were stunted in their growth, their hideous faces bedaubed with white paint, their skins filthy and greasy, their hair entangled, their voices discordant, and their gestures violent. Viewing such men, one can hardly make oneself believe that they are fellow-creatures, and inhabitants of the same world. It is a common subject of conjecture what pleasure in life some of the lower animals can enjoy: how much more reasonably the same question may be asked with respect to these barbarians! At night, five or six human beings, naked and scarcely protected from the wind and rain of this tempestuous climate, sleep on the wet ground coiled up like animals. Whenever it is low water, winter or summer, night or day, they must rise to pick shell-fish from the rocks; and the women either dive to collect sea-eggs, or sit patiently in their canoes, and with a baited hair-line without any hook, jerk out little fish. If a seal is killed, or the floating carcass of a putrid whale discovered, it is a feast; and such miserable food is assisted by a few tasteless berries and fungi.

A severe earthquake on the coast of Chile, February 1835

February 20th. – This day has been memorable in the annals of Valdivia, for the most severe earthquake experienced by the oldest inhabitant. I happened to be on shore, and was lying down in the wood to rest myself. It came on suddenly, and lasted two minutes, but the time appeared much longer. The rocking of the ground was very sensible. The undulations appeared to my companion and myself to come from due east, whilst others thought they proceeded from south-west: this shows how difficult it sometimes is to perceive the direction of the vibrations. There was no difficulty in standing upright, but the motion made me almost giddy: it was something like the movement of a vessel in a little cross-ripple, or still more like that felt by a person skating over thin ice, which bends under the weight of his body.

A bad earthquake at once destroys our oldest associations: the earth, the very emblem of solidity, has moved beneath our feet like a thin crust over a fluid; – one second of time has created in the mind a strange idea of insecurity, which hours of reflection would not have produced.

ALFRED RUSSEL WALLACE
(1823–1913)

English naturalist. Beginning his career as a schoolmaster in Leicester, Wallace was inspired by reading the works of von Humboldt and Darwin to set off in 1848 to Brazil. His companion, Henry Walter Bates, was similarly inspired and together they travelled up the Tocantins, a 1680-mile-long river that rises on the central plateau of Brazil. The next year they went up the Amazon, travelling separately, and thereafter each man explored on his own. From his studies, Wallace evolved a concept of evolution similar to Darwin's.

A boa-constrictor for four shillings and sixpence, August 1848

We received a fresh inmate into our verandah in the person of a fine young boa constrictor. A man who had caught it in the forest left it for our inspection. It was tightly tied round the neck to a good-sized stick, which hindered the freedom of its movements, and appeared nearly to stop respiration. It was about ten feet long, and very large, being as thick as a man's thigh. Here it lay writhing about for two or three days, dragging its clog along with it, sometimes stretching its mouth open with a most suspicious yawn, and twisting up the end of its tail into a very tight curl. At length we agreed with the man to purchase it for two milreis (4s. 6d.), and having fitted up a box with bars at the top, got the seller to put it into the cage. It immediately began making up for lost time by breathing most violently, the expirations sounding like high-pressure steam escaping from a Great Western locomotive. This it continued for some hours, making about four and a half inspirations per minute, and then settled down into silence, which it afterwards maintained unless when disturbed or irritated.

The advantages of a stay at Javita on the Rio Negro

I would . . . strongly recommend Javita to any naturalist wishing for a good unexplored locality in South America. It is easily reached from the West Indies to Angostura, and thence up the Orinooko and Atabápo. A pound's worth of fish-hooks, and five pounds laid out in salt, beads, and calico, will pay all expenses there for six months. The traveller should arrive in September, and can then stay till March, and will have the full benefit of the whole of the dry season. The insects alone would well repay any one; the fishes are also abundant, and very new and interesting; and, as my collections were lost on the voyage home, they would have all the advantage of novelty.

HENRY WALTER BATES
(1825–1892)

English naturalist and explorer. A clerk in a brewery at Burton-on-Trent, he went to Brazil with Alfred Russel Wallace in 1848. When he returned eleven years later he had collected more than 14,000 zoological specimens, 8000 of which were hitherto unknown.

The tropical day at Para, Brazil

We used to rise soon after dawn, when Isidoro would go down to the city, after supplying us with a cup of coffee, to purchase the fresh provisions for the day. The two hours before breakfast were devoted to ornithology. At that early period of the day the sky was invariably cloudless (the thermometer marking 72° or 73° Fahr.); the heavy dew or the previous night's rain, which lay on the moist foliage, becoming quickly dissipated by the glowing sun, which rising straight out of the east, mounted rapidly towards the zenith. All nature was fresh, new leaf and flower-buds expanding rapidly. Some mornings a single tree would appear in flower amidst what was the preceding evening a uniform green mass of forest – a dome of blossom suddenly created as if by magic. The birds were all active; from the wild-fruit trees, not far off, we often heard the shrill yelping of the Toucans (Ramphastos vitellinus). Small flocks of parrots flew over on most mornings, at a great height, appearing in distinct relief against the blue sky, always two by two chattering to each other, the pairs being separated by regular intervals; their bright colours, however, were not apparent at that height. After breakfast we devoted the hours from 10 a.m. to 2 or 3 p.m. to entomology; the best time for insects in the forest being a little before the greatest heat of the day.

The heat increased rapidly towards two o'clock (92° and 93° Fahr.), by which time every voice of bird or mammal was hushed; only in the trees was heard at intervals the harsh whirr of a cicada. The leaves, which were so moist and fresh in early morning, now become lax and drooping; the flowers shed their petals. Our neighbours the Indian and Mulatto inhabitants of the open palm-thatched huts, as we returned home fatigued with our ramble, were either asleep in their hammocks or seated on mats in the shade, too languid even to talk. On most days in June and July a heavy shower would fall some time in the afternoon, producing a most welcome coolness. The approach of the rain-clouds was after a uniform fashion very interesting to observe. First, the cool sea-breeze, which commenced to blow about ten o'clock, and which had increased in force with the increasing power of the sun, would flag and finally die away. The heat and electric tension of the atmosphere would then become almost insupportable. Languor and uneasiness would seize on every one; even the denizens of the forest betraying it by their motions. White clouds would appear in the east and gather into cumuli, with an increasing blackness along their lower portions. The whole eastern horizon would become almost suddenly black, and this would spread upwards, the sun at length becoming obscured. Then the rush of a mighty wind is heard through the forest, swaying the tree-tops; a vivid flash of lightning bursts forth, then a crash of thunder, and down streams the deluging rain. Such storms soon cease, leaving bluish-black motionless clouds in the sky until night. Meantime all nature is refreshed; but heaps of flower-petals and fallen leaves are seen under the trees. Towards evening life revives again, and the ringing uproar is resumed from bush and tree. The following morning the sun again rises in cloudless sky, and so the cycle is completed; spring, summer, and autumn, as it were, in one tropical day.

FREDERICK JAMES
STEVENSON
(1835–1926)

Scottish traveller. An engineer, he worked on the construction of the Kennet and Avon Canal and the Grand Trunk Railway in Canada, where he gave Thomas Edison his first job (as a train newspaper boy). In 1867–9 he explored Brazil, Peru, Argentina, Patagonia, Chile and Bolivia, enjoying countless hairsbreath escapes and surviving dreadful perils. In August 1868 he witnessed the terrible earthquake and tidal wave that devasted the west coast of South America.

A dilemma

On hearing of the outbreak of a revolution in Monte Video I had some idea of returning there by the first steamer, hoping to be in time to see something of any street-fighting that might still be going on. But on consulting Mr. Haycroft, he strongly advised me not to go, as the affair would most likely be settled and all fighting over before I got there, and I would probably miss a much more important revolution that is expected here in Buenos Ayres, 'which would be an awful sell for you.'

Looting a map of Bolivia in the debris of Arica, Chile, after its destruction by a tidal wave

I now struggled painfully on until at about 3 o'clock I came well in sight of the bay on the shores of which Arica ought to have been, but where now nothing was visible except a half-ruined church tower, and two portions of a rather large wooden building lying some distance apart, but which I found later on to be the two halves of the Hotel de Europa, in which I had slept just a week ago. . . .

Tired as I was, and ravenously hungry as well as thirsty, I hurried down to the Playa, where a drunken mob of hundreds of lawless riff-raff from the late town, as well as Indians and half-breeds from the neighbouring districts, were engaged in looting and fighting over the spoils of the catastrophe. The first thing I noticed was the peculiar grey hue of the sandy shore, caused, as I now found, by countless thousands of paraffin candles and enormous numbers of dead silvery-scaled fishes – killed probably by some great submarine volcanic eruption, and cast upon the shore by the series of earthquake waves that for over two hours had come rolling in from the Pacific Ocean. . . .

At the point where I reached the Playa, I found a bank of wreckage 10 to 15 feet high, composed mostly of fragments of wrecked ships, broken-up wooden houses, doors, window-frames, smashed furniture – amongst which I noticed a cradle, and near it a battered locomotive and the crumpled-up remains of a railway truck and carriages – also a 68-pounder gun (probably from the wrecked U.S. store-ship *Fredonia*) and many heavy iron columns from the large Custom-House building. And on the sands, between this extraordinary bank of wreckage and the sea, scattered about amongst the paraffin candles and the dead fishes, were innumerable smaller and lighter articles of domestic use, and great numbers of boxes and packing-cases of merchandise and stores – mostly broken open and the contents turned out on the sand – amongst them cases of English ale in bottles, a few of which were still unopened, to my infinite relief and refreshment.

Here also I found what was of very considerable importance to me, namely, a large map of Bolivia, mounted on linen and rollers, and nicely coloured and varnished. I had long been enquiring at every considerable town I had visited for a good map of Bolivia, for use in my proposed visit to that country, but always without success, and I had given up all hope of finding one, as I expect to be on my way into the interior in a few days. As I had already, to my great satisfaction, looted somebody's beer, I thought I might as well go a little further, and so without hesitation I annexed that invaluable map of Bolivia, and with as much secrecy as was possible in broad daylight, I carried it back to the railway and buried it carefully in the sandy bed of a dry ditch by the side of the track. I was glad to think that I had not been observed by any of the other looters, who were too busy with their own nefarious proceedings to pay any attention to me, and I returned to the Playa to prosecute my enquiries and search for my friends, rather pluming and congratulating myself on my cleverness and good luck.

I now noticed that a group of looters engaged in breaking open a large packing-case were curiously habited, their ponchos instead of hanging in more or less graceful folds all round their bodies, projecting stiffly and awkwardly from their shoulders, and on closer inspection I was surprised to find that every man of them was wearing a map of Bolivia, torn from its rollers, as a poncho, with the printed, coloured and varnished side outward. The maps being 5×4 feet were just right for size, and with a slit in the middle to poke the head through, made excellent rainproof and highly interesting and instructive, though by no means graceful ponchos.

CECIL GOSLING
(1870–1944)

English diplomat. In his time he held the posts of Honorary Attaché to the Legation at Guatemala, Vice-Consul at Havana, and Envoy Extraordinary and Minister Plenipotentiary to the Republic of Bolivia.

The piranha

Perhaps the most dangerous inhabitant of Paraguayan waters is the *piraña*, which I suspect of causing more loss of life to man and beast than alligators, *surubìs*, or *mangarujùs*, and such like aquatic monsters. The *piraña* is a scaled fish, similar in shape to our European perch, only the head is of more aggressive appearance, the mouth being armed with a most formidable set of teeth, more like those of a wild animal than a fish. With these, and aided by his powerful jaws, there is literally nothing that he will not bite through. I have put a lead pencil into the mouth of one, and seen it bitten clean off, and I have also seen him bite off the edge of a keenly tempered knife. His ferocity is equally developed, and one has to be very careful in handling these demons when caught, and when getting the hooks out of their mouths. When taken out of the water they make a barking noise.

A friend of mine, a police inspector, while bathing, was attacked by a shoal of them, which mutilated him in such a manner that he at once swam back to the bank to the spot where his clothes were, picked up his revolver, and blew out his brains.

ELLERY S. SCOTT
(fl. 1902)

American ship's officer. On the morning of 8 May 1902 he witnessed the eruption of Mount Pelée, Martinique. His ship was destroyed by a rain of volcanic fire and ashes in the harbour of St Pierre. The only survivor in the port was a prisoner in the town jail.

The eruption of Mount Pelée

The saloon and the after end of the ship blazed up at once. The *Roraima* was lying with a heavy list to starboard, pointing towards the shore. Hot ashes fell thick at first. They were soon followed by a rain of small, hot stones, ranging all the way from the size of shot to pigeons' eggs. These would drop in the water with a hissing sound; but where they struck the ship's deck they did little damage, for the decks were protected with a thick coating of ashes from the first outburst. After the stones came a rain of hot mud, lava apparently mixed with water, of the consistency of very thin cement. Wherever it fell it formed a coating, clinging like glue, so that those who wore no caps it coated, making a complete cement mask right over their heads. For myself, when I saw the storm coming I snatched a tarpaulin cover off one of the ventilators and jammed it down over my head and neck, looking out through the opening. This saved me much, but even so my beard, face, nostrils, and eyes were so filled with the stuff that every few seconds I had to break it out of my eyes in order to see. This mud was not actually burning, but it steamed, and there was heat enough in it to dry on the head and form a crust so that it fitted like a plaster cast. . . .

Everybody was not on deck at this time. Some of the passengers were dressing, some still in their bunks. In some cases they were poisoned almost instantaneously by the noxious gas. In others they were drowned by the water which swept in hot through the open port-holes of the submerged staterooms on the starboard side.

The darkness was appalling, only lit by the flames from the after-end of the ship and by the lurid glare of the conflagration on shore when some big warehouse caught fire, and the great puncheons of rum burst with a loud report and shot their blazing contents into the air. At this time I went to the lower bridge, feeling my way along, in order to find the captain. There on the bridge I almost stumbled on a crouching figure with a hideous face, burned almost beyond recognition.

'Who are you?' I cried, for I did not know him, crouched there in the darkness.

The man looked up, his face terrible to see.

'Mr. Scott,' he said, 'don't you know me?'

I said, 'My God, it's the captain!'

ALDOUS HUXLEY
(1894–1963)

English novelist and essayist. During the 1920s he travelled widely in Europe, Asia and America. His 1933 journey to the West Indies, Guatemala and Mexico is described in *Beyond the Mexique Bay* (1934).

The disappointing pitch lake of Trinidad

My conception of the pitch lake of Trinidad was formed in child-hood and had been modified by no subsequent accession of knowledge. I had only to shut my eyes and murmur the words, 'pitch lake of Trinidad,' to see a black tarn, boiling hot, and surrounded by appalling precipices. My private pitch lake looked, in fact, like one of Doré's illustrations to the *Inferno*. Imagine, then, my disappointment with the real, the public pitch lake. For the real pitch lake is simply about two hundred asphalt tennis courts, in very bad condition, set in the midst of some gently undulating green meadows. I felt inclined to ask for my money back.

SYBILLE BEDFORD
(1911–   )

English writer. Her books include *A Legacy*, the biography of Aldous Huxley, and a delightful account of a journey to Mexico, *A Visit to Don Otavio*.

Mexico City

The first impact of Mexico City is physical, immensely physical. Sun, Altitude, Movement, Smells, Noise. And it is inescapable. There is no taking refuge in one more insulating shell, no use sitting in the hotel bedroom fumbling with guide books: it is here, one is in it. A dazzling live sun beats in through a window; geranium scented white-washed cool comes from the patio; ear-drums are fluttering, dizziness fills the head as one is bending over a suitcase, one *is* eight thousand feet above the sea and the air one breathes is charged with lightness. So dazed, tempted, buoyed, one wanders out and like the stranger at the party who was handed a very large glass of champagne at the door, one floats along the streets in uncertain bliss, swept into rapids of doing, hooting, selling. Everything is agitated, crowded, spilling over; the pavements are narrow and covered with fruit. As one picks one's way over mangoes and avocado pears, one is tumbled into the gutter by a water-carrier, avoids a Buick saloon and a basin of live charcoal, skips up again scaring a tethered chicken, shies from an exposed deformity and bumps into a Red Indian gentleman in a tight black suit. Now a parrot shrieks at one from an upper window, lottery tickets flutter in one's face, one's foot is trodden on by a goat and one's skirt clutched at by a baby with the face of an idol. A person long confined to the consistent North may well imagine himself returned to one of the large Mediterranean ports, Naples perhaps: there are the people at once lounging and pressing, there is that oozing into the streets of business and domesticity; the show of motor traffic zigzagged by walking beasts; the lumps of country life, peasants and donkey carts, jars and straw, pushing their way along the pavements; there are the over-flowing trams, the size and blaze of the Vermouth advertisements, the inky office clothes, the rich open food shops strung with great hams and cheeses, and the shoddy store with the mean bedroom suite; the ragged children, the carved fronts of palaces and the seven gimcrack skyscrapers. Nothing is lacking: monster cafés, Carpet Turks, the plate-glass window of the aeroplane agency, funeral wreaths for sale at every corner and that unconvincing air of urban modernity. One looks, one snuffs, one breathes – familiar, haunting, long-missed, memories and present merge, and for a happy quarter of an hour one is plunged into the loved element of lost travels. Then Something Else creeps in. Something Else was always here. These were not the looks, not the gestures. Where is the openness of Italy, that ready bosom? This summer does not have the Southern warmth, that round hug as from a fellow creature. Here, a vertical sun aims at one's head like a dagger – how well the Aztecs read its nature – while the layers of the air remain inviolate like mountain streams, cool, fine, flowing, as though refreshed by some bubbling spring. Europe is six thousand miles across the seas and this glacier city in a tropical latitude has never, never been touched by the Mediterranean. In a minor, a comfortable, loop-holed, mitigated way, one faces what Cortez faced in the absolute five hundred years ago: the unknown.

The newest hotel in Guadalajara

We pulled up in front of a large and beautiful sixteenth-century palace. 'Hotel Guzman,' said Anthony. 'Don't worry, it's all fixed up new inside. You've never seen such bathrooms. Solid black marble.'

We all shot up in a small, fast lift. The manager flung open a door and ushered us into a splendid apartment full of divan beds and somebody's clothes.

'Why that's *my* room,' said Anthony.

'Yes, Sir. I had beds for the ladies moved in while you were absent.'

'Now, see here . . .' said Anthony.

E. took over. 'We do not want to be three in a room,' she said gently.

'No room for three? But the gentleman said he was expecting two ladies.'

'Yes, and here we are. But you see we don't want all three to share one room.'

'That is all right, Señora. It is a large room. In Holy Week when there are many travellers we would have a family of seven, nine persons in such a room. And their servants in the bathroom.'

'But this isn't Holy Week.'

'It is not, Señora. In Holy Week there would be a family and servants in every room, now it is only one gentleman and two ladies. It costs more in Holy Week, too.'

'Look here,' I said, 'we have strange habits and we want two, or at least one other room. Have you got them?'

'Yes, yes, many rooms. We are the newest hotel in Guadalajara.'

'Well, can we see them?'

'They are very new, Señora. More new than this room. We are still working on the newness.'

After a good deal more of this, a bed for Anthony was moved into a cupboard leading out of our room. The cupboard had a window, but it opened into a corridor. Ours had an open view over red-tiled roof tops and a brilliant nocturnal sky. The night was warmer than it had been in Morelia. We were very hungry.

A cry of distress from E. in the bathroom. 'My dear, I can't make the water run. Do try.'

Indeed: hot tap, cold tap, tub and basin, not a drop. There was a telephone on the wall, I picked it up.

'There doesn't seem to be any water in our bathroom.'

'Of course not, Señora. It has not been laid on. One thing after another. Perhaps next year? Yes, certainly next year. If we do well. You will recommend us?'

Ready first, I proceeded to go downstairs. I walked up the corridor, none too well-lit, then saw, caught myself, and knees buckling reeled a step backward, collapsed against a wall and howled for Anthony.

He came running. 'What's the matter?'

'THERE ARE NO STAIRS.'

'Well, what d'you want stairs for?'

'I was about to go down.'

'What's wrong with the elevator?'

'Oh God, Anthony, don't be so yourself. And don't let's have a Mexican conversation. Go and see . . . No, don't go! Be careful!'

Anthony went a few steps up the corridor. 'Jesus Christ,' he said.

The corridor ended in space. Seventy feet below, at the bottom of the crater left by flights of marble recently ripped out, lay invisible in a dim pool of light the reception desk, the leather armchairs and the spittoons of the entrance hall. Between, a void. They had begun working on the newness on the top floor. Anthony and I fetched E. from the room and we all went down in the lift.

RICHARD BISSELL
(1913–   )

American writer and playwright. After graduating from Harvard University he worked as a seaman on a freighter. He later became the only author since Mark Twain to have secured a pilot's licence on the Upper Mississippi. After retiring from the river he worked in a pyjama factory; his book about his experiences there, *A Gross of Pyjamas*, became the hit musical *The Pajama Game*.

The ruins of Pachácamac, Peru

Chumpitazi took us to Pachácamac in his Pontiac taxicab. It is twenty miles from Lima. Chumpitazi said he would take us there and back for 100 soles. Chumpitazi grinned horribly. I was afraid that Chumpitazi was a bandit. But he was a nice man; under his ferocious moustache and beak he spoke Spanish C-L-E-A-R-L-Y and S-L-O-W-L-Y so that all members of the class could understand exactly what Chumpitazi was saying. *Nos gustaba mucho Chumpitazi.*

As ruins go, Pachácamac is undoubtedly the most ruinous. Frankly, it's a mess. Once a terraced temple rising high above the Pacific beach and the Lurin River valley, it is now a gigantic pile of dust and rubble and stone walls. After leaving Chumpitazi in the Pontiac blissfully puffing an American cigarette, we walked up and up to the summit through meadows of dust; we were ankle deep in bones, shards of pottery, and fragments of mummy wrappings. No one is in attendance, there are no guards, and one's pockets seem to fill mysteriously with human jaw fragments, finger bones, and strips of ancient winding sheets as one literally wades through acres of funerary remains. In a few places pieces of wall outcrop in the midst of general desolation, revealing the original stucco in rose-red, chrome-yellow and blue. From the summit there is an astonishing view. With your shoes full of sand and powdered Incas dead five hundred years, you look out over another queer-scape. Sands, gloomy dusty fine-grained sands, stretch all round about. Then, facing west, you see the Pacific far below, its waves breaking in long rollers. To the south is a green river valley, while over in the east rise the Andes.

There is really nothing that I have heard of like this combination of haunted desert, sea, ruins, river and mountains anywhere in the world but in Peru. Another answer to Why I Like Peru. Besides, it is so astonishing to be here. One *expects* to find oneself sometime or other staring goggle-eyed with sentiment at Paris from the Eiffel Tower, one knows that of course some day one will be on the Gorner Grat, in Piccadilly, Pisa, Trondheim and Tilsit; but one does NOT expect to be in Peru.

Chumpitazi apologized for Pachácamac. He said it wasn't his fault that it was all busted. On the way back to Lima we saw Indian women sitting by the road in piles of picked cotton; they were pulling out the seeds by hand. Yes, they have heard of cousin Eli Whitney, but nobody has got the dough to buy a cotton gin. And if they have the dough they don't spend it on a cotton gin anyway because it would give the workers wrong ideas.

PATRICK LEIGH FERMOR
(1915–   )

English traveller, soldier and writer. (See p. 186.)

Arrival at Pointe-à-Pitre, Guadeloupe, c. 1948

Half an hour later the *Colombie*, that congenial ship, was preparing to weigh anchor, and we were sitting in the lounge of the Hôtel des Antilles. We had followed the elderly Negro who pushed our luggage up the main street of Pointe-à-Pitre. The heat was so intense that our clothes had stuck to our arms and legs; nearly everybody, we observed, was wearing open shirts and shorts or cotton trousers. The brilliance of the sunlight made all the shadows appear black and profound, and the change of temperature when walking into the shade was as welcome as a waterfall. All the way to the hotel we had not passed one white person. This, and the dazzling robes of the older women, the hundreds of black faces, the sound on every side of the odd new language, most of whose words were French but whose tenor was incomprehensible, this, and the murderous heat, invested the place with an atmosphere of entire strangeness. Even at eleven in the morning a heavy tropical languor weighed on the air. The streets had grown emptier every moment.

With slow enjoyment we ate the fruit we had bought in the market. The bananas were gigantic but commonplace. The soursops were about the size of a child's football, tapering into the shape of a pear, and covered with a dark rind roughened with innumerable little hooked briers. The fruit inside was semi-liquid and snow white, expelling an aroma faintly resembling peardrops, and wringing our dusty palates with a delicious and slightly acid astringency. The paw-paw, which we next opened, was roughly the same size, but the soft rind was a smooth, patchy gold in colour, mottled with green and rusty brown. We halved it lengthways, and discovered two deep oblongs of a dewy, coral-coloured fruit of a consistency miraculously poised between solidity and liquescence; much sweeter than the soursop, and, I thought, even better. Its sweetness is mitigated and, as it were, underlined by the faintest tang of something sharper – was it creosote or turpentine? – but so slight that one loses the identity of the taste while attempting to define it. Pushing the ruins aside, we each chose an avocado pear: dark green or violet globes the size of cricket balls, enclosed in a hard and warty carapace. The knives made a sharp tearing noise as we opened them. In the centre, loose in their hollows, lay big round stones, completely spherical and smooth and very heavy. I hated throwing them away, they seemed so perfect and neat, and somehow important, but except as embryonic avocado trees, they are useless . . . The pale green fruit clung to the shell with a consistency half-way between butter and plasticine.

Our ejaculations of delight must have been unusual, for two wide-eyed Guadeloupean waitresses made occasional bird-like titters. They were a mahogany colour, barefoot, and dressed in white, with aprons and turbans of marmalade-coloured tartan. They talked to each other in the same lingo as our porter, but addressed us in a prim rather old-fashioned French mysteriously lacking in R-sounds.

The world outside the windows had by now become a calcinated desert from which the perpendicular sun had driven every inch of shade. The palm trees, overtopping the corrugated iron roofs, stood motionless in a pale blue haze. The two maids showed us upstairs to our rooms, large wooden barns with no furniture except the beds under their milky tents of netting. I climbed inside and began cutting the pages of the memoirs of Père Labat, a French Dominican who lived in these islands at the end of the seventeenth century, but even the lively prose of this extraordinary monk failed to keep me awake for long. . . . I was about to fall asleep when a metallic uproar in the street brought me to the window. It was the rattle of rain on the roofs of Pointe-à-Pitre. The street had become a river of slime, bubbling and swirling under a wavering wall of water. But it was soon over and in five minutes the sun had dried up every trace of moisture, and all was arid and dusty again.

SEBASTIAN SNOW
(1928–   )

English traveller and explorer. One of the last of the truly amateur adventurers, he has made some epic solo journeys in South America. On his first trip he followed the Amazon from source to mouth; next he climbed Cotopaxi, the highest volcano on earth, and Chimborazo, the highest mountain in Ecuador. Later, in 1968, he attempted to recreate the epic journey made 425 years before by Francisco de Orellana, who had crossed South America from west to east at its widest point. It was a journey Snow was lucky to survive.

'There are no brakes on a raft' – going down the Coca River, Ecuador, 1968

But then, perhaps repenting of its indulgence on the 13th, Fate struck the cruellest – and most decisive – blow of all. Clambering up an eight-foot slippery black rock on the foreshore, I fell backwards and twisted my leg. When I got up and tried to walk, the leg collapsed under me and sent me sprawling on the ground. It felt as if somebody was skewering my flesh with red-hot needles. I had in fact torn a group of tendons below my right knee.

I rested and tried to walk again. But every time my weight fell on the injured leg, I ended up in an undignified heap on the ground. It was particularly frustrating because I was going well at the time.

I urged Romulo to leave me there and send back help as soon as he reached Coca. It was the only sensible thing to do!

Nevertheless, I felt a surge of relief when he categorically refused. He was that sort of man.

Obviously, since I could no longer walk and it was impossible to carry me along the river bank, there was only one solution: we must take to the river again! The current looked dangerously strong, but the Coca made a right-angled turn a couple of hundred yards ahead. From my experiences on the Marañon, I deduced that, beyond it, the river would very probably widen out into a flat reach of comparative tranquillity. Once more, the Indians set about constructing a raft, in which they had little faith and less option – brave men.

This time they did find some balsa – not enough for a whole raft, but sufficient to give us five stout poles. We added four more of the harder *perchica*, lashed our remaining possessions aboard and dragged ourselves on after. It was April 17th, and my prognostications about the probable course of the river around the bend could not have hardly been further from reality.

As soon as the raft floated away from the bank, it was drawn into the maw of a whirlpool near the littoral. We described three complete circles, the Indians paddling furiously and in vain before the craft tore itself free and spun off into the main current.

The raft seemed comfortably stable after our last effort but there was no time for the slightest complacency. We were being swept along at what seemed a terrifying speed, probably fifteen to twenty miles per hour, and all my companions' efforts were powerless to affect our course.

Within seconds we were heading straight for a sentinel boulder embedded in the stream. We hit it with a jarring crunch, lurched off to one side, spun round, and were then carried on downstream.

Somehow, the tough flexible creepers held and the raft did not break up immediately. But then, as we swirled around the corner of the gorge at a near ninety-degree angle, I saw that we were doomed.

Instead of the broad Thames-like reach I had postulated, we were faced with a considerable cataract – a roar and a rush of foaming white horses leaping high into the air between narrowing walls of rock and jungle.

There are no brakes on a raft. We could not get off. We were absolutely committed (an uneasy feeling), powerless to alter course with the rough-hewn paddles, now mere symbols of 'despair'. For a few crazy seconds, we rode the storm, bucking and jumping in the inferno of waters like a steer unleashed at its first rodeo. Then came a particularly violent shock and the raft shuddered as if stricken. I was hurled headlong to the outer edge of the poles. I lost my grip and the thunder of the river came up to meet me.

V. S. NAIPAUL
(1931–   )

Trinidadian novelist and essayist. Of Indian parentage, he settled in England in 1950. He has travelled widely in the West Indies, North and South America, India and Africa. In 1960 he returned to Trinidad, and then travelled on to British Guiana, Surinam, Martinique and Jamaica, recording his observations in *The Middle Passage* (1962).

Port of Spain, Trinidad:
the noisiest city in the world

Port of Spain is the noisiest city in the world. Yet it is forbidden to talk. 'Let the talkies do the talking,' the signs used to say in the old London Theatre of my childhood. And now the radios and the rediffusion sets do the talking, the singing, the jingling; the steel bands do the booming and the banging; and the bands, live or tape-recorded, and the gramophones and record-players. In restaurants the bands are there to free people of the need to talk. Stunned, temples throbbing, you champ and chew, concentrating on the working of your jaw muscles. In a private home as soon as anyone starts to talk the radio is turned on. It must be loud, loud. If there are more than three, dancing will begin. Sweat-sweat-dance-dance-sweat. Loud, loud, louder. If the radio isn't powerful enough, a passing steel band will be invited in. Jump-jump-sweat-sweat-jump. In every house a radio or rediffusion set is on. In the street people conduct conversations at a range of twenty yards or more; and even when they are close to you their voices have a vibrating tuning-fork edge. You will realize this only after you have left Trinidad: the voices in British Guiana will sound unnaturally low, and for the first day or so whenever anyone talks to you you will lean forward conspiratorially, for what is being whispered is, you feel, very secret. In the meantime dance, dance, shout above the shuffle. If you are silent the noise will rise to a roar about you. You cannot shout loud enough. Your words seem to be issuing from behind you. You have been here only an hour, but you feel as exhausted as though you had spent a day in some Italian scooter-hell. Your head is bursting. It is only eleven; the party is just warming up. You are being rude, but you must go.

You drive up the new Lady Young Road, and the diminishing noise makes it seem cooler. You get to the top and look out at the city glittering below you, amber and exploding blue on black, the ships in the harbour in the background, the orange flames issuing from the oil derricks far out in the Gulf of Paria. For a moment it is silent. Then, above the crickets, whose stridulation you hadn't noticed, you begin to hear the city: the dogs, the steel bands. You wait until the radio stations have closed down for the night – but rediffusion sets, for which there is a flat rental, are never turned off: they remain open, to await the funnelling of the morning noise – and then you wind down into the city again, drowning in the din. All through the night the dogs will go on, in a thousand inextricably snarled barking relays, rising and falling, from street to street and back again, from one end of the city to another. And you will wonder how you stood it for eighteen years, and whether it was always like this.

HUNTER S. THOMPSON
(fl. 1966–   )

American writer and journalist. He began his career as a sports journalist, then worked in the Caribbean and South America before joining the subject of his first book, the Hell's Angels of California. He is best known for that unorthodox book of travel writing, *Fear and Loathing in Las Vegas* (1971).

The first tourist in Puerto Estrella, Colombia

I arrived at dusk on a fishing sloop from Aruba. And since there is no harbour I was put ashore in a tiny rowboat. Above us, on a sharp cliff, stood the entire population of the village, staring grimly and without much obvious hospitality at Puerto Estrella's first tourist in history.

In Aruba, the Guajiro Indians are described as 'fierce and crazy and drunk all day on coconut whisky'. Also in Aruba you will hear that the men wear 'nothing but neckties, knotted just below the navel'. That sort of information can make a man uneasy, and as I climbed the steep path, staggering under the weight of my luggage, I decided that at the first sign of unpleasantness I would begin handing out neckties like Santa Claus – three fine paisleys to the most menacing of the bunch, then start ripping up shirts.

As I came over the brink of the cliff, a few children laughed, an old hag began screeching, and the men just stared. Here was a white man with twelve Yankee dollars in his pocket and more than $500 worth of camera gear slung over his shoulders, hauling a typewriter, grinning, sweating, no hope of speaking the language, no place to stay – and somehow they were going to have to deal with me. . . .

There is not much for the tourist in Puerto Estrella, no hotels, restaurants, or souvenirs. Nor is the food palatable. Three times a day I faced it – leaves, maize, and severely salted goat meat, served up with muddy water.

The drinking was a problem too, but in a different way. At the crack of dawn on the day after my arrival I was awakened and taken before a jury of village bigwigs. Its purpose was to determine the meaning of my presence. These gentlemen had gathered in the only concrete-block house in town, and before them on the table was a cellophane-wrapped bottle of Scotch whisky.

After an hour or so of gestures, a few words of Spanish, and nervous demonstrations of my camera equipment, they seemed to feel a drinking bout was in order. The Scotch was opened, five jiggers were filled, and the ceremony began.

It continued all that day and all the next. They tossed it off straight in jiggers, solemnly at first and then with mounting abandon. Now and then one of them would fall asleep in a hammock, only to return a few hours later with new thirst and vigour. At the end of one bottle they would proudly produce another, each one beautifully wrapped in cellophane.

As it turned out, three things made my visit a success. One was my size and drinking capacity (it was fear – a man travelling alone among reportedly savage Indians dares not get drunk); another was the fact that I never turned down a request for a family portrait (fear, again); and the third was my 'lifelong acquaintance' with Jacqueline Kennedy, whom they regard as some sort of goddess. . . .

Trying to leave can turn a man's hair white. You are simply stuck until one of the Indians has to run some contraband down the peninsula to Maicao.

There is nothing to do but drink, and after fifty hours of it I began to lose hope. The end seemed to be nowhere in sight; and it is bad enough to drink Scotch all day in any climate, but to come to the tropics and start belting it down for three hours each morning before breakfast can bring on a general failure of health. In the mornings we had Scotch and arm-wrestling; in the afternoons, Scotch and dominoes.

The break came at dusk on the third day, when the owner of a truck called the Power Wagon rose abruptly from the drinking table and said we would leave immediately. . . .

The drive from Puerto Estrella to Maicao is ten to twelve hours, depending on which rut you take, but it seems like forty days on the rack. On top of the heinous discomfort, there is the distinct possibility of being attacked and shot up by either bandits or the law. As far as the *contrabandista* is concerned, one is as bad as the other.

We rumbled into Maicao at three in the afternoon. They dropped me at the airport, where my luggage was thoroughly searched by a savage-looking gendarme before I was allowed on the plane for Barranquilla. An hour later, there was another search at the Barranquilla airport. When I asked why, they replied I was coming from an area called Guajira, known to be populated by killers and thieves and men given over to lives of crime and violence.

I had a feeling that nobody really believed I had been there. When I tried to talk about Guajira, people would smile sympathetically and change the subject. And then we would have another beer, because Scotch is so expensive in Barranquilla that only the rich can afford it.

BRUCE CHATWIN
(1940–   )

English travel-writer and novelist.

Welsh Patagonia

I took the night bus on to the Chubut Valley. By next morning I was in the village of Gaimán, the centre of Welsh Patagonia today. The valley was about five miles wide, a net of irrigated fields and poplar windbreaks, set between the white cliffs of the barranca – a Nile Valley in miniature.

The older houses in Gaimán were of red brick, with sash windows and neat vegetable gardens and ivy trained to grow over the porches. The name of one house was *Nith-y-dryw*, the Wren's Nest. Inside, the rooms were whitewashed and had brown painted doors, polished brass handles and grandfather clocks. The colonists came with few possessions but they clung to their family clocks.

Mrs Jones's teashop lay at the far end of the village where the bridge crossed over to the Bethel. Her plums were ripe and her garden full of roses.

'I can't move, my dear,' she called through. 'You'll have to come and talk to me in the kitchen.'

She was a squat old lady in her eighties. She sat propped up at a scrubbed deal table filling lemon-curd tarts.

'I can't move an inch, my darling. I'm crippled. I've had arthritis since the flood and have to be carried everywhere.'

Mrs Jones pointed to the line where the floodwater came, above the blue-painted dado, on the kitchen wall.

'Stuck in here I was, with the water up to my neck.'

She came out nearly sixty years ago from Bangor in North Wales. She had not left the valley since. She remembered a family I knew in Bangor and said: 'Fancy, it's a small world.'

'You won't believe it,' she said. 'Not to look at me now you won't. But I was a beauty in my day.' And she talked about a laddie from Manchester and his bouquet of flowers and the quarrel and the parting and the ship.

'And how are the morals back home?' she asked. 'Down?'

'Down.'

'And they're down here too. All this killing. You can't tell where it'll end.'

Mrs Jones's grandson helped run the teashop. He ate too much cake for his own good. He called his grandmother 'Granny' but otherwise he did not speak English or Welsh.

I slept in the Draigoch Guest House. It was owned by Italians who played Neapolitan songs on the juke box late into the night.

AUSTRALIA AND
NEW ZEALAND

JAN CARSTENZOON
(fl. 1623)

Dutch navigator. In 1623 he commanded the Dutch East India Company's ships *Pera* and *Arnhem* on a voyage of discovery from Batavia. He crossed the Torres Strait and entered the coastal waters of the Cape York Peninsula, discovered in 1606 by Willem Jantszoon while sailing in a small yacht, the *Duyfken*.

An early encounter with Australian aborigines, Cape Keerweer, Cape York Peninsula, 18 April 1623

. . . The boats having come back, we were informed by the skipper [of the *Pera*], when he had landed with the party, a great lot of blacks (some of them armed and others not) came up to them, and were so forward and appeared so bold that they grasped the muskets of our men and wanted to take them from their shoulders and everything they saw was attractive to them; therefore they were enticed with some iron and corals, and so our people seeing their opportunity, caught a black by a string which was attached round his neck and brought him on board; the rest, who remained on the beach, made a great clamour and hubbub, and others, who were still in the bushes, stayed there; the aforesaid people are pitch black, thin of body and quite naked, with a woven basket or net on their head, and furthermore in hair and stature like the blacks of the Coast of Coromandel, but, so it seems, not so hostile, bold and vicious in disposition as the blacks of the west part of North Guinea. . . .

On the 19th the wind south-east we stayed there, and as the vessels were quite out of firewood, the skipper of the Pera landed with both boats duly manned and armed, and, while the men were chopping, they saw a very large party of blacks, more than 200, coming to them and they were seen to use every device to surprise and beat our men, so that it was necessary to fire two shots, wherefrom they fled and retreated, as one was hit and fell: so our men went some way inland, where they saw some of their weapons and brought them as a novelty. Also while they were marching they saw many human bones in various places, whence it can be firmly presumed that the blacks along Nova Guinea are cannibals and when hungry do not spare others.

ABEL JANSZOON TASMAN
(1603?–1659)

Dutch navigator. He made several voyages of exploration in the Pacific and Indian Oceans in the service of the Dutch East India Company. In 1642 he discovered Tasmania and New Zealand, touched the Tonga Islands and returned to Batavia, having circumnavigated Australia.

Tasmania: the first report, 2 December 1642

. . . They [the sailors sent ashore] had heard certain human sounds, and also sounds nearly resembling the music of a trump, or a small gong, not far from them, though they had seen no one.

. . . They had seen two trees about 2 or 2½ fathom in thickness, measuring from 60 to 65 feet from the ground to the lower-most branches, which trees bore notches made with flint implements, the bark having been removed for the purpose. These notches, forming a kind of steps to enable persons to get up the trees and rob the birds' nests in their tops, were fully 5 feet apart, so that our men concluded that the natives here must be of very tall stature, or must be in possession of some sort of artifice for getting up the said trees. In one of the trees these notched steps were so fresh and new that they seemed to have been cut less than four days ago.

. . . On the ground they had observed certain footprints of animals, not unlike those of a tiger's claws.

WILLIAM DAMPIER
(1652–1715)

English explorer, navigator and buccaneer. In January 1688, while engaged on a buccaneering expedition, he visited the north-western coast of Australia. In May he was marooned, on the Nicobar Islands in the Bay of Bengal. Returning to England in 1691 he published an account of his experiences which brought him wide fame. In 1699 the Admiralty appointed him commander of an expedition to the South Seas and he became the first Englishman to explore the west coast of Australia.

The unfriendly, unfrightened natives of Australia,
31 August 1699

There were 10 or 12 of the Natives a little way off, who seeing us three going away from the rest of our Men, followed us at a distance. I thought they would follow us: But there being for a while a Sand-bank between us and them, that they could not then see us, we made a halt, and hid our selves in a bending of the Sand-bank. They knew we must be thereabouts, and being 3 or 4 times our Number, thought to seize us. So they dispers'd themselves, some going to the Sea-shore, and others beating about the Sand-hills. We knew by what Rencounter we had had with them in the Morning that we could easily out-run them. So a nimble young Man that was with me, seeing some of them near, ran towards them; and they for some time, ran away before him. But he soon over-taking them, they faced about and fought him. He had a Cutlass, and they had wooden Lances; with which, being many of them, they were too hard for him. When he first ran towards them I chas'd two more that were by the Shore: But fearing how it might be with my young Man, I turn'd back quickly, and went up to the top of a Sandhill, whence I saw him near me, closely engag'd with them. Upon their seeing me, one of them threw a Lance at me, that narrowly miss'd me. I discharg'd my Gun to scare them, but avoided shooting any of them; till finding the young Man in great danger from them, and my self in some; and that tho' the Gun had a little frighted them at first, yet they had soon learnt to despise it, tossing up their Hands, and crying Pooh, Pooh, Pooh; and coming on afresh with a great Noise, I thought it high time to charge again, and shoot one of them, which I did. The rest, seeing him fall, made a stand again; and my young Man took the Opportunity to disengage himself, and come off to me. . . .

JAMES COOK
(1728–1779)

English explorer and navigator. The son of a farm labourer, he joined the Royal Navy in 1755. After service in Canada, where he explored the St Lawrence and the coasts of Newfoundland and Labrador, in 1768 he sailed on an expedition to the Pacific to chart the transit of

Venus. When he returned in 1771 he had not only circumnavigated the world, but also explored and charted the coasts of New Zealand and eastern Australia. In 1772 he commanded another expedition to the South Pacific, exploring the Antarctic Ocean and the New Hebrides and disproving the rumour of a great southern continent. He returned to England in 1775, having lost only four men in the 70,000-mile voyage. Less than a year later Cook set sail again, this time his aim being to search for a passage from the Pacific to the Atlantic round North America. After exploring as far as the coasts of Alaska and northern Siberia, he turned for home, but was killed by natives at Hawaii. Cook was a genius: capable, reserved, determined, he was a typical officer of the Royal Navy. The only erratic thing about him was his spelling.

The Maoris demonstrate their cannibalism on board the Resolution, Queen Charlotte Sound, South Island, November 1773

Tuesday 23rd November. Calm or light airs from the Northward so that we could not get to Sea as I intended, some of the officers went on shore to amuse themselves among the Natives where they saw the head and bowels of a youth who had lately been killed, the heart was stuck upon a forked stick and fixed to the head of their largest Canoe, the gentlemen brought the head on board with them, I was on shore at this time but soon after returned on board when I was informed of the above circumstances, and found the quarter deck crowded with the Natives. I now saw the mangled head or rather the remains of it for the under jaw, lips &c were wanting, the scul was broke on the left side just above the temple, the face had all the appearance of a youth about fourteen or fifteen, a peice of the flesh had been broiled and eat by one of the Natives in the presince of most of the officers. The sight of the head and the relation of the circumstances just mentioned struck me with horor and filled my mind with indignation against these Canibals, but when I considered that any resentment I could shew would avail but little and being desireous of being an eye wittness to a fact which many people had their doubts about I concealed my indignation and ordered apiece of the flesh to be broiled and brought on the quarter deck were one of these Canibals eat it with a seeming good relish before the whole ships Company had such effect on some of them as to cause them to vomit. . . . That the New Zealanders are Canibals can now no longer be doubted. . . .

An embarrassing present, New Hebrides, South Pacific, June 1774

Tuesday 28*th* June. I was no sooner return'd from the Pond the first time I landed that this Woman and a Man presented to me a young woman and gave me to understand she was at my Service. Miss, who probably had received her instructions, I found wanted by way of Handsel a Shirt or a Nail, neither the one nor the other I had to give without giving her the Shirt on my back which I was not in a humour to do. I soon made them sencible of my Poverty and thought by that means to have come off with flying Colours but I was mistaken, for I was made to understand that I might retire with her on credit, this not suting me neither the old Lady began first to argue with me and when that fail'd she abused me, I understood very little of what she said, but her actions were expressive enough and shew'd that her words were to this effect: Sneering in my face and saying 'what sort of a man are you thus to refuse the embraces of so fine a young woman', for the girl certainly did not [lack] beauty which I could however withstand, but the abuse of the old Woman I could not and therefore hastned into the Boat, they then would needs have me take the girl on board with me, but this could not be done as I had come to a Resolution not to suffer a Woman to come on Board the ship on any pretence whatever and had given strict orders to the officers to that purpose. . . .

JACQUES-JULIEN HOUTOU DE LA BILLADIERE
(1755–1834)

French naturalist. He accompanied the Chevalier d'Entrecasteaux on his voyage to the Indian Ocean, Tasmania, Australia and the South Seas in 1791. Unfortunately, although assiduous (he collected more than 4000 specimens during the voyage), he was a disagreeable, quarrelsome man and became very unpopular with his shipmates.

Aborigines on the east coast of Tasmania, 1792

We got ready a few cartridges as fast as we could, and set out towards the place where we had seen the aborigines. It was now only nine o'clock. We had gone only a few steps before we met them. The men and the youths were ranged in the front, nearly in a semicircle; the women, the children and then the older girls, were a few paces behind. As their manner did not indicate any hostile design I hesitated not to go up to the oldest, who accepted, with a very good grace, a piece of biscuit that I offered him, of which he had seen me eat. I then held out my hand to him, as a sign of friendship, and had the pleasure of seeing that he understood my meaning very well, he gave me his hand also, at the same time inclining himself a little sort of bow, at the same time as he did this he raised his left foot, which he carried backward in proportion as he bent his body forward. All these motions were accompanied by a very pleasant smile.

My companions seeing this, also advanced up to the other males of the tribe, and immediately the best understanding prevailed. They received with a show of great joy the neckcloths that we offered to them. Then the young people approached near to us, and one of them had the generosity to give me a few small shells, of the welk kind, pierced near the middle, and strung like a necklace. This ornament, that he seemed to call 'canlaride', was the only one that he appeared to possess, and it had been worn round his head. A handkerchief supplied the place of this present, gratifying the utmost wishes of his savage heart, when he advanced towards me I tied it round his head for him, and his countenance expressed the greatest joy, as he lifted up his hand to feel it again and again. . . .

. . . It appeared very astonishing to us that at that high latitude, where, at a period of the year so little advanced as the present, we needed all the clothing that we could wear, that they did not feel the necessity for wearing clothes. Even the women for the most part were entirely naked, as well as the men. Some of the women only had the shoulders, or part of the back, covered with a kangaroo's skin, worn with the hair next to the body, only two had this form of a covering, and each of these had an infant at the breast. . . .

I had given several things to them without thinking, or expecting, anything in return; but I wished to get a kangaroo's skin. Among the aborigines that were around us I could see only one girl who had one. I made signs that implied that if she gave it to me she could have a pair of pantaloons instead, but she ran away to hide herself in the woods. The other aborigines appeared truly hurt at her refusal to give it to me, and called several times for her to come back. At length she yielded to their entreaties, and came to bring me the skin. Perhaps it was from timidity only that she could not prevail on herself to part with the 'garment'. In return she received the pantaloons, less useful to her, according to the customs of the ladies of this country, than the skin, which served to cover the shoulders, which are the particular part, at least among the females, that have to be hid. We showed her the manner of wearing the pantaloons; but notwithstanding this, it was necessary for us to put them on for her ourselves. To this she yielded with the best grace in the world.

FABIAN GOTTLIEB VON BELLINGSHAUSEN
(1779–1852)

Russian naval officer and navigator. Between 1819 and 1821, on an expedition ordered by Tsar Alexander I, he crossed the Antarctic Circle (the first to do so since Cook), penetrating to within twenty miles of the Princess Martha Coast on the Antarctic mainland. He reached the most southerly point so far attained: 69°52'S.

The Russians remark the sobriety of the Maoris, Queen Charlotte Sound, New Zealand, 1820

The old man to whom I had made such lavish presents on the previous day appeared to us to be the Chief. I received him with all the courtesies of the South Sea Islands; we embraced and, by rubbing noses, confirmed our mutual friendship, which we maintained on both sides throughout our stay in Queen Charlotte Sound. As it was our dinner hour, I invited the Chief to come into the cabin and dine with us. We seated him in the place of honour between Mr Lazarev and myself. He examined with astonishment all the table utensils and fingered them, but would not make use of them to eat with until someone gave him an example; then he very cautiously and clumsily began to put his food into his mouth with a fork. He did not seem to care to drink the wine. After dinner we renewed our assurance of friendship for one another by signs and by means of the few words that I knew. But when, wishing to give him a further proof of my good will, I made him a present of a beautiful, well-polished axe, he jumped up from the table overjoyed, and asked to go on deck, whither I accompanied him. There he rushed at once to his compatriots and then embraced me with great delight shouting, 'toki! toki!' (axe! axe!).

We regaled the other New Zealanders on the quarter-deck with biscuits, meat, gruel and rum. They all ate very heartily, but one glass of rum was sufficient for all of them. Such sobriety serves to prove that they can only have been visited rarely by the enlightened Europeans who, wherever they settle, always teach the natives to drink alcoholic liquors, and to smoke and chew tobacco; then, when these ignorant people begin to show the bad effects of strong drink, they start to explain to them how disgraceful it is to give way to drunkenness and other evil habits.

JOHN JOHNSON
(1794–1848)

English doctor. Johnson was New Zealand's first Colonial Surgeon, one of the half dozen officials appointed to assist William Hobson when he was sent to acquire sovereignty over New Zealand and set up British government there in 1840. In 1846–7 Johnson made a journey to the Central Lakes, leaving a detailed account of the trip.

The hot springs of Rotorua, 1847

Jan. 6. We rose at daybreak, and on going out found the whole pa enveloped in vapour, which was rising from the numerous *ngawha*, and we could hear the voices and the splashing, though we could not see the persons, of a number of people in the lake below, who were enjoying the luxury of a bath, in the common bathing-place. Thither we descended and found it nothing less than an arm of the lake, occupying at least an acre in extent, which was heated to a temperature of 96°, both by the streams that flow into it from the *ngawha*, as well as from a large boiling spring in its centre, by approaching, or keeping at a distance from which, the temperature may be varied at pleasure, but in the summer season it is never below what I have stated.

On reaching the edge of the basin, a scene, certainly unique of its kind, presented itself. About a hundred and fifty people of all ages were engaged in bathing, all in a state of nature, with the exception of the women, who, beyond a certain age, wore the *bouraki*, a species of kilt made of flax, reaching from the waist to the knee. In one corner might be seen a group of young women with dripping tresses, like so many Stygian Naiads – in another, a swarm of young urchins, sporting about like so many imps in Dante's Inferno. Here were a party of the seniors of the pa, seated in the water, quietly enjoying their morning pipe – and there, a family from grand-father to grand-child, and mothers with infants at the breast, enjoying this agreeable luxury; but the strangest scene of all was a row of young men sitting up to their necks in water, in front of whom was squatted a man who was asking questions, which were answered by the *posse* in full chorus. I found, on enquiry, that these were a set of young noviciates aspiring to an entrance into the Christian field, who were repeating the *ten commandments* to their teacher, as an initiatory rite.

CHARLES STURT
(1795–1869)

Australian explorer. Having fought in the Peninsular War, Sturt was sent to Australia in charge of a convict escort. In 1828 he discovered the Darling River, then in 1829–30 explored the Murrumbidgee and Murray Rivers, on an expedition which he and his companions were lucky to survive.

A vast concourse of Aborigines, the Murray River, January 1830

We had proceeded about nine miles, when we were surprised by the appearance in view, at the termination of a reach, of a long line of mangnificent trees of green and dense foliage. As we sailed down the reach, we observed a vast concourse of natives under them, and, on a nearer approach, we not only heard their war-song, if it might so be called, but remarked that they were painted and armed, as they generally are, prior to their engaging in deadly conflict. Notwithstanding these outward signs of hostility, . . . I continued to steer directly in for the bank on which they were collected. I found, however, when it was almost too late to turn into the succeeding reach to our left, that an attempt to land would only be attended with loss of life. The natives seemed determined to resist it. We approached so near that they held their spears quivering in their grasp ready to hurl. They were painted in various ways. Some who had marked their ribs, and thighs, and faces with a white pigment, looked like skeletons, others were daubed over with red and yellow ochre, and their bodies shone with the grease with which they had besmeared themselves. A dead silence prevailed among the front ranks, but those in the back ground, as well as the women, who carried supplies of darts, and who appeared to have had a bucket of whitewash capsized over their heads, were extremely clamorous. As I did not wish a conflict with these people, I lowered my sail, and putting the helm to starboard, we passed quietly down the stream in mid channel. Disappointed in their anticipations, the natives ran along the bank of the river, endeavouring to secure an aim at us; but, unable to throw with certainty, in consequence of the onward motion of the boat, they flung themselves into the most extravagant attitudes, and worked themselves into a state of frenzy by loud and vehement shouting.

It was with considerable apprehension that I observed the river to be shoaling fast, more especially as a huge sand-bank, a little below us, and on the same side on which the natives had gathered, projected nearly a third-way across the channel. To this sand-bank they ran with tumultuous uproar, and covered it over in a dense mass. Some of the chiefs advanced to the water to be nearer their victims, and turned from time to time to direct their followers. With every pacific disposition, and an extreme reluctance to take away life, I foresaw that it would be impossible any longer to avoid an engagement, yet with such fearful numbers against us, I was doubtful of the result. The spectacle we had witnessed had been one of the most appalling kind, and sufficient to shake the firmness of most men; but at that trying moment my little band preserved their temper coolness, and if anything could be gleaned from their countenances, it was that they had determined on an obstinate resistance. But at the very moment, when my hand was on the trigger, and my eye was along the barrel, my purpose was checked by M'Leay, who called to me that another party of blacks had made their appearance upon the left bank of the river. Turning round, I observed four men at the top of their speed. The foremost of them as soon as he got ahead of the boat, threw himself from a considerable height into the water. He struggled across the channel to the sand-bank, and in an incredibly short space of time stood in front of the savage, against whom my aim had been directed. Seizing him by the throat, he pushed him backwards, and forcing all who were in the water upon the bank, he trod its margin with a vehemence and an agitation that were exceedingly striking. At one moment pointing to the boat, at another shaking his clenched hand in the faces of the most forward, and stamping with passion on the sand. . . . The reader will imagine our feelings on this occasion: it is impossible to describe them. We were so wholly lost in interest at the scene that was passing, that the boat was allowed to drift at pleasure. For my own part I was overwhelmed with astonishment, and in truth stunned and confused; so singular, so unexpected, and so strikingly providential, had been our escape.

In August 1844 Sturt left Adelaide on his last expedition, an attempt to reach the centre of the continent. On 27 January 1845 he set up a camp at Depot Glen, near Milparinka, and in temperatures of 132°F in the shade and 157°F in the sun, waited for the rains to break.

Rain at Depot Glen, New South Wales, July 1845

On the 11th the wind shifted to the east, the whole sky becoming suddenly overcast, and on the morning of the 12th it was still at east, but at noon veered round to the north, when a gentle rain set in, so gentle that it more resembled a mist, but this continued all the evening and during the night. It ceased however at 10 a.m. of the 13th, when the wind shifted a little to the westward of north. At noon rain again commenced, and fell steadily throughout the night, but although the ground began to feel the effects of it, sufficient had not fallen to enable us to move. Yet, how thankful was I for this change, and how earnestly did I pray that the Almighty would still farther extend his mercy to us, when I laid my head on my pillow. All night it poured down without any intermission, and as morning dawned the ripple of waters in a little gully close to our tents, was a sweeter and more soothing sound than the softest melody I ever heard. On going down to the creek in the morning I found that it had risen five inches, and the ground was now so completely saturated that I no longer doubted the moment of our liberation had arrived.

PETER EGERTON
WARBURTON
(1813–1889)

Australian explorer. After more than twenty years' service in the army, he became a commissioner of police in
Australia. In April 1873, having already covered more
than a thousand miles from Adelaide, he set off from
Alice Springs with his son, a cook, a surveyor, two
Afghan camel drivers, an Aborigine boy called Charley
and seventeen camels. His aim was to reach the Indian
Ocean. After crossing a terrible plain covered with spinifex, they entered the Great Sandy Desert. There their
camels began to die from eating poisonous plants or from
sheer weakness, and they themselves suffered dreadfully
from thirst. They finally reached human habitation on
the Oakover River on 21 January 1874, the first men to
cross the continent from east to west.

The hand of Providence, 5 November 1873

A strong east wind is blowing. We are compelled to give up smoking
whilst on short allowance of water. It is a deprivation, for smoke
and water stand in the place of food. We started west-south-west at
6.30 p.m., and made twenty-five miles, though we had most trying
sand-hills to cross. I became quite unable to continue the journey,
being reduced to a skeleton by thirst, famine, and fatigue. I was so
emaciated and weak I could scarcely rise from the ground, or
stagger half a dozen steps when up. Charley had been absent all day,
and we were alarmed about him when he did not return at sunset. I
knew not what to do. Delay was death to us all, as we had not water
enough to carry us through; on the other hand, to leave the camp
without the lad seemed an inhuman act, as he must then perish. It
was six against one, so I waited till the moon was well up, and
started at 9 p.m. We made about eight miles, and whilst crossing a
flat heard, to our intense delight, a 'cooee', and Charley joined us.
Poor lad, how rejoiced we were to see him again so unexpectedly!
The lad had actually walked about twenty miles after all the fatigue
of the previous night's travelling; he had run up a large party of
natives, and gone to their water. This news of more water permitted

us to use at once what we had with us, and the recovery of Charley put us in good spirits. It may, I think, be admitted that the hand of Providence was distinctly visible in this instance. I had deferred starting until 9 p.m., to give the absent boy a chance of regaining the camp. It turned out afterwards that had we expedited our departure by ten minutes, or postponed it for the same length of time, Charley would have missed us; and had this happened there is little doubt that not only myself, but probably other members of the expedition would have perished from thirst. The route pursued by us was at right angles with the course taken by the boy, and the chances of our stumbling up against each other in the dark were infinitesimally small. Providence mercifully directed it otherwise, and our departure was so timed that, after travelling from two to two hours and a half, when all hope of the recovery of the wanderer was almost abandoned, I was gladdened by the 'cooee' of the brave lad, whose keen ears had caught the sound of the bells attached to the camels' necks. To the energy and courage of this untutored native may, under the guidance of the Almighty, be attributed the salvation of the party. It was by no accident that he encountered the friendly well. For fourteen miles he followed up the tracks of some blacks, though fatigued by a day of severe work, and, receiving a kindly welcome from the natives, he had hurried back, unmindful of his own exhausted condition, to apprise his companions of the important discovery he had made. We turned towards the native camp, and halted a short distance from it, that we might not frighten them away. I was so utterly exhausted when we camped, at 3 a.m., that it was evident I never could have gone on after that night without more food and water. I would therefore thankfully acknowledge the goodness and mercy of God in saving my life by guiding us to a place where we got both. . . .

Eating a camel

No shred was passed over. Head, feet, hide, tail all went into the boiling pot. . . . The tough, thick hide was cut up and parboiled. The coarse hair was then scraped off with a knife and the leather-like substance replaced in the pot and stewed until it became like the inside of a carpenter's glue pot, both to the taste and the smell. . . .

ANTHONY TROLLOPE
(1815–1882)

English novelist, best known for his 'Barsetshire' novels.
Until 1867 he worked for the Post Office in whose service
he travelled extensively. In 1871–2 he visited Australia
and New Zealand.

Blowing

I may, perhaps, take this opportunity of saying one word as to
colonial character which must be in the nature of censure, – though
of censure of the mildest form. And I beg my friends on the Darling
Downs, should this book ever reach so far, to understand that the
reference is not made to them, but is altogether general in its nature.
Colonists are usually fond of their adopted homes, – but are at the
same time pervaded by a certain sense of inferiority which is for the
most part very unnecessary. But it exists. Men and women will
apologize because they cannot do this or that as it is done in
England. But this very feeling produces a reaction which shows
itself in boasting of what they can do. And soon the boast becomes
much louder than the apology, – and very much more general. It
arises, however, as does all boasting, from a certain dread of
inferiority. In the Australian colonies it has become so common,
that the salutary fear of being supposed to boast does not produce
that reticence as to self which is considered to be good manners at
home. You are told constantly that colonial meat and colonial wine,
colonial fruit and colonial flour, colonial horses and colonial fruit
and colonial flour, colonial horses and colonial sport, are better
than any meat, wine, fruit, flour, horses, or sport to be found
elsewhere. And this habit spreads from things national to things
personal; and men boast of their sheep, their cattle, and their
stations; – of their riding, their driving, and their prowess. When
one man asserts that he has shot a hundred and fifty wild horses in a
day, it is natural that another man should have shot two hundred.
And so the thing grows, and means perhaps not a great deal. The
colonists themselves have a term for it, and call it – 'blowing.' I met
a gentleman who had once shot a bushranger. He had not been in
my company five minutes before he had told me, – nor an hour

without his mentioning it half-a-dozen times. He always 'blows' about that, said a friend who was with me; – and those who heard him thought no more of it than if he bit his nails, or had a trick of stroking his beard. That gentleman always 'blew.' Now if I was sending a young man to the Australian colonies the last word of advice I should give him would be against this practice. 'Dont blow,' – I should say to him.

EDWARD JOHN EYRE
(1815–1901)

English colonial administrator and explorer. He went to Australia in 1833 to work as a sheep and cattle driver. In 1840–41 he crossed the continent from east to west, setting off from Fowler's Bay, South Australia, on 25 February 1841 with an overseer, John Baxter, three aboriginal boys, nine pack horses, a pony and a foal, six sheep and what he hoped would be enough food.

The death of Baxter, 28 April 1841

The night was cold, and the wind blowing hard from the south-west, whilst scud and nimbus were passing very rapidly by the moon. . . . It was now half past ten, and I headed the horses back, in the direction in which I thought the camp lay, that I might be ready to call the overseer to relieve me at eleven. Whilst thus engaged, and looking steadfastly around among the scrub, to see if I could anywhere detect the embers of our fires, I was startled by a sudden flash, followed by the report of a gun, not a quarter of a mile away from me. Imagining that the overseer had mistaken the hour of the night, and not being able to find me or the horses, had taken that method to attract my attention, I immediately called out, but as no answer was returned, I got alarmed, and leaving the horses, hurried up towards the camp as rapidly as I could. About a hundred yards from it, I met the King George's Sound native (Wylie), running towards me, and in great alarm, crying out, 'Oh Massa, oh Massa, come here,' – but could gain no information from him, as to what had occurred. Upon reaching the encampment, which I did in about five minutes after the shot was fired, I was horror-struck to find my poor overseer lying on the ground, weltering in his blood, and in the last agonies of death.

Glancing hastily around the camp I found it deserted by the two younger native boys, whilst the scattered fragments of our baggage, which I left carefully piled under the oilskin, lay thrown about in wild disorder, and at once revealed the cause of the harrowing scene before me.

Upon raising the body of my faithful, but ill-fated follower, I found that he was beyond all human aid; he had been shot through the left breast with a ball, the last convulsions of death were upon him, and he expired almost immediately after our arrival. The frightful, the appalling truth now burst upon me, that I was alone in the desert. He who had faithfully served me for many years, who had followed my fortunes in adversity and in prosperity, who had accompanied me in all my wanderings, and whose attachment to me had been his sole inducement to remain with me in this last, and to him alas, fatal journey, was now no more. For an instant, I was almost tempted to wish it had been my own fate instead of his. The horrors of my situation glared upon me in such startling reality, as for an instant almost to paralyse the mind. At the dead hour of night, in the wildest and most inhospitable wastes of Australia, with the fierce wind raging in unison with the scene of violence before me, I was left, with a single native, whose fidelity I could not rely upon, and who for aught I knew might be in league with the other two, who perhaps were even now, lurking about with the view of taking away my life as they had done that of the overseer.

MARY TAYLOR
(*fl.* 1845–1857)

English traveller. A close friend of Charlotte Brontë, she was the original of Rose Yorke in *Shirley*. In 1845 she emigrated to the new colony of New Zealand, settling in the small town of Wellington. She returned to England in 1857.

A letter from New Zealand

DEAR CHARLOTTE,

About a month since I received and read *Jane Eyre*. It seemed to me incredible that you had actually written a book. Such events did not happen while I was in England. . . . After I had read it I went on to the top of Mount Victoria and looked for a ship to carry a letter to you. There was a little thing with one mast, and also H.M.S. *Fly*, and nothing else. If a cattle vessel came from Sydney she would probably return in a few days, and would take a mail, but we have had east wind for a month and nothing can come in. . . .

. . . I mention the book to no one and hear no opinions. I lend it a good deal because it's a novel, and *it's as good as another!* They say 'it makes them cry.' They are not literary enough to give an opinion. If ever I hear one I'll embalm it for you. . . .

. . . My life here is not disagreeable. I have a great resource in the piano, and a little employment in teaching. Then I go in to Mrs Taylor's and astonish the poor girl with calling her favourite parson a *spoon*. She thinks I am astonishingly learned but rather wicked, and tries hard to persuade me to go to chapel, though I tell her I only go for amusement. She would have sense but for her wretched health, which is getting rapidly worse from her irrational mode of living.

I can hardly explain to you the queer feeling of living, as I do, in two places at once. One world containing books, England, and all the people with whom I can exchange an idea; the other is all that I actually see and hear and speak to. The separation is as complete as between the things in a picture and the things in the room. The puzzle is that both move and act, and I must say my say as one of each. The result is that one world at least must think me crazy. I am just now in a sad mess. A drover, who has grown rich with cattle dealing, wanted me to go and teach his daughter. As the man is a widower I astonished *this* world when I accepted the proposal, and still more because I asked too high a price (£70) a year. Now that I have begun, the same people can't conceive why I don't go on and marry the man at once, which they imagine must have been my original intention. For my part I shall possibly astonish them a little more, for I feel a great inclination to make use of his interested civilities to visit his daughter and see the district of Porirua. If I had a little more money and could afford a horse (she rides), I certainly would. . . .

It is a pity you don't live in this world, that I might entertain you about the price of meat. Do you know, I bought six heifers the other day for £23, and now it is turned so cold I expect to hear one-half of them are dead. One man bought twenty sheep for £8, and they are all dead but one. Another bought 150 and has 40 left, and people have begun to drive cattle through a valley into the Wairau plains and thence across the straits to Wellington, etc., etc. This is the only legitimate subject of conversation we have, the rest is gossip concerning our superiors in station who don't know us on the road, but it is astonishing how well we know all their private affairs, making allowance always for the distortion in our own organs of vision.

I have now told you everything I can think of except that the cat's on the table and that I'm going to borrow a new book to read – no less than an account of all the systems of philosophy of modern Europe.

JOHN McDOUALL STUART
(1815–1866)

Scottish-born explorer. Emigrating to South Australia in 1838, he entered the government survey department and joined Sturt's 1844 expedition. Between 1858 and 1862 he led six expeditions from Adelaide. In 1860 he was the first to reach the centre of Australia, and in 1862 the first to cross the continent from south to north. He reached his goal only at great cost to his health. He lost the power of speech and went blind, before dying four years later.

Reaching the centre, April 1860

Sunday, 22nd April, Small Gum Creek, under Mount Stuart, Centre of Australia: – To-day I find from my observations of the sun, 111°00′30″, that I am now camped in the centre of Australia. I have marked a tree and planted the British flag there. There is a high mount about two miles and a half to the north-north-east. I wish it had been in the centre; but on it to-morrow I will raise a cone of stones, and plant the flag there, and name it 'Central Mount Stuart'. . . .

Monday, 23rd April, Centre. – Took Kekwick and the flag, and went to the top of the mount, but found it to be much higher and more difficult of ascent than I anticipated. After a deal of labour, slips, and knocks, we at last arrived on the top. . . . Built a large cone of stones, in the centre of which I placed a pole with the British flag nailed to it. Near the top of the cone I placed a small bottle, in which there is a slip of paper, with our signatures on it, stating by whom it was raised. We then gave three hearty cheers for the flag, the emblem of civil and religious liberty, and may it be a sign to the natives that the dawn of liberty, civilization, and Christianity is about to break upon them. . . .

Reaching the sea, July 1862

Thursday, 24th July, Thring Creek. Entering the Marsh. Started at 7.40, course north. I have taken this course in order to make the sea coast, which I suppose to be distant about eight miles and a half, as soon as possible; by this I hope to avoid the marsh. I shall travel along the beach to the north of the Adelaide. I did not inform any of the party, except Thring and Auld, that I was so near to the sea, as I wished to give them a surprise on reaching it. . . . At eight miles and a half came upon a broad valley of black alluvial soil, covered with long grass; from this I can hear the wash of the sea. On the other side of the valley, which is rather more than a quarter of a mile wide, is growing a line of thick heavy bushes, very dense, showing that to be the boundary of the beach. Crossed the valley, and entered the scrub, which was a complete network of vines. Stopped the horses to clear a way, whilst I advanced a few yards on to the beach, and was gratified and delighted to behold the water of the Indian Ocean in Van Diemen Gulf, before the party with the horses knew anything of its proximity. Thring, who rode in advance of me, called out, 'The Sea!' which so took them all by surprise, and they were so astonished, that he had to repeat the call before they fully understood what was meant. Then they immediately gave three long and hearty cheers. . . . After all the party had had some time on the beach, at which they were much pleased and gratified, they collected a few shells; I returned to the valley, where I had my initials (J.M.D.S.) cut on a large tree, as I did not intend to put up my flag until I arrived at the mouth of the Adelaide. Proceeded on a course of 302° along the valley; at one mile and a half, coming upon a small creek with running water, and the valley being covered with beautiful green grass, I have camped to give the horses the benefit of it. Thus have I, through the instrumentality of Divine Providence, been led to accomplish the great object of the expedition, and take the whole party safely as witnesses to the fact, and through one of the finest countries man could wish to behold – good to the coast, and with a stream of running water within half a mile of the sea. From Newcastle Water to the sea-beach, the main body of the horses have been only one night without water, and then got it within the next day. If this country is settled, it will be one of the finest Colonies under the Crown, suitable for the growth of any and everything. . . .

CHARLES HEAPHY
(1820–1881)

English-born painter, surveyor, soldier and traveller in New Zealand. He came to New Zealand in 1839 and worked for the New Zealand Company, eventually becoming chief surveyor. In 1846 he made two expeditions with Thomas Brunner; the first was 'something of a picnic', the second – round the west coast of South Island to Arahura and back – was definitely not. In 1867 Heaphy won New Zealand's first Victoria Cross, for bravery under fire.

Seafood

The mutton fish, or *pawa*, although resembling india rubber in toughness and colour, is very excellent and substantial food for explorers, both European and native; and when it can be obtained, which is only at low water, spring tides, is much prized by those gentlemen. The sea urchin tastes like spider crab, and, though very palatable, would be much improved by vinegar and condiments. But the sea anemone is the most *recherché*. Half animal, half vegetable, as we unscientific people must describe a zoophyte, it is the most extraordinary food that ever afforded nutriment to the human body, and must be eaten to be comprehended. Suffice it to say that in its capture it must be jerked quickly from its holding on the rock, or it contracts itself into a small lump and nearly disappears in the crevice from which it grows. In cooking it, care should be taken to keep it apart from other victuals, and in eating it the eyes should be kept closely shut. It has a decidedly suspicious appearance, and is not a favourite food of Scotch terrier dogs.

Disturbed at night by morning service

5th. Heavy N.E. gale with rain. Forded the Okari creek and proceeded on by the sand beach to the Totara river, three miles distant, and finding it much flooded were obliged to encamp upon the northern bank. Notwithstanding the rain, which poured unintermittingly, we soon had a capital house built, and had raised a fire large enough to roast an ——. I will not mention what, as our provisions were not of that kind; but had soon a kettle of hot penguin soup, which would be a capital mess were it not so fishy. . . .

7th. The natives, by their chattering during the night, prevented our getting any sleep. They passed it in an incessant row of singing, chanting, and talking; one only giving over and lying down to be followed by the commencement of another. When they had exhausted the news and finished their songs, for want of other occupation they commenced anew with the recital of the morning service, not for purposes of devotion, but merely as a pastime, and perhaps, to show their proficiency. Before morning we thus heard repeated four litanies, and the whole collection of their version of the Psalms, together with three or four creeds and a marriage service. These were repeated with every variety of intonation of voice; and finally they recited the whole morning service in grotesque pronunciation and manner of delivery, which with these natives is a species of never-tiring amusement.

ERNEST GILES
(1835–1897)

English-born explorer. He came to Australia to work in the goldfields. Between 1872 and 1882 he made six expeditions through central South Australia and Western Australia, in the course of which he twice traversed the continent. In August 1873 he set off on an expedition into what was later to be named the Gibson Desert, west of the Petermann Range, in Western Australia. When his companion, Alfred Gibson, perished, Giles went on alone, carrying a 45 lb keg of water on his shoulders for sixty miles. In 1875 he crossed the continent from Port

Augusta to Perth, then re-crossed it on his way back, making another terrible journey through the Gibson Desert.

Coming out of the Gibson Desert, April 1874

About the 29th I had emptied my keg, and was still over twenty miles from the Circus. Ah! who can imagine what twenty miles means in such a case? But in this April's ivory moonlight I plodded on, desolate indeed, but all undaunted, on this lone, unhallowed shore. At last I reached the Circus, just at the dawn of day. Oh, how I drank! how I reeled! how hungry I was! how thankful I was that I had so far at least escaped from the jaws of that howling wilderness. . . . Just as I got clear of the bank of the creek, I heard a faint squeak, and looking about I saw, and immediately caught, a small dying wallaby, whose marsupial mother had evidently thrown it from her pouch. It only weighed about two ounces, and was scarcely furnished yet with fur. The instant I saw it, like an eagle I pounced upon it and ate it, living, raw, dying – fur, skin, bones, skull and all.

Under the eye of God, June 1876

The flies were still about us, in persecuting myriads. The nature of the country during this march was similar to that previously described, being quite open, it rolled along in ceaseless undulations of sand. The only vegetation besides the ever-abounding spinifex was a few blood-wood-trees on the tops of some of the red heaps of sand, with an occasional desert oak, an odd patch or clump of mallee trees, standing desolately alone, and perhaps having a stunted specimen or two of the quandong or native peach-tree, and the dreaded Gyrostemon growing among them. The region is so desolate that it is horrifying even to describe. The eye of God looking down on the solitary caravan, as with its slow, and snake-like motion, it presents the only living object around, must have contemplated its appearance on such a scene with pitying admiration, as it forced its way continually on; onwards without pausing, over this vast sandy region, avoiding death only by motion and distance, until some oasis can be found. Slow as eternity it seems to move, but certain we trust as death; and truly the wanderer in its wilds may snatch a fearful joy at having once beheld the scenes, that human eyes ought never again to see. On the 15th of June we found a hollow in which were two or three small salt-lake beds, but these were perfectly dry; on the 16th also another solitary one was seen, and here a few low rises lay across a part of the eastern horizon. On the 17th a little water left in the bottom of a bucket overnight was frozen into a thick cake in the morning, the thermometer indicating 18°. The nights I pass in these fearful regions are more dreadful than the days, for 'night is the time for care, brooding o'er days misspent, when the pale spectre of despair comes to our lonely tent;' and often when I lay me down I fall into a dim and death-like trance, wakeful, yet 'dreaming dreams no mortals had ever dared to dream before.'

. . . The place might well be termed the centre of silence and solitude; despair and desolation are the only intruders here upon sad solitude's triumphant reign. Well may the traveller here desire for more inhabited lands; rather to contend with fierce and warlike men; to live amongst far noisier deaths, or die amid far louder dangers! . . .

SAMUEL BUTLER
(1835–1902)

English novelist. Author of *Erewhon* and *The Way of All Flesh*. In 1859, refusing to become a clergyman like his father and grandfather, he emigrated to New Zealand and set up as a sheep farmer. He called his sheep run, in Rangitata Valley, 'Mesopotamia'. Butler's *A First Year in Canterbury Settlement* (1863) was compiled by his father from his journal and letters. A very amusing and not uncritical view of the colony, it may have been one of the reasons why Butler returned to England in 1864.

Mount Cook

No one can mistake it. If a person says he *thinks* he has seen Mount Cook, you may be quite sure that he has not seen it. The moment it comes into sight the exclamation is, 'That is Mount Cook!' – not 'That *must* be Mount Cook!' There is no possibility of mistake. . . .

I am forgetting myself into admiring a mountain which is of no use for sheep. This is wrong. A mountain here is only beautiful if it has good grass on it. Scenery is not scenery – it is 'country,' *subauditâ voce* 'sheep.' If it is good for sheep, it is beautiful, magnificent, and all the rest of it; if not, it is not worth looking at. I am cultivating this tone of mind with considerable success, but you must pardon me for an occasional outbreak of the old Adam.

The decidedly inferior wildlife of New Zealand

As for the quadrupeds of New Zealand, they are easily disposed of. There are but two, a kind of rat, which is now banished by the Norway rat, and an animal of either the otter or beaver species, which is known rather by rumour than by actual certainty.

The fishes, too, will give us little trouble. There are only a sort of minnow and an eel. This last grows to a great size, and is abundant even in the clear, rapid, snow-fed rivers. In every creek one may catch eels, and they are excellent eating, if they be cooked in such a manner as to get rid of the oil.

> Try them spitchcocked or stewed,
> They're too oily when fried,

as Barham says, with his usual good sense. I am told that the other night a great noise was heard in the kitchen of a gentleman with whom I have the honour to be acquainted, and that the servants, getting up, found an eel chasing a cat round about the room. I believe this story. The eel was in a bucket of water and doomed to die upon the morrow. Doubtless the cat had attempted to take liberties with him; on which a sudden thought struck the eel that he might as well eat the cat as the cat eat him; and he was preparing to suit the action to the word when he was discovered.

The insects are insignificant and ugly, and, like the plants, devoid of general interest. There is one rather pretty butterfly, like our English tortoise shell. There is a sprinkling of beetles, a few ants, and a detestable sandfly, that, on quiet, cloudy mornings, especially near water, is more irritating than can be described. This little beast is rather venomous; and, for the first fortnight or so that I was bitten by it, every bite swelled up to a little hard button. Soon, however, one becomes case-hardened, and only suffers the immediate annoyance consequent upon its tickling and pricking. There is also a large assortment of spiders. We have, too, one of the ugliest-looking creatures that I have ever seen. It is called 'weta,' and is of tawny scorpion-like colour with long antennæ and great eyes, and nasty squashy-looking body, with (I think) six legs. It is a kind of animal which no one would wish to touch: if touched, it will bite sharply, some say venomously. It is very common, but not often seen, and lives chiefly among dead wood and under stones. In the North Island, I am told that it grows to the length of three or four inches. Here I never saw it longer than an inch and a half. The principal reptile is an almost ubiquitous lizard.

Summing up, then, the whole of the vegetable and animal productions of this settlement, I think that it is not too much to say that they are decidedly inferior in beauty and interest to those of the old world.

D. H. LAWRENCE
(1885–1930)

English novelist, poet and essayist. (See p. 173.)

'Really a weird show' – Australia in 1922

If you want to know what it is to feel the 'correct' social world fizzle to nothing, you should come to Australia. It *is* a weird place. In the *established* sense, it is socially nil. Happy-go-lucky, don't-you-bother, we're-in-Australia. But also there seems to be no inside life of any sort: just a long lapse and drift. A rather fascinating indifference, a *physical* indifference to what we call soul or spirit. It's really a weird show. The country has an extraordinary hoary, weird attraction. As you get used to it, it seems so *old*, as if it had missed all this Semite-Egyptian-Indo-European vast era of history, and was coal age, the age of great ferns and mosses. It hasn't got a consciousness – just none – too far back. A strange effect it has on one. Often I hate it like poison, then again it fascinates me, and the spell of its indifference gets me. I can't quite explain it: as if one resolved back almost to the plant kingdom, before souls, spirits and minds were grown at all: only quite a live, energetic body with a weird face.

JACK GORDON HIDES
(1906–   )

Australian administrative official in Papua New Guinea. He was one of the men who made some remarkable journeys into the mountainous interior of Papua New Guinea between the wars, discovering unsuspected areas of dense population. In 1935 Hides led a party of native police into the Wen country, between the headwaters of the Strickland and Purari Rivers.

The gentlemanly natives of Bangalbe, Papua New Guinea

We had not gone more than two hundred yards when a terrific din of yodelling arose on all sides of us, and the whole line was attacked. It all happened with remarkable suddenness, but every man was ready for them, and Borege was the only one to take an arrow. I fired in front of me and at the back of me, at men not fifteen feet away, rushing with short stabbing spears. The poor carriers got new strength; they yelled and screamed and threw their steel tomahawks at the attacking natives. To give some idea of how these people regarded us, and how closely they attacked, Constable Badua, rushed at close quarters by spearmen, started swinging his rifle instead of firing. He was pulled to the ground, a man with a battle-axe on top of him; and had I not heard Badua's call for help, and seen the incident, he would have been killed by two other natives assisting his assailant. I shot one of them as I rushed to Badua's assistance and, pulling his assailant off him, after hitting him with the butt of my rifle, allowed him to run off. The struggle was over by then; it had only lasted about fifteen seconds. The thunder of the rifles had brought silence in the country around us, and we walked out of the timber into cultivations again.

Our attackers came to meet us with presents of food. They stood and offered the bunches of bananas and bundles of spinach; but the food was thrown back at them, and I explained that we did not take presents from people who tried to murder us; and further, that when we were ready for the food, we would take it. They stood like down-hearted schoolboys, and for all their treachery, my heart went out to them. So that when a little later about twenty venerable old men met us, and with great difficulty and care explained by gestures that this was not the section that had attacked us, I pretended to believe their story. At the same time I told them that we would now take the food we wanted.

Their answering gestures could have been read as: 'Go to it, old man.'

We killed two pigs in a pen nearby, dug what potatoes we wanted, and then handed the old men axes, which they all smilingly accepted. Then with large fires going, and food cooking, we gorged ourselves to contentment.

The attitude of these people was extraordinary. Within an hour or so of the attack, fully three hundred men, all of them genuinely friendly, were sitting around the party; and it would have been indelicate, I thought, to have even suggested to them that only a short time before we had been fighting with them. They seemed to treat a fight like a football match. They could be treacherous, but they could also be gentlemen.

JAN MORRIS
(1926–   )

Welsh writer and traveller. (See p. 189.)

The aborigines of Sydney in the 1980s

Most of the aborigines of these parts were exterminated, by imported disease or by brute force, within a few decades of the first white settlement. Yet two centuries later a few hundred cling to their roots in Sydney, at the very site of the European coming. They are called 'coories' here, and like the water of the harbour, like the exotic foliage of the parks and headlands, they are a reminder of stranger, older things than Kev and his kind can conceive. To some Australians the aborigines are a blot on the conscience, to others just a pain in the neck: still, in the end most people thought the coories were worth feeling sorry for, and feel sorry for them I did.

Though their community has produced some celebrities in its time, notably boxers, they live mostly in more luckless quarters of the town, and do not show much as a rule. As it chanced, however, while I was in Sydney this time they celebrated Aboriginal Day. The aboriginal flag of gold, black and yellow flew, to the consternation of Old Australians, side by side with the national flag on Sydney Town Hall, and a march through town was announced, to be followed by a rally at Alexandria Park. Alas, all this went sadly awry. Nobody seemed to know where the march was to begin, or when, somebody pulled the flag down from the Town Hall, not everyone seemed to have mastered the rally chant – *What do we want? Land rights! What have we got? Bugger all!* – and the arrangements ran so late that when the time came for speeches everyone had gone home. 'They are a *random* people,' was the convincing explanation I was given, when I asked if this was true to coorie form.

By the time I reached Alexandria Park Aboriginal Day seemed to have fizzled out altogether, and all I found was a small huddle of dark-skinned people around an open bonfire, surrounded by litter on the edge of the green. They greeted me with a wan concern, offering me beer out of an ice-bucket, sidling around me rather, and occasionally winking. A small thin boy with cotton wool stuffed in one ear wandered here and there leading a black puppy on a string. Others kicked a football about in the gathering dusk, and around the fire a handful of older men and women looked sadly into the flames. A strong smell of alcohol hung over us, and the man with the bucket urged me quietly, again and again, to have one for the road, dear. Had the rally been a success? I asked. 'Yeah,' they said, and looked into the fire.

I *did* feel sorry for them. They were like last wasted survivors from some primeval holocaust, whose memories of their own civilization were aeons ago expunged. Did they have a Sydney all their own, I wondered, long ago near the beginnings of time? Did their flag fly braver then? When I said goodbye and drove away ('Go on, dear, just one') the lights of the downtown tower blocks were shining in the distance: but in the shadows at the edge of the park the bonfire flames were dancing still, and the frail figures of the indigenes moved unsteadily in the flicker.

THE ARCTIC AND
THE ANTARCTIC

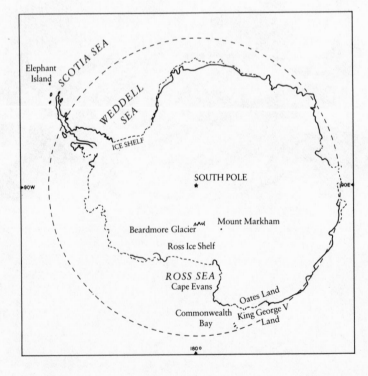

The Arctic

CHRISTOPHER HALL
(fl. 1576)

English sea captain. Master of the *Gabriel*, one of the ships in Martin Frobisher's 1576 expedition to discover the North-West Passage to China.

An early view of the Eskimos in what is now Frobisher Bay, Baffin Island, July 1576

The 19. day in the morning, being calme, and no winde, the Captaine and I tooke our boate, with eight men in her, to rowe us a shoare, to see if there were there any people, or no, and going to the toppe of the Island, we had sight of seven boates, which came rowing from the East side, toward that Island: whereupon we returned aboord againe: at length we sent our boate with five men in her, to see whither they rowed, and so with a white cloth brought one of their boates with their men along the shoare, rowing after our boate, till such time as they sawe our ship, and then they rowed a shoare: then I went on shoare my selfe, and gave every of them a threadden point, and brought one of them aboord of me, where hee did eate and drinke, and then carried him on shoare againe. Whereupon all the rest came aboord with their boates, being nineteene persons, and they spake, but we understoode them not. They bee like to Tartars, with long blacke haire, broad faces, and flatte noses, and tawnie in colour, wearing Seale skinnes, and so doe the women, not differing in the fashion, but the women are marked in the face with blewe streekes downe the cheekes, and round about the eyes. Their boates are made all of Seales skinnes, with a keele of wood within the skin: the proportion of them is like a Spanish shallop, save only they be flat in the bottome, and sharpe at both ends.

529

HENRY MORGAN
(fl. 1586)

English sailor. Purser of the *Sunshine*, one of the ships in the fleet of John Davis on his second voyage to discover the North-West Passage. Davis sent the *Sunshine* and the *North Star* to seek a passage between Greenland and Iceland, while he explored the waters around Baffin Island.

Football with the Eskimos of Baffin Island, August 1586

The 21. of August the Master sent the boate on shore for wood with sixe of his men, and there were one and thirtie of the people of the countrey which went on shore to them, & they went about to kill them as we thought, for they shot their dartes towards them, and we that were aboord the ship, did see them goe on shore to our men: whereupon the Master sent the pinnesse after them, and when they saw the pinnesse comming towards them, they turned backe, and the Master of the pinnesse did shoote off a caliver to them the same time, but hurt none of them, for his meaning was onely to put them in feare. Divers times they did wave us on shore to play with them at the football, and some of our company went on shore to play with them, and our men did cast them downe as soone as they did come to strike the ball. And thus much of that which we did see and do in that harborough where we arrived first.

GERRIT DE VEER
(fl. 1596–1597)

Dutch seaman and explorer, chronicler of Willem Barents' third expedition in search of a North-East Passage. In August 1596 Barents' ship was beset by ice on the coast of Novaya Zemlya, and he and his men spent the winter there – the first expedition to do so in the Arctic. The wooden house they built was still standing in 1871, when it was found by a Norwegian fisherman. On 13 June

1597, the party, who had suffered terribly from scurvy, set off in two open ship's boats through the still abundant drift ice, from time to time hauling their boats out onto the ice. The survivors eventually reached Amsterdam in November.

Trouble with a bear

The 6 of September, some of our men went on shore upon the firme land to seeke for stones, which are a kinde of diamont, whereof there are many also in the States Island: and while they were seeking ye stones, 2 of our men lying together in one place, a great leane white beare came sodainly stealing out, and caught one of them fast by the necke, who not knowing what it was that tooke him by the necke, cried out and said, Who is that that pulles me so by the necke?

The death of Barents, 20 June 1597

. . . We sat talking one with the other, and spake of many things, and William Barents read in my card which I had made touching our voiage, and we had some discussion about it; at last he laid away the card and spake unto me, saying, Gerrit, give me some drinke; and he had no sooner drunke but he was taken with so sodain a qualme, that he turned his eies in his head and died presently, and we had no time to call the maister out of the [other] scute to speake unto him; and so he died before Claes Adrianson [who died shortly after him]. The death of William Barents put us in no small discomfort, as being the chiefe guide and onely pilot on whom we reposed our selves next under God; but we could not strive against God, and therefore we must of force be content.

SIR ALEXANDER MACKENZIE
(1764–1820)

Scottish fur-trader and explorer. (See p. 402.) In July 1789 he reached the Arctic Ocean at the mouth of the Mackenzie River, after a journey of 2990 miles.

Indians on the Mackenzie River, North-West Territories, July 1789

They amused us with Songs of their own & some in Imitation of the Eskmeaux, which seemed to enliven our new Guide, so much that he began to dance upon his Breech in his small Canoe & we expected every Moment to see him upset but he was not satisfied with his confined Situation. He paddled up along Side of our Canoe & asked us to embark him (which a little before he had refused) we allow'd him & immediately he began to perform an Eskmeaux Dance upon our Canoe when every Person in the Canoe called out to him to be quiet which he complied with & before he sat down pull'd his *Penis* out of his Breeches laying it on his hand & telling us the Eskmeaux name of it. In short he took much Pains to shew us that he knew the Eskmeaux & their Customs.

SIR JOHN FRANKLIN
(1786–1847)

English naval officer and Arctic explorer. Entering the Navy in 1801, he fought at the Battle of Trafalgar. In 1819 he was sent to explore the northern coast of Canada eastward from the mouth of the Coppermine River. His party mapped the coast as far as Cape Turnagain, 175 miles from the mouth of the river, although in order to do so they actually sailed 640 miles. Rapids on the Hood River made it impossible for them to return by that route and they were forced to make a terrible journey overland to Fort Providence. The survivors owed their lives to friendly Indians. Franklin disappeared in 1847 on a voyage in search of a north-west passage.

Hunger on the Barren Grounds, 65°N, 112°W, October 1821

[5/6 October] In the afternoon we had a heavy fall of snow, which continued all the night. A small quantity of *tripe de roche* [edible lichen] was gathered; and Crédit, who had been hunting, brought in the antlers and back bone of a deer which had been killed in the summer. The wolves and birds of prey had picked them clean, but there still remained a quantity of the spinal marrow which they had not been able to extract. This, although putrid, was esteemed a valuable prize, and the spine being divided into portions, was distributed equally. After eating the marrow, which was so acrid as to excoriate the lips, we rendered the bones friable by burning, and ate them also.

On the following morning the ground was covered with snow to the depth of a foot and a half, and the weather was very stormy. These circumstances rendered the men again extremely despondent; a settled gloom hung over their countenances, and they refused to pick *tripe de roche*, choosing rather to go entirely without eating, than to make any exertion.

The want of *tripe de roche* caused us to go supperless to bed. Showers of snow fell frequently during the night. The breeze was light next morning, the weather cold and clear. We were all on foot by day-break, but from the frozen state of our tents and bed clothes, it was long before the bundles could be made, and as usual, the men lingered over a small fire they had kindled, so that it was eight o'clock before we started. Our advance from the depth of the snow was slow, and about noon coming to a spot where there was some *tripe de roche*, we stopped to collect it, and breakfasted. . . .

The distance walked to-day was six miles. As Crédit was very weak in the morning, his load was reduced to little more than his personal luggage, consisting of his blanket, shoes, and gun. Previous to setting out, the whole party ate the remains of their old shoes, and whatever scraps of leather they had, to strengthen their stomachs for the fatigue of the day's journey. . . .

Three of the party were left behind with a tent. Franklin and the survivors continued.

[7 October] . . . Not being able to find any *tripe de roche*, we drank an infusion of the Labrador tea plant, (*ledum palustre*), and ate a few morsels of burnt leather for supper. We were unable to raise the tent, and found its weight too great to carry it on; we, therefore, cut it up, and took a part of the canvass for a cover. The night was bitterly cold, and though we lay as close to each other as possible, having no shelter, we could not keep ourselves sufficiently warm to sleep. . . .

[11 October] At length we reached Fort Enterprise, and to our infinite disappointment and grief found it a perfectly desolate habitation. There was no deposit of provision, no trace of the Indians, no letter from Mr. Wentzel to point out where the Indians might be found. It would be impossible for me to describe our sensations after entering this miserable abode, and discovering how we had been neglected: the whole party shed tears, not so much for our own fate, as for that of our friends in the rear, whose lives depended entirely on our sending immediate relief from this place.

ELISHA KENT KANE
(1820–1857)

American doctor and Arctic explorer. In 1853, Henry Grinnell, president of the newly formed Geographical Society of New York, organized an expedition to search for Sir John Franklin, who had not been heard of since the end of July 1845. Kane, who had already taken part in a previous expedition (also organized by Grinnell) in 1850, was appointed commander. The expedition went north-ward through Smith Sound at the head of Baffin Bay, discovered and explored the Kane Basin, and discovered Kennedy Channel beyond. One of the expedition's sledge parties reached 81°10′N. In May 1855 they abandoned their brig, the *Advance*, and set off on a terrible journey to Upernavik, Greenland. With rations for only 36 days, they survived the 83-day journey only with the help of the Etah Eskimos. Kane's account of the expedition, *Arctic Explorations* (1856), became a well-deserved bestseller.

Etah Eskimos, North-West Greenland, 1855

It was quite late in the evening when I drew near Etah. . . . I had not quite reached the little settlement when loud sounds of laughter came to my ear; and, turning the cape, I burst suddenly upon an encampment of the inhabitants.

Some thirty men, women, and children, were gathered together upon a little face of offal-stained rock. Except a bank of moss, which broke the wind-draught from the fiord, they were entirely without protection from the weather, though the temperature was 5° below zero. . . .

Rudest of gypsies, how they squalled, and laughed, and snored, and rolled about! Some were sucking bird-skins, others were boiling incredible numbers of auks in huge soapstone pots, and two youngsters, crying, at the top of their voices, 'Oopegsoak! Oopegsoak!' were fighting for an owl. It was the only specimen (*Strix nyctea*) that I had seen except on the wing; but, before I could secure it, they had torn it limb from limb, and were eating its warm flesh and blood, their faces buried among its dishevelled feathers. . . .

The scene was redolent of plenty and indolence, – the *dolce far niente* of the short-lived Esquimaux summer. Provision for the dark winter was furthest from their thoughts . . .

Baron Nils Adolf Erik Nordenskjöld
(1832–1901)

Swedish Arctic explorer. Having led two unsuccessful expeditions to the North Pole, he determined to force the North-East Passage. Between the summers of 1878 and 1879, in the 300-ton ship the *Vega*, he sailed from Tromsö to Japan via the north of Asia. Nordenskjöld and his men, who included a zoologist, O. Nordquist, who was also a member of the Russian Imperial Guard, were the first to achieve the North-East Passage.

A report by an officer of the Imperial Guard on a night with Chukchis, natives of north-eastern Siberia

At night the children were completely undressed; the adults had short trousers on, the man of tanned skin, the woman of cloth. In the oppressive heat, which was kept up by two train-oil (blubber-oil) lamps burning the whole night, it was difficult to sleep even in the heavy reindeer-skin dresses. Yet they covered themselves with reindeer skins. Besides the heat there was a fearful stench – the Chukchis obeyed the calls of nature within the bed-chamber – which I could not stand without going out twice to get fresh air. When we got up next morning our hostess served breakfast in a flat tray, containing first seals' flesh and fat, with a sort of sourkrout of fermented willow-leaves, then seals' liver, and finally seals' blood – all frozen.

ROBERT EDWIN PEARY
(1856–1920)

American naval officer and Arctic explorer. After a number of Arctic journeys, Peary tried three times to reach the North Pole, succeeding on his third attempt. On 5 April 1909, with his Negro companion Matthew Henson and four Etah Eskimos – Ootah, Eginwah, Seegloo and the sixteen-year-old Ookeah, who had volunteered to prove to a girl he loved that he was of the stuff that good Eskimos are made – Peary reached the Pole. The entire Etah Eskimo community had given themselves to Peary's service: the women made the clothing which enabled him and his party to survive; their men drove the sledges, built the snow houses, hunted for him and laid down their lives for him. Although another American explorer, Frederick A. Cook, claimed to have got there first, Peary is generally regarded as the first man to have reached the North Pole.

Crossing the top of the world

. . . In a march of only a few hours, I had passed from the western to the eastern hemisphere and had verified my position at the summit of the world. It was hard to realise that on the first miles of this brief march we had been travelling due north, while on the last few miles of the same march we had been travelling south, although we had all the time been travelling precisely in the same direction. . . .

East, west and north had disappeared for us. Only one direction remained, and that was south. Every breeze which could possibly blow upon us, no matter from what point of the horizon, must be a south wind. Where we were, one day and one night constituted a year, a hundred such days and nights constituted a century. Had we stood in that spot during the six months of the Arctic winter night we should have seen every star of the northern hemisphere circling the sky at the same distance from the horizon, with Polaris practically in the zenith.

FRIDTJOF NANSEN
(1861–1930)

Norwegian Arctic explorer, statesman and scientist. In 1888 he crossed Greenland on skis. He then conceived a plan for reaching the North Pole by drifting in the ice across the polar basin. His specially-designed ship left Oslo in June 1893, and eventually drifted to a point 400 miles south of the Pole. In March 1895 Nansen and Hjalmar Johansen set out to complete the journey by sledge. After twenty-three days of dreadful hardship they reached latitude 86°13′N, 160 miles further north than any man had reached previously and 240 miles from the Pole, but could go no further. They began the long retreat to Franz Josef Land, reaching it in August 1895. They spent the winter in a stone hut, heating it with walrus blubber and living on bear meat, unaware that another expedition, led by Frederick Jackson, was encamped only 94 miles away.

'By Jove! I am glad to see you!', Cape Flora, Franz Josef Land, 17 June 1896

A long time passed, and nothing was to be heard but the noise of the birds. Again arose doubt as to whether it was all an illusion. Perhaps it was only a dream. But then I remembered the dogs' tracks; they, at any rate, were no delusion. But if there were people here, we could scarcely be on Gillies Land or a new land, as we had believed all the winter. We must after all be upon the south side of Franz Josef Land, and the suspicion I had had a few days ago was correct, namely that we had come south through an unknown sound and out between Hooker Island and Northbrook Island, and were now off the latter, in spite of the impossibility of reconciling our position with Payer's map.

It was with a strange mixture of feelings that I made my way in towards land among the numerous hummocks and inequalities. Suddenly I thought I heard a shout from a human voice, a strange voice, the first for three years. How my heart beat, and the blood rushed to my brain, as I ran up on to a hummock, and hallooed with all the strength of my lungs. Behind that one human voice in the midst of the icy desert, this one message from life, stood home and she who was waiting there; and I saw nothing else as I made my way between bergs and ice-ridges. Soon I heard another shout, and saw, too, from an ice-ridge, a dark form moving among the hummocks farther in. It was a dog; but farther off came another figure, and that was a man. Who was it? Was it Jackson or one of his companions, or was it perhaps a fellow-countryman? We approached one another quickly; I waved my hat: he did the same. I heard him speak to the dog, and I listened. It was English, and as I drew nearer I thought I recognised Mr. Jackson, whom I remembered once to have seen.

I raised my hat; we extended a hand to one another, with a hearty 'How do you do?' Above us a roof of mist, shutting out the world around, beneath our feet the rugged, packed drift-ice, and in the background a glimpse of the land, all ice, glacier, and mist. On one side the civilised European in an English check suit and high rubber waterboots, well shaved, well groomed, bringing with him a perfume of scented soap, perceptible to the wild man's sharpened senses; on the other side the wild man, clad in dirty rags, black with oil and soot, with long, uncombed hair and shaggy beard, black with smoke, with a face in which the natural fair complexion could not possibly be discerned through the thick layer of fat and soot which a winter's endeavours with warm water, moss, rags, and at last a knife had sought in vain to remove. . . .

Jackson: 'I'm immensely glad to see you.'

'Thank you, I also.'

'Have you a ship here?'

'No; my ship is not here.'

'How many are there of you?'

'I have one companion at the ice-edge.'

As we talked, we had begun to go in towards land. I took it for granted that he had recognised me, or at any rate understood who it was that was hidden behind this savage exterior, not thinking that a total stranger would be received so heartily. Suddenly he stopped, looked me full in the face, and said quickly:–

'Aren't you Nansen?'

'Yes, I am.'

'By Jove! I am glad to see you!'

And he seized my hand and shook it again, while his whole face became one smile of welcome, and delight at the unexpected meeting beamed from his dark eyes.

EJNAR MIKKELSEN
(fl. 1910)

Danish Arctic explorer. In 1910 Mikkelsen and Iver Iversen set out in search of diaries and maps believed to have been left behind in the course of the unsuccessful Greenland expedition of 1906–8 led by Mylius Erichsen. The two men spent 865 days together after the expected ship failed to arrive to take them off.

Resisting temptation on the way to Danmark's Fjord, autumn 1910

Now and again . . . hunger did come to the surface and drive all other sensations from our consciousness: we felt it then as a physical pain, an overwhelming desire for food.

Again Iver came up alongside me, and for some minutes we walked in silence close together, swaying on our feet, stumbling and bumping shoulders; it was impossible to continue like that. 'Either behind or in front, Iver, I don't mind which; but we can't walk close together, however much we would like to.'

Iver dropped behind and I could hear his unsteady footsteps on the frozen ground, his occasional stumbles over a stone, his grunts when the pain became too great to be borne in silence. Then there he was alongside me again.

When this had happened several times, I halted and we sat down on a stone.

'What is it Iver?' I asked. 'Is it the valley again?'

He did not say much. He just sat and stared out into the distance and shook his head: 'No,' he said, 'it isn't the valley. I'm famished, I can't do much more.'

I too was famished and not able to do much more; but there was nothing to be done about it. We had food in Danmarks Havn and there was no chance of anything edible before that, unless we ran into a bear and could shoot it.

Shoot? I looked at Iver, who was carrying the rifle, and a thought came into my head: 'Tell me honestly, Iver: is it the rifle you are afraid of?'

He nodded despairingly, looked at me steadily and held out the rifle: 'Take it and give me something of yours to carry. I can't have the rifle any longer – it's dangerous.'

So then I knew, and I refused to carry the rifle: 'Keep it, Iver,' I said, 'carry it as you have been doing and don't think too much. But if it will help your peace of mind, I can tell you that I see you in front of me the whole time. And when hunger dulls pain, weariness and reason, my thoughts are no doubt the same as yours: if he should drop and die, what then? Will you, or won't you, eat a bit of what is no longer Iver?'

Iver nodded assent and said: 'Yes, but I've got the rifle.'

'I know that, Iver,' I said. 'But keep it. After all our struggles we can walk on together, till we can walk no farther; and we can struggle on together, till we can struggle no more – or have come to our journey's end.'

VILHJAMUR STEFANNSSON
(1879–1962)

Canadian Arctic explorer. Of Icelandic parentage, he led several expeditions in the Arctic, adopting the Eskimo way of life. In 1913–18 he undertook the most prolonged polar exploration in history by remaining north of the Arctic Circle for an unbroken period of more than five years.

A man's best friend

After a day of high living on the one caribou ham, eight bear-paws, and five Canada jays we were down to a diet of skins and oil again. We also ate our snow-shoe lashings and several fathoms of other raw-hide thongs – fresh rawhide is good eating; it reminds one of pig's feet, if well boiled. It occurs to one in this connection (seriously speaking) that one of the material advantages of skin clothing over woolens in Arctic exploration is that one can eat them in an emergency, or feed them to one's dogs if the need is not quite so pressing. This puts actual starvation off by a week or so. As for eating one's dogs, the very thought is an abomination. Not that I have any prejudice against dog-meat, as such; it is probably very much like wolf, and wolf I know to be excellent. But on a long, hard sled trip the dogs become your friends; they work for you single-mindedly and uncomplainingly; they revel with you in prosperity and good fortune; they take starvation and hard knocks with an equanimity that says to you: 'We have seen hard times together before, we shall see good times again; but if this be the last, you can count on us to the end.' To me the death of a dog that has stood by me in failure and helped me to success is the death of a comrade in arms; to eat him would be but a step removed from cannibalism.

The Antarctic

CHARLES WILKES
(1798–1877)

American naval officer and Antarctic explorer. On 19 January 1840 Wilkes made what he thought was the first sighting of the Antarctic continent; it later transpired that the French explorer Dumont d'Urville had made a sighting on exactly the same day. Wilkes subsequently circumnavigated the globe. An impetuous man, he was twice court-martialled and, during the American Civil War, nearly provoked a war between the Union and Great Britain.

Icebergs off Oates Land, 21 January 1840

Some of the bergs were of magnificent dimensions, one-third of a mile in length, and from one hundred and fifty to two hundred feet in height, with sides perfectly smooth, as though they had been chiselled. Others, again, exhibited lofty arches of many-coloured tints, leading into deep caverns, open to the swell of the sea, which rushing in, produced loud and distant thunderings. The flight of birds passing in and out of these caverns recalled the recollections of ruined abbeys, castles and caves, while here and there a bold projecting bluff, crowned with pinnacles and turrets, resembled some Gothic keep. . . . If an immense city of ruined alabaster palaces can be imagined, of every variety and shape and tint, composed of huge piles of buildings grouped together, with long lanes or streets winding irregularly through them, some faint idea may be formed of the grandeur of the spectacle. The time and circumstances under which we were viewing them, threading our way through these vast bergs, we knew not to what end, left an impression upon me of these icy and desolate regions that can never be forgotten.

HENRIK JOHAN BULL
(b. 1844)

Norwegian Antarctic explorer. In 1894 the shipowner Svend Foyn sent his whaler *Antarctic* to the Antarctic whaling grounds. On 24 January 1895, the ship's captain Leonard Kristensen, and two young Norwegians, Bull and Carsten Borchgrevink, became the first men to set foot on the Antarctic continent.

Strange and pleasurable

The sensation of being the first men who had set foot on the real Antarctic mainland was both strange and pleasurable, although Mr Foyn would no doubt have preferred to exchange this pleasing sensation on our part for a right whale, even of small dimensions.

CARSTEN EGEBERG BORCHGREVINK
(1864–1934)

Norwegian-Australian Antarctic explorer. He emigrated to Australia in 1888. In 1898 he led an expedition to Antarctica, anchoring his ship, the *Southern Cross*, in Robertson Bay, near the place where he had landed in 1895 with H. J. Bull. It was the first anchorage ever made in Antarctica. The *Southern Cross* then sailed away, leaving ten men to endure the darkness and blizzards of the southern winter. Borchgrevink and his party proved that it was possible to winter on the continent, thus opening the way for the attack on the South Pole.

Watching ourselves grow old

During the gradual shortening of the days we experienced great depression, as if watching ourselves grow old. We were getting tired of each other's company and began to know every line in each other's faces. . . . The darkness and the silence weighed heavily on one's mind. The silence roared in our ears; it was centuries of heaped-up solitude.

An Antarctic picnic

At 11 p.m. we camped. Savio, whose turn it was to prepare a meal, laid different utensils and tinned food on the top of a sleeping-bag, without noticing that Ole Must was within. It was bitterly cold, and so tired was Ole that he did not notice when I suddenly sat down upon his head, remaining there whilst I had my meal, thinking all the while I was sitting on a Dutch cheese, of which we had some with us, but which froze so hard that undoubtedly they would have been useful projectiles for a cannon.

ROBERT FALCON SCOTT
(1868–1912)

English naval officer and Antarctic explorer. After various Antarctic expeditions, Scott set out for the South Pole in 1910. His ship, the *Terra Nova*, reached the Ross Sea in January 1911. In November he and four companions set out for the Pole, pulling their own sledges. They arrived on 18 January 1912 to find Amundsen's Norwegian flag already flying there.

An awful place

Wednesday, January 18, 1912
. . . Great God! This is an awful place and terrible enough for us to have laboured to it without the reward of priority. . . .

Now for the run home and a desperate struggle. I wonder if we can do it.

*Scott and his companions were in poor shape for the
800-mile journey to Cape Evans. Both Captain Oates and
Petty Officer Evans were suffering from frostbite. Evans
died on 17 February. On 2 March the survivors reached
their depot east of Mount Markham to find that their vital
fuel oil had leaked away, leaving scarcely enough to reach
the next depot. In the event, they never reached it. Temperatures were down to −40°F at night and Captain Oates was
forced to confess that both his feet were terribly frostbitten.
By 6 March gangrene had set in and he could no longer pull
a sledge.*

'It seems a pity. . . .'

Friday, March 16 or Saturday 17. – Lost track of dates, but think
the last correct. Tragedy all along the line. At lunch, the day before
yesterday, poor Titus Oates said he couldn't go on; he proposed we
should leave him in his sleeping-bag. That we could not do, and we
induced him to come on, on the afternoon march. In spite of its
awful nature for him he struggled on and we made a few miles. At
night he was worse and we knew the end had come. . . .

. . . This was the end. He slept through the night before last,
hoping not to wake; but he woke in the morning – yesterday. It was
blowing a blizzard. He said, 'I am just going outside and may be
some time.' He went out into the blizzard and we have not seen him
since. . . .

Monday, March 19. – Lunch. We camped with difficulty last
night, and were dreadfully cold till after our supper of cold pemmi-
can and biscuit and a half a pannikin of cocoa cooked over the
spirit. Then, contrary to expectation, we got warm and all slept
well. To-day we started in the usual dragging manner. Sledge
dreadfully heavy. We are 15 ½ miles from the depôt and ought to get
there in three days. What progress! We have two days' food but
barely a day's fuel. All our feet are getting bad – Wilson's best, my
right foot worst, left all right. There is no chance to nurse one's feet
till we can get hot food into us. Amputation is the least I can hope for
now, but will the trouble spread? That is the serious question. The
weather doesn't give us a chance – the wind from N. to N.W. and
−40° temp. to-day.

Wednesday, March 21. – Got within 11 miles of depôt Monday
night; had to lay up all yesterday in severe blizzard. To-day forlorn
hope, Wilson and Bowers going to depôt for fuel.

Thursday, March 22 and 23. – Blizzard bad as ever – Wilson and Bowers unable to start – to-morrow last chance – no fuel and only one or two of food left – must be near the end. Have decided it shall be natural – we shall march for the depôt with or without our effects and die in our tracks.

Thursday, March 29. – Since the 21st we have had a continuous gale from W.S.W. and S.W. We had fuel to make two cups of tea apiece and bare food for two days on the 20th. Every day we have been ready to start for our depôt *11 miles* away, but outside the door of the tent it remains a scene of whirling drift. I do not think we can hope for any better things now. We shall stick it out to the end, but we are getting weaker, of course, and the end cannot be far.

It seems a pity, but I do not think I can write more.

R. Scott.

Last entry.
For God's sake look after our people.

ROALD AMUNDSEN
(1872–1928)

Norwegian explorer and navigator. The first man to reach both Poles and the first to negotiate the North-West Passage. He reached the South Pole on 14 December 1911, after a dash by dog team and skis across the Bay of Whales, thirty-five days before Captain Robert F. Scott. To reach the North Pole he used an airship, the *Norge*, crossing the Pole on 11 May 1926.

'Good grounds for mutual respect' at the South Pole

At three in the afternoon a simultaneous 'Halt!' rang out from the drivers. They had carefully examined their sledge-meters, and they all showed the full distance – our Pole by reckoning. The goal was reached, the journey ended. I cannot say – though I know it would sound much more effective – that the object of my life was attained. That would be romancing rather too bare-facedly. I had better be honest and admit straight out that I have never known any man to be placed in such a diametrically opposite position to the goal of his desires as I was at that moment. The regions around the North Pole

– well, yes, the North Pole itself – had attracted me from childhood, and here I was at the South Pole. Can anything more topsy-turvy be imagined?

We reckoned now that we were at the Pole. Of course, every one of us knew that we were not standing on the absolute spot; it would be an impossibility with the time and the instruments at our disposal to ascertain that exact spot. But we were so near it that the few miles which possibly separated us from it could not be of the slightest importance. It was our intention to make a circle round this camp, with a radius of twelve and a half miles (20 kilometres), and to be satisfied with that. After we had halted we collected and congratulated each other. We had good grounds for mutual respect in what had been achieved, and I think that was just the feeling that was expressed in the firm and powerful grasps of the fist that were exchanged. After this we proceeded to the greatest and most solemn act of the whole journey – the planting of our flag. Pride and affection shone in the five pairs of eyes that gazed upon the flag, as it unfurled itself with a sharp crack, and waved over the Pole.

SIR ERNEST HENRY SHACKLETON
(1874–1922)

English Antarctic explorer. Born in Ireland, he made his first Antarctic expedition with Scott in 1901–4. He then commanded the expedition (1907–9) that located the south magnetic pole in 1906. In 1914 he set off on an expedition to cross the Antarctic from the Weddell Sea to the Ross Sea, by way of the Pole and the Beardmore Glacier. His ship was crushed in the ice in 1915, but he led his men to safety at Elephant Island. He then decided to try to reach South Georgia, a voyage of 800 miles across the Scotia Sea, among the wildest waters in the world. With five companions, he made the journey in sixteen days – a feat of extraordinary courage and seamanship. Leaving three men on the uninhabited south-west coast of South Georgia, Shackleton and his companions Worsley and Crean crossed the completely unexplored mountain ranges of the interior to Stromness Bay. The twenty-two men left on Elephant Island, and the three on the South Georgian coast, were eventually rescued.

'The world is mad' – Stromness whaling station, May 1916

Shivering with cold, yet with hearts light and happy, we set off towards the whaling-station, now not more than a mile and a half distant. The difficulties of the journey lay behind us. We tried to straighten ourselves up a bit, for the thought that there might be women at the station made us painfully conscious of our uncivilized appearance. Our beards were long and our hair was matted. We were unwashed and the garments that we had worn for nearly a year without a change were tattered and stained. Three more unpleasant-looking ruffians could hardly have been imagined. Worsley produced several safety-pins from some corner of his garments and effected some temporary repairs that really emphasized his general disrepair. . . .

. . . We came to the wharf, where the man in charge stuck to his station. I asked him if Mr. Sorlle (the manager) was in the house.

'Yes,' he said as he stared at us.

'We would like to see him,' said I.

'Who are you?' he asked.

'We have lost our ship and come over the island,' I replied.

'You have come over the island?' he said in a tone of entire disbelief.

The man went towards the manager's house and we followed him. I learned afterwards that he said to Mr. Sorlle: 'There are three funny-looking men outside, who say they have come over the island and they know you. I have left them outside.' A very necessary precaution from his point of view.

Mr. Sorlle came out to the door and said, 'Well?'

'Don't you know me?' I said.

'I know your voice,' he replied doubtfully. 'You're the mate of the *Daisy*.'

'My name is Shackleton,' I said.

Immediately he put out his hand and said, 'Come in. Come in.'

'Tell me, when was the war over?' I asked.

'The war is not over,' he answered. 'Millions are being killed. Europe is mad. The world is mad.'

SIR DOUGLAS MAWSON
(1882–1958)

Australian Antarctic explorer. In September 1912 he set off with Lieutenant B. E. S. Ninnis, a British army officer, and Dr Xavier Mertz, a Swiss mountaineer and skiing champion, to explore King George V Land. With them they took three sledges and seventeen dogs.

The death of Ninnis, 14 December 1912

When next I looked back, it was in response to the anxious gaze of Mertz who had turned round and halted in his tracks. Behind me nothing met the eye except my own sledge tracks running back in the distance. Where were Ninnis and his sledge?

I hastened back along the trail thinking that a rise in the ground obscured the view. There was no such good fortune, however, for I came to a gaping hole in the surface about eleven feet wide. The lid of the crevasse that had caused me so little thought had broken in; two sledge tracks led up to it on the far side – only one continued beyond.

Frantically waving to Mertz to bring up my sledge, upon which there was some alpine rope, I leaned over and shouted into the dark depths below. No sound came back but the moaning of a dog, caught on a shelf just visible one hundred and fifty feet below. The poor creature appeared to have a broken back, for it was attempting to sit up with the front part of its body, while the hinder portion lay limp. Another dog lay motionless by its side. Close by was what appeared in the gloom to be the remains of the tent and a canvas food-tank containing a fortnight's supply.

We broke back the edge of the hard snow lid and, secured by a rope, took turns leaning over, calling into the darkness in the hope that our companion might be still alive. For three hours we called unceasingly but no answering sound came back. The dog had ceased to moan and lay without a movement. A chill draught rose out of the abyss. We felt that there was no hope.

It was difficult to realise that Ninnis, who was a young giant in built, so jovial and so real but a few minutes before, should thus have vanished without even a sound. It seemed so incredible that we half expected, on turning round, to find him standing there.

And of Mertz, 7 January 1913

[31 December 1912] On talking things over with Mertz, I found that, though he had said little on the subject in the past, he had found the dog meat very disagreeable and felt that he was getting little nutriment from it. He suggested that we should abstain for a time from eating any further of this meat and draw solely upon the ordinary food of which we still had some days' supply carefully husbanded. This plan was adopted as it was expected to act beneficially on our health. I will always remember the wonderful taste that the food had in those days. Acute hunger enhances the taste and smell of food beyond all ordinary conception. . . . Cocoa was almost intoxicating and even plain beef suet, such as we had in fragments in our hoosh mixture, had acquired a sweet and aromatic taste scarcely to be described. . . .

Later in the day I had another surprise finding that Mertz had lost appreciation of the biscuit; it was then that I first began to realise that something really serious was the matter and that his condition was worse than my own.

Snow continued to fall all day long throughout New Year's day and the light remained as bad as ever. We waited anxiously for a glimpse of the sun to give us direction, in the meantime we decided not to attempt a move as Mertz was not up to his usual form and the rest might recuperate him. . . .

At length in the evening of January 3 the clouds broke and the sun peered through for a time. We were not long in packing and getting on the way. It was an exceptionally cold night and the wind pierced our emaciated frames like a knife. Alas, before five miles were covered we were again in camp for Mertz had suddenly developed dysentery. To make matters worse his fingers had been badly frost-bitten, which for a moment he himself could scarcely believe, for so resistant to cold was he that he had never before suffered in this way. To convince himself he bit a considerable piece of the fleshy part off the end of one of them. . . .

The morning of January 7th opened with better weather, for there was little wind and no snow falling; even the sun appeared gleaming through the clouds.

In view of the seriousness of the position it had been agreed overnight that at all costs we would go on in the morning, sledge-sailing with Mertz in his bag strapped on the sledge. It was therefore a doubly sad blow that morning to find that my companion was again touched with dysentery and so weak as to be quite helpless. After tucking him into the bag again, I slid into my own in order to kill time and keep warm, for the cold had a new sting about it in those days of want. . . .

There was no prospect of proceeding so I settled myself to stand by my stricken comrade and ease his sufferings as far as possible. It would require a miracle to bring him round to a fit travelling condition, but I prayed that it might be granted.

After noon he improved and drank some thick cocoa and soup.

Later in the afternoon he had several more fits and then, becoming delirious, talked incoherently until midnight. Most of that time his strength returned and he struggled to climb out of the sleeping-bag, keeping me very busy tucking him in again. About midnight he appeared to doze off to sleep and with a feeling of relief I slid down into my own bag, not to sleep, though weary enough, but to get warm again and to think matters over. After a couple of hours, having felt no movement, I stretched out my arm and found that my comrade was stiff in death. He had been accepted into 'the peace that passeth all understanding.'

It was unutterably sad that he should have perished thus, after the splendid work he had accomplished not only on that particular sledging journey but throughout the expedition. No one could have done better. Favoured with a generous and lovable character, he had been a general favourite amongst all the members of the expedition. Now all was over, he had done his duty and passed on. All that remained was his mortal frame which, toggled up in his sleeping-bag, still offered some sense of companionship as I threw myself down for the remainder of the night, revolving in my mind all that lay behind and the chances of the future.

Mawson cut his sledge in half, jettisoned all non-essential equipment and set out on the 100-mile journey to Commonwealth Bay, where the expedition's ship was supposed to be waiting. On the way he fell into a crevasse but was held, dangling at the end of a fourteen-foot rope, by his sledge. 'Fired by the passion that burns the blood in the act of strife', he hauled himself out and went on. At the end of January he found some food left by a search party. When he finally reached Commonwealth Bay he had the terrible experience of seeing his ship steaming away. Fortunately, five men had been left behind, and he was saved.

RICHARD EVELYN BYRD
(1888–1957)

American naval officer, aviator and polar explorer. In 1926, with Floyd Bennett, he was one of the first men to fly over the North Pole. In 1933–4 Byrd spent four and a half months alone in a 12′ × 9′ hut, 125 miles south of the Ross Ice Shelf. On 11 May 1934, in the middle of a fierce blizzard, he left the hut to visit the instrument shelter. When he returned he found he was unable to open the entry hatch.

Reason fled

Panic took me then, I must confess. Reason fled. I clawed at the three-foot square of timber like a madman. I beat on it with my fists, trying to shake the snow loose; and, when that did no good, I lay flat on my belly and pulled until my hands went weak from cold and weariness. Then I crooked my elbow, put my face down, and said over and over again, You damn fool, you damn fool. Here for weeks I had been defending myself against the danger of being penned inside the shack; instead, I was now locked out; and nothing could be worse, especially since I had only a wool parka and pants under my wind-proofs. Just two feet below was sanctuary – warmth, food, tools, all the means of survival. All these things were an arm's length away, but I was powerless to reach them.

There is something extravagantly insensate about an Antartic blizzard at night. Its vindictiveness cannot be measured on an anemometer sheet. It is more than just wind; it is a solid wall of snow moving at gale force, pounding like surf. The whole malevolent rush is concentrated upon you as upon a personal enemy. In the senseless explosion of sound you are reduced to a crawling thing on the margin of a disintegrating world; you can't see, you can't hear, you can hardly move. The lungs gasp after the air sucked out of them, and the brain is shaken. Nothing in the world will so quickly isolate a man.

Half-frozen, I stabbed toward one of the ventilators, a few feet away. My mittens touched something round and cold. Cupping it in my hands, I pulled myself up. This was the outlet ventilator. Just why, I don't know – but instinct made me kneel and press my face against the opening. Nothing in the room was visible, but a dim patch of light illuminated the floor, and warmth rose up to my face. That steadied me.

Still kneeling, I turned my back to the blizzard and considered what might be done. I thought of breaking in the windows in the roof, but they lay two feet down in hard crust, and were reinforced with wire besides. If I only had something to dig with, I could break the crust and stamp the windows in with my feet. The pipe cupped between my hands supplied the first inspiration; maybe I could use that to dig with. It, too, was wedged tight; I pulled until my arms ached, without budging it; I had lost all track of time, and the despairing thought came to me that I was lost in a task without an end. Then I remembered the shovel. A week before, after levelling drift from the last light blow, I had stabbed a shovel handle up in the crust somewhere to leeward. That shovel would save me. But how to find it in the avalanche of the blizzard?

I lay down and stretched out full length. Still holding the pipe, I thrashed around with my feet, but pummelled only empty air. Then I worked back to the hatch. The hard edges at the opening provided another grip, and again I stretched out and kicked. Again no luck. I dared not let go until I had something else familiar to cling to. My foot came up against the other ventilator pipe. I edged back to that, and from the new anchorage repeated the manœuvre. This time my ankle struck something hard. When I felt it and recognized the handle, I wanted to caress it.

Embracing this thrice-blessed tool, I inched back to the trap-door. The handle of the shovel was just small enough to pass under the little wooden bridge which served as a grip. I got both hands on the shovel and tried to wrench the door up; my strength was not enough, however. So I lay down flat on my belly and worked my shoulders under the shovel. Then I heaved, the door sprang open, and I rolled down the shaft. When I tumbled into the light and warmth of the room, I kept thinking, How wonderful, how perfectly wonderful.

SOURCES
AND ACKNOWLEDGEMENTS

ADVICE ON TRAVELLING

SAMUEL JOHNSON: (1) *A Journey to the Western Islands of Scotland*, London, 1775; (2) letter to Mrs Thrale, 12 August 1773; (3) quoted in James Boswell, *The Life of Samuel Johnson*, London, 1791.

PRINCE HERMANN PÜCKLER-MUSKAU: *Regency Visitor: The English Tour of Prince Pückler-Muskau Described in His Letters, 1826–1828*, trans. Sarah Austin, ed. E. M. Butler, London, 1957.

SIR FRANCIS GALTON: *The Art of Travel*, 3rd ed., London, 1860.

W. B. LORD and THOMAS BAINES: *Shifts and Expedients of Camp Life*, London, 1876.

MURRAY'S HANDBOOK OF TRAVEL TALK: London, 1874.

FRANK TATCHELL: *The Happy Traveller: A Book for Poor Men*, London, 1923.

MEMBERS OF THE ROYAL GEOGRAPHICAL SOCIETY: *Hints to Travellers*, 11th ed., London, 1938. Reprinted by permission of the Royal Geographical Society.

HORACE KEPHART: *Camping and Woodcraft*, New York, 1916.

V. G. RAGAM: *Pilgrim's Travel Guide*, Part 2: North India with Himalayan Regions, n.d.

JOHN HATT: *The Tropical Traveller*, London and New York, 1982; revised ed. 1985. Reprinted by permission of Pan Books and Hippocrene Books, Inc.

AFRICA

SUETONIUS PAULINUS: *The Natural History of Pliny the Elder*, Vol. 5, trans. J. Bostock and H. T. Riley, London, 1857.

FIDELIS: Quoted and translated by John Wilkinson in *Jerusalem Pilgrims before the Crusades*, Warminster, Wilts, 1977. Reprinted by permission of Aris & Phillips Ltd.

IBN BATTUTA: *Travels in Asia and Africa 1325–1354*, trans. and selected by H. A. R. Gibb, London, 1929.

ALVISE DA CADAMOSTO: *The Voyages of Cadamosto*, ed. and trans. G. R. Crone, Hakluyt Society, 2nd Series, Vol. 80, 1937. Reprinted by permission of the Hakluyt Society.

VASCO DA GAMA: *A Journal of the First Voyage of Vasco de Gama, 1497–1499*, ed. and trans. E. G. Ravenstein, Hakluyt Society, 1st Series, Vol. 99, 1898.

LEO AFRICANUS: *The History and Description of Africa*, trans. J. Pory, ed. R. Brown, Hakluyt Society, 1st Series, Vol. 92, 1896.

ANONYMOUS ENGLISHMAN: *Hakluyt's Principal Voyages*, London, 1598–1600.

ANDREW BATTEL: *Purchas His Pilgrims*, London, 1625.

JAMES BRUCE: *Travels to Discover the Source of the Nile*, London, 1790.

MUNGO PARK: (1 & 2) *Travels*, London, 1799; (3) *Journal of a Mission to the Interior of Africa in the Year 1805*, London, 1815.

WILLIAM J. BURCHELL: *Travels in the Interior of South Africa*, London, 1822.

JOHANN LUDWIG BURKHARDT: *Travels in Nubia*, London, 1819.

AUGUSTUS EARLE: *A Narrative of a Nine Months' Residence in Tristan D'Acunha, an Island Situated between South America and the Cape of Good Hope*, London, 1832.

HUGH CLAPPERTON: D. Denham, H. Clapperton and W. Oudney, *Narrative of Travels in Northern and Central Africa in 1822–24*, London, 1826.

RÉNÉ CAILLIÉ: *Travels through Central Africa to Timbuktoo . . .*, Vol. 2, London, 1830.

RICHARD LEMON LANDER: *Records of Captain Clapperton's Last Expedition*, London, 1829.

GÉRARD DE NERVAL: *Journey to the Orient*, trans. Norman Glass, London, 1972; reprinted by Michael Haag, 1984. Reprinted by permission of Peter Owen Ltd.

FRANCIS OWEN: *The Diary of the Rev. Francis Owen M.A.*, ed. Sir G. E. Cory, the Van Riebeck Society, Cape Town, 1926.

ALEXANDER KINGLAKE: *Eothen*, London, 1844.

JOHANN LUDWIG KRAPF: *Travels, Researches and Missionary Labours during an Eighteen Years' Residence in East Africa*, London, 1860.

WILLIAM MAKEPEACE THACKERAY: *Notes of a Journey from Cornhill to Grand Cairo*, London, 1846.

DAVID LIVINGSTONE: *Missionary Travels and Researches in South Africa . . .*, London, 1857.

ROUALEYN GORDON CUMMING: *The Lion Hunter of South Africa*, London, 1850.

LUCIE DUFF GORDON: *Letters from Egypt*, London, 1865; reprinted by Virago Press, 1983.

HEINRICH BARTH: *Travels and Discoveries in North and Central Africa*, London and New York, 1857.

SIR SAMUEL WHITE BAKER: *The Albert N'Yanza, Great Basin of the Nile*, London, 1866.

GUSTAVE FLAUBERT: From *Flaubert in Egypt: A Sensibility on Tour*, ed. and trans. F. Steegmuller, London, 1972. Reprinted by permission of Academy Chicago.

SIR RICHARD FRANCIS BURTON: *The Lake Regions of Central Africa*, London, 1860.

JOHN HANNING SPEKE: *Journal of the Discovery of the Source of the Nile*, London, 1863.

GEORG AUGUST SCHWEINFURTH: *Heart of Africa: Three Years' Travels and Adventures in the Unexplored Regions of Central Africa*, London, 1873.

HENRY MORTON STANLEY: *How I Found Livingstone in Central Africa*, London, 1872.

JOSEPH THOMSON: *Through Masai Land: A Journey of Exploration among the Snowclad Volcanic Mountains and Strange Tribes of Eastern Equatorial Africa*, London, 1885; reprinted by Frank Cass, 1968.

MARY KINGSLEY: *Travels in West Africa*, London, 1897; reprinted by Virago Press, 1982.

EDITH WHARTON: *In Morocco*, London, 1920; reprinted by Century Publishing, London, and Hippocrene Books, Inc., New York, 1984. Reprinted by permission of Mr W. R. Tyler and Hippocrene Books, Inc.

COLETTE: *Places*, trans. David Le Vay, London, 1970. Reprinted by permission of Peter Owen Ltd.

EVELYN WAUGH: *When the Going was Good*, London, 1946. Reprinted by permission of A. D. Peters & Co. Ltd.

GRAHAM GREENE: *Journey without Maps*, London, 1936. Reprinted by permission of Laurence Pollinger Ltd and Viking Penguin, Inc. Copyright © 1961 by Graham Greene.

SIR CECIL BEATON: *The Parting Years, Diaries 1963–1974*, London, 1978. Reprinted by permission of Weidenfeld & Nicolson Ltd and the Literary Executors of Sir Cecil Beaton's Estate.

GEOFFREY GORER: *Africa Dances*, London, 1935; reprinted by Penguin Books, 1983. Reprinted by permission of David Higham Associates Ltd.

SIR LAURENS VAN DER POST: *Venture to the Interior*, London, 1952; reprinted by Penguin Books, 1984. Reprinted by permission of the author and Chatto & Windus Ltd.

PETER MAYNE: *The Alleys of Marrakesh*, London, 1953. Reprinted by permission of John Murray Ltd.

JOHN HILLABY: *Journey to the Jade Sea*, London, 1964. Reprinted by permission of Constable & Co. Ltd.

GEOFFREY MOORHOUSE: *The Fearful Void*, London, 1974. Reprinted by permission of the author and Hodder & Stoughton Ltd.

PATRICK MARNHAM: *Fantastic Invasion: Dispatches from Contemporary Africa*, London, 1980. Reprinted by permission of the author and Jonathan Cape Ltd.

EUROPE

HANNIBAL: Polybius, *The Histories*, trans. W. R. Paton, London and New York, 1922.

LUITPRAND OF CREMONA: *Historia*, quoted in *The Journey of William of Rubruck to the Eastern Parts of the World*, Hakluyt Society, 2nd Series, Vol. 4, 1900.

BENVENUTO CELLINI: *The Autobiography of Benvenuto Cellini*, trans. J. A. Symonds, London, 1949. Reprinted by permission of Phaidon Press Ltd.

GEORGE TURBEVILLE: *Hakluyt's Principal Voyages*, op. cit.

GILES FLETCHER: *Hakluyt's Principal Voyages*, op. cit.

OTTAVIANO BON: *Purchas His Pilgrims*, London, 1625.

THOMAS CORYATE: *Coryats Crudities*, London, 1611. Reprinted by James MacLehose & Sons, 1905.

WILLIAM LITHGOW: *The Totall Discourse, of Rare Adventures, and painfull Peregrinations of long nineteen yeares travayles*, London, 1632.

THOMAS DALLAM: 'Diary, 1599–1600' in *Early Voyages and Travels in the Levant*, ed. J. T. Bent, Hakluyt Society, 1st Series, Vol. 87, 1893.

JOHN EVELYN: *The Diary of John Evelyn*, Vol. 1, London, 1906.

MADAME DE SÉVIGNÉ: *Letters from Madame La Marquise de Sévigné*, selected and trans. by V. Hammersley, London, 1955. Reprinted by permission of Secker & Warburg Ltd.

JAMES DRUMMOND: *Letters from James Earl of Perth to His Sister, The Countess of Erroll*, ed. W. Jerdan., Camden Society, London, 1845.

LADY MARY WORTLEY MONTAGU: *The Letters and Works of Lady Mary Wortley Montagu*, ed. Lord Wharncliffe, London, 1837.

HENRY FIELDING: *Journal of a Voyage to Lisbon*, London, 1892.

LAURENCE STERNE: *A Sentimental Journey*, London, 1768.

THOMAS GRAY: *Letters of Thomas Gray*, selected by J. Beresford, Oxford, 1951.

HORACE WALPOLE: *The Letters of Horace Walpole, Fourth Earl of Orford*, ed. P. Cunningham, Edinburgh, 1857–9.

PHILIP THICKNESSE: *A Year's Journey through France and Part of Spain*, Dublin, 1777.

TOBIAS SMOLLETT: *Travels through France and Italy*, London, 1766.

EDWARD GIBBON: *The Autobiography of Edward Gibbon*, London, 1796.

JAMES BOSWELL: (1) *Boswell in Holland*, ed. F. A. Pottle, London and New York, 1952; (2) *Boswell on the Grand Tour*, ed. F. A. Pottle, London and New York, 1953. Printed with permission of Yale University, the McGraw-Hill Book Company and William Heinemann Ltd.

LADY ANNA MILLER: *Letters from Italy*, London, 1776.

ARTHUR YOUNG: *Travels in France*, London, 1792.

JOHANN WOLFGANG VON GOETHE: (1) *Goethe's Travels in Italy, together with His Second Residence in Rome and Fragments on Italy*, trans. A. J. Morrison and C. Nisbet, London, 1892; (2) *Letters from Goethe*, trans. M. von Herzfeld and C. Melvin, Edinburgh, 1957.

WILLIAM BECKFORD: *Italy with Sketches of Spain and Portugal by the Author of 'Vathek'*, 2nd ed., London, 1834.

MICHAEL KELLY: *Reminiscences*, London, 1826.

EDWARD DANIEL CLARKE: (1) *Travels in Various Countries of Europe, Asia and Africa*, Vol. 9, London, 1824; (2) Ibid., Vol. 1, London, 1816.

WILLIAM HAZLITT: *Notes on a Journey through France and Italy*, London, 1856.

STENDHAL: *Rome, Naples and Florence in 1817*, London, 1818.

BENJAMIN ROBERT HAYDON: *Autobiography and Journals*, ed. T. Taylor, London, 1853.

LORD BYRON: *Letters*, Everyman edition, London, 1936.

PERCY BYSSHE SHELLEY: *The Letters of Percy Bysshe Shelley*, ed. R. Ingpen, London, 1909.

MARQUIS DE CUSTINE: *The Empire of the Czar*, London, 1843.

RICHARD FORD: *Gatherings from Spain*, London, 1846.

GEORGE BORROW: *The Bible in Spain*, London, 1843.

JULIA PARDOE: *Beauties of the Bosphorus*, London, 1839.

ALEXANDER KINGLAKE: *Eothen*, op. cit.

ROBERT CURZON: *Visit to the Monasteries in the Levant*, London, 1849.

EDWARD LEAR: *Journals of a Landscape Painter in Greece and Albania*, London, 1851.

JOHN RUSKIN: *Praeterita*, London, 1885.

JOHN MACGREGOR: *A Thousand Miles in the Rob Roy Canoe*, London, 1866.

EARL OF DUFFERIN: *Letters from High Latitudes*, London, 1857.

MARK TWAIN: *The Innocents Abroad*, Hartford, Conn., 1869.

FREDERICK BURNABY: *A Ride to Khiva: Travels and Adventures in Central Asia*, 2nd ed., London, 1876.

W. H. MALLOCK: *In an Enchanted Island*, London, 1889.

ROBERT LOUIS STEVENSON: *Travels with a Donkey in the Cévennes*, London, 1879.

THOMAS STEVENS: *Around the World on a Bicycle*, London, 1887.

C. E. MONTAGUE: *The Right Place*, London, 1926.

JOHN FOSTER FRASER: *Round the World on a Wheel*, London, 1899; reprinted by Chatto & Windus, 1982.

NORMAN DOUGLAS: *Old Calabria*, London, 1915. Reprinted by permission of the Society of Authors as literary representative of the Estate of Norman Douglas.

ROSE MACAULAY: *A Pleasure of Ruins*, London, 1953. Reprinted by permission of Thames & Hudson Ltd and Holt, Rinehart & Winston, Inc.

D. H. LAWRENCE: *The Letters of D. H. Lawrence*, ed. A. Huxley, London, 1932. Reprinted by permission of Laurence Pollinger Ltd, the Estate of Mrs Frieda Lawrence Ravagli and Viking Penguin, Inc. Copyright 1932 by the Estate of D. H. Lawrence. Copyright renewed © 1960 by Angelo Ravagli and C. M. Weekley, Executors of the Estate of Frieda Lawrence Ravagli.

WALTER STARKIE: *The Road to Santiago*, London, 1957. Reprinted by permission of John Murray Ltd.

SIR VICTOR PRITCHETT: *The Spanish Temper*, London, 1954. Reprinted by permission of the author, Chatto & Windus Ltd and A. D. Peters & Co. Ltd.

CYRIL CONNOLLY: *The Unquiet Grave*, London, 1948. Reprinted by permission of Deborah Rogers Ltd.

EVELYN WAUGH: *Labels*, London, 1946. Reprinted by permission of A. D. Peters & Co. Ltd.

SIR CECIL BEATON: (1) *The Wandering Years, Diaries 1922–39*, London, 1961;

(2) *The Strenuous Years*, London, 1973. Reprinted by permission of Weidenfeld & Nicolson Ltd and the Literary Executors of Sir Cecil Beaton's Estate.

ROBERT BYRON: *First Russia then Tibet*, London, 1933. Reprinted by permission of A. D. Peters & Co. Ltd.

GEORGE MILLAR: *Horned Pigeon*, London, 1946. Reprinted by permission of Laurence Pollinger Ltd.

SIR FITZROY MACLEAN: *Eastern Approaches*, London, 1949. Reprinted by permission of the author and Jonathan Cape Ltd.

WILLIAM SANSOM: *Blue Skies, Brown Studies*, London, 1961. Copyright © William Sansom 1961. Reprinted by permission of Elaine Greene Ltd.

LAWRENCE DURRELL: *Prospero's Cell*, London, 1945. Reprinted by permission of Faber & Faber Ltd, the author and his agent, James Brown Associates, Inc.

PATRICK LEIGH FERMOR: *Mani: Travels in the Southern Pelopponese*, London, 1958. Reprinted by permission of John Murray Ltd.

EDITH TEMPLETON: *The Surprise of Cremona*, London, 1954; reprinted by Methuen, 1985. Reprinted by permission of Curtis Brown Ltd, London.

JAN MORRIS: *Cities*, London, 1963. Reprinted by permission of the author.

COLIN THUBRON: *Among the Russians*, London, 1983. Reprinted by permission of William Heinemann Ltd.

GREAT BRITAIN AND IRELAND

PYTHEAS: Diodorus, V, 21, quoted in M. Cary and E. H. Warmington, *The Ancient Explorers*, London, 1929.

STRABO: *Geography*, trans. H. L. Jones, London and New York, 1930.

GIRALDUS CAMBRENSIS: *The Journey through Wales (Itinerarium Cambriae)*, trans. L. Thorpe, London, 1978. Copyright © the Estate of Lewis Thorpe, 1978. Reprinted by permission of Penguin Books Ltd.

JOHN LELAND: *The Itinerary of John Leland*, ed. L. Toulmin Smith, London, 1907.

EMANUEL VAN METEREN: *Nederlandtsche Historie*, 1614, quoted in *England as Seen by Foreigners*, ed. W. B. Rye, London, 1865.

FYNES MORYSON: *An Itinerary Containing His Ten Yeeres Travell . . .*, London, 1617.

PETER MUNDY: *The Travels of Peter Mundy*, Vol. IV, ed. R. C. Temple, Hakluyt Society, 2nd Series, Vol. 55, 1925.

MARTIN MARTIN: *A Description of the Western Islands of Scotland*, London, 1703.

DANIEL DEFOE: *A Tour through the whole Island of Great Britain*, London, 1724–6.

CELIA FIENNES: *The Journeys of Celia Fiennes*, London, 1888.

CÉSAR DE SAUSSURE: *A Foreign View of England in the Reigns of George I and George II: The Letters of Monsieur César de Saussure to His Family*, trans. and ed. Madame van Muyden, London, 1902.

JAMES BOSWELL: *Boswell's Journal of a Tour to the Hebrides*, London and New York, 1936. Printed with permission of Yale University, the McGraw-Hill Book Company and William Heinemann Ltd.

JAMES WOODFORDE: *Woodforde: Passages from the Five Volumes of the Diary of a Country Parson, 1758–1802*, selected and ed. J. Beresford, Oxford, 1924. Reprinted by permission of Oxford University Press.

CARL PHILIP MORITZ: *The Travels of Carl Philip Moritz in 1782*, London, 1924.

WILLIAM COBBETT: *Rural Rides*, London, 1830.

FRANCOIS DE LA ROCHEFOUCAULD: *A Frenchman in England, 1784*, ed. J. Marchand, trans. S. C. Roberts, Cambridge, 1933.

HSIEH CH'ING-KAO: From Kenneth Ch'en, *Monumenta Serica*, Vol. 7, 1942, quoted in Jeannette Mirsky, *The Great Chinese Travellers*, London, 1965.

LOUIS SIMOND: *Journal of a Tour and Residence in Great Britain during the Years 1810 and 1811*, Edinburgh and London, 1817.

CHEVALIER DE LA TOCNAYE: *A Frenchman's Walk through Ireland 1796–7*, trans. J. Stevenson, Belfast and Dublin, 1917; reprinted by The Blackstaff Press, Belfast, 1984.

DOROTHY WORDSWORTH: *Recollections of a Tour Made in Scotland, A.D. 1803*, ed. J. C. Shairp, Edinburgh, 1874.

PRINCE HERMANN PÜCKLER-MUSKAU: *Regency Visitor*, op. cit.

GEORGE BORROW: *Wild Wales*, London, 1862. Reprinted by Century Publishing and Hippocrene Books, Inc., 1984.

FANNY KEMBLE: *Record of a Girlhood*, London, 1878.

WILLIAM MAKEPEACE THACKERAY: *The Irish Sketch Book*, London, 1843.

ALEXANDER HERZEN: *My Past and Thoughts*, trans. C. Garnett, London, 1968. Reprinted by permission of Chatto & Windus Ltd and Alfred A. Knopf, Inc.

ALPHONSE ESQUIROS: *The English at Home*, trans. and ed. L. Wraxall, London, 1861.

QUEEN VICTORIA: *Leaves from the Journal of Our Life in the Highlands*, London, 1868.

BAYARD TAYLOR: *Views Afoot*, New York, 1846.

HIPPOLYTE TAINE: *Taine's Notes on England*, trans. E. Hyams, London, 1957. Reprinted by permission of Thames & Hudson Ltd.

HENRY JAMES: *English Hours*, London, 1905; reprinted by Oxford University Press, 1981.

EDITH WHARTON: *A Backward Glance*, London and New York, 1934. Reprinted by permission of Constable & Co. Ltd and Charles Scribner's Sons.

NIKOS KAZANTZAKIS: *England*, New York, 1965; London, 1970. Reprinted by permission of Athena G. Damis.

KAREL CAPEK: *Letters from England*, trans. P. Selver, London, 1924. Reprinted by permission of the Estate of Karel Capek.

H. V. MORTON: *In Search of England*, London, 1927. Reprinted by permission of Methuen London Ltd.

CYRIL CONNOLLY: *The Unquiet Grave*, op. cit. Reprinted by permission of Deborah Rogers Ltd.

JOHN HILLABY: *Journey through Britain*, London, 1968; reprinted by Paladin Books, 1983. Reprinted by permission of Constable & Co. Ltd.

HEINRICH BOLL: *Irish Journal*, trans. L. Vennewitz, New York, 1967. Reprinted by permission of the McGraw-Hill Book Company and Secker & Warburg Ltd.

NEAR ASIA

XENOPHON: *Anabasis*, trans. C. L. Brownson, London and Cambridge, Mass., 1932. Reprinted by permission of the Loeb Classical Library and Harvard University Press.

ST PAUL: *The Shorter Bible*, Acts 27, 39–44 and 28, 1–15.

ST WILLIBALD: Quoted and translated by John Wilkinson in *Jerusalem Pilgrims before the Crusades*, op. cit. Reprinted by permission of Aris & Phillips Ltd.

ODORIC OF PORDENONE: *Cathay and the Way Thither*, trans. and ed. Col. Sir H. Yule, Hakluyt Society, 2nd Series, Vol. 33, 1913.

LUDOVICO DI VARTHEMA: *The Travels of Ludovico di Varthema*, trans. from the original Italian ed. of 1510 by J. Winter Jones, Hakluyt Society, 1st Series, Vol. 32, 1863.

GEFFREY DUCKET: *Hakluyt's Principal Voyages*, op. cit.

JOHANN LUDWIG BURCKHARDT: *Travels in Syria and the Holy Land*, London, 1822.

ALEXANDER KINGLAKE: *Eothen*, op. cit.

SIR RICHARD BURTON: *The Personal Narrative of a Pilgrimage to El Medinah and Mecca*, London, 1855.

CHARLES MONTAGU DOUGHTY: *Travels in Arabia Deserta*, Cambridge, 1888; definitive edition, London, 1936.

EDWARD GRANVILLE BROWNE: *A Year among the Persians*, London, 1893. Reprinted by Century Publishing, 1984.

DAVID GEORGE HOGARTH: *A Wandering Scholar in the Levant*, London, 1896.

GERTRUDE BELL: *Letters*, London, 1927.

T. E. LAWRENCE: *The Seven Pillars of Wisdom*, London, 1935. Reprinted by permission of the Seven Pillars Trust, Jonathan Cape Ltd and Doubleday and Company, Inc. Copyright 1923, 1935 by Doubleday and Company, Inc.

BERTRAM THOMAS: *Arabia Felix*, London, 1932. Reprinted by permission of the Estate of Bertram Thomas, Jonathan Cape Ltd and Charles Scribner's Sons. Copyright 1932 Charles Scribner's Sons, copyright renewed © 1960 Cynthia Thomas and Bessie Mary Thomas.

DAME FREYA STARK: *The Journey's Echo*, London, 1963. Reprinted by permission of John Murray Ltd.

EVELYN WAUGH: *When the Going Was Good*, op. cit. Reprinted by permission of A. D. Peters & Co. Ltd.

ROBERT BYRON: *The Road to Oxiana*, London, 1937. Reprinted by permission of A. D. Peters & Co. Ltd.

WILFRED THESIGER: *Arabian Sands*, London, 1959. Copyright © Wilfred Thesiger 1959. Reprinted by permission of the author.

GEOFFREY BIBBY: *Looking for Dilmun*, London, 1970. Reprinted by permission of William Collins Ltd and Alfred A. Knopf, Inc.

DERVLA MURPHY: *Full Tilt*, London, 1965. Reprinted by permission of John Murray Ltd.

PAUL THEROUX: *The Great Railway Bazaar*, London and New York, 1975. Copyright © 1975 by Paul Theroux. Reprinted by permission of Mr Gillon Aitken and Houghton Mifflin Company.

JONATHAN RABAN: *Arabia through the Looking-Glass*, London and New York, 1979. Reprinted by permission of William Collins Ltd and Simon & Schuster, Inc. Copyright © 1979 by Jonathan Raban.

MIDDLE ASIA

ALEXANDER THE GREAT: Arrian, *The Life of Alexander the Great*, trans, A. de Selincourt, London, 1958. Copyright © the Estate of Aubrey de Selincourt 1958. Reprinted by permission of Penguin Books Ltd.

NEARCHUS: Arrian, *Indica*, Book 8, trans. E. Ilif Robson, London and Cambridge, Mass., 1949.

MEGASTHENES: *The Geography of Strabo*, Vol. 7, trans. H. L. Jones, London and New York, 1930.

ODORIC OF PORDENONE: *Cathay and the Way Thither*, op. cit.

MARCO POLO: *The Book of Ser Marco Polo*, ed. Col. Sir H. Yule, London, 1903.

IBN BATTUTA: *Travels in Asia and Africa*, op. cit.

GONZALEZ DE CLAVIJO: *Narrative of the Embassy of Ruy Gonzalez de Clavijo to the Court of Timour at Samarcand A.D. 1403–6*, trans. C. R. Markham, Hakluyt Society, 1st Series, Vol. 26, 1859.

THOMAS CORYATE: From *Early Travels in India 1518–1619*, ed. Sir W. Foster, London, 1921.

PIETRO DELLA VALLE: *The Travels of Pietro della Valle in India, 1664*, Hakluyt Society, 1st Series, Vol. 84, 1892.

EDWARD TERRY: Ibid.

ALEXANDER VON HUMBOLDT: Quoted, from a Russian source, by George Kennan in *Siberia and the Exile System*, London, 1891.

THOMAS MANNING: *Narratives of the Mission of George Bogle to Tibet and of the Journey of Thomas Manning to Lhasa*, ed. Sir C. Markham, Hakluyt Society, 1876.

JOSEPH WOLFF: *Travels and Adventures*, London, 1860.

EMILY EDEN: *Up the Country*, London, 1866. Reprinted by Virago Press, 1983.

JOHN WOOD: *Personal Narrative of a Journey to the Source of the River Oxus*, London, 1841.

EVARISTE REGIS HUC: *Travels in Tartary, Thibet and China 1844–1846*, trans. W. Hazlitt, London, 1851.

LUCY ATKINSON: *Recollections of the Tartar Steppes and Their Inhabitants*, London, 1863; reprinted by Frank Cass, 1972.

MRS R. M. COOPLAND: *A Lady's Escape from Gwalior*, London, 1859.

ARMINIUS VÁMBÉRY: *Travels in Central Asia*, London, 1864.

HARI RAM: *Records of the Survey of India, Vol. 7, Part 1: Exploration in Tibet and the Neighbouring Regions*, Dehra Dun, 1915.

FREDERICK BURNABY: *The Ride to Khiva*, op. cit.

SIR GEORGE SCOTT ROBERTSON: *The Kafirs of the Hindu Kush*, London, 1896.

GEORGE NATHANIEL CURZON: *Tales of Travel*, London, 1923.

ANTON CHEKHOV: *The Selected Letters of Anton Chekhov*, trans. S. K. Lederer, London, 1955. Reprinted by permission of Pan Books Ltd and Farrar, Straus, Giroux, Inc.

SIR FRANCIS YOUNGHUSBAND: *The Heart of a Continent*, rev. ed., London, 1937.

SVEN HEDIN: *My Life as an Explorer*, London, 1926.

ALEXANDRA DAVID-NEEL: *Magic and Mystery in Tibet*, London and New York, 1967. Reprinted by permission of Souvenir Press Ltd and Librairie Plon.

FREDERICK M. BAILEY: *No Passport to Tibet*, London, 1957. Reprinted by permission of Anthony Sheil Ltd.

J. R. ACKERLEY: *Hindoo Holiday*, London, 1932; revised ed. 1952; reprinted by Penguin Books, 1983. Reprinted by permission of David Higham Associates Ltd.

ELLA MAILLART: *Turkestan Solo: One Woman's Expedition from Tien Shan to the Kizil Kum*, New York, 1934, London, 1938. Reprinted by permission of David Higham Associates Ltd.

PETER FLEMING: *News from Tartary*, London, 1936. Reprinted by permission of the Estate of Peter Fleming, Jonathan Cape Ltd and Charles Scribner's Sons.

HEINRICH HARRER: *Seven Years in Tibet*, trans. R. Graves, London, 1953. Reprinted by permission of the author.

ERIC NEWBY: *A Short Walk in the Hindu Kush*, London, 1972; reprinted by Picador, 1981. Reprinted by permission of the author.

ROGER ST MARTIN O'TOOLE: *A Stag at Large*, London, 1968, New York, 1969. Reprinted by permission of the author.

FAR ASIA

FA-HSIEN: *A Record of Buddhistic Kingdoms*, trans. and ed. J. Legge, Oxford, 1886.

HSUAN-TSANG: *The Life of Hiuen-Tsiang by the Shaman Hwui Li*, London, 1884; reprinted by Academica Asiatica, Delhi, 1973.

GIOVANNI DE PIANO CARPINI: *The Texts and Versions of John de Plano Carpini and William de Rubruquis*, ed. C. R. Beazley, Hakluyt Society, 1903.

WILLIAM OF RUBRUCK: *The Journey of William of Rubruck to the Eastern Parts of the World, 1253–55*, trans. and ed. W. W. Rockhill, Hakluyt Society, 2nd Series, Vol. 4, 1900.

MARCO POLO: *The Book of Ser Marco Polo*, op. cit.

SOURCES AND ACKNOWLEDGEMENTS

ODORIC OF PORDENONE: *Cathay and the Way Thither*, op. cit.

IBN BATTUTA: *Travels in Asia and Africa*, op. cit.

MA HUAN: *Ying-yai sheng-lan (The Overall Survey of the Ocean's Shores)*, 1433, trans. and ed. Feng Ch'eng-Chün, Cambridge, 1970. Reprinted by permission of Cambridge University Press.

LUDOVICO DI VARTHEMA: *The Travels of Ludovico di Varthema*, op. cit.

ANONYMOUS ENGLISHMAN: In *Memorials of the Empire of Japon in the Sixteenth and Seventeenth Centuries*, ed. T. Rundall, Hakluyt Society, 1st Series, Vol. 8, 1850.

MATSUO BASHO: *The Narrow Road to the Deep North and Other Travel Sketches*, trans. Nobuyuki Yuasa, London, 1966. Copyright © Nobuyuki Yuasa, 1966. Reprinted by permission of Penguin Books Ltd.

ENGLEBERT KAEMPFER: *The History of Japan, Together with a Description of the Kingdom of Siam, 1690–92*, trans. J. G. Scheuchzer, Glasgow, 1906.

ISABELLA BIRD: *Unbeaten Tracks in Japan*, London, 1880. Reprinted by Virago Press, 1984.

NIKOLAI MIKAILOVICH PREJEVALSKY: *Mongolia, the Tangut Country and the Solitudes of Northern Tibet: Being a Narrative of Three Years' Travel in Eastern High Asia*, trans. E. D. Morgan, London, 1876.

THOMAS STEVENS: *Around the World on a Bicycle*, op. cit.

BEATRIX BULSTRODE: *A Tour in Mongolia*, London, 1920.

MILDRED CABLE and FRANCESCA FRENCH: *The Gobi Desert*, London, 1942; reprinted by Virago Press, 1984. Reprinted by permission of Hodder & Stoughton Ltd.

SIR OSBERT SITWELL: *Escape with Me*, London, 1939. Reprinted by permission of David Higham Associates Ltd.

JOHN MORRIS: *Traveller from Tokyo*, London, 1943. Reprinted by permission of A. D. Peters & Co. Ltd.

S. J. PERELMAN: *The Most of S. J. Perelman*, London, 1959. Reprinted by permission of A. D. Peters & Co. Ltd and Simon & Schuster, Inc.

PETER FLEMING: *One's Company*, London, 1934. Reprinted by permission of the Estate of Peter Fleming and Jonathan Cape Ltd.

NORMAN LEWIS: *A Dragon Apparent*, London, 1951; reprinted by Eland books, 1982. Reprinted by permission of Eland Books.

OLIVER STATLER: *Japanese Pilgrimage*, London, 1984. Reprinted by permission of Pan Books Ltd and William Morrow Inc. Copyright © 1983 by Oliver Statler.

JAMES KIRKUP: *Japan behind the Fan*, London, 1970. Reprinted by permission of the author.

GAVIN YOUNG: *Slow Boats Home*, London, 1985. Reprinted by permission of Century-Hutchinson Ltd and Mr Gillon Aitken.

REDMOND O'HANLON: *Into the heart of Borneo*, Edinburgh, 1984, New York, 1985; reprinted by Penguin Books, 1985. Reprinted by permission of A. D. Peters & Co. Ltd and Random House, Inc.

NORTH AMERICA

LEIF ERICSSON: *The Vinland Sagas*, trans. M. Magnusson and H. Palsson, London, 1965. Copyright © Magnus Magnusson and Hermann Palsson, 1965. Reprinted by permission of Penguin Books Ltd.

CHRISTOPHER COLUMBUS: *The Journal of Christopher Columbus*, trans. C. Jane, New York, 1960. Copyright © 1960 by Clarkson N. Potter, Inc. Reprinted by permission of Clarkson N. Potter, Inc.

GIOVANNI DA VERRAZANO: *Cellere Codex*, trans. E. H. Hall, in the *Fifteenth Annual Report of the American Scenic and Historic Preservation Society*, Albany, N.Y., 1910.

JACQUES CARTIER: *The Voyages of Jacques Cartier*, trans. H. P. Biggar, Ottowa, 1924.

PETRO DE CASTANEDA: *The Journey of Coronado, 1540–1542*, trans. and ed. G. P. Winship, New York, 1904.

PHILIP AMADAS: *Hakluyt's Principal Voyages*, op. cit.

JOHN WHITE: *Hakluyt's Principal Voyages*, Vol. III, London, 1600.

JOHN SMITH: *Travels and Works of Captain John Smith, President of Virginia and Admiral of New England, 1580–1631*, ed. E. Arber, Edinburgh, 1910.

CLAUDE JEAN ALLOUEZ: *The Jesuit Relations*, Cleveland, 1896–1901.

HANNAH SWARTON: 'A Narrative, Containing Wonderful Passages, Relating to Her Captivity and Her Deliverance' in Cotton Mather, *Magnalia Christi Americana: The Ecclesiastical History of New England*, London, 1702.

JOHN LAWSON: *History of North Carolina*, ed. F. L. Harriss, London, 1714.

PETER KALM: *Travels into North America*, trans. J. R. Foster, London, 1772.

WILLIAM BARTRAM: *Travels through North and South Carolina, Georgia, East and West Florida . . .*, Philadelphia, 1791.

ALEXANDER HENRY: *Travels and Adventures in Canada and the Indian Territories between the Years 1760 and 1776*, London, 1809.

JOHN GOTTLIEB ERNESTUS HECKEWELDER: 'Account of the History, Manners and Customs of the Indian Nations, Who Once Inhabited Pennsylvania and the Neighbouring States', American Philosophical Society, 1819.

MÉDERIC LOUIS ÉLIE MOREAU DE SAINT-MÉRY: *Voyage aux États-Unis de l'Amérique, 1793–1798*, ed S. L. Mims, New Haven, Conn., 1913.

SIR ALEXANDER MACKENZIE: *Voyages from Montreal on the River St Lawrence and through the Continent of North America to the Frozen and Pacific Oceans in the Years 1789 and 1793*, London, 1801.

MERIWETHER LEWIS and WILLIAM CLARK: *History of the Expedition under the Command of Lewis and Clark*, New York, 1893 (first ed. 1814); reprinted by Dover Publications, 1965.

JANET SCHAW: *Journal of a Lady of Quality*, ed. E. W. Andrews and C. M. Andrews, New Haven, Conn., 1921.

JOHN FREDERICK REICHEL: Quoted in *Travels in the American Colonies*, ed. N. D. Mereness, New York, 1916.

FRANCES TROLLOPE: *Domestic Manners of the Americans*, London, 1832.

FANNY KEMBLE: *Journal by Frances Anne Butler*, London, 1835.

JOHN CHARLES FREMONT: *Report on the Exploration of the Country Lying between the Missouri River and the Rocky Mountains*, New York, 1843.

G. D. WARBURTON: *Hochelaga, or England in the New World*, London, 1846.

HENRY DAVID THOREAU: *The Maine Woods*, Boston, 1864.

FRANCIS PARKMAN: *The Oregon Trail Journal, 1846*, in *The Journals of Francis Parkman*, ed. M. Wade, London, 1949.

ALONZO DELANO: *Life on the Plains and among the Diggings*, New York, 1854.

GEORGE AUGUSTUS SALA: *My Diary in America in the Midst of War*, London, 1865.

FREDERICK WHYMPER: *Travel and Adventure in the Territory of Alaska*, London, 1868, New York, 1869.

ISABELLA BIRD: (1) *An Englishwoman in America*, London, 1856; (2) *A Lady's Life in the Rocky Mountains*, London, 1879; reprinted by Virago Press, 1982.

JOHN WESLEY POWELL: *Explorations of the Colorado River of the West*, 1875.

R. M. BALLANTYNE: *Hudson's Bay*, Edinburgh and London, 1848.

JOHN MUIR: *A Thousand Mile Walk to the Gulf*, New York, 1916.

BRUCE SIBERTS: *Nothing but Prairie and Sky: Life on the Dakota Range in the Early Days*, recorded by W. D. Wyman from the original notes of Bruce Siberts, Norman, Oklahoma, 1954. Copyright © 1954 by the University of Oklahoma Press.

W. H. Davies: *The Autobiography of a Super-Tramp*, London, 1908.
Andy Adams: *The Log of a Cowboy*, New York, 1903.
Chief Buffalo Child Long Lance: *Long Lance: The Autobiography of a Blackfoot Indian Chief*, New York, 1928, London, 1956; reprinted by Abacus, 1976. Reprinted by permission of Holt, Rinehart & Winston, Inc.
Henry Miller: *The Air-conditioned Nightmare*, New York, 1945, London, 1947. Reprinted by permission of Laurence Pollinger Ltd and New Directions Publishing Corporation. Copyright © 1954 by New Directions Publishing Corporation.
John Gunther: *Inside USA*, London, 1947. Reprinted by permission of Mrs Jane Gunther.
John Steinbeck: *Travels with Charley in Search of America*, London and New York, 1962. Reprinted by permission of William Heinemann Ltd and Viking Penguin, Inc.
Sir Cecil Beaton: *The Wandering Years, Diaries 1922–1939*, London, 1961. Reprinted by permission of Weidenfeld & Nicolson Ltd and the Literary Executors of Sir Cecil Beaton's Estate.
Jack Kerouac: *On the Road*, London, 1958. Reprinted by permission of Andre Deutsch Ltd.
Norman Levine: *Canada Made Me*, London, 1958. Reprinted by permission of Putnam & Co. Ltd.
Hood River Blackie: 'Home on the Rails: A Veteran Hobo Turns Historian in Recalling His Favourite Characters from the Heyday of Rail-Riding', *Quest Magazine*, August/September, 1978.
John McPhee: *The Survival of the Bark Canoe*, New York, 1975. Reprinted by permission of Farrar, Straus, Giroux, Inc. Copyright © 1975 by John McPhee.
Jonathan Raban: *Old Glory*, London and New York, 1981. Reprinted by permission of William Collins Ltd and Simon & Schuster, Inc. Copyright © 1981 by Jonathan Raban.

CENTRAL AND SOUTH AMERICA and THE CARIBBEAN

Amerigo Vespucci: *Letter to Piero Soderini, Gonfaloniere*, trans. and ed. G. Tyler Northup, Princeton, N.J., 1916.
Ferdinand Magellan: *The First Voyage Round the World*, translated from the accounts of Pigafetta and other contemporary writers by Lord Stanley of Alderley, Hakluyt Society, 1st Series, Vol. 52, 1874.
Bernal Diaz de Castillo: *The True History of the Conquest of Mexico*, trans. M. Keatinge, London, 1927.
Hans Stade of Hesse: *The Captivity of Hans Stade of Hesse in A.D. 1547–1555, Among the Wild Tribes of Eastern Brazil*, trans. A. Tootal, Hakluyt Society, 1st Series, Vol. 51, 1874.
Francis Fletcher: *The World Encompassed by Sir Francis Drake* (1628), Hakluyt Society, 1st Series, Vol. 16, 1854.
Sir Walter Raleigh: *The Discovery of the Large, Rich, and Beautiful Empire of Guiana, etc. Performed in the Year 1595 by Sir Walter Raleigh Knt*, London, 1596; reprinted by the Hakluyt Society, 1st Series, Vol. 3, 1848.
John Chilton: *Hakluyt's Principal Voyages*, op. cit.
Miles Philips: Ibid.
Samuel Fritz: *Journal of the Travels and Labours of Father Samuel Fritz in the River of the Amazons between 1686 and 1723*, trans. and ed. Rev. G. Edmundson, Hakluyt Society, 2nd Series, Vol. 51, 1922.
Janet Schaw: *Journal of a Lady of Quality*, op. cit.
Alexander von Humboldt: *Personal Narratives of Travels in the Equinoctial Regions of America*, trans. T. Ross, London, 1851.

CHARLES WATERTON: *Wanderings in South America*, London, 1825.

HENRY NELSON COLERIDGE: *Six Months in the West Indies in 1825*, London, 1826.

MADAME CALDERON DE LA BARCA: *Life in Mexico during a Residence of Two Years in that Country*, London, 1843.

JOHN LLOYD STEVENS: *Incidents of Travel in Central America, Chiapas, and Yucatan*, New York, 1841.

CHARLES DARWIN: *Voyage of the Beagle*, London, 1839.

ALFRED RUSSEL WALLACE: *A Narrative of Travels on the Amazon and Rio Negro . . .*, London, 1853.

HENRY WALTER BATES: *The Naturalist on the River Amazon*, London, 1863.

FREDERICK JAMES STEVENSON: *A Traveller of the Sixties*, ed. D. Timins, London, 1929.

CECIL GOSLING: *Travel and Adventure in Many Lands*, London, 1926.

ELLERY S. SCOTT: 'The Tragedy of Martinique', *Strand Magazine*, September 1902.

ALDOUS HUXLEY: *Beyond the Mexique Bay*, London, 1934. Reprinted by permission of Mrs Laura Huxley, Chatto & Windus Ltd and Harper & Row, Publishers, Inc.

SYBILLE BEDFORD: *A Visit to Don Otavio*, London, 1953; reprinted by Eland Books, 1982. Reprinted by permission of Eland Books.

RICHARD BISSELL: 'Lima I Love You – Oddly Enough', *Holiday* Magazine, June 1964.

PATRICK LEIGH FERMOR: *The Traveller's Tree*, London, 1950. Reprinted by permission of John Murray Ltd.

SEBASTIAN SNOW: *Half a Dozen of the Other*, London, 1972. Reprinted by permission of John Farquharson Ltd.

V. S. NAIPAUL: *The Middle Passage*, London, 1962. Reprinted by permission of Mr Gillon Aitken.

HUNTER S. THOMPSON: *The Great Shark Hunt*, New York, 1979, London, 1980 (first published in the *National Observer*, 6 August 1962). Reprinted by permission of Deborah Rogers Ltd and International Creative Management. Copyright © 1979 by Hunter S. Thompson.

BRUCE CHATWIN: *In Patagonia*, London, 1977. Reprinted by permission of the author, Jonathan Cape Ltd and Summit Books, Inc.

AUSTRALIA AND NEW ZEALAND

JAN CARSTENZOON: Quoted in J. E. Heeres, *The Part Borne by the Dutch in the Discovery of Australia*, London, 1889.

ABEL JANZOON TASMAN: *An Account of Several Late Voyages to the South and North, by Sir John Narborough, Captain Jasmen Tasman, Captain John Wood, and Frederick Marten of Hamburgh*, London, 1694.

WILLIAM DAMPIER: *A Voyage to New Holland in the Year 1699* (1703/9), in *Dampier's Voyages*, ed. J. Masefield, London, 1906.

JAMES COOK: *The Explorations of Captain James Cook in the Pacific as Told in His Own Journals, 1768–1779*, ed. G. Price, New York and London, 1971.

JACQUES-JULIEN HOUTOU DE LA BILLADIERE: *The Voyage of La Perouse 1791–1794*, Paris, 1800, quoted in D. Davies, *The Last of the Tasmanians*, London, 1973.

FABIAN GOTTLIEB VON BELLINGSHAUSEN: *The Voyage of Captain Bellingshausen 1819–21*, Hakluyt Society, 2nd Series, Vols 91 and 92, 1945.

JOHN JOHNSON: *New Zealander*, 22nd September – 29 December 1847, reprinted in *Early Travellers in New Zealand*, ed. N. M. Taylor, Oxford, 1959.

CHARLES STURT: *Narrative of an Expedition into Central Australia*, London, 1849.

PETER EGERTON WARBURTON: *Journey across the Western Interior of Australia*, London, 1875.
ANTHONY TROLLOPE: *Australia and New Zealand*, London, 1873.
EDWARD JOHN EYRE: *Journals of Expeditions of Discovery into Central Australia and Overland from Adelaide to King George's Sound in the Years 1840–41*, London, 1845.
MARY TAYLOR: Quoted in H. Bolitho and J. Mulgan, *The Emigrants: Early Travellers to the Antipodes*, London, 1939.
JOHN MCDOUALL STUART: *The Journals of John McDo'uall Stuart during the Years 1858, 1859, 1860, 1861 and 1862*, ed. W. Hardman, London, 1864.
CHARLES HEAPHY: *Nelson Examiner*, 5 September–17 October 1846, reprinted in *Early Travellers in New Zealand*, op. cit.
ERNEST GILES: *Australia Twice Traversed...*, London, 1889.
SAMUEL BUTLER: *A First Year in Canterbury Settlement*, London, 1863.
D. H. LAWRENCE: *The Letters of D. H. Lawrence*, op. cit. Reprinted by permission of Laurence Pollinger Ltd, the Estate of Mrs Frieda Ravagli Lawrence and Viking Penguin, Inc.
JACK GORDON HIDES: *Papuan Wonderland*, Glasgow, 1936. Reprinted by permission of Blackie & Son Ltd.
JAN MORRIS: *Journeys*, Oxford and New York, 1984. Reprinted by permission of Oxford University Press. Copyright © 1984 by Jan Morris.

THE ARCTIC AND THE ANTARCTIC

CHRISTOPHER HALL: *Hakluyt's Principal Voyages*, op. cit.
HENRY MORGAN: Ibid.
GERRIT DE VER: *The Three Voyages of William Barents to the Arctic Regions*, ed. K. Beyren, Hakluyt Society, 1st Series, Vol. 54, 1876.
SIR JOHN FRANKLIN: *Narrative of a Journey to the Shores of the Polar Sea...*, London, 1823.
SIR ALEXANDER MACKENZIE: *Voyages...*, op. cit.
ELISHA KENT KANE: *Arctic Explorations in Search of Sir John Franklin*, New York, 1856.
BARON NORDENSKJÖLD: *Voyage of the Vega*, trans. A. Leslie, London, 1885.
ROBERT EDWIN PEARY: *The North Pole*, New York, 1910.
FRIDTJOF NANSEN: *Farthest North*, Vol. 2, London, 1898.
EJNAR MIKKELSEN: *Two Against the Ice*, trans. M. Michael, London, 1957.
VILHJAMUR STEFANNSSON: *My Life with the Eskimo*, New York, 1913.
CHARLES WILKES: *Narrative of the U.S. Exploring Expedition by Authority of Congress, during the Years 1838–42*, Philadelphia, 1845.
HENRIK JOHAN BULL: *The Cruise of the Antarctic*, London, 1896.
CARSTEN BORCHGREVINK: *First on the Antarctic Continent*, London, 1901.
ROBERT FALCON SCOTT: *Scott's Last Expedition: The Personal Journals of Captain R. F. Scott, CVO, RN, on his Journey to the South Pole*, London, 1923.
ROALD AMUNDSEN: *The South Pole*, London, 1912.
SIR ERNEST HENRY SHACKLETON: *South: The Story of Shackleton's Last Expedition*, London, 1917, New York, 1920.
SIR DOUGLAS MAWSON: *The Home of the Blizzard*, London, 1938.
RICHARD EVELYN BYRD: *Alone*, New York, 1938, London, 1958.

ILLUSTRATIONS

The illustrations that appear on the fly-leaves are taken from the following sources:

ADVICE (p. 13) and THE ARCTIC AND THE ANTARCTIC (p. 527) from *Shifts and Expedients of Camp Life* by W. B. Lord and T. Baines, London, 1876.

AFRICA (p. 29) from *Illustrated Travels*, ed H. W. Bates, London 1869–75.

EUROPE (p. 103) from Barnard's *Sketches in Switzerland*.

GREAT BRITAIN AND IRELAND (p. 193) from the *Illustrated London News*. Reproduced by permission of the *Illustrated London News*.

NEAR ASIA (p. 249), MIDDLE ASIA (p. 293) and FAR ASIA (p. 343) from *Around the World with General Grant*, New York, 1879.

NORTH AMERICA (p. 379) from *Echoes from the Rocky Mountains* by John W. Clampitt, New York, Paris and London, 1888.

CENTRAL AND SOUTH AMERICA AND THE CARIBBEAN (p. 451) from *Vom Amazonas und Madeira* by Franz Keller-Leuzinger, Stuttgart, 1874.

AUSTRALIA AND NEW ZEALAND (p. 497) from *Journey Across the Western Interior of Australia* by Colonel Peter Egerton Warburton, London, 1875.

INDEX